The Professional Selling Process

John C. Hafer

University of Nebraska–Omaha

The Professional Selling Process

John C. Hafer

University of Nebraska–Omaha

WEST PUBLISHING COMPANY

MINNEAPOLIS/ST. PAUL · NEW YORK · LOS ANGELES · SAN FRANCISCO

▶ Production Credits

Copyediting: Marilynn Taylor
Art: DBA Design and Illustration
Text Design: Roslyn M. Stendahl, Dapper Design
Cover Design: Three Fish Design
Composition: Beacon Graphics
Production, Prepress, Printing, and Binding: West
      Publishing Company

Thanks to Hamline University Bookstore, St. Paul, MN, for
allowing us to shoot photos in their facility.

Photo Credits follow the index.

West's Commitment to the Environment

In 1906, West Publishing Company began recycling materials left over from the production of books. This began a
tradition of efficient and responsible use of resources. Today,
up to 95 percent of our legal books and 70 percent of our
college texts are printed on recycled, acid-free stock. West
also recycles nearly 22 million pounds of scrap paper annually—the equivalent of 181,717 trees. Since the 1960s, West
has devised ways to capture and recycle waste inks, solvents,
oils, and vapors created in the printing process. We also recycle plastics of all kinds, wood, glass, corrugated cardboard,
and batteries, and have eliminated the use of styrofoam book
packaging. We at West are proud of the longevity and the
scope of our commitment to our environment.

Library of Congress Cataloging in Publication Data

Hafer, John C.
    The professional selling process / John C. Hafer.
       p.   cm.
    Includes bibliographical references and index.
    ISBN 0-314-01164-1 (Student Edition)
    ISBN 0-314-01176-5 (Instructor's Annotated Edition)
    1. Selling.   2. Industrial marketing.   I. Title.
HF5438.25.H33 1993
658.8′5—dc20   92-24867
                                               CIP

▶ To Gail, who endured the sound of clicking keys far into the night and every weekend. I owe her more than a simple dedication.

Contents in Brief

Contents

Part II KNOWING YOUR CUSTOMER **142**

Part III   MAKING A SUCCESSFUL SALE   **279**

Part IV ADDITIONAL DIMENSIONS OF SELLING   **454**

COLOR INSERT IV
Sales Management
and Technology

The Continually Evolving Profession

Selling is evolving as an ever-more professional, technical, challenging, and complex profession. Every salesperson faces greater competition and buyers who are far more sophisticated than they have ever been. Salespeople are expected to be familiar with the latest technology, computers, and software. Even in the traditionally simple retail transaction, a computer and scanner now replace the cash register. Fax machines, cellular phones, computer ordering, and data base marketing have made the field of selling a more professional arena than it has ever been. This trend will continue at an increasing rate. Today's professional salesperson is expected to know about psychology, servicing customers, working in partnership, and adapting sales presentations to customers with different personalities and social styles. Finally, salespeople are increasingly expected to be business consultants and problem solvers. This trend will continue with even greater demands for creativity and innovation in the future. In short, selling is one of the most dynamic, vibrant, challenging, and future-oriented professions.

The Selling Process

This book approaches selling as a process, a series of interrelated activities that work together. Topics are not discrete blocks of information with one having little connection to the next. This book was conceived in such a way that the topics and issues build one upon the other. It was designed to follow the natural sequence of events that occurs in the selling process. The central focus is the adaptive selling process. The sales training programs used today focus on creating relationships with customers by understanding them and their needs then adapting to their social style and particular business circumstances. This is exactly what this text does. In doing so, it provides students with a realistic view of what they would get in a corporate sales training program. By taking the adaptive selling process perspective, students will realize that anyone can be highly successful in the profession if he or she observes, adapts, and follows the right steps in the process of selling to the unique needs of each customer. The focus specifically adopted here emphasizes a process or systems orientation. This has become the cornerstone of operating in today's global, highly integrated, and interdependent markets.

A Book From Which It Is Easy to Learn and to Teach

This book is written *for* students interested in the study and practice of selling and marketing. The writing style is conversational, and the contents are a mix of the necessary theoretical underpinnings and applications or examples which illustrate the theory. It is pedagogically designed *for* students. In each chapter, specific learning objectives are identified in the beginning, highlighted where they appear in the text, and finally reinforced in the chapter summary. Each major section of a chapter ends with "Follow-up Questions," which students can use to judge their comprehension of that section's contents. At the end of each chapter key terms are defined and review questions are presented for homework assignments or for students to use as markers to evaluate their understanding of the chapter's contents.

Major facts, techniques, and how-to features are listed in bulleted tables that are placed in easily identifiable boxes to provide visual diversity and to clearly identify major points. The boxes distinguish application techniques from theoretical and other discussion material. Material from such sources as *Sales and Marketing Management* magazine and *Personal Selling Power* are incorporated throughout the text. Such authors as Tom Peters, Gary Karras, Mack Hannan, and Howard Stevens are cited since they are authorities read by today's salespeople and managers in order to stay ahead in the profession of selling.

Advantages Over Competitive Texts

While there are several fine competing texts, *The Professional Selling Process* covers not only the basics, but also offers the advantage of including subjects others neglect. This text contains extensive material on contract law, negotiating tactics used by buyers and sellers, recognizing and adapting to different buyers' social styles, technological applications, and dealing with sexual harassment, just to name a few.

This text separates itself from others by its depth of treatment of legal issues. No other text provides the extent of discussion of contract and sales law that this one does. This treatment of the legal side of sales transactions and contracts was specifically included to give students an understanding of the legal obligations a salesperson has when completing a sales contract and delivering it. Specific references are made to the Uniform Commercial Code, contract law, sales law, and the obligations of salespeople when they act as agents or bailees.

In addition, a chapter on not-for-profit and service selling is unique to this text. With the continued growth of the service sector in our economy, a selling book deficient in this area would leave the student ill-prepared to enter the selling profession.

Integrated into the chapters are discussions or sections on ethics, international sales, and technology. Also included in each chapter are a variety of experiential features. Highlighted boxed items, such as "Case In Point," provide illustrations of the application of textual material. The feature "What Would You Do If..." places the student in particular selling situations calling for solutions. These can be used as the basis for class discussions. A unique feature of this text is another boxed item titled "When Things Go Right/When Things Go Wrong." In this, actual selling situations are related, some with successful outcomes and some showing that no matter what is tried, sometimes nothing works. These features are included for the student's and the instructor's benefit. They all can serve as homework exercises or the focus for class or group discussions.

The Professional Selling Process Package

This book offers students and instructors a totally self-contained learning package. The pedagogical elements in the text provide variety and challenge. Cases are included in each chapter, some long and some short, to give the instructor the maximum flexibility. Each chapter also contains suggestions for group and individual presentations in class. Once again, these are unique to this text and provide instructors with numerous teaching options.

An extensive and innovative *Student Activity Manual* is available. In it are numerous application exercises, scenarios, suggestions for activities outside of class, role-play exercises, and ideas for in-class group activities for each chapter. Multiple-choice questions are also included for each chapter. The *Student Activity Manual* is keyed to the specific objectives of each chapter so students have a tightly knit package in which the text and the activity manual directly reinforce each other.

Also available is the *Sales Presentation Manual* by David Reid. This role-playing simulation has sample buyer and seller cards, contracts, ads, and its own instructor's manual for an office copier sales exercise.

This total-system approach to providing students with a complete, provocative, fun, and state-of-the-art package will produce students who have learned more of the personal selling process in both theory and application, and they will have learned it faster.

For the instructor, the text package offers a mix of the proven ancillaries and high-tech augmentations. A test bank and instructor's manual are the foundations of the ancillary package. The special instructor's annotated edition text contains an abbreviated instructor's manual for quick reference and suggestions for integrating the entire ancillary package with the text. Transparency masters are also provided in hard-copy form. For instructors with Harvard Graphics 3.0 capability, the transparencies are provided on disk for use with multimedia or computer projection facilities. The transparencies on the disk are filed by chapter "shows" and are in color with animation. Lecture points can be made with such attention-getters as moving arrows and bullets, fade-in and fade-out, and screen wiping. Instructors can use the disk as is or as a foundation for customizing their own multimedia or high-tech lectures.

The instructor's package also includes the most complete set of videos available with any selling book on the market. All adopters will receive a set of interactive video vignettes keyed to parts of the text. Additionally, qualified adopters will receive the actual tapes used by major corporations to train their salespeople. These videos are the actual tapes used by major corporations for training their own salespeople.

The complete collection of ancillaries surpasses competitive offerings. The ancillary package offers both new instructors and the most seasoned professors a package complete enough and flexible enough to be readily compatible with existing instructional regimens, or easily customized for each new school term. The ancillary package is the most complete, flexible, creative, contemporary, and high-tech system available.

In conclusion, this total learning package offers instructors a learning system not available elsewhere. The suggestions of many experienced people have created this unique package.

Acknowledgements

I would like to thank everyone who has had a part in this book's creation. Foremost are Arnis Burvikovs and Susan Smart, the editors at West Educational Publishing who shepherded this book along in an orderly, systematic, and generally sane manner. In addition, this book would never have come to completion without the insightful and creative comments of the reviewers and contributors. Specifically, my thanks go to:

Thomas H. Stevenson
University of North Carolina

Gordon J. Badovick
University of Wisconsin-Oshkosh

William Bryant Smith
Georgia Southern College

Dick Klawiter
University of Wisconsin-Platteville

Guy Devitt
Herkimer County Community
College

Gary M. Donnelly
Casper College

Ramon A. Avila
Ball State University

Myron J. Leonard
Western Carolina University

Barbara Rosenthal
Miami-Dade Community College

Rosemary R. Lagace
University of South Florida

Raghu Tadepalli
North Dakota State University

Richard L. Jones
Marshall University

David C. Carlson
New Mexico State University

Alicia G. Lupinacci
University of Texas-Arlington

Robert J. Boewadt
Georgia College

Marc H. Goldberg
Portland State University

Steven B. Castelberry
University of Georgia

Timothy Hartman
Ohio University

Harry J. Moak
Macomb County Community College

Joseph D. Chapman
Ball State University

Dan C. Weilbaker
Bowling Green State University

Don Frederick
Mankato State University

Kenneth E. Stover, Jr.
Manatee Junior College

John F. Tanner, Jr.
Baylor University

David A. Reid
University of Toledo

O. Karl Mann
Tennessee Tech University

John C. Hafer
December 1992

The Professional Selling Process

The Profession of Selling

Objectives

After completing this chapter you will be able to:

1. Define the role of selling in the marketing function.

2. Identify the three major benefits to society of the selling process.

3. Explain the five categories of sales careers.

4. Describe the attractions (advantages) and aversions (disadvantages) of the profession of selling.

5. Describe briefly the four major elements of the adaptive selling process.

6. Define in detail the major steps in the selling process.

7. Discuss the four different selling environments in which most selling jobs occur.

The Professional Selling Question

What makes a good salesperson?

Two Famous Sales Experts Respond

Fran Tarkenton is a successful businessman. Before that he was a professional quarterback. During his years as a quarterback, he gained the respect of his fellow players and established himself as one of the great people in the game. Tarkenton's sales success has been even brighter than his exploits on the field. He is the owner and super salesman for Knowledgeware, a computer software firm. When he bought it for $3 million dollars in 1985 it was a loser. Now its sales are over $120 million and Tarkenton's personal share in the company is over $60 million.

In Tarkenton's view, six things make a good salesperson and a career success.

1. The enthusiastic desire to serve others. The key word here is enthusiastic.
2. The ability to establish trust. For a successful career in sales, the salesperson must believe in the product and communicate that to customers.
3. The ability to perform effectively. Customers link the performance of the product to the performance of the salesperson. If the salesperson isn't performing well, the product probably won't either.
4. Success at negotiating. A successful salesperson negotiates by trying to arrive at a win-win situation.
5. Refusal to take "no" for an answer. A "no" is only a temporary setback.
6. The ability to work through the disappointing times. The bad times cause you to stretch to new levels of creativity.[1]

Another sales expert is John Cleese, star of the famed "Monty Python's Flying Circus." John Cleese has turned his talents to the practical applications of selling. He is featured in a series of sales training tapes which are some of the most popular in the industry. Cleese has been quoted as saying that inexperienced salespeople want to coat themselves with imaginary armor because they are scared. A good salesperson doesn't put on a false front because the more one does that, the more it will tend to repel customers. A sales presentation is a bit like a performance. You get comfortable in the role you have by rehearsing it. Cleese believes that you learn about audiences (and customers) by getting out there in front of them. You rehearse, do your show, and then analyze the audience feedback to perfect your craft.[2]

Introduction

Selling is the most vital function of a business. Without selling, exchanges do not occur and there is no business. Selling fits into a firm's strategic plan as the chief instrument for generating income, serving customers, and providing the essentials for a firm to survive—profitable sales. Salespeople make it all happen.

Everyone is a salesperson in some way.

Selling comes in many forms. There are retail salespeople, salespeople who sell products or services to businesses, salespeople who sell to resellers, salespeople who strictly open accounts, and salespeople who sell to institutions and the government. Because there are so many different types of selling, it is an attractive career. Some people choose a selling career for the unparalleled opportunity and freedom. Others like the variety and challenge, or the compensation potential. Still others choose it as a route to upper management positions.

In this chapter we will explore numerous aspects of the profession, delve into what separates successful from unsuccessful salespeople, introduce you to the concept and application of adaptive selling, and acquaint you with the selling process. You will get an overview of the exciting and dynamic world of the professional salesperson.

Case in Point

The Professional Salesperson

The national sales director of a large company asked one of her top salespeople to speak at a meeting of 300 sales representatives at Chicago's McCormick Square. At the meeting, the speaker approached the podium and said, "I do not know why Mrs. Smith asked me to talk to you people about selling, because I have never *sold* a thing in my life. But I have helped a lot of people *buy.*"

Marketing and Selling Functions in the Economy

Marketing is a host of separate but intertwined activities which culminate in the sale of something to consumers, companies, governments, or even nations. The "something" can be a tangible product—something you can actually touch, like this book—or an intangible service having no physical manifestation. Intangible services are exemplified by a vacation arranged by a travel agent, a bank's services in writing wills, or even your dental exam.

Selling serves the marketing process by facilitating exchanges. You may read many definitions of marketing. For our purposes, *marketing is a system that delivers satisfaction to customers and thus is responsible for the distribution, pricing, promotion, and creation of products or services that households, individuals, and businesses buy to deliver the standard of living we enjoy.*

◄ ◄ ◄ ◄ ◄ ◄ ◄ ◄

Learning Objective 1: The role of selling in the marketing function

Everyone is selling something to someone, and through the exchange both sides benefit. You sell yourself in a job interview, your teacher is selling you an education, and someone sold your school the chair you are sitting on. When you try to get a date, you are trying to sell yourself. You hope to persuade the other person that an evening out would leave both of you better off (or one of you better off and the other at least no worse for the experience).

Selling's Role in Marketing's Functions

Selling is one of the three universal functions of marketing. *The universal functions of marketing are the activities that create and deliver satisfying products to customers.* These functions can be separated in the following ways:

The Universal Functions of Marketing

Exchange Function	Physical Distribution Function	Facilitation Function
Buying	Transportation	Grading or quality control
Selling	Storage	Financing
		Risk transfer
		Market information

Exchange is when a buyer and seller agree to make a trade. In developed economies, the buyer trades money for the seller's goods or services. In some economies, barter is the exchange vehicle. Selling represents one half of the exchange function, buying represents the other.

Physical distribution is another function of marketing that involves salespeople. *Physical distribution is the actual transportation and storage of products.* Salespeople often arrange for transportation and storage and are responsible for making sure the delivery is on time with goods undamaged. They can directly help their own companies and their customers' cost containment by closely monitoring the many details of physical distribution.

Salespeople are key links between their companies and industrial customers using Just in Time (J.I.T.) inventory management. With J.I.T., customers carry little if any inventory, so deliveries must not only arrive on the day promised, but usually at a specific time of the day. If the salespeople can monitor, control, and intercede to assure the accurate and timely delivery, then their functioning in the physical distribution aspect of selling helps build strong relationships with customers.

Facilitation is also part of a salesperson's job. Salespeople facilitate exchanges by helping to arrange financing. A real estate agent is a salesperson but also helps new homeowners find and secure the best mortgage loan. Salespeople facilitate exchanges by being a primary source of market information. Who better to ask about what's going on in a market than the salespeople who serve it? Finally, salespeople facilitate exchanges by reducing the customer's risk through negotiated terms. Negotiating graduated payment plans, staggering delivery dates, and offering guarantees are ways salespeople act as risk reducers. Selling crosses all the boundaries of marketing.

▶ ▶ ▶ ▶ ▶ ▶ ▶ ▶ ▶ ▷

Learning Objective 2: Selling benefits society three ways: Creates satisfaction, creates efficiency, creates opportunities

Selling benefits society in three ways. First, it helps create satisfaction by bringing customers who have wants and needs together with others who have the products and services to satisfy those wants and needs. Second, selling creates efficiency and lower prices. By allowing for specialization of labor, manufacturers and suppliers can concentrate on what they do best and the salespeople can do what they do best. Finally, selling creates opportunities. By bringing buyers and sellers together, society benefits by having more goods available to more people. Let's discuss each benefit separately.

Selling Creates Satisfaction

Selling is a natural process we all use to create satisfaction. Salespeople look upon their jobs as facilitators for increasing their customers' well-being. They sell them products or services which satisfy their needs or solve their problems. If you had everything you needed, there would be no necessity for selling or marketing. We know this is not the case.

About noon your stomach tells you of a need which should be fulfilled. Feeling that need, you seek out something to fill it. There are businesses (restaurants, vending machines, grocery stores, etc.) which have addressed themselves to filling that need, but they need money to operate. You have money but you cannot eat that; they have food, and as a result of their having something you want and you having something they want, an exchange occurs. You both give up something of lesser value for something of greater value. Both of you come away from the exchange better off than you started. This small marketing encounter has served to create satisfaction for you both. If you think about all of the activities it took to get that food where you wanted it, when you wanted it, and at a price you felt was fair, you can see that marketing and selling are a tremendously synchronized set of endeavors that do only one thing: serve the customer—YOU!

Figure 1-1 **Selling Benefits Society**

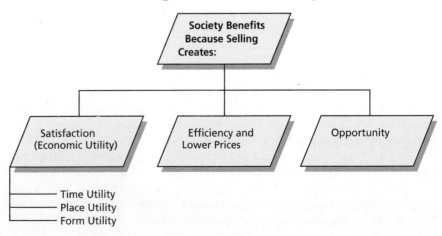

Selling's Benefits to Society

Society Benefits Because Selling Creates:

Satisfaction (Economic Utility) — Time Utility, Place Utility, Form Utility

Efficiency and Lower Prices

Opportunity

Salespeople help create our standard of living.

Selling Creates Efficiency and Lower Prices

Let's step back in time for a second and think of a world without selling. Suppose you needed a new pair of shoes. You would have to spend time finding the materials and making the shoes. If you were doing that, you could not be doing something else, like growing food. If a group of people worked together as a team to do nothing but make shoes, shoes could be produced in quantity; and because this team could specialize, it could make a pair of shoes much cheaper than you. If a salesperson, a specialist in selling shoes, were to find customers and make sales, the team could concentrate on doing what it does best, the unit cost would go down, and the total profits of the team (company) would go up. Selling allows the whole economy to take advantage of this specialization of labor.

Selling enhances the firm's ability to produce at lower cost and creates a better standard of living for everyone. Think about it: every economy in the world with a high standard of living has a well-developed and well-defined system for selling products and services. All this has come about because some people elected to specialize in selling so others could specialize in what they do best—producing the product.

Selling Creates Opportunity

Selling directly and indirectly creates opportunities for many people. Since the products and services sold by salespeople are the culmination of all business activities, salespeople's efforts create jobs for other people. This means salespeople are on the front line of business and without them, there would be no need for accountants, truck drivers, or manufacturing workers.

The profession of selling is the major catalyst for most other jobs. When a car salesperson sells an automobile, she sells the labor of factory workers, truck drivers, manufacturers, and miners (not to mention bankers, lawyers, ad agencies, importers, and cargo ship captains). Without that car sale, all these people's jobs are at risk.

1. How do the activities of salespeople create jobs for other people?
2. How does selling benefit the economy?
3. How do selling activities fit into marketing?

Learning Objective 3: The diversity of sales careers

The Diversity of Sales Careers

Sales careers fall into five categories:

1. Retail sales,
2. Selling to resellers,
3. Selling to businesses for their use,
4. Selling to institutions, and
5. Missionary sales.

The last four are often collectively called "industrial sales." Figure 1-2 represents the family tree of sales careers. We shall discuss the categories to give you a better idea of what each is like.

Retail Sales

Retail sales are the sales made to the final end-user consumer, the customer who ultimately gets the satisfaction out of the product or service. Retail sales jobs represent the largest proportion of all selling jobs. The retail salesperson's job is assisting the customer in making choices from a wide variety of merchandise. With "in-store retailing," the customer comes to the salesperson rather than the salesperson searching for the customer. In "nonstore retailing," like

Figure 1-2 **The Family Tree of Selling**

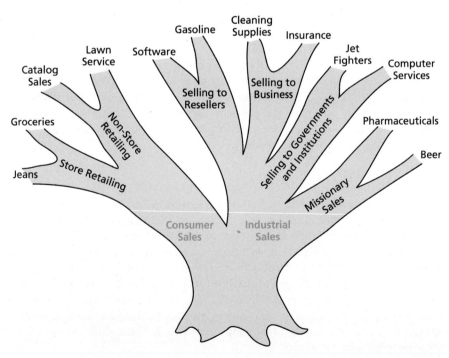

Mary Kay or Tupperware, the retail salesperson goes directly to the customer. This is referred to as "direct sales." Nonstore retailing encompasses vending, direct mail, and catalog sales as well, but those are not personal selling activities so they will not be discussed here.

Retailing is the last and most important link between the manufacturer, wholesaler, and consumer. Retail salespeople are key individuals in any manufacturer's marketing plan, and without them many manufacturers would go out of business. In-store retail selling represents the predominant vehicle for most of the consumer products we buy.

Selling to Resellers

Selling to resellers is done by manufacturers who sell to wholesalers and retailers, and by wholesalers who sell to retailers. The main function of a wholesaler's salesperson is to sell products to the retail store buyers whose stores or outlets will then resell to the public. After the sale is made, the wholesaler's salespeople often arrange for transportation, inspect the product upon delivery, and deal with any resulting problems. They are responsible for keeping the buyers informed of advertising campaigns, discounts and allowances, and the general useful information.

The number of salespeople in wholesaling are far fewer than the number of persons in retail sales. According to the 1980 census there were 1.91 million people in wholesale sales occupations compared to 7.35 million in retail sales.[3] Today there are great career opportunities for women in this area of selling. More women (on a percentage basis) than men are entering wholesale selling careers. Between 1979 and 1982 there was a 60 percent increase of females in wholesale sales compared with a 9 percent increase of males. During the same period the number of females working as salespeople for manufacturers increased only 13.5 percent, and the number of male salespeople working for manufacturers decreased by 10 percent.[4]

Salespeople who sell to resellers want to establish and maintain lasting business relationships with their customers. They must know the specific needs of each, the buying process each goes through, the special characteristics of the buyer's personality, and the way the customer's company does business. The following Case in Point gives insights into this type of selling.

Case in Point

Selling to Safeway Stores, Inc.

Safeway is a major grocery retailer with thousands of stores located mainly in the western United States. Safeway operates its stores through a series of geographically established divisions, each with its own buyers. It also operates a network of national buying offices that have the authority to make purchases for any division in the nation.

In the national buying office in Dallas, salespeople made presentations only on Monday mornings from 8:00 A.M. to noon. The presentations had a 15-minute time limit, after which the buyers would

Continued

Selling to Businesses

We will consider selling to businesses different from selling to resellers. Here, *selling to businesses is sales not meant for direct resale*. Yes, when General Motors buys tires for its cars, you ultimately take possession of those tires. The difference is that you did not buy tires per se, you bought the car and the tires were part of it.

All businesses are customers, whether they buy for resale or for their own use. Think about the number of parts in your car. Most are purchased by, rather than made by, the automaker. Now think about the number of cars, trucks, and tractors assembled each year. You quickly become overwhelmed with the enormity of this type of sales. Business-to-business sales is an area most people are not aware of when they consider a sales occupation. Someone sold the paper these words are printed on and the ink that makes them visible. Someone in the printing company sold their services to the publisher. Someone sold the printing presses to the printer to do the printing.

Selling to Government and Institutions

The government, at all levels, is the single largest buyer of products and services in the nation. Governments have unique buying situations and offer a variety of selling opportunities. Someone sells the government missiles, aircraft carriers, concrete, postal trucks, and much more. The quantities governments buy are usually large, so that one sale may be a salesperson's single transaction for a year or more.

Governments usually buy on the basis of competitive bids, according to specifications they set. Salespeople often have a hand in helping government purchasing agents determine the specifications for the products they buy, and write bids rather than actual orders. Often the salesperson never sees the buyer and simply submits a bid in writing through the mail.

Selling to institutions, like schools or state and county hospitals, is similar to selling to the government because they buy in large quantities and often on a specification basis. Most of the buying goes through a purchasing department with the buyer and seller seldom coming together. In such situations the salesperson's job is to make an initial call on the purchasing agent, hoping to become a listed supplier. Once listed, orders come automatically as they are processed through the purchasing office. Your school buys tons of paper each year, yet the paper salesperson and the school's purchasing agent seldom meet face-to-face to make the sale.

Missionary Sales vs. the Traditional Sales Role

Missionary salespeople do not take orders directly from customers but persuade them to buy from the distributors and wholesale suppliers they work for.[6] In the brewing industry, a distributor's salespeople call on tavern owners to persuade them to buy the brands of beer the distributor is licensed to sell. These missionary salespeople take no orders, but offer such inducements as signs, promotional materials, and services. The distributor's truck drivers take and fill the orders. The missionary salesperson's primary job is to increase business from current and potential customers by providing them with product information and other personal selling assistance.

When Things Go Right

A Patient Approach to Government Selling[7,8]

Selling to the government is easy, jokes Bob Hollingshead, president of Hollingshead International, Santa Fe Springs, California. "All you have to do," he says, "is have the patience of a saint."

He speaks from long, hard experience. Last month, seven years after he first approached the U.S. Navy, he signed a contract to do repairs on several fighter jets. He is replacing the racks that hold the jets' black boxes, which hold the electronic intelligence that controls and monitors various functions of the aircraft. If the boxes are not held securely in place, they can send out false signals that cause the planes to malfunction.

Hollingshead holds more patents for such avionic support equipment than anyone else, and he had already filled a large order for his racks for Lockheed's L-1011 aircraft. Despite his expertise, he found that in order to sell his talents to the government, he first had to sell the navy on the idea that the trouble it was having with its jets was being caused by subpar racks, not faulty black boxes. This took all of Hollingshead's powers of persuasion. The navy only now recognizes support structures as a separate entity. It was a classic "catch-22" situation.

"To show you how neglected the area is," says Hollingshead, "there's no work order in the military or on the commercial side that defines a racking problem. Consequently, when a box does not function, if it's the fault of the rack and not the box, they have to report the failure against the box because there's no place on their forms for rack failures."

It took 60 trips to Washington and visits with 200 individuals in the navy and Defense Department to convince the decision makers to see things his way. He used flip charts loaded with engineering and performance data as well as product demonstrations—his own structures compared to those manufactured by major airframe companies. When talking about minute measurements, he whipped out a micrometer to illustrate his point.

"Eventually," says Hollingshead, whose only prior sales experience was knocking on doors for the Fuller Brush Company, "I gave up the charts completely. I found I couldn't stand there and do flip charts and give out numbers because people tended to fall asleep."

Hollingshead's ultimate sales tool was an offer to refit three of the navy's jets at his own expense. It cost him around $450,000 to prove his point. Though the navy accepted his offer, it did not do so with breakneck speed. Hollingshead made his proposal in 1978. He was given planes for repair in late 1981 and eary 1982. Test results on the refitted planes convinced the navy.

Would he go through it all again?

"Yes," says Hollingshead. "The government is out there to buy products and they've got a lot of money to buy with. I'm overwhelmed by the amount of money they have. Anyone with a good product can sell to them, but you just have to keep plowing at it. Once you hit it, it starts squirting like a gusher."

Another industry where missionary selling occurs is in pharmaceuticals. Pharmaceutical salespeople, called "detail people," call on pharmacies, clinics, and hospitals, and persuade physicians to prescribe their company's prescription products. The products are sold to the pharmacy through a whole-sale druggist, and through a pharmacy to you.

Service Selling

Businesses buy services as well as products. Service salespeople range from your doctor to the crew that mows your grass. Computer service bureaus do payroll computing, inventory control, and accounts receivable/payable. They can do it less expensively and more efficiently than if it were done by their customers in-house.

Services are often customized, tailored to the individual wants and needs of each customer. The customer has direct interaction with the production, operations, physical resources, support functions, and with other customers, as well as with the individuals selling the service. These interactions become part of the total customer contact process and involve many functions. Personal selling opportunities abound during these direct interactions.

▶ ▶ *follow-up question*

1. What are the differences between the various types of selling careers?

The Attractions and Aversions of Selling

The opportunities of professional selling attract many people. However, many others are averse to a career in sales. Table 1-1 lists the reasons most frequently given for and against a sales career.

The Attraction

There are five reasons for choosing a sales career.

◀ ◀ ◀ ◀ ◀ ◀ ◀ ◀
Learning Objective 4: The attractions and aversions of selling

Freedom of action   Many salespeople get to set their own hours, almost like they are running their own businesses. Some, like residential real estate salespeople, do most of their business on weekends. Others, like insurance salespeople, work mostly in the evenings. There is a sales job to fit any lifestyle. Salespeople will tell you that one of the attractions to their job is the freedom they have to set their own schedules. They are not tied to a desk or cooped up in an office all day. They can work as much or as little as their income, advancement, and success goals motivate them.

Table 1-1   **The Attractions and Aversions of Selling**

Selling Attracts People Because of:	Selling Repels People Because of:
▶ Freedom of Action	▶ Self-Doubt
▶ Variety and Challenge	▶ Rejection
▶ Professional Growth and Advancement	▶ Hard Work
▶ High Compensation	▶ Travel and Relocation
▶ Mobility and Stability	▶ Low Status and High Stress

Variety and Challenge Another attraction is the variety and challenge that selling offers. If you have mastered the techniques and skills of selling, you can carry them with you to any company selling any type of product. Good salespeople can change jobs and still be successful because they have mastered the craft of helping people buy.

Selling jobs are seldom boring. Each customer offers a new situation and a new challenge, providing a level of excitement many people enjoy. Salespeople have a great variety of duties in the normal performance of their jobs, and are responsible for far more "executive" activities than ever before. In a 1990 survey in which over 10,000 salespeople responded, actual face-to-face selling time comprised only one-third of the daily activities. The rest of the work week was consumed by meetings, administration, travel, account servicing, and telephone selling (see Figure 1-3).[9]

Professional Growth and Advancement Selling is often the steppingstone to management. Managers should know the company's products, its customers and their problems, the competitors, the problems the salespeople face, and the characteristics of the markets they serve. There is no better training ground than in the sales force. From sales, two career paths are open. One is to stay in the sales area and become a sales manager, another is to move into nonselling areas like product management or marketing management. Success in sales is often a prerequisite to advancing into management.

High Compensation Without compensation, selling would not be a highly sought-after profession. Compensation is more than just wages alone, however. For a field salesperson, the compensation package usually includes a car, expense account, and profit sharing and stock options. According to a survey by *Sales and Marketing Management,* in 1985 the average compensation for a sales trainee selling industrial products was $24,335 and for a sales supervisor it was $48,863.[10] Earnings for trainees have been increased about 10 percent, and for the more experienced salespeople as much as 39 percent since 1985. Figure 1-4 shows the average annual compensation for salespeople, trainees, and supervisors. These are averages, of course, but there are many salespeople making six-figure incomes. Selling can be both a finan-

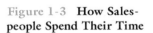

Figure 1-3 How Salespeople Spend Their Time

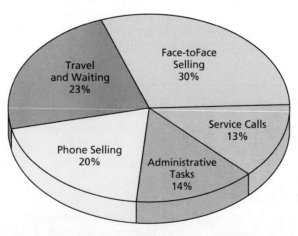

Source: *Sales and Marketing Management,* Vol. 143, No. 7, pg. 77.

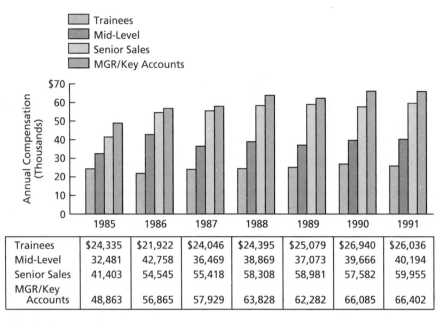

Figure 1-4 **Average Compensation for Salespeople**

	1985	1986	1987	1988	1989	1990	1991
Trainees	$24,335	$21,922	$24,046	$24,395	$25,079	$26,940	$26,036
Mid-Level	32,481	42,758	36,469	38,869	37,073	39,666	40,194
Senior Sales	41,403	54,545	55,418	58,308	58,981	57,582	59,955
MGR/Key Accounts	48,863	56,865	57,929	63,828	62,282	66,085	66,402

Source: *Sales and Marketing Management*, Vol. 143, No. 7, June 17, 1991, pg. 73., and Vol. 144, No. 7, June 22, 1992, pg. 68.

cially and a professionally rewarding career. Table 1-2 compares the starting pay of sales trainees having bachelor's degrees and master's degrees, from the classes of 1979 and 1992.

Increases in starting pay have advanced each year for both B.A. and M.B.A. groups. If this trend continues, you could reasonably expect to receive a starting compensation package worth almost $60,000 in 2000!

Mobility and Stability   Good salespeople are seldom unemployed. Because their skill is transferable between products and companies, salespeople have a high degree of mobility and stability. There are employment opportunities in all parts of the nation. Salespeople can change companies or industries, and move to new locations. Having mastered their selling skills and customer partnering techniques, they can find a job just about anywhere they want.

The Downside of Sales Occupations

Selling has many advantages, but there are also disadvantages.

Table 1-2 **Starting Salaries of Sales Trainees**			
Field of Study and Degree	**Class of 1992**	**Class of 1979**	**Percent Change**
B.S./B.A.—Sales and Marketing	$27,144	$13,092	+107.3%
B.S./B.A.—Business Administration	$27,024	$13,464	+100.7%
M.B.A.			
With technical degree	$42,612	$19,812	+115.1%
With nontechnical B.A.	$44,796	$18,468	+142.6%

Source: *Sales and Marketing Management,* Vol. 143, No. 7, pg. 75 and Vol. 123, No. 8, pg. 67.

Self-Doubt   Selling jobs require people to be constantly sharpening their selling skills and product knowledge. However, even the most experienced salesperson suffers self-doubt at some time. Many people avoid a sales career because *they* do not think *they* can sell. It is not uncommon for novices to think, "Why would the customer want to buy my product?" Or, lacking the confidence that comes with training and experience, they might think, "I'm not sure I can sell anybody anything. I have never done anything like that before!"

People who are not "salespeople" tend to think they are not in sales. In reality, they have to sell their ideas to other people, they have to sell themselves in job interviews, they must convince others of their opinions. This is all selling! Self-doubt destroys good salespeople and keeps promising people from pursuing a sales career. It also is a hurdle that keeps many people from achieving their dreams and goals regardless of their occupation.

Self-confidence and self-esteem remove self-doubt. While self-doubt causes many people to avoid a career in sales, it is really an unfounded aversion. It can be overcome with training, with the coaching of a good sales manager, and with time plus experience. So, while everyone at one time or another suffers from self-doubt, successful salespeople (or successful people in any job, for that matter) analyze why they are in a slump and suffering from self-doubt; then they set about practicing, training, and working on their weaknesses and bolstering their strengths.

Hard Work   Selling is hard work! It takes time to find new customers, develop them, and solve their problems. Paperwork accompanies all sales and it must be done correctly and on time. This is demanding and meticulous work that is often frustrating, but it is part of the job. Selling often requires physical labor. Many products are installed, tested, and repaired by the salesperson. It can be physically exhausting to make calls and handle deliveries, repairs, and installations all in one day. Selling requires hard mental work as well. Good salespeople spend a great deal of time researching information in libraries, tracing problems over the phone, and talking to customers before a sales call is even planned. Anyone who is good at selling will tell you it requires more physical and mental stamina than most people anticipate, but that the rewards for that effort can be excellent!

Rejection   Rejection goes with the territory. Salespeople get rejected every day, because not all customers buy. Salespeople must be resilient, and confident in their ability to serve their customers. They cannot let rejection get them down. Salespeople learn to look on rejection positively and make it work for them. There is a saying: "It takes ninety-eight noes to get two yeses. Therefore, every no is just one step closer to a yes." If you look at it this way, every no is a motivator, not a demotivator. Rejection must be accepted as a normal, everyday occurrence, not as a personal affront.

Travel and Relocation   Travel and relocation are common in many selling jobs. Positions in real estate sales, life insurance, and stock brokerage require little, if any, overnight travel, but selling industrial products, pharmaceuticals, and textbooks often has extensive travel requirements. International sales positions require even more travel; spending many hours in airports, on planes, and in hotels.

Not all sales are free from stress.

Travel requirements can vary depending on the job. A publisher's representative (the person who sold your instructor this book) travels extensively during the fall and spring, when schools select textbooks. During the winter and summer, travel is minimal.

Relocation is also common. It usually means bigger territories, more responsibility, and career progression. Willingness to relocate is used as a criterion by many firms in their promotion and hiring process. Relocation decisions, though, can be difficult because of family pressures and community ties. Buying a house, selling a house, transferring children to different schools, leaving old friends and a familiar setting make relocation a difficult decision. But it can also be the beginning of a new opportunity!

Low Status and High Stress   Unfortunately, many firms place a lower status on salespeople than they should. Salespeople are often viewed as being on the periphery of the firm, out of sight, off doing whatever it is they do. Some sales jobs can be stressful. The need to make quotas, call on prospective customers, handle problems from existing customers, and do the necessary paperwork makes selling a job that requires good organizational skills and good time management. Salespeople need to balance the needs of the firm and of their families. This is particularly true when travel or relocation requirements create changes in the family's short-term and long-term plans. While these are stresses related to selling, they are also faced by all successful corporate employees on their way to top management positions.

▸▸ *follow-up questions*

1. Which of the downside items listed above do you think is the one most responsible for turning people off to a selling career? Why?
2. Why do people choose a career in selling?
3. If you had to rank the reasons given for choosing a sales career, how would you rank them for yourself and why?

Adaptive Selling[11]

Adaptive selling is the theme of this book. The fundamental idea in adaptive selling is to manage four things: selling behavior, selling resources, the buying task of the customer, and the nature of the sales relationship.[12] When using adaptive selling, the outcome of a sales interaction is contingent upon adapting the sales presentation to the selling situation. This means learning the tools and techniques of selling and understanding the psychological/social aspects of both sales and purchasing.

The book will teach you the tools of selling along with the personal relationship side of sales. It is equally important to understand the customer's buying process, personality, motives, and attitudes when making a purchase. Figure 1-5 illustrates the adaptive selling framework. A brief discussion of its elements will illustrate how a salesperson can become proficient at "adaptive selling."

Salesperson's Behavior

The salesperson completes a sale by interacting with a prospective customer. How the salesperson and customer each handle their roles determines the outcome. Salespeople must adapt to customers and try to influence their thinking.

Learning Objective 5:
Elements of the adaptive selling process

Adapting to Customers There are a variety of social styles, each requiring or causing specific behaviors. Adaptive salespeople learn to modify their behavior as conditions dictate. Later in this book, we will devote extensive time to four different social styles and the sales approach that works best with each.

Case in Point

Serving the Client's Needs

Mr. Palmer, a music teacher at a leading university, went to Radio Shack and purchased his first VCR. After reading the complicated instructions, he was unable to get it to work. He phoned Radio Shack and the clerk said, "We have a video tape that shows you how to hook it up. Come in and get it." Mr. Palmer asked to speak to the manager, who said, "Where do you live? I can stop by on my way home and connect it for you. That way you won't have to make the trip back here." Because of this interest in serving the client's needs, Mr. Palmer has purchased all of his electronic equipment from this store and even more for his music classes at the university.

Establishing an Influence Base Salespeople need to establish and develop a sense of credibility, legitimacy, and reliability in the buyer's mind. This is what the customer or purchasing agent expects of professionals. Salespeople presenting themselves as knowledgeable professionals with technical expertise and experience will be more successful when the customer's purchase decision is complex or technical. When the sale is relatively simple, like the straight reorder of a familiar product, operating in a more social and friendly

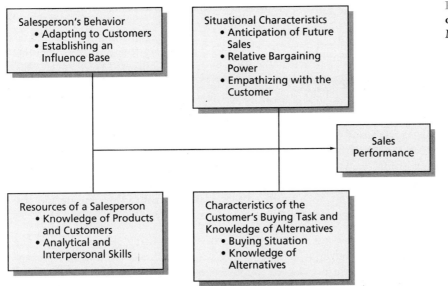

Figure 1-5 **Elements of Adaptive Selling Methodology**[15]

manner leads to more sales. Salespeople influence customers because they have established a base of trust, reliability, credibility, technical expertise, or familiarity.[13]

Resources of Salespeople

The resources of salespeople are their knowledge of products and customers, plus their analytical and interpersonal skills. These come through education, training, experience, and knowledge of the customer's field of interest. The more experiences salespeople get and the longer they stay in the profession, the more resources they accumulate and the greater the chances for success.

Knowledge about Products and Customers The greatest asset salespeople have is the knowledge of their products and customers. Product knowledge allows comparisons between your company's products and the competitor's products. Customer knowledge permits the salesperson to draw upon vital insights into the customer's behavior, needs, personality, and buying process. Lack of product knowledge is one of the major causes of failure in selling, yet knowledge is one of the easiest to assets to acquire.

Analytical and Interpersonal Skills Analytical skills pair the ability to deduce the customer's problems or needs with the ability to offer solutions. Interpersonal skills deal with how people interrelate. Some people are more at ease than others with meeting new people. Some are better communicators and can make new acquaintances quickly feel at ease. Analytical skill can be enhanced through training and education. In many companies, when technical analysis (like analysis of engineering specifications) is required, the salesperson calls on specialists for help. Similarly, interpersonal skills can be sharpened and enhanced through training, observation, role playing, and experience.

Situational Characteristics: The Buyer/Seller Relationship

Clearly, the ability to adapt to the situation and to the buyer's style makes for a more successful salesperson. The salesperson who can accurately identify the situational problems at hand, anticipate the business or personal interactions that will occur, assess the relative power to negotiate terms, and empathize with the customer's problems will be more adaptable and have a better chance of making the sale.

Anticipation of Future Sales   More loyalty and interdependence exist between buyers and sellers who anticipate a long-term working relationship. This loyalty translates into continual orders and greater difficulty for competitors to make inroads. Also, if salespeople expect future business with a customer to expand, they approach that customer from a different perspective than if the reverse is expected.

Relative Bargaining Power   The relative bargaining power of both the salesperson and buyer affect the selling situation. Major customers who represent a significant portion of the salesperson's business have greater power to negotiate better deals and influence the terms they get on the sales agreement than do small volume customers. When the relative bargaining power is in favor of the customer, the salesperson may have to make concessions on such things as discounts, delivery dates, minimal order quantities, or the way the product is packed or shipped. Similarly, if the relative bargaining power is in favor of the salesperson, fewer or less significant concessions would be made to the smaller customer than to the larger one.

Characteristics of the Customer's Buying Task and Knowledge of Alternatives

As an adaptive salesperson, you must remember that no sale occurs unless the correct selling process coincides with the buying situation. The knowledge of alternatives for both the buyer and salesperson affects the salesperson's success. There are three buying situations.

New Buying   New buying situations exist when the buyers are in the market for products they have never before purchased. The buyers know nothing about the vendor's firm or its products, and might not even know what products or services they need from the vendor. They lack information about products, services, guarantees, and the outcomes to expect. Because of these unknowns, they perceive the risks to be high.

Modified Re-buying   A modified re-buy is a variation of what has been bought before, but the customers are still buying basically the same product. This requires less risk to the buyers and probably less information. Changing an order from one colored item to another would be an example.

Straight Re-buying   A straight re-buy is simply ordering the same product bought in the past. The buyers' risk is low and their informational needs are minimal. Many firms buying on a straight re-buy basis program their computers to automatically print purchase orders when inventory levels get to a predetermined amount.

Not only does the type of buying situation influence how and what the adaptive salesperson presents, but the "buying center" may differ between companies. *A buying center is a term usually referring to the group of people who have input into the buying decision; it is where the alternatives are evaluated and the decisions are made.* In some companies, the individual buyer's information is the only input, and he or she has total control over the purchase decision. In other companies, purchasing agents present information supplied by salespeople to a buying committee (a type of buying center) which makes the decision. In some cases, the salesperson, not a purchasing agent, must address the committee and try to persuade the group rather than one individual. In such a situation there are "multiple buying influencers." This can occur when selling consumer products as well. Retail salespeople often must address the concerns of everyone in the family when trying to make a sale. It is important for them to know how the buying decision is actually made as it will affect the process and content of the sales presentation.

▶▶ *follow-up questions*

1. What are the major elements of the adaptive selling approach?

2. How would you prepare a presentation for a buying committee as opposed to a presentation for an individual?

3. Are consumers' household purchases ever made by a "buying committee?" What would be an example?

What Would You Do If...?

You have just graduated from college and have little sales experience outside of the training for your new job with the Apex Office Equipment Company. For the past three months you have read your product manuals and have gone through several role-playing exercises with your sales manager. You have accompanied her and watched her make presentations but today is your solo flight. You are making a call on a buyer you have never met before.

After getting in to see the buyer, you begin to tell her the types of problems your products can solve and ask her if she has experienced any of those problems. She begins to tell you about her company's difficulties in securing products and how she hasn't found anybody who can really meet her specific needs. You begin to probe the specific nature of those needs, but she gives only vague and confusing replies to your questions.

You are beginning to wonder if *she* really knows what her problem is. Is she telling you about the symptoms in hopes that you can somehow solve the problem and make her look good? Is she just testing your creativity to see what alternatives you could offer?

▶ Question: Now is the time to call upon all of your personal resources. What type of influence base do you think would work best here? Will you need more analytical or interpersonal skills to handle this one? Explain the reasoning behind your answers.

Understanding the Selling Process—A Look Ahead

Throughout this book we will be explaining the selling process. In this section of the chapter, we will give you a glimpse of the selling process so you get an idea of where we are going.

The Steps in Selling

The steps actually involved in making the sale will be fully dealt with later in their own separate chapters, but for now let's introduce them.

Learning Objective 6: Steps of the selling process

1. **Prospecting**. Prospecting generates the list of names the salesperson will use as an initial potential customer list. Lists can come from many sources, but before any high-probability prospects—"leads"—are identified, the salesperson must determine who can and cannot use the product or service.

2. **Qualifying**. Qualifying is the process of determining if the prospective customer meets the criteria to warrant a presentation. Qualifying, then, is the system of matching prospective customers to established criteria, making them viable candidates to become customers.

3. **Presentation**. In the presentation the salesperson asks questions and presents the features, advantages, and benefits of the product or service. There are a variety of presentation techniques ranging from "scripted" to customized.

4. **Answering Objections**. This is the stage of the selling process inexperienced salespeople fear the most and experienced salespeople anxiously await. Experienced salespeople anticipate objections and are prepared to show the buyer why objections are really benefits.

5. **Closing**. Closing is when the salesperson asks for the order. Closing can take place at any time during the presentation, not just at the end. If prospective customers are properly qualified, have been given a good presentation, and have had their objections answered, closing is the easiest part of the selling process.

6. **After-Sale Service**. After-sale activities may involve arranging delivery and making sure it is done on time, at the right location, and invoiced. After-sale activities also include customer relations. Customer relations means keeping in touch, making sure that everything is working smoothly, and simply checking that there are no problems.

The selling process is a series of well-defined steps. First is prospecting, getting the names of potential customers. Prospecting is sometimes considered a marketing activity and sometimes part of the selling process. Here we will consider it part of the selling activity. Second is qualifying. Qualifying separates prospects to weed out the names of people who do not have a need for what we sell or who cannot buy for some reason. Third is making the presentation. This is the time when the salesperson presents the product's features, advantages, and benefits to the qualified prospect. Fourth is dealing with objections. Most customers raise some objections during the presentation and the salesperson must effectively overcome these objections if the sale is to be made. The most common objection is price related. Fifth is closing, when the salesperson asks for the order. Last is after-the-sale service. This encompasses follow-up activities such as installations, service, or instruction.

The Four Selling Environments

The selling processes occur in four general selling environments. They are:

1. A consultative environment,
2. A closing environment,
3. The relationship selling environment, and
4. Display sales.

The Consultative Selling Environment[14] In consultative selling, the function of the salesperson is more like that of a business consultant. The salesperson works closely with the prospective customer, sometimes at the customer's site for long periods, to develop solutions to unique and often complex problems. An example is selling computer mainframe applications to your school. The salesperson would have to spend time with administrators, faculty, and students in order to understand the types of reports and data the computer would be expected to deal with.

Learning Objective 7: Four selling environments

The Closing Environment In the closing environment, the customers already know about the products and their features, so the basic function of the salesperson is to close the sale. Amway, WearEver, and Kirby home demonstrations are good examples. It is critical for the salesperson to qualify, present, answer objections, and then proceed to close the sales on as many products as possible as quickly as possible. The salesperson must also manage the environment of this selling situation by keeping it fun, entertaining, and lively. While the selling techniques used are quite direct, they can be soft and subtle at the same time. The customer is much more prone to buy if the sales encounter is an enjoyable personal as well as business experience.

Relationship Selling In the relationship selling environment, the goal is to develop and manage the buyer/seller relationship. Relationship selling is most common in service sales. For example, when you visit your lawyer to make out a will, transfer title on property, or initiate litigation, it is a foregone conclusion the lawyer will get your business. What is important is applying skill and knowledge to your problem and beginning the client/ counselor relationship. Relationship selling is becoming more and more of

Route salespeople are the most obvious examples of the display sales environment.

a mainstay in industrial sales. Businesses are finding that with increased competitive pressures, particularly from foreign competitors, building a successful, mutually profitable relationship often makes the difference between long-term growth and survival, and the alternative.

Display Sales   In display sales, the salesperson focuses on keeping the buyer in stock and making sure that price and convenience concerns are met. A specific example would be a route salesperson for Coca Cola. The order is written up and the product is delivered to the shelves. Occasionally the salesperson may be required to explain new products to buyers, but for the most part the major function here is to keep the buyer in stock.

Table 1-3 provides examples of typical products or services sold using each selling approach. The critical role of the salesperson in the closing environment is to qualify, present, answer objections, and, of course, close the sale. In the consultative environment, the critical role is to make the presentation, answer objections, and continue the customer salesperson relationship. In relationship and display selling it is important to focus on continuing the relationship, providing extensive customer service, and continually doing follow-up activities to enhance greater resale possibilities.

▸ ▸ *follow-up questions*

1. How does the closing environment differ from display sales in the way a person goes about the selling process?

2. More and more firms selling industrial products are becoming "relationship oriented." Why would a firm selling something like machine lubricants be interested in emphasizing relationships?

3. If you were selling stereo equipment, in which selling environment would you probably find yourself? Could you change that environment?

	Closing	Consultative	Relationship	Display
Table 1-3 Typical Products Sold with Each Selling Strategy				
Examples	*New or unique products or services (Often "trends")*	*High or new tech products system or services*	*Accepted and widely used products/ services*	*Commodities*
Computers	Original Univac	Original IBM accounting systems	NCR/point-of-sale terminals for retailing	Radio Shack Computer Land
Medical		Specialized surgery	Family physician	Nonprescription drugs
Apparel	Custom designers	Custom tailors	Boutiques	K-Mart
Commercial	Tax shelter sales Venture consultants	Investment consultants	Banks	Credit cards
Packaging	Bubble packs	Special Christmas liquor boxes Consumer medical products boxes	Auto parts boxes	Standard bakery boxes Packing material Styrofoam shells
Building		Architects	Contractors	Building supply
Advertising	Inflatable balloons Special directories	Ad Agencies	Trade magazines	Newspaper classified
Typical products/ services	▸ Tupperware ▸ Positive mental attitude seminars ▸ One-of-a-kind designer fashions ▸ Vacation homes ▸ Diet foods ▸ Tax shelters	▸ Consumer seminars ▸ Architectural services ▸ Management information ▸ Custom software ▸ High tech medical equipment ▸ Advertise business legal service ▸ Corporate insurance	▸ Drugs and medical supplies ▸ Tooling ▸ Auto parts ▸ Family physicians ▸ Family insurance ▸ Contract services ▸ Travel agencies ▸ Special or boutique retail ▸ Business to business standard services	▸ Fast foods ▸ Supermarkets ▸ Gasoline ▸ Health clubs ▸ Air travel ▸ Office supplies ▸ Most general retail

Source: The H. R. Chally Group, division of SSS Consulting, Inc. Dayton OH.

Summary

Selling's role in business is to facilitate exchanges between customers needing products and services and the people or firms that can supply them (Learning Objective 1). The economy thrives on these exchanges. The universal functions of marketing are the exchange, physical distribution, and facilitation activities which must be accomplished to create and deliver satisfying products to customers.

Selling creates satisfaction and a better standard of living by making it possible for customers to get a variety of goods and services to satisfy their every need. Because of selling, businesses get what they need to carry on and make a profit, thus providing not only goods for the economy but employment as well. Through the selling profession, firms are more efficient and lower prices actually result. By having a sales force, a firm can take advantage of specialization of labor, which in turn creates operational efficiency and lower costs. Finally, selling creates opportunities. Without salespeople making sales, there would be no need for managers, truck drivers, factory workers, etc. Salespeople create the revenues that employ everyone else (Learning Objective 2).

Salespeople's careers can be grouped into one of the five categories:

1. Retail sales,
2. Selling to resellers,
3. Selling to businesses,
4. Selling to institutions, and
5. Missionary sales.

Most people in selling naturally fall into retail sales because retailing is the largest industry in the nation. Other types of selling careers offer unique challenges, ranging from selling to small businesses to working with the largest customer of all, the government (Learning Objective 3).

Selling offers a great many attractions. Professional salespeople have a great deal of freedom from being tied to a desk and they enjoy the variety and challenge. There are great opportunities for personal and professional growth, and through that growth salespeople can be highly compensated. Many enjoy the mobility that can go with sales positions, but salespeople in general are reassured by the fact that a good salesperson is never without a job.

Sales careers are not without their disadvantages. Self-doubt, hard work, rejection, travel and relocation, stress, and low status in many firms are part of the job. Anyone going into a sales career should be aware of both the upside and downside of the profession (Learning Objective 4).

Adaptive selling will form the foundation of this book. Adaptive selling has four main elements in its implementation and offers a variety of opportunities in making sales presentations. First, it requires skill in recognizing the clues given by prospective customers and in recognizing your own style, strengths, and weaknesses. Salespeople must adapt to the customer's style and establish an influence base. Second, salespeople must draw on their own resources, such as product and customer knowledge, analytical tools, and interpersonal skills. Third, adaptive salespeople evaluate the situational characteristics. These include expected future sales, relative power to negotiate terms or conditions, and empathizing with the customer's situation. Finally, adaptive salespeople examine the nature of the customer's buying situation and closely fit together a feasible set of alternatives to fit that customer's specific needs (Learning Objective 5).

The selling process itself is a series of well-defined steps. The mechanics of selling are:

1. Prospecting,
2. Qualifying,
3. Presentation,
4. Answering objections,
5. Closing, and
6. After-sale servicing.

Knowledge of the selling processes will lead you to success regardless of which of the four selling environments you work in (Learning Objective 6).

Salespeople can find a place in one of four selling environments. In a consultative environment, you would work closely with the customer, acting more as a business consultant than a salesperson. In the closing environment, the main objective is to close the sale as quickly as possible. The relationship environment has a more personal goal, establishing a close working relationship, because a long-term commitment is the norm rather than the exception. The display sales environment is the most common as typified by in-store retail sales (Learning Objective 7).

In future chapters you will learn how to sell to a variety of people in a variety of selling situations. The techniques you master now, from this course and this book, will serve you throughout the rest of your life.

Key Terms

Universal functions of marketing   The universal functions of marketing are the activities that create and deliver satisfying products to customers.

Marketing   Marketing is a system that is responsible for the distribution, pricing, promotion, and creation of products or services that households, individuals, and businesses buy. It ultimately sets the standard of living in a country.

Exchange   Exchange is when a buyer and seller agree to make a trade. It can be barter or the exchange of goods and services for money.

Physical distribution   Physical distribution is the actual transportation and storage of products.

Retail sales   Retail sales are the sales made to the final consumer.

Missionary salespeople   Missionary salespeople do not take orders directly from customers but persuade them to buy from the distributors and whole-sale suppliers they work for.

Selling to resellers   Selling to resellers is done by manufacturers who sell to wholesalers and retailers, and by wholesalers who sell to retailers. It is the sale of goods destined for resale to another customer in the marketing chain.

Empathy   Empathy is being able to put yourself in the other person's shoes and see the problem from that perspective.

New buying   New buying situations exist when the buyer is in the market for products not previously purchased.

Modified re-buying   A modified re-buy is a variation of what was bought before, but still basically the same product.

Adaptive selling   Adaptive selling is an approach to the sales interaction, focusing on the premise that in order to be successful a salesperson must recognize and adapt to each customer type. Adaptive selling means managing selling behaviors and selling resources, while adapting to the buying task of the customer and the nature of the sales relationship.

Closing   Closing is when the salesperson asks for the order.

Customer relations   Customer relations means keeping in touch, making sure that everything is working smoothly and simply expressing concern that there are no problems.

Consultative selling environment   In consultative selling, the function of the salesperson is more like that of a business consultant whose main function is to solve a complex problem by offering a variety of alternatives or solution.

Closing selling environment   In the closing approach, the customers usually know about the products and their features. The basic function of the salesperson is to close the sale.

Relationship selling   In the relationship selling approach, the goal is to develop and manage a relationship.

Display sales   In display sales, the salesperson focuses on keeping the buyer in stock and making sure the price and convenience concerns of the buyer are met.

Discussion Questions

1. Besides the ones listed in the chapter, what are other services sold to consumers? What would be examples of services sold to businesses?
2. How can we make the statement that through the efforts of salespeople, other people have jobs?
3. How does a career in selling prepare a person for jobs in management?
4. Why are communication skills so important for becoming successful in sales?
5. Why do people not succeed in sales careers?
6. At a Tupperware home party, which type of selling environment strategy would work the best and why?
7. Several times in the chapter the word *empathize* was used. What does it mean and why is it an important attribute of successful salespeople?

Application Exercise

Reread the boxed item entitled "A Patient Approach to Government Selling," then answer the questions below:

1. What is Bob Hollingshead's selling environment?

2. What would be the most difficult aspect of his job selling to the navy?

3. Would you consider Bob's selling environment to be more "consultative" or "relationship" in nature? Why?

Class Exercises

Group Exercise

Many people (even students in business and marketing) have preconceptions about sales and personal selling. Separate into groups of three to six members, with one member taking notes, and brainstorm the following ideas:

▸ When the word "salesperson" is mentioned, what adjectives come to mind first?

▸ In order to be successful in sales you must _____ .

Task

1. Group your responses into the journal below.

Positive	Negative

2. Which list is longer and why?

3. Where do we collect our perceptions about salespeople? Why do we consider them accurate?

Individual Presentation

Prepare a brief presentation on one of the major categories of sales careers.

Task

1. Describe the category, including details on the variety of jobs within it.

2. Interview people in three different selling jobs. Ask them about how they make their sales and how they interact with customers.

3. Present to the class a comparison of what you found in #2 above.

Cases

He Sells But Really Isn't a Salesman?

Diane and Adrian were looking at the jobs posted outside the career placement office at school. Most were targeted toward marketing and management majors and some listed "any business major" without stipulating a specialty. Of the twenty posted, fifteen were entry level sales positions.

Diane said to Adrian, "There's nothing here worth looking at! The only things here are sales jobs. If I'd wanted to go into sales, I certainly wouldn't have needed to spend all this time in school. Besides, I'm no salesperson. I want to go into management, not sales. Let's go to class. If I want to be depressed, I'll go pick up my mid-term from my accounting prof."

As they walked to class Adrian said, "I thought your dad was in sales." Diane said, "Yes, but that's different. He's not like a salesman. He helps businesses solve their problems. He spends a lot of time with his clients, then sells them the computer software they need."

Adrian thought about what Diane had just said. It seemed to be somewhat inconsistent. Did or didn't her father sell? "Doesn't he like his job?" she asked.

Diane said, "Oh yes, he thinks it's great. I'd like to do what he does, but he's not really in sales."

Questions

1. What does Diane's father do in his job? Is he in sales?
2. Do quite a few people think like Diane? Why?
3. Would you like a job like the one Diane's father has? What might make it attractive to you?

The New Company Venture

Irene and Heather were ardent and talented seamstresses. They had displayed many of their creations at craft shows and had done well selling them. Heather thought their customers might like more time to look over the merchandise and maybe ask some questions, but were unable to at the crowded craft shows. She talked to Irene about a new business venture, doing home parties like Tupperware does. The craft and handmade merchandise might get better consideration if it could be shown without all the other competing craft merchants close at hand.

Irene liked the idea, but didn't think just their products would offer a wide enough selection. Irene suggested that the two of them take other people's merchandise on consignment and sell it along with theirs at these in-home parties. Heather liked that idea and the new business venture was launched.

In their consignment sales, Heather and Irene would take merchandise from other people and sell it for a 25 percent commission. They contacted numerous people who made craft products and managed to have a good offering for their first party. Having a good source of supply, they have come to you for help in formulating a strategy of how to sell. But before you give them a winning strategy, you need to think a little more about their whole concept.

1. How will Irene and Heather's in-home parties allow their suppliers to be more efficient?
2. Are their sales retail, wholesale, or business-to-business?
3. What type of influence techniques do you think would work best at the in-home parties?

Take-It-Or-Leave-It Loses a Customer

Craig wanted to build a deck on his beach house in South Carolina. He needed thirty-six decking planks and went to a lumber yard that had them on sale. The lumber was on strapped stacks. The only unstrapped pile had been picked over, and the remaining decking planks were mostly crooked and unusable. Craig asked the lumber yard manager if he could select his lumber from a strapped pile because he needed straight ones for his deck. The yard manager said, "We cannot cut the straps on the new ones until all the crooked ones are gone." Craig walked out and the lumber yard lost a sale.

Questions

1. How could the policy have been improved to prevent the lost sale?
2. What should the yard manager have said to Craig to preserve his good will?
3. What basic element of customer relations was violated in this case?

References

1. Gerhard Gschwandtner, "Fran Tarkenton, Knowledgeware's $60 Million Champion," *Personal Selling Power,* 11 (1991): p. 20.
2. L. B. Gschwandtner, "John Cleese Brings His Unique Body Language Savvy to the Sales World," *Personal Selling Power,* 9 (1989): 8–11.
3. Census of Population Subject Report Occupation by Industry, no. C-3.223/18:980/vol. 2/part 7C (Washington, D.C.: Government Printing Office).
4. "For Saleswomen, Wholesale Pays," *Sales and Marketing Management,* 133 (1984): 19.
5. Adapted from Bill Kelley, "Selling in a Man's World," *Sales and Marketing Management,* 143 (1991): 28–35.
6. Gilbert A. Churchill, Neil M. Ford and Orville C. Walker, Jr., *Sales Force Management* (Homewood, Ill.: Richard D. Irwin, 1985), pp. 6–7.
7. "A Patient Approach to Government Selling," *Sales and Marketing Management,* 134 (1985): 60–61.
8. RFP in this story refers to "Request for Proposals."
9. William A. O'Connell and William Keenan, Jr., "The Shape of Things to Come," *Sales and Marketing Management,* 142 (1990): 39.
10. Survey of Selling Costs, *Sales and Marketing Management Magazine,* 142 (1990): 76.
11. *Adaptive selling* is a term introduced by Barton Weitz in "Effectiveness in Sales Interactions: A Contingency Framework," *Journal of Marketing,* 45 (1981): 85–103.

12. Barton A. Weitz, "Effectiveness in Sales Interactions: A Contingency Framework," *Journal of Marketing,* 45 (1981): 85–103.
13. Modified from Weitz, pp. 85–103.
14. Barton Weitz, "A Critical Review of Personal Selling Research: The Need for Contingency Approaches," *Research Perspectives on the Performance of Salespeople: Selected Readings,* ed. Ford, Walker, Churchill (Cambridge: Marketing Science Institute (1983): 181–182.

The Sales Professional

2 What Makes a Person Successful in Sales

Objectives

After completing this chapter, you will be able to:

1. Identify and explain the factors that determine success in professional selling.

2. List and explain the five steps in creative problem solving.

3. Define the foundational principles in successful selling and explain how salespeople put them into action.

4. List and explain three major guidelines to building trust with the customers.

5. Outline the essential elements of a good sales training program.

The Sales Professional and the Process of Selling

◄ Cold calling, or canvassing, is a common method of making an initial contact with a new prospect. To be successful in this time-consuming task, the salesperson organizes a logical strategy for selecting prospects. For example, this textbook representative organizes leads by text subject matter.

► Being successful at prospecting is the result of persistent effort, an intelligent approach, exploring opportunities and disqualifying potentially poor prospects. Training and experience dictate how long a salesperson should search out and pursue productive leads.

◄ Through qualifying, the salesperson judges which leads to pursue and which to pass. Determining the product needs and interest of the key person is a vital step in qualifying. Thoroughly qualifying prospects leads to a successful presentation and, ultimately, to a closed sale.

▲ Once a prospect is qualified, the salesperson begins the precall planning process. This consists of fact-finding, creating an account profile, preparing a call planner, and mapping out an approach strategy. Possible product offerings and key players are determined prior to the initial presentation.

▲ Product knowledge is multi-faceted. The salesperson must know the pricing, available credit terms, and distribution alternatives for her product. To be truly successful, she must also research the competition to know their products, pricing, distribution, market share, and their strengths and weaknesses.

◄ By asking questions, listening and observing, the sales representative gains competitive intelligence. A textbook salesperson visits bookstores as part of the job not only to provide service, but also to inspect competing texts and obtain feedback from store customers who are text users.

► A phone call to confirm on the day before the sales appointment serves as a reminder to the prospect, and is a courtesy as well as a time-saver.

◄ After introducing herself and presenting her business card, the salesperson will thank the prospect for the appointment. She must be certain before reaching her destination that she has all of her sales support materials ready for her presentation.

► In textbook sales, a sales representative could use either the needs-satisfaction or formula type of presentation. Both are suitable for developing a long-term, sustainable business relationship.

▶ Prospects really buy solutions to their problems. It is the salesperson's task to question and listen to the prospect to determine the problem. She can then discuss the possible solution—her company's product, and its benefits and features.

◀ The adaptive salesperson modifies her presentation to the prospect's social style. This potential buyer is an Analytical, and the salesperson must be prepared, straightforward, and business-like in order to work most effectively with him.

▶ The salesperson is always ready to answer questions and to use the minor yes or other trial close to determine if this decision-maker is ready to close the sale and complete the transaction.

◄ During the presentation, the prospect may expresses objections. Since the prospect was thoroughly qualified and willing to grant the appointment, possible objections in this situation would most likely concern the product or the price, and not hidden objections or stalling for time.

► A salesperson need not feel intimidated by objections, but should welcome them—no objections can mean no buying decision. In handling the objections of this Analytical prospect, the salesperson provides facts and figures and remains calm and pleasant.

◄ The final decision in this sale will not be made until after a group presentation.

▲ A group will usually consist of a mix of social styles, and the salesperson cannot adapt to each at once. She might respond to this challenge by adapting to and managing the presentation environment.

▲ In this case, since she cannot control the physical environment, this salesperson instead will manage the emotional and perceptual impact of the presentation. Her demonstration will stress the product's advantages, benefits and features. If software or videos accompany the textbook, she will demonstrate these, as well.

◄ This salesperson uses visual aids to enhance the buying environment, and the flow of the presentation. A visual presentation must be simple, concise and understandable and should amplify and reinforce the features, advantages and benefits of the product or service.

◀ A positive mental environment is important to making the sale. The adaptive salesperson recognizes and enhances the positive emotions of her prospects, and works to disspell the negatives.

▶ Objections and questions have been successfully addressed. The salesperson has observed the buyers' verbal and non-verbal signals throughout the presentation. The group has discussed the product and made definite statements of interest, and the salesperson has used the direct close to complete this part of the sale.

◀ The next step is the after-sale follow-up to verify the order and answer any new questions. The salesperson will later follow up to make sure the order has been filled and meets the customer's expectations.

◄ Closing the sale is only the beginning of the buyer-seller relationship. Now the salesperson must maintain this relationship if she wishes to keep a repeat customer.

◄ To build a better relationship between the buyer and the seller, this sales representative acts as a liaison between her firm and the customer. She keeps up on new product or service developments that can be beneficial to the customer. She also relays information from the customer to her firm to help improve the quality of the product and its related services.

► It is important to customer relations for the salesperson to be available for problem-solving, and to help the customer even though it may not result in a sale. This salesperson will be rewarded for her attention to such detail with new leads and customer loyalty.

The Professional Selling Question

How important is salespeople's attire to their successfully making sales?

Sales Experts Respond

John T. Molloy wrote a book titled *Dress for Success* several years ago. Since then, the topic of the "proper business uniform" has been cussed and discussed. Everyone has his or her own thoughts on the topic. Proper dress is important, there is no denying that. But what is proper? The typical answer to that is dress conservatively, but this is by far not the final word.

Attire is important. Customers do notice. Inappropriate attire makes the job harder.

Many companies used to have dress codes. A salesperson could wear only a certain colored suit and a specific type of shirt or blouse, and some firms had restrictive policies on hair length. Beards and moustaches were generally not acceptable at all. Today, things have changed to some extent. While restrictive dress codes are not as prevalent as they once were, they still exist.

Richard Rindels, a real estate agent, changes from the typical business suit to his blue jeans and boots when he is showing agricultural land from the back of a horse or four-wheeler. Don Quinn from Exide Corporation in Kansas has a simple rule he follows: dress formally when you go through the front door and more casually when you come in the back door. Since people in some selling occupations also get involved in installing and demonstrating products, work clothes can be the order of the day. Wanda Brown, a sales consultant from Minneapolis, recommends dressing in a manner comfortable to the client.

Jordan Adler of America West says that dressing appropriately is extremely vital, especially on the first call. He says the initial call is where salespeople establish their image and set the stage for the relationship. Paul E. Sussman of Hancock Securities cautions salespeople that if they don't look the part of a professional salesperson, they probably won't even get in to see the client.

While Molloy says dress codes vary region by region and industry by industry, he still insists on the uniform of universality. Recently, he was hired as a consultant by a small San Diego accounting firm that was opening a Los Angeles office. Its principals firmly believe potential entertainment business clients distrust accountants in suits. "They even call them 'suits,'" Molloy said.

But at his urging, the accountants donned the uniform. "Now they have nineteen offices," Molloy said, "and they only have one rule: suits." The moral of the story? "People who wear gold chains won't give their money to people who wear gold chains."[1]

Introduction

The Myth of the Natural-Born Salesperson

In the late 1850s, Marshall Field left the farm for Pittsfield, Massachusetts, and a clerk's position in a dry goods store. In 1856, the lure of the West drew him to the frontier town of Chicago and a local dry goods store's salary of $400 per year. By 1864, Field had a $260,000 interest in the store. By the time of Field's death in 1906, *his* store was grossing $68 million per year. During his years as a salesperson and manager, he developed ten fundamental values for all his salespeople to follow:

1. Time—Time can make a million out of a dime. It determines whether you are a salesperson or a loafer.

2. Perseverance—You will always find the greatest sales at the end of the street, the end of the day, and after ringing many doorbells in vain.

3. Work—Without work, your days are empty and satisfaction flies. There is no pleasure like work.

4. Simplicity—A sincere attitude does not need words. Simplicity is compelling selling.

5. Kindness—The service you provide does not hide behind the mask of friendliness, for kindness cannot be counterfeited.

6. Example—The greatest influence you have is built by what you do.

7. Duty—Your sense of duty whispers to you through your conscience. People who don't listen to their conscience act like people without a conscience.

8. Talent—Wise salespeople know their abilities and talents and continually strive to train, expand, and improve them.

9. Character—The word of some salespeople is greater than the bond of others. Character is so dominant and self-evident that it needs no advertising.

10. Originating—A salesperson's foremost duty is to point out to prospects new joys and possibilities. Salespeople originate new visions and sell through them.[2]

Case in Point

The Right Clothes Are No Substitute for the Right Words

A young man wrote Ann Landers as follows:

> I am a salesperson who is having problems getting purchasing agents to pay attention to what I tell them. I dress properly, am clean and neat, always wear a fairly new suit, and polished shoes and my socks match my ties. I even wear an expensive watch and yet no one seems to pay any attention to my sales pitch. Why?

Ann Landers answered:

> Perhaps you don't say anything the customer is interested in!

What Separates Successful from Unsuccessful Salespeople[3]

Selling will remain a profession of risk and reward. As the risk remains relatively high (compared to, for example, that faced by an accountant), the rewards will also remain high. Sales professionals will have the opportunity to make a substantial living as long as there are customers who need products and services. However, you can reduce the risk and increase the reward if you know what it takes to be successful and particularly what customers and sales managers are looking for in a salesperson.

Today's successful salesperson and definitely the salespeople of the future will need greater analytical and interpersonal skills than ever before. The emergence of more and more sophisticated computer hardware and software will require salespeople to have advanced technical knowledge. The ability to call up, analyze, and use information to satisfy the buyer's needs will become more specific. This means sales representatives and sales managers will have to become more specialized within the sales function. More vendors will focus in on specific customers by developing salespeople with greater knowledge of specialized products, markets, and customers.

Salespeople will also be encouraged to spend more time with decision makers in developing stronger personal bonds as a method of increasing sales. Thus, the demand for increased productivity will require greater personal and professional goal orientation.

What Do Buyers Want in a Salesperson?

You may hear statements like "salespeople are born, not made" or that a person is a "natural-born salesman." This simply is not true. What makes someone successful in sales is being able to satisfy the buyers and help them solve problems. Let's examine a recent study in which 205 purchasing agents revealed their likes and dislikes. The results are in Table 2-1. The boxed item titled "Salespeople Speak Back" has the responses of salespeople to the survey. It makes for an interesting comparison.

Determinants of Success in Sales

Attributes that distinguish successful salespeople from the unsuccessful ones are noted in Figure 2-1 on page 37. The first and maybe the most important of these for a salesperson is oral and written communications skills.

Oral and Written Communication Skills Selling is a business of communicating, and the most effective communicators will be the most successful salespeople. Some people feel more comfortable communicating on a one-to-one basis; others prefer getting up in front of groups. Sales offers opportunities for both. One thing is certain, success in persuading and convincing customers, managers, and other people who interact with salespeople hinges on the ability to talk with and listen to people. Being a good communicator reflects self-confidence, another characteristic of successful salespeople.

Self-confidence Self-confidence comes from knowing you can handle the situation at hand. It is the result of training and experience. One common reason people give for not considering a sales career is that they do not think they can sell. With the right training, anyone can learn to sell and become self-confident in doing it. Research has repeatedly shown that self-esteem and self-confidence directly relate to selling success. People who *think* they *can* be successful will be successful. Nothing creates self-confidence and

◄ ◄ ◄ ◄ ◄ ◄ ◄ ◄
Learning Objective 1: Determinants of success in selling

Table 2-1   **What Purchasing Agents Like and Dislike about Salespeople**[4]

What Customers Like	What Customers Do Not Like
Reliability/credibility	*Specific comments:*
Professionalism/integrity	"No follow-up"
Product knowledge	"Not making appointments"
Innovative problem solving	"Begins calls by talking sports"
Presentation/preparation	"Puts competitor's products down"
Specific Comments:	"Poor listening skills"
"Honesty"	"Too many phone calls"
"Lose a sale graciously"	"Lousy reputation"
"Admits mistakes"	"Fails to ask about my needs"
"Problem solving capabilities"	"Lacks product knowledge"
"Friendly but professional"	"Wastes my time"
"Dependable"	
"Adaptable"	
"Knows my business"	
"Well prepared"	
"Patient"	

Source: Anonymous, "PAS Examine the People Who Sell to Them," *Sales and Marketing Management* 135 (1985): 40–41.

self-esteem more than a completed sale. Successful salespeople usually do what failures will not do.

Problem Analysis Skills   Selling revolves around solving problems. The better a person is at determining what the problem is, why it occurred, and what solutions are possible, the better that person will be able to offer innovative solutions. In most selling situations, the problems you might expect to encounter fall into a reasonably predictable distribution. Your ability to recognize the problem (and that you may have dealt with it before) and offer a creative solution makes you valuable to both your company and your customer.

Creativity is an essential part of being successful. It means being innovative. Often, simply putting combinations of products or services together in innovative ways is enough. Innovative delivery schedules or packaging may also do the trick. Creativity can be learned, but many people confuse creativity and inspiration. There are steps you can take to increase your creativity.

Generating ideas, the basis for creative problem solving, can be broken into five steps:[5]

Learning Objective 2: Steps to creative problem solving

1. *Gather raw material.* Raw material is the research done on clients and their problems. It is also the reservoir of experiences salespeople have developed through their dealings with similar clients or situations.

2. *Work over the raw material in your mind.* Think about what the problem is, what you already know, and what you have gathered through research.

3. *Incubate.* In this stage, wipe the entire matter from your conscious mind. Let your subconscious take over. Do whatever stimulates your imagination: go to a movie, listen to music, and so on.

Figure 2-1

4. *Get the idea*. If you have done the first three steps, you can almost bet that at least one idea will emerge. Usually, though, many more pop up!

5. *Implementation*. Write your idea down so you can see it in front of you, then determine how it might be implemented. During this stage, the idea is modified to its final form.

People lack creativity because they do not gather enough raw material or because they try to force ideas. They get stymied by shortsightedness in

Trade journals can be a valuable source of raw material for generating ideas.

forming the innovative combinations of alternatives or new relationships. Many people have difficulty even thinking of alternatives, which can be a tremendous source of innovation. Think of innovativeness as constructing a building—every architect chooses from among the same materials: bricks, steel, glass, concrete, and so on. New and exciting structures result from innovative ways of combining the same old materials.

Six Methods for Creative Inspiration[6]

The following are some suggestions on generating creative inspiration from Derry Daly, a past manager for the J. Walter Thompson advertising agency:

▶ **Put yourself in the prospect's position.** Try to think like the prospect and ask yourself: "What makes this product different from its competitor's? Why should I be interested? What benefits does the product or service offer?" Ask your prospect, "If you could have any feature on this product, what would it be?"

▶ **Talk to friends or associates who are prospects for a product.** When developing material for the Marine Corps to recruit high schools students, I consistently try to talk to 17- and 18-year-old boys to understand their interests, attitudes, and way of stating things.

▶ **Learn from other salespersons.** There are a surprising number of ways to do the same thing. Innovation is often the result of adapting someone else's way of doing something to your situation.

▶ **Try to use the client's product or service.** Personal experience with the client's product, if possible, can produce a number of insights much quicker than having someone tell you what it does, how it tastes, and so on.

▶ **Meet with the client's customers.** They are often a source of new insights about the product or company that can be useful in generating new ideas.

▶ **When you get stuck, reexamine the problem.** Something may have been overlooked, misinterpreted, oversimplified, or overemphasized.

Planning and Organizational Skills   For most field salespeople, planning and organizational skills center around managing time. Successful salespeople are able to allocate and plan their time to get the most from it. Nick DiBari retired at the age of 39 from COMDISCO. He earned over $7 million in commissions between 1976 and 1983. His commissions totaled over $1.3 million alone in 1983. DiBari said, "Usually, it (time management) is the last thing salespeople work on. They just show up for a call and open their book. They are not prepared and the customers know it. Identify target accounts, then identify monthly objectives, then design a weekly itinerary. Finally, get it down to each day. My rule was that the whole working day would be spent calling on customers, which meant that paperwork was reserved for nights and weekends. When I began selling, I would start my day off at 8:00 A.M. by writing on a yellow pad. I would list my sales calls, and under each, I'd write every question I could think of related to that customer's needs and problems. Once in the door, I would not leave until I had all my questions answered."[7]

Enthusiasm and Persuasiveness   Enthusiasm is a strong excitement for an activity. It is effusive and contagious. Enthusiastic people get customers enthused. It has been said that "enthusiasm is the *outward* expression of an *inner* desire." Enthusiasm creates a general level of excitement conducive to closing sales. It is a bulwark against rejection. Enthusiastic salespeople persist and establish themselves with all but the most difficult customers. This leads to more sales and greater confidence, two items shown to be powerful motivators to success.

Enthusiastic salespeople create enthusiasm among their fellow salespeople. They help bolster morale and motivate their co-workers, which in turn creates a better working environment. Research has shown that morale, motivation, and a positive work environment are directly related to job satisfaction and sales performance. Individual salespeople, as well as customers and co-workers benefit from enthusiasm.

Salespeople must be enthusiastic about their products, company, and themselves. Customers prefer to deal with someone who is enthusiastic. Can enthusiasm be taught? The answer is yes! Good training and confidence in how the product and services benefit customers ultimately result in enthusiastic salespeople and customers.

Persuasiveness sways opinions or attitudes. Salespeople convince prospects that the benefits of making a purchase outweigh the costs. Salespeople must be skillful at convincing buyers to at least listen and consider what they have to say. Clearly, persuasiveness and enthusiasm are related.

Empathy   Empathy is being able to put yourself in other people's shoes and see the problem from their perspective. Empathy is understanding customers' problems, their industry and its problems, and their personal stake in the decision at hand. Let's look at an example. Many people buy IRAs (individual retirement accounts). Some buy them for savings and security, some for tax avoidance. Since the tax law was changed a few years ago, more people are buying IRAs for savings than for tax avoidance. The salesperson must discover the buyer's motives. Clearly, if you are empathetic, you understand the problem from the customer's viewpoint and can tailor your solution to that customer's specific need. If customers want the benefits of tax avoidance from an IRA, then selling them on the benefits of savings and security will not satisfy them. Sell them on the benefits of tax avoidance. Understanding the benefits they want and expect to receive is the result of empathizing with them.

Salespeople Speak Back[8]

In Table 2-1, we learned what purchasing agents liked and disliked about salespeople. But what do salespeople have to say about it? The ones *Sales and Marketing Management* magazine contacted, like their purchasing counterparts, were surprised at some responses, expected others, and were more than willing to comment on them.

Continued

Continued—"There still is the car-salesman, insurance-salesman image," says Kathe Sparacino, executive director of Sales and Marketing Executives of Los Angeles, reacting to the list of offensive sales characteristics. "But the old aggressive types are on their way out."

The "pushy" salesperson, she says, is usually the poorly trained and poorly educated one whose idea of a good selling technique is getting a foot in the door. "Selling is more than just asking for the order, and the newer groups of salespeople are turning this image around."

Like the others, former president of the Sales and Marketing Club of Philadelphia Lou Nolan was not surprised that reliability/credibility and professionalism/integrity were one and two and theorizes that they were ranked so high because buyers found them lacking in salespeople. "A lot of buyers have a low opinion of salespeople," he says.

The real surprise to him, however, was the comparatively low marks given to product knowledge. "If a salesman doesn't have product knowledge, what does he have?"

Others agreed but said that product knowledge is not a black-and-white issue. Says Turner Warmack, vice president, sales, Ziegler Tool, an Atlanta distributor, "That all depends on what you're selling; if it's a commodity, you obviously don't need it."

Gerald Clapp, eastern region manager for the Neenah Division of Kimberly-Clark, feels that buyers think product knowledge is important but find other qualities even more pressing. "They [buyers] probably feel that if a salesman has integrity, he's O.K." However, he adds, it's not just, "O.K." for his salespeople." If they don't have it they're gone."

The personality paradox was not surprising to salespeople. They expect buyers to give personality a low rating, yet complain about the types of salespeople with whom they have to work.

"It's like dating," says Judy Buckley, a sales manager with Marriott, Stamford, Connecticut. "When you ask people, they always say it's a good personality and sense of humor they want. They'll never say it's looks!"

Adaptability Salespeople must be able to adapt to each selling situation they face. Let's look at an example of how this might occur. If you were sell-

Case in Point

What Students Think Are the Most Desirable and Undesirable Personal Qualities for a Salesperson

A professor in the marketing department of a leading university in Columbus, Ohio, started teaching a class in "Professional Salesmanship" in 1976. At the first class meeting of each trimester, he asked the students to list what they believed were the personal qualities for success in selling and what aspect of selling as a career they believed was the most difficult or most undesirable.

From 1976 to 1988, over 900 students told the professor what they thought of selling as a career. The chart below lists the top ten most-mentioned personal qualities and most difficult aspects.

Continued

ing cars to individuals, you would certainly go about it differently than if you were selling a fleet of cars to Hertz. Similarly, you might use different tactics in selling to Hertz than you would use in selling to Avis. And, to carry this one step further, you might even use different tactics when selling to different buyers from Hertz.

Successful salespeople must be able to "read" the signs sent by prospective buyers and their surroundings. After reading the signs, salespeople must adapt their selling techniques to fit the situation. This means always being prepared for any circumstance, being ready with a solution, innovative idea, or unique approach to fit the situation.

▶ ▶ *follow-up questions*

1. In your estimation, what is the major determinant of success in selling?

2. Why is being adaptable so important?

What Would You Do If...?

As part of the sales team in an insurance agency, your tasks involve selling policies and servicing existing policyholders. Today, your manager asked you to go to the local college and interview seniors for a position that has just opened in your agency. This is the first time you will have done anything like this. To begin, you sit down with a tablet and plan out what questions you will ask and what attributes you want in the new employee.

▶ Questions: What attributes would you look for?
▶ How much information regarding these attributes would come from the resumé and how much would have to come from the interview?

Success in Sales—"The Foundational Principles"[9]

▶ ▶ ▶ ▶ ▶ ▶ ▶ ▶ ▶ ▷
Learning Objective 3:
Principles of successful selling

The relationship between salespeople and customers should be based on the principles of specialization, creating niches, and differentiation. Salespeople accomplish this by providing top-quality customer service, being extraordinarily responsive, creating the perception of uniqueness, and being obsessed with listening.

Specialize, Create Niches, and Add Value

Successful salespeople strive to create the perception of being specialists. Customers come to depend on salespeople's expertise in solving problems when salespeople are creative, responsive, and customer-oriented, when they create the notion that "We are the ones that *specialize* in solving your specific type of problem."

Case in Point

Selling a Special Service Becomes a Full-time Business

Angelica Martinez, a camera store salesperson for about three years, became interested in photography. She developed considerable skill in outdoor photography, especially taking pictures of people engaged in sports. She had some success photographing boys and girls at summer camps, which employed her to do this. Angelica's work had been excellent, and soon she wanted to be a full-time "camp photographer," establish a reputation, and employ other photographers to offer this service nationally.

Angelica is now on contract with over ten camps to teach young people how to properly use a camera. She also provides a camcorder to teach picture composition.

Comment: This is an example of creating customers by providing a service never before offered. Selling can serve customers' needs.

Creating superior service has meant big money in selling services.

Successful salespeople are constantly seeking to create new market niches. They hunt for new customers who could be but are not, using their products. They hunt for new ways to use and sell products to existing and potential customers (which, of course, opens entirely new markets that competitors have not thought of!).

Don Beaver of the New Pig Corporation took corn cobs and created a multimillion dollar business with them. He found that ground cobs are tremendously absorbent and that, stuffed in a cloth "sock," they could be used to absorb chemical spills. He opened a niche, and his product is now comfortably ensconced in a thriving and growing market.

Many salespeople are blind to features that can add to a product's value. For example, suppose you are selling yellow forklifts. The creative salesperson emphasizes the color as an advantage over the competitor's gray machine. The benefits of a yellow forklift? Simple, it is easier to see, which is likely to reduce accidents. And that means fewer insurance claims, less damaged merchandise or equipment, and lower operating costs! By using the color as a benefit, the salesperson created value, justified the price, and gave the buyer one more reason to buy. The unsuccessful salesperson probably would not even pay attention to something as simple as color.

Provide Top Quality as Perceived by the Customer

What can a salesperson do about the quality of the product or service? Salespeople enhance the perception of quality through the caliber of their presentations. Being prepared and organized, having anticipated questions, using visuals to demonstrate benefits, listening, and being genuinely concerned for the customer all enhance the quality of a presentation. Can a salesperson enhance the quality of the product itself? The answer is yes. Customers provide feedback on the product's performance—or lack of it. Listening to a customer saying, "What I'd like to see is a machine that would . . ." and communicating this to engineers or designers can result in improved performance. Through such indirect intelligence, products get developed, improved, and modified for new applications. Salespeople have a direct impact on and input to improving the quality of products.

Provide Superior Service and Emphasize Intangibles[10]

Customers perceive superior service as the ratio between what they expected and what they experienced. Customers' experience, and therefore their perception of superior service, can be enhanced by the salesperson doing the little things, using callbacks, underpromising and overdelivering, and treating customers as appreciating assets.

First, little things mean a lot. AT&T instituted a "thank you for using AT&T" campaign. Why did it have to wait for competition to force it into saying thank you? Other little things that can create and hold a customer, besides saying thanks, include returning phone calls the same day, trying to help customers even if it means referring them to a competitor, and using good telephone manners.

Callbacks are powerful tools successful people use. A callback is simply keeping in touch. Good salespeople know the power of callbacks in creating customer loyalty and devotion. Callbacks communicate the salesperson's concern for, and specific interest in, the customer's well-being. Every call is made for a reason, sometimes for an important reason, sometimes not. Since the salesperson often has no way of knowing the reason, all calls must be treated as important. Taking the initiative to call a customer just to confirm an appointment, inquire about a product's performance, or check for possible problems communicates concern that buyers appreciate. Such concern nurtures the sense of partnership that is vital to strong buyer-seller relationships. Ruth Nilson, the purchasing agent for Copely Pharmaceuticals, says that she judges salespeople on their ability to follow up after the sale. She appreciates a salesperson who personally inspects shipments for quality and makes sure products are shipped on time, arrive on time, and are not damaged in transit.[11]

Underpromise and overdeliver is the opposite of what most unsuccessful salespeople practice. Lofty promises and apologetic deliveries are tantamount to death in sales. Successful salespeople promise what they *know* they can do, then deliver more than they promise.

Finally, treat the customer as an appreciating asset. The following example makes this point: "My little 25-person firm runs about a $1,500-a-month Federal Express bill. Over a ten-year period, that will add up to $180,000.... If our courier has 40 regular stops at businesses my size (which would be normal), she is managing each day a 'portfolio' of customers worth 40 times $180,000, or...over $7 million in ten years."[12] Successful salespeople know the value of customers: they are and should be treated as appreciating assets.

Be Extraordinarily Responsive

Being totally responsive to customers requires viewing them as partners in progress. Being extraordinarily responsive means treating every customer inquiry, request, or question as though it is an emergency. Treat customers as though your business life depends on it because it does! In today's business world, firms are electronically linked to customers and production, delivery, and order-processing people. This allows instant access to vital information for extraordinarily fast response. Linking electronically with your customers allows you to respond to them better and differentiates you from competitors.

Even firms that cannot link up electronically can be extraordinarily responsive. Setting response-time targets is a first step. Establishing goals based on customer input can build relationships through service customization and catering to the customer's actual needs. Responsiveness goals for order processing, delivery, product alterations, repairs, and claim resolution improve response times and build customer loyalty.

Create the Perception of Uniqueness

"Can you state your uniqueness in 25 words or less? Test the level of agreement, randomly and regularly with … employees, suppliers, distributors and customers. Is your uniqueness, as practiced day to day, clear to all of these participants in your business?"[13] Successful salespeople and their company should be able to clearly distinguish what makes them and their offering unique. After all, if you cannot tell a customer how you are different, how and why should the customer distinguish you from competitors?

Be Obsessed with Listening

Successful salespeople are good listeners. They let the customer talk and ask questions. They listen with their brains, concentrating on what is being said—not thinking about what they are going to say next, when they are scheduled for their next appointment, or what else they have on their day's agenda. They pay attention. Try a simple test: As you sit in class, take notes and tape record the instructor's lecture. After class, ask three classmates about some particular point in the lecture. You'll probably find three different interpretations, or confusion, and one may not even remember the point being made. In a sales situation, if these three classmates were salespeople, each would have solved the same problem differently. How many "right" solutions would have resulted? Which one would have really satisfied the customer's need? Being obsessed with listening requires paying attention and asking for explanations if something is not clear.

> If You Don't Pay Attention …
>
> … You'll Never Learn.

You Only Do Business with Your Friends—Gaining the Customer's Trust

You only do business with your friends. Business is conducted on a basis of trust, mutual respect, and give-and-take, like a friendship. Trust is built up through a series of interactions between salespeople and buyers. Trustworthiness depends on the experiences between buyer and seller, the salesperson's ability to provide accurate information quickly, the ability of the salesperson to influence the selling firm on the buyers' behalf, the salesperson's abilities do what was promised, and the buyer's trust in the seller's firm.[14] Let's expand on these and develop some guidelines.

◄ ◄ ◄ ◄ ◄ ◄ ◄ ◄
Learning Objective 4:
Guidelines for building trust

> Guideline 1—The more positive interactions buyers and sellers have, regardless of the size or magnitude, the greater the trust that is developed.

Murata Beats Fujitsu with the Right Attitude and Being Flexible

Murata is not a household name in the copier business—or in the facsimile machine business, for that matter. A company less than twenty years old, it is now making headway through such aggressive dealers as R. Michael Franz's Murata Business Systems based in Dallas, Texas. Sales of facsimile machines are not overwhelming. Franz says three or four machines sold to any one company is a good order and dealers go crazy if an order for 100 or more machines ever appears.

A big sale for Franz was an 800-machine order (at $2,200 each) to Sir Speedy, a franchise printing company. Fujitsu was the leader for Sir Speedy's business. In fact, Sir Speedy had 18 Fujitsu machines installed in Southern California outlets on a test basis. Franz managed to get a meeting with Don Lowe, CEO of Sir Speedy. The night before the first meeting, Franz held a meeting with the team that would visit Lowe the next morning. "Going into the first meeting," says Franz, "we realized we had to quickly understand what situation they were in and what their plans were for putting the network in place. The first impression was absolutely essential. There would be no second meeting if the one didn't go well."

Bill McCue, consultant to Lowe, says, "Fujitsu's problem was attitudinal. Their equipment is basically the same and in the same price range, but there was such a difference between the two (Fujitsu and Murata) in working out solutions to price breaks and support, I had to reassess my evaluation of Fujitsu. Fujitsu's management people who came to close the deal—not the salespeople we had been dealing with and who were doing a good job—would either not acknowledge there was a problem, saying 'No problem, no problem,' or ignore it and go on to another feature of their equipment. Murata's attitude was, 'What's the problem? Let's solve it.'"

Murata got the order for over $1.7 million. Why did Lowe go with Murata? "Several things: One, I liked the people. There are a lot of fax machines out there, all manufactured in Japan. All specifications look the same, sound the same, read the same. You can pick any price point you want and you can find at least ten or twelve machines with the same specs for the same price. What we looked for was a company we thought would shoot straight. Since we do not know a heck of a lot about the facsimile business, we were looking for someone who would share their expertise with us, and after meeting with the people at Murata, we thought they would do that."

As for Fujitsu blowing the deal, Lowe says, "I think Fujitsu could have done everything we wanted them to, but they would not. They were not that flexible."

*Source: Liz Murphy, "Building a Million-Dollar Business Deal at the Last Minute," *Sales and Marketing Management Magazine,* 40 (1988): 36–41.

Obviously, the experiences between buyers and sellers are important. Successful salespeople know they actually teach buyers to trust them through their actions. In a recent study, the salesperson's dependability was found to be the most important factor in building trust between buyers and sellers.[15]

Case in Point

Courtesy Always Contributes to a Positive Interaction

Marisa just returned from a tour of Europe. A friend asked to see her pictures. Marisa checked her projector and found she needed a new lamp. She went to a neighborhood photo shop and asked the clerk, "Do you have a new lamp like this one?" The clerk said yes and took one from the shelf. Marisa asked the clerk the price of the lamp. The clerk said, "Twenty-four dollars."

Marisa said, "Twenty-four dollars!!!!—the last one I bought was only $14, and I thought that was high!" The clerk said, "Well, do you want it or not?" Marisa said, "I have no choice! I have 300 slides to show and no light source. I also need a slide tray. Do you have any?"

The clerk handed Marisa three 98-slide trays and said, "Cash or charge?" He took Marisa's credit card and ran it through the machine, and Marisa left the store with her purchases, grumbling as she went.

Marisa sat in her car for a few moments reflecting on what had just transpired. She was not happy.

Comment: Why was Marisa unhappy? What did the clerk do to create an unfriendly customer? Remembering that customers return to stores based on what they experienced the first time, do you think Marisa would be likely to go back? Would you? The clerk lost this customer, but even worse, Marisa will no doubt tell her friends about the experience.

Guideline 2—Constantly study and learn about your product, industry, competitors, and customers. Seek all the professional certifications in your field.

The greater the ability of the salesperson to provide accurate and timely information to the buyer, the greater the attribution of trust. Some suggest that buyers attribute this ability to the salespeople's formal education, company training and technical support, years of experience with their company, product, and/or industry, and certification or licensing where appropriate. Charles Romono, purchasing director for Okonite Company, a New Jersey manufacturer of cable and wire, says smart salespeople make the most of the information Okonite's purchasing agents provide. By knowing more about Okonite, they can know how to provide the best service. Romono says most sellers are order takers, not professional salespeople. Most do not fully understand their own products or how Okonite uses them. Anyone can come in and ask for the order; it takes a *salesperson* to offer new services, applications, and cost savings.[16]

Guideline 3—Promise what you know you can do and do what you promise.

Gaining a customer's trust is the result of doing what you promise. The greater the consistency and reliability the buyer sees, the greater the trust (and, of course, business). Buyers not only observe the ability of salespeople to do what they promise, but they also distinguish between the accomplishment of regular tasks and emergency services. Buyers develop trust much more quickly in salespeople who always come through in the clutch. Salespeople who perform well at the regular business but drop the ball in emergencies become little more than residual suppliers. Paul Taxworth, who buys for Hotsy Corporation, a $30-million-a-year cleaning equipment manufacturer, says good salespeople are ones you can give a list to and the job gets done. They get back to you and make sure it happens. Where there is a problem with delivery, quality, or design, the salesperson is there to make the necessary corrections.[17]

Successful salespeople catch on quickly to what distinguishes success from failure, and they usually find it amounts to simple things that are easily overlooked. Remember, not everyone is successful in sales, but everyone can be successful if he or she *really* wants to strongly enough.

in 1982. In the past five years, Paul has held various positions in sales and sales management, starting with retail sales specialist in Houston and moving to account executive and retail unit manager in Jacksonville, Florida, before his present position.

One of the key reasons Paul joined Black & Decker was its commitment to employee development.

Paul believes that for any salesperson to be successful, he or she must have two things. The first is product knowledge. The customer relies heavily on the expertise of the salespeople when making a decision to buy. They must have the right product to meet their customers' needs and job applications. At Black & Decker, the goal is to make every sales representative a "power tool expert" through classroom as well as on-the-job training. Black & Decker salespeople out there selling power tools and accessories know that to get ahead of the competition, they must offer customers better service, and through product knowledge, they do just that.

The second thing a salesperson must have to be successful is selling skills. These skills include how to communicate and listen effectively and how to make presentations. The bottom line is that each salesperson must have the skills necessary to both sell and manage his or her territory effectively. At Black & Decker, Paul and the other trainers spend a good deal of their time training salespeople not only on how to sell the company's products to the accounts but also on how they can help their accounts sell the product through to the end user.

Black & Decker's commitment to the development of its sales force is just one example of how it is putting its theme, "The Customer Is King," to work.[18]

▶ ▶ *follow-up questions*

1. List the principles discussed in this section.

2. Which of the principles of success do you think is the most important to a real estate salesperson? To a retail salesperson? To a salesperson for a textbook publisher?

3. Can you think of situations you have experienced when one of the guidelines for building trust has been broken? How did you feel when it happened? How did you react? If it was in a buying situation, how did it affect your future relations with the salesperson or the firm?

Dress for Success—Is Appearance All That Important?

The answer is most definitely yes. Salespeople must make two sales. They sell themselves first and their product or service second. Can this person be trusted? Does this person appear to be honest? Do I relate to this person? Would I want to do business with someone who looks like that? What kind of a company would let their salespeople dress like that? Regardless of how

Dressing appropriately means fitting into the customer's environment but always remembering you carry the firm's image.

much we try to be liberal and tolerant, we still base our first impressions on how a person looks and acts. If you are asking strangers to buy a product from you, you are asking them to take a risk—to give up their money on a chance of making more or saving more. A big portion of any selling job is to convince customers to take the risk, and this means they must trust the salesperson. As irrational as it may seem, people seem to trust people who *look trustworthy*. Clothing and grooming make up the image you project for yourself and your firm. To the customer, you *are* your company.

Appearance is how salespeople package themselves. Clothing communicates both the firm's and salespeople's overall image. The key word in dressing for success is appropriateness. Generally, a good rule to follow is dress like your customers would expect you to dress. Another rule is simply when in doubt, err on the conservative side, rather than the extravagant side. When asked one day about the reason IBM stressed conservative dress, a salesperson said, "It's hard enough to sell computers. There are more than enough hurdles to jump in making the sale; trying to overcome a bad first impression because of your clothes is something we just do not need."

The appropriate dress for salespeople is set by two standards: the customer's and the company's. These are seldom far apart. "All people with money and power act, walk, talk, and dress in the same style," says John Molloy, the author of *Dress for Success* (Warner, 1975). "There is very little difference at the top," he says.[19]

Women in sales have a greater degree of latitude, but the message is still the same. From a survey of 6,000 women in business, Michael Solomon and Susan Douglas of New York University concluded that "looking right" means being comfortable, accepted, and approved of. They emphasize being conservatively fashionable, rather than exceptionally stylish or trendy.[20] Jewelry and makeup should be stylish but conservative. Overdoing these defeats the image you are trying to convey. This does not mean you have to take the "plain Jane" approach; it simply means moderation is best.

Dress Codes at Work: Admit It or Not, They Exist

When Jeff Leston was a salesman at IBM, no one told him the company had a dress code, but, he said, "You got the message." So he dressed in dark suits, conservative ties, and white shirts with button-down collars. "Your collars couldn't be too long or too short," Mr. Leston said.

Then came the day he rebelled. His boss eyed the blue shirt Mr. Leston had chosen to wear and said, "Jeff, are you selling to the Air Force this morning?"

"There are ways to apply pressure to people," said Mr. Leston, who is now a financial management consultant.

"If you are in a service business, the client wants to feel you can be trusted," said Jerry Fields, president of Jerry Fields Associates, an advertising and executive search firm. "In business in general, in banking, insurance, steel, automobiles, the image is set by top management, not in writing, not by edict, but by everyone saying 'Do as they do. Let's not make waves.' "

Source: Michael Gross, "Dress Codes at Work: Admit It or Not, They Exist," *New York Times,* 15 January 1986. Reprinted with permission.

▶ ▶ *follow-up questions*

1. Does appearance contribute to the customer's perception of a salesperson's trustworthiness? Explain.

2. John Molloy was quoted in this section from his first book on dressing for success written in 1975. Do you think his words still hold true today? Discuss why or why not.

3. Do you believe the dress code for women is more liberal than that for men? Why or why not?

Training Makes Salespeople Successful

Salespeople are not born; they are trained. Selling is a learned skill. You learned to throw a ball, play the piano, drive a car, and get through school. Selling takes training, observing, trying, making mistakes, and trying again until it becomes second nature.

Firms spend on the average $3,737 on training per salesperson, and many spend $10,000 or more. They invest both money and time. In a survey of 1,554 companies, large companies (sales over $500 million) reported their median training cost was $3,673 per person. Smaller companies (sales under $25 million) had a median training expense of $976 per person. Figure 2-2 shows the median amount spent on training by small through large firms.[21]

Figure 2-2

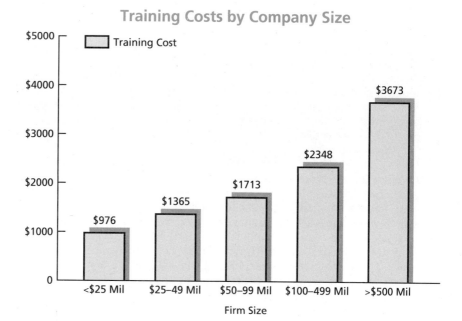

Training Costs by Company Size

Source: William Keenan, Jr., "Are You Overspending on Training?"
Sales and Marketing Management 142 (1990): 58.

B–Practical

Competence and confidence comes with training. Anyone can be successful in selling if he or she remembers the following acronym: *B-PRACTICAL*

B..Basic techniques

PR..PRactice the basic techniques

A..Analyze failures and successes

C..Change behavior: use what works, avoid what doesn't

T..Try again

I..Improve

C..Commit to success

AL..Allow time for learning

B..Basic Techniques   Basic selling techniques involve prospecting, qualifying, making presentations, handling objections, and closing. These are all taught during sales training. As athletes know, mastering the basics is essential before a player progresses to the more elaborate techniques. Sales training programs give the novice a foundation in these basic skills—without which there is no base of support for later success. Many books, training programs, and seminars on basic sales techniques are available for novice and experienced salespeople.

PR..PRactice the Basic Techniques   Practice is essential. Practice creates memory: getting the "feel" of what is right and doing it without thinking. Practice does not mean doing it until you get it right; it means doing it right until you get it. Practice is essential, but there is no substitute for the real

Training builds
competence and
confidence.

thing. People give up selling because they do not give it enough on-the-job practice. Successful salespeople never stop practicing. They practice the basics, they practice new techniques, they break in new types of openings, closings, and ways of presenting the same product. They are continually looking for improvement and an edge to make more sales.

A.. Analyze Failures and Successes   Analyzing successes and failures is the key to learning. Studying the failures highlights what *not* to do. Studying the successes reinforces what to repeat. Salespeople analyze successes and failures so when they make a presentation that does not seem to be going right, they can adopt plan B, and if that does not work, they can turn to plan C, and so on.

C.. Change Behavior: Use What Works, Avoid What Doesn't   Changing behavior in the face of success or failure is a mark of the successful person. After trying a variety of selling techniques, successful salespeople change their behaviors to take advantage of what was learned through analyzing their successes and failures. Companies constantly work to change the behaviors of their salespeople because customers and markets are constantly changing. What worked yesterday may not work today, so selling techniques and the manner in which they are applied must be continually updated.

T.. Try Again   Successful salespeople never accept failure. Sure, they have disappointments, but they look on them as simply sales for a later date or the result of something traceable and correctable. A successful salesperson once said she got nine no's for every one yes. With each no, she got one step closer to a yes. Soon, the no's are out of the way with nothing but yesses remaining.

I.. Improve   Improvement is the goal all good salespeople strive for. It is best accomplished by setting small achievable goals; successful salespeople do not try to improve on everything at once but rather take it one step at a time.

C.. Commit to Success   Commitment is the cornerstone of success in selling. Wanting success is the driving force in all outstanding salespeople.

Think of it this way: if you do not commit to success, then you are automatically committing to the opposite, which spells failure in sales or anything else.

AL..Allow for Learning   Allow time for learning. Success comes from practice, mistakes, and analysis. It takes time for all of these to occur, and a significant cause of turnover in young salespeople is simply that they do not give themselves enough time.

What Does a Good Training Program Teach?

Selling is a skill, a craft that anyone can learn. Training programs differ between firms. Figure 2-3 indicates the results of the annual *Sales and Marketing Management* magazine survey about training. New salespeople selling industrial or consumer products should expect training programs to last three to six months.[22] The figure shows the average training periods for new hires in several industries.

▶ ▶ ▶ ▶ ▶ ▶ ▶ ▶ ▶
Learning Objective 5: What you learn in sales training

"The focus of a sales training program is likely to be the actual 'selling,' that is, helping salespeople identify methods that will effectively result in sales. The most useful kind of knowledge is detailed knowledge of sales situations, customers and selling procedures."[23] Training programs have at least four modules. The largest is product knowledge. Next is selling techniques. Third is market or industry orientation, and last is company policies.

Product Knowledge Module   Product knowledge involves how the product is made, how it functions, typical problems it might have, and why it is designed as it is. Product knowledge is essential if a buyer's questions are to be accurately answered. Product knowledge also involves knowing similar information about competitor's products. Salespeople who know as much about the competitor's products as their own can make comparisons and show their product's superiority.

Figure 2-3

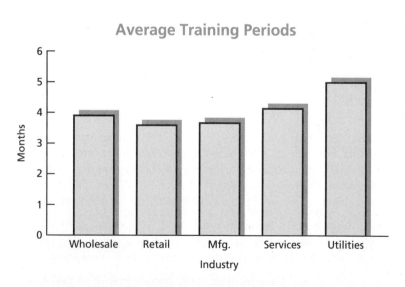

Average Training Periods

Source: Complied from *Sales and Marketing Management* 142 (1990): 81.

Selling Techniques Module   Selling techniques center on such things as approaches, presentation styles, objection-handling techniques, and closing methods. As the selling environment changes, new strategies and techniques will result from the pressures of industry trends. Table 2-2 identifies future trends that will affect selling techniques.

Industry or Market Orientation Module   In orienting salespeople to their industry or market, the size and growth of the market, the potential in the market, and the trainee's firm's market position are commonly discussed. Trainees learn about their competitors' market strength and how they are positioned. The economics of the industry—for example, its normal cycles, whether it has seasonal sales, and how changes in government regulations would affect it—is another favorite topic.

Company Policy and Procedures Module   Companies establish policies to guide employees in selling, to govern intracompany activities, and to regulate their relationships with customers and competitors. Trainees learn about potential legal and ethical issues, such as customer requests that violate laws or company policy. Ignorance of the rules or the law is never an excuse. Laws have been enacted that guide pricing procedures, packaging and labeling, and the types of incentives or inducements salespeople can offer customers. Salespeople should know about these laws in general, at least enough to know when they *might be* in violation of them. Many firms rigorously test trainees on the rules and laws to ensure adequate familiarity.

During the company policy and procedures module, trainees learn about the ever-present forms and paperwork. Order forms, claim forms, forms for returns and allowances, shipping manifests, call reports, expense reports, and insurance forms are but a sample of the necessary paperwork that accompanies a sale.

Table 2-2   Trends for the 1990s and Beyond[24]

Trend	Strategic Necessity
Increased Competition	Differentiate and distinguish; add value through service
Consolidated Buying Groups	Consultative and more team selling
Technological Breakthroughs	Dealing with a more sophisticated buyer; putting together groups of products to form solutions
Elongated Sales Cycles and Shortened Product Life Cycles	Greater need for product awareness, patience, persistence, and prospecting for new customers
Greater Service Orientation	More consultative selling and differentiation through services more than products
Deregulation	Greater competition in many industries; greater differentiation through service; price and value will be key issues in selling strategies; price shopping will increase

▶ ▶ *follow-up question*

1. Why do training programs stress product knowledge more than anything else?

Summary

Many factors influence success. Regardless of which sales career you choose, success depends on your oral and written communication skills, self-confidence, problem analysis skills, planning and organizational skills, enthusiasm and persuasiveness, empathy, and adaptability (Learning Objective 1).

Creativity is a precursor to success. The steps to stimulating the creative process are:

1. Gathering the raw material,
2. Working over that material in your mind,
3. Gestating the entire matter,
4. Getting the idea, and
5. Shaping and developing the idea into practical usefulness.

Industry knowledge and staying ahead of competitors, as well as keeping in tune with the customer's industry, are important for success. Trade associations and private and public publications are excellent sources of facts about your industry and your customer's (Learning Objective 2).

The seven principles for success are:

1. Specialize, create niches, and add value;
2. Provide top quality as perceived by the customer;
3. Provide superior service and emphasize the intangibles;
4. Be extraordinarily responsive;
5. Create the perception of uniqueness;
6. Be obsessed with listening; and
7. You only do business with your friends. (Learning Objective 3).

You must gain the customer's trust to be successful. Trust is built up through positive interactions, no matter how large or small. Trust also comes because the salesperson has the knowledge and expertise to handle the customer's problems. Finally, trust develops from never making promises that cannot be fulfilled (Learning Objective 4).

Dress is an important component of success, but appropriateness is the central issue, rather than any one style. There is no one best way to dress in selling because selling situations are so varied.

Training creates successful salespeople. The better the training program a salesperson goes through, the better are his or her chances of success. Training programs usually consist of four modules and are offered through classroom sessions, on the job, home study, and specialized classes. The four modules of most training programs cover a combination of product knowledge, selling skills, company policies and procedures, and industry or market orientation (Learning Objective 5).

Key Terms

Enthusiasm Enthusiasm is a strong excitement for an activity.

Empathy Empathy is being able to put yourself in the other people's shoes and see the problem from their perspective.

Product Knowledge Facts and operating characteristics of the product or services sold; a major component of sales training programs.

Company Policy The rules the company has established to guide its employees in selling and management tasks.

Discussion Questions

1. Why is dressing the part essential for success? What is appropriate dress?
2. What does it mean to say aptitude is "task specific"?
3. In the B-PRACTICAL acronym, what does the A stand for, and why is it so important?
4. When does sales training end for a salesperson?
5. The discussion of the seven principles of success included ways salespeople can improve their dealings with customers. Could one of these be considered as the *most important* principle? Discuss.
6. Can creativity be learned? Can it be enhanced? If so, how, and if not, why not?
7. What are the top five factors, in order, that sales managers look for as indicators of future success?
8. People come to rely on others they trust. What builds trust between a salesperson and customer, and how can a salesperson lose the trust of a customer?

Application Exercise

Go back into the chapter and reread the "When Things Go Right ..." about Murata and Fujitsu, then answer the following questions:

1. Which of the foundational principles did Fujitsu forget and Murata remember that made the difference between getting and losing the Sir Speedy account?
2. Was it interpersonal skill or technical skill that landed the Sir Speedy account for Murata?

Class Exercises

Group Exercise

In groups of three to six, discuss and record the group's responses to the phrase "Perception is reality" as it relates to:

▸ Ford versus Honda
▸ Personal resumés

- ▸ Getting a first date
- ▸ Insurance salespeople

Be aware that 1) each person has his or her own perceptions and 2) sales-people have to *adapt* to any situation.

Individual Presentation

You will prepare ahead to discuss the following:

1. Personal selling qualities successful salespeople must and must not have.
2. The most difficult aspects of professional selling from your point of view.
3. A plan for becoming successful in professional selling, given your answers in numbers 1 and 2 above.

Cases

Does the Resumé Reflect the Criteria?

Kelly Wexler is a sales rep for a direct-selling company. She recruits women of all ages and backgrounds to sell the firm's products. In general, she has done well. Some years, she has made over $53,000, and in a couple of bad years, she made in the twenties.

Kelly has developed a plan that has worked well for recruiting women more or less like herself. Kelly recruits through word of mouth and ads in the newspaper. Sometimes, people call her asking if she has an opening. Kelly now needs more people. Business has grown, and she finds herself in a dilemma: she needs more time for recruiting and more for selling. She has decided to use an employment agency to help her recruit new salespeople.

On Tuesday, she met with Mary Jenkins of the agency, who asked Kelly what kind of person she was looking for. Kelly said, "You know, someone with a lot of personality, excitement, and drive." Kelly had never done anything like this before and felt she knew what she was looking for but couldn't explain it very well. Mary gave Kelly a list of ten attributes often used by managers to evaluate salespeople and asked Kelly to rank them. Kelly handed her back the list shown below:

1. Enthusiasm	1
2. High verbal skills	4
3. Organized	8
4. Specific selling experience	2
5. Ambition	3
6. Recommendations	9
7. High persuasiveness	5
8. Follows instructions	7
9. General sales experience	6
10. Sociability	10

Mary had a resumé of a person she thought might work out and gave it to Kelly. The resume of Gail Bloomquist is shown here:

Gail Bloomquist
111 Cottonwood Plaza, P1
Minneapolis, MN   68164
402/490-3944

OBJECTIVE

A sales position with a growing firm where I can apply my extensive selling and human relations skills, ultimately leading to a sales management position.

QUALIFICATIONS IN BRIEF

— Demonstrated ability in planning/implementing programs.
—Strong organizational aptitude.
—Work effectively with wide range of personalities.
—Excellent written, verbal, and listening skills.

EDUCATION

| M.S. | University of Minnesota | 1986 |
| B.S. | University of Nebraska at Lincoln | 1981 |

PROFESSIONAL EXPERIENCE

Buyer, Midwest Fashion Stores
Minneapolis, MN, 1986–91.

—Analyzed sales and inventory records.
—Trained store personnel in selling and merchandising techniques.
—Planned and supervised promotions.

Assistant Manager/Sales Associate, Goldstein-Chapman Co.
St. Cloud, MN, 1981–1986.

—Interviewed, trained, and supervised 20-member sales staff.
—Communicated department business with management and central merchandising staff.
—Prepared weekly work schedule for sales staff.

REFERENCES WILL BE FURNISHED ON REQUEST

Questions

1. Does this resumé match the criteria set forth by Kelly?

2. How does this resumé show the factors most important to Kelly? Would this person have a good chance at being successful as one of Kelly's salespeople? Why or why not?

There's the Phone Book, Barry—Have at It!

Barry Williams recently graduated from business school and had just accepted his first selling job. He was excited as he began his first day on the job with a local firm that leases construction and heavy equipment. Though he had no background or experience with this type of equipment, he figured he could grow into the job, and the owner felt he could, too.

2.2

The company leased equipment such as graders, backhoes, ditchers, payloaders, and bulldozers to construction companies, contractors, and landscapers. It also leased such construction equipment as scaffolds, air compressors, and pneumatic equipment.

The owner greeted Barry on his first day and told him that his job would be to get the equipment leased, handle the paperwork on the leases, and take care of any customer problems. But, the owner told Barry, "your main job is to go out and get those long-term leases. Those are the ones that make us the most and what most of your bonus will be based on." When Barry looked around and saw nobody else in the office except a secretary, he asked how he was going to be trained to sell the leases. The owner looked at him out of the corner of his eye, reached down into his desk, and tossed Barry the phone book, saying, "There's your prospect list. Now go get 'em!" Three weeks later, Barry was looking for another job.

Questions

1. Why was Barry looking for another job so soon?
2. What was wrong with the training program?
3. How would you design a training program for this firm so that new salespeople would be successful?

References

1. Michael Gross, "Dress Codes at Work: Admit It or Not, They Exist," *New York Times,* 15 January 1986. Reprinted with Permission.
2. "Marshall Field's Ten Virtues of a Successful Salesperson," *Personal Selling Power,* 8 (1988): 31.
3. David J. Good, "Sales in the 1990's and Beyond: A Decade of Development," *Review of Business,* 12 (1990): 3–7.
4. Anonymous, "PAs Examine the People Who Sell to Them," *Sales and Marketing Management* 135 (1985): 40–41.
5. Derry Daly, "Direct Marketing Creativity—Minus the Mystique," *Direct Marketing Association Manual* (New York: Direct Marketing Association, Release 300.1, May 1979).
6. Ibid.
7. James A. Snyder, "What Made Supersalesman Nick DiBari Call It Quits?" *Sales and Marketing Management,* 132 (1984): 47–49.
8. *Sales and Marketing Management,* 135 (1985): 41.
9. The following discussion draws heavily upon and has been slightly modified from Tom Peters, *Thriving on Chaos* (New York: Alfred A. Knopf, 1988).
10. Ibid., p. 98.
11. Edith Cohen, "A View from the Other Side," *Sales and Marketing Management,* 142 (1990): 118.
12. Peters, *Thriving on Chaos,* pp. 98–99.
13. Ibid., p. 136.
14. John E. Swan et al., "Measuring Dimensions of Purchaser Trust of Industrial Salespeople," *Journal of Personal Selling and Sales Management,* 8 (1988): 1–10.
15. Ibid.
16. Cohen, "A View from the Other Side," pp. 108–14.
17. Ibid., p. 120.
18. Contributed by Paul Boitmann, 10 January 1988.
19. Gross, "Dress Codes at Work: Admit It or Not, They Exist."

20. Michael R. Solomon and Susan P. Douglas, "The Power of Pinstripes," *Savvy*, March 1983, pp. 59–62.
21. William Keenan, Jr., "Are You Overspending on Training?" *Sales and Marketing Management*, 142 (1990): 56–60.
22. This is based on the firms reporting to the *Sales and Marketing Management* magazine survey published in 1988. Variations will exist from year to year, depending on the number and types of firms reporting.
23. Barton A. Weitz, Harish Sujan, and Mita Sujan, "Knowledge, Motivation, and Adaptive Behavior: A Framework for Improving Selling Effectiveness," *Journal of Marketing*, 50 (October 1986): 174–91.
24. Anonymous, "Selling Today," *Training and Development Journal*, March 1988, pp. 38–41.

3 Communication Skills
Necessary for Success

Objectives

After completing this chapter, you will be able to:

1. Explain the communication process and its elements.

2. Define and give an example of selective decoding of messages.

3. Create more powerful sales presentations by using power words.

4. Identify the major elements of nonverbal communication.

5. Identify and know how to deal with body language cues that could occur during a presentation.

6. Develop strategies to react to various body language cues.

7. Define the elements of persuasive communication.

8. Explain how to build rapport with a prospective customer.

9. Discuss barriers to effective communication.

10. Categorize questions to help formulate an effective communication approach with a prospect.

11. Explain in detail the four social styles people exhibit and explain why knowing them is so important to making a successful sale.

The Professional Selling Question

How do good salespeople use their knowledge of nonverbal communication to make more and bigger sales?

A Salesperson Responds

Christine Christman, senior faculty member with Communique Exhibitor Education, Inc., feels body language is one of the most important communication tools a salesperson has. She says, "In his book *Texas*, James Michener describes an ancient Spanish tradition called *paseo*. It was a courting tradition where young men and women met their future partners. Here's how it works. The young people gathered in the town square with the women forming a circle in the open plaza. The young men form a concentric circle outside of the women's. The two pass one another in a parade-like fashion. The interesting thing about all of this is that the women and men *never* talk to one another. Conversation would be considered too forward. Instead, they could identify their interests through eye contact and nonverbal gestures.

"When I read that, my first thought was, 'Boy, is that ever archaic.' Then I began to think about some of the bars I went to in college and some of the parties I had attended. Don't we still use nonverbal communications in much the same way?

"Well, in a business setting, nonverbal communication, though used differently, is equally powerful. In selling, we use nonverbal communication to:

▶ Identify the customer's comfort level in the interaction.
▶ Evaluate his or her *real* interest in what we are selling.
▶ Tell us if the customer is in agreement with what has been said and if it is safe to proceed.
▶ Determine if it is time to close the sale.
▶ Tell us if we are probing a sensitive area.

"Typically, 93 percent of what is communicated is done so without words. Nonverbal gestures account for 55 percent of what is communicated. Tone of voice accounts for 38 percent of a message and words, only 7 percent of what is really meant in an interaction. In my experience, observing thousands of salespeople in action, I would say that sensitivity to nonverbal communications is one of the key factors that separates the average salesperson from the top performer.

"In a study conducted by Communispond, Inc., a New York-based management consulting firm, corporate buyers who were surveyed identified communication skills as a major deficiency for most salespeople. Of those surveyed, 49 percent listed "too talky" as the salesperson's primary problem, and 87 percent said salespeople do not ask the right questions about the buyer's needs.[1]

"Sensitivity to nonverbal signals allows salespeople to pick up on the cues from the customer about whether or not they are on track. But the best salespeople are very aware of what they are communicating to customers nonver-

bally. What does your eye contact, hand gestures, tone of voice, and facial expressions communicate about your message? It may speak volumes more than the words that come out of your mouth. Body language plays a vital role in your sales presentation strategy and its success."[2]

Introduction

Selling is an exchange of ideas through language before it is ever an exchange of goods or services for money. If I have something you need, I must first communicate that I have it and then that I am willing to exchange it. You must communicate to me that I have what you want and that you are willing to give me something for it. If there is a lack of communication, an incorrect message, or a misunderstanding, it is difficult and sometimes impossible for buyers and sellers to get together.

The basic communication process entails the mechanics of how people transmit meaning, facts, emotions, and desires. An understanding of this process is useful for determining why one sales presentation was successful and another a failure. If you have ever been in a conversation and felt the other person was saying one thing but meaning something else, you have experienced the effect of verbal and nonverbal signals. This is particularly relevant for selling situations because often more things are communicated through nonverbal messages than through words.

Word selection is vitally important in selling. A crossword puzzle is an ingeniously tessellated, essentially heterogeneous concatenation of verbal, synodic similitudes, replete with internal inhibitors especially designed to promote fulminative vituperation, to dispel hebetudinosity, and to develop introspective cogitation by means of psychic gymnastics. This definition of a crossword puzzle is technically correct, but it may not rate high as an example of effective communication. Communication is a social relationship between individuals in which a message emanating from one to the other reduces the uncertainty of misunderstanding.

Selecting the right words creates the image and builds the perception in the prospect's mind, which is so vital to success. Any conversation, sales presentation, or letter can be improved and strengthened by using more powerful and imaginative vocabulary. The power words identified in this chapter will make a presentation more impressive and successful.

Communication is both what is said and how it is said. Barriers to effective communication have recognizable signs that arise before the breakdown actually takes place. Barriers occur at the source of the message, in the message itself, in the media used as the vehicle of the message, and with the receiver. Many of the barriers are avoidable through listening and questioning.

To be an effective communicator, one must adapt to the social style of the message recipient. The four social styles, each with different communication requirements, will be explained in this chapter. Let's begin with the requirements for effective communication.

Requirements for Effective Communication

The word *communication* comes from the Latin word *communis,* which means "common." The word communication would literally mean "common understanding," which implies that the words used to communicate would have the same meaning to both the sender and the receiver. But more important than words is the effect a communication has on the behavior of the person receiving it. The desired effect may be one of increasing knowledge, comprehension, or action on the part of the receiver. Communication employs many of the human senses, plus emotions. We all live in a sea of constant communication signals, and our response to this constant input determines our behavior. Our reaction to a communication signal is influenced by our attitude and our sincere interest in the action the signal is designed to stimulate. A communication signal may be a simple stimulant requesting a single response (a stop sign) or a complex group of signals requesting an involved change of behavior (a banner that says "Prevent Air Pollution").

Communication is the selling skill to which all others are subordinate. You cannot make a presentation or close a sale without communicating. You certainly cannot overcome an objection without understanding the two-way communication that is a prerequisite to a closed sale. Let's begin by understanding the communication process, how it works, how you can use it to your advantage, and how it helps explain communication failures.

The Communication Process

The communication process has seven parts. First is the sender: the person or firm wanting to convey a message and create a meaning. Second is the sender's encoding process: the words, pictures, or body language selected to express the meaning. Third is the channel or vehicle that will carry the message. Fourth is noise, which is anything that interferes with the communication (such as static on the radio or a snowy TV picture). The fifth and sixth parts center on the receivers and their decoding process. The seventh part is feedback: the way a receiver reacts to a message. We will explain each of these in detail. The communication process is diagrammed in Figure 3-1.

◀ ◀ ◀ ◀ ◀ ◀ ◀ ◀
Learning Objective 1: The communication process

Figure 3-1   **The Communication Process**

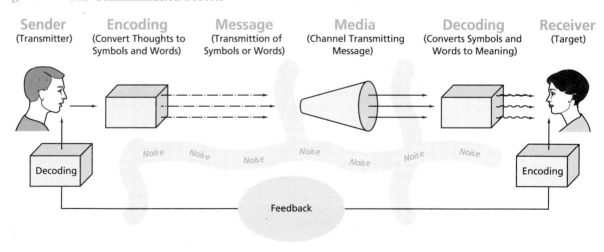

Source: Christopher H. Lovelock and Charles B. Weinberg, *Marketing for Public and Non-profit Managers,* (New York: John Wiley & Sons, 1984), p. 388.

Sender   *The **sender** is a person or institution that has a message to convey.* This message creates an image, a base of information, a degree of knowledge, or a level of expertise in the receiver's mind. Through it, the sender (salesperson) hopes the prospective buyer will have a change of attitude and buy rather than reject, listen and consider rather than dismiss, or be a conduit to persuade others to buy. The sender's message can be personal or nonpersonal. A brochure, TV ad, radio spot, or billboard can help communicate the salesperson's message.

The message   *The **message** is the intent or meaning the sender wants to convey.* The message, or meaning the sender wants to impart, is dependent on his or her interpretation. *Encoding* is the sender's interpretation of the message. The accumulation of facts, their prioritization, and their structure all depend on the sender's interpretation of the message. Let's look at two conversations based on the same facts and determine if multiple messages are being sent.

Here are the facts:

▸ The product weighs two tons
▸ It is made of steel
▸ It travels along the road at 75 miles per hour
▸ It is green
▸ It costs $12,000

Salesperson A's use of facts:

> "This is quite a piece of equipment, fast and lightweight. It will travel down the road at 75 miles per hour without so much as a whisper. And durable? Why, the totally steel construction makes it almost indestructible. The green color creates a pleasant sensation for the eye, and at only $1,000 per month, you cannot pass it up!"

> Things are not usually as they seem: we encode, the customer decodes; sometimes we lose the idea we want to convey!

Salesperson B's use of the facts:

> "Comfort and durability are the main features. Comfort to the eye and comfort to the wallet. At three dollars per pound and with all-steel construction, it's hard to beat. It will go faster than most others—75 miles per hour—and it is one of the lightest in its class!"

What were the impressions you drew from these two salespeople? What message was the first salesperson trying to get across? What about the second? As you read these two paragraphs, what product did you think each was describing? Could it have been a car, a trailer, or an army jeep? The selection of the facts and terminology is a significant part of encoding.

Accuracy and detail make the meaning clearer as well. In our sales scenarios above, both salespeople stated the product would do 75 miles per hour. This is explicit and conveys an identically clear meaning to both buyer and seller. Relative terminology, such as *big, fast, heavy,* and *slow,* is words that create meaning relative to the buyer's or seller's frame of reference. This makes the meaning subject to interpretation. To say the car is fast, big, and

INCREASE YOUR SALES AND PROFITS...

With Laptop Computer Systems/Solutions
from the HUGH CARVER GROUP℠
"The Portable Productivity People"

Some messages are meant to be very obvious.

luxurious creates a relative meaning that depends on whether you drive a Fiat or a Rolls Royce.

As a final point, the sender's own attitudes, perceptions, values, education, judgment, and biases all affect the encoding process. Ten people can take the same facts and translate them into ten different messages implying ten different meanings. Sales trainers recognize this, which is why some firms use "scripted presentations." By training and drilling salespeople to say exactly the same thing with the same voice intonations and gestures, the trainers are sure the same meaning and message will be sent every time. This is one reason telephone sales agents follow the same script in each call they make.

An important part of the message is **paralanguage**—the characteristics of the voice. The verbal element centers on *what* is said; paralanguage focuses on *how* it is said. Paralanguage refers to:

▸ The rate of speech   ▸ Pacing

▸ Diction   ▸ Pitch

▸ Tone and rhythm   ▸ Style

▸ Volume   ▸ Accent or emphasis

Paralanguage conveys the reaction and emotions of the speaker. When excited, people speak faster, choppier, and louder. When bored, they slow down and have an almost sing-song quality in their voice. Salespeople communicate their enthusiasm through paralanguage. A cheerful and vibrant "Good morning, Mrs. Smith" may start the day. After ten calls and ten rejections, the "Good afternoon, Mrs. Smith" may come out reflecting rejection and dejection. It may reflect an attitude of "It may be a good afternoon for you, Mrs. Smith, but it's not for me." Salespeople must guard against unwittingly creating a negative impression via their paralanguage. Paralanguage is the vocal mirror of emotions, so how you say what you say carries as much meaning as what you actually express.

The Communications Channel *The **communications channel** is the conduit or vehicle that carries the message.* Personal channels include verbal and nonverbal vehicles, such as body language. Nonpersonal channels include written memos, letters, advertisements, brochures, and sales promotion pieces. The nonpersonal channel can be electronic as well. As computer linkages become more prevalent in businesses, electronic mail (E-mail) will develop into an ever increasing popular communications channel. Table 3-1 illustrates the variety of vehicles that salespeople and their customers can use to communicate.

Deciding which channel to use has important ramifications. In face-to-face communication, words carry a portion of the meaning, but the voice intonation carries another and more subtle part. Think of all the different meanings that could be communicated in the following simple sentence:

Buyer: "What price are you going to charge me for this drill press?"

Scenario 1: "What price are *you* going to charge me for this drill press?"

Scenario 2: "What price are you going to charge *me* for this drill press?"

Scenario 3: "What price are you going to charge me for *this* drill press?"

> It is not so much what you say but how you say it.

In the first scenario, the buyer is asking what the salesperson will do, maybe relative to a competitor. In the second scenario, she wants to know what her price will be—not the list price but what special deal the seller will make for her. In the last scenario, the question implies there may be several drill presses and the buyer is inquiring about the one to which she is pointing.

Nonpersonal channels are a predominant way of communicating in marketing today. These channels encompass letters, bids, contracts, brochures and promotional pieces. Their content must be precise enough to create both

In other communications, the message may be more subtle.

Table 3-1	Communications Channel Matrix	
	Personal Conveyance	**Nonpersonal Conveyance**
N O N V E R B A L	Personal letter Body language Appearance Point-of-purchase material	Brochure Specification sheet Print advertisements
V E R B A L	Speech/discussion Sales presentation by salesperson	Videotape Audiotape TV and radio

the explicit and the perceived meaning. Specific facts are expressed in the verbal message, but nonverbal signals also send a message. Any personally directed written communication is read for content, but style is also important. There is no more glaring communication error than a business letter with misspelled words, poor grammar, or inappropriate style.

Noise **Noise** means anything that distorts or interferes with or is a barrier to communication. Noise exists in telephone calls, other conversations, and computer or machine noise. These create confusion, and when confusion occurs, meaning gets lost, distorted, and misinterpreted. Mental distractions are a form of noise preventing total attention and concentration. Thinking about picking the kids up at school, the next appointment, or how close it is to quitting time interferes with communication.

Receiver The **receiver** is the message's target. The receiver should come away from a communications encounter with the message the sender wanted to project. In most selling situations, the receiver (customer) is a busy person in a noisy situation with limited time. This affects how well the message gets through. As the sender selects facts, interprets those facts, and formulates a goal-specific communication, so the receiver formulates meaning through a similar interpretation process. Decoding means deriving meaning from a message.

Feedback **Feedback** is the verbal or nonverbal way the receiver responds to the sender's message. Feedback can consist of questions, statements, or body language cues. The response depends on the receiver's understanding of the message. Feedback is the way a salesperson tests the message for correct content and meaning. If the salesperson is trying to communicate that his or her company only takes credit cards and the customer asks about the credit terms and length of payment period, the customer hasn't understood the message. As salespeople gain experience, they know what kind of feedback to expect. When something unexpected comes back, it is a signal the communications process has faltered. At that point, the problem must be corrected.

People Selectively Decode Messages to Get Meaning

People receive communications from different channels. They draw meaning from the melange of signals their brain translates. This is **decoding.** If I say "The plane is coming," you are ambivalent. If I jump up and down, point above me, then fall to the ground, covering my head, and yell, "The plane is coming!", your brain tells you something very specific. The receiver's brain admits the verbal and nonverbal signals into its central processor and matches each signal against meanings it already knows. It sorts through possible meanings and tells the receiver what the specific signal means. This becomes the receiver's perception of the communication. Ideally, the meaning in the receiver's brain matches the one the sender (the salesperson) wanted to convey. The decoding process, that is, the creation of meaning from communication signals, is a function of selective reception (what part of the message receivers choose to listen to), selective perception (how and what they choose of the message to believe), and selective retention (what portions they choose to remember).

▶ ▶ ▶ ▶ ▶ ▶ ▶ ▶ ▶
Learning Objective 2: The selective decoding of messages

Selective Reception **Selective reception** means the brain filters only the parts of the message (or signals) it wants to receive. With some message parts rejected, part of the intent is lost, and the resulting meaning is changed:

Salesperson: From today until next week, when you buy five, you get the rest of your order at half price.

Buyer *(listening to the statement above, when the phone rings):* Keep talking, I can do two things at once. *(Key words buyer's brain heard: "_____ _____ _____ next week _____ _____ _____ _____ you get _____ _____ _____ your order at half price.")*

Buyer *(hangs up the phone):* Say, that sounds great I'll take 100, and we will send you the purchase order tomorrow.

Problem: The salesperson writes the order for delivery this week charging the full price for five units and half price for the rest. However, buyer's purchase order calls for delivery next week with 100 units at half price. Noise was a contributing factor, and selective reception did the rest.

Selective Perception **Selective perception** means the receiver's brain now takes the bits of the message it chose to admit for processing and interprets those parts according to any criteria, bias, experience, or rational, or irrational methods it chooses. Through selective perception, the receiver judges the message as true, accurate, false, incoherent, prejudicial, nonsensical, relevant, or totally obtuse. Salespeople have no control or influence over how a customer will selectively perceive the message. Salespeople can only probe for preconceived notions, request feedback on the buyer's interpretations, or ask questions. Through any of these, salespeople get a glimpse into the buyer's brain regarding what perception is forming.

Selective Retention **Selective retention** means the receiver's brain only chooses to remember what it wants to remember. The brain retains only a portion of the messages it receives, and the criteria for selection depend on the individual. What is retained, for whatever reason, directly affects selective perception because it adds to the base of knowledge or experiences that form future selection criteria, biases, and so on.

In summary, decoding creates the meaning from the messages. The meanings guide the behaviors of salespeople and buyers alike. From the discussion of these parts of communication process, it should be apparent that miscommunication can occur for a variety of reasons. The verbal and nonverbal elements of communication will be discussed in the next two parts of this chapter.

▸ ▸ *follow-up questions*

1. What are the three activities a sender must do prior to initiating a presentation to a buyer?
2. What causes messages to be misinterpreted?
3. What is meant by *noise* in a communication channel? Identify four sources of this noise.

Verbal Communication and Perception

When salespeople meet prospective customers for the first time, there is a natural strangeness between them that is diminished through questions and answers on both their parts. This interplay of questions and answers forms communication signals that tend to pull the prospects and the salespeople together. As the discussion continues, the prospects' and salespeople's fields of interest start to overlap. This overlap is where true communication takes place; the salespeople and the customers now have something in common (from the Latin *communis*).

Verbal messages can be weak or powerful, image-evoking or sleep-inducing. Imagine one of your aspiring dates calls you this week and says, "Wanna go to a movie, then do something after that?" Then a second calls and says, "I've got tickets to that new movie everyone is trying to see and I would like you to go with me, then afterward get a sinfully rich dessert. Would you like to go?" Which one will get the date? Which one used power words? Using power words, rather than weak ones, creates excitement, enthusiasm, meaning, and the image the user wants to convey.

Power Words Create the Perception

Words convey facts and emotions. They create images and evoke passions. Choosing the right word is the difference between creating excitement, interest, and enthusiasm and boring customers to death. Terms that encourage acceptance, rather than evoke rejection, are the stock-in-trade of successful salespeople.

Learning Objective 3: Using power words creates a more powerful sales presentation

People seldom make decisions on totally rational grounds. Successful salespeople know how to create an atmosphere that excites customers to want to buy. Visuals, such as slides, charts, and product demonstrations, create the physical environment conducive to buying. Verbal communication creates the mental and psychological environment. Rejection words have negative connotations.

Is it just a common blender or is it the start of a luscious dessert? Power words create a perception.

Compare: "If I can get the cost of this $12,000 service contract spread over six years, will you sign the contract?"

To: "Would you authorize an agreement if the monthly investment in guaranteed quality service were only $167?"

Note how $12,000 creates the image of a large expenditure, how *cost* implies a cash outlay that will make you poorer as a result of the deal, and how six years sounds like forever! Signing a contract connotes legal implications—contracts, stipulations, and breech of contract.

In the second version, notice how the power word *authorize* makes the buyer feel more important. An *agreement* is something between friends. The *monthly investment* creates the image of something that will make you richer and increase in value, and *$167 per month* sounds like pocket change relative to $12,000. No one wants to "buy at a cost of _____," they would rather "own an investment valued at _____." Using the former terminology is certain to cue negative images, while the latter cues positive images. Let's compare sample phrases to illustrate the image-creating effect of power words.

Mediocre: "You'll enjoy your new boat."

Image-creating: "Imagine how envious your friends will be seeing you in *this* boat at the lake."

or

"Visualize *this* sitting in your dock where the *old* one was."

or

"The pride in owning a *ski boat like this* is something only a few really get to experience."

Power words and phrases stimulate the buyer's mind to create images far grander than any detailed description the salesperson might create. In the first example above, prospective buyers will probably imagine a far greater degree of envy on their friends' part than will exist. "Visualize this..." say's yesterday's dependable old standard of family recreation is now, in the prospects' mind, an outdated, dull, and thoroughly behind-the-times barge. "The pride of owning..." says the buyer is special, one of the elite. These powerful images are created by simply substituting a few selectively received words and letting them do their job cuing up selectively retained images to create the right meanings.

In Table 3-2, power words are compared to their mundane, rejection-inducing counterparts.

▶ ▶ *follow-up questions*

1. What are three power words that could be used to replace the word *price* in a sales presentation?
2. How do power words create sales and how do rejection words create rejection?

Powerful Nonverbal Communication

Nonverbal communication is the sum of kinesics and proxemics. *Kinesics relates to body motions as communication signals,* which are commonly called

Table 3-2	**Power Words That Create Sales**	
Rejection Words	**Power Words**	
Cost	Investment	Available at
Price	Valued	Total investment
Charges	Worth	Invoiced at/for
Fees	Offered at	
Payment	Total investment	
Down payment	Initial investment	
Spend	Investment	
Outlay	Monthly investment	
Contract	Agreement, permission	
Stipulations	Promise	
Commitment	Guarantee	
Sold	Confirmation	
Deal	Pledge	
Negotiate	Understanding	
Sign	Authorization	
Buy	To own	

Source: Adapted from Tom Hopkins, *How to Master the Art of Selling* (New York: Warner, 1982), Chap. 4.

body language. **Proxemics** refers to the way people use space around them. Both are essential elements in the communication process. They give salespeople clues to the buyer's thoughts and behaviors.

Elements of Nonverbal Communications

Nonverbal communication is conveyed in five ways:

Learning Objective 4:
Elements of nonverbal
communication

1. eye contact,

2. mannerisms,

3. the way the salesperson shakes a prospect's hand,

4. the salesperson's body movements, and

5. the space between the salesperson and the prospect.

Eye Contact   Eye contact communicates to the buyer sincerity, trustworthiness, strength of character, and self-confidence. People feel uncomfortable when there is too little eye contact and when they are being stared at. What is your impression of someone who will not look you in the eye? If you are like most people, it gives you the feeling the speaker isn't trustworthy. By the same token, many people begin to feel defensive if they believe they are being stared at. While there is a balance of eye contact that the salesperson and a buyer will feel comfortable with, the salesperson should always maintain plenty of eye contact during a presentation.

Eye contact is also important because eye movements give away what a person is really thinking about. The boxed feature "Eyes Are Windows to the Mind" explains how eye movements reveal thoughts.

Most people give their thoughts away through their eye movements. For example:

WHEN THEY LOOK:	THEY ARE:
▶ Up and left	visualizing something from the past as if they are picturing it in their minds
▶ Up and to the right	constructing an image of what something *will* look like
▶ Down and to the right	recalling or imagining *feelings*
▶ Sideways to the left	hearing sounds from the past in their minds
▶ Sideways and right	constructing a future conversation in their minds, thinking of the right words or how they are going to tell you something
▶ Down and left	talking things over with themselves

Mannerisms *Mannerisms are the little things people do, which they may not even be aware of. They result from nervousness, habits, or subconscious (or conscious) attitudes.* Some people wring their hands or pace when they make presentations, others fidget with their neckties or jewelry. Many people don't know what to do with their hands; they put them in their pockets, fold them on their lap, or wave them around. Mannerisms will quickly communicate to the buyer nervousness, self-confidence, and comfort.

Personal mannerisms can communicate confidence, nervousness, low self-esteem, or any number of inner thoughts.

The Handshake   First impressions come from a person's general appearance, degree of eye contact, facial expressions, and handshake. Some people have a limp-fish handshake, and others like the pump-handle style. Still others try to crush your hand, while some master the grab and twist. A good handshake is firm, brief, and accompanied with direct eye contact.

Body Position   Body positions and movements are powerful communicators. They transmit information and clues about the customer's state of mind or readiness to buy. People subconsciously transmit their feelings through their body angle, facial expressions, arm position or movements, hand position or movements, and leg positions. *Body language* is the term often used to

◂ ◂ ◂ ◂ ◂ ◂ ◂ ◂
Learning Objective 5: Body language cues that occur during a sales presentation

describe the messages sent via the body movements. These messages fall into three categories. First, is the "Yes, I'm interested" signal. The second type of message is the skeptical "I'm not so sure," or caution signal. The last is the "rejection" signal.

"Yes, I'm interested" signals indicate interest and a desire or willingness to listen. The greater the interest, the more the prospect will relax and lean forward, not frowning or appearing concerned or perplexed. Interested customers show a greater degree of openness and acceptance. They nod in agreement and are more receptive and interested. They communicate this by "opening up." These signs give the salesperson a clear signal to continue with the presentation or close the sale.

"Proceed with caution" signals indicate skepticism or disbelief. When skeptical or cautious, the customer will lean away, tilting back. The prospect may even turn so as not to face the salesperson directly. This is a defensive position. Eye contact breaks, or little is maintained. The face may be somewhat frowning, the brow wrinkled, or have a puzzled appearance. The arms may be fully closed and the hands showing signs of distraction and nervousness. Legs, too, may be crossed and turned away, and the person's head may make nervous movements, looking from side to side while giving the appearance of shaking in disbelief.

These signals may appear suddenly. In this situation, the salesperson should ask the prospect if there is a problem or a question or if the prospect is "just thinking it over?" The question here is, "Do I deal with this signal now or wait until later?" Deal with it now. The prospect may not have understood what the salesperson said, or the message may not have been clear. It is important to clear up any doubt, skepticism, or misunderstanding immediately. Not doing so will lead to further communication breakdown or outright rejection.

What do adaptive salespeople do when the "proceed with caution" signals appear? Here are five guidelines:

Learning Objective 6:
Strategies for reacting to body language cues

1. Stop or slow down; adjust and clarify your presentation.
2. Ask if there any questions.
3. Pose a direct question, preferably an open-ended one, that asks for something more than a one-word answer.
4. Acknowledge the customer's skepticism and show why it is unfounded.
5. Change your body language to reflect interest and acceptance. Lean forward, be more open with your arms, legs, and hand positions, and above all, show positive facial expressions.

"Rejection" signals indicate the prospect either does not believe the salesperson or has totally lost interest. These are serious signals. Deal with them immediately. Customers may lean back or even turn completely away from the salesperson with their shoulders pulled back. Their face is definitely tense, frowning, and with a wrinkled brow. They maintain little, if any, eye contact. Their arms may be crossed tightly over their chest, forming a wall between them and the salesperson. Their hands may be clenched or open with fingers up and palms turned toward the salesperson, as if to push him or her away. To deal with them, one can use the same techniques as with the "proceed with caution" signals. Below is a scenario involving a salesperson and her prospect.

Salesperson *(sitting across the desk from the prospect while making good eye contact, legs crossed, upright posture and holding a sample of the product):* Not only does the Z-35 weigh less than any of our competitor's hydraulic pumps, it generates the same pressures and we are priced 35 percent less than even the foreign competition.

Buyer: It sounds like something we would be interested in investigating further. *(Note that the buyer has given a strong positive verbal signal to continue—a "tell me more" response.)*

Salesperson *(leaning a little more forward and definitely smiling at this point):* We feel our pump is superior and our one-year service contract is an additional feature that is well worth the money.

Buyer *(now beginning to lean back, turning slightly to the salesperson, crossing his legs, and beginning to break eye contact):* What do you mean by a service contract that is 'well worth the money'? *(At this point, several possibilities must be considered. First, a chord was struck when the service contract was mentioned. Second, what signals did the buyer send? They were certainly not "safe to proceed" signals. Third, how serious could it be? Could the problem be that there is a separate contract, rather than service being part of the whole product package? Is it that the contract is only a one-year contract? Or is it that the contract is not free? How to proceed from here is the big question. What would you do at this point?)*

Salesperson *(continuing to lean slightly forward, concerned expression on face, puts sample down):* I sense you have a question or concern about the service contract.

Buyer *(turning back toward the salesperson and leaning forward):* This service contract, it's only good for one year?

It is now clear that the buyer has some questions about the length of the contract and has communicated the message of "Yes, I'm still interested if you can explain why the contract's limit is only one year." Table 3-3 summarizes a number of body language cues and what they communicate. After reviewing the table, read the "What Would You Do If...?" feature and determine the signals being sent and what you should do.

The Salesperson's and the Buyer's Space

Proxemics is how salespeople use their space and the buyer's space. It comes from *proximity*. Everyone subconsciously has a proximity comfort zone. A distance of about two feet represents the *intimate zone*. Only the closest of friends enter this area. Another two feet out is the *personal zone*. This is about the distance spanned by a desk in a sales presentation. Next is the *social zone*. It extends from about four to ten feet out. Most business is transacted in this zone. Last is the *public zone*. It extends beyond ten feet and is a comfortable distance when making group presentations. On a cold call, the prospect may know nothing of the salesperson, or the selling company. The salesperson may know little more about the prospect. They both are somewhat apprehensive and cautious, so they probably will elect to stay in the social zone. The distance gets reduced to the personal zone with greater familiarity.

Body position and proxemics are closely linked. As people lean forward, they reduces the space between them and another. This may mean moving

Body language and proxemics are powerful communicators.

Table 3-3	Body Language Cues and What They Communicate		
Interpretation	**Body Angle**	**Face**	**Arms**
"Rejection"	Sitting astride chair	Piercing eye contact	Hands on hips
	Exaggerated leaning over	Head down	Hands to face, hair
	Standing while others sit	Minimum eye contact	Rubbing back of neck
	Fidgeting	Constant blinking	Arms crossed
	Shifting from side to side	Negative shake of head	Finger under collar
	Turning body away	Lips pursing	
		Eyes squinting	
		Chin thrusting out	
		Frown	

	Hands	**Legs**	
	Hands behind neck	Leg over chair	
	Steepling (fingers touching)	Feet on desk	
	Wringing hands	Legs crossed	
	Fist		
	Finger pointing		
	Hands gripping edge of desk		

Interpretation	**Body Angle**	**Face**	**Arms**
"Proceed with caution"	Head in palm of hand	Lack of eye contact	Touching nose while speaking
	Moving body away	Looking at door, at watch, out window	Pulling ear while speaking
	Sideways glance	Blank stare	Pinching bridge of nose
	Crossing arms or legs with body forward	Avoiding eye contact	Tugging at clothes

Continued

Table 3-3 — *Continued*

Interpretation	Body Angle	Face	Arms
"Proceed with caution"	Pacing back and forth	Eyes squinting Head down or tilted Biting lip Eyes shifting left and right	Scratching head

	Hands	Legs	
	Playing with object on table	Tapping feet	
	Shuffling papers toward exit	Feet pointing	
	Drumming on table	Look of concentration while tapping feet	
	Fingers crossed		

Interpretation	Body Angle	Face	Arms
"I'm interested..."	Head tilted slightly	Slight blinking of eyes	Hand gripping chin
	Ear turned toward speaker	Eyes squinting	Putting glasses in mouth
	Leaning forward in seat	Eyebrows raised	Putting hands to chest
	Sitting far up in chair	Nodding	Free movement of arms and hands
		Good eye contact	
		Slight blinking	
		Smile	

	Hands	Legs	
	Putting index finger to lips	Kicking foot slightly	
	Open hands	Legs uncrossed	
	Palms toward self	Feet flat on floor	

Source: Modified from Carlton Pederson, Milburn Wright, and Barton Weitz, *Selling Principles and Methods* (Homewood, Ill.: Richard D. Irwin, 1988), pp. 184–85.

from social space into personal space. Leaning back means the opposite. Prospective buyers communicate greater trust and acceptance as they reduce the space across the desk. Similarly, leaning back increases the space. Salespeople can test the degree of buyer acceptance by subtly adjusting their proximity to the buyer. For example, as the presentation is progressing, the salesperson can scoot the chair a little closer to the buyer's desk and leaning slightly forward, reducing the space. If the buyer retreats, the communication is clear, "I'm not ready to trust you or your product enough to get too close." Adaptive salespeople are keenly aware of these space concepts.

In summary, body language and proxemics are powerful communicators. The adaptive salesperson recognizes the signals and interprets their correct meaning. The signals and actions recommended here are guidelines. Body language signals may not be as clear as described here. Such signals are subject to misinterpretation, but through training and practice, salespeople can become skillful at recognizing and reacting to the signs. Knowing how to send nonverbal signals is also important to communicate the right message to the buyer.

▶▶ *follow-up questions*

1. How do proxemics and kinesics combine to create nonverbal communication?

2. How would a buyer or a seller communicate interest in what is being said without ever saying a word?

Persuasive Communication

Persuasive communication has only one goal—to change someone's attitude or behavior. A person can be persuaded through facts, logic, emotion, rationalizations, personal appeals, or any number of ways. Success at persuasive communication comes from using words evoking the desired emotions and mental images from the buyer. Persuasive communicators don't just sell, they don't just convey information; they make the customer's mind and imagination come into the interaction.

Persuasive Communication Defined

Persuading is trying to change someone's attitude or opinion to cause a behavioral change. It is the culmination of gathering information, communicating an understanding of the problems, and offering viable, beneficial alternatives. Persuasion is a process where responses are encouraged and guided by using four techniques, the first three of which are elements of active listening. Active listening behaviors communicate that you are paying attention and have heard (and understood) the message.

◀ ◀ ◀ ◀ ◀ ◀ ◀ ◀

Learning Objective 7: Elements of persuasive communication.

Atmospherics and Personal Selling Research Findings[4]

Atmospherics is a new term encompassing both the spatial and architectural features of the selling environment (office design, proxemics, etc.) and the physical characteristics of the salesperson.

Research has shown:

1. Invading personal space causes customers to react negatively, hostilely.
2. Good news, when presented up close to a person, is received more positively than when presented at a distance; the opposite holds true for bad news.
3. Similarity and/or appropriateness of dress evokes positive responses. Dissimilarity evokes uncertainty, caution, and avoidance behavior.
4. Attractive individuals are given more personal space.
5. Attractive females are viewed less positively if they are selling masculine stereotyped products or services.

Summary: Dress the part, look the part, and when you tell them about a price reduction, get nice and close; when it's a price increase, keep a healthy distance!

Technique 1—Echoing Echoing is simply repeating a word or phrase spoken by the prospect. For example, the prospective buyer might say, "Price and delivery have been our two biggest headaches." The salesperson could echo and encourage an explanation by saying, "Price *and* delivery?"

Technique 2—Acknowledging Acknowledging is simply a verbal or nonverbal indication of understanding and agreement. Nodding is the most common outward behavior people use to acknowledge they are listening and understanding.

Technique 3—Reflecting Reflecting restates what was said, but in the receiver's own words. An example of a reflecting statement is "You've mentioned three problems, but it sounds to me like your greatest concern is with _____." Reflecting is a way of confirming you have heard and understood.

Technique 4—Advocating Advocating acknowledges that needs exist, then provides solutions to satisfy those needs. People are not persuaded to change their behaviors unless there are definite and recognizable benefits in doing so.

Asking great questions and encouraging and guiding responses won't persuade anyone unless a clearly beneficial outcome will result from changing behavior. A good rapport between the customer and the salesperson facilitates persuasion. The greater the rapport, the greater the chances the persuasion will be effective.

Building Rapport with Customers[5]

Learning Objective 8: The rapport-building process

Building rapport is essential for success in sales. Building rapport begins with speaking the customer's language. The salesperson must also consider posture (legs crossed, leaning back, relaxed), voice tone (excited, relaxed, loud), gestures (hand motions, smiles, frowns, head movements), and other clues. The salesperson must follow word or behavior patterns as subtly as possible to create harmony, not dissonance. Creating an atmosphere of

Figure 3-2 **The Rapport Cycle and the Selling Cycle**

Source: William G. Nickles et al., "Rapport Building for Salespeople: A Neuro-Linguistic Approach," *Journal of Personal Selling and Sales Management,* 3 (1983): 1–7.

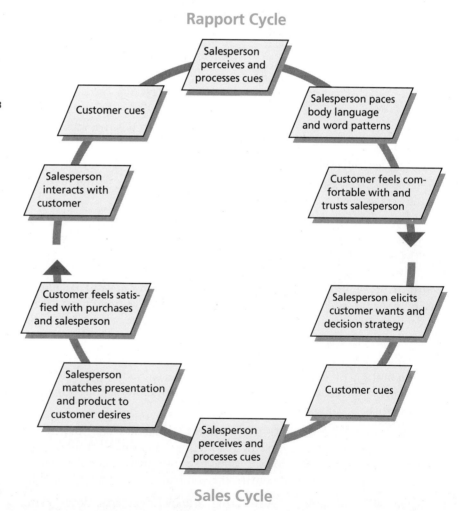

commonality, a feeling of unity, or mutual interest and understanding, is the first step toward creating behavioral change (or in the case of selling, making a sale). Even difficult prospects are responsive to this type of selling encounter.[6]

Rapport building and the selling cycle, that is, the cycle of events from the initial contact until the sale is concluded, are closely interwoven. The rapport cycle and the selling cycle interact as shown in Figure 3-2. The sales-person reacts to the customer's cues by developing a pace and communication style that matches the buyer's. The buyer then feels more comfortable, rapport increases, and the result is more sales. After repeated interactions, sales-people know how to react to and deal with each buyer. This is the essence of adaptive selling.

Case in Point

Communication Skills Success

Lynn Hicks works for West Educational Publishing as a college textbook sales representative. Lynn has traveled college campuses with great success as a rep for two years. In January of 1992, Lynn was honored as the Co-Rep of the Year after increasing dollar volume in her New Mexico-based sales territory by 28% over the previous year.

When asked about the importance of communication skills, Lynn had this to say:

In most cases I usually have the opportunity to visit with a professor at least 2-3 times before a textbook decision will be made. Therefore, most of my time is spent during the first visit establishing a rapport with a professor, then trying to establish his/her textbook needs. I rarely attempt a presentation during this first visit unless I feel that I may not have another opportunity to meet with the professor before the decision is made.

Obviously getting off to a good start is extremely important. I try to be polite and courteous and address the professor by name. Offering a firm handshake, I will introduce myself and explain why I am there. I think it is especially important to ask for their time as it shows respect for their position and puts the professor in a position to invite you to continue. I will always smile and maintain good eye contact. It is very difficult to be rude to a smiling person.

Most people are comfortable with someone who is similar to themselves, so in many ways I try to mimic the style and personality of the professor I am meeting with. For example, if a professor speaks quietly, I will lower my voice. If that person is short and to the point, I will try to keep my questions more focused. Some professors really like having someone to talk to and others have a no nonsense approach. If I can respond with a similar style it will be much easier to develop a trusting relationship and subsequently they will be more willing to share information about what they really want and need in a textbook.

The biggest communication problem I face is not getting an open and honest discussion with the professor. This could happen for a lot of

Continued

Lynn Hicks

▶ ▶ *follow-up questions*

1. What do atmospherics have to do with selling and persuasion?

2. Is building rapport an important part of a retail salesperson's selling technique? Why or why not?

3. Is there one or more places in the rapport cycle where the customer has an advantage over the salesperson? Where the salesperson has an advantage over the customer?

Barriers to Effective Communication

Learning Objective 9: Barriers to effective communication

*A **barrier to communication** is anything that blocks the flow of the message or makes its meaning difficult to transmit and/or understand.* A source barrier is one that originates with the sender. Barriers can also result from problems with the message itself. In this case, the receiver may have difficulty not with how the message is communicated or the credibility of the salesperson but with what is being communicated. A channel barrier is a problem, often mechanical in nature, with transferring the message. Finally, the barrier can be at the receiving end. The receiver may misinterpret the message because of a lack of understanding, selective distortion, selective retention, or lack of education, sophistication, or experience. Table 3-4 identifies the causes of communication barriers.

Barriers at the Source

When salespeople lack product knowledge, trying to present the product's features, advantages, and benefits and to answer questions can make communication difficult. This communicates to prospective customers a lack of preparation and training and heightens their anxiety about buying.

A barrier may occur simply because the salesperson is unable to communicate effectively and concisely. In addition, talking to the wrong person is not only a barrier to communication, it is also an embarrassment and a reflection of a salesperson who has done a poor job of determining who the

Table 3-4   Causes of Barriers to Effective Communication

	Source Barriers	Message Barriers	Channel Barriers	Receiver Barriers
1.	Lack of product knowledge	Too technical	Noise, no language in common	Lack of sophistication
2.	Inability to communicate effectively	Poorly stated	Wrong channel	Distractions
3.	Talking to the wrong person	Poorly timed	Too many people in channel	Buying pressure
4.	Wrong body language	Information overload	Physical layout	Turf protecting
5.	Bias/perception problems	Prejudices	Misinterpretations	Stereotyped thinking
6.	Selling pressure	Lack of rapport	Limited use of appropriate channels	Sales resistance
7.	Credibility gap	Prior expectations	Channel wearout	Past performance

right person is. This can happen to anyone, but there is no excuse for not clarifying that the person the salesperson is about to meet is the right one.

Another barrier to communication can arise because of "body language washout." This occurs when verbal and nonverbal messages conflict. The verbal message may be engaging, and the customer might even be verbally indicating interest in what the salesperson has to sell. However, the prospect's body language may be saying exactly the opposite. The sender's attitude affects on not only *what* is said but *how* it is said, and the receiver's attitude, and thus his or her body language, directly affects the messages conveyed back to the sender.

The pressure to make a sale can create a communication barrier. This pressure can cause the salesperson to hurry the presentation, fail to respond to questions from the buyer, give incorrect or inaccurate answers, or simply create the impression of desperation.

Finally, a credibility gap may exist as a result of the reputation of the salesperson's firm or experiences the buyer has had with the salesperson, the firm, or the product. The customer may not believe the salesperson's claims or the company's promotional material. The credibility gap can stem from any number of sources, but the affect is generally the same.

Message Barriers

Barriers to effective communication may result from problems with the message itself. In this case, the receiver may have no difficulty with how the message is communicated or the credibility of the salesperson. *What* is being communicated may be causing the problem. The message may be too complex or beyond the expertise of the receiver. An observant salesperson notes the customer's reactions to what is said and speaks in terms the customer understands. If, through observing customers' body language and listening to their questions, it is clear they do not understand some or all of what has been said, the salesperson must shift to more familiar terms and phrases. Salespeople can quickly find themselves using technological buzzwords instead terms familiar to the receivers. This breaks the communication process, leaving customers confused or drawing the wrong conclusions because they

Eye contact and other nonverbal messages communicate uneasiness or acceptance.

have translated (incorrectly) the buzzwords to what they think they mean. Watching customer body language is particularly important here. People communicate their uneasiness and lack of understanding in their posture and their nervousness by lack of eye contact. They break eye contact, lean back, furrow their brow, and get that "I-haven't-the-foggiest-notion-what-you-just-said" look.

Timing is important in communication. A poorly stated or poorly timed message creates a barrier. This is true in oral as well as written communication. Bad grammar, spelling, and organization, illogical flow, and sloppiness create a poorly stated message. There is a time in the sales presentation when it is the customer's turn to ask questions and the salesperson's turn to sit quietly and listen. Poorly timed questions and premature answers to anticipated questions may cause more problems than they solve and severely inhibit further communication. A good sense of timing comes through training, practice, and experience.

A barrier also may result from information overload. Certain types of people like to know *everything* there is to know; others want just the "bottom line." The salesperson's job is to determine what information is needed and wanted by a prospective buyer. When prospects begin to suffer information overload, they tune out the salesperson.

When Things Go Wrong

The Case of the Poorly Timed Message

"Picture the setting. There I was, propped up between two pillows, slightly elevated in the hospital bed. My lung had collapsed, I had double pneumonia and a 103-degree temperature. I had tubes in my nose, needles in my arms, and a big sign on the door saying "NO VISITORS." I had been admitted to the hospital the day before and was about half conscious with sedatives. Even my wife was not permitted to visit. It didn't matter, since at the moment I wasn't even aware I was married. Suddenly the lights in the darkened room came on and I thought I was hallucinating, because standing before me was a young man in a tuxedo. He wore rouge and lipstick and was carrying a dozen helium balloons. "Jim Lavenson?" he asked. I guess I nodded, although I wasn't sure of the right answer. He then let fly the balloons to the ceiling, stretched out his arms à la Al Jolson, and began to sing: "You look swell! You look grand! We're all here to strike up the band!"

"By the time I reached for the emergency cord above the bed to summon either a nurse or the police, he had left. When a nurse did arrive, she was sure I was having a bad dream and gave me another shot.

"The next day, I found a card on one of the balloons. The song the balloon man had sung was reprinted there, advising me that this special messenger was sent by my insurance agent!"

"I'm going to wait a full year before acknowledging his 'thoughtfulness.' It's my way of teaching him about timing."

Source: Jim Lavenson, "No Bedside Manner for Selling," *Sales and Marketing Management Magazine,* 135 (1985): 12.

Prejudice and lack of rapport are obvious barriers. If one has a built-in intolerance for communicating with someone or no desire to establish a relationship, communication is barred before it starts.

Prior expectations also acts as a message barrier. If either the sender or the receiver has unrealistic expectations, then the outcome will be less than at least one party expected. Salespeople avoid creating unrealistic expectations by not making grandiose promises and always keeping the customer informed with current, accurate information, regardless of whether it is good or bad.

Barriers in the Channel

Barriers to communication can also develop in the channel itself. Noise, such as distractions, can interfere with communication and create a barrier.

Using the wrong channel creates a barrier. Talking to the wrong person, sending a brochure when a personal presentation was needed, or making a personal presentation when the customer wanted only written information creates barriers. Many have had the experience of requesting information about life insurance, for example, only to find that the brochure they thought they were going to get turned out to be a personal visit from an agent who wanted 30 minutes of their time.

The third cause of a communication barrier can be too many people involved in the channel. When several people receive and interpret the message, then communicate it to the intended receiver, the problems of selective perception and retention are compounded. The greater the number of relayers in the channel, the greater the chances for miscommunication.

The physical layout at the customer's site can also be a barrier. An office may be arranged such that it forces the salesperson to sit too far away from the customer to effectively demonstrate a product. The customer's location may not be large enough to do the demonstration, or getting to the site may be impossible.

Misinterpretations occur as a result of the channels used and bar communications. Customers may feel slighted when they receive a computer-generated form letter stating the current product offering and prices when they felt a personal letter would be more appropriate for a "regular customer doing the volume with them that we do." The customers interpret the form letter as communicating that they are insignificant.

Limited use of an appropriate channel may also inhibit communication. Failing to call important customers with the latest information ignores the verbal channel customers may feel they deserve. Failing to confirm such calls with letters or memos has the same effect. Lack of innovation is another barrier. For example, using videotape in a presentation to a customer who is used to just seeing the salesperson go through the standard presentation can make a big communication impact. Doing the same old thing in the same old way numbs the receiver, doesn't spark any interest, and convinces the customer of the salesperson's lack of creativity.

Finally, channel barriers come from wear-out. This occurs when the salesperson uses the same channel so much it has no effect any more. For example, consistent use of a form letter to announce prices teaches the customer to simply open the envelope, pull out the price letter, and pass it on.

Announcements of new products or personnel changes would probably go unnoticed if they were included with the form letter. In essence, customers get trained to look for the letter to communicate one thing, and they don't look to that channel for anything more. A separate mailing would work better.

Barriers at the Receiving End

The final source of communication barriers is at the receiving end. The first of these source barriers comes from a lack of receiver sophistication. Just as the seller can erect a barrier by having a presentation that is too technical or complex, a buyer's lack of sophistication can set up one, too. A successful, adaptive salesperson matches the buyer's level of sophistication to prevent confusion.

Distractions create a barrier if they draw the receiver's attention away from the communication. This is the noise in the channel referred to earlier.

The third barrier is the pressure to buy. This may put the salesperson in the situation of being shut off before important material can be presented. It heightens the problem of selective retention and selective reception leading to misunderstanding and buyer dissatisfaction.

Turf protecting can also create barriers. Customers, like everyone else, feel a certain sense of "turf" or territory when it comes to their job and business. Salespeople communicating that they know more, are more sophisticated, or have greater expertise than their customers often find communications failing because they have just invaded the customers' turf. The customers, correctly or incorrectly, know best what they want and need. Business customers know more about their business than the salespeople calling on them, so when salespeople communicate that they know more about the customers' business needs than the customers do, turf protecting will likely result.

Many salespeople are the victims of stereotyped thinking, another barrier to communication. When dealing with a customer who thinks all salespeople are the same, the salesperson is challenged to change that perception. When dealing with a buyer who has stereotyped the salespeople and their products, the salespeople must back up and look at the messages they need to communicate. Breaking the stereotype starts the communication anew. If the customer is accustomed to salespeople who are responsive, articulate, and knowledgeable about product application, the communication would be very different than if the stereotype is negative or at best one of mediocrity.

Finally, sales resistance and past performance are barriers to communications that must be addressed. They often go together. A customer may show resistance to any communication attempts because of the salesperson's or the firm's past performance. Failing to deliver on promises, not addressing the customer's needs, and generally being a poor salesperson create resistance to further communications.

▶ ▶ *follow-up questions*

1. How would you, as a typical customer, react to an information overload? How would a buyer to whom you are making a presentation react?

2. How can pressure to buy or sell create a barrier to communication?

Effective Communication Skills Can Be Learned

Anyone can become a better communicator. Most communication barriers are easily overcome through training, experience, common sense, and consideration for the receiver. Sharp listening and questioning can help resolve most problems. Improving listening skills permit salespeople to comprehend what is said directly and between the lines. Questioning skills enable salespeople to draw information from prospective customers. Remember, buyers will generally tell salespeople everything they need to know to make the sale, if the salespeople just listen carefully.

Listening Skills

Developing good listening skills is essential to good communication. People can listen to more than 500 words per minute, but they can only speak about 150 words per minute at best. Since the mind can absorb words faster than someone can speak them, it wanders off thinking about other things in that 350 words of "spare time." Tom Peters, the famous management consultant and author, recommends treating the customer as a foreigner. Pretend the customer doesn't speak the language or doesn't speak it well. You know how much more intensely you listen when someone who is not fluent in the language speaks. Your mind concentrates on the conversation. Why should it be any different when listening to customers? When salespeople do not pay close attention, vital points slip by. Vital points communicating "Here's my problem," "Here's how I want you to solve it," and "Here's why your competitor did not make the sale" go unnoticed. The box below has six suggestions to help improve listening skills.

Six Suggestions on Listening That Will Boost Sales[7]

Listening is a skill. While you have been doing it all your life, you may find it is a skill that can be improved.

▶ *Resist the temptation to monopolize the conversation.* Before you speak, be sure the customer has made his or her point. People tend to think aloud, and if you are talking when you should be listening, you'll miss what the customer is revealing.

▶ *Avoid judging the speaker too soon.* Instead of thinking about *how* the customer is speaking, think about what message you should be getting from this conversation.

▶ *Don't fake attention.* Attentive listeners remain alert and maintain eye contact. Simple gestures—nodding, raising eyebrows, leaning forward—all convey the message that "I am interested and listening to what you are saying."

▶ *Listen for ideas as well as facts.* People tell you facts and their dreams or aspirations. They tell you their problems and how they want those problems solved. If you are not listening and paying attention, you miss out on the key to opening a relationship.

Continued

> ▶ *Continued — Be alert to nonverbal cues.* Body position, facial expressions, and voice intonations are signals we often give without realizing it. They can be the window to the customer's mind.
>
> ▶ *Use the speed of thought.* You think faster than you talk or listen. The speed of thought is a valuable asset. When the customer is finished talking, you can gain thought time by restating the main points or saying something like "Do I understand you correctly to mean...?"

Questioning Skills

Questions are marvelous tools when used properly. Questions have two basic functions: to discover something—information, attitudes, or readiness to buy, and to lead prospects toward a close or conclusion by focusing their attention. In some cases, the same question will aim to both lead and discover. Using questions has three benefits. First, questions gather information. Next, they keep the prospective buyer involved and focused on the presentation. Third, they provide the questioner with time to think. The brain works very rapidly. In the time it takes for the salesperson to ask the question and the receiver's brain to hear and formulate an answer, the salesperson can gain valuable seconds of thinking time. Other benefits of good questioning are:

▶ Questions may help the prospect make some useful discoveries. For example, the prospect may say, "We haven't done business with your firm for over 20 years and don't see any reason to start now." The salesperson may simply say, "Why is that?" The answer may point to a problem that occurred 20 years ago as a result of design, delivery, or accounting problem that has long since been cleared up.

▶ Questions demonstrate genuine interest and keep the prospect involved.

▶ Questions give the salesperson the opportunity to discover and correct misperceptions or incorrect information.

▶ Questions help the salesperson remain in control of the pace and direction of the presentation.

▶ Questions help the salesperson start the prospect on the flow of yesses that ultimately lead to a buying decision.

▶ Questions can be used to arouse and direct emotions.

▶ Questions help isolate problems or objections that normally occur during the presentation and help answer objections.

▶ Questions help determine the general and specific needs and benefits the prospect is seeking.

▶ Questions test the tension, trust, and progress of the presentation.[8]

▶ ▶ ▶ ▶ ▶ ▶ ▶ ▶ ▶

Learning Objective 10: Categories of questions salespeople use to enhance communication

Categories of questions salespeople use The two broad categories are closed-ended and open-ended questions. Figure 3-3 shows the main and subcategories of questions. **Closed-ended questions** direct responders toward a specific, direct answer. They are specific and direct themselves. **Open-ended questions** direct the responders to expound and tell their story. Think of the closed-ended question as analogous to a multiple-choice test question and the open-ended question as an essay-type question.

Closed-ended questions will generate brief answers. Using too many of them causes an information gap; the buyers don't get to tell their story. The

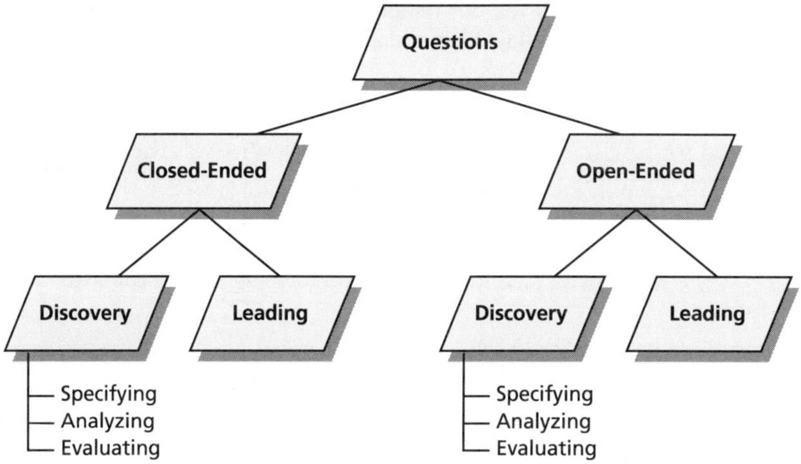

Figure 3-3
**Categorizing the
Types of Questions
Salespeople Use**

result is salespeople miss important information the customers need and want to share. Also, extensively using closed-end questions may mean the right question is not asked. The questioner makes the assumption that all of the questions are the right ones, but they may not cover everything the buyer has to contribute. Finally, extensively using the closed-ended question makes the salesperson carry the bulk of the conversation. This can be physically and mentally draining. If salespeople come out of presentations wondering why prospects didn't seem very talkative, it could be they didn't give them a chance!

The open-ended question makes the prospect say more than yes or no. What good salespeople learn early in their careers is to keep the prospect talking. Using the open-ended question takes the physical and mental burden of carrying the conversation off the salesperson. When responding, customers always give more information than they think they do. Below are some examples of using open- and closed-ended questions to create the "sales conversation." The first involves closed-ended questions:

Seller: How many Z-34 pumps do you use now?
Buyer: Fifteen.
Seller: Have you had problems with leaky gaskets?
Buyer: No.
Seller: Any problems with the bearings?
Buyer: No.
Seller: Cracks in the housings?
Buyer: No.

You see how this could go on forever. Now let's look at how using closed-ended plus open-ended questions discovers the buyer's service problem:

Seller: How many Z-34 pumps do you use now?
Buyer: Fifteen.
Seller: I'm going to be talking to our engineers later on. If you could meet with them instead of me and talk about our pump, what would you tell them?
Buyer: I would tell them the hose fittings are too small and this causes hoses to leak under pressure. What is really aggravating is that when this happens, it takes your service people two days to get here and fix them!

Seller: I'm going to need to tell our people about that. How many times have you had to wait two days? What do you estimate that costs you?

In the second conversation, the seller used both types of questions and found the pump had a mechanical problem, which if corrected, would eliminate the need for service calls. He also discovered service was the major problem this buyer faced.

Open- and closed-ended questions can discover information or lead the prospect. Discovery questions can be further divided into questions asking the prospect to specify, analyze, or evaluate. These are the functions of questions.

Six Questions that Can Save the Salesperson

	Closed-ended	Open-ended
What?	What did it cost?	What happened?
When?	When do you need it?	When that occurred...?
Who?	Who used it?	
Where?	Where do we deliver?	
Why?		Why did you choose this?
How?	How many?	How did that happen?

Let's look at an example of how questions can be converted from nonproductive to productive tools.

▶ **Nonproductive Question Scenario**

Salesperson *(approaching a customer in a clothing store):* May I help you?

Customer: No thanks, I'm just looking. *(Salesperson usually turns and walks away or at most, the customer may get the following offer.)*

Salesperson: Well, if you find something you like, I'll be over there.

▶ **Productive Question Scenario**

Salesperson *(approaching a customer in a clothing store):* Are you looking for something for yourself or a gift for someone? *(Note that the customer cannot say the standard, "No, I'm just looking.")*

Customer: I'm looking for a dress for myself. *(Salesperson now has a focus.)*

Salesperson: Will it be for casual wear, parties or for wearing around the house? *(Note that the question both gathers information and leads the customer to an even sharper focus.)*

Customer: I'm looking for a dress to wear to a casual party Saturday night. *(The salesperson now knows the dress is for a special occasion, but it is a casual occasion, and there is a sense of urgency—it's not for sometime in the future but for this coming Saturday night.)*

The first lesson from this scenario is always to try and make a question do double duty. The more functions the question can perform, the more efficient it is. The second lesson is to avoid "say no" questions. When given the chance, people will say "no" more than 50 percent of the time. It doesn't put them in a decision-making situation, and it's safer.

The discovery function of a question can also be used in response to a question. For example:

Customer: Can we get the same discount if we order 500 cases, instead of 1,000?

Salesperson: That would save you quite a bit. Why don't we place the order for 500 cases just to hold them for you, and I'll work on getting the discount.

Here the salesperson has used a question in response to a question. The result will either be a closed sale or the customer will divulge other desires or problems standing in the way of the closed sale.

Categories of discovery questions are specifying, analyzing, and evaluating.

Specifying questions seek specific information, for example:

"How many people work here?"

"What days do you set aside to take deliveries?"

"How many are you thinking about buying?"

"Are you buying similar products now?"

"Are your suppliers mostly foreign or domestic?

Analyzing questions probe needs, concerns, or values. These types of questions ask the prospects to give information based on their interpretation. Some examples of analyzing questions are:

"If you increase the size of your plant, how will this affect our delivery schedule to you?"

"If you are going to use this VCR mostly for playing back only, why are you so concerned about three heads versus four heads?"

"How will the changes in exchange rates affect your sales?"

Evaluating questions ask customers for an evaluation or comparison. They can be very effective when used with specifying questions as a way to get prospects to give both detailed, factual information and their personal feelings or assessments.

For example:

"What do you see as the biggest advantage of leasing over owning?"
    "Which one do you like the best?"

"Do you think your customers will think this is a significant advancement?"

"Which option do you think will be the most useful in your situation?"

Leading questions help focus the presentation or bring it from generalities to specifics. They can also help the prospect come to a decision (remember the earlier explanation of the types of questions used to persuade people). The purpose of the leading question is to advance the sale. Below are some typical leading questions:

"Would you rate buying from a dealer known for service as important in your decision?"

"Quality is always an important feature in what you sell to your customers, isn't it?"

"If you had to rate price in your buying decision on a scale from one to ten, where would you place it?"

Before making a sales presentation, develop a strategy for asking effective questions. It should include:

1. *Planning*

   ▸ What do you need to know?

   ▸ What do you want the prospect to know?

2. *Prioritizing*
   ▸ What are the "must ask" questions?
3. *Sequencing*
   ▸ Will you sequence questions from general to specific or from specific to general?
4. *Framing the question's presentation*
   ▸ Body language to support questions.
   ▸ Paralanguage to support questions.
5. *Preparing your questions*
   ▸ Check for the use of power words.
   ▸ Do the words match prospect's style?
   ▸ Is there a balance between open- and closed-ended questions?
   ▸ Is there a balance between leading and discovery questions?
6. *Testing*
   ▸ Role-play.
   ▸ Read the questions aloud and listen to how they sound; check for duplication.

Case in Point

Use Questions to Focus the Prospect on the Future as Well as the Present

Most of the prospects salespeople calls on are already using a product similar to the one they are selling. This means two things must be considered: first, how to convert a prospect away from the competition; and second, how to create the impression that the salesperson will be able to satisfy this prospect's need both now and in the future. Helping with the future may be the greatest lever to current sales.

The editors of *Personal Selling Power,* a publication subscribed to by many top salespeople, have the following suggestions:

> To help your prospect define future needs, a comprehensive questioning strategy is the best tool. Once you get your prospect talking about his or her current business practices, carefully lead the conversation to the future by asking questions like: "What are your expansion plans for the coming year?" "Where do you see the most significant growth taking place?" "What problems do you anticipate when you get over _____ dollars in sales?"

Such questions are designed to focus the prospect's attention on future problems. Once he or she has explained what the future looks like and where the problems are going to crop up, begin to suggest possible ways your product might help solve these problems. While you are making subtle suggestions, talk about the prospect's stated problems and relate your solutions to specific scenarios. Once your prospect knows he or she can count on you for solutions to future problems, you are more likely to get current and future orders.

Source: Adapted from *Personal Selling Power,* January-February 1988, p. 6.

▶ ▶ *follow-up questions*

1. Why would a salesperson be forever asking questions of a buyer? How does the salesperson benefit from the questions?
2. What is an open-ended question and what are its benefits, compared to a closed-ended question?

Knowledge of Social Style

Adaptive salespeople are alert to the nuances of verbal and nonverbal communication. Through the insights into the buyer's social style that these nuances provide, salespeople can customize the sales presentation to the buyer's style.

Social Style

A **social style** is a combination of the effects of thinking, feeling, and behaving. It is the way in which people interact. Some people are assertive, while others are meek. Some are very emotional, and others show no emotions at all. There are four social styles—Analyticals, Amiables, Expressives, and Drivers—which are based on assertiveness and responsiveness.[9]

Learning Objective 11: Communicating with four different customer social styles

Analyticals are detail-oriented people, deliberate, efficient, and well organized. They are careful and avoid risk. Analytical buyers want alternatives complete with all the facts and figures. They appreciate a systematic approach to everything, and before deciding, they will want to know all about the salesperson and his or her qualifications, the vendor's firm, products, services, and track record. In a word, analyticals are careful to the utmost. Analytical buyers are sensitive to the systematic organization of the presentation. They are as turned off by an unorganized, disjointed presentation as they are by inaccurate facts and figures.

Analyticals are conservative in their dress, speech, and mannerisms. They are not given to initiating close personal involvement with vendors and want to keep everything on a business-like footing. They are careful to meet their company's needs first. They are both cautious and deliberate in committing funds. Analyticals will make buying decisions based on reason and practicality, using cost-benefit logic. They make a commitment only when convinced their decision represents the best, most logical, most efficient, safest, and cost-justified of the alternatives.

In communicating with Analyticals, salespeople can become frustrated by these buyers' need for details. They always want more facts and information. Analyticals are slow to reach a decision, so salespeople must be patient in trying to close the sale.

Drivers are forceful and controlling people. Drivers want to know what the results will be; they are "bottom-line" people more concerned with outcomes than procedures. Drivers are urgent people.

Drivers want salespeople to give them alternatives. Don't tell them what to do. Salespeople dealing with Drivers soon learn they are in control, or at least want to be. Drivers will act quickly once they know their options.

Drivers are straight-forward and communicate their expectations clearly from the very start. They focus on the objective at hand and bring the sales presentation back to center anytime it drifts. These people want action and

Analyticals are detail oriented.

Drivers are control-oriented people.

don't have a great deal of patience. This means quick reaction time is essential if the salesperson wants to make the sale.

Expressives are emotional and "big picture people." People who have this third social style want salespeople to communicate the whole concept, not the minute details that are demanded by Analyticals. Expressives like to talk and brainstorm. They are free and open with information and often provide salespeople with additional information to help the sale. They are creative and relatively easy to sell to once they grasp what the product can do for them. Expressives appreciate creativity and innovation and are not afraid to take risks.

Dealing with Expressives requires taking a different approach than with either Drivers or Analyticals. Expressives want the best solution. Giving them all the alternatives will only make them restless and anxious. These are fast-lane people who are outgoing and always enthusiastic, so don't be surprised if they have a short attention span when it comes to details. Give them the big picture, then the solution, and save the details for later.

The fourth social style is found in people called **Amiables**. Amiables are extremely relationship-oriented. They only buy from their "friends." This is important to understand because once they feel the bond of friendship, they develop strong loyalties that competitors find hard to break.

How the salesperson has communicated friendship and camaraderie influences their decision making. Salespeople who expect the quick decision making of the Drivers with these people will be frustrated. Amiables want input from all the buying influences before making decisions. With an Amiable, salespeople will want to provide enough brochures, pamphlets, and so on for both the buyer and staff. You also will want to use such phrases as

Expressives have a "big picture" orientation.

Amiables are casual, open, and relationship oriented.

Communication in the Sales Profession

◄ One of the important nonverbal signals to the salesperson is the eye contact between her and the prospect. The prospective buyer sends messages about his interest in the seller and the product through a combination of eye contact, eye movement and body language. Such nonverbal signals work both ways, and the salesperson must also engage in an appropriate balance of eye contact.

► Here the prospect looks up and to the left. This indicates that he is visualizing something from the past in his mind.

◄ When the prospect's eyes move up and to the right, it indicates that he is constructing an image of what something will look like.

◄ The face alone, with a number of cues at once, can signal the prospect's state of mind. This man's eyes are squinted, his head is tilted, chin slightly lowered, and he is avoiding eye contact. These cues communicate a message to the salesperson to proceed with caution or even back up in the presentation.

▼ Here the prospect not only verbalizes his interest, but also expresses it in his face. His eyebrows are raised, he exhibits good eye contact, his head is raised and he leans toward the salesperson as he speaks.

◄ Mannerisms are physical actions which people perform unconsciously, usually from habit, nervousness or subconscious attitudes. This prospect fidgets with his tie; it may be too tight, or he may have a nervous habit, or it could be a reaction to something the salesperson said.

► One combination of cues which can be interpreted as meaning rejection is when the prospect avoids eye contact, leans away from the salesperson and clearly appears skeptical.

◄ While this prospective buyer may really be concerned about the time, he may also be indicating that he would like the appointment to be over. This prospect is sending unequivocal signals to the salesperson.

▶ The salesperson must exhibit positive body language as she demonstrates her product. She is relaxed as she leans slightly toward the prospects and opens her hands. This is the end of her presentation and she is interested in and open to any questions her clients may have.

◀ The open palms and slight smile of this prospect say, "I'm interested. . . . "

▶ This buyer is leaning away from the salesperson, her chin is thrust forward, her hand is at her face. She is sending "proceed with caution" signals. Her eyes are looking sideways and to the right; she is constructing a future conversation in her mind, mentally preparing the objections she is about to raise.

◄ The buyer's frown and crossed arms quickly communicate "rejection" to the salesperson.

▲ In a group presentation, the salesperson must interpret the body language cues of several people at once. This group appears skeptical, expectant and grim. It will be a challenge for the salesperson to project a relaxed and positive attitude and win them over.

◄ Another important factor in body language is proxemics, the use of space. The social zone extends from a little over two feet away to about ten feet. It is the acceptable space in which two people who are acquaintances feel comfortable.

► A married couple are comfortable in each other's intimate zones, but the sales representative remains within the bounds of the social zone.

◄ As the salesperson leans toward the prospects, the woman leans away to maintain the acceptable social distance.

◄ Communication extends to others in the salesperson's field. Often sales representatives learn more through informal discussions with each other than through formal training.

◄ Salespeople discuss business at lunch and will form friendships or informal working relationships which will enhance their networking.

► Many sales situations are carried on outside of the sales office and require salespersons to adapt their presentation and manner to the physical surroundings of the potential buyer.

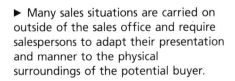

◀ Retail salespersons are generally on their own "turf," with an ample supply of their inventory available to them. Still, they must adapt to each customer's style and be able to communicate effectively.

▼ The appropriate dress requires donning a hard-hat in this industrial sales situation.

"You and your staff...". Being patient is a virtue when dealing with Amiables. Not only will they seek input from staff, they will want to feel their decisions are acceptable and fit well with the "team spirit" of the firm.

Adapting to the social style of the buyer is essential for the salesperson to be successful. Social style becomes apparent after dealing with the buyer, but what about the first meeting? What do salespeople look for?

The following are signs of the buyer's social style:

Analyticals	Drivers
▸ Printouts, data, etc. stacked on or around desk	▸ Always appear to be in mid-crisis
▸ Probably a dirth of pictures, decoration in the office; an all-business atmosphere	▸ Conservatively dressed, but probably in a "sleeves rolled up" operating fashion
▸ Order and neatness in everything from personal dress to books on the shelves	▸ Will have several piles of things to do on desk, file cabinet, credenza
▸ Likes individual leisure activities, such as reading, golf	▸ Achievement awards on walls
▸ Technical background	▸ Likes group activities
	▸ Desk placed so contact is across the desk, rather than beside the desk

Amiables	Expressives
▸ Pictures of kids, family, pictures drawn by their kids	▸ Lots of flash and pizzazz
▸ Casual atmosphere, warm and friendly	▸ Trophies and awards
▸ Slower paced, soft spoken	▸ Vibrant, excitable, given to emphatic gestures and exaggeration
▸ Liberal arts background	▸ Liberal arts background
▸ Personal mementos on walls	▸ Motivational slogans on walls
▸ Desk placed for open contact, rather than across the desk	▸ Desk cluttered, unorganized
	▸ Desk placed for open contact, rather than across the desk
	▸ Flamboyant dress

When Things Go Wrong

Canning the Wrong Fish

Miquel is in the market for a telemarketing system for his sales office. He has already requested literature from a number of vendors and made a rather thorough analysis of what was sent. He feels confident that he knows what he wants and decides to call in Roger, the salesperson for Teletalk Inc. He wants Roger to answer a few questions and see what he will do on the price. He wants to know if there are some features the literature might not have covered.

Continued

Canning the Wrong Fish — Continued

Roger's system is pretty straightforward, will do what Miquel wants, and is competitively priced. Roger begins his presentation the next week in Miquel's office. It is not overly furnished and offers Roger a comfortable environment for his presentation. He begins by explaining all the technical features and each feature's advantages and benefits to Miquel. As he is progressing through his presentation, Miquel interrupts with requests such as "That's all great stuff, but just tell me what this thing can and can't do." Roger fends off these requests by saying that understanding all it will do is difficult without understanding the technical nature of the system and how it operates. After a few minutes of this, Miquel gets noticeably restless. He asks Roger who else in town is now using the system. Roger says he has sold the system "to many businesses around town" and then continues on with his technical presentation. He never gives Miquel any names. He begins again with "Now where was I?"

Miquel, visibly impatient now, says, "Roger, thanks for stopping by. Why don't you leave your literature with me and I'll decide and let you know?" Roger thanks Miquel for his time and leaves. Miquel mumbles, "I hate canned shows," then throws the literature in the wastebasket and calls up another company.

▶ Question: Where did Roger go wrong?

▶ ▶ *follow-up questions*

1. How are Analyticals different from Expressives?
2. How would you alter your selling style when going from a Driver to an Amiable?
3. What would an Expressive salesperson have to do to adapt to an Analytical buyer?

Summary

This chapter has focused on the communication process. The process starts with a sender who devises or encodes a message. The message gets transmitted over a channel, which can be verbal or nonverbal and personal or nonpersonal (Learning Objective 1). The receiver is the target and he or she decodes the message signals to interpret a meaning. Selective perception, selective retention, and selective reception affect the meaning taken from the message (Learning Objective 2).

Verbal and nonverbal signals are the primary modes of communication. Power words make for more convincing sales presentations by creating more positive images in the customer's mind. *Authorize*, rather than *sign, agreement*, rather than *contract*, are less threatening and therefore more powerful, results-oriented words (Learning Objective 3). Nonverbal signals consist of eye contact and movement, mannerisms, the handshake, and body position. Body position cues and their meaning were explained as indicators of rejection, caution, and interest (Learning Objectives 4 and 5).

If the customer's body language is communicating caution or rejection signals, attentive salespeople have a variety of options for responding: they could slow the presentation down because the customer may not understand what is being said, or they could directly ask if there is a problem. Several more options were presented (Learning Objective 6). If the signals are positive, the salesperson can reasonable assume it is safe to proceed. Understanding body language cues can be coupled with the four persuasive communication techniques of echoing, acknowledging, reflecting, and advocating. If used when caution or rejection signals occur, the salesperson can usually solve communication inconsistencies before they become communication problems (Learning Objective 7). Proxemics was discussed, along with its contribution in nonverbal communication. How close salespeople are allowed to approach reflects the customer's trust in them.

Rapport building was presented as something salespeople should strive for. Rapport is established and nurtured through building a harmonious relationship with customers. This is done by matching customers' thinking mode, as reflected in their rate of speech, tone, and body movements. (Learning Objective 8).

The chapter next explained how barriers to communication can exist with either the sender or receiver, or even the channel. Barriers arise for numerous reasons. They are predictable and when apparent, easy to avoid or surmount (Learning Objective 9).

Listening and questioning skills were discussed next. Informal and formal listening techniques were presented. Questions were categorized broadly as open- and closed-ended. Those two categories were subdivided into discovery and leading questions. Discovery questions were further segregated into specifying, analyzing, and evaluating questions. A plan for developing a questioning strategy was presented (Learning Objective 10).

Social styles were explained in detail. These social styles are Amiables, Drivers, Expressives, and Analyticals. Each social style represents a generalized description of how people react and interact with each other. The characteristics of each type provide salespeople with a clue to their buyer's personality. This leads to adapting and customizing the presentation to fit the buyer's social style. Adapting to the social style increases rapport and gives buyers the type of presentation they want and are most comfortable with (Learning Objective 11).

Key Terms

Sender   The person or firm that has a message to convey.

Message   The intent or meaning the sender attempts to convey.

Encoding   The interpretation of the message by the sender.

Paralanguage   What people convey simply by the way they speak, that is, through intonation, pitch, rate of speech, and so forth.

Communications channel   The conduit or vehicle that carries the message.

Noise   Anything that distorts or interferes with the transmission of a message.

Receiver   The person to whom the message is directed.

Feedback   The verbal or nonverbal way the receiver responds to the sender's message.

Decoding The way the receiver of a message draws meaning from the melange of signals communicated by the sender.

Selective reception The brain's selection of only the parts of the message (or signals) it wants to receive.

Selective perception The bits of the message the receiver's brain chooses to admit for processing and interpretation according to any criteria, bias, past experience, or rational or irrational method it chooses.

Selective retention What the receiver's brain chooses to remember.

Proxemics The way people use space around them.

Persuasive communication A communication that has only one goal—to change someone's attitude or behavior.

Barrier to communication Anything that blocks the flow of the message or makes its meaning difficult to transmit and/or understand.

Closed-ended questions Questions that direct the person responding toward a specific direct answer.

Open-ended questions Questions that direct the responder to expound and tell his or her story.

Social style A combination of the effects of thinking, feeling, and behaving.

Analyticals A social style characterized as being critical, detail-oriented, and wanting to know all the facts and analyze them before making a decision.

Drivers A social style characterized by a desire for control, a bottom-line orientation, and a greater interest in results than process.

Expressives A social style identified as being flamboyant, emotional, even theatrical. People with this style are futuristic and holistic thinkers who want to see the big picture more than the details.

Amiables A social style of person who depends to a great degree on personal relationships and trust when making business decisions.

Discussion Questions

1. What is meant by encoding, decoding, and paralanguage?

2. If you were a salesperson planning a presentation, how could you include all categories of personal and nonpersonal and verbal and nonverbal communications in your plan?

3. What effect can the three types of selectivity mentioned in regard to decoding have on the accuracy of the decoded message in the receiver's brain?

4. Identify four elements of nonverbal communication and explain how each contributes to sending a nonverbal message.

5. Suppose you were giving a sales presentation and began receiving "caution" signals? First, what would these be, and second, what would you do?

6. During your presentation, you are sitting across the desk from a prospective buyer. As you lean forward onto the desk, the buyer leans back. What message(s) should you discern from this?

7. Define rapport building. How would you explain it to a salesperson, and why it is important to know about?

8. Which of the barriers to communication described in the chapter do *you feel* is the greatest?

9. How could a salesperson prevent the mistake of making a message too technical or complex?

10. Why would a Driver-type salesperson become frustrated trying to sell to an Amiable buyer?

Application Exercise

Reread the section on the communication process at the beginning of the chapter and then try this application exercise: Make up a brief sales presentation about your personal calculator. Identify three of its calculating functions. Then, write out how, without having the calculator there to demonstrate them, you would explain these functions to a prospective customer. Before doing so, think about the following:

1. What must the customer know about those functions?

2. What is the customer's level of expertise?

3. How will you know if the customer has understood your descriptions?

4. When you have finished, could the customer, without help from you, calculate the square root of 47 or correctly divide 128 by 37.2?

Class Exercises

Group Exercise

Based on the information you have read about social styles:

1. Identify your social style and the social style of the classmate sitting on each side of you.

2. In groups, identify each individual member's social style and compare your findings with the results from question 1 above.

3. List any discrepancies between the results in questions 1 and 2 and present possible explanations for them.

4. How does information gathered in questions 1 through 3 enhance your individual abilities to adapt to any selling situation?

Individual Presentation

Using a controversial current economic or social issue chosen by the instructor, for example, sexual harassment or fraudulent sales techniques, list *four* questions you would pose to the instructor as the "expert" on this issue.

Two of these questions should be open-ended and *two* should be closed-ended.

You will be allowed to ask *one* of each type of question, as you choose.

Questions

1. Compare the *amount* and *quality* of information you have gathered from the open-ended questions and the close-ended ones.

2. What does this finding in question 1 above tell you about the need for effective questioning skills in selling?

Cases

The Frustrating Sales Calls

Case 3.1

Cameron Taylor came back into the office after calling on accounts all day and went straight to see his manager, Jack Peschke. Cameron looked exhausted and discouraged. Jack asked what the problem was, and Cameron said, "I'm beat! I've been calling on accounts all day and feel like I have been pulled through the wringer! I talk to these prospects, ask them questions, but they never seem to have much to say. I ask them every question I can think of—you know, trying to probe their needs like you taught me in training two weeks ago, but it just seems like they won't open up."

Jack thought about what Cameron was saying and said, "Let's go over your presentation plan. Take me through your plan of attack for making the presentation." Cameron thought for a minute and began to talk about what he did, but it became clear to Jack that Cameron really didn't formulate a plan for making his presentations. Jack asked, Cameron, do you plan *what* questions you are going to ask? How do the prospects react?" Cameron looked a little puzzled but answered, "Questions? Well you know, the standard 'What are you using now?', 'How many?', 'How often?', 'Is it working okay for you?', 'Are you satisfied with the competitor's prices?'...that sort of stuff." Cameron thought a little more and added, "What do you mean, how do they react? For the most part, they just sit there and don't say anything accept grunt out yesses and no's."

Jack said, "Well, do they tend to lean forward and seem interested, or are they off in never-never land while you are talking?" Cameron lit up: "Yeah, you've got it! I feel like I'm talking to that plant over there most of the time when I'm talking to these guys."

Jack smiled and said he thought he might have some suggestions for this new and enthusiastic but somewhat frustrated salesman.

Question

1. If you were Jack, what would you suspect are several of Cameron's problems and what would be your suggestions to Cameron?

Mary Ann Sells to a Doubting Alice

Case 3.2

Mary Ann Buchmeier was making a presentation to one of her regular clients. In the copier business, buyers are either very sophisticated or are getting their first machine and really know very little about copiers. Alice Mackenzie was the office manager for Smith and Soncini, a law firm. Though Smith and Soncini had several copiers, Mary Ann was making a presentation to Alice of a new model. The XJ45 was a top-end copier with many new features. It also had a high price tag because of all those features. Smith and Soncini, while prominent, was not the type of firm that would spend money on a new copier just to get new features. It was a conservative firm and didn't believe in spending any more money than it had to for anything. Alice was willing to listen to Mary Ann, but she was unsure whether the firm needed another copier, particularly one selling for top dollar.

As Mary Ann started her presentation, Alice became quite interested. Though she had explained the conservative nature of the firm, Alice was interested enough to ask questions and appeared to be becoming more intrigued with the XJ45. As Mary Ann was explaining her product's features, advantages, and benefits, Alice began to react unexpectedly. She turned at her desk and, rather than facing Mary Ann head-on, began to look at her from the side. She picked up a pencil and rolled it between her fingers while looking more at it than at Mary Ann. She asked very few questions at this point, and her eye contact became less pronounced.

Mary Ann became concerned but continued on with her presentation. She could see Alice becoming more distracted as the presentation progressed.

Questions

1. What is Alice communicating to Mary Ann?
2. If you were watching this scene on videotape with Mary Ann and stopped the tape at this point, what would you tell Mary Ann to do next?

Selling in the Middle of a Three-Ring Circus

Malcolm Bell sat down after he and Mr. Maxwell greeted each other and shook hands. As Malcolm exchanged pleasantries with his prospect and began to transition into the presentation, Mr. Maxwell's assistant came into the room to ask about a shipment of steering wheel inserts. Mr. Maxwell discussed the shipment with the assistant, but as soon as the assistant left, the phone rang. Mr. Maxwell answered it and after about a three-minute conversation, apologized and asked Malcolm to continue. Just then Mr. Maxwell's secretary came in and handed him some papers. Mr. Maxwell glanced at them and told her to file them under Ishiguro Ltd. Malcolm started again, but this time Al Hunt came in, apologized for interrupting, but said it was important that Mr. Maxwell get a message right away.

After two more interruptions, Malcolm folded his arms, crossed his legs, and leaned back in his chair while Mr. Maxwell again took a short phone call. Malcolm's voice became agitated, and his temper was beginning to rise.

Questions

1. What communication barriers are occurring?
2. What message is Malcolm sending Mr. Maxwell?
3. What mistake is Malcolm getting ready to make?
4. How should Malcolm deal with this situation?

References

1. Adapted from *Business Magazine,* December 1989, p. 17.
2. Christine Christman, 1990, used with permission. Christman is a senior faculty member with Communique Exhibitors Education, Inc. She has trained thousands of sales personnel on interpersonal communications skills for selling at trade shows and has observed a host of selling interactions. Her most recent book is *The Complete Handbook of Successful Trade Show Selling,* published by Prentice-Hall.
3. William G. Nickles, et al., "Rapport Building for Salespeople: A Neuro-Linguistic Approach," *Journal of Personal Selling and Sales Management,* 3 (1983): 3.
4. James C. McElvoy et al., "The Atmospherics of Personal Selling," *Journal of Personal Selling* 10 (1990): 31–43.
5. Nickles, "Rapport Building for Salespeople," pp. 1–7.
6. Ibid., pp. 3–4.
7. Fred Pryor, "Listening for More Sales," *Personal Selling Power,* January-February 1988, p. 6.
8. Adapted from Nido Qubein, "The Power of Asking Questions," *Personal Selling Power,* pp. 20–21, and Tom Hopkins, *How to Master the Art of Selling* (New York: Warner Books), pp. 39–40.
9. Roger Wenschlag, *The Versatile Salesperson* (New York: John Wiley, 1987), p. 54.

4 Knowledge Is a Key to Success

Objectives

After reading this chapter, you will be able to:

1. Explain how a company's goals and objectives affect the individual salesperson.

2. Elaborate on how personal selling interfaces with other promotional tools.

3. Define in detail the elements of product knowledge needed to sell effectively.

4. List and explain the various pricing methods encountered in the selling process and be able to calculate prices based on cost and selling prices, with and without discounts.

5. Identify the various forms of credit available in helping to create sales.

6. Give three examples of power politics in the channels of distribution.

7. Give three examples of the types of conflict occurring in the channels of distribution.

8. Identify the types of competitive intelligence a salesperson needs to know and how to get it.

The Professional Selling Question

What is the most important bit of knowledge you would pass on to a novice salesperson and why?

Sales Experts Respond

In answering this question, many sales and marketing executives have specific pieces of advice. Brad Poulos of Wampole Laboratories in Arizona says that persistence is the best thing a novice salesperson can develop. He also says that it is essential to remember that rejection is just part of the game and a salesperson must learn not to give up. Roy Daugherty of Complete Protection Alarms in Michigan echoes this thought by saying good salespeople must take rejection and continue on without letting it get the best of them.

Todd Spare from Pennsylvania-based The Triad Group feels that the best advice for a salesperson is to remember that selling is 80 percent face-to-face time. He says that if salespeople aren't in front of customers at least that much of the time, they really aren't selling. A thread running through the advice of many sales executives is to never give up and be persistent, even in the face of rejection.

Other executives offer always being enthusiastic as their best advice. Diane Vehar of Bigler-Ketchim asserts that if salespeople are not enthusiastic about what they are selling, they should think real hard about getting out of the business. Karen Zivan of New York-based Les Trois Petit Cochons repeats that sentiment. She says enthusiasm comes before the salesperson meets the customer. Enthusiasm comes from being prepared and confident.

The two last pieces of advice come from Louis B. Fournier of Groundwater Technology in Pennsylvania and Karen McFadden of Roche Biomedical Laboratories in New Jersey. Fournier offers novice salespeople the wisdom that silence is golden: Too many salespeople don't listen, they just make their pitch. Fournier says clients will tell you what you need to know to tailor your presentation to them. McFadden says, "Be honest, make it fun, and get off your rear and just do it!"

Source: Bristol Voss, "This Month's Question," *Sales and Marketing Management* 142 (1990): 2–8.

Introduction

The greater the knowledge salespeople have, the greater their edge over the competition. What salespeople draw from their knowledge base determines how strongly they can compete and excel in selling. Good salespeople never stop learning. They take every opportunity to learn about their products, their competitor's products, and their customers and their problems. A salesperson has both factual and intuitive knowledge. Factual knowledge is bona fide knowledge: that a gallon of water weighs 8.8 pounds is bona fide knowledge because it can be measured. Intuitive knowledge is inferred

The greater knowledge salespeople have, the greater their edge over the competition.

information; you mentally compare what you observe with patterns observed in the past, then derive a conclusion. This is your hunch, your gut feeling, your intuition, your inexplicable common sense that tells you what to do. Unfortunately, common sense is not *too* common!

Company-imparted knowledge is what sales trainees learn through formal or informal training programs. It forms the foundational information about the company, its practices, and its policies—information through which salespeople determine their roles in the salesforce and firm. Company-imparted knowledge provides the salesperson with the company vision, which communicates what the firm stands for and its corporate culture.

Case in Point

The Professional Salesperson Is Knowledgeable

Purchasing agents must know a great deal about the products and services they depend on to successfully achieve their firm's goals and challenges. These purchasing executives learn much about the world economy, the competitive atmosphere, development trends in a specific field, and research in process, all of which may affect their future. They learn much of this from the salespeople who call on them.

Today's company sales representatives must, as never before, become a member of the customer's marketing team. Salespeople no longer survive in today's competitive marketplace by merely pitching

Continued

their product's features. Providing the quantity needed, delivery, service, a dependable flow of goods or services, and a realistic and reliable price structure—this all involves the salesperson!

Comment: The professional sales representative is vital to our economy—and to the purchasing agents of organizations everywhere.

Salespeople Know Their Company's Goals and Objectives

Mission Statement Sets the Company Philosophy

Goals and objectives give salespeople a sense of perspective and form their frame of reference. The firm's mission statement contains the general goals or guiding vision of the company. In it, the firm states its philosophy or purpose and gives all the salespeople a sense of the company's direction. Mission statements may be long or quite short, general or very specific. Table 4-1 contains the mission statement from NCR Corporation. As you read it, ask yourself, "If I were a new hire, what would I interpret this to mean? What does this firm want to accomplish and what does it value?"

Table 4-1   Mission Statement from NCR Corporation*

NCR's Mission: Create Value for Our Stakeholders

NCR is a successful, growing company dedicated to achieving superior results by assuring that its actions are aligned with stakeholder expectations. Stakeholders are all constituencies with a stake in the fortunes of the company. NCR's primary mission is to create value for our stakeholders.

▶ We believe in building a mutually beneficial and enduring relationships with all of our stakeholders, based on conducting all business activities with integrity and respect.

▶ We take customer satisfaction personally: we are committed to providing superior value in our products and services on a continuing basis.

▶ We respect the individuality of each employee and foster an environment in which employees' creativity and productivity are encouraged, recognized, valued and rewarded.

▶ We think of our suppliers as partners who share our goals of achieving the highest quality standards and the most consistent level of service.

▶ We are committed to being caring and supportive corporate citizens within the worldwide communities in which we operate.

▶ We are dedicated to creating value for our shareholders and financial communities by performing in a manner that will enhance the return on their investments.

*NCR is the name and trademark of NCR Corporation. Copyright NCR Corporation, 1987. Reprinted by permission.

Personal Performance Goals

▶ ▶ ▶ ▶ ▶ ▶ ▶ ▶ ▷

Learning Objective 1: How company goals affect individual salespeople

A company wants its salespeople to know specific as well as the general goals and objectives for the long and short run. Specific objectives usually relate to quantifiable tasks for the whole company, the sales region, the local branch office, and, ultimately, the individual. Specific goals that salespeople or their sales branches receive are:

- ▶ Sales forecast goals
- ▶ Market share goals
- ▶ Sales quotas
- ▶ Activity quotas

Sales forecast goals   The **sales forecast** is the projection a company or sales branch makes about expected sales. It is usually a projection for the upcoming year, but it can be shorter, even to daily sales goals. The sales forecast can be for total dollar or unit sales. It is an extremely vital goal because it forms the firm's basis for projecting its revenues and profits. From sales goals, firms assume the forecasted revenue is forthcoming and plan their expenditures accordingly. Part of those expenditures affect salespeople's salary and even the number of salespeople employed. Inaccurate sales forecasting or not achieving the forecasted amount can seriously impact salespeople's futures.

Market share goals   A **market share** goal is the target percentage or the share of the business the sales unit is expected to capture. Studies have shown that market share and profitability are directly linked. The supposition is that as market share grows, so does profitability.

Sales quota goals   A **sales quota** is a minimum amount of sales required. The quota can be for a division of the company, a product line, an individual product, a sales branch office, or an individual salesperson. Achieving (or not achieving) this goal is the basis for merit raises, bonuses, promotion, demotion, or termination. Management uses it as a yardstick to measure individual performance.

Activity quotas   The activity quota is a goal slightly different from the two above. Like the sales quota, it prescribes a minimal level of performance deemed necessary. The activity quota focuses on the variety of activities salespeople perform, rather than a sales outcome. **Activity quotas** are placed on such tasks as the number of calls per day, prospecting calls, displays set up, or cold calls a salesperson is required to make. The object is to direct the salespeople to perform a prescribed number of activities. The assumption is that sales will result from these activities.

These are but a sampling of the goals and objectives salespeople regularly face. Management directs the salesforce through the use of such goals. The goals management sets impact salespeople in two ways. First, goals tell them what management wants accomplished. If they know there is a big push to sell the model XYZ copier rather than the ABC model, the goal affects what models they present to prospects. Second, the goals and the rewards for hitting them affect the salesforce's morale and motivation. Reasonable and attainable goals that have an adequate reward are powerful incentives. Being able to accomplish the goals makes the salespeople feel more self-assured and professional. The spiral of goal-accomplishment-motivation continues upward.

1. How is a mission statement different from the personal goals and quotas assigned to salespeople?

2. Can activity quotas be measured by sales managers?

3. How do you think salespeople would react to a sales quota they feel is not attainable?

Policies and Procedures

Policies Set the Procedural Guidelines

Company policies and procedures were introduced in Chapter 3 as part of what a training program teaches new employees. Policies directly affecting salespeople would involve order-form completion, product demonstrations, pricing, delivery, entertainment, gifts, expense accounts, customer complaint resolution, and handling returned or damaged goods. Each firm wants sales order forms filled out according to a specified format, orders called in by a certain time, or reports in on a certain day. Many firms have established procedures for demonstrating their products to prospective customers. Retailers often have procedures for properly displaying merchandise.

The firm's pricing policy, for example, may be as simple as "Prices are not negotiated and discounts are not allowed." If the salesperson knows this, then when a prospective buyer attempts to haggle on a price, the salesperson simply says price dealing is against company policy (it may also be illegal, violating the Robinson-Patman Act or any of a host of laws established to maintain fair competition).

In some firms, the salesperson is subject to both internal and external policies and procedures. Stock brokerage firms, banks, and savings and loans are all subject to regulations imposed by federal, state, and local governments. Salespeople working in one of these organizations must know both their firm's policies and the government's regulations. The insider-trading scandals on Wall Street of the late 1980s, where salespeople from several prominent brokerage firms were sent to prison and heavily fined, are a testament to what can happen through either intentional or accidental violation of company and governmental policy.

▶ ▶ *follow-up questions*

1. Why is it important for a company to have its salespeople following the same procedures for submitting orders?

2. Do all companies enforce their policies and procedural guidelines? Why do you think they do or do not?

Salespeople Know How Advertising and Sales Promotion Support Their Selling Efforts

◀ ◀ ◀ ◀ ◀ ◀ ◀ ◀

Learning Objective 2: How personal selling interfaces with other promotional tools

The firm's promotional tools that interface with personal selling are advertising, sales promotion, and publicity. Knowing how personal selling is supported by other sales promotion efforts gives the salesperson an over-all perspective of how the company orchestrates its different promotional operations.

The point of personal selling is to directly contact a customer to make a sale. Salespeople are the firm's front-line contact with customers and competitors. Like the soldiers of an army, salespeople need support to do their jobs. The firm must educate salespeople about the promotional support they will receive and how to use it effectively.

Case in Point

Joyce Nardone: AMFAX's Sales and Advertising Mixing Together

Joyce Nardone is a 24-year-old salesperson selling AMFAX copiers and fax machines. She is adept at cold calling but adds a little more to both her selling job and her promotional activity. She says, "I have over 100 clients, and I consider them my friends. Most salespeople do not bother to go back [after the sale] but I'll bring them a free roll of paper or fax them a Hanukkah or Christmas card." As a result, customers often refer other companies to Nardone, so she has a steady stream of new business. She also coordinates AMFAX's advertising schedule with newspapers and arranges for the company to exhibit at local trade shows. "Actually, I'm creating my own job," says Nardone.

Source: Martin Everett, "Selling's New Breed: Smart and Feisty," *Sales and Marketing Management* 141 (1989): 52–64.

Advertising

Advertising is used to remind, persuade, and inform. It serves as a vehicle to contact a large number of people simultaneously through paid messages over a variety of media. Advertising media can be electronic (TV, radio, computer network, movies), print (newspapers, magazines, direct mail), or display (billboards, bus signs, skywriters). It supports salespeople by stimulating customers to want to buy or to seek information as a prelude to buying.

Retail ads target household consumers. Retailers and manufacturers often team up to do co-operative (co-op) advertising in which they share the cost of the ad. Retailers benefit by either having as much as 50 percent of the cost of the ad borne by the manufacturer or by being able to double the advertising they can do with the same money. The manufacturer is assured of getting retailers to promote the product.

Retailers, wholesalers, and distributors (known collectively as "trade channel members") are also ad targets. Manufacturers advertise directly to them through the mail or in trade magazines. For example, a publication most retail grocers and their wholesalers subscribe to is *Progressive Grocer*. If Heinz wanted to tell retailers about a new product, it would place ads in *Progressive Grocer* several weeks prior to a consumer ever seeing an ad for the product in the newspaper or on TV. Trade advertising and direct mail often have the industrial buyer presold before the salesperson arrives. The salesperson can more efficiently handle larger numbers of customers because of this preselling effect. The result is a build-up of customer interest so when salespeople make their first presentation, the product is already known to the customer. Such advertising supports the salespeople and makes their job a little easier.

Firms teach salespeople how to coordinate their presentations with ads. Salespeople learn about the timing of sales presentations, when ads appear in trade magazines, on TV or radio, or in newspapers, and how to coordinate their efforts with the ads to increase sales.

Sales Promotion

Like advertising, sales promotion is directed toward consumers and trade channel members. Sales promotion's purpose is to offer potential customers an inducement or to excite their curiosity. Trade channel members get promotions, such as contests, discounted prices, or free merchandise (called "premiums"). **Consumer sales promotion** uses such devices as coupons, free samples, contests, buy-one-get-one-free deals, and in-store demonstrations to promote sales.

One particular type of sales promotion device popular with retailers is **point-of-purchase (P-O-P) material.** P-O-P materials are banners, window signs, displays, shelf coupons, floor stands, dump displays, inflatable characters, and so forth. The purpose of P-O-P materials is to draw attention to the merchandise and stimulate impulse purchases while reinforcing planned purchases. The aim of sales promotions is to provide that extra little incentive to tip the undecided customer in your direction. For the customer who is on the fence, that coupon, contest prize, or free sample might just be enough to do the trick. For the customer who has already decided to buy, the sales promotion item acts as an unexpected reward, a little extra bonus.

Publicity

Publicity is the free TV, radio, or print exposure a firm receives because of something newsworthy about itself or its product. A drug company, for example, gets a promotional boost when it announces a new drug that lowers the risk of heart attack. Firms control much of the publicity they get through press releases issued to the media. In this way, they tell the media what they want them to know. Publicity is usually planned but may occur inadvertently when the media generates a news story, which, of course, can be good publicity or bad.

▶ ▶ *follow-up questions*

1. Some people say advertising wastes money. If we had less advertising, we could have lower prices. How would you argue *for* advertising on the basis of its relationships to salespeople and their jobs?
2. How do advertising and public relations differ?

Product Knowledge

Salespeople have a professional responsibility to maintain their knowledge about what they sell and not wait for the company to require attendance at training sessions. Successful salespeople implement a self-imposed product knowledge refresher regimen. This is done by:

▸ Keeping abreast of all product-related literature and publicity;

▸ Attending all training sessions offered by the company;

▸ Seeking out information on all competitor's products and any sources where comparisons are made between products (in *Consumer Reports,* for example);

▸ Personally using and comparing competitor's products, if possible;

▸ Asking customers about how the products they use perform under a variety of situations and how the competitors' do, as well; and

▸ If possible, visiting the company's production plant to see how the product is made. (Travel agents are often given free cruises so they can tell clients about their first-hand experience.)

Salespeople need to know everything about their product from its inception to its most probable malfunctioning component.

The Four W's of Selling

Salespeople must know the four W's of their product:

1. What is it?,
2. What will it do?,
3. Why will it do it?, and
4. What are its advantages and disadvantages?

The four W's are a combination of a product-oriented and a customer-oriented description. Before salespeople can talk about the product and its benefits to the customer, they must *know* the product.

To be adequately prepared, a salesperson must be prepared to answer the buyer's questions about the product and its history, what it will do, how is it made and from what, how do we get it, how is it packed, who will do the servicing.

What is the Product and Its History?

Learning Objective 3: Elements of product knowledge a salesperson must know

What is it? This is a simple and very frequently asked question. All too often, the reply to it does not really answer the customer's question. Some salespeople fail to tell their customers what it is they are selling. For example:

A *pen* is a *writing instrument.*

A *stereo* is a *high-quality sound system.*

A *power mower* is *effortless lawn care.*

Such descriptions create a mental image of being "better off" through the product's purchase. By answering this question, the salesperson is also set

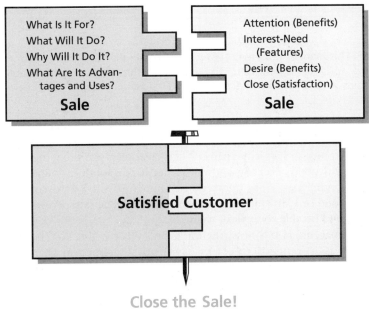

Fit Your Product Into Your Customer's Needs and. . .

What Is It For?
What Will It Do?
Why Will It Do It?
What Are Its Advantages and Uses?
Sale

Attention (Benefits)
Interest-Need (Features)
Desire (Benefits)
Close (Satisfaction)
Sale

Satisfied Customer

Close the Sale!

to establish and elaborate on the product's benefits—what the customer is *really* interested in.

Other forms of the "What is it?" question are, "How did it come into being and when?", "Why did it come into being?", "What stage of the product's life cycle is it in?", and "Has the product always been packed like this, looked like this, or been used in this way?" Knowing the answers to these questions helps address customers' questions.

Customers naturally ask such questions as "How long has this product been on the market?", "Why do you want to sell me this new model when the old one I have works just fine?", or "I'm not familiar with that product. Has it ever been called something different or been packed differently?"

Here's a small application exercise: Suppose you are selling a personal computer word processing program and the customer asks, "Where do the terms *uppercase, lowercase* and *font* come from?" Do you know the answer?[1] Knowing the history of your product helps answer many of the customer's questions (it's also just interesting to know!).

What Will It Do?

This may seem like a naive question. Can't most buyers see what it is and what it will do? No! Buyers seldom see all the things a product really does.

For example, read the dialogue below and decide which food blender you would want:

Customer *(looking at blender)*   What all does this do?

Salesperson: This blender does all eight of the functions you see here: blends, chops, purees, liquefies, etc.

or

Customer *(looking at blender)*   What all does this do?

Salesperson: This blender does everything from simple blending at 400 rpm to liquefying food at 13,000 rpm. To accomplish this, the double-insulated motor spins a solid chrome shaft supported by lifetime-guaranteed sealed bearings.

In this scenario, the customer knew the blender's basic functions but lacked the details. The first salesperson was of little help, but the second filled in the customer's knowledge gaps. When customers are shopping for a tax-free municipal bond, do they know whether it is a single-, double-, or triple-exempt bond? Does it pay quarterly or annually? Is it a zero-coupon, deep-discount bond or a sinking-fund debenture type? The salesperson must know the facts and be able to explain them.

In the pharmaceutical business, the question "What will it do?" is vital. Physicians really ask two questions of a pharmaceutical salesperson when they ask, "What will it do?" The first is "What will it do...to solve the problem?" and the second is "What are the side effects?" Physicians don't want to prescribe a drug that will cure patients' ills but proves to be fatal because of the side effects. Being able to fully answer "What will it do?" requires extensive product knowledge.

In answering the "What will it do?" question, the salesperson needs to concentrate the explanation on the product's benefits to the customer whenever possible. These benefits should be ones the customer surely wants and ones the salesperson can prove.

How Is It Made and from What?

Touring production facilities, knowing product specification sheets, and attending product training sessions are the best ways to understand a product's components. Knowing how a product is made means knowing about the quality of materials going into it and the care taken to make it. Salespeople need to know this for two reasons: first, they must be able to adequately address the product's features (its physical characteristics) to the customer during the presentation. It is a selling point if the salespeople know that their product is made from chrome vanadium steel, rather than high carbon steel, but it's only a selling point if *they know that!* Second, knowing how the product is made and what it is made from is tremendously helpful when dealing with customer complaints about faulty quality, improper assembly, or operational malfunction. Did the company really make it incorrectly, or did the customer just put it together wrong?

By knowing what the product is made of and how it works, a salesperson is prepared for the tough but always welcomed question, "So what makes yours better than theirs?" Successful salespeople are always prepared for that one because they know exactly of what and how both their own and the competitor's products are made.

Salespeople will want to tell the prospective customer not only what their product will do but *why* it will do it—the two cannot be separated:

a. Explain why it will do what is claimed.

b. Show the product and relate its features to why it will do what is claimed.

c. Offer proof through demonstrations, testimonials, sampling, or trial use.

The fourth W deals with the product's advantages over competitors' products or over not buying. The salesperson will naturally be asked at some-time during the presentation about what makes this product better than others on the market. Through a clear knowledge of all the product's features, advantages, and benefits, this fourth "W" is easily answered. Customers will express interest by asking more questions the salesperson needs to be prepared for. The next one is "How do we get it?"

How Do We Get It?

A salesperson needs to know all the aspects of product distribution. Products are distributed through a variety of channels. Retailers need to know if the product is distributed through wholesalers or sold directly from the manufacturer. This is important because they must know with whom to place the order and whom to pay. Industrial products, such as pipes, valves, and fittings, are sold and delivered through distributors. Plant engineers would ask if they should order replacement valves from the manufacturer or the distributor. While this might seem simple enough, the manufacturer and the distributor could have salespeople covering the same territory and both calling on the same engineers. The salespeople must know if this is the case and tell the engineers where to place the order.

How Is It Packed?

This question involves two issues—damage or breakage prevention and inventory control. Knowing how a product is protected against the traumas of shipping is a powerful selling tool to a customer plagued with broken or damaged merchandise on delivery. When products are damaged on delivery it means filing claim forms, waiting for credit from the vendor, and the aggravation of disposal.

Packing refers to the numbers of units a vendor sells per "shipper" or case. If a customer orders one case of product, it is important from an inventory control perspective to know if that case is a 6-pack, 12-pack, 24-pack, or 36-pack. How a product is packed is a vital issue when selling in foreign markets. The standard 48″ × 40″ wooden pallet used by domestic trucks and trains is not the standard around the world. If the product is shipped on such a pallet, it won't be unloaded from the ship or train in some countries, or if it is, the seller will be changed for the expense. Salespeople incorporate knowledge of packing into their overall product knowledge to ensure that customers' needs will be accommodated.

Who Will Do the Servicing?

Many products at one time or another require service. Some require technical installation, and others need both technical installation and customer training. Of course, there is the question of who will fix it if it breaks or won't work. Part of a salesperson's product knowledge is knowing the service aspects of the product. Will the vendor provide service? If the answer is no, then the buyer has a problem to solve, that is, who will do the servicing? Some firms offer both full-line sales and service. Sears and local contractors both sell heating products and install as well as fix them. The real estate agent who sold you your house offers you no repair service on that house, however. Once you own it, whatever breaks is your problem, not the agent's.

Servicing can also be handled through service contracts. These are either arranged by the salespeople using their own firm's service people or through a servicing firm. General Electric and Maytag are two firms that use "authorized" service representatives to install and fix their products.

The salesperson's ability to incorporate knowledge of the service arrangements can make or break a sale. Successful, adaptive salespeople are quick to use their knowledge of service contracts when pricing a product. They will often use it as leverage to close an overly price-conscious buyer. This means they might reduce the price of the service contract or extend its terms in order to close the sale. An item priced at $1,000 with an annual service contract costing $100 actually ends up costing its owner $2,000 after 10 years! By manipulating the product's or the service contract's price, the salesperson can create a salable package.

When Things Go Right

Molex Trains Engineers to Sell

When Molex's Tim Moore took the job of training director, he found himself up against a classic problem—a sales force made up of engineers who were good at technical expertise but lousy at selling. He sent questionnaires to all 110 salespeople and found:

- When asked what they were selling, that is, performance, quality, price, delivery or service, none of the salespeople agreed.
- When asked how well the company had prepared them for the job, 23 percent said "very well", 45 percent said "less than adequately," and 9 percent said they had no preparation at all.

From the results of the survey, Tim decided the salesforce needed training in basic selling skills, sales management procedures, and product and application information. Existing product training had not focused on applications. He decided to do the applications training in-house and buy an off-the-shelf selling program from an outside supplier.

Three months after everyone had completed the 25-hour training, program results were evaluated. "Comparing monthly sales, adjusted for economic shifts and seasonal efforts, before and after training, we discovered an increase of $237,000/month in sales which projected out to just less than $3 million over the year. This was a 37:1 return-on-investment for the training," said Tim. After a second three-month period, measurements were taken again and the monthly figure had climbed to $264,000 in sales, or a 40:1 return on investment. Increasing the salesperson's knowledge about products, procedures and selling skills paid off handsomely.

*Source: Arthur Bragg, "When the Problem Is Skill, Start from Scratch," *Sales and Marketing Management* 139 (1987): 90–91.

We have discussed the range of topics related to product knowledge. Now, let's explain how salespeople use pricing alternatives to close more sales.

▶ ▶ *follow-up questions*

1. How does product knowledge make a salesperson more competitive?
2. Name several products where the question of who will service them is as important as the product's price.
3. Why is the packaging question so important to a customer?
4. Why is it important for a salesperson to know about the four W's when planning a sales presentation?

Pricing Knowledge

Being able to determine a profitable price the customer can live with involves knowing about the variety of discounts and allowances. Pricing knowledge falls into two major categories: pricing methods and price adjustments. Salespeople must know how to calculate the net prices and delivered prices of their products. When selling to resellers, such as wholesalers and retailers, salespeople must know how those resellers determine the prices they charge *their* customers. Some salespeople have full latitude over the prices they quote, but others are rigidly locked into the prices set by their company.

Pricing Methods

A pricing method refers to the way a firm determines the price it will charge. Four types of prices are commonly used. These reflect the costs incurred in making and delivering the product and a return for the risk the seller has borne. The four types of prices are:

▶ **List price**—The normal standard price charged to all customers. List prices are based on the cost of the goods sold plus a markup. The list price is often called the "suggested retail price" or the "suggested list price."

Salespeople must be knowledgable about pricing methods and adjustments.

- ▶ **Net price**—The list price minus all discounts and allowances.
- ▶ **Zone price**—The same price charged to everyone in a defined zone. A good example of zone pricing is the way UPS charges customers. It divides the nation into zones and sets one price to ship to anywhere in a zone.
- ▶ **FOB price**—FOB stands for "free on board." "FOB destination" means the seller pays all the shipping costs. "FOB orign" means the buyer pays. It also designates the title's transfer point, that is, the point where ownership changes.

Case in Point

Eight Timeless Truths about Pricing

Truth No. 1: Pricing strategy has got to be tied to market share strategy. If the strategy is to increase market share, prices must reflect whatever it will take to do it.

Truth No. 2: Pricing must always consider some kind of cost strategy. A salesperson must consider the cost of his or her products and what a reasonable profit is when quoting a price. Making unprofitable sales is the quickest way out of selling.

Truth No. 3: Pricing must be a derivative of the price performance equation of your product versus those of your competition. If your product delivers no-frills performance, appearance and appeal, you're going to have a tough time getting more than a bargain-basement price. You sell "up" to the performance in the product, not "down" to somebody else's price.

Truth No. 4: Pricing must always consider the target-market customer. If the market is not concerned about price, do not sell on a price basis. Premium price where you can, discount where you must. In a survey of air travelers, price ranked fourteenth on the list of why they choose the airline they do—most important was the variety of schedules.

Truth No. 5: Upward price leverage requires continuous investment in brand equity. This means you can only raise prices successfully if customers are loyal to the product and unwilling to switch because they perceive no other substitute will do the job as well.

Truth No. 6: Astute pricing requires marketers know and understand how to design a sound price discount program. A good discount program should stimulate buying that generates significant profits and/or volumes such that cost savings counterbalance reduced prices.

Truth No. 7: Pricing plans should be easy to understand. A discount or pricing plan no one can interpret means mistakes, misunderstanding and too much of the salesperson's time is spent trying to educate the customer on something that should be obvious to both.

Truth No. 8: Pricing is one of the least measured of the marketing activities that are measured. Unfortunately, pricing often takes a back seat to more glamorous things, such as advertising, product

Continued

Markup   **Markup** *is also called margin, but it simply is the profit.* The markup represents a dollar amount or a percentage over cost. It can be expressed as either a dollar amount or percentage of the selling price. The selling price is the sum of the product's cost and the profit, or markup, the vendor puts on it. So:

◀ ◀ ◀ ◀ ◀ ◀ ◀ ◀
Learning Objective 4: Pricing methods salespeople use

$$\$ \text{ Cost} + \$ \text{ markup} = \$ \text{ selling price}$$

$$\text{Cost \%} + \text{markup \%} = 100\%$$

If the product's cost is used as the calculation basis, then the markup (profit) is calculated as a percentage of the product's cost:

$$\% \text{ markup on cost} = \$ \text{ markup}/\$ \text{ cost}$$

For example, if it costs a hotel $40 to make up a room, pay the overhead, and account for the variables costs, and it charges guests $75 for the room, then it is making a $35 profit, or marking the room up $35 over costs. Its percentage markup on cost is $35/$40 = 87.5 percent. If it decided to change its markup to 90 percent, what would it have to charge?

$$\text{New Room Price} = \$X/\$40 = .90 \rightarrow X = \$36$$

$$\$36 + \$40 = \$76$$

The hotel would need to raise its room rate by one dollar, to $76. The shortcut to figuring markup based on cost is to add 1 to the markup percentage and multiply it by the cost figure. For example:

$$\text{Cost} + \text{Markup} = \text{Selling Price}$$

$$\$15 + 15\% \text{ over cost} = \text{Selling price}$$

$$\$15 \times 1.15 = \$17.25 \text{ is the } \textit{New Selling Price}$$

Sometimes, vendors use selling price as the base, rather than costs, to calculate their markups. You are probably wondering how a markup could be based on selling price when it is the selling price we are trying to determine! The secret is to remember that the cost represents a percentage of the selling price and that the markup is the necessary percentage to make the sum of the two total 100 percent. Therefore, if you want a 30 percent markup on selling price, then the cost must equal 70 percent of the selling price, since the two together must equal 100 percent. If the cost is to be 70 percent of the selling price, then use this formula to determine the selling price:

$$\$ \text{ Cost}/\text{Cost \%} = \text{Selling Price}$$

Going back to our hotel room, the cost was $40. If we wanted a markup (profit) of 35 percent of the selling price, then the cost would be 65 percent of the selling price. Since the cost was $40, then the selling price for the room would be:

$$\$40/65\% = \$61.53 \text{ new room price}$$

The hotel would make a profit of $21.53. To check: $21.53 should be 35% of the selling price.

Retailers generally use selling price because all of their sales and mark-downs are reductions in selling price. Wholesalers, manufacturers, and distributors use cost as their basis since they very seldom use reductions and markdowns. Salespeople must know this because if they say, "This is a good price that will allow you a 25 percent markup," it will mean different things to different buyers, depending on whether they use cost or selling price as the base.

Discounts and Allowances

Salespeople use quantity discounts, cash discounts, trade discounts, seasonal discounts, advertising allowances, and damage allowances. **Quantity discounts** are price reductions for buying larger quantities. Such discounts encourage buyers to place bigger orders because they lower the per-unit price. Quantity discounts are prevalent in all types of selling and all types of products. A quantity discount might be quoted as "5 percent off for orders over 500 units." Buyers would automatically reduce the price by 5 percent if they bought 500 or more units.

The **cash discount** *is an incentive for buyers to pay their bill early.* Cash discounts are stated like "2/10 n 30," which means "take 2 percent off the price if you pay the whole bill in 10 days; if you do not pay in 10 days, the full amount is due in 30 days." This discount represents a substantial saving to the customer. Not taking a 2/10 n 30 cash discount amounts to charging yourself 36 percent interest per year![2]

Trade discounts *are manufacturer's suggested markups to wholesalers and retailers.* Trade discounts are also called **chain discounts.** These discounts are suggested reductions from a manufacturer's *suggested retail list price.* Here is an example of how a trade discount works. The manufacturer states on the invoice sent to the wholesaler (see invoice on page 121):

The suggested retail price is $12 and the suggested retailer markup over the wholesaler's price is 33.3 percent and the wholesaler's markup over the manufacturer's price is 15 percent. But how much does the wholesaler pay the manufacturer? The answer is $6.80/dozen figured as ($12 − $4) = $8 − $1.20 = $6.80. The $4 is 33 percent off the suggested retail list price, and the $1.20 is 15 percent off the suggested wholesale price of $8. The manufacturer expects to be paid $6.80 per dozen and suggests the wholesaler sell to the retailer at $8 and the retailer sell to consumers for $12 per dozen.

What if the retailer is large enough to buy direct from the manufacturer? The retailer pays $6.80 because it is assuming both the wholesaling and retailing functions. The wholesaler is not required to sell to the retailer at $8, nor is the retailer required to sell to the public at $12. These are what the manufacturer suggests, but each channel member can charge more or less than that.

```
                            INVOICE
                   XYZ Manufacturing Company
                      Littletown, USA 68114
   Sold to:    Bob Smith Wholesalers
   Ship to:    Same
               114 Elm St.
               Middletown, Ohio

   Quantity:   100 Dozen Golden Bear Widgets

               List price $12.00 per dozen
               less trade discounts of 33.3% and 15%

```
(note the discount chain here)

```
   100 Doz @ $12 = $1,200
           Less trade discount of 33.3% and 15%

   Amount due = $680
```

Seasonal discounts encourage off-season purchases. Many products have seasonal sales patterns. From the seller's perspective, the seasonal discount encourages commitments in advance of the busy season. This helps the seller's scheduling, cash flow planning, and transportation booking. For example, a seasonal discount would be offered to Christmas tree buyers if they placed orders before May 1.

Advertising allowances *are a reward for advertising the product.* Manufacturers often reward retailers for promoting their products in ads. For example, a hot dog manufacturer gives a large retailer three dollars per case off if the retailer agrees to advertise the hot dogs during a specified time period. The retailer submits an ad allowance claim form to the manufacturer, along with proof of the ad, and a check is issued for the three dollars. Sometimes the three dollars is simply deducted from the face of the invoice after the proof of advertising has been submitted. Advertising allowances are common in retailing. They represent an incentive to the retailer to promote the product as well as encourage lower prices to consumers.

Another discount is the **damage allowance.** Used in only a few industries, the purpose of this discount is to save time and expense for both the buyer and the vendor. If the manufacturer knows that statistically, 1 percent of its products will be faulty, it allows buyers to automatically deduct 1 percent of the invoiced amount for damages. This saves everyone the cost of dealing with the claims. Sometimes the buyer doesn't have any damaged merchandise but gets the allowance anyway, and sometimes goods are damaged. Such allowances tend to even out over the long run and benefit everyone involved.

Finally, there is the **direct rebate.** *Direct rebates give customers cash back with proof of purchase.* Rebates effectively lower the price paid without having to adjust the list price. Rebates are an effective form of temporary price reductions that can be started and stopped at the seller's discretion. Rebates have become popular on everything from liquor to railroad car shipments to airline tickets (frequent flyer programs). In the late 1980s, Chrysler's rebate plan started the giant automaker back on the road to financial recovery from what had appeared to be certain death.

Discounts are pricing tools, a way of changing the actual price without changing the listed price! With all the discounts discussed here, lowering them increases the actual amount the vendor receives, and raising them decreases the actual price. In the Case in Point below a typical transaction with discounts and mark-ups is described.

Case in Point

Why the Salesperson Must Know How to Figure Prices and Discounts—A Retailing Example

You have just completed the sales presentation with Fred O'Brien of XYV Stores Inc. Fred has agreed to buy 150 units of your toddler toy called Slinky Worm. Fred says, "You quoted a price of $15.50 FOB our warehouse. With the cash discount of 2/15 n 45, the 10 percent break we get on everything over 100 units and the seasonal discount of $1.50 each, do you think we'll have trouble selling them if we put our normal 75 percent markup on cost on these? Is that the retail price you've seen most of the competition charging?" As the salesperson, you must be quickly able to figure what retail price Fred O'Brien is talking about. Which of the following retail prices is correct:[3]

a. $13.69   c. $23.13
b. $18.73   d. $10.88

▶▶ *follow-up questions*

1. Which of the discounts discussed above are the ones the customer can take and which ones are given by the vendor?

2. What is a 20 percent markup on cost equivalent to in terms of a markup on selling price?

3. If your firm were the only vendor of ceiling fans to a manufacturer, why would you even think about offering a discount(s) to it?

Understanding about Credit Helps Create Sales[4]

Many sales are credit sales. Businesses as well as consumers often prefer to buy on credit when they can. They maintain their cash liquidity longer, budget payments into their costs of doing business, and pay off the debt in the future. Credit terms are a good way of making a formidable purchase affordable. When the payments are stretched over several weeks, months, or years, the price becomes less of a factor. For example, when most people buy a car or house, they are more concerned about the size of the monthly payments than the total price.

Credit terms offer vendors two advantages: they make expensive purchases more affordable for customers so vendors can sell more products and credit terms are accompanied by a finance charge that generates additional revenue as a reward to the vendor for taking the risk of the customer not paying. Credit also creates problems, the biggest being collecting. With credit sales, the people who made the sales may become bill collectors. Salespeople can reduce credit problems through understanding credit and credit alternatives. Credit can be handled in several ways: consignment sales, dating terms, performance letters of credit, progressive payments, third-party financing, and installment loans.

Consignment Sales

Consignments sales call for payment only after the product is resold, rather than when it is delivered. Title to the product usually remains with the owner until the consignee actually sells it. For the consignee, this means products are not paid for until they are actually resold, thus the payment is made when the cash from the resale is received. For the owner, the sale is carried as an account receivable, but it may take days, weeks, or months before the money from the sale reaches the till. The solution to this is using timed consignment sales terms—"We will sell it for you on a 30-day consignment." At the end of 30 days, the customer pays up for what was sold and returns the unsold merchandise.

Learning Objective 5: Forms of credit salespeople use to help customers buy products and services

---

Case in Point

Creative Credit and Pricing Allows More Customers to Buy

A representative of a national pharmaceutical company was having difficulty competing on the price of a particular product. The competitors had a "contract" and received the "contracted price" based on quantity purchases of one particular product. The representative's company had the usual "quantity price" break on the product needed by a local hospital, but the buyer stated she did not have storage for large quantities—nor did she want her money tied up in inventory. The rep personally designed a plan he called the "E.A.N. agreement" that involved the buyer estimating her annual need and getting the quantity price break on that estimate. The customer would order when she needed and not have to take a large shipment all at once to get the special price. The hospital would be invoiced at the special price.

  Advantages:

▸ No inventory holdings (cost savings)
▸ Fresh merchandise always on hand
▸ Unit price reduced to less than the competition was charging.

Should the hospital for any reason not purchase the quantity agreed upon, it would be charged the price nearest the quantity price on all the previous orders. The plan worked so well that it became a model for the rest of the company's reps across the country.

Comment: This is an example of how knowledge about pricing and the industry and being creative paid off for the customer, the vendor, and the salesperson.

Dating Terms

Credit can be extended through creative dating terms. For example, an oil refiner could sell fuel oil to local distributors before the heating season by setting the payment's due date after the heating season begins, when the distributors have the money to pay for it. The sale may take place in May, but the date for the payment would be March of the next year. This would allow the refiner to get the inventory of fuel oil off its hands and free up production facilities and storage space for other products. It could also carry the sale as an account receivable (an asset) and benefit from such dating as long as the cost to store it in its inventory is greater than the cost of delaying the payment from the customer. The customers secure the oil they need but avoid paying for it until after their busy season.

Using Performance Letters of Credit

A performance letter of credit is a letter from the customer's bank saying, in essence, that if the customer does not pay the seller within a certain time, and the seller sends a statement to that effect to the bank and demands that the bank pay, the bank will pay the seller. This guarantees that the seller will get paid. The bank either draws the money against the customer's account at the time it gives the seller the performance letter or requires the customer to place enough funds on deposit to cover the bill. Vendors use this tool when dealing with poor credit risks, customers with a history of not paying on time, or foreign companies.

Progressive Payments

Progressive payments are used to spread the risk and payments. A progressive payment schedule is common in service sales, that is, construction, legal service, landscaping contracts, or dental work. Simply, a progressive payment

Knowing how to handle credit transactions helps create sales.

schedule is a way of extending credit by saying that the customer will pay a certain percentage of the total due at specified times, such as when the order is written, when half the work is completed, and when the job is finished. The buyer gets to extend the payments, and the seller gets some money up-front, reducing the risk of not getting paid.

Third-Party Financing

Third-party financing means having a third party (usually a bank) make the payment, rather than the customer. The vendor ships the product but gets paid by the bank (the third-party guarantor). Cars and houses are normally sold this way. You buy your house from the builder, but the builder gets his/her money from the mortgage company, which you pay off. This is the preferred method of financing for many large-ticket items.

Installment Loans

Installment loans are loans paid back over a number of periods. Most credit terms are written this way by third-party financiers, and most consumer credit purchases are made this way. Credit card financing is an installment loan. The customer pays the debt as a series of installments but owes a finance charge in the process. Installment loans can substantially raise the total cost of the product when the interest cost is included. If salespeople are going to use credit as a selling point, they need to know its full impact on the customer.

Customers benefit three ways from such a credit purchase. First, they get to keep their money to use for other things, thus maintaining liquidity. Second, paying out only a portion of the total is easier on the pocketbook and thus maintains a healthier cash flow. Finally, the interest paid is usually tax deductible (depending on the current tax regulations).

Using credit allows customers to make purchases that would otherwise be impossible. Another alternative salespeople should have knowledge of is leasing. Leasing offers some of the benefits both of outright purchase and of installment buying.

Leasing Arrangements

Large-ticket items are often leased, rather than sold. Leasing arrangements offer considerable advantages to the customer and are great selling points. When a firm leases a product to another, it is actually providing a financing function—a way for the customer to acquire the product without having to pay the full price up front. A lease is not a disguised installment sale.

Customers enter into leasing agreements for several reasons. First, they may not have the money to make the purchase outright. Second, leasing has significant tax advantages. Third, customers may anticipate technological advances, style changes, or potential obsolescence and do not want to own a product that would have no future salvage value. With a lease, the product goes back to the vendor when the lease is up. Computers are often leased for this very reason—as new models emerge, old models are replaced by simply letting their leases run out and sending them back to the manufacturer. Table 4-2 lists the advantages and disadvantages of leasing.

Table 4-2	**Advantages and Disadvantages of Leasing**	
Advantages	**Disadvantages**
Maintains liquidity	High implicit interest
Form of 100 percent financing	No salvage value to lessee
Limits creditor's claims	No product modifications without lessor's consent
Avoids obsolescence	
High degree of flexibility	

Leases offer several advantages over direct purchase. Customers can obtain the product when they cannot or are not willing to make the total financial commitment. By leasing, customers maintain their liquidity.

A second advantage is that leases offer the option of 100 percent financing. In credit or outright purchases, some if not all of the price of the product is required up-front. Many leases require no such up-front payment so the purchase is totally financed by the vendor.

The third advantage is the limit on claims in the event of bankruptcy or reorganizations. Bankruptcy laws have limited creditors' claims to a maximum of three years' worth of lease payments. In the case of an outright purchase, creditors can sue for the full amount owed. Salespeople should check with local, state, and federal tax authorities before making specific claims regarding this benefit of leasing.

There are disadvantages to leasing. The lessor (vendor) can build in a high interest cost as part of the payment. A lease does not have an explicit interest cost like a loan, so the lessor incorporates whatever amount of implicit interest it wants. Second, there is no salvage value for the lessee (customer). When customers own a product then wish to replace it, they can capture a salvage value when selling it off. With the lease, any salvage value belongs to the lessor. Finally, since the product is owned by the lessor, the lessee cannot alter it in any way without the lessor's permission. For example, if a firm leased a large sheetmetal stamping machine and wanted to make minor modifications to it so it would more efficiently fit into its new production process, it could not do so without the lessor's permission.

The specifics of leases and the mechanics of making them an element of the sales presentation are part of the knowledge a salesperson gains through training and experience.

▶▶ *follow-up questions*

1. A salesperson quotes a price and terms to a customer by saying, "The price is $4,700. We can finance that over 5 years at 8 percent interest." The customer says, "What does that make the monthly payments?" What's your answer?[5]

2. Why would people want to use an installment loan if the product just ends up costing them more in the long run than if they paid cash up-front?

3. Can you give an example of a third-party payment plan?

Politics in Trade Channels

Knowledge of the political and power relationships in channels of distribution helps salespeople recognize and capitalize on opportunities and avoid problems.

Power in the Channels

Power is the ability to influence others. In channels of distribution, competitive and cooperating firms are always trying to influence each other. Being profit-oriented, each firm attempts to exert influence over the others. The power in a channel gives salespeople knowledge about which firms can influence and which must be submissive. Table 4-3 defines the five bases for political and economic power.

Power bases and the power of politics in channels partially explain why firms do business with each other. For example, if the buyer says, "Why should I switch wholesalers and buy from your firm? We have been buying from XYZ for a lot of years and have been satisfied with the way they have treated us," the astute salesperson should recognize two clues: "for a lot of years" (probably a referent power base) and "have been satisfied with the way they have treated us" (probably a reward power base). A referent power base indicates a degree of friendship and loyalty. The inept salesperson would lose all chances on this sale by degrading the competitor. The astute salesperson would acknowledge the existence of the friendly relations and use an "I want to be your friend, too" approach. If the base is in reward power, an appeal could be directed toward the prospect of even greater rewards. By understanding power and how it is used, the salesperson can be more successful.

◄ ◄ ◄ ◄ ◄ ◄ ◄ ◄

Learning Objective 6: Power politics in channels of distribution

Conflicts in Channels

Conflicts in channels naturally occur. Conflicts are usually the result of miscommunication or direct competitive attempts to alter channel relationships. There are three kinds of conflict:

▶ Role conflict

▶ Conflicting goals

▶ Communication conflicts

Table 4-3 Power Bases Firms Use to Influence Each Other

Coercive power is the ability to punish.

Reward power is the ability to grant rewards.

Referent power comes from a feeling of friendship, mutual like and interest, and mutual respect.

Legitimate power means one firm has a legitimate or legal right to influence another. Franchisors influence franchisees because the contract between the two says the franchisee will do what the franchisor says.

Expert power is the ability to influence because of a special skill, knowledge, or technical expertise.

Role conflicts   Role conflict occurs when channel members do not live up to their roles and don't do what is normally accepted or expected of them. Traditional channel relationships are based on past behaviors and the division of duties that led to the evolution of a channel. For example, ABC Wholesalers has traditionally sold only to retailers, and BDN is a retailer. Should ABC begin to sell directly to consumers, BDN's traditional market, a role conflict would result between the two. The salesperson selling to BDN and ABC could be caught in the middle, with both saying, "If you deal with the other guy, you can kiss my business good-bye."

Goal conflicts   Each firm in the channel has a specific agenda of its own, but it is tied to the agendas of other participants in the channel. A retail firm can only expand up to the ability of its wholesalers to supply, and a wholesaler can expand only to the limit of its retail customers' ability to buy. So while a wholesaler's goal may be to double sales over the next seven years, it can do so only if the retailers can increase their sales. Goal problems occur in franchisee-franchisor channel relationships. When the goals of the franchisor (McDonald's, as an example) are at odds with those of the individual franchisee (the McDonald's outlet by your house), then a conflict occurs. The corporation may set a goal to double the number of Big Macs sold, but the franchisee cannot hit that goal because Big Macs don't sell in its market. As a representative for the franchisor, you would be caught between the company goals and those of a valued franchisee.

What Would You Do If...?

As a relatively inexperienced salesperson calling on the major wholesaler, you have made good inroads and are getting an increasing amount of business. This wholesaler is a major force in the channel and commands a good share of the retail customers who ultimately sell your product to final consumers.

The wholesaler also has been dealing with one of your competitors for a number of years. This wholesaler alone could account for 30 percent of your firm's total business if you could get it all. The chances of that happening are slim, but you dream about it. Your company is a national concern with many offices across the nation. However, the company's sales have been off over the last couple of years, and management has said the key to gaining new business is to bend over backwards to help customers. Policies have not changed, however, and there is still a ban on price cutting—everyone gets charged the same, regardless of size of company or of order.

Yesterday, you called on the wholesaler and were floored when the general manager said, "We are thinking of switching away from our present supplier and we would like to give all of our business to you and your firm. The problem is the price. For us to make our customary margins, you would have to shave your prices by 5 percent. In return, you will get all our business, and you know how much that amounts to."

This is too big of a decision for you to make alone so you decide to take it up with your sales manager. She listens to what you have to say then says, "What do you think we should do?"

▶ Question: What would you recommend?[6]

Communication conflicts The largest single source of conflict arises from communication problems. As you learned in the last chapter, there are numerous barriers to accurate communications. Channel conflicts are often traceable to such barriers or to problems of media, message, and understanding in general. Communication conflicts often stem from a channel member lacking necessary information. Information sharing on such topics as prices, demand, availability, upcoming promotions, and transportation problems is vital to efficient and profitable operations.

▶▶ *follow-up questions*

1. A firm can exert power or influence in five ways. What is referent power and how does it differ from expert power?
2. How would role conflict come about in a channel of distribution?

Competitive Intelligence

Successful, adaptive salespeople need to know as much about the competition as they do about their own company and products. Salespeople sell against the competitor's features, advantages, and benefits. Salespeople must be able to answer the hard but often asked question, "How does your product out perform theirs?" To answer this, more than just product knowledge is required. Competitive intelligence means knowing all the facets of the competitor's product, service, successes, failures, good ideas, and bad ideas.

What You Need to Know

Competitors' strategy A good place to start learning about competitors' strategy is with their four P's: *product, price, promotion,* and *place or distribution*. Salespeople must know the operational features of the competition's *products* if they are to sell successfully against them. Knowing about their products is fairly easy in most industries. In the consumer goods industries (grocery, department, and drug store items, for example), all competitors have their products displayed on the shelf. It is a simple task to go buy a competitor's product and try it. For industrial products, it can be more complex. Some buyers give salespeople samples of the product they are now using to make comparisons. Testing laboratories test and compare products then publish their findings.

It helps to know the competitors' *prices* and discount plans. Some prices are public information. With consumer goods, the prices are on the items and out for everyone to see. Car dealers have the stickers on the windows of their cars. Buyers sometimes provide the prices charged by competitors. Salespeople may not know the competitor's exact offering price, but knowing their prices are generally competitive, lower, or higher is often enough.

Promotion is a part of the marketing mix that is hard to hide. Ads, flyers, billboards, and direct mail pieces are highly visible. With little difficulty, buyers and sellers alike have easy access to each other's promotional materials and can observe their strategies in action.

The fourth element is *place or distribution*, and like promotion, distribution practices are highly visible. In consumer goods, a simple phone call or a

Learning Objective 8:
Competitive intelligence—
what you need to know and
how to get it

trip to a store identifies the channels of distribution a firm uses. For industrial distribution, observation or a phone call to a distributor will produce the same results.

With a little creativity, hard work, and some detective zeal, salespeople can easily learn about competitors' four P's. They then can make comparisons for the prospective buyer between how "they do it" and how "we do it." This is vital knowledge for the salesperson.

Successes and failures   Salespeople must know the successes and failures of both their products and the competition's. A salesperson often makes recommendations to the buyer about which product to use and which one to avoid. This can only be done successfully if the salesperson knows the best product to recommend. Salespeople are often called in to sell a product as a replacement for a competitor's product that did not perform as promised. They must be familiar enough with the competitor's product to avoid making a similar mistake and recommending a product that will not stand up to the buyer's applications.

Salespeople must be aware of the failures that occur as well. Failures may come from using products in applications for which they were not designed. Salespeople must know where their own products fail. This allows them to warn buyers ahead of time that certain uses of the product will not be successful and to steer buyers toward products that will do the job. However, professional salespeople never degrade a competitor's products nor do they take the buyer's time to berate the competitor's failures. Salespeople's time with the customer is best spent talking about what their product will do, not what the competitor's product won't do.

Goals and strategies   A salesperson should know the competitor's goals and strategies to determine the best defenses against each competitor. When Wendy's saw McDonald's installing salad bars in its stores, the strategy was apparent, and Wendy's followed suit. The makers of disposable plates, knives, forks, spoons, refrigerated salad bar fixtures, and many other products reformulated their strategies in light of this new strategy evolving in the fast-food industry. The salespeople for these firms knew their strategy must be one of speed, price, and service. The one getting to the fast-food firm first had the best chance. Since plastic plates and utensils are commodity items, price would be a big part of the salespeople's selling strategy. Finally, service before and after the sales would tell the story for repeat business.

Knowing the strategies competitive firms employ tells adaptive salespeople two things. First, it says what is going to happen and where changes will be made. And second, it tells them the degree of change to expect. When Coca Cola changed its original formula to match more closely Pepsi's flavor, Pepsi did not resort to changing its formula; it simply did nothing—except advertise Coke's changes and its own success with its taste tests, thus taking advantage of Coke's strategic error. Knowledge of the competitor's goals and strategies is extremely useful to salespeople.

Competitors' strengths and weaknesses   Competitors' strengths and weaknesses are part of the competitive intelligence package. Knowing these is knowing where competitors are vulnerable. Firms are not strong in all areas. For example, IBM has never been known as a leader in product innovation. While its computers are some of the best in the industry, one of its greatest strengths lies in its marketing capability. A competitor may be strong in product design but weak in service, installation, or training. Salespeople facing this competitor would want to stress product quality equal to the competitor's but hit hard their firm's superiority in service, installation, and training (the competitor's weakest areas.) One of the most basic of all strategies is to attack from a position of strength and target a point of weakness.

Keeping track of competitive intelligence A good procedure for recording competitive intelligence is to create a competitor analysis worksheet. It should contain all the elements necessary to provide a profile of the competition's past, present, and expected moves. Figure 4-1 contains an example of such a worksheet.

How to Gather Competitive Intelligence

While a company training program is a way to gather knowledge about competitors, only so much can be taught. After training, salespeople must depend on their own ability and creativity to gather competitive knowledge. For most salespeople, what they learn about the competition, they learn through their own initiative. There are several ways of gaining competitive intelligence.

Ask questions, observe, and listen The best way to gather competitive intelligence is by asking questions, observing, and listening. Salespeople live in a sea of information available for the taking. They call on buyers that have information about what competitors are doing. In retailing, they can easily

Dimension	Weaknesses	Strengths	Opportunities	Threats
Products (New, Old)				
Distribution (Current, Past, Changes)				
Promotion (Print, TV, Radio)				
Price (Discounts, Allowances)				
Service				
Market Position				
Target Customers				
Market Share (Current, Changes)				
Market Potential (Markets served, Not served)				
Current Vendors (Local, Regional, National, International)				
Growth Potential				
Management Changes				
Marketing Changes				

Figure 4-1 **Example of a Competitor Analysis Worksheet**

Case in Point

95 Percent of What You Need to Know Is Public Information

Gathering competitive intelligence isn't the cloak-and-dagger work one might think. Most of the information a salesperson needs is in the public domain, but you must know where to look. Most of the "spies" are market analysts, researchers, and salespeople. A competitive intelligence specialist says he likes to talk to his contacts in the South, rather than the North—they are far more approachable and friendly than in the North. Some of the basic dos and don'ts are:

DO use business school libraries. Wealthy business families often endow business schools and their libraries so they are good places to gather information that might not be available elsewhere.

DO attend trade shows. Attend trade shows for your industry and that of your customers. Trade show attendees are notoriously talkative and eager to tell you all they know about what they're doing and how things are going.

DO check out the town assessor's office. Companies must file tax, ownership, and zoning information. It's a good place to start when researching the competition.

DO read Dunn & Bradstreet Credit Reports. They analyze the company and often have information about key personnel.

DO contact the state economic development office in the state capitol. It often has detailed, public information about a firm or industry.

DO contact country clubs, Welcome Wagons, or local charitable institutions. They often have a wealth of information about key business leaders that can be very helpful.

DON'T call for information on Mondays. No one seems to want to talk on Monday.

DON'T be afraid to be too aggressive on the phone. It may take six or seven tries.

Source: Kathleen Behof, "The Right Way to Snoop on the Competition," *Sales and Marketing Management* 136 (1984): 46–48.

observe the competition. Channel members and intermediaries also have information. Buyers and sellers trade information on the events and people in their industries everyday. Buyers are as curious about the goings-on of their competitors as the salespeople are of their competitors. Buyers and sellers often trade information on each other's competitors as part of their regular business conversation.

Developing listening skills helps salespeople gather competitive intelligence. Buyers often and unknowingly pass along competitive intelligence in the objections they give and through general conversation. The following conversation illustrates how to glean competitive intelligence from a presentation:

Salesperson: We like to think our service is one of the strongest selling points we have to offer.

Buyer: Service is something we consider essential from our vendors and one of the reasons we are talking to other vendors.

Salesperson: Service has been a problem with your current vendor?

Buyer: Yes, XYZ has not been doing the job they used to, and we just cannot depend on them lately.

Salesperson: When did you start having trouble?

Buyer: After they decided to move their warehouse to Cincinnati, their ability to take care of our needs like they used to fell off. They just seemed to have trouble getting things straight, you know, sending us the wrong items, wrong quantities, late, etc. They promised things would not change, but they did, and they have had so much trouble with their new computer billing system, it has been one headache for us after another. We just cannot do business that way, it costs us too much money. When we brought it up to their new salesperson, she said there was not much she could do but she would try. It just hasn't worked out.

What did you learn from the conversation? You should have determined the following:

▶ The old vendor has fallen down in service (weakness).

▶ The old vendor was XYZ.

▶ XYZ has opened a new warehouse in Cincinnati, and since then, things have not been working well. This is strategically important because other customers served out of that new warehouse may also be dissatisfied (an opportunity).

▶ Problems are not singular: they are having trouble with accuracy in quantity and selection and scheduling deliveries. Problems appear to be both internal to this new warehouse and external, too (another opportunity).

▶ XYZ has just installed a new computer billing system, and it isn't working (something the salesperson's top management would want to know!).

▶ XYZ has a new salesperson who is proving to be ineffective or doesn't have the power to get things corrected, maybe the result of a change in managerial policy (an opportunity and something the salesperson's top management would want to know).

Adaptive salespeople would go back to the office and make a list of all firms like the one they just called on. These firms are probably having the same trouble, and their dissatisfaction with XYZ offers an opportunity to steal them away. The salesperson now knows the selling points to use. S/he can talk about their firm's accuracy in filling orders, delivering, getting the billing straight, and responding to customer needs. All this competitive intelligence came from less than a minute's worth of conversation. Being a good listener can pay a handsome dividend.

Reading news publications   Successful salespeople stay abreast of their markets, industry, customers, and competitors by reading as much as they can in news publications. Local newspapers are excellent sources of local trade and competitive information. Most major newspapers have business sections that contain feature stories about local businesses. This can be a fertile field for gaining timely and locally important information. It can also be a source of ideas. A bank president once told your text's author that many of his new product ideas came from the newspapers of the cities he traveled in.

He would read the business section, search for products offered by the local banks and savings and loans, then take them home and use them in his bank.

National publications are also excellent sources of competitive intelligence. The *Wall Street Journal, Business Week,* trade association magazines, and similar publications provide a more global perspective from which salespeople can learn of events and developments at their customers' and competitors' corporate level.

Specialty information and data Salespeople often need special information or data for sales presentations. For example, such facts as the average sales per square foot for hardware retail stores would be important for a salesperson helping a new store owner determine an inventory level. Another example would be average labor costs for a beer distributor. This would be important for a business software salesperson helping a new distributor set up a computer program.

Such specialized facts come from at least three sources. A major source is trade association data. There are literally hundreds of trade associations. One of their major functions is to lobby the government, and to do that effectively, they collect data of every kind imaginable. This data is available to association members and often to anyone who asks. Data that would be used in the two examples above come from trade associations. The *Encyclopedia of Trade Associations,* available in most libraries, lists all the trade associations in the United States, along with their addresses and phone numbers.

Government reports are also valuable sources of information and data. The *Statistical Abstract of the United States,* published annually and available in all libraries, is a highly condensed version of just some of the data gathered by the federal government. Starting there will put you on the trail of other governmental publications for even more in-depth data.

Purchased market intelligence is the third source. Commercial marketing research firms collect, condense, and interpret trade association and governmental data, which they then sell. Using these sources can be expensive, but can save valuable time. While the average salesperson probably cannot afford these services, it's good to know there are professionals available, should the need arise. The American Marketing Association in Chicago provides a list with most of the marketing research firms in the United States.

Salespeople must know all they can about everything even remotely linked to their businesses. Selling is a learning profession, and the good salesperson is constantly learning new ways to do things and important facts and information to make it easier and more fascinating.

▶▶ *follow-up questions*

1. What is meant by "competitive intelligence"?
2. If you were selling TV sets for Hitachi to TV and electronic retail stores, what competitive intelligence would you want and what sources would you use to get it?

Summary

In this chapter, we began by explaining about a firm's goals and objectives. These affect the salesperson by providing a broad performance guide. Company goals ultimately get translated into goals and quotas for salespeople. The goals most directly impacting salespeople revolve around capturing some portion of the market potential. This portion was called market share (Learnng Objective 1).

Personal selling was discussed in relationship to the other promotional elements firms use: advertising, public relations, and sales promotion. Personal selling was presented as an integral part of the whole promotional strategy. Emphasis was placed on how personal selling must work in concert with other promotional elements to coordinate the effective communication and sale of products through the channels of distribution to end users and consumers (Learning Objective 2).

Salespeople learn such things as product knowledge, selling skills, and pricing techniques through company training programs. Product knowledge involves all aspects of the product's history, construction, performance, packaging, and service (Learning Objective 3).

Pricing techniques are based on cost and selling price. Markups are figured on a dollar or a percentage amount of either the cost paid or the selling price sought. Prices are quoted in any combination of list, zone, net, and FOB prices.

Prices are adjusted down to the net price by using quantity, cash, trade, or seasonal discounts. Also, some firms have allowances for damaged goods or advertising, that effectively lower the list price. Quantity discounts represent rewards for buying in large quantities. The cash discount rewards the customer for paying early, and the seasonal discount is an inducement to buy in the off-season. Trade discounts are often suggested by manufacturers to channel members based on the services they perform and the manufacturer's suggested markups. Through such discounts, a firm can effectively alter its net price without adjusting its list price (Learning Objective 4).

Various types of credit tools salespeople use were explained. Salespeople often extend credit through installment payments, forward dating, consignment selling, or leasing. Extending credit is a way of making a product affordable to a broader base of customers who otherwise would not have the money to pay the full price all at once. Cars, homes, appliances, and most business equipment are all regularly purchased through some sort of credit terms arranged by the salesperson (Learning Objective 5).

The nuances of channel politics and power bases were discussed to explain why salespeople must understand how and why firms try to influence salespeople (Learning Objective 6). Salespeople are often put in conflict situations by trying to accommodate the policies of customers, other channel members, and their own firms. Understanding power and political relationships can help salespeople capitalize on opportunities and avoid problems, which usually stem from miscommunication, role conflicts, or conflicts in goals (Learning Objective 7).

Competitive intelligence was defined as essential information about competitors. Competitive intelligence should be gathered in a systematic way, and a worksheet was presented as a tool to organize this information. Basic competitive intelligence contains product, service, strategic, and success-failure information. This information helps the salesperson determine the competition's strengths and weaknesses. Competitive intelligence can be gathered through such obvious means as asking questions, reading newspapers and magazines, and observing. Specialized sources of competitive intelligence include trade publications, governmental reports, and purchased consulting reports (Learning Objective 8).

Key Terms

Sales forecast   The projection a company or sales branch makes for its expected sales.

Market share   The target percentage or share of the total business in the market.

Sales quota   A minimum amount of sales required, usually expressed as a target amount of either dollar or unit sales for the upcoming year.

Activity quota   The number of calls per day, prospecting calls, displays set up, cold calls, and so on a salesperson is expected to make. It is a target level for a specific selling activity.

Consumer sales promotions   The coupons, free samples, contests, buy-one-get-one-free deals, and demonstrations you see all the time in stores and newspapers and on packages.

Point-of-purchase material   The banners, window signs, displays, shelf coupons, floor stands, dump displays, inflatable characters, in short, all of the promotional materials used to encourage interest at the point of purchase.

List price   The normal standard price charged to all customers.

Net price   The price the customer actual pays; the list price minus any discounts, allowances, and refunds.

Zone price   All customers in the same geographic zone are charged the same price for a product.

FOB price   FOB stands for "free on board." The price is related to who will pay the shipping costs. "FOB destination" means the seller pays the freight charges; "FOB origin" means the buyer pays.

Markup   Also called margin, it simply is the profit.

Quantity discount   A reduction from the list price given to encourage buying larger quantities.

Cash discount   A discount the seller gives to buyers for paying their bills early.

Trade discounts   Suggested reductions from a retail price the manufacturer thinks the product should sell for. The discounts are based on the normal costs of channel members.

Seasonal discounts   Reductions used to encourage off-season purchases.

Advertising allowances   Discount awarded to retailers for advertising the product.

Damage allowance   An automatic deduction for damaged goods used only in a few industries.

Direct rebate   Cash allowances paid to customers with proof of purchase.

Discussion Questions

1. What is the purpose of a firm's mission statement and how does its contents affect the field salesperson?
2. Differentiate between a sales forecast and a market share goal.
3. Why would a salesperson encourage a customer to pay now and take the cash discount?
4. Which of the elements described under competitive intelligence would *you* say is the most important and why?
5. How do the different types of promotional tools serve to help salespeople do their jobs?
6. Why would a company want to offer a seasonal discount? What are the pros and cons of the seasonal discount for both the selling firm and the purchasing firm?
7. What advantages does a firm get from using zone pricing? What are the advantages to the buyer?
8. If you were the manager of the local Goodyear tire store and wanted to determine your share of the passenger car tire market for this year, what data would you already have, what would you want, and where would you get it?
9. If a product was purchased by a wholesaler from you for $12.99, then sold to a retailer who marked it up to $21.99, what was the retailer's cost if he marked it up by 37 percent on selling price? What would his cost have been if he had marked it up 37 percent on cost?
10. If a customer wanted to finance a purchase through credit terms and your firm did not grant credit, what alternatives could you offer that customer?
11. Explain how using progressive payments is a form of credit to the customer and how it really amounts to an interest-free loan.
12. What is meant by a firm's "discount policies"?
13. What are four types of prices salespeople regularly use?
14. What credit tool could Christmas tree farms use when selling trees in July to the local Optimist Club for its annual tree sale?

Application Exercise

Go back and read the boxed feature about Molex's training program, then answer the following questions:

1. Do the results Tim Moore got back after surveying his 110 salespeople indicate a deeper problem than just a lack of training? If yes, what could it be?
2. What do you think would be most important for sales engineers to learn from a training program? Why?
3. Do you think all training programs have such a healthy return on investment? How could a firm determine its return on investment for training?

Class Exercise

Group Exercise

The class will be divided into groups, each of which will be a sales organization that sells educational supplies, equipment, and textbooks to community colleges and universities.

In preparing for an upcoming sales presentation, the sales manager reviews the product line, which is composed of:

- overhead projectors
- desks
- pencils and pens
- heavy-duty staplers
- computer hardware

For each product listed above, the groups will identify:

1. Unique features
2. Unique benefits to the customers
3. The competitive edge gained by its unique features and benefits.

Create a work sheet like the one below to help you organize your thoughts.

Work Sheet No. 1 Unique *Features* of your product or service	Unique *benefit* of your product or service	Competitive edge gained
1.		
2.		
3.		
4.		
5.		
6.		

Individual Presentation

Step 1. Each student will identify what he or she feels is a salable product or service for today's marketplace. Be as creative as possible.

Step 2. The student will then present to the class an outline of his or her ideas on how the product will be promoted, advertised, and priced.

Step 3. The student will then describe, in detail, the personal selling process for this product or service, given the factors identified in Step 2.

▼ ▼ ▼ ▼ ▼ ▼ *Cases* ▼ ▼ ▼ ▼ ▼ ▼

How To Handle Henry?

On Tuesday Candace De Souza was thinking about the presentation she had scheduled for the end of the week with the H. J. Ogleby Company. Ogleby, a wholesaler for beer and wines, has most of the retailers in town as its accounts and is by far the leader in market share of the wholesale liquor and spirits trade in the area. Candace knew Henry Ogleby only by reputation. He was purported to be fair but tough and a hard bargainer. He was a no-nonsense person that would see salespeople almost any time but would not give them more than a few minutes to make their pitch.

Candace began mentally planning for this call. She decided what social style she thought Henry was and figured that service and price would be the two hooks she would use in her presentation. She figured that she would need to know more about H. J. Ogleby Company and that she must be sharp and quick when it came to discussing price with Henry. She decided she would have her presentation focus on Gallo's new blush chablis wine. It's packed twelve bottles in a case and has a wholesale list of $28.66 per case. This month Candace's firm offers a seasonal discount of 3 percent, plus its standard 6 percent reduction for purchases of 150 or more cases. Naturally, it also offers a cash discount. Candace set a personal goal of selling Henry 300 cases of the wine. She still needed to find out more about Henry's company, so she decided she would work on that the rest of the week in addition to making her regular calls.

Questions

1. If you were Candace, what other information would you want before calling on Henry? Where would you get it?

2. If Henry is a hard bargainer, he will want proof that the new Gallo wine is going to be a good seller. If you were Henry, what questions would you be asking Candace during the interview. If you were Candace, what questions would you prepare for?

3. If Henry asked for the bottom line price for the 300 cases, what would Candace quote?

Benner's Security

J. J. Benner and David Esrati were about to complete the sale of a security system to Benner's chain of jewelry stores. Benner has 42 stores in the chain and will realize substantial insurance savings if he installs the security system before the end of the year. Benner also stands to gain substantial tax savings by doing it now, in December, rather than waiting until next year. The total cost to outfit each store with a system is $6,247 per store, or a total sale for Esrati of $262,374. This represents a major sale for David and one he doesn't want to lose. Benner and Esrati have agreed on the needs to be filled and the price. Benner now throws Esrati a curve:

Benner: Well, David, things look pretty good. I'd like to get this deal wrapped up before the end of the year. If we can work out an arrangement to make the invoice show the purchase in next year, you have yourself a deal.

Esrati: I don't see any problem with that. The only thing we need to finalize is the payment. Should we invoice you directly for the 42 units?

Benner: Dave, we are talking about a lot of money here. What can you come up with in terms of credit arrangements? I cannot lay out over $262,000 all at once.

Esrati: Mr. Benner, I know that's quite a lot of money. I anticipated your idea for credit arrangements. Let me give you some ideas that would make this affordable to you.

With that, David offered several alternatives.

Questions

1. What alternatives would you offer if you were David?
2. If you helped Benner arrange financing at a local bank for a loan at 9.5 percent compounded over three years, what would Benner's monthly payments be?
3. What would the total system end up costing Benner, considering the interest in addition to the principle?[7]
4. How would a tax savings help Benner pay for the 42 systems? Would this be a selling point Esrati could use?

References

1. *Uppercase* and *lowercase* are printer's terms. In the old days of hand-set type, each letter's impression was made with steel or wooden type. These pieces of type were kept in two separate boxes, or cases, at the composer's table—capital letters in the upper case, which was set above the case in which other letters were kept; hence, the terms *uppercase* and *lowercase*. *Font* refers to a metal striking or forging. The italics *font* means the individual pieces of type were forged, that is, hammered, into the characteristic italics shape.
2. There are 18 20-day periods in a year. If you fail to take the discount of 2 percent for each of them, that amounts to 2 percent × 18, or 36 percent per year. It is even cheaper to borrow the money at 20 percent to pay early, rather than pass up the cash discount.
3. The correct answer is $23.13. The first 100 units you sold him were at the full price of $15.50, but the next 50 were at 10 percent off $15.50. So ($15.50 × 100) + ($13.95 × 50) = $2,247.50. He gets $1.50 per unit off for the seasonal discount, which totals to $225. At this point, you are looking at a sale of $2,022.50. If he pays within the 15 days as stipulated by the cash discount of 2/15 n 45, he can deduct another $40.45, leaving him with a cost of $1,982.05 or $13.21 per unit. If he marks up the $13.21 by 75 percent, his final retail price would be $23.13.
4. R. D. Rutherford, "Make Your Sales Force Credit Smart," *Sales and Marketing Management,* 141 (1989): 50–56.

5. Hint: call a local bank and ask what the payments would be. Banks all have payment schedule books that allow them to determine the monthly payment for any size loan over any span of time for any amount.

6. Blaise Bergeil and G. Glenn Walters, *Marketing Channels* (Dallas: Scott, Foresman, 1982), chap. 18.

7. There are several issues here. One is channel power. This is obviously a powerful wholesaler whose business you would like to have. It could substantially increase your market share. Another issue is the discount. It is only asking for 5 percent. Still another is the ethical dilemma—a policy that says no and a directive that says do all you can for the customer. Ethically, should a wholesaler try to pressure you and force you to cut your price? Third, how reliable will this wholesaler be? It is getting ready to dump its current supplier. If you were to take it on and as a major share of your business, what would happen if it dumped you as easily? Lastly is the personal perspective. Getting this account would mean a substantial increase in your salary and a definite promotion. Weighing all of that, what would you recommend?

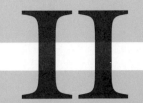

Knowing
Your Customer

5 Behavior and Motives of Individual and Organizational Customers

Objectives

After completing this chapter, you will be able to:

1. Differentiate between consumer's and organizational buyer's motives, behaviors, and situations.

2. Categorize consumers into four major types.

3. Categorize organizational buyers into five major types.

4. Identify three key motives that enter into the final buying decision.

5. Define three levels of problem solving in the buying process.

6. List and explain the psychological factors affecting the buying process.

7. List and explain the environmental factors affecting the buying process.

8. State the six principles of influence that affect the buying decision.

9. Apply the knowledge of the six steps of the purchase decision process to a simple buyer-seller encounter.

10. Apply the knowledge of behavior and motives to the steps of benefit selling.

Salespeople always want to know what reasons a person has for making a buying decision. If salespeople knew that, then they could use that information to create better appeals. What are the basic reasons people buy?

Sales Experts Respond

The answers to this question come from Homer D. Smith, a marketing consultant and author of *Selling through Negotiations,* and Gerhard Geschwandtner, publisher of *Personal Selling Power.* People buy for profit or gain. They want to save money or make money or they want to be better off than they are. Convenience is another motive for buying. People also buy out of fear of possible loss or for security. People want a guarantee that they won't lose. The loss can be financial or personal. If the salesperson can show customers that their risk is eliminated or reduced, the sale is half-way made. People buy for other emotional reasons, such as comfort or pleasure (and avoidance of pain or discomfort). Enjoyment, beauty, feeling good, and delighting in the ownership and use of possessions and services are basic to satisfaction. Everything that is alive seeks to avoid discomfort. For customers, discomfort can be physical or mental, real or anticipated. Love or affection are two more emotional reasons. Everyone likes to be liked and to receive social approval of themselves and their accomplishments. The purchasing agent for a major corporation wants her boss to commend her for a job well done. The guy next door likes to hear the praises heaped on his new convertible. In short, people like to feel that they have made the right decision and that the decision has gained them social acceptance. Other emotional reasons are pride (also ego) and prestige. Honors, recognition, and advancement all feed the ego. A pur-

Every Person Buys:

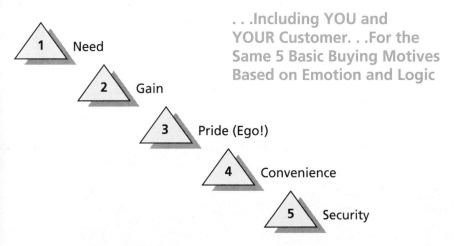

. . .Including YOU and YOUR Customer. . .For the Same 5 Basic Buying Motives Based on Emotion and Logic

1 Need
2 Gain
3 Pride (Ego!)
4 Convenience
5 Security

Figure 5-1 **Basic Buying Motives**

chase can enhance customers' pride and prestige, and customers do not forget who helped them get the ego boost. (See Figure 5-1.)

Understanding buyers' behavior includes understanding what prevents them from buying. People fear spending money on the unknown. A new product or service represents a risk. Customers also fear change. Everyone gets comfortable and content with things the way they are. Asking customers to change is asking them to break away from the familiar. People also fear being duped or taken advantage of, being made to look bad. This damages egos and is often professionally demeaning. Finally, customers fear the negative opinions of others. They have a nagging concern about what the other guy will think. Self-image plays an important part in any transaction, and if it appears the purchase could or has caused the buyer to lose face, the salesperson has a major obstacle to overcome.[1]

Introduction

To be successful at adaptive selling requires understanding that customers make purchases to solve problems; some are routine and others are extensive. Closing a sale only happens when buyers feel the purchase provides the best solution to the problem, given the constraints of time, money, available alternatives, and risk.

Think about the last purchase you made. It may have been a soda from the vending machine at the gas station on your way home. It may have been a burger and fries after class last night. In each case, little risk or money was involved. In fact, there was so little risk, there wasn't even a need for a salesperson! But now think about another buying decision. Your company is about to install a new 30-ton press that will stamp out metal parts. You can buy the foreign-made press for 20 percent less than a domestically made press. This would save your company $500,000 and probably get you a promotion. The foreign-made press, however, has a poorer safety record than the domestic press. Do you go for the savings and the promotion, or do you spend the additional money and give up the promotion?

Buyers make a variety of decisions every day. While some take little or no thought—routine purchases—others carry a heavy burden of risk and responsibility with significant and possibly negative ramifications. The successful salesperson must know how to effectively handle customers when they are making low-risk, low-involvement purchases and when they are making purchases that put the safety, health, and well-being of others on the line. Professional buyers daily make decisions that affect other people. Wrong decisions have far-reaching consequences. Understanding this and other aspects of the buying process makes selling much easier.

In this chapter, we will focus on the buying decisions of consumers and organizational buyers. By understanding what influences the buying process, the adaptive salesperson can choose the most effective selling techniques for a given situation. We will begin this chapter by discussing the different categories of consumers and organizational buyers. After that, the principles of influence that affect the buying decision will be explained in detail. Then, we will narrow the focus to the actual steps in the decision making process. The chapter will conclude with tips on how to identify buyers' needs and a brief introduction to benefit selling.

The Two Arenas of Selling

Salespeople work in two selling arenas: (1) consumer sales and (2) business to business sales, sometimes called organizational selling. Professional buyers dominate the organizational arena, which includes the government, industrial firms, wholesalers, and retailers. The adaptive salesperson must effectively tailor the sales presentation to the customer. To do this, the salesperson must understand who influences the decision-making process and how. A customer record sheet is an invaluable aid in tracking this information. Below is a brief version of one that can be kept on a note card and used as a quick reminder about a customer and what has transpired to date.

The Customer Record Sheet

Every sales person should have same kind of Customer Record sheet on which are recorded all vital information and dates of contact, products or services purchased, and so forth. Below is a suggested format:

Name _____ Company _____ Phone _____

Address _____ Primary Type of Business _____

Company policy info _____   SPECIAL DATA _____

Buyer Social Style _____

Secretary _____ Office hrs _____ Yrs in business _____

Dates of Interviews	Product/Service Discussed	Reception to Presentation	Potential Sales in $

Sales Rep _____

Categorizing Consumers for Better Selling Effectiveness

Salespeople face a variety of buying situations everyday. A buying situation encompasses the environment and the personal pressures that affect the decision-making process. We will be using the term *consumer* to mean the ultimate consumer—the person whose buying motive is personal consumption, not buying for resale or for use in making another product.

Consumers buy goods and services they and their families will use. Advertising, salespeople, other consumers, and trends or fads in their social reference group influence their choices. Some purchases are impulsive, and others are planned well in advance. Some consumers buy whatever is new simply because it is new; others wait until everyone is using the product before they will try it. Some consumers are avid shoppers and compare prices; others do not.

The key characteristics a salesperson must remember about consumers are:

◀ ◀ ◀ ◀ ◀ ◀ ◀ ◀
Learning Objective 1:
Consumers' buying motives
and behaviors

▶ Consumers get personally involved in gathering information, and they get it from many sources, some reliable and accurate and some questionable.

▶ Consumers evaluate information based on their values, judgment, perception, experience, and education.

▶ Consumers alone are responsible for their decisions, which are emotional in many cases.

▶ Consumers are at some personal degree of risk because they will be using the product or service themselves.

Consumers have different buying habits. Fortunately, research has shown that consumers can be grouped into categories that provide information about their buying patterns and help salespeople adapt their presentations accordingly. There are four consumer categories: Innovators, Early Adopters, Majority, and Laggards. No one fits exclusively into one group, but the descriptions of each are broad enough to allow the salesperson to understand customers' general buying behaviors and make initial categorizations. Figure 5-2 illustrates when these different buyers enter the product's life cycle.

◀ ◀ ◀ ◀ ◀ ◀ ◀ ◀
Learning Objective 2: Four
types of consumers

Innovators Innovators are the small percentage of customers who are the most venturesome and risk-taking. They buy new products when they first come on the market. Innovators tend to be younger, better educated, and more professionally mobile than other consumers. They rely on impersonal information sources, such as articles, technical data, or ads in special interest publications, for their product knowledge. The salesperson's input to an Innovator's decision-making process may be limited to providing facts and information, rather than trying to persuade or influence.

Early Adopters Early Adopters are somewhat more cautious than innovators. They depend on salespeople and mass media sources for most of their

Figure 5-2 **Consumer Categories and Their Entry Into a Product's Life Cycle**

Innovators and early adopters are the first two types of customers to try new products.

product information. Early Adopters are often the community or social opinion leaders and for this reason are very important to salespeople. They are an excellent source of referrals and word-of-mouth promotion for the salesperson and the product.

Majority People in this category are the majority of consumers. They observe the experiences of innovators and early adopters before they venture into the market. They are somewhat more skeptical and take a wait-and-see attitude. Proof is an essential element when dealing with them. References or testimonials from satisfied customers are powerful tools with these people. They tend to buy only established products and brands with track records. The salesperson serves to inform, persuade, and reassure this type of customer.

Laggards Laggards generally enter the market only after the product has been adopted by everyone else. Laggards are tradition-bound and cling to the status quo. You know the type: "If it was good enough for Grandpa, it's good enough for me." They make up only a small segment of the market and may not be worth the time and trouble it would take to sell to them. Most firms do not even consider this group in their marketing plans, but sometimes conditions change that convert Laggards into good customers. See the Case in Point below for just such a situation!

Case in Point

Becoming an Innovator Creates Selling Opportunities

The salesperson for the Good Paint Company has been calling on a Mom-and-Pop hardware store in a small town near a large city. After

Continued

Categorizing Organizational Buyers

Organizational buyers are professional purchasing agents for businesses, institutions, or government. Organizational buyers have many responsibilities. In retailing, they are often responsible for determining the store's merchandise mix and setting the retail prices. In industrial companies, organizational buyers often fill the purchasing requests submitted by production managers, engineers, or buying committees. An organizational buyer is the salesperson's contact and easily represents a variety of departments, interests, and budgets in the firm. The salesperson must deal with the organizational buyer in the event of problems, and the organizational buyer is the person whom people in his or her company call if there is any trouble with the product or service.

The organizational buyer is often the quality-control expert. In this role, the organizational buyer must be completely familiar with the company policy on quality and with the vendor's claims and rejections policy. All too frequently, the buyer's company accepts delivery of a product, then later finds it is not what it expected, and tries to pressure the salesperson into taking the product back and refunding the money. What would you do in that situation? You may want to read the following "What Would You Do If...?"

What Would You Do If...?

What would you do if you were a salesperson for a major meat packing firm and had to deal with the following?

Early one morning, you get a call from a buyer for the largest grocery store chain in the market, one of the largest in the world. It has over

Continued

As an adaptive salesperson, your goal is both to sell your firm's products and establish a long-term, profitable "partnering" relationship with the organizational buyer. A partnering relationship produces an understanding of the common goals of both firms and the buyer's and seller's personal agendas. The following Case in Point gives ten rules for better partnering.

Case in Point

Ten Rules for Partnering with Buyers

Developing a partnered relationship between buyers and sellers means following these rules:

1. Add value to each other: teach each other new ways to be more productive.
2. Be supportive, not competitive, with each other.
3. Avoid surprises: keep each other informed and plan ahead.
4. Be open and honest.
5. Enter into each other's frame of reference: learn each other's perspectives, opinions, and attitudes.
6. Be reliable.
7. Anticipate opportunities and capitalize on them.
8. Do your homework: know what is happening and what might happen.
9. Treat each other as people, not merely as functionaries.
10. Enjoy the relationship: nobody likes doing business with people he or she doesn't enjoy.

Source: Adapted, with permission of the publisher, from *Consultative Selling* © 1985 Mack Hanan. Published by AMACOM, a division of the American Management Association. All rights reserved.

Purchasing agents seldom make impulse purchases. Their buys are almost always planned well in advance of the actual authorization of an order. While consumers buy for their own use, the organizational buyer is usually detached from how, when, or where the purchases are used. The key characteristics a salesperson must remember about organizational buyers are:

▶ Organizational buyers are seldom the sole decision maker in the purchase.

▶ Organizational buyers are often given product specifications and must find vendors who can fill them.

Learning Objective 1 (cont'd): Characteristics of organizational buyers

- Organizational buyers are detached from the actual use of the product.
- Organizational buyers are professionals; they may see hundreds of salespeople in a month, so their time is limited and very valuable.
- Organizational buyers want long-term relationships with vendors. In many cases, purchasing agents have only a few sources of supply.
- Asking price may not be a major decision factor. The organizational buyer evaluates the life-cycle cost, which includes purchase price, repair and service costs, and productivity losses due to downtime, production slowdowns, and late deliveries.
- Packaging, mode of transportation, freight rates, foreign currency valuations, and current laws or changes in laws affect organizational buyers' decisions far more than they do consumers'.

Salespeople find it advantageous to classify organizational buyers because developing a profile of how a particular buyer does business means a more successful sales-call strategy. There are five "types" of organizational buyers (see Table 5-1). As you read the descriptions of these groups, think about how you would sell to each.

The Hard Bargainer Selling to the Hard Bargainer would involve giving a brief presentation focusing on price, savings, or the deal the buyer would be getting. It is tough to sell this buyer new products that don't have an established track record. This buyer haggles, so point out such things as volume and seasonal discounts and how those affect the overall price. Salespeople should expect to hear comments referring to the buyer's ability to get the same thing from the competition for a lower price (which may be simply a ploy to get salespeople to drop their price). The Hard Bargainer may even try to pit competitors against each other by telling what each seller has quoted.

◄ ◄ ◄ ◄ ◄ ◄ ◄ ◄
Learning Objective 3: Four types of organizational buyers

The Sales Job Facilitator These are easy customers to deal with. They may be hard to sell at first, being cautious and loyal to their present suppliers. But

---

Table 5-1 Categories of Organizational Buyers

The Hard Bargainer Likes to negotiate. Is resistant to buying new products. Has price as the main buying criteria. Uses several sources of supply for the same product. Tends to be very conservative.

The Sales Job Facilitator Uses one, or very few, sources of supply for the same item. Rarely asks for free samples. Does not spring unexpected requests on salespeople.

The Straight Shooter Doesn't hesitate to ask for concessions from salespeople. Doesn't try to get a lower price only to use it as lever against current supplier. Rarely uses his or her power to force concessions from salespeople.

The Socializer Likes to make small talk during the salesperson's presentation. Wants to socialize after hours. Willingly accepts and expects free gifts.

The Considerate Is compassionate, empathetic, and warm-hearted. Knows a lot about products purchased. Is willing to accept substitute products if necessary. Understands the problems salespeople face in doing their jobs.

Source: Alan J. Dubinsky and Thomas Ingram, "A Classification of Industrial Buyers: Implications for Sales Training," *Journal of Personal Selling and Sales Management* (Fall/Winter 1982): 46–51.

this can be an advantage. Once the salesperson is established as a supplier, the relationship will be sustained with continuous sales. This buyer enters into a partnering relationship very easily and will always give salespeople plenty of advanced notice of any changes in company policy, product request, specifications, or delivery schedules.

The Straight Shooter   This person is a combination of the Hard Bargainer and the Sales Job Facilitator. These buyers try to get as many concessions as possible but do not try to force salespeople to do anything. They do not abuse the power they may have but try to get all they can in terms of samples, promotional materials, or sales assistance.

The Socializer   Selling to the Socializer will require considerable small talk as a prelude to formally starting the sales presentation. Socializers look for a free lunch or tickets to the ball game and in general expect entertainment on the salesperson's expense account.

The Considerate   Considerates are easy to do business with. They understand salespeople are there to do a job and will try to make the selling job easier. This does not mean they are an easy sale, but they do not badger, demean, or belittle salespeople. Considerates look upon the salesperson as an equal. Forcing concessions through the abuse of power does not even enter their mind. Considerates are very flexible and will readily accept substitute products. They will make their decisions on a variety of factors and consider the value of the offering, not just the price.

Adaptive salespeople must be adept at quickly determining the type of buyer they are dealing with and adjust their presentation style accordingly. Keeping these categories in mind will prove to be a valuable aid in selling. Also remember, buyers may not fit snugly into each category; they may exhibit some of the characteristics of two or more groups. The adaptive salesperson must determine through observation, listening, and questioning which style is predominant.

▶ ▶ *follow-up questions*

1. Does it make sense to try to categorize customers? After all, everyone is different, so why do this? Explain your answer.
2. If you were going to sell your calculator to a Hard Bargainer, what would you use as your selling points? What if you were selling to a Socializer?
3. How would a presentation to an Early Adopter differ from one to a Laggard?

The Complexity of the Buying Decision

Each purchase represents a problem someone is trying to solve, and problems can range from the simplest to the most complex. The complexity of the buying decision, regardless of whether it is by a consumer or organizational buyer, influences the decision process. The adaptive salesperson must understand what the buyer's concerns are and use this information to close the sale.

Buying Motives

Emotional, rational, and patronage motives stimulate customers to begin the buying process. All three motives enter into the final buying decision.

Emotional motives   **Emotional motives** are part of any buying decision. Each purchase represents a bundle of emotional motives based on the customer's feelings of pride, fear, love, despair, and belonging. Emotional motives may be subconsciously stimulated for reasons that are difficult to explain or justify on rational grounds. The reason people select the colors they do is a subconscious and seriously powerful motive. If you want a blouse in blue, and the store does not have it, will any color do? Probably not, and you will shop somewhere else, somewhere that has it in blue. Not being able to satisfy that emotional motive can lose sales. Emotional motives are psychological. People buy cars for transportation, to make a statement about their success, and to match either their self-image or the image they want to project.

Learning Objective 4: Key motives entering into the buying decision.

Rational motives   **Rational motives** involve such attributes as dependability, durability, efficiency, economy, flexibility, or performance characteristics. Most consumers hate to admit it, but they buy out of emotional motives and try to justify their purchases on rational grounds. Teenagers buy a motorcycle for emotional reasons but usually try to justify it to their parents on its gas mileage, how they won't be borrowing the car any more, and they must have transportation to get a job to pay for the bike. Large companies are no less vulnerable to emotional buys that are justified on rational grounds. Is the purchase of a country club membership for the company president *really* economically justified?

Patronage motive   **Patronage motives** stem from the relationship between the buyer and the vendor. People get comfortable buying from the same salesperson or company and want their supplier to succeed. Price, locational advantage, reputation, variety of offering, services, or the salesperson's or firm's personality initially attracts the buyers. They just like doing business with a certain salesperson or firm. The psychic satisfaction of working with the rep or company is perceived as such a benefit that the customer will pay a premium price or be willing to overlook minor inconveniences to obtain it.

Successful salespeople realize they must target their presentation to all three motives. Being sensitive to real and perceived motives means being aware of what stimulates people to want to buy.

Problem Solving

Each purchase represents a solution to a problem for the buyer. It is the salesperson's job to solve that problem by selling a product that has benefits with which the buyer is comfortable and satisfied. Customers commonly face routine, moderate, or extensive problem-solving situations.

Routine problem solving   An example of a consumer's **routine problem-solving** situation would be buying a blank tape for a VCR. Industrial cleaning supplies or copier paper would be examples of routine problem-solving purchases of an industrial product. Such purchases are often called straight rebuys by purchasing agents. The salesperson's function may be merely to

Learning Objective 5: Three levels of problem solving customers face

take the order, without ever visiting the buyer or making any presentation. Larger companies are now committing many of these buys to computers, which monitor the inventory level and print out the purchase order when the stock on hand reaches a predetermined point.

Moderate problem solving   An example of a consumer's moderate problem-solving situation would be the purchase of a business suit. It is certainly not a routine purchase since it represents a sizable cash outlay and usually entails making comparisons with other suits. There are many styles, colors, and materials to consider.

In moderate problem-solving decisions, salespeople have greater responsibility to try to reduce the customer's uncertainty and apprehension through providing facts, demonstrations, and guarantees of after-the-sale service. To satisfy the customer, the salesperson should make every attempt to determine the purpose of the purchase, that is, is the suit for special occasions or everyday wear? Does the buyer sit at a desk or move around a lot? All of these questions help the salesperson determine the fabric, cut, and style that will give the customer the greatest wear and satisfaction.

For an industrial example, suppose a purchasing agent were considering the purchase of ten new typewriters for the office staff. In this situation, the buyer will not be the user but must buy typewriters that will satisfy the users and not exceed her budget. She would ask the secretaries who will use these machines about the brands they prefer; the features they need, such as correctable ribbon and express carriage return; and any other special features they would like. Her dilemma comes if the model with all of the necessary features is too expensive.

Extensive problem solving   An example of an **extensive problem-solving** situation is buying a car or a house. Such major purchases are not easily reversible and may offer many alternative choices. In addition, the first-time

Some purchases represent extensive commitment and a long-term obligation.

buyer may have little, if any, information with which to make the buying decision.

In extensive problem-solving situations, salespeople can be of greatest help by presenting themselves as a source of knowledge and expertise and by exhibiting an enthusiastic willingness to be available to answer any questions. Providing the prospective buyer with references of satisfied customers also helps allay the buyer's apprehension. The information needed, the risks, the number of influencers to consult, and the time the buyer needs just to think it over means the selling cycle may be very long. The **selling cycle** is the time span from initial contact to completion of the sale, and completing the sale may extend beyond signing the order by including all of the after-sale service.

Buyers in the retail clothing industry face extensive problem-solving decisions because they buy so far in advance. They must guess what the customers will like a year from now, how many garments will sell, how many will get discounted, and which assortment and quantity of sizes will match the customers coming into the store. The buyers' job—and the survival of the store—depends on their ability to be right. The characteristics of each of the buying situations are listed in Figure 5-3, and the "Problem-Solving Guide" in the following box gives helpful hints to understanding the problems buyers face.

Problem-Solving Guide

1. *Project objectives*
   a. Collect all available pertinent data.
   b. Organize and analyze data.
   c. Isolate major needs.
   d. Write up a simple statement of *what* must be done. (This becomes the *objective* of your program.

2. *Relate logical standards to objectives.*
   a. Prepare a simple *statement of acceptable results.* (This becomes the *standard* by which you will judge success or failure.)
   b. Make the *standard* logical and attainable *within the immediate future.* (Set time limits.)

3. *Outline procedures to be followed.*
   a. List *how* results are to be achieved (your personal plan of action).
   b. Define tools and techniques to be used.
   c. Solicit help and advice when necessary.
   d. Plan for adequate follow-up.

4. *Balance results routinely.*
   a. Check attainment against expectations (standards).
   b. Recognize success or failure.
   c. Change program as necessary for success.

Figure 5-3 Character-
istics of Problem-
Solving Situations

	Routine Problem Solving	Moderate Problem Solving	Extensive Problem Solving
Risk	little/none	acceptable	affects decision
Salesperson influence	little/none	provides information	extensive
Information need	little/none	some	extensive about company, product, service, technical applications
Sacrifice	inconsequential	limited	high; personal, professional, and financial
Postpurchase anxiety	none	little but not inconsequential	high probability of extensive stress

▶▶ *follow-up questions*

1. What are the functions an organizational buyer may perform besides buying?

2. What are the categories of consumers and organizational buyers, and what are the characteristics of each?

Factors Affecting the Buying Decision

Salespeople must understand the forces, both personal and environmental, that influence the prospective buyer's decision. This awareness helps salespeople adapt their sales presentation to the customer and understand customers' objections, questions, and apprehensions.

When Things Go Wrong

When a Routine Purchase Turns Out to Be Extremely Stressful

At the end of a business trip, a customer called Continental Airlines to confirm the departure time of his flight from New Orleans to New York. He was assured it was on time and left for the airport about an hour later. By the time, he got there, the flight had been canceled. He waited in line to speak to the ticket agent to find out what had happened. The ticket agent told him she didn't know why the flight was canceled, and there was nothing she could do about it anyway. When the customer asked to speak to the agent's supervisor, he was told to move out of the way.

Word spread among passengers that the flight was so overbooked that Continental had canceled it rather than have to decide who could get on—a rumor the staff member couldn't substantiate. The customer who now will never trust Continental again, wrote Frank Lorenzo, CEO of Texas Air, Continental's parent company, for an explanation and is still waiting for a response.

Source: Bill Kelley, "Damn Right the Customer Isn't Always Right," *Sales and Marketing Management* 140 (May 1988): 51–54.

Psychological Factors

Psychological factors are the rational or emotional thought processes that cause buyers to act or react in the ways they do. Salespeople consider a variety of psychological factors in formulating a selling strategy. They must consider the buyer's motivation, self-concept, perception, learning, and stage of life.

◄ ◄ ◄ ◄ ◄ ◄ ◄ ◄

Learning Objective 6: The psychological factors that influence the buying decision

Motivation Motivation is a psychological factor that stimulates people to do something or keeps them at it. Two persons offered the same set of facts in identical presentations may arrive at different conclusions—making a purchase in one case and deciding not to do so in another case. One buyer is not "right" and the other "wrong"; they have simply processed the information differently. Some explanations for the differences lie in motivation theory. One theory often cited is **Maslow's hierarchy of needs,** represented in Figure 5-4. Before people try to achieve a higher-level need, they must satisfy the need below it first. The adaptive salesperson can use this concept to probe a prospective customer's purpose for making the purchase.

Salespeople should recognize that buyers have personal and emotional motives. Three personal motivators on the buyer's private agenda interact to influence the decision: power, achievement, and affiliation.[3]

The power motive is two-dimensional: it is both personal and social. Dominance-submission or a win-lose type of interaction is the basis for a personal power relationship. Social power is used to make others feel confident and competent so they can achieve common objectives.

The achievement motive is the drive to achieve for its own sake. This motive influences buyers to try to excel in making the best and shrewdest deals possible. It is also a driving factor in their personal career goals. Achieving as an organizational buyer means greater achievements to come.

The third motive is affiliation. Buyers want to maintain strong interpersonal relationships with the salespeople that call on them. This does not mean, however, they must be close personal friends, but rather they want a relationship of trust and dependability, regardless of their personal interactions. This human need for relationships with others enters into every decision process. The adaptive salesperson realizes no sale is ever made without considering it.

Self-concept theory Self-concept theory explains an additional psychological factor. It says people have a four-dimensional view of themselves:

▶ *"Real Self"*— the way you really are: short, fat, tall, thin, beautiful, or ugly, happy, depressing, the life of the party, or the wallflower. This is your actual personality and behaviors.

▶ *"Ideal Self"*— the image you want to portray to others.

Highest Need Level	Product/Service
Self-Actualization	Painting lessons; wilderness trek
Esteem	BMW; country club membership
Acceptance	Popular fashion
Safety	Insurance; burglar alarm
Physiological	Food; clothes; shelter
Lowest Need Level	

Figure 5-4 **Maslow's Hierarchy of Needs with Products That Exemplify Need Levels**

People buy products that reflect their self-image or the image they want to project.

▶ "*Self-image*"— the way you see yourself in your own mind.

▶ "*Other Self*"— what you think others think of you.

Adaptive salespeople need to understand the nature of their product and to which "self" it most appeals. Matching the product's features, advantages and benefits to the correct "self" is a key to successful selling. The ideal self, for example, is the target for health club memberships and diet plans.

Perception   Perception is another psychological factor. Perception is the meaning people draw from the information presented to them. Perception influences behavior because people's perceptions are always accurate and true—from their perspective. How people perceive something is the result of their attitudes, which act as mental gatekeepers. Buyers' attitudes control what they accept and reject as fact. The buyers' attitudes are the result of learning, which may have occurred formally or through experience.

Learning   Learning occurs when people accept information from credible sources or through experiences that in turn changes their behavior. Buyers learn from salespeople, from their own experiences, and from the experiences of others. Salespeople are often the teacher, and with every successful sale, they teach buyers about their dependability, sincerity, veracity, and empathy. Buyers then modify their behavior to depend more on these salespeople and less on others.

Stage of life cycle   The buyers' life-cycle stage influences their behavior. At different stages in their life cycle, people have different needs and priorities. To a single person just starting a career fresh out of college, a financial plan geared toward a son's or daughter's college education has little appeal. However, soon after becoming a parent, that same person will actively shop the market for financial plans based on life and income-protection insurance. As the family grows, health insurance becomes a priority item, and as retirement approaches, Medicare supplements are high on the priority list. As this brief example makes clear, understanding the linkages between life cycle, Maslow's hierarchy of needs, and self-concept enables salespeople to select more effective product selling points, ask better questions, and more effectively deal with objections to close more sales.

Learning Objective 7: Factors in the environment affect the buying decision

Environmental Factors

Multiple buying influences   The number of participants who influence the buying process affects the ultimate decision. The key task for the adaptive salesperson is to determine who the players are and their respective roles. Sales are often made by directing the presentation to the supporting cast members because they are trusted advisors and information analysts for the ultimate buyer. A presentation made to a group of people who can influence the buying decision is sometimes called **group selling.**

Six roles are associated with a consumer's or organization's buying decision. These roles are not mutually exclusive, and one person can play all six. Salespeople often lose sales by directing their efforts to the wrong person. Table 5-2 explains the different roles.

Buying center   The organizational buyer's job is to purchase goods and services for a company, institution, or agency. The salesperson may be faced

A person's stage of life influences buying decisions.

with a buyer operating in a reference group called a buying center. This group may be a combination of influencers, buyers, initiators, users, and deciders. The adaptive salesperson needs to identify who is playing what role. The most effective presentation may be to the influencers, rather than the actual buyer. *Back-door selling* is the term used when the focus of the sales presentation is on the influencers. It means convincing the influencers to sway the decider toward the salesperson's product before he or she makes a formal presentation to the decider.

Table 5-2	Roles Involved in Consumer and Business Purchases

Initiators—the people who start the buying process by recognizing an unfulfilled need or want in themselves or someone else.

Influencers—the people who have the ability to sway the decision process and have an affect on gathering and evaluating information, selecting alternatives to be considered, and, of course, making the final decision.

Deciders—the people who are ultimately responsible for accepting or rejecting a sales offer.

Buyers—the people who go through the mechanical processes of completing the actual transaction. For business purchases, this is often the person who actually issues the purchase order and places the order with the salesperson.

Users—the people who will ultimately operate or consume the product.

Gatekeepers—the people who control access to any of the above individuals or groups. Secretaries are often gatekeepers for purchasing agents, and purchasing agents are often gatekeepers for influencers and deciders.

Source: Adapted from Philip Kotler, *Marketing Management: Analysis, Planning and Control,* 4th ed. (Englewood Cliffs, N.J.: Prentice-Hall, 1980) pp. 134, 174–75.

Culture Prospective buyers' culture govern their buying decision and decision process. The term *culture* represents the whole of a person's beliefs, attitudes, and ways of doing things. A combination of learned attitudes and beliefs and personal experiences directs what a person feels is important or insignificant when evaluating a product's features, advantages, and benefits.

Social class A social class encompasses people who have about the same social status. Understanding social class differences impacts selling strategies. The upper class likes exclusive treatment with personal service and recognition. The middle class constitutes the mass market, which is very home- and family-oriented; people in this class view many of their purchases as social symbols of success or future success. People in the lower class are generally less educated and more tradition-bound. They rely on advertising more than the other groups and are usually more concerned with price than quality.[4]

Reference group A customer's reference group is the set of persons the customer looks to for direction when making or considering a purchase. A primary reference group usually includes family and close personal friends. A secondary reference group is often work or school associates, namely, peers. Reference-group influence is one of the reasons why referrals and word-of-mouth are so effective. For organizational buyers, the primary reference group would be other buyers in the firm, members of the professional purchasing managers' association, or the buying influencers with whom they work.

Economic The final factor to consider is economic. This encompasses the customer's current and expected economic state. The economic factor will show itself in the sales presentation through the customer's use of phrases like "we can't afford it," "we can't afford it now," and "it's too much for our budget." While these may be just objections to get the salesperson to lower the price, they can reflect an economic condition that the salesperson cannot overcome. Salespeople must consider the prospective customer's current and future economic state when that customer makes a big-ticket purchase. Individuals will often make major purchases in anticipation of a pay raise, a promotion, or some future event that will affect their income. Businesses will often vary their purchase requirements based on their projections of what the economy or interest rates will do.

▶ ▶ *follow-up questions*

1. Is there a difference between perception and learning? Are they related?
2. What would be the organizational buyer's primary purchasing motive?

The Principles of Influence[5]

Creating sales is a matter of influencing the right people in the right ways to predispose them to change their behaviors in the *correct* manner, that is, to buy, rather than to avoid buying. The box below contains the six principles of influence.

The Principles or Rules of Influence

▸ *Reciprocation:* people repay, in kind, what others have done for or given to them

▸ *Commitment and Consistency:* once people have made a choice, they will be reluctant to change, wishing to behave in a consistent manner with their commitment

▸ *Social Proof:* people think what is correct is based on what they observe others thinking or doing; society has proven it to be correct through their actions

▸ *Liking:* a recognition and acceptance based on a degree of personal similarity or mutual need; the "chemistry" of a relationship

▸ *Authority:* the power to influence derived from opinion, respect, or esteem

▸ *Scarcity:* the scarcer something is, is thought to be, or could become, the greater its value; people will be more motivated to act if something they want is perceived as scarce, rather than abundant.

Reciprocation

The **rule of reciprocation** says people repay, in kind, what others have done for or provided to them.[6] It means that to get people to do something for you, you have to do something for them first. The free sample is a classic application of the reciprocity rule. The fact that a person gave you a free sample of Geno's pizza during your last trip to the grocery store created an obligation on your part to at least consider buying a Geno's pizza. Salespeople often use sales promotion devices to exploit the rule of reciprocation. Such sales promotion devices can be as simple as pens, pocket calendars, or letter openers, but regardless of the size or value, the recipient still feels an obligation to

Learning Objective 8: The six principles of influence salespeople need to know and use to be successful

return the favor. A variation of the rule of reciprocation is the **rule of reciprocal concession.** This means if you make a concession to people, they feel obliged to make a concession to you.[7]

Case in Point

The Three-Dollar Set of Wooden Steps

Eric Berger was hired to deliver a $500,000 cabin cruiser from Connecticut to Florida. Eric and his crew of four stopped overnight in the city marina in Beaufort, South Carolina, where he had the cruiser fueled with 800 gallons of high-grade diesel fuel. Before leaving, a crew member thanked the dock manager for his cooperation and especially for the three-step stool he provided to help everyone embark and disembark comfortably. The manager said, "That little step stool cost me only three dollars to make. It has returned me hundreds of dollars in sales and gratuities."

Comment: Customers will remember you if you do something to show your personal interest in their welfare.

Commitment and Consistency

Commitment and consistency influence prospective buyers. Research has shown that obtaining compliance on even the smallest request significantly enhances commitment to a larger request.[8] This is known as the "foot-in-the-door technique" — getting your foot in the door by a positive decision, on even a small, insignificant request. It becomes the wedge that eventually opens the door for more. Look at it this way, when people sign an order for merchandise, even though the profit is so small it hardly compensates the salesperson for the time and effort of making the call, they are no longer prospects, they are customers.[9]

Consistency is really quite simple. Once people have made a choice, they will be reluctant to change, wishing to behave in a consistent manner with their commitment (even if that commitment is decidedly and obviously wrong!). In fact, so strong is the need for consistency and commitment that after making a decision, most people will alter their behavior to match their decision. Even if the decision was a poor one, they hope their behavior will somehow make it right.

Social Proof

The **social proof** principle states that people believe "correctness" is determined by what others think or do. People like to act in accordance with what is socially acceptable, and what others do provides the social proof of acceptability. After all, if everyone is doing it, it can't be all bad, can it? How can they go wrong if they are doing what others are doing? Buyers do not really require an answer to these types of questions because they ask them to justify or rationalize their purchase.

Realizing the prospect's desire for similarity, an adaptive salesperson emphasizes either who has already purchased the product or the prestige of current customers. Testimonials, reassuring statements, or simply telling prospects how many people have already purchased conveys the social proof to influence the prospect to buy.

Liking

Liking is a recognition and acceptance based on a degree of personal similarity or mutual need, the "chemistry" of a relationship. The power and use of liking in a selling scenario is the mainstay of home-party sales. Friends approach friends both to have parties and to attend. At your friend's home, you feel compelled and obligated to buy—you wouldn't want to turn your friend down, would you? The rule is very simply understood when you realize it is harder to turn down a request from someone you like than from a stranger.

Authority

Authority influences people's behavior. People are taught from childhood that it is proper and right to follow the directions of those in authority. There is a degree of safety and reduced risk in doing so. Advertising commonly uses authority figures or authoritative testimonials, such as "aspirin doctors give to their children" and the "motor oil used by racing professionals."

Titles and symbols are tools to create and communicate authority. *M.D., Ph.D., D.D.S.,* and *C.L.U.* are symbols designating a degree of authority. Clothes designate authority. To illustrate the point, a man dressed in work clothes jaywalked across a busy street. The same man returned later in a business suit and did it again. Three and a half times as many people followed the suited jaywalker across the street than followed the "worker."[10]

Scarcity

The last principle of influence is scarcity. The scarcer something is, thought to be, or could become, the greater its value. "Going out of business sale," "limited time offer," or "while quantities last" are standard phrases in newspaper ads and TV commercials. The perception of scarcity is a powerful motivator to closing sales and is the basis for a closing technique discussed later in this book.

▶ ▶ *follow-up questions*

1. What is the difference between the rule of reciprocation and the rule of reciprocal concession?

2. Why do people stay committed to a decision, even though it may be a bad one?

3. How would a salesperson use the rule of social proof when selling a stereo system to a teen-age customer?

The Six Steps of the Purchase Decision Process

A customer usually follows six steps in making a buying decision:

1. recognizing or arousing needs and wants,

2. searching for information,

3. evaluating information,

4. evaluating purchase alternatives,

5. making the choice, and

6. avoiding postpurchase anxiety.

Learning Objective 9: Six
steps of the purchase decision

Step 1: Recognizing or Arousing Needs and Wants

Needs—such as for food, clothing, shelter, affiliation, or reproduction—are basic forces stimulating action. Wants are desires. In most selling situations, wants are the prime motivators. One stimulus for entering the buying process is dissatisfaction with current products. UPS, Emery Air Freight, Purolator Courier, and other such services grew out of a realization that businesses wanted something better than the U.S. Postal Service could offer.

New technology creates desired and previously unavailable benefits that make existing products obsolete. Good examples are the benefits of the microwave oven, personal computers, and FAX machines.

Step 2: Searching for Information

The more complex the product, the higher the price, the greater the personal involvement, and the less a prospective buyer knows, the greater will be the time spent searching for information before making a decision. Adaptive salespeople determine the information needs of the prospective buyer and supply that information. Salespeople who fail usually do so because they simply do not pay attention to the buyer. They give too much information about things the buyer is not interested in and too little about what is crucial to solving the buyer's problem.

Consumers get information from ads, salespeople, or their friends. Organizational buyers get information from many more sources. A study of over 300 purchasing agents revealed the five most important sources of information for them were information systems departments, the department using the product, top management, vendor's salespeople, and users. Their complete ranking is shown in Table 5-3.

Step 3: Evaluating Information

Prospective buyers must feel they have both adequate quantity and quality of information. Factual accuracy and the credibility of the source are two measures of information quality. Some consumers are sophisticated enough to know factually correct from factually incorrect information. If they are not certain of the factual accuracy, their perception of the salesperson's credibility is their guide. Credibility of the source is extremely important. Salespeople create the perception of credibility through their product knowledge, appearance, presentation skills, symbols of credibility (C.L.U., Ph.D., M.D., D.D.S., etc.), and environmental surroundings.

Personal priorities enter the decision process through the conscious and subconscious filtering of information. This filtering causes selective bits of the information to be retained and selectively interpreted. Selective interpretation means coming to conclusions about what was meant more often than what was said. A good salesperson also understands how personal priorities affect the time spent searching for or accepting information. Only the facts

Rank	Source	Rank	Source
1	Information systems department	9	Stories in trade publications
2	Using department	10	Trade association data
3	Top management	11	Trade shows
4	Vendor salespeople	12	Ads
5	Users	13	Outside consultants
6	Sales literature	14	Purchasing departments
7	Colleagues in other firms		
8	Rating services		

Table 5-3 **Perceived Importance of Information Sources**

Source: Rowland Moriarity and Robert E. Spekman, "An Empirical Investigation of the Information Sources Used During the Industrial Buying Process," *Journal of Marketing Research*, 21 (May 1984): 137–47.

interest some people, while others base their decisions more on personal dimensions. The factually oriented person scrutinizes the amount of information and its technical accuracy, while other people may rely on information because it comes from someone they know they can trust.

Urgency is a mitigator in evaluating information. Decision making in urgent situations simply does not permit the luxury of gathering the ideal amount and quality of information. Adaptive salespeople should always keep their facts, features, advantages, and benefits categorized as "essentially important—need to know," "important and should be known," and "important minor points." By doing this, they are ready for the buyer who faces an urgent situation and wants just the most essential information with no fluff or frills.

Step 4: Evaluating Purchasing Alternatives

Theoretically, an alternative set includes all possibilities. Realistically, the set is narrowed to the feasible set after evaluating enough information. The feasible set of alternatives:

▷ Adequately solves the problem at hand;

▷ Does not create more problems than it solves;

▷ Has a reasonable time frame;

▷ Can be incorporated into the current operation without insurmountable difficulty; and

▷ Is affordable.

Let's look at a fictitious set of alternatives an auto buyer might consider. Table 5-4 lists a set of cars along with the customer's rankings on the looks, power, and styling dimensions.

If styling were the major criterion, then the set narrows to the Bond and the Pismo. If low price were the sole criterion, the set narrows to only the

Table 5-4	New Car Purchase Alternatives			
Make	**Price**	**Looks**	**Power**	**Styling**
Bond	$7,900	3	4	pretty
Pismo	$7,800	1	2	pretty
Rapier	$8,200	2	1	OK
Labelle	$8,100	1	3	OK
Volta	$7,700	5	6	plain
Asti	$8,400	4	5	plain

Source: David L. Kurtz, H. Robert Dodge, and Jay E. Klompmaker, *Professional Selling* (Plano, Texas: Business Publications, 1982), p. 53.

Volta. To arrive at a decision, buyers use evaluation methods like the "offsetting" approach, the "dictionary" approach, the "good-enough-on-all-factors approach," and the "good-enough-on-at-least-one-factor" approach.[11]

The "offsetting" approach rates each factor for each alternative, then sums all ratings for each alternative. The alternative with the highest overall rating is chosen. This assumes all factors to be of equal importance. But buyers often do not weigh all factors equally; they use implicit weights for each factor and multiply the rating on each factor times that factor's implicit weight. If the auto buyer in our example weighted price five times more important than either looks or power and almost twice as important as styling, the choice is clearly the Volta. Most buyers use a preference or priority scheme in considering the attributes of a product or service.

In using the "dictionary" approach, where attributes are categorized and mentally arranged from best to worst or A to Z, the buyer focuses on the most important attribute and uses others only if there is a tie between alternatives. In our car example, if price were the most important attribute, the choice would be obvious. If it were styling, there would be a tie, and the ranking on some other attribute would then break the tie.

The "good-enough-on-all-factors" approach requires the product or service to meet at least a minimum threshold level of acceptance on all attributes. If the buyer determined that the cars had to score at least a 2 on all factors, then none of these would qualify, and a new set of cars would be considered. Industrial buyers who purchase parts or structural components by specifications often use this method. The parts are tested and get rejected if they do not meet at least minimum specifications on all attributes.

Last is the "good-enough-on-at-least-one-factor" approach. This is a short-cut to the "good-enough-on-all-factors" approach. A buyer concentrates on the most important attribute and makes the determination based on it meeting a minimum standard.

The salesperson who understands these decision strategies can ask questions and, through observation, determine what is most important to the buyer, then focus the selling effort on that. The salesperson can tailor the presentation to the buyer's specific needs.

Step 5: Making the Choice

Rarely do buyers use only one of the above methods for evaluating and selecting alternatives, and rarely do they make up their minds at the same speed. Everyone takes time to cogitate, that is, to formulate the decision. Before formally committing, the option to back out still exists, but afterward, withdrawing may have serious legal and/or financial implications. The salesperson who understands a buyer's reluctance to commit anticipates that reluctance and offers the assurances, guarantees, satisfied customer references, and so on that will dispel the prospect's reluctance. Risk-averse buyers need much more assurance than do people who have a greater propensity toward risk.

Step 6: Avoiding Postpurchase Anxiety

Postpurchase anxiety is sometimes called buyer's remorse or cognitive dissonance. It defines the apprehension buyers feel after making or committing to a purchase. Postpurchase anxiety is not a regular part of the decision process, and if salespeople do their job effectively, it should not occur. Since it does happen occasionally, we must discuss it as a part of the decision process.

Postpurchase anxiety may occur because buyers feel their purchase did not live up to expectations or was not the best available; they feel they may have, in fact, rejected the best one. This anxiety is particularly prevalent when buyers have two alternatives that are very close or have too many choices. Too many choices boggles the customers' mind. They either do not make a choice or make what amounts to little more than a random selection, then wonder if it was the best one.

Alleviate postpurchase anxiety before it occurs and create a customer in the process. The first rule of selling is do not promise what you cannot deliver. Postpurchase anxiety will not occur if the promises are congruent with the expectations. If postpurchase anxiety is caused by fear of having not chosen the best alternative, the salesperson can anticipate the anxiety by assuring customers that their decision is the best, by concentrating on the positive aspects of the chosen alternative and the negative aspects of the rejected ones, and by minimizing the positive aspects of the rejected alternative.

▶ ▶ *follow-up questions*

1. What are the six steps in the buying decision process?
2. Explain two of the four methods for evaluating alternatives and arriving at a decision.
3. Define postpurchase anxiety and give two examples of how salespeople can head it off.

Applying the Knowledge of Behavior and Motives to Benefit Selling

Buyers purchase expected performance from a product. They cannot truly judge the wisdom of their purchase until after they use the product. Salespeople should represent their product or service accurately and use the discovery method to identify and adequately satisfy buyers' needs and wants.

Free samples encourage people to buy because of the rule of reciprocation.

How to Identify Buyers' Needs—The L-O-C-A-T-E Acronym

One technique that can help in discovering the prospective buyer's needs is to use the L-O-C-A-T-E acronym, which stands for: Listen, Observe, Canvass, Ask questions, Talk to others, and Empathize.

Listening implies the obvious: paying attention. It also means being sensitive to the nuances in voice, tone, word selection, and body language. These tell the skilled salesperson both what is being said and what should be communicated in the verbal and nonverbal disclosure.

Observe what is going on. Observe the surroundings, what is occurring with regard to your product's sales volume and that of your competitors. Observe such things as managerial changes and changes in the amount or timing or type of advertising done by the customer's firm. In retail clothing sales, for example, if a woman is looking at men's shirts, it's a good bet she is buying for someone else.

Canvass means to pore over, seek out, or scrutinize. In essence, this means gathering information from as many sources as possible. The information can come from the newspaper, trade publications, other salespeople (both your colleagues and competitors'), other customers, secretaries or receptionists in the prospect's office, or other sources.

Talk to others. Mark McCormick, noted businessman and deal maker for celebrities, says, "Most people are only too happy to tell you everything you need to know about the company they work for, such as how it is structured and who reports to whom. Without much coaxing (and by knowing when to remain silent), you can learn almost anything else you want to know—the company's priorities, its problems, its strengths and weaknesses, internal squabbles, power struggles, and so on. This kind of information is useful because a company's real decision-making process is rarely the way it is on an organizational chart. Another excellent source of information is anyone who has successfully dealt with that company before and therefore has some insights into its bureaucratic secrets."[12]

Empathizing means to be sympathetic, sensitive, and responsive to buyers and their problem or dilemma. It is often paraphrased as being able to put yourself in the other person's shoes. Understanding the buyers' situation and what they face helps shape the sales presentation and provides that little extra consideration that will sway a buyer.

The Steps in Benefit Selling

Benefit selling means focusing on what the customers' expected benefits will be, which are, in essence, their true reason for buying. Benefit selling may actually have little to do with the product's features. The quintessence of benefit selling is stressing the product's benefits that are complimentary to the customer's perceived benefit needs. It is really the art of perception management and has five steps.

◀ ◀ ◀ ◀ ◀ ◀ ◀ ◀
Learning Objective 10: The steps in benefit selling

Step 1: Positioning   Noted consultant Mark McCormick defines positioning as a matter of determining what people are really buying when they purchase a product or service and then conveying those impressions and motivations to them. This is simply positioning yourself and the facts to get the desired results.[13] It does not mean selling prospects something they do not want; on the contrary, it means selling them exactly what they want. If the car buyer's primary motive is transportation, then a straightforward utilitarian automobile will do. A Mercedes buyer is motivated by prestige over dependability, so focus on prestige. The same car may be sold to another buyer on the basis of its dependability. It is still the same car; the only thing different is the buyer's motivations. Thus, the selling focus changes to match.

Salespeople should offer themselves as the customer's business consultant as part of the products' total benefit package.[14] This is done through increasing the personalization and professionalization of the buyer-seller relationship and the customer's participation in the relationship.

Increasing the personalization results in greater trust and information sharing, which ultimately leads to buyers and sellers becoming more involved in each other's business goals. Increased customer participation means a greater flow of factual knowledge from the customer to the salesperson so the salesperson can more effectively prescribe the best solution. Increasing professionalism translates to converting a customer into a client. A client relationship exists when the buyer begins to rely on the salesperson as the only source of supply, the expert, and will neither search for nor want another vendor. A client relationship is like the one you have with your family doctor.

Step 2: Sell benefits they want   Remember that prospective buyers are making purchases based on their needs and problems. To be successful, sell them the benefits *they want, not what you want* to sell. Each product and service represents a constellation of benefits, some of which are important to a buyer and some not. Adaptive salespeople must determine the buyer's real benefit priorities and sell to those. Henry Ford sold Model T's in any color— as long as it was black. Cadillac found people wanted something other than black and offered its cars in a variety of colors. Ford sold what he wanted to sell, not giving customers any choices. But back when he built his first cars, there were few alternatives, so Ford had buyers over a barrel.

Step 3: Sell value People always buy value. Price and value are different. Price is a number related to costs and profit. Value is psychological and a function of perception. Value is the difference between expected benefits and expected sacrifices (time, money, effort, risk, etc.). To a true baseball fan, a baseball with Babe Ruth's autograph on it may be beyond price. Its value is in its historical or nostalgic significance. To someone who does not care about baseball, it is simply an old baseball.

Value may hinge on an emotional motivation, an urgency factor, a one-time offer, uniqueness, or special considerations. The important thing to remember is that value is far more psychological and perceptual than is price. AT&T has sold against its more competitively priced competitors by simply stating, "You get what you pay for," and Curtis-Mathis, the electronics manufacturer, stated it's product was "the most expensive TV you could buy, and darn well worth it." Even as competitors cut prices, these two firms succeeded because they were selling value, not price.

Step 4: Convince with advantages Successful salespeople sell a match between the benefits sought and the benefits their product delivers. The buyer is convinced by the product's advantages. Advantages are highlighted by salespeople through comparing their product to a competitor's. While two products may offer the same benefits, the salesperson's may be more advantageous because it is easier to use, can do it faster, offers greater flexibility, and so forth. Advantages can be perceptual and emotional, like benefits.

Advantages can be presented both positively and negatively; in essence, the same thing can carry different perceptual meanings to the buyer by how it is described. For example, saying a product will allow longer production runs carries a different meaning than saying it won't break down, but essentially the same thing is being said. In the seller's mind, these two may be equivalent statements but to buyers who have been plagued by stoppages due to mechanical failure, the latter statement carries a perception that directly addresses their major problem. Buyers often are more interested in what a product won't do than what it will do!

Step 5: Deliver with features Successful salespeople sell benefits, convince with advantages, and deliver with features. Features are the attributes of the product or service, the firm making the product, and the firm or person selling the product. "You won't get tired feet (benefit) because the shoe soles are softer (advantages), thanks to the new crepe rubber construction (product feature), and if you are dissatisfied, our shoe store offers a money-back guarantee" (vendor feature). The features of the product are the vehicles that deliver the benefits sought.

Features attributed to the seller are as much a part of the total product's features as are those of the actual product itself. Most grocery stores sell Green Giant green beans and for about the same price. The product features are the same regardless of where it is bought, but the fact that it is bought in a particular store reflects features of the store, such as carry-out service, location, hours of operation, or variety of products. The buyer purchases tangible and intangible benefits that are delivered through a combination of product, manufacturer, and seller features.

1. Explain how adaptive salespeople can use the L-O-C-A-T-E acronym to discover buyer's wants and needs.
2. Explain benefit selling.
3. How does value differ from price?

Summary

In this chapter, we have presented some of the factors that help to explain what influences buyers to make the decisions they do. Consumers make purchases mostly for their own consumption. Their decisions are more emotional because they will be the ones who use and enjoy the product. Organizational buyers, the professional purchasing agents that buy for businesses, government, and institutions, are more concerned with product performance, meeting specifications, the economics of the purchase, and the returns the product will generate. Organizational buyers who buy for resale don't use the products they buy. Their major concerns center on how the product will perform for the ultimate customer, the amount of profit they can make on the resale, and the number of times they can turn their inventory (Learning Objective 1).

Consumers and organizational buyers can be classified based on their buying behaviors. By knowing about these classifications, salespeople can formulate better sales strategies. Consumers tend to fall into one of four categories: Innovators, Early Adopters, Majority, or Laggards (Learning Objective 2). Organizational buyers can be classified according to their buying style: Hard Bargainers, Sales Job Facilitators, Straight Shooters, Socializers, and Considerates (Learning Objective 3).

Any buying decision, regardless of its consumer or industrial nature, has emotional, rational, and patronage motives (Learning Objective 4). These motives initiate and influence the whole buying process. Motives also interact with the nature of the buyer's problem-solving situation, which may be routine, moderate, or extensive. The more complex the problem, the more the salesperson can be an influencing or deciding factor in the customer's ultimate decision (Learning Objective 5).

Psychology plays a significant part in the buying decision. Motivation theories of power, achievement, and affiliation help explain why buyers behave in a certain, and to some extent, predictable way. Self-concept and stage-of-life cycle theories are also useful when trying to understand buying behaviors (Learning Objective 6.) Environment also affects which decision is made. In many companies, there are multiple buying influences and maybe even a group of people called a buying center. For both consumers and organizational buyers, culture, social class, reference group influences, and economics all enter into the final buying decision (Learning Objective 7).

The complexity of the buying situation influences how buyers search out and use information and what input they expect from salespeople. Salespeople must be aware of both the personal and environmental pressures customers feel. With this in mind, six principles or rules of influence were presented (Learning Objective 8).

Prospective customers go through a six-step process in making any type of buying decision. They realize they have a need, search for information on alternatives that could satisfy that need, evaluate that information, determine a set of feasible alternatives, make a choice among them, and occasionally worry if they made the right decision. By knowing this, an adaptive salesperson can recognize the stage the prospect is in and tailor the sales presentation to that specific stage (Learning Objective 9).

Knowledge of buyer behavior is used to implement the idea of benefit selling. In benefit selling, positioning yourself and your product as the ones that most specifically address the benefits sought by the buyer leads to increased sales and more satisfied customers. The L-O-C-A-T-E acronym was presented as a tool to help salespeople determine the buyer's needs and benefits sought (Learning Objective 10).

By understanding the mental steps and processes a customer uses to make a decision, the adaptive salesperson can make more sales more effectively and more easily.

Key Terms

Organizational buyer   Buyers for businesses, institutions, or government.

Selling cycle   The time span from initial contact to completion of the sale, which may extend beyond signing the order to include all of the after-sale service.

Emotional motives   Buying motives stimulated for emotional reasons, some of which are sentimental, the result of cognitive stimuli, subconscious needs or wants, or such pure emotions as love, hate, fear, despair or belonging.

Rational motives   Rational motives involve such attributes as dependability, durability, efficiency, economy, flexibility, or performance characteristics.

Patronage motives   Motives stemming from the relationship between the buyer and the vendor. People get comfortable buying from the same salesperson or company and want to patronize that firm.

Routine problem solving   Purchase decisions made on a regular basis requiring little risk, search effort, or information on the buyer's part.

Extensive problem solving   Decisions putting the buyer under stress, usually due to price, risk, or lack of familiarity with the product.

Maslow's hierarchy of needs   A theory of motivation suggesting people strive to achieve five basic needs in a hierarchical order, those needs are physiological, safety needs, acceptance, esteem, and finally, self-actualization.

Rule of reciprocation   We try to repay, in kind, what another person has provided to us.

Rule of reciprocal concession   If you make a concession to people, they feel obliged to make a concession to you.

Commitment and consistency   A principle of influence that means people are hesitant to be inconsistent with either a previously made decision or stay committed to a decision in order to avoid having to repeat the decision-making process required to change.

Social proof A principle of influence that says people are influenced by what they see as acceptable in their society; if everyone is doing it, it must be okay.

Postpurchase anxiety Also called buyer's remorse, it is the feeling that the wrong purchase decision has been made.

Liking A recognition and acceptance based on a degree of personal similarity or mutual need; the "chemistry" of a relationship.

Authority The power to influence derived from opinion, respect, or esteem.

Scarcity The scarcer something is, is thought to be, or could become, the greater its value; people will be more motivated to act if something they want is perceived as scare, rather than abundant.

Discussion Questions

1. What are the categories of consumers and organizational buyers and the characteristics of each?

2. How do the criteria for making a purchase decision differ between consumers and organizational buyers?

3. If you were just leaving a sales call having dealt with a Hard Bargainer and were going to your next call with a Considerate what differences would you expect and how might you adjust your presentation?

4. What is "life cycle cost" and why does the organizational buyer take it into consideration when making a buying decision?

5. What would be an example of a routine, a moderate, and an extensive problem-solving buying decision? What might be the salesperson's input into the decision in each case?

6. How does the complexity of the buying decision affect the length of the selling cycle?

7. What are the subsets of personal factors that affect the buying decision?

8. Explain how understanding Maslow's hierarchy of needs and the self-concept theory could make you a better salesperson.

9. Which "self" do tanning salons sell to? How about cosmetic surgeons?

10. Explain how a free sample is an example of the rule of reciprocation.

11. What is meant by the term *reciprocal concession?*

12. How can using the rule of social proof help sell to a Laggard?

13. What are the subdimensions of liking?

14. Explain how a corporate culture can influence an organizational buyer's decision-making process.

15. Explain how a reference group can influence a customer's purchasing behavior.

16. Define *buying center* and how it relates to back-door selling.

17. What is the partnering concept in selling? Give an example of how you could use it in selling clothing to a organizational buyer for J.C. Penney.

18. What are the six steps in the buying decision process?

Application Exercise

Reread the box called "Ten Rules for Partnering," then answer the following questions:

▸ Does partnering apply only to industrial buying situations? How would it apply if you were selling stocks and bonds to investors?

▸ Thinking back to what you read in chapter 1, would partnering be applicable in display sales? In closing sales? Explain the reasoning behind your answers.

Class Exercises

Group Exercise

In pairs, develop a *script* for a role play between a funeral home director and a member of the deceased's family. No previous plans were made for the burial of the deceased, including choice of plot, headstone, or type of casket.

The script must include consideration of:

1. Emotional buying motives
2. Rational buying motives
3. The nature of the services rendered
4. Urgency of the product or service sale

Each written role play will be placed in a box from which the instructor will select one for presentation by the authoring pair. Comment on the dynamics of the role play in regard to:

▸ How role-playing helps define such concepts as buying motives.

▸ How well the participants presented the role play as a selling situation.

Individual Presentation

Recall a recent purchase or conjure up a planned purchase of a durable good, such as a stereo, car, TV, or washer. Take such a purchase through the six steps of the decision process, as outlined in this chapter. Concentrate on how *you* would make the decision. In addition, justify (sell) your ideas to the class.

 Cases ▼ ▼ ▼ ▼ ▼ ▼ ▼

The Big TV Woes

Suppose you are a retail TV salesperson. A person has just come through the door of your store, and as you approach her to offer assistance, something like the following occurs:

The customer begins to ask questions about your big-screen TV sets, and you can hear in her voice and see in her facial expressions a defensive tone. She asks several times if there will be a delivery charge, should she decide to buy. She also wants to know your name and that of the store's manager, if the TV is in stock, and how soon it can be delivered. After answering her questions and feeling it is time to close the sale, you ask her if she would like to pay for the set now and have it delivered the next day. On hearing that, she becomes quite tense, shaking her finger at you and saying she is never again going to pay for something before it is delivered and that if you have to have your money before she has her TV, you can forget your sale, now and forever!

Questions

1. What clues did the customer give that you might use to understand her attitude and statements?
2. What type of buying decision might this represent and how might you use the L-O-C-A-T-E acronym to help you understand her needs and the source of her defensive attitude?
3. How might you use the influence principles of social proof and authority to help calm her down and close the sale?

Better Late Than Never [15]

While delayed departures are commonplace these days, one customer felt that American Airlines went a little too far; her flight left six and a half hours after its scheduled departure time. Upset, she wrote a letter to the director of consumer relations: "I've been flying for approximately thirty-five years and have always tried to find an American Airlines flight. However, I've just experienced the worst flight of my life."

The letter went on to document the problems she encountered because of the late flight, including getting home at about 3 A.M., instead of 8:30 P.M., and having to get up a few hours later to go to work. But what she found most annoying was the cavalier attitude displayed: "Once on the plane, there was no attempt to make amends or make things more pleasant—just an announcement that they (American) were sorry for the inconvenience."

She closed by saying she is a loyal American customer but may think twice about using the airline again.

Questions

1. If you were a representative for American Airlines asked to respond to this customer, what would you do?
2. Has this customer suffered postpurchase anxiety? If you were talking to her on the phone, what would you say to her?
3. Which of the six principles of influence would work best with this customer now that she has had this bad experience?
4. How would you apply the ten rules of partnering to this situation? [15]

Losing a Well-Charged Sale

Jeff needed a new battery for his boat and went to the automotive department of a large retail store, where boat batteries were displayed. Selecting one, he put it in the cart and went to the checkout desk in the department. No one was there. A sign on the glass door leading to the garage read, "If you need help, press buzzer." Jeff did so, and a man rushed to the door, quickly opened it, and said gruffly, "What do you want?" Jeff said, "I want to buy this $87 battery and want to know if you have one charged up so I could take it home with me and use it in my boat this afternoon."

The service clerk said, "Can't talk to you now, I have another customer. Come back in ten minutes." Ten minutes later, Jeff came back and pressed the buzzer again. The same man rushed to the door, opened it quickly, and said, " I told you I couldn't talk to you right now." With that, he closed the door in Jeff's face.

Jeff left the battery, a plastic case, and a small charger he would have purchased for more than $100 in the cart and walked out of the store.

Questions

1. If you were Jeff, how would you feel about the store?
2. If you were the manager of this automotive department and learned of this lost sale, what would you do?

References

1. Adapted from Gerhard Geshwandtner and Donald J. Moine, "Selling Without Anxiety, Fear or Worry," *Personal Selling Power,* 10 (1990): 60; Homer D. Smith "How to Identify the Six Basic Buying Motives," *Personal Selling Power,* 9 (1989): 7.
2. This was an actual situation. The meat packer picked up the meatballs, gave back the money, and formulated a company policy that no product over 30 days old could be returned for any reason. This is an example of the power one member of the channel of distribution can have. How far would you be willing to go to jeopardize a multimillion-dollar account for $3,900 worth of meatballs?
3. Mack Hanan, *Consultative Selling* (New York: American Management Association, 1985), pp. 126–27.
4. E. Jerome McCarthy and William D. Perreault, Jr., *Basic Marketing* (Homewood, IL: Richard D. Irwin, 1987), pp. 211–12.
5. Adapted from Robert B. Cialdini, *Influence* (New York: William Morrow, 1984).
6. Ibid., p. 29.
7. Ibid., pp. 47–49.
8. Robert A. Hansen and Larry Robinson, "Testing the Effectiveness of Alternative Foot-in-the-Door Manipulations," *Journal of Marketing Research,* 17 (1981): 359–64. See also, Chris T. Allen, et al., "More on Self-Perception Theory's Foot Technique in the Pre-Call/Mail Survey Setting," *Journal of Marketing Research,* 17 (1980): 498–502.
9. Hansen and Robinsin, "Testing the Effectiveness," citing the *American Salesman,* 1965.
10. Cialdini, *Influence,* pp. 220–21, citing a 1955 study by Lefkowitz, Blake, and Mouton.
11. David L. Kurtz, H. Robert Dodge, and Jay E. Klompmaker, *Professional Selling* (Plano, TX: Business Publications, 1982), pg. 53.
12. Paraphrased from Mark H. McCormick, *What They Don't Teach You at the Harvard Business School* (New York: Bantam Press, 1984).
13. Ibid., pp. 121–25.
14. Hanan, *Consultative Selling,* pp. 17–45.
15. Bill Kelley, "Damn Right the Customer Isn't Always Right," *Sales and Marketing Management,* 140 (1988), 51–54. American Airlines wrote her two

weeks later, saying, "It is not possible for us to guarantee our schedules or to be responsible for the expenses that result when a flight does not operate as planned. This situation you described, however, warrants an exception to this policy. A $50 voucher is enclosed that we hope will encourage you to fly with us again. I'm confident we can demonstrate the kind of schedule dependability you expect."

Chapter

6

Prospecting and Qualifying: How to Find the Right Buyers

Objectives

After completing this chapter, you will be able to:

1. Define prospecting.

2. Identify the four steps in the buying cycle.

3. List and describe four preconditions for successful prospecting.

4. Identify and discuss sources of leads.

5. Explain what qualifies a lead to be a prospect.

6. Discuss the steps used to qualify leads.

7. Explain how salespeople use prospect control systems.

8. Apply the 80-20 rule to determine the size of the prospecting and qualifying effort.

The Professional Selling Question

Telemarketing is becoming a tool increasingly used to qualify leads. How does qualifying leads through telemarketing differ from traditional methods?

A Sales Expert Responds

Lead qualification through telemarketing uses inexpensive phone procedures to separate the names of high-probability prospects from low-probability ones. Using the phone to qualify prospects can reduce selling costs and make the field salesperson calling face-to-face on the customer more effective and efficient.

"The purpose of lead qualification is to ask enough probing questions to determine if we should continue our investment in time and dollars with this prospect," says Lee Van Vechten, publisher of the *Van Vecten Report,* a telephone marketing newsletter. Using telephone lead qualification, a sales manager can determine if the prospective customer is too small to warrant a visit from a field salesperson but would warrant contact by the inside salesforce. Qualifying over the phone makes the job of the visiting field salesperson easier because it identifies who the decision maker is and who else might be involved.

Qualifying leads over the phone usually requires the in-office qualifying technician to follow a script to make sure every prospective customer is asked the same questions in the same way. Van Vechten cautions, "Lead qualification programs should not be read to the prospective customer. They should be structured but casual and given with confidence as well as in word phrases that are comfortable."

Van Vechten adds, "Don't lose sight of your overall business objective. Usually qualifying routines are designed to allow other business activities to happen. If it is costing your company $200 a call using outside sales reps, then you want them calling on viable, qualified accounts, not suspects but prospects." You may want to use the call-mail-call program. In this, you make the first call a qualifying call. If the prospective customer meets your criteria, then a full package of literature about your firm or products is mailed out on the day of the call. The second call is then the selling call where you ask if the customer has had a chance to review the material and go into making your presentation.[1]

Introduction

How many times do you suppose salespeople get told no before they ever get a "yes, I will buy" answer? How many jobs have you interviewed for and been turned down? In each case, the more prospective opportunities you have, the better are your chances. However, having just more opportunities is not enough; they need to be opportunities with a high probability of paying off.

Beginning with this chapter, we enter into the actual steps of the selling process. Before salespeople can make a presentation, they must have a prospective customer. Salespeople need a large enough set of potential customers to yield a profitable base of active purchasers. Since there is a natural attrition of active customers, new prospects are needed to replenish the pool. Qualifying of potential customers assures only high-probability prospects get in the pool. Prospecting and qualifying are the life blood of selling. Without a constant inflow of new customers, salespeople cannot survive in this dynamic profession.

Understanding how successful prospecting and qualifying makes the job of selling easier is important. For novice salespeople, or persons considering a sales career, one of their recurring concerns is how to develop a customer base. In this chapter, you will learn about a variety of sources of names and a step-by-step procedure for qualifying them. Having a large pool of names and rigorously qualifying them makes success in sales much more certain. The poor salesperson spends too little time qualifying and a lot of time making presentations to disinterested prospects. The successful salesperson spends more time qualifying and makes more presentations to prospects who are good candidates to become new customers.

Prospecting for Leads

Why Prospect?

Learning Objective 1: What prospecting is

Prospecting is the process of creating a pool of possible customers from a target group of people or businesses that could have a need for the salesperson's product or service. The names in this pool are called leads. This pool of possible customers (still leads at this point) is then filtered through the qualification process to create a smaller set of high-probability potential customers called prospects. It is from this smaller pool that salespeople develop their customer base.

Why does a salesperson prospect? The answer is survival. Think of a bucket of water having a small hole in the bottom. Some water is always lost, and without replenishment, the bucket soon runs dry. Salespeople need to keep bringing in new customers to replace ones that leak away. Prospecting is essential even to the most successful and experienced salesperson. It is the only activity that develops the customer base, and the quality of the customer base is direclty related to the quality of the prospecting efforts.

Asset value of the customer base   The customer base is one of the most essential elements for success for every salesperson. It is much like a salesperson's personal financial assets. How wealthy a salesperson is (or wants to be) depends on the sales coming from the customer base. Salespeople can calculate the asset value of their customer base by comparing the amount of sales or profits made to each customer and the costs to make those sales. They can also calculate the potential asset value of a customer base and determine which customers should get more effort and which ones less. Table 6-1 is a schedule of such a calculation.

The base can be measured in two ways: (1) by the number of customers and (2) by potential or current business. In Table 6-1, the current customer

Table 6-1 Asset Value of a Customer Base

Customer	Current Value (Sales/Year)	Potential Business	Gain	Probability of Getting	Future* Asset Value
XYZ CO.	$100,000	$175,000	$75K	.60	$145,000
ABC INC.	$ 75,000	$ 85,000	$10K	.10	$ 86,000
JJJ INC.	0	$110,000	$110K	.20	$ 22,000
JCH LTD.	0	$ 50,000	$50K	.75	$ 37,500
LMN CO.	0	$100,000	$100K	.05	$ 5,000
ZZZ CO.	$125,000	$175,000	$50K	.95	$172,500
TOTAL	$300,000	$695,000	$395K		$468,000

*(Gain × Probability) + Current Value

base has three members. The potential base has six (the three already buying plus the three who are not). The current dollar base is $300,000 and the potential base is $695,000. Our salesperson has a 43 percent penetration rate. She has realistically estimated the chances of getting the additional business from each customer and concluded the best she can get is $468,000.

Stages in the buying life cycle A salesperson prospects because different customers are at different stages in the four-stage buying life cycle. This **buying life cycle** represents the cycle of time the buyer is in the market and actively purchasing (see Figure 6-1). The cycle begins with the *investigation stage*. Prospective customers gather information from salespeople, existing customers, or industry sources (trade publications, advertising, etc.) These prospects are interested but are neither committed nor currently purchasing the product, at least not from these salespeople.

◀ ◀ ◀ ◀ ◀ ◀ ◀ ◀
Learning Objective 2: Stages in the buying life cycle

Next is the *trial stage*. Customers often purchase on a trial basis from several vendors, searching for the one(s) that most satisfies their needs. After doing business in the trial stage, buyers generally settle on a selected vendor or group of vendors; this is called the steady buying stage.

The 4 Stages of the Buying Life Cycle

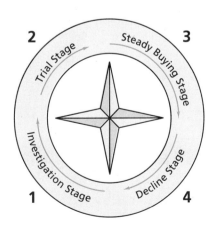

Figure 6-1 **The 4 Stages of the Buying Life Cycle**

During the *steady buying stage,* customers come to rely on this group of vendors as their major suppliers, and these vendors look to this customer for reliable repeat business. A strong loyalty between buyer and seller results in this stage, and it is difficult for competitors to break in.

The last stage is the *decline stage.* As a result of many factors, vendors and customers begin to part company. Decline comes about because of personnel changes, product obsolescence, market abandonment, technological changes, or simply changes in needs and/or desires.

Notice that there has been no mention of a time dimension. These stages may be short or long. Some buyers sustain the steady buying stage for many years, some for only a few months. New prospects replace old ones that fall into decline. Figure 6-2 illustrates three customers, each in a different stage of the cycle. Customer A is in decline, B is still in the trial stage but becoming a steady customer, and C has just entered the trial stage. Without prospecting, the salesperson would see business decline, were it not for the new customers B and C.

What It Takes to Be Successful at Prospecting

▶ ▶ ▶ ▶ ▶ ▶ ▶ ▶ ▶

Learning Objective 3:
Activities necessary for
successful prospecting

Being successful at prospecting is the result of a consistent and persistent effort, an intelligent approach, exploring every opportunity, and eliminating unproductive prospects.

A consistent and persistent effort A consistent and persistent prospecting effort must be a routine activity. Some sales managers require a portion of their salespeople's day to be spent on prospecting calls. Prospecting is not something just new salespeople do; it is not abandoned after a customer base has been established.

An intelligent approach Prospecting should be approached intelligently and systematically. Separating out the high-potential prospects depends on a logical process. Both deductive and inductive systems of prospecting can work. A deductive system starts with a large pool of prospective customers, such as from a rented mailing list, then eliminates all but the high-probability ones.

Figure 6-2 **Buying Life Cycles of Three Customers**

An inductive process starts with information about a specific customer, such as zip code and age, then works up to an expanded list of high-probability prospects. From this information, for example, a salesperson could reason that if one person of that age and in that zip code area bought, there must be more in that zone who are about the same age who would also buy. The salesperson could get a mailing list of those people and go from there.

Prospecting based on logical relationships can be very successful. For example, if a person owns a personal computer, does that make them a good prospect for buying commodity futures from stockbrokers? Very possibly, and here's the logic: ownership of a personal computer means a higher level of discretionary income. A higher level of discretionary income means a higher level of income in general. It also means greater sophistication and education, a higher tax bracket, and a need to find investment opportunities. Now we have it! By working from a list of personal computer owners, the stockbrokers develop a list of persons whose probability of buying stocks or bonds is greater than those they would have found if they had made random calls from the phone book. Is this logic infallible? No, of course not. Does it improve the salespeople's chances over random calling? Definitely!

Exploring every opportunity Successful prospecting requires exploring every opportunity. Successful salespeople never stop exploring. They explore what worked in the past, what other salespeople have used with success, and new sources of relationships that point to new prospects.

Eliminating unproductive prospects Salespeople have limited time and must weigh the time investment in prepurchase activity against the profit potential of the prospect. The higher the profit potential, the greater the upfront time commitment can be. Some salespeople make decisions based on their experience, that is, if after several calls where interest was apparent, the prospect still won't buy and the salespeople have learned why, the prospect is eliminated. Training and experience dictate how long a salesperson should stay with prospects before abandoning them. It is simply a matter of efficiency and opportunity cost. Time spent chasing an unproductive lead is time taken away from a profitable one.

▶ ▶ *follow-up questions*

1. What is the difference between the inductive and deductive approaches to prospecting?
2. Why do salespeople prospect?

Lead Generation

The most frequently asked question by novice salespeople is "Where do you come up with your leads and prospects?" The answer is "Everywhere!" Before customers are prospects, they are first leads.

Leads versus Prospects

A **lead** is a person who might become a prospect but has not yet matched the qualifying criteria. Leads that qualify as having the *willingness, ability,* and *authority* to buy become prospects. A **prospect,** then, is a qualified lead.

Prospecting success and converting prospects to customers is a matter of percentages. If 10 percent of all prospects become customers, then 30 prospects per month should convert to three new customers. The salesperson pursuing 100 prospects will have ten new customers. The more leads salespeople generate, the better their chances of creating a larger customer base.

Sources of Leads

▶ ▶ ▶ ▶ ▶ ▶ ▶ ▶ ▶

Learning Objective 4: Sources of leads

Generating enough leads is a matter of using any of the 15 proven sources of leads shown in the box below.

15 Sources of Leads

1. Past customers
2. Referrals
3. Networking
4. Centers of influence
5. Cold calls
6. Current customers
7. Libraries/directories
8. Advertising leads
9. Direct response
10. Telemarketing
11. Seminars
12. "Bird dogs"
13. Noncompeting salespeople
14. Trade and professional associations
15. Civic and business groups

Past customers   Strange as it may seem, past customers can be good prospects. They did business with a salesperson in the past, so there must have been something they liked. They stopped doing business with the salesperson, so there must have been a reason for that, too. They may have stopped buying because the salesperson forgot about them, because of a problem that occurred years ago, or because they got lost in the shuffle of a personnel change. Past customers are often orphaned once they cease buying. Such accounts may be good possibilities for creative, adaptive salespersons. And it costs must less to reinstate an inactive customer than to establish a new one.

Referrals   Referrals are the best source of quality leads. This is the word-of-mouth recommendation all salespeople want. Referrals can be voluntary, that is, a satisfied customer gives the salesperson's name to some one else, or they can come through the **endless chain referral** method, which is also called the daisy chain referral. An endless chain referral is one in which a satisfied customer gives the salesperson names of acquaintances who might be interested. The adaptive salesperson asks customers for the name of someone else who might benefit from the product. Too many salespeople overlook this great opportunity.

Endless chain prospecting yields better prospects and increases the chances of making a sale because the salesperson can say "Carmen referred me to you." The relationship between the referring customer and the new lead starts the salesperson off on a good footing. The endless chain referral process has several benefits:

▶ The salesperson gets the name of someone who probably has the same needs or problems as the satisfied customer.

▶ The salesperson can use the satisfied customer's name when calling on the referral. New leads will probably be more inclined to listen to a presentation if the salesperson has been referred by someone they know, trust, and can call on.

▶ The salesperson does not have to dig up more leads to chase; satisfied customers provide them.

Networking   New salespeople should network as much as possible. Only your imagination limits the number of networking possibilities, some of which are[3]:

▶ friends from a previous job

▶ school and college acquaintances

▶ people known through hobbies or sporting events

▶ acquaintances made through civic activities

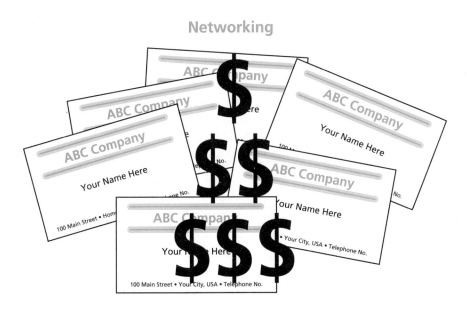

Networking

Give each of your customers serveral calling cards. Have a supply with you at all times. Include your cards (2) with every mailing. Don't leave home without them! Be sure everyone knows who you are, what you sell, and the company you're with. Get on the guest-speakers list of the service clubs in your area.

- neighbors
- friends from church, PTA, or social activities
- acquaintances in professional associations

Effective networking is simply knowing and keeping in touch. It is knowing and being known. William W. Holes offers this tip[4]:

> "The most successful networkers make it a point to help people, even ever so little, before they try to sell them something."

Once you have gotten to know your target prospects, give them a helpful idea or two. This approach is a polite and kind one. The prospects who will be most interested in you are the ones you make feel interesting themselves. By showing the prospects *you* are interested, you make them able to trust in you. They are likely to remember to do business with you and give you referrals."

Center of influence   **Center of influence** describes anyone who can exert a degree of influence and predispose a prospective customer to buying. Heads of households, immediate supervisors, siblings, governmental dignitaries, bankers, clergy, community leaders, and celebrities are examples of centers of influence. They carry the degree of authority and credibility that makes them powerfully influential. They can leverage many new sales and make the selling job easier. Persons with this power are opinion leaders and, with a simple reference, can open many doors. By developing such centers of influence as customers, salespeople quickly and easily gain profitable referrals.

The center-of-influence method of prospecting requires two steps. The first is identifying persons who are truly centers of influence. Such persons need not be community or business leaders. A foreman in a factory could be a center-of-influence for a tool salesperson trying to sell the line workers ratchet wrenches. The second step is having that influential person agree to

What Would You Do If . . . ?

Here's a chance for you to test your creativity. Suppose you just graduated from college and have taken your first selling job. The job is selling rental contracts for industrial heavy equipment, such as backhoes, forklifts, trenchers, and mobile utility cranes. Your manager has just come into your office and said, "We need to get you out in the field selling. Let's plan on making some calls day after tomorrow. Plan a list of five prospects to call on, then call and make appointments for us. Let me see your preliminary list before you schedule appointments."

▶ Question: What would you do?

Suppose you are being sent to Idaho to open a new sales branch. Your firm has never done business there before. Without knowing any more than that, what *process* would you devise for assembling a list of leads you might want to start qualifying once you get there?[5]

▶ Question: What would you do?

help identify new prospects. This is the real key to the center-of-influence prospecting method. Not every influential person is going to commit to helping, but it only takes one good one to generate numerous high-quality leads.

Cold calling Cold calling is the oldest prospecting method. It is also called canvassing. It is simply calling on a prospect with whom no previous contact has been made. Salespeople use cold calling to introduce themselves, their company, and their product or service to a prospective customer. At that time, no sale is planned, but rather the purpose is to identify prospects, then interest them in scheduling a full presentation.

Cold calling has a low probability of success and can be very time-consuming. To be successful, salespeople need to have a logical strategy in selecting the people or businesses they plan to call on. Selecting candidates for cold calling is based on probable need. A tree removal service can knock on every door in the neighborhood, but it would be more successful by calling on the homes with dead trees in their yard.

In cold calling, make several assumptions:

▶ The prospects probably do not know who you are.

▶ They do not know who you represent.

▶ They do not know what you sell.

▶ They are probably highly skeptical of you and your motives.

▶ They are not likely to give you much time.

Given these assumptions, you can see how important it is to establish a rapport very quickly, then get to the reason for your call. In cold calling, the salesperson must make a positive impression and hit upon the product benefits the prospect needs very quickly.

Current customers Current customers must always be considered prospects for even more business. Since they are already customers, they know the salesperson, the firm, and some of the products offered. Note the word *some*. All too often, salespeople become complacent and fail to consider that the customer may want other products in the their firm's line. But the customer may not know what the salesperson has for sale. Salespeople can get a new lead by simply asking if other divisions in the customer's firm might use some of what they have to sell.

Libraries and directories Libraries and directories are sources of prospect lists. Even very small towns have libraries, and numerous types of directories can be found in them. Many associations publish membership directories. *The Encyclopedia of Associations* lists most of the professional and trade associations in the nation. Such directories are valuable because they identify the individual or company with a common link, the association.

Also useful is the telephone directory. In addition to regular phone directories, some cities have business-to-business directories.

Specialized directories, such as the R. L. Polk City Directory, are often helpful. The R. L. Polk City Directory lists households and residents by address and relative location. Through this directory, salespeople can get the name and address of every household on a block, every other household, just the names of persons living on the left (or right) side of the street, or the names and addresses zigzagging left and right, missing every other household.

Salespeople use library resources as sources of new business.

Directories of corporations identify the locations of home offices; sales, production, or assembly branches; and the names of key management personnel. Such directories are useful in system selling, for example, where a computer installation would be used by many divisions of a company.

Governments provide directories. State economic development departments publish free or low-cost directories of manufacturers, retailers, dealers, and wholesalers. A directory of manufacturers, for example, will be organized by alphabet, location, or type of business. A sample page from a directory is shown in Figure 6-3.

Advertising leads Advertising creates leads for salespeople. This is particularly true in retailing. Retailers run ads to get prospective customers to come in. The numerous ads for Lazy-Boy recliners, Amana microwave ovens, Buicks, and Kinney Shoes do two things. First, they inform prospective customers about a special price or promotion, and second, they tell them where to buy the product.

Retail salespeople know that a person who comes in the store has some degree of interest in buying. Another advertising-related prospecting method involves using reply cards, like those in magazines. A form of reply card is the magazine "bingo card," on which readers circle the numbers corresponding to products or services advertised in the magazine and send the card to the publisher. Local salespeople get readers' names from these reply cards, then contact them through the mail or over the phone.

Advertising-related prospecting is a powerful way of getting the names of literally thousands of interested prospects at once. Using advertising to generate leads must be done judiciously, however. If so many names are generated that the salesforce cannot handle them, the prospective customers are left with the impression that the company does not need their business.

Direct response Direct response is a prospecting tool used to generate a direct reply from a potential customer responding to an ad, a mailed letter, brochure, or promotional piece, a magazine tip-in or bind-in card, or a tele-

Figure 6-3 **Sample Page from a State Directory**

Restorative Health Services C
   5601 North 103 Street 68134
   493-6384
   Joel A. Larimore, President
   *8049 Rehabilitation services (09)

Richardson, Larsen, Schroeder & Associates, P. C. C
   11235 Davenport Street 68154
   333-6600
   Robin Richardson, Managing Partner
   *8931 Accountants (09)

Richman Gordman Stores .... H
   12100 West Center Road 68124
   333-3400 (9 locations)
   A. D. Gordman, Chairman
   *5311 Department store (07)

Riekes Equipment Company C
   2910 Cuming Street 68131
   341-1181
   Duncan Murphy, President
   *5084 Material handling equipment (06)

Rigel Corporation .... E
   7545 Pacific Street 68124
   392-2904
   Vincent Morrissey, Co-Owner
   John Chisholm, Co-Owner
   *5812 Restaurant (07)

Rigle-Chix (Kentucky Fried Chicken) .... F
   4315 Frances Street 68105
   (Home office: Louisville, KY)
   558-0330 (12 locations)
   Jack D. Wagaman, President
   *5812 Restaurant (07)

Riley Advertising Company .... E
   301 South 74 Street 68114
   390-9119
   H. Douglas Riley, President
   *2641 Manufacture pressure sensitive labels (04)

Ring Transfer & Distribution C
   828 1/2 South 17 Street 68102
   342-4269
   Al Ring, Manager
   *4214 Trucking & distribution (05)

Rite Way Oil & Gas Company, Inc. .... D
   8400 I Street 68127
   331-6400
   Rex Ekwall, President & Owner
   *5541 Service station (07)

Rite-Style Optical Co. ....
   19102 Bedford 68134
   571-0976
   George P. Lee, President
   *3851 Prescription optical lenses, finished glasses,
   contact lenses (04)

River City Drywall .... D
   4619 South 136 Street 68137
   (Div. of Eliason & Knuth)
   895-1012
   John Eliason, President
   *1742 Drywall contractors (03)

Roadway Express, Inc. .... D
   10626 I Street 68127
   339-9200
   Bob Rich, Terminal Manager
   *4213 Long distance trucking (05)

Roberts & Dybdahl, Inc. C
   1109 South 19 Street 68108
   341-3246
   Mike Hecker, Manager
   *5031 Lumber - wholesale (06)

Roberts Dairy Company .... E
   2901 Cuming Street 68131
   (Div. of Prairie Farms Dairy, Carlinville, IL)
   344-4321
   Ron Richardson, General Manager
   *2023 Ice milk mix (04)
   *2026 Milk products
   *2033 Fruit drinks

Roe Machine & Pattern Works, Inc. C
   1808 Ogden Street 68110
   453-6777
   Harold Schulte, Owner
   *2752 3-dimension planographing (04)
   *3361 Aluminum castings
   *3462 Gears
   *3544 Tool & die work

Rollheiser, Holland, Kahler Associates, Inc. C
   11248 John Galt Boulevard 68137
   592-7300
   Jay Rollheiser, Chairman
   Jeffrey R. Kahler, President
   *7311 Advertising & public relations (09)

Ronco Construction Company C
   1717 North 74 Street 68114
   397-9109
   Don Bassler, President
   *1521 General contractor - residential (03)
   *1542 General contractor - nonresidential

Rose Bowl Of Omaha, Inc. C
   1110 North Saddle Creek Road 68132
   (Div. of All American Bowling Corp., Atlanta, GA)
   556-7212
   Bill Hughes, General Manager
   *7933 Bowling alley (09)
   *5812 Snack bar
   *5813 Lounge
   *5941 Bowling equipment & accessories

Ross's Steak House, Inc. .... E
   909 South 72 Street 68114
   393-2030
   Sandra Lorello, President
   Ross Lorello, Jr., Vice President
   *5812 Restaurant (07)

Rotellas Italian Bakery, Inc. .... D
   1105 South 24 Street 68108
   341-5125
   Louis J. Rotella, Sr., President
   *2051 Bread, cake & related products (04)

Royal Insurance C
   Suite 300
   7000 West Center Road 68106
   (Home office: New York, NY)
   392-2855
   Danny Mize, Branch Manager
   *6411 Multi-line insurance (08)

Employment Code: F - 250-499; G - 500-999; H - 1000-2499; I - 2500 or more

When Things Go Wrong (Part 1)

Leads, Leads Everywhere, But How to Handle Them?

Jim Dauw became advertising and promotion manager for Huck Manufacturing and decided to visit some of the salespeople specifically to ask about the advertising lead program. When he visited one salesperson, the salesperson opened a bottom desk drawer and said, "Here they are, six months' worth of leads. Do you want 'em?"

Continued

QUALIFIED LEAD

Shown below is a QUALIFIED LEAD produced from our advertising and publicity efforts. Material was mailed to the prospect originally and he now needs more information.

Please follow up this lead. Complete and return this form to:

Please complete and return this card to Huck Manufacturing Company

What type of business is your company in?
- ☐ Transportation
  Specify:_____
- ☐ Electronics
- ☐ Distribution
- ☐ Construction
- ☐ Other_____

Is your project need:
- ☐ Immediate
- ☐ 1 to 6 months
- ☐ More than 6 months
- ☐ Information only

Do you:
- ☐ Recommend
- ☐ Specify
- ☐ Have final approval

For immediate information:
*Huck Manufacturing Company
Industrial Fastener Division
Waco, TX
817-776-2000*

FORM HWB 855

What additional information would you like?
_____
_____
_____

What is your application?
_____
_____
_____

Phone Number   Ext   Best time to call

Date contacted_____ ☐ In person, ☐ By phone
Lead Quality ☐ Excellent, ☐ Good, ☐ Fair, ☐ Poor
Purchase possibility: ☐ Immediate, ☐ 3 Months, ☐ 6 Months
☐ Longer, ☐ None, ☐ Current Customer
Add to mailing list: ☐ Yes, ☐ No
End product or application_____

Other products he's interested in_____

Comments_____

Follow up date_____ Salesman_____

phone solicitation. One of the most widely used forms of direct response is direct mail. Direct mail can be aimed at business prospects or consumers. With the cost of an industrial sales call approaching $200 per call, using direct mail to generate leads can mean dramatic cost savings. It can also improve the sales-to-call and profit-to-call ratios by generating a greater number of high-quality leads.

Direct mail prospecting gets names from house lists, rented lists, and warrantee cards. A **house list** contains the names of the firm's own customers. These may be both active and inactive customers. Businesses rent other firm's customer lists or compiled lists from list brokers. For example, a salesperson could rent the names of subscribers to *Field and Stream* magazine. An example of a compiled list taken from public information is a list of motor vehicle owners in California. It would only cost a salesperson about $500 to get a list of 10,000 names of Cadillac owners from California. If only 1 percent of them (100) became customers and bought only five dollars worth of merchandise, the $500 has been returned!

Warrantee cards are another direct mail source of names. Each time consumers send in a warrantee card on any product or service, the firm has their name. Salespersons can call and try and sell them more, or their name can be rented out unless they specifically state, in writing, that their name is not to be included on a company's rented or leased address list.

Telemarketing Telemarketing is one of the fastest growing lead-generation tools in selling today. **Telemarketing** is done by either inbound or outbound calling. Inbound refers to prospective customers calling in, usually to an 800 number. In outbound telemarketing, a firm makes calls to individuals soliciting their interest in having a salesperson call on them.

Many firms are combining print and TV ads with toll-free 800 numbers. This combination can generate thousands of leads for a firm's salespeople. Mutual of Omaha is known for its animal show "Mutual of Omaha's Wild Kingdom." Through this show and the 800 number used in its ads,

Many companies use telemarketing "800" numbers to generate leads for field salespeople.

thousands of names are generated for Mutual's salespeople around the nation. It is a tremendously successful tactic.

Outbound calling is becoming more widely used and can be done very inexpensively. Telemarketing agents call prospects to schedule appointments for face-to-face meetings with salespeople or to do prenotification prospecting, that is, sending literature to the prospect that the salesperson later follows up on. Using outbound telemarketing to do prenotification prospecting has been shown to be very effective at increasing the number of appointments granted a salesperson and resulting sales.[6]

Prenotification prospecting is an application of the foot-in-the-door technique, that is, gaining commitment to a major request by first gaining compliance to a minor one. In the Case in Point below, the foot-in-the-door technique is being applied by asking the prospect to permit the caller to simply send information. A call from a sales representative would follow in a few days.

When this technique was applied and compared to calls directly asking for appointments, the results showed prenotification telemarketing increased the number of scheduled appointments from 1 in 16.3 calls to 1 in 4 calls and the number of resulting presentations from 1 in 1.5 to 1 in 1.3, while the number of closed sales was doubled![7]

Seminars A popular method of generating leads, particularly in the real estate development, vacation property, and financial investment industries, is

Caller: Hello! Is this Mr./Ms. _____? I hope I didn't disturb your (lunch, dinner). Mr./Ms. _____, I actually called to introduce myself. My name is _____ and I'm working on a unique assignment with an organization known as _____. Perhaps you've seen some of our trucks? We're one of the major burglar alarm companies in the _____ area.

I'll tell you why I called *you.* Just recently, we've been installing a substantial number of residential security systems rather close to where you live. And so we thought it might be a good idea to distribute literature to people, perhaps like yourself, who live nearby.

We *had* planned to mail it to you and a number of other neighbors so that if and when you ever decide to link into residential security, at least one company name would be familiar to you. But I don't want to clutter up your mailbox with something you might consider junk mail...so I thought it would be polite to call first and get your permission to mail the literature. May I drop the information in the mail?

Good! I'll mail it tomorrow and you'll recognize the name _____. Are you still at (*address*)? Oh, I do need your zip code. Please have everyone at home look it over very carefully. And with your permission, I'd like to give you a call in a few days to see what questions you'll have. Will that be okay? Good! I'll drop the material in the mail.

Goodbye, Mr./Ms. _____.

Objections: I'm Not Ready to Buy a Burglar Alarm

Caller: Mr./Ms. _____, let me make myself clear. My job is to send you the information. What you do with the information is up to you. Some people will never install a burglar alarm. Others will decide to install a system right away, and many people will decide to install a system sometime in the future. I have no idea which category you're in. But we have found most people welcome the information. Is that true in your case?

(If lead still refuses, thank them for their time and hang up.)

Source: Marvin A. Jolson, "Prospecting by Telephone Prenotification: An Application of the Foot-in-the-Door Technique," *Journal of Personal Selling and Sales Management,* 6 (1986): 40.

through seminars. Ads are placed in newspapers or magazines or on TV promoting a free seminar. During the seminar, the salespeople make their presentation and attempt to either close sales on the spot or schedule appointments. The beauty of the seminar approach is that the salesperson can make one introductory presentation to hundreds of potential customers at once. This is simply another way of generating prospects efficiently.

"Bird dogs" Bird dogs are used by hunters to run ahead and point out the quarry. Some salespeople use prospecting "bird dogs" the same way. **Bird dogs** are persons hired to get leads for the salesperson to follow up on. Using bird dogs is often necessitated by economics. It is more efficient to pay some-one to make the calls while the salesperson closes the sales.

Noncompeting salespeople   Noncompeting salespeople can be sources of leads. It is not uncommon for a customer, particularly a purchasing agent, to buy numerous types of products from a host of vendors. Vendors who make personal sales calls on customers often wait in a lobby or waiting room and exchange conversation about business. It would not be out of the question for an industrial solvents salesperson to pass along the name of a prospective cus-tomer to a salesperson selling floor maintenance equipment. Noncompeting salespeople should be considered as much a part of a salesperson's networking activities as prospective clients.

Trade and professional associations   Trade and professional associations are great places to make contacts. A home builder's association has both building contractors and building products suppliers as members. Trade and professional association members include businesses and individuals directly or indirectly involved in the trade or profession. Examples of such organiza-tions are Sales and Marketing Executives International, the Society of Chemical Engineers, and the American Restaurant Association. The alert salesperson skilled in talking to audiences should get on the speakers list of such associations. This is a good way of making more contacts and becoming better known in both the salesperson's own and the customer's industry.

Most industries hold trade shows at which members set up displays to promote their product or service. Also attending trade shows are vendors who sell to the industry members. In fact, vendors usually comprise the bulk of the exhibitors. Trade show leads are very efficient, in that the vendors can convert a trade show lead to a closed sale with fewer sales calls after the show than they would normally have to make with other leads. The Trade Show Bureau reports that 3 percent of the contacts made at trade shows actually placed orders at the show and 54 percent placed orders after the show. Of

Trade shows offer products to prospective customers and are a good source for new business.

those placing orders after the show, 54 percent did so by phone, 22 percent by mail, and 10 percent through local distributors or dealers. The bureau reported that leads generated through trade shows require only one to two calls to close the deal, compared to 5.1 calls to convert a lead to a closed sale when that lead was generated through some means other than a trade show.[8]

Civic and business groups   Civic and business groups are a fertile field of leads. Such organizations as the Rotary Club, the Elks Lodge, the Optimists International, the Chamber of Commerce, and the Lions Club are populated by business people, all of whom could be leads or sources of leads. Members have access to membership directories. Like professional and trade associations, these groups should definitely be included in the salesperson's network of possibilities.

Case in Point

Strange as It Seems, Some Salespeople Resent Sales Leads!

Some salespeople may resent leads they didn't create because they:

▸ May think it reflects on their ability to identify leads on their own: "If I get a sale from a lead I didn't create, it shows I'm doing a poor job of identifying prospective customers."

▸ Feel leads are awkward to follow up because they mean making cold calls.

▸ Are given too many to handle. It is impossible to follow up on all of them, so why bother at all?

▸ Feel leads generated by mail, shows, and so on are poor quality, that is, only about 10 percent ever amount to anything.

▸ Feel the time lag between when leads originated and when they are told of them and have time to call back means the leads get cold and never pan out.

Source: Allen Konopacki. Cited in *Sales and Marketing Management,* "Why Salespeople Resent Sales Leads," 130 (1983): 76.

▸▸ *follow-up questions*

1. How has telemarketing made salespeople more efficient?
2. Distinguish between a house list and a compiled list of names.
3. How does the center-of-influence method of prospecting differ from the referral method?

Who Is a Prospect?

Leads become prospects when they are ready, willing, and able to buy; when they have been successfully qualified. This means everyone is a prospect for something. Salespeople often refer to an individual who is ready to buy now as a hot prospect.

◂ ◂ ◂ ◂ ◂ ◂ ◂ ◂
Learning Objective 5: What qualifies a lead to become a prospect

> A prospect is someone who:
>
> 1. Needs and/or wants what is offered
> 2. Has the ability to buy
> 3. Has the authority to buy

A Prospect Needs or Wants What Is Offered

A prospect must perceive a need for the vendor's product: the greater the need, the hotter the prospect. Needs or wants are transient and temporal. This means a person's needs are fleeting and what prospects want today may not be what they want tomorrow.

A Prospect Has the Ability to Buy

The ability or inability to buy may be constrained by monetary and nonmonetary factors. Prospects should have the financial, physical, and mechanical capability of buying.

Financial ability   Making a presentation to someone who cannot afford the offering is a waste of time, the salesperson's and the prospect's. Financial ability means prospects must be able to afford the product. Note the word *afford*. Most people buy goods they cannot pay for all at once. Part of the salesperson's job is to make the purchase affordable. This may mean lowering the price in return for immediate payment (as with a cash discount) or arranging financing over several years. Adaptive salespeople must be able to arrange creative methods of financing for prospects, such as the numerous credit and leasing alternatives discussed in the previous chapter. These can put seemingly unaffordable product well within the customer's financial reach.

Physical ability   Physical ability means such things as storage space and transportation. The prospect may have the money and the desire but no storage space. Similarly, there may be no way to get the goods to the buyer so purchasing now would be of no benefit. This becomes a particularly relevant factor when selling in foreign countries, where physical facilities compatible with the vendor's shipping practices may not exist. In such cases, alternative shipping methods must be arranged, or the sale may have to be abandoned.

Mechanical ability   Mechanical ability means the buyer must be able to complete the mechanics of the transaction. For example, if you go into a store that only takes cash and Visa cards and you have no cash and only an American Express card, you and the merchant cannot complete the transaction. Anything that impedes the mechanical consummation of the sale eliminates the prospect from consideration unless the impediment is overcome.

A Prospect Has the Authority to Buy

The authority to buy means legal, organizational, or social authority. Legal authority must be considered in all sales. The sale of alcoholic beverages to minors is prohibited in most states. While they may have the desire and mechanical ability, minors are not authorized under the law to buy such beverages.

The organizational authority to buy is, in many firms, granted only to purchasing agents. While other persons in the organization may direct the purchasing agent to make the formal purchase (issue the purchase order), only the purchasing agent may have the organization's authority to buy. This is often the case in large corporations.

Social authority is the power bestowed on someone by default, custom, or social, cultural, or family position to buy. Parents have the authority to buy for their children and slowly relinquish that authority as their children get older. In some households, women relinquish buying authority to men for some items and vice versa.

In summary, prospects must exhibit **effective demand,** which means they have the need, the ability to buy, and the authority to make the purchase. When any one of these is missing, a person is not a prospect, at least not at that point in time.

▶ ▶ *follow-up questions*

1. Some mechanical reasons that would impede a sale were mentioned. Can you name two more?

2. Why is it important for a salesperson to know if a prospect has the legal authority to buy? What could be the consequences of selling to someone who does not have legal authority?

3. How would a salesperson determine who has the authority to buy?

Qualifying the Prospect

Qualifying is the process a salesperson uses to determine if prospects meet the criteria indicating they will become a customer.

The Purpose of Qualifying

From qualifying, the salesperson judges which leads to pursue and which to pass. A degree of risk always exists that the wrong lead will be pursued and the truly great one will slip through. Think of qualifying as a "funnel of success," like the one shown in Figure 6-4.

Successful salespeople extensively qualify their leads because it benefits them in several ways:

▶ Qualifying permits them to be more efficient by determining which leads will likely be the most productive.

▶ Salespeople gain additional information from qualifying, thus permitting sales presentations that are more directly focused on that customer's specific needs or problems.

▶ The information gained from qualifying gives salespeople an idea of what objections will be raised so they can be prepared for them.

▶ Qualifying saves time for selling. An hour spent qualifying may well save salespeople numerous hours making unproductive calls.

▶ Qualifying makes the productive calls more so. If salespeople are calling on a poorly qualified lead, they cannot be calling on a hot lead. They are thus wasting too much time on a long shot and not enough time on the sure thing.

Figure 6-4 **Qualifying Is a Funnel of Success**

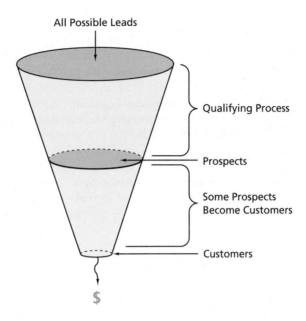

Salespeople must look at qualifying as an investment in success—an investment that is often hard for novices to see because they think the secret to success is making sales calls. They are only half right: the secret is making sales calls on leads that will become active customers. The qualifying process is shown in Figure 6-5.

Qualifying Steps

Learning Objective 6: Steps in the qualifying process

Not all leads represent qualified buyers. Think of qualifying leads as a filtering process. The screen through which qualified applicants pass can be as fine or coarse as necessary. The more stringent the qualifications, the fewer prospects result, but those who remain have a higher probability of buying. Qualifying is simply asking the right people the right questions.

Step 1: Find the key person Every salesperson searches for the one person among the buying influences who has the greatest sway over the decision. In most sales, this key person is easily identified. However, making any assumptions is still not safe. It is better to ask questions to determine the identity of this key person. In retail sales, the conventional wisdom used to be that the male head of the household was the key person for major purchases. Cars, major appliances, insurance, lawn services, water softener systems, and so on were assumed to be his domain. The woman of the household was assumed to be the key person for child-related purchases, home decorating items, and most of the home's routine purchases. Times have changed! These traditional assumptions are no longer applicable.

In business-to-business sales, discovering who the key person may be a problem and require investigation. A good place to start qualifying is with the secretary or receptionist. This person can direct the salesperson to the right contact with whom the salesperson can use probing questions to determine if a meeting and presentation is in order. Qualifying leads before a face-to-face meeting is called prequalifying or self-qualifying.

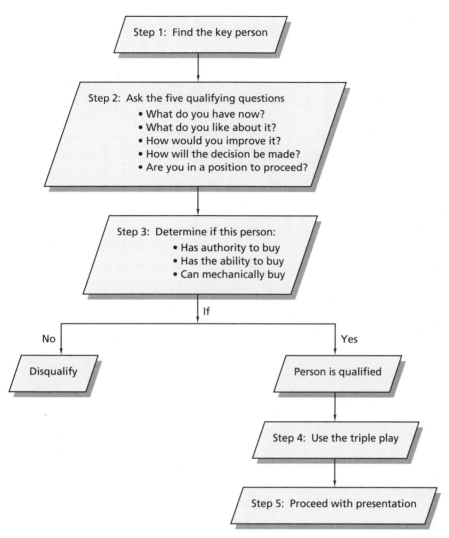

Figure 6-5 **The Lead Qualifying Process**

Step 1: Find the key person

Step 2: Ask the five qualifying questions
- What do you have now?
- What do you like about it?
- How would you improve it?
- How will the decision be made?
- Are you in a position to proceed?

Step 3: Determine if this person:
- Has authority to buy
- Has the ability to buy
- Can mechanically buy

If

No

Disqualify

Yes

Person is qualified

Step 4: Use the triple play

Step 5: Proceed with presentation

With prequalifying, the salesperson or person acting as a "bird dog" contacts the lead and asks a series of standard qualifying questions. If done by mail, the lead is asked to complete an interest survey or return a business reply card. An example of a direct mail piece used in prequalifying is shown in Figure 6-6. When the agents receive a completed pamphlet, they have a prospect, not a lead. They then make a phone contact to schedule an appointment and deliver the requested material. Depending on the interest of the respondents, the agents may even try to close them on a listing agreement to sell their house or schedule a model-home viewing. The agents investigate the respondents' relocation intentions, planning horizon for relocating, financial situation, and the specifics they want in a new home.

Self-qualification is another means of qualifying a lead in which the potential customer takes the initiative to contact the vendor. Self-qualifying dominates most retail store sales; that is, when customers walk in the door, they have declared an interest in purchasing. A form of self-qualifying occurs in industrial sales during trade shows and conventions. Attendees at these events qualify themselves as leads simply by their presence.

Step 2: Ask the five qualifying questions[9]   *Question 1: What do you have now?*   A good rule to remember in solving any problem is to begin with what you know and work toward what you don't. Before trying to sell prospects on a product or service, determine what they are using now. It is a good starting place and a way to quickly probe their needs, desired benefits, and buying history. Buyers are often eager and proud to explain the product or service they currently use. Some prospects, however, are reluctant to divulge any information. If this is the case, salespeople must resort to indirect questioning techniques and use their powers of observation to deduce the needed information.

Question 2: What do you like about it?   A natural extension of Question 1 is what prospects likes about the products they are using. Here is where a good salesperson probes for as much detail as possible. The greater the detail, the greater the information and number of selling points the salesperson has when it comes time to close the sale. In this second step of qualifying, develop an extended line of questioning, and of course, pay attention with all senses to both verbal and nonverbal clues.

An extended line of questioning flows from a prospect's answer. Below is a conversation to illustrate the point (the salesperson, Rodney, is talking to a prospective boat buyer):

Prospect: Rodney, why don't you take a run out here and give me your opinion as to how much I could get for my boat on today's resale market? You could make the round trip in a couple of hours."

Rodney: I'd like to do that. Tell me what you have and what you like best about it.

Prospect: I'm currently sailing an Acme X28, a pretty good old boat, and well, I guess what I like most about it would be its seaworthiness. It's kind of a slow old tub, but I wouldn't be afraid to ride out a hurricane in it.

Rodney: A fast boat can put you back in the harbor before the weather gets bad!

Prospect: Yeah, if your engine doesn't quit. My boat is almost a motorsailer—it has a steadying sail that could get me home in a blow if the mill stops grinding.

Rodney: How old is your boat?

Prospect: A little over ten years old now.

Rodney: Have you had any trouble with the motor over the ten years?

Prospect: Not much, and that's the way I like it. I'm no mechanical engineer, and I have neither the patience nor the inclination to be fooling around with some supersophisticated piece of hardware that's temperamental.

Notice how Rodney asked a few astute questions and used the prospect's responses as a springboard for more questions. Rodney sells speed boats and high-performance craft, exactly what the prospect *does not* want! Rodney can eliminate this lead.

Rodney later said, "If I'd have rushed out to see this prospect and his 'slow old tub,' I would have missed the chance at a sale to someone wanting a high-performance boat. Don't waste your time working with people who want what you don't have. If you spend your time that way, you'll have the bad luck to be out every time the business comes in. Concentrate on finding and working with people you can help enjoy the benefits they want. You'll be working with buyers who have precommitted themselves to what you do have. They will literally be sold before you even demonstrate, and when you do demonstrate, your demonstration will simply be a confirmation that they've got to have it."[10] Too many novice salespeople spend time trying to convert a "nonwanter" into a "wanter." This is like pushing a string up hill! The purpose of qualifying is to separate the "wanters" from the "nonwanters".

Question 3: How would you improve it? The third question is called the fantasy question. It works in conjunction with the previous two questions and goes something like this, "What would you like to see altered or improved in your present _____?" Very few buyers can't think of something they would like to see improved. Everyone would like "it" to be faster, cheaper to operate, easier to use, more dependable, better, or more quickly repaired if it breaks. This question is called the fantasy question because prospects can always imagine something better than what they are now using.

Suppose Rodney, our boat salesperson, was qualifying another customer. He has just asked the fantasy question, and the lead said, "I would like the sails to be easier to raise and lower. These old-fashioned cranks and pulleys are getting me down." Rodney would have even further evidence to support his conclusion that this customer does not want what he has to sell. But, suppose the prospect said, "Rodney, sails are great, but even though they are dependable, I would like a little more speed available if I would need it." Rodney could then ask if this prospect felt sails were a necessary item on her next boat. If the prospect said they were, then Rodney would tell the prospect he is in the power boat business and can't help the prospect if she is looking for a sailing craft. If the prospect says sails are not a requirement for her next boat, Rodney knows he has a reasonable chance and can proceed to close the sale.

The fantasy question works with difficult prospects equally as well. Where a salesperson is making a cold call on a less-than-cooperative prospect, the fantasy question can be a useful tool to break the ice. Look at an excerpt of a conversation below and notice how the salesperson uses the fantasy question to find a selling opportunity.

Seller *(a stock broker making a prospecting call over the phone):* What type of investments do you currently have?

Prospect: The standard mix, I guess you would say: Some stocks, several bonds and some money in CDs. I know why you are calling and I am totally satisfied with the stocks and the broker I now have.

Seller: I'm sure you are, but just let me have a few more seconds of your time for a couple of questions. With that portfolio of yours, which financial instruments do you like the best?

Prospect: Bonds. They are safe and dependable.

Seller: Think about those bonds you have. What would you like to see improved with your bond holdings?

Prospect: Nothing, they are just fine. But I'd like to see a bond paying twice the interest with the same or better security.

Seller: Wouldn't we all? But would you be interested in listening to me about bonds that pay 8.75 percent, are guaranteed by the U.S. Treasury, and cost $190 for a $1,000 bond?

Prospect: One hundred and ninety dollars—totally safe and backed by the treasury?

The qualifying questions used in sequence told the salesperson what the prospect is looking for in an investment and what the prospect's favorite investment is and created a possible customer from a disinterested lead.

Question 4: How will the decision be made? Salespeople must know if they are talking to the right person. Also, they must know if they are not talking to the right person but rather with a person who has a degree of influence with the right person. By simply asking, "In addition to yourself, who will make the final decision?" the salesperson has proceeded in the qualifying process and determined the degree of influence this person has in the buying process. If prospects respond by saying they are the decision maker, the salesperson need go no further; if the response is "We decide as a group about the product we buy," the salesperson now has more information for further qualification. Questions like "Does the group have a chairperson?", "Are you that person?", "How many people are in the group?", "How often does the group meet?", and "Has everyone been satisfied with the performance of the product you are using now?" all further the qualification process.

Question 5: Are you in a position to proceed? The fifth qualifying question asks prospects if they would be in a position to consummate the deal if the details were worked out to their satisfaction. The specific question goes like this: "If we were fortunate enough today to find the right _____, would you be in a position to proceed?"[11] A more subtle approach is to ask prospects if they are "in the market to actively purchase today (or soon)." Where long selling cycles are common, prospects may not be actively in the market for several months. They may just be gathering information now, and the purpose of the salesperson's call may be simply to supply that information. The salesperson must know if buyers are ready for a presentation, wanting information, or just shopping vendors.

Case in Point

Wickes Machine Tool Group
Ranks Prospects after Qualifying

Wickes Machine Tool uses a system of ranking qualified prospects according to the time horizon in which they intend to purchase. They use a "1-4 system," defined as:

▸ No. 1 Prospect: project is funded and plans to buy in one to two months; salesperson to contact within two weeks.

▸ No. 2 Prospect: project is funded and plans to buy in two to six months; salesperson to contact in 30 days or less.

▸ No. 3 Prospect: project is funded and plans to buy in six to twelve months; salesperson to contact in one to two months.

▸ No. 4 Prospect: may or may not be funded but does not plan to purchase in the next 12 months.

Source: Rayna Skolnik, "For Wickes, Qualifying Begins with a Handshake"; "*Sales and Marketing Management,* 130 (1983): 68.

The salesperson does not want to overly pressure prospects. The situation needs to be handled as though prospects are usually in a position to proceed but perhaps just this once may need to wait. Prospects who are part of a buying group and must okay the purchase, consult with others in their family, or review their finances will generally reveal such information at this point. Of course, the best answer is "Yes, if we can work out details, I'm in a position to buy." Regardless of the answer, the salesperson gets more information about this prospect. Figure 6-7 summarizes the information gained from the five questions.

Step 3: The ability to pay   As we discussed in the section on "Who Is a Prospect", the salesperson needs to determine if the customer has the authority, the ability, and the need to buy. Without any of these criteria, the person can not be considered a viable prospect at this time. If the person does meet these criteria, move on to the following step.

Step 4: The triple play   The "triple play" specifically qualifies prospects by giving them three choices. The choices can be almost anything—three different models, colors, prices, sizes, shapes, or features, advantages, or benefits. In the triple play, salespeople narrow the discussion to the three choices they think will do the job best, given the information they have. In doing this, they frame what they believe to be the best choice with the other two. Let's look at how Janelle uses the triple play for some fine-tuned qualifying.[16]

Janelle: Our copiers do three things: copy, separate, and collate. Of these, which is the most important to you?

Figure 6-7 **Informa-
tion Gained from
the Five Qualifying
Questions**

Question	What Salespeople Learn
What do you have now?	1. Product currently used 2. Who competition is 3. What they are up against
What do you like about it?	1. Important features, advantages, benefits 2. Selling points to stress 3. What they don't say!
How would you improve it?	1. Additional needs and/or wants 2. Areas of dissatisfaction 3. Buyers' vision and/or hopes 4. Emotional or rational nature of the decision
How the decision will be made?	1. The decision process 2. Who the players are 3. Time it will take to get an answer 4. If prospects are players (talking to right person?) 5. Mechanics of how paperwork will be handled
Are you in a position to proceed?	1. Prospects' readiness to buy 2. Objections to closing 3. Need for more information 4. Time horizon for the sale

Prospect: Collating. It's something we do a lot of and something our present machine does not do. *(Note: Janelle used the triple play and the importance question together and before any others. Also notice, the prospect volunteered the anwer to the fantasy question. Janelle could probe the fantasy question answer further to discover what else the prospect's current copier lacks or just go on from here. She also can eliminate all models that do not collate because of what the qualification process has told her.)*

Janelle: We also have machines that make up to 400 copies per minute, models that do between 200 and 400 per minute, and a model that makes 200 copies per minute. What is the speed of your current machine?

Prospect: I think 200 copies per minute, but that is really more than we need. *(Janelle can make a choice here to narrow her offering down to a machine of similar speed. She may realize the prospect was probably sold more machine than needed and offer a slower machine that would satisfy the prospect's needs and maybe even save money.)*

Janelle: I notice your office decor is primarily done in blues. Should the color of your next machine match or contrast this?

Step 5: Proceed with presentation   Janelle determined the speed, color, and important features this prospect wanted in a new copier. The important thing to note is that she has not only qualified the prospect to determine if the prospect was interested but also determined some of the desired specifics of the product. She can now proceed to make a presentation, schedule an appointment with the key people to make that presentation, or attempt to close the sale now. In the presentation, she will concentrate on the models with the specifics this prospect wants.

1. What is the purpose of the fourth qualifying question?
2. What is meant by "an extended line of questioning"?
3. If you were to use the five qualifying questions, what would you be listening for in the answers?

Prospect Control Systems

What Are Prospect Control Systems?

Prospect control systems are procedures for managing leads and prospects. A **prospect control or lead management system** is an organized method for recording, modifying, and recalling information about a prospect or lead. A good prospect control system will allow the salesperson to follow the history of a lead from initial contact through every phone call and letter and the sale.

Computerized lead-handling systems can cut the in-house cost of promotion in half and triple the return on a firm's promotional dollar.[12] These database management systems have been around since the early 1980s and are now becoming standard equipment with salespeople as computers are appearing side-by-side with the salesperson's sample case.

Before computers and such programs as dBase and Lotus 1-2-3, prospecting systems used file cards and manual sorting and recording of data. Computerized lead management systems permit extensive data storage, retrieval, and sorting. An example of the variety of data that computerized systems can store is shown in Figure 6-8.

Computerized prospect control systems benefit salespeople by:

▶ Allowing them to process more inquiries faster.

▶ Permitting prescreening so only the most promising leads are pursued.

▶ Linking the leads generated to specific promotional campaigns by the company.

▶ Tracking the success of leads back to their source of origin, allowing the replication of successful lead-generation activities and the avoidance of unsuccessful attempts.

A good, off-the-shelf prospect control program should include word processing for letters and mass mailings and be capable of producing reports identifying:

▶ Prospect's Company name and dept.
▶ Sales rep's name
▶ Source of the lead
▶ Credit rating
▶ Standard Industrial Classification code
▶ Date of first, last, and next call
▶ Annual sales to date
▶ Potential sales
▶ Comments

▶ Address and phone
▶ Territory or region
▶ Specific ad promotion
▶ Market segment
▶ Best time to call
▶ Call rate per year
▶ Number of employees
▶ Competitors
▶ Product interests

Source: From "Saleseye, Sales Lead Management System," sold by High Caliber Systems, 165 Madison Avenue, New York, N.Y. Version 2.0 published in 1985.

```
              **  DATA SCREEN # 1 - INITIAL CONTACT DATA  **
     DATE (MM/DD/YY) :11/23/92:    SALESPERSON :JCH:        FILE = B:PROSPECT
                                                           ACTIVE LEAD
     NAME- FIRST   :HARRY     :    LAST :SMITH             :
           TITLE   :PRESIDENT               :
           FIRM    :XYZ CORPORATION INTERNATIONAL :
           ADDRESS :123 WELLS STREET          :
                   :                          :
           CITY    :CINCINNATI           :
           STATE   :OH:         ZIP :55555        :

     LEAD SOURCE        :A:          PRODUCT OF INT. #1 :TRINKETS:
     TYPE OF INQUIRER   :    :       PRODUCT OF INT. #2 :       :

     DESCRIPTION OF BUSINESS :IMPORTER OF IMPORTED CONSUMER PRODUCTS  :
     PRINCIPAL COMPETITION   :MANGELSON'S    :

     REMARKS :HARRY IS INTEREESTED IN SEVERAL OF OUR IMPORTED NOVELTY ITEMS.2 :
             :                                                              :
E)dit  S)ee codes  I)nactivate  H)istory  2)nd data screen  G)o back
D)one  M)ain menu  R)eactivate  T)ickler  P)rint           K)eep looking  :?:


              **  DATA SCREEN # 2 - FOLLOW-UP DATA  **
              FIRM - XYZ CORPORATION INTERNATIONAL         FILE = B:PROSPECT
     NEXT CONTACT - FIRST NAME :HARRY      :               ACTIVE LEAD
                    LAST  NAME :SMITH              :
                    TITLE :PRESIDENT                :
                    FORM LETTER PHRASE :Dear Harry        :
                    PHONE :513-555-1212        :

     NEXT CONTACT  (MM/DD/YY)  :12/12/92:
     LAST CONTACT  (MM/DD/YY)  :11/23/92:

           LAST ACTION       :G:      DOLLARS BUDGETED  :12000      :
           LEAD QUALITY      :1:      NO. OF EMPLOYEES  :1500       :

     -------------  SALES ACTIVITY SUMMARY FOR THIS PERIOD  -------------

           TOTALS TO DATE - CALLS : 45:
                          - HOURS : 68.0:    ANTICIPATED - HOURS :  72.0:
                          - SALES :   5000:               - SALES :   6000:

E)dit  S)ee codes  I)nactivate  H)istory  1)st data screen  G)o back
D)one  M)ain menu  R)eactivate  T)ickler  P)rint  A)utodial  K)eep looking  :?:
```

How to Use Prospect Control Systems

▶ ▶ ▶ ▶ ▶ ▶ ▶ ▶ ▷

Learning Objective 7: How salespeople use prospect control systems

Lead and prospect management systems increase salespeople's productivity. By using such a system, salespeople can sort their data for any number of uses. Referring to Figure 6-8, salespeople would start their day by sorting on the "next contact date" field and generating a list of everyone to be contacted that day. If they wanted a list of all the hot prospects, a simple sort on the "lead quality" field would do the job. In seconds, rather than hours, literally thousands of leads get sorted. Sorting leads for further contacts is just one use of this type of a system.

Lead management systems also help determine the level of activity to devote to a prospect and monitor the activity that has already occurred. Note the sales activity summary at the bottom of Figure 6-8. By tracking calls, hours spent, and sales to date, salespeople can determine the value of the lead. This information allows them to decide whether to continue pursuing the lead or drop it.

Lead management systems are particularly useful to inside salespeople, such as stock brokers, who work over the phone. Many computerized systems link directly to modems. When prospects' files are retrieved, their phone number is automatically dialed. While salespeople are speaking with a prospect, the past account activity, along with the date of last contact, is displayed for them to review. This keeps them current and able to answer questions about past sales or inquiries.

Lead management or prospect control systems don't have to be computerized, but they must be systematized (see the figure below). This requires certain activities be done automatically and sequentially to assure everything gets done properly and in its proper order. Read the "When Things Go Right" which follows, a continuation of the earlier one about Huck Manufacturing, to see how Jim Dauw systematized his lead management system.

The Prospector Customer Record Sheet

An example of a non-computerized lead management system.

Name of Company _____ Contact Title _____ Class _____
Address _____ Phone _____ Section _____
Nature of Business _____ Trade Assn. Member _____
Products Service Major Interest? _____
Prospect's Annual Potential _____

Contact	Phone	In-Person	Product-ServiceDiscussed

Profile _____
_____

Class:
   A. Present customer, Major potential
   B. Excellent prospect
   C. Could be developed
   D. Weak potential

(the Class will change
as you develop your
customer base)

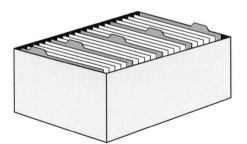

• Renew each card before you call.

• Record each call.

• This record sheet could be your
   constant work companion.

Note: These cards are working cards to be used prior to the sales interview, written on after the interview, carried in the car, and reviewed each evening while preparing your report. You may find the record sheet very simple and easy to use.

His system reduced the number of inquiries to really qualified leads the salespeople could contact with a high degree of assurance a sale would result.

▶▶ *follow-up questions*

1. In what ways would a prospect control system help a new salesperson be more successful?
2. How does being connected to a modem make a prospect control system more effective?

When Things Go Right (Part II)

Lead Qualifying at Huck Manufacturing

Jim Dauw needed a way of handling the 2,600 reply cards the company got each year. He instituted the following system:

▶ Cards are mailed directly to him, not the salespeople.
▶ He codes them to the product group and the ad campaign that generated the inquiry.
▶ His office sends out any literature or information requested on the reply card.
▶ The name and phone number is sent to the local salesperson, who makes a follow-up call during the next two weeks.
▶ Forty days after the first reply card is received at Huck, Dauw sends back a follow-up card asking if the literature was received and if the respondent wants more information. Replies to this mailing are sent to local salespeople.

The result of Dauw's system is that salespeople now deal with only a dozen or so advertising generated leads per month, and about 20 percent turn into sales. All these advertising leads are qualified, and the salespeople know what to focus their sales call on. A sample reply card and follow-up mailing letter are shown below. Huck receives the business reply card, the salesperson receives the "Qualified Lead" form, and 40 days later, the respondent gets the "We Need Your Opinion" letter.

Please complete and return this card to Huck Manufacturing Company

What type of business is your company in?
☐ Transportation
  Specify:_____
☐ Electronics
☐ Distribution
☐ Construction
☐ Other:_____

Is your project need:
☐ Immediate
☐ 1 to 6 months
☐ More than 6 months
☐ Information only

Do you:
☐ Recommend
☐ Specify
☐ Have final approval

For immediate information:
Huck Manufacturing Company
Industrial Fastener Division
Waco, TX
817-776-2000

HUCK A Federal-Mogul Company

FORM HWB 855

What additional information would you like?
_____
_____
_____

What is your application?
_____
_____

Phone Number   Ext   Best time to call

Continued

Lead Qualifying at Huck Manufacturing

We need your opinion!

Several weeks ago we sent product information to you regarding specific Huck Fastening systems. We hope that the package is beneficial and our service satisfactory to you. If not, we need to know how to improve. Please take a moment to complete and return this postage paid questionnaire. You will help us deliver, "The promise that holds."™

1. Did you receive the information package? ☐ Yes ☐ No

2. Was this information complete enough for your needs? ☐ Yes ☐ No

3. What additional information would you like? _____

4. Were you contacted by a Huck representative? ☐ Yes ☐ No

5. If not, would you like to be? ☐ Yes ☐ No

6. What is your phone number (___) _____ Ext _____ and when is the best time to contact you? _____

7. Would you like to participate in a product demonstration? (Other people are welcome) ☐ Yes ☐ No

8. If you have purchased or if you plan to purchase a fastening system, please state the manufacturer and type: _____

9. Is your requirement ☐ Immediate ☐ 1-6 months ☐ 6+ months ☐ Longer

10. Do you: ☐ Recommend ☐ Specify ☐ Have final approval ☐ Purchase

11. If you have decided on purchasing, what factors determined your decision? _____

Please refold this form to expose the postage paid address, tape or staple shut and return to us. We welcome any additional comments and appreciate your participation toward improving our service to you.

Sincerely,

Jill Dauw

James E. Dauw
Corporate Communications Manager

Huck Manufacturing Company
World Headquarters
6 Thomas
Irvine, California 92718
(714) 855-9000

HUCK A Federal-Mogul Company

*Source: Bill Kelley, "Picking the Best from the Rest," *Sales and Marketing Management*, 141 (1989): 30–31.

The 80-20 Rule

One of the oldest axioms in business is that 80 percent of the business comes from 20 percent of the customers. While this may or may not be true in all situations, the 80-20 phenomenon is something to consider. If salespeople prospect with the assumption that 20 percent of the prospects will convert into lasting customers, then by calculating backwards they can determine how many prospects are needed for success. The following example illustrates how to determine the size of the prospecting and qualifying effort. Assume:

$$\text{Average sale per account} = \$5,000$$

$$\text{Salesperson's annual sales quota} = \$500,000$$

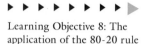

Learning Objective 8: The application of the 80-20 rule

With this information, the salesperson needs on average at least 100 accounts ($500,000 sales per year/$5,000 sales per account per year). Using the 80-20 rule as a starting point, to get the 100 necessary accounts, 500 prospects must qualify to become customers (100 accounts/20% chance of getting an account). Again, assuming only 20 percent of the leads qualify, then 2,500 lead names must be generated (500 prospects/20% chance of a lead converting to a prospect). If a salesperson works 250 days per year (5 days per week × 50 weeks), then the salesperson must average 10 qualifying calls each day. Clearly, there are many assumptions in this example, and indeed, the 80-20 rule is an assumption. However, it is a place to start; the salesperson's performance will modify the assumptions.

Summary

In this chapter, we defined prospects, identified sources of prospects, differentiated them from leads, and discussed qualifying. A salesperson must always prospect for new business to replenish and expand the customer base (Learning Objective 1). Replenishment must occur because customers are at four different stages in their buying life cycles. For some customers, the length of their buying life cycle with a vendor may span many years. For others, it may cease in the investigation stage (Learning Objective 2).

Successful prospecting requires a constant and persistent effort, an intelligent, systematic approach in which every opportunity is explored, and the judgment to eliminate unproductive prospects (Learning Objective 3).

Prospects exist among past customers, referrals, friends and relatives, centers of influence, persons met during cold calling, present customers, directories in libraries, advertising leads, through direct response techniques, among seminar attendees, and finally from names gleaned by "bird dogs" (Learning Objective 4).

Good prospects have the financial, physical, and mechanical ability to buy. They must also have the legal, organizational, or social authority to make purchases. They must, in essence, reflect what is called effective demand. Merely wanting or needing the product is not enough to qualify people to be serious prospects; however, they may, and often do, become serious prospects in the future when they meet these three preconditions (Learning Objective 5).

Qualifying was referred to as a "funnel of success." It is a process of filtering out a small number of qualified potential buyers from a relatively large pool of leads. Qualifying is done to identify the key individual players in the buying decision. This is aided by using the five qualifying questions: "What do you have now?", "What do you like about it?", "How would you improve it?", "How will the decision be made?", and finally, "Are you in a position to proceed?" (Learning Objective 6)

Managing an extensive prospecting activity requires a prospect control system. Computerized versions help salespeople sort names, store data, and recall information on prospecting activities (Learning Objective 7).

Finally, we discussed the 80-20 rule. It means that 80 percent of the business usually comes from 20 percent of the customers. While this is not a hard-and-fast rule, it is generally true that most of a firm's business comes from only a relatively small percentage of its customer base. Only through good qualifying can that 20 percent be quickly and efficiently identified and sold (Learning Objective 8).

Key Terms

Buying life cycle   The cycle of time the buyer is in the market and actively purchasing.

Lead   A lead is a person or business that might become a prospect.

Prospect   A qualified lead.

Endless chain referral   A process in which one customer provides names of more prospects.

Center of influence   Anyone who can exert a degree of influence on or predispose a prospective customer to buying.

Cold calling   Calling on a prospect with whom no previous contact has been made.

Direct response   A prospecting tool used to generate a reply from a potential client directly from an ad, mailed letter, magazine tip-in or bind-in card, or telephone solicitation.

House list   A list of customers the firm already has.

Telemarketing   Using the phone through either inbound or outbound calls to generate leads or make sales.

Bird dogs   Persons hired to get leads for the salesperson to follow up on.

Effective demand   Prospects who have the need, the ability to buy, and the authority to make the purchase.

Prospect control or lead management system   A system for recording modifying, and recalling prospect information.

Discussion Questions

1. Explain how a customer base is like a bank account or financial asset.
2. What is a buying life cycle, and how does it relate to the customer base?
3. Why do some buyers never get into the "steady buying stage" of the buying life cycle?
4. What can cause a customer's buying life cycle to sink into decline?
5. How long does a buying life cycle last?
6. Identify the various aspects of a customer's ability to buy.

7. How many types of authority to buy should a salesperson be prepared to encounter? Explain each.

8. What is meant by a prospect having "effective demand"?

9. When it was said that selling success is a matter of percentages, what did that mean?

10. How could a current customer be considered a prospect?

11. How can inbound and outbound telemarketing be used to generate leads?

12. Why are leads qualified? What is the relationship between the number of qualifying criteria that must be met and the number of qualified prospects produced?

13. What are the steps in qualifying a lead?

14. Explain the purpose of the fantasy question.

15. What is the triple play in qualifying?

16. List the five qualifying questions.

Application Exercise

Go back and reread the boxes about the Huck Company, then answer the following questions:

1. If the average customer bought $12,000 worth of product per year from Huck, and Huck only responds to 15 percent of the 2,600 inquiries it gets per year, how much potential business is it passing up?

2. Look over the correspondence the salesperson receives from Dauw's office about the respondents to the ad campaigns Huck runs. How would you change it to make it better?

3. Could Huck have computerized this system to make it even better? How?

Class Exercises

Group Exercise

Every salesperson needs a constant source of leads. As an individual class member, you will be asked to write down *the name of one idea* for a new product or service that you feel is salable.

Your class will separate into groups as assigned by your instructor and pick at random from your members' choices one of these products or services.

1. Brainstorm all possible sources of leads for selling your group's product or service.

2. Select the top three sources and present them to the class, along with the rationale for your choices.

3. Ask the class for consensus on the one best lead source for your particular product or service idea.

4. Have a group spokesperson summarize the link between lead generation and the type of product or service you want to sell.

Individual Presentation

You are the membership chairperson for the student chapter of the local Sales Executives Club. Your job is to increase membership in the organization from 50 to 75 members by the end of the current year.

Prepare a plan for possible presentation to the class to increase this membership base.

1. Regarding your *sources of leads* for your chapter:
   a. Where and how would you start?
   b. How would you compile (gather and organize) a list of leads?
   c. What would be your criteria for qualifying these leads as chapter prospects?
2. Summarize your reactions to this process.

Denzel Mitchell Calls a Prospect

Denzel Mitchell started his day as usual. He came into the office, opened the mail, and, finding nothing particularly earth-shattering, looked at his daily planner. Most of the day was going to be taken up with calling on prospects. The process of qualifying leads and scheduling appointments with those who qualified would take most of the morning.

Denzel, who had some success in his new-found career as a financial planning salesperson, was hoping to expand his business. He had been in the job now for about four months and was considered by his manager as progressing at an average rate. He showed some signs of progress but was not the top performer. Lately, his success with getting prospects to close had fallen off, even though he had been using the same sales presentation that had worked in the past and the one he had been taught. Sara Hovan, the new salesperson across the desk from Denzel, had been having better luck.

Sara seemed to make fewer presentations and spend less time on them, but her sales were increasing. Denzel assumed Sara was obviously calling on the high rollers and getting bigger orders. Denzel and Sara talked about it, and Denzel found Sara was calling on the same type of person that he called on. Sara told Denzel, "I don't make a presentation to people who are low-probability buyers. I make fewer presentations than you do, but I guess I just have better luck." Denzel wondered if he was spending too much time on low-probability buyers.

Denzel is planning on coming to you for advice on how to turn his situation around. If that turnaround doesn't happen soon, he will probably quit.

Question

1. What advice would you give Denzel?

Prospects, Prospects Everywhere

Valley Manufacturing of Valley, Nebraska, is one of the largest manufacturers of center pivot irrigation systems in the world. A center pivot irrigation system is a water sprinkling system that works off a well head in the middle of a field; the sprinkling system literally moves in a circle around it on large wheels. One center pivot system can irrigate about 200 acres. They cost between $80,000 and $100,000 each, depending on options.

A center pivot system is superior to letting water run down ditches dug between the crop rows because the amount of water applied can be precisely controlled. While the volume of water showering from the many nozzles is constant, the speed at which the unit travels its circle can be varied. The more water that is needed, the slower the unit travels. It also has the ability to move over rolling terrain. This means a center pivot irrigation system waters up the hills and down, something ditch irrigation can't do. When it was first introduced, it represented a major technological advancement. Farms that could not be irrigated before could now show dramatically increased yields owing to the ability to get water on previously inaccessible areas.

Before Valley sends salespeople into a state, it wants to have a list of possible buyers. Every farmer or rancher in a state is not a possible customer; only those who meet the qualifying criteria will suffice.

Questions

1. If you were going into Montana as a Valley field sales representative, how would you get the names of prospective buyers?

2. What criteria would you establish to produce qualified leads (those with a high probability of buying)?

References

1. Lee Van Vechten, "Lead Qualification, an Essential Telemarketing Task," *Personal Selling Power,* 8 (1988): 16.
2. Ibid.
3. Ronald B. Marks, *Personal Selling, An Interactive Approach* (Needham Heights, Mass.: Allyn and Bacon, 1988), p. 193.
4. William W. Holes, "Effective Networking," *Personal Selling Power,* 9 (1989): 12.
5. This situation is vague by design. However, there are still three alternatives. The first is to review lists of current customers. While they would not be in Idaho, the type of business those customers are in would help identify prospects there. For example, if current customers were retail florists, then retail florists likely would be customers in Idaho. A list of retail florists in Idaho could be rented or bought. Another alternative is state directories available from state economic development agencies. Of course, a third alternative is the phone book. Simply looking in the Yellow Pages would help enormously. The point of this question is to make you think about and identify possible alternatives even when there is the scantiest of information to start with.
6. Marvin A. Jolson, "Prospecting by Telephone Prenotification: An Application of the Foot-in-the-Door Technique," *Journal of Personal Selling and Sales Management,* 6 (1986): 39–42.
7. Ibid., p. 41.

8. Reported in *Sales and Marketing Management*, 8 (1983): 72, citing the Trade Show Bureau, *Research Report No. 18,* April 1983.

9. This section borrows heavily from Tom Hopkins, *How to Master the Art of Selling* (New York: Warner Books, 1982), chap. 12.

10. Ibid., pp. 181–82.

11. Ibid., p. 183.

12. John B. Kennedy, "Want Higher Sales Productivity? Start with a Data Base," *Sales and Marketing Management,* 131 (1984): 66–68.

7 Fact-Finding: Step 1 of Precall Planning

Objectives

After completing this chapter, you will be able to:

1. Identify the four steps in precall planning.

2. List and explain the six objectives of fact-finding.

3. Build a WOTS summary for determining a prospect's current situation.

4. Apply at least four tools salespeople use to uncover the facts they need.

5. Determine a plan for when to gather facts.

6. Create an account profile for a hypothetical customer.

The Professional Selling Question

How important is fact-finding to a successful sales presentation? How does a salesperson go about finding the facts needed to put together a winning sales plan?

A Salesperson Responds

The answers to these questions come from Edward D. Walsh, a veteran of 30 years in sales and marketing. He is executive vice-president of Tech 3 in Boca Raton, Florida. Walsh says that the more information a person can collect while doing preplanning, the better the end results will be. Some of the most important information to gather during precall planning is competitive information.

Walsh recommends competitive information be sought out from all possible sources and accumulated and cataloged on a regular basis. He says such an effort will point out the competitions' strengths and weaknesses and, over time, show the quality and quantity of their communications. Keeping such a file will, in his words, "point up the opportunity gaps, positioning gaffes, and misconceptions your company may be able to exploit."

The information salespeople need is, to some degree, readily available— if they take the time to find it. Most of the information is free in public libraries, newspapers, and professional or trade associations. Walsh says, "Some publications also cover media sales, providing useful industry data. And don't be shy about pursuing information in publications; the best publishers invest a lot in their own research and are proud to share knowledge about the market they serve with other organizations."

Trade associations that use "blind reporting" are particularly good sources. In blind reporting, a trade association contracts with an outside source, usually an accounting firm, to gather data on the association's members from its members. This information is then reported to the association by the outside firm for all the members to see. In this way, very specific data can be collected with a guarantee of anonymity to the suppliers. This data is then made available to any interested party. It is valuable information a salesperson can use when trying to understand about a specific customer or industry.[1]

Introduction

Imagine you are a busy executive with a fully planned day. At 10:00 A.M., your appointment calls to confirm she will be there at 10:15 as scheduled. You are impressed by this thoroughness and courtesy. At 10:15, your secretary brings her into your office. She introduces herself and launches into her presentation explaining how you will benefit from her line of copiers. They will copy faster, more accurately, and cheaper than the XYZ model you are now using.

At this point, you stop her and explain that while you do operate an office supply store, the copier she is selling against (the one you are now using) is one that you are licensed as a dealer to sell! What would you think of this salesperson? Had she done her homework more thoroughly, she would have discovered you are her direct competitor. It is painfully clear she did qualify you as a user of copying equipment but did not do enough fact-finding before making the call. What should she have done before scheduling the call?

In the last chapter, you learned how prospects were identified and qualified from numerous leads. The qualifying process gave you some information about them but still not enough to be prepared for a presentation. In this chapter, we will focus on the first half of the precall planning process called fact-finding. The accuracy of salespeople's presentations depend on the accuracy of their facts about the customer. Everything is finally in place to make a presentation only after the facts are gathered, analyzed, and the presentation strategy is planned.

Objectives of Fact-Finding

▶ ▶ ▶ ▶ ▶ ▶ ▶ ▶ ▶ ▶

Learning Objective 1: The four steps in precall planning

Precall planning is a four-step process. The first step is *fact-finding*. Fact-finding should produce enough information about the customers so the salesperson feels well acquainted with them. Next is creating an *account profile*. This is a detailed outline containing all the pertinent information about each customer. The account profile is useful in planning sales calls and as a reference file for future calls or other salespeople who may call on the account.

The third step in precall planning is creating a *call planner*. This is a brief plan for the call itself; an outline of what the salesperson will do during the call. The last step in precall planning is mapping out an *approach strategy*. This encompasses all the tasks from making the appointment to that first minute of the actual presentation. Steps three and four will be covered in the next chapter.

Fact-finding is different from qualifying. Qualifying determines if leads meet the necessary conditions to qualify them as potential buyers. **Fact-finding** is gathering facts to use when formulating a strategy for, and actually making, the sales presentation. These facts help adaptive salespeople build a presentation with a high probability of being successful. Using these facts, they become totally familiar with the prospect prior to the presentation. As the saying goes, "Forewarned is forearmed"; the more salespeople know going into the presentation, the better equipped they are to handle it. Fact-finding has at least six objectives, as shown in Figure 7-1.

Figure 7-1 **Six Objectives of Fact-Finding**

1. Determine the prospect's current situation.
2. Build a historical perspective.
3. Anticipate the prospect's problems.
4. Anticipate problems in making the presentation.
5. Anticipate which products (solutions) will fit the prospect's problems.
6. Determine who the players are.

Objective 1: Determine the Prospect's Current Situation

It is vital to know as much as possible about the prospect's current situation. With an industrial customer or for a reseller (a wholesaler or retailer), this would involve knowing the answer to such questions as: Whom do they now serve and whom they compete with? Where do they currently do business? Through what channels? Using what promotional media? Who are the strongest and weakest competitors and how many are there? How much of a market force are they? Is their position (image or market share) in the market increasing or decreasing? By knowing what prospects are up against, salespeople can sell them products to improve their competitive advantage.

◀ ◀ ◀ ◀ ◀ ◀ ◀ ◀

Learning Objective 2: Six objectives of fact-finding

Salespeople should try to determine who the prospect's current vendors are. Knowing who the competition is permits salespeople to more effectively plan the call because they know the features, advantages, and benefits of the competitive vendor's products. The salespeople can then concentrate on their own product's features, advantages, and benefits. For example, if a prospect was doing business with the Ajax Corporation, which was noted for low prices but slow service, the salesperson could guess what the prospect's main interest is! If a prospect was dealing with the highest-priced vendor, but the vendor with the highest quality, the salesperson would know to stress value and quality. Knowing who is currently selling to the prospect gives the salesperson an insight into the prospect's buying mentality.

A good salesperson always tries to discover the prospect's current vendors for long-range planning purposes. Competitors in the same industry and market all know each other through trade association interactions, professional meetings, the grapevine, and by watching each other. In retailing, for example, all the current competition cookie salespeople face is displayed on the grocery store's shelf! One trip to the store tells them who they are up against. Knowing who is in the game permits salespeople to take advantage of opportunities. If it is well known that XYZ Corporation is in financial trouble and may not be able to make its promised deliveries, all the competitive salespeople will be calling on XYZ's customers to let them know how

Sometimes it's easy to determine who your competitors are.

they pride themselves on delivery. Good, adaptive salespeople keep on top of what is happening in their own industry as well as their customers' industries. This knowledge pays off in the long run and lets them establish a planning horizon to coincide with opportunities that arise, such as a competitor's future delivery problems.

▶ ▶ ▶ ▶ ▶ ▶ ▶ ▶ ▶ ▶
Learning Objective 3:
Building a WOTS summary is an essential product of fact-finding

By determining the prospect's current situation, the salesperson can construct a WOTS summary. WOTS is an acronym for *Weaknesses, Opportunities, Threats,* and *Strengths.* A WOTS summary could be done on prospective customers, their competitors, the salesperson's own firm, or its competitors. Such summaries are done to compare the weaknesses, opportunities, threats, and strengths of customers compared to their competitor. A prospect could be strong in distribution while its major competitor is weak in that area. WOTS comparisons between the selling firm and the prospective customer's firm are also helpful. This would point out how the salesperson's products would help prospective customers in an area where they are weak. For example, the selling firm's strength in facility design would compliment a customer that is weak in that area. Figure 7-2 illustrates some of the areas a WOTS summary covers.

Salespeople plan presentations to bolster the prospective customers' weaknesses, help them capitalize on their opportunities, reduce the threats they face, and enhance their competitive strengths. This is the way salespeople become trusted partners in the prospect's business operations, partners competitors find hard to dislodge. In the example that follows, a sales rep forgot to investigate the prospect's current situation. The salesperson needs to understand the current situation, as well as the history of the prospective customer.

When Things Go Wrong

Lack of Fact-Finding Turns a KOOL Idea into a Frigid Reply

It seemed like a cool idea at the time. Julie Silver, a new sales rep for Denver's KOOL-FM radio station, hit upon the notion of selling Polaroid Corporation on a promotion linking the station's summer rock concert with Polaroid's Cool Cam instant camera. So, during her first week on the job, Ms. Silver calls on Donald Sortino, Polaroid's district manager in Denver.

"I knew he was interested in radio promotions," Ms. Silver explains. "So I presented our KOOL concert promotion to him. He seemed to be excited about it and said he was interested in sending it along to Polaroid management for approval."

Then Ms. Silver handed Mr. Sortino her business card, which is embossed with the logo of Shamrock Holdings Inc., the Burbank California holding company of the Roy E. Disney family and the parent of KOOL-FM.

Recalls Ms. Silver: "He says, 'You're with Shamrock?! Well, we can't do business with you.... Your company is trying to take over our company.'"

Ms. Silver said she wasn't aware of Shamrock's protracted hostile takeover battle for Polaroid. She knows all about it now.

Source: "Too Bad She Showed Her Business Card," *Wall Street Journal,* 24 March 1989, p. B1.

Figure 7-2 **WOTS Summary for Fact-Finding**

Investigate Weaknesses Opportunities Threats Strengths relative to:		
Product	Price	Promotion
Distribution	Finance	Management
Customers	Morale	Stockholders
Vendors	Lawsuits	Politics
Foreign competitors		

Objective 2: Build a Historical Perspective

Fact-finding should produce a brief history of prospects and their firms. This may be simply how long they have been in business, or it may be a detailed account of their history and growth. Publicly held corporations document this in their annual reports, which are available on request. Understanding prospective customers' histories sheds light on why they operate the way they do. Understanding their business explains their philosophy, mission, goals, and corporate culture.

Understanding history and culture is essential for salespeople selling in foreign countries. Knowing the historical influences that have shaped the current business environment helps salespeople create a presentation that both respects and uses that history. Territorial, political, cultural, and religious events shape a nation and the way firms in that nation do business. Failure to understand the impact of historical events can mean not only the loss of an immediate sale but also the impossibility of future sales.

Objective 3: Anticipate the Prospect's Problems

By now, the salespeople should know prospects' current situation and what has occurred in the past to propel them to that situation. This knowledge has a three-fold purpose. It allows salespeople to anticipate prospects' problems, the problems they will face in the presentation, and which products to offer.

Salespeople must anticipate prospects' problems to be prepared when those problems surface during the sales presentation. Some problems are rather universal: low markups, slow turns on the inventory, rising expenses, and lack of storage or shelf space. Some problems, however, are specific to the prospect. Some customers need special financing arrangements, and some need custom-designed products or services. Anticipating prospects' problems prior to the sales presentation gives salespeople an extra edge of preparedness.

Objective 4: Anticipate Problems in Making the Presentation

The code of behavior for the adaptive salesperson should read "Be prepared." A good salesperson will anticipate all the problems that might occur in making the presentation and be ready for them. Problems in making the presentation can be grouped into three rubrics. First are the objections prospects might raise. Second are the physical or mechanical problems. Third are people and personality problems.

Objections   It is fairly easy to anticipate prospects' objections. In a later chapter, you will learn about objections and how to handle them. For now, it is enough to know the most common objections are the product, price, no-need, stalling, or hidden objections. Knowing the most common objections raised, salespeople are ready to deal with them when they occur during the presentation. This can be a tremendous confidence builder. If you, as a new salesperson, made a presentation anticipating all the objections and discovered you were not only right about which would come up but were successful in overcoming them as you had planned, you would feel self-confident and self-assured.

Physical and mechanical problems   In anticipating physical and mechanical problems, a good rule is "Make no assumptions!" If a product demonstration needs electricity, the salesperson must not assume that prospects have an outlet close to their desk—or an extension cord. When making a group presentation, salespeople must not assume that prospects will furnish an overhead projector for visuals. Salespeople should bring along their own and always have paper copies to hand out in case overhead projection cannot be used.

Salespeople should be sure their demonstration does what it is supposed to do. If they are going to demonstrate the durability of unbreakable dishes by hitting one with a hammer, they had better do a test before the presentation to make sure they don't break. A good salesperson never takes anything for granted when it comes to a demonstration during a presentation. The quickest way to lose credibility (and the sale) is to build a presentation around a product's feature, then have the demonstration go haywire. It shows the prospect that neither the salesperson nor the product is performance-tested.

People and personality problems   The third type of problem to anticipate is that caused by other people who create distractions. Salespeople must expect an interruption during the sales presentation. It may come from a phone call, a secretary or someone else coming in. It may come from the prospect. The important thing to remember is that any interruption causes the prospects to lose their train of thought and the salesperson to break the selling rhythm. These must be regained if the presentation is to be successful. In the case of intrusions or phone calls, adaptive salespeople follow a plan like this:

1. Determine if the prospect wants you to leave the room. Simply asking "Should I leave?" is sufficient.

2. Don't waste time while the prospect is on the phone. Mentally reflect on what you have said, what the prospect has (or hasn't) said, where you are in your presentation, and, where you plan to go.

3. When the interruption is over, restate what you were talking about and what you both have agreed on to that point to get the prospect back on track. Use a statement such as "Let me continue talking about our _____ " or "You were asking me about the _____ ."

4. Another tactic to regain prospects' interest is to handing them something. Put a sample in their hands, give them your literature; get them involved!

5. Watch for the verbal and nonverbal cues, regardless of whether you ask a question, make a statement, or put something in their hands. Only proceed farther into the presentation if you are sure interest has been regained.

Personality problems are important to anticipate. Good, adaptive salespeople are aware of their social style and adjust to the buyer's social style and personality. Incompatible personal or social styles can cause problems, and unless the salespeople adjust their style, personality problems will hinder the sales presentation. Tolerance, understanding, and empathy are always necessary for adaptive salespeople.

Anticipating problems is one of the most strategic success factors salespeople can learn. Having anticipated the problems and planned the appropriate reactions, salespeople always remain calm, professional, and in control. This projects the feeling of self-confidence all buyers want to see. After all, who wants to do business with someone who can't remain cool, calm, and in control? By predicting the customer's problems, a salesperson is better prepared to offer realistic and timely solutions. Being prepared by anticipating problems, salespeople use presentation time more efficiently. When a problem crops up, an answer or solution is at hand. Customers often have technical questions. Anticipating a technical problem question, the well-prepared salesperson has the technical manual, specification sheet, or performance report at the ready.

Objective 5: Anticipate Which Products Will Fit the Prospect's Problems

The products and services customers purchase represent solutions to problems. Fact-finding helps determine which product or services would be most likely to solve prospects' problems. Most salespeople sell a variety of products in a line, but most buyers only want a selected few. Part of being a good salesperson is being able to discern the products that will satisfy the customer and focus the presentation on those.

Determining which product or service to offer helps the salesperson reduce the buyer's cognitive dissonance. Keep in mind that buyers who have difficulty in making decisions or who face high-risk or extensive problem-solving situations appreciate the salesperson's product-related suggestions. During the presentation, it will become clear which product or service best fits the prospect's specific needs. But by narrowing the field during fact-finding, the salesperson is better prepared for the presentation.

Anticipating a prospect's product or service needs facilitates cross-selling. By asking a few questions, the salesperson can direct the presentation to take advantage of preplanned cross-selling opportunities. Examine the following dialog:

(A salesperson in a retail men's clothing store approaches a prospect who has just entered the store.)

Salesperson: Good afternoon, are you looking for something for yourself or for a gift? *(Fact-finding question. If a gift, probable sale of under $50. Possible product alternatives: shirt, tie, belt, accessories, sweater. Cross-selling opportunities: few. If for the customer, probable sale hard to determine at this point.)*

Prospect: Good afternoon. I'm looking for something for myself.

Salesperson: Will this be for dress, work, or casual? *(Fact-finding question. Depending on the answer, the salesperson will direct the prospect to the appropriate department of the store.)*

Prospect: I need a suit for work.

Salesperson: Do you work in an office, or are you out of the office a lot? *(Important question. If answer is office, a lighter-weight fabric could work. if out of the office, a more durable, heavier fabric might be better for heavier wear.)*

Prospect: I work in an office, just sitting at the desk most of the day. *(The salesperson is now mentally narrowing down the suits she will present to the prospect. Cross-selling opportunities are shirts, ties, shoes, and accessories.)*

Salesperson: Let me show you something in a worsted wool. Something with pleated trousers to give you added comfort at your desk. I'll also show you some of our lighter-weight suits, some that have been very popular with many of our clients.

While the prospective customer is trying on several suits, the salesperson is selecting coordinating shirts and ties. The prospect doesn't have to worry about selecting shirts and ties from the hundreds of combinations possible because the salesperson has narrowed the product alternatives down for him. The sale is finally made: a suit, two shirts, and four ties. The entire time for this conversation above may have been no longer than five to ten minutes. The salesperson followed a logical process of narrowing down alternatives to the most feasible choices as facts were gathered. Cross-selling was enhanced, and the customer bought more than he originally planned because of the salesperson's suggestions. The customer was freed from having to make decisions about shirts and ties from the all possible combinations. The result was a satisfied customer who appreciated being served in an efficient and professional manner. Anticipating product or service alternatives before the presentation is the hallmark of a professional, customer-oriented salesperson.

Objective 6: Determine Who the Players Are

Proper fact-finding indicates who the players are in the buying decision. This is important for designing an effective presentation strategy. In most retail sales presentations, the salesperson deals with only one person. In business-to-business sales, the salesperson commonly encounters several buying influences in the buying center. Imagine the shock of planning on a presentation to only one person, then walking into the meeting and facing a group of six!

Determining who the players are helps salespeople in several ways. First, by simply knowing the number of persons involved, they come prepared with enough handout material or samples. Second, it provides insights into the importance the buyer's firm is placing on the purchase. When system selling, such as computer systems or communications systems, salespeople commonly make a major presentation to half a dozen individuals because the nature of the purchase is so large. Knowing the ranking of the players in the customer's organization indicates the importance of the decision to that firm. If the presentation involves everyone from the vice-president of procurement to the junior purchasing agent, it is a good bet the firm looks on this buy as a major, long-term investment. The presentation had better be top-notch!

Fact-finding produces information regarding who the facilitators are. Facilitators, while not directly involved in the decision, can make the job of getting to see the right people simple or impossible. A good salesperson never overlooks nor underestimates the power and help to be found in people like secretaries, receptionists, assistants, aides, advisors, and consultants.

Keep in mind that fact-finding may take months of research or only a few minutes, depending on the nature of the sale and the customer. Regardless of that, fact-finding is a vital part of every successful salesperson's plan of attack. Preparedness is essential, and it comes through persistent effort and work.

▶ ▶ *follow-up questions*

1. What is the purpose of fact-finding?

2. Why would salespeople do a WOTS analysis of their own company, their prospect's company, and a competitive firm?

3. How does fact-finding apply to retail salespeople? Is it really necessary in retailing?

4. What sort of problems should fact-finding prepare the salesperson for during the presentation?

Tools for Fact-Finding

Where does a salesperson find the facts about prospective clients, how they do business, and their general situation? Successful salespeople do not rely on just one source. Sources depend on the nature of the clients. In this part of the chapter, a variety of sources will be explained. We will start with reports professional salespeople could use.

Annual Reports

Annual reports are published by publicly held corporations. They provide extensive information about what the corporations did and did not do over the course of the year. This information consists of a status report from the corporate officers, facts about the firm's product or service lines, and financial information. Annual reports contain statements about the firm's goals and its success at achieving them.

Learning Objective 4: Tools salespeople use to uncover facts

The status report from the officers is particularly useful because it summarizes the firm's current situation. The officers explain about the sales, compare sales levels to previous years', and explain the reasons for growth or decline. If the corporation is multinational, sales by country are often presented. Profits and sales are compared to past levels. Present sales figures are often reported on by product line, division, or country. Annual reports commonly explain about sales in specific product or service lines. The Coleco Corporation reported the success of its Cabbage Patch dolls in 1986 and 1987, while sales were skyrocketing (along with its stock price). In 1988, it reported dismal sales of the doll and the introduction of a new line of dolls. The lack of success in both was reported in its next annual report, and its stock price fell dramatically. Indications of product or service introductions or deletions are significant facts to consider in fact-finding. When Nord Resources announced its expansion into gold mining, mining equipment suppliers around the world had the green light to call.

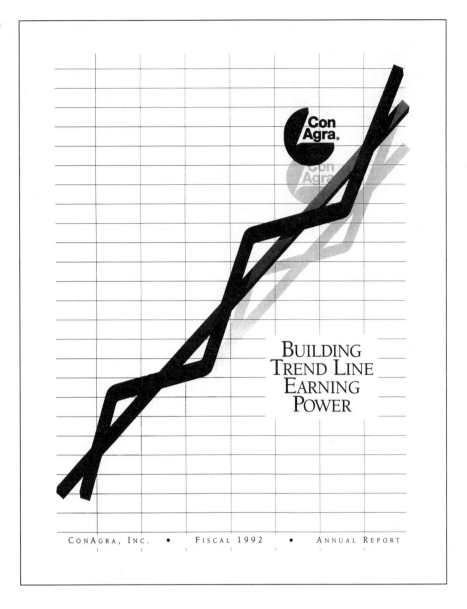

CONAGRA, INC. • FISCAL 1992 • ANNUAL REPORT

BUILDING TREND LINE EARNING POWER

Salespeople use annual report information to develop a historical perspective about the firm's performance. Knowing the fluctuations in sales and profits tells them about the potential for business in the firm. If the officers' report indicates losses are occurring, they may want to avoid the firm. On the other hand, if growth is occurring, opportunities for selling to the firm are brighter.

The officers' report indicates where the firm's expansion plans are focused, which could be from a product, service, or geographic perspective. If the officers were reporting expansion of production facilities into North Carolina, salespeople in North Carolina wanting to do business with the firm would be more excited about the future business potential than salespeople in California.

The financial section of annual reports provides salespeople with data necessary to the success of a call. Not only do they learn about the firm's financial health, but they get information on inventory levels and stock-turn rates. Increasing inventory levels, for example, may signal a slowdown in orders, declining sales, a tighter financial condition, and generally a tougher selling environment.

Commercial Directories[2]

Commercial directories are available in public and university libraries. Larger libraries have business departments staffed by business reference librarians who can be tremendously helpful in finding the right directories. Some of the more common directories are described in Table 7-1.

Trade and professional associations make directories available to members and sell them to the public. They are sources of information about member firms and often list the names of key persons in those firms. The membership directory of the American Marketing Association lists the thousands of professional, academic, and business members. If you were selling computer software for writing marketing plans, this would be a good list to use for prospecting, qualifying, and fact-finding.

Salespeople use directories in tandem when fact-finding. A specific firm name and address may be found in the Dun & Bradstreet directory with similar firms in the *Thomas Register*. For example, let's say you have a service applicable to ball-bearing manufacturers. In the *Thomas Register*, you find several bearing manufacturers listed for the sales territory you work. In the *Standard & Poor's Directory*, you would find the names of their corporate officers and some personal data about each of them. With this data in hand, you would know something about their organizational chart and who is responsible for purchasing. You could consult the *Robert Morris Annual Statement Report* to learn about the financial condition of typically similar firms.

Table 7-1   **Directories Salespeople Commonly Use**

Dun & Bradstreet Million Dollar Directory. This lists companies having a net worth of over $1 million and gives some background on each firm, along with the names of the top directors and officers.

Thomas Register of American Manufacturers. This enormous work, with more than dozen volumes, lists both small and large firms under product/service headings. It provides addresses and descriptions of the firms and their products.

Standard and Poor's Directory. This directory lists thousands of small, medium, and large corporations and the names of key people. A companion volume lists the names of officers, directors, and principals, along with personal information, such as home addresses and phone numbers and often even the college they attended.

Robert Morris Annual Statement Report. This report gives the financial situation of "standard" firms arranged by SIC codes.[3] It gives the norm for a typical firm and financial information for typical smaller and larger firms in that SIC code. It is extremely useful for comparing the financial health of a business relative to others in its industry.

With this information, you would have the beginnings of a profile for this firm and its industry.

Organizational Charts

Organizational charts give salespeople a diagram of a firm's structure, a schematic of who reports to whom. This can be vital in determining who the buying influencers are and at what levels a buying decision may occur.

Charts showing complex and highly structured organizations can foretell a long selling cycle as permission to purchase may require authorizations through the chain of command. It may also indicate opportunities. More than one division might be interested in the salesperson's products. For example, a computer salesperson might have an opportunity to sell mainframes to the corporate management information system division and smaller units, such as PCs, to the marketing, advertising, logistics, or accounting departments.

Knowing the organizational structure can facilitate servicing the account when problems arise. In retail grocery chains, the procurement division is often separate from the retail operations group. Knowing products are bought by procurement and sold through the retail division can explain the time delays in both making sales and learning about customer complaints. Salespeople need to understand how their product will be handled through the customer's firm. Customer satisfaction is the result of satisfying everyone involved with the product or service after the sale, not just the buyer at the time of the sale; that's why knowing the organizational chart is important to planning the call. The organizational chart helps determine who the players are, or will be.

Asking Questions

Without a doubt, the best fact-finding method is simply asking questions. Asking the receptionist whom to call on will identify the specific contact person. That receptionist can explain the policies followed when salespeople call, what to expect, and the procedures for scheduling an appointment.

The salesperson may get a chance to talk directly to the buyer before making a formal call. This can prove to be extremely helpful. Questions about time limits on calls, how and where presentations are made, how the buying process works, and what to bring along can all be answered by a preliminary discussion with the buyer. Why would a buyer provide this information to a salesperson or even take the time to talk before the presentation itself? The answer is simple: efficiency and effectiveness. A salesperson saves the prospective buyer time by coming to the presentation adequately prepared. A buyer would rather spend 10 minutes doing preappointment coaching than waste 30 minutes of presentation time on someone who did not know what to bring, what to leave behind, and what was acceptable.

A successful salesperson asks questions of other salespeople who have called or are calling on the same account. Several salespeople from the same firm often call on the same customer when the selling firm is organized by product and service lines. By tapping the experience of others, important information can be learned quickly and easily. Novice salespeople taking over the accounts of retiring or promoted veterans find their tips and insights to be the difference between success and failure.

What Would You Do If...?

Suppose you were a salesperson for West Publishing Company. You are new to the territory, and it has some rather large schools in it. Today, you are planning on making a call at the university's college of business to see several of the faculty there. If you could get the marketing faculty members, Professors Armani and Coleman, to adopt your *Professional Selling Process* textbook, it would mean an adoption of around 2,500 books per year. This is a major adoption, one that would make you one of the top West reps in the area.

Armani and Coleman are somewhat hard to reach. They are quite busy with classes, grading tests, and team-teaching an honors course. You are determined to get in to see them. Before you go over to the university, you need to get all the information you can about them, their courses, and what they have done with West in the past.

▶ Question: Who would you talk to before the call and what would you want to know?

▶ What would you do to get this information?[4]

Successful salespeople make a list of everyone who could have useful information, then talk to as many of them as possible before scheduling the appointment. Who to ask depends on the source of the original lead. If the lead came through a referral, they ask the referring person for all the information they can get. That person can often tell them almost everything they want to know. If the lead was generated through a "bird dog," successful salespeople make it a practice to contact that person to gather as much information as possible.

Listening

Successful salespeople listen to conversations of other people, secretaries, other salespeople—everyone. They listen to the radio and TV. A news story could provide valuable information. News about local firms are always good conversation starters. Businesses often announce major policy changes, plant expansions, closings or new products or services through the media. Personnel changes are also announced this way if they involve top-ranking people. In small towns, listening to the conversation in the local cafe over a cup of coffee or lunch can mean the difference between knowing enough about the customer to make or lose the sale. Listening at every opportunity is a successful salesperson's fact-finding axiom.

Case in Point

If You Don't Pay Attention, You Will Never Learn

Almost everything you need to know about selling to a customer will come from that customer! Passive listening will teach little, while active listening will provide the knowledge you must know about your

Continued

customer's needs and wants, the industry information essential for you to know, and the competitors you are facing.

Customers' answers to the questions you ask determine the direction your sales presentation must take. You compliment your customers when you pay attention to what they are saying. They will tell you their interests, goals, desires, needs, risks, fears, future, benefit sought, competition, problems, plans for growth, budget restrictions, and their expectations of your product, your company, and you.

Comment: A customer once said, "If you would stop talking, I would like to give you my order!"

Case in Point

Listening Is a Good Place to Start a Sale

Salespeople spend much of their time giving the presentation and sometimes neglect the importance of *listening* to the customer. You learn much about your customers' needs, desires, and wants if you give them a chance to tell you what they want.

There are ten guides to good listening:

1. *Listen* for the customers' area of interest, (if you stop talking, they will tell you!) When you listen to customers, you are showing them great courtesy. We like people who listen to us!

2. Judge prospects not on the basis of their delivery, but rather on the content of what they say.

3. Don't interrupt your customers—even if you are anxious to get on with your sales story.

4. Be flexible: allow customers to tell you what they think or want from you.

5. Listening is hard work. Don't merely listen with your ears but with your eyes and your sincere attention. If you don't pay attention, you'll never learn.

6. Keep your opinions to yourself. Don't cut in on customers' speaking by saying, "Yes, but we have _____ and _____ and _____."

7. Keep an open mind. Customers may tell you how you can present an efficient presentation. Usually, they will give you a profile of their basic interests that you could never find anywhere else.

8. When you present a product or service benefit, listen to the customers' response, and if the benefit is of interest to them, quickly agree and present proof.

9. Don't wait for customer objections. *Ask* for them. When faced with an objection, respond with "If I were you, I would feel as you do. How can this problem be corrected?"

10. Listen for the sound of *agreement,* one of the most interesting sounds to the professional salesperson.

Making Joint or Team Calls

Another approach to fact-finding is making team calls. While not the norm, this method is used for first-time cold calls, when the sales manager feels the call may require more than one level or type of expertise, or when novice salespeople are in training. Joint calling improves fact-finding because it simply spreads the work to two sets of ears and brains, rather than one. One salesperson often hears something the other misses. Such team calls allow salespeople the chance to trade off between asking questions and listening to the responses. While it can make fact-finding more productive, that productivity comes at a higher cost per call.

▶▶ *follow-up questions*

1. If you were planning a call on the Dynamo Ball Bearing Company in your town, what directory(ies) would you use to determine the name of the chairman of the board, the types of products it makes, and who its direct, local competitors are?

2. How would you obtain a copy of RJR-Nabisco's annual report? What would you as a salesperson use it for?

3. If you were selling textbooks to high schools, how would you gather the necessary facts, and from where, before calling on the textbook buying manager?

When to Do Fact-Finding

Fact-finding is continuous! Salespeople never stop gathering facts about customers, competitors, and prospects. Salespeople gather most of their

Learning Objective 5: When to do fact-finding

Fact finding can be done by sales teams.

facts during prospecting, qualifying, "get-acquainted" cold calls, and the presentation.

During Prospecting

During prospecting, only elementary information is available, but usually there is enough to determine if the lead should be pursued and qualified. During the prospecting process, the salesperson gathers the necessary background on the company's size, the nature of the business, and the names of key people. In a retail sale, the salesperson would ask the customer about the purpose for buying (gift, personal use, business use, etc.), if the product is familiar to the prospect, and if the prospect has ever had any experience with it.

During Qualifying

More facts are uncovered in the qualifying process. Salespeople try to gather as many facts as possible during prospecting and qualifying. Using these facts, they determine the prospect's qualifications to be a customer, but more importantly, they zero in on the prospect's wants, problems, and product or service needs. From this information, they evaluate the prospective customer's potential and decide to either pursue or drop the prospect. If the decision is to pursue, a data file of important facts has already begun to take shape.

During the "Get-Acquainted" Cold Call

Where the fact-finding is done on an existing account, an informal get-acquainted call can be the most expeditious way of updating the customer's account file. Many novice salespeople get their prospects and first accounts from existing customer lists. In this case, someone has probably been calling on these accounts. The accounts' records should be a wellspring of facts, containing data on previous sales, past calls, and problems. Armed with this information, salespeople can make get-acquainted calls to introduce themselves, update existing information on the account, refresh the file with new information, and explain any new policies or events the buyer needs to know about.

A get-acquainted call on new accounts is a good time for fact-finding. Salespeople can simply ask to stop by the prospect's place of business to introduce themselves. In that first casual meeting, a wealth of information flows from the conversation and observation of the surroundings. The surroundings tell the observant salesperson such things as the number of buyers, the size of office staff, the level of activity in the office, and the number of phone lines and computers in the office. All of this helps the salesperson learn about the prospect's business.

During the Presentation

The most significant fact-finding occurs during the presentation itself. This is when the salespeople and the prospects focus on solving the problem at hand, when prospects make decisions regarding their trust in the salespeople and how much information to divulge.

During the sales presentation, prospects may (but not always) explain in depth their situation, problems, and possible solutions. In a retail sale, almost all the relevant facts are uncovered during the presentation because qualifying, fact-finding, and the presentation are usually done simultaneously.

Fact-finding during the presentation is best accomplished by asking open-ended questions and listening intently. At this stage of the presentation, it is important to keep the prospect talking as much as possible. In a later chapter on making a presentation, we will discuss in detail how to uncover problems using successful questioning techniques.

Having gathered the necessary facts, the next step is to build a customer data base called an *account profile*. Such profiles help salespeople plan calls more effectively and serve as a reference in the developing salesperson-buyer relationship.

▶ ▶ *follow-up questions*

1. What are the objectives of fact-finding?
2. What types of problems should salespeople anticipate when fact-finding?

Creating an Account Profile of Business Customers

Building an **account profile** means organizing the data gathered during fact-finding for quick and easy reference. Figure 7-3 is an outline of a business account's profile. It has four parts. The first is a business outline, and the second is a description of the prospect's environment. This is followed by an estimate of the prospect's budget and, finally, specific buying criteria. This is a generic example of an account profile. Some firms require their salespeople to gather more personal than business-related information. Others want their salespeople to do just the opposite. It all depends on the type of information deemed the most useful for the selling situation.

Figure 7-3 represents a good starting point for any salesperson to build on.

◀ ◀ ◀ ◀ ◀ ◀ ◀ ◀

Learning Objective 6: Sample structure of an account profile form

Figure 7-3 **Outline of a Business Account's Profile**

Section 1: Business Outline

a. Description of prospect's business
b. Demographics
c. Business operations
d. Financial health

Section 2: Prospect's External Environment

a. Description of problems and needs
b. Markets served
c. Competitors
d. Vendors and their products
e. Business constraints

Section 3: Prospect's Budget

Section 4: Buying Criteria

a. Timing
b. Specifications to be met

Section 1: Business Outline

Salespeople need to understand the prospect's business to understand where it has been and where it is going. The business outline has a description of the prospect's business, demographic information, data on how it operates, and its financial health.

Description of prospect's business This should contain:

1. What it makes, sells, provides, or uses.
2. Its industry, for example, retail clothes, steam pipe distribution, direct marketing, or car dealership.
3. From 2 above, its SIC (Standard Industrial Classification) code.
4. A brief history of the firm.
5. The firm's key personnel and the people the salesperson will encounter.

The description of the prospect's business can range from a paragraph to a lengthy dissertation. A simple yet sufficient description of a firm selling refrigerated display cases to retail grocers might look like this:

> ABC Corporation is a *retail grocery* firm dealing in limited and *exclusive lines of gourmet foods*. Its SIC code is *2101,* and it operates similar to other firms in that code. It has distinguished itself with extremely *high levels of customer service* and, through *four of five stores,* has one of the *premier business catering operations* in the markets served. It has been in operation for *25 years,* since *Simon Jackson founded* it. It is owned and *operated by his son Daniel,* who has increased the number of stores from two to five. *Daniel is the key individual* in all buying decisions, but all *adoptions must go through a buying committee.*

This simple paragraph gives the salesperson a feel for the client's operation and enough knowledge to make intelligent conversation during the sales call. Note the key pieces of data in italics. While this description is not lengthy, it does the job. There are eleven key pieces of data in one paragraph!

Demographics **Demographics** refers to vital statistics. These would include, but not be limited to, such data as:

1. Size of the business, numbers of employees, value of sales, or value of shipments.
2. Number of branches, factories, or subsidiary companies it owns.
3. Plant, store, warehouse, shipping, or receiving sites.
4. Size of facilities.
5. Data on equipment the firm uses.

Continuing with the description of the ABC Corporation, a demographic profile would be:

> ABC Corporation has operated five stores for the past six years, with the fifth store opened in 1989. ABC employs approximately *150 retail employees* and *six central office managers* and has a *fleet of four truck drivers.* It has a small *warehouse facility in the downtown* area, which receives all shipments for distribution to stores. The stores are located in *Redding, Highland Heights, Kettering, Troy, and Oakdale.* They have a combined retail show floor *space of 125,000* square feet. The largest store is in *Redding, with 35,000* square feet. The other stores

are approximately equal in size. Two stores, *Kettering and Troy, have just undergone remodeling* to increase their frozen food *capacity by 15 percent*. They are currently using Hussman refrigerated display cases in all stores, but *most need replacing,* as they are original equipment. No formal plans to replace them have been announced, but from their apparent condition, *replacement must occur this year or next*. Our *model 123-z in the 12-foot* length would probably be the best candidate to present to Daniel.

As before, the pertinent information is italicized. The salesperson would have a good idea where to start when planning the call to ABC. A salesperson would come up with all this detailed information through simple observation and asking store managers a few questions!

Business operations   This defines how the firm operates. The following would be essential data:

1. Form of business, such as sole proprietorship, partnership, or corporation (closely held or public).
2. How and when it pays its accounts payable.
3. Amount of advertising and favorite media.
4. When it takes deliveries.
5. When it sees salespeople.
6. Fiscal year dates.
7. Budgeting schedule, if any.
8. Purchasing patterns, if any.

An account profile for ABC's business operations would be as follows:

ABC is a *public corporation* whose stock is traded on the local exchange; current price, $12.50. It offers no dividends, and most stock is held by Daniel. It *pays bills on the first* of the month and always *takes all discounts*. Weekly newspaper ads consume its total ad budget, but this is of little consequence to us. Deliveries are always accepted on Wednesday, Friday, and Monday for perishables and alternate days for nonperishables. Tuesday is a light delivery day: *plan on any deliveries of equipment for Tuesday. Salespeople are seen only on Mondays, unless by special appointment*. Plan informational meeting on Monday with main purpose being setting up a scheduled appointment. It's *fiscal year ends on June 30,* and budgeting for the next year is done between April and June. *Plan on making a call during first week of April*.

Financial health   Financial health is always important because it indicates success in managing and doing business. Such information can be obtained through credit checks and references. The necessary information would include:

1. Financial ratio data.[5]
2. Credit problems.
3. Dates and details on bankruptcies or foreclosures, if any.
4. Financial condition of parent company, if dealing with subsidiary, or subsidiary, if dealing with parent.
5. Past, present, and expected sales, profits, loans, and general debt situation.

This part of ABC's profile could be as simply stated as:

ABC has had *no record of credit problems.* It is well capitalized, and its current stockholders report indicates a *growth in sales and profit of 4 percent annually since 1978.* Major expansions and equipment purchases have been *financed through First National Bank,* its banking associate. The firm is in *excellent financial condition* with an *asset to debt ratio of 3:1.*

ABC has grown, been well financed, and is in an excellent position to afford a major equipment purchase. We have a good idea about the nature and operating characteristics of this business. The next segment of the profile describes the prospect's external environment.

Section 2: Prospect's External Environment

The external environment section of the account profile briefly outlines the significant problems and needs faced by prospective customers, the markets they serve, their competitors, and their current vendors (our competitors). It should also define any business constraints and estimate prospects' purchasing budget.

Description of problems and needs   Good salespeople recognize that their job is to help customers solve problems. Account profiles may not be able to specifically identify the details of prospective customers' problems, but they should at least state the salespeople's interpretation of, or intuitive guess about, the problems they will be helping the prospects to solve. While this may seem like a formidable task, common sense goes a long way here. Think like a customer (Daniel Jackson, in this case) for a moment. The needs Jackson at ABC might have are:

- ▶ Greater margins
- ▶ Credit terms
- ▶ Quick delivery
- ▶ Ability to place add-on orders

- ▶ Faster turn on inventory
- ▶ Easy handling at stores
- ▶ Advertising support
- ▶ Shipment information

This is no magical list determined by hours of research. This is what all retailers want! The salesperson planning this call could start with what all buyers want and go from there. This list would give the salesperson eight needs to think about before even making a face-to-face visit with the buyer! By thinking like a buyer, the salesperson anticipates problems and prepares for them. Having anticipated the problems the buyer faces, it is reasonable to go one step farther and examine the markets the buyer serves. This can help illuminate the nuances of the buyer's situation and flesh out the account profile.

This part of ABC's profile would read as follows:

In ABC's gourmet retail business, *inventory turn tends to be slow;* at best, four turns per year. This means *margins are critically* important to it. Since we cannot help it sell its products, we can *focus on cost reduction* as selling points. Credit will be very important to it, as will delivery. It would also be *sensitive to the downtime* any *equipment installation* might cause. Long-term ownership cost, rather than initial purchase price, is probably a point of interest. *Need to stress value over the life of our equipment.*

This description is a good estimation of ABC's concerns, which could be deduced through what we know about the firm and some common sense.

The salesperson would use this to organize the presentation and prioritize his or her products' selling points.

Markets served A major concern is the markets (or customers) served by prospective customers if they are not buying for their own use. This section of the account profile would describe from a number of perspectives where prospects are doing business. A description of these markets would include:

1. Geographic details: national, local, regional, and international.

2. Psychographic information on markets.

3. Census data on population, manufacturers, retailing, wholesaling, agriculture, housing, and so on.

4. Usage information: who uses what we sell? How do they use it? Where? In what quantities?

Knowledge of the market served is an important part of the account profile.

A description of ABC's served market would be:

> While having stores located in all major suburbs, the specialty nature of the business causes customers to come from the entire metropolitan area. However, *most business occurs in a trade area of a ten-minute drive* of each store. The customer is an *upscale, well-informed shopper, generally from middle- to high-income households of professional and upper managerial occupations.* ABC caters to and gets the *carriage trade,* and it prices accordingly. Most customers are less concerned about price than *selection, service, and quality.* Less than the best is not tolerated. ABC's customers would be considered "*yuppies,*" highly fashionable, and *trend conscious,* wanting major brands and *imported items.*

This helps us empathize with Daniel by knowing about *his* customers. Dealing with upscale, demanding customers could be a signal that Daniel Jackson might be the same way. In his market, money is less of a concern than service and quality. A good line of conversation during the presentation would center around giving Daniel just what he gives his customer. He can relate to that.

Competitors Building an external environmental description also means considering prospects' competitors. We want to know as much about them as we can. This might be easier to do than you think. If you were in a firm selling to retail grocers, like ABC, you would know all the grocers, including ABC. Because of this, little outside fact-finding would be needed. However, in dealing with larger firms or multinationals, extensive data gathering would be essential. Competitor data would identify:

1. Who they are.

2. Where they are located.

3. Their current share of market—an indication of the strength and pressure they are putting on the prospect.

4. WOTS, (as described earlier).

Our profile of ABC would have the following competitive analysis:

> ABC is facing increased competition from *Safeway Stores,* Inc. Safeway has built *new stores across the street from three ABC stores.* While still maintaining its share, ABC is finding it tougher as a result of Safeway's incursion. The next major competitor is *Giant Foods.* In ABC's markets, the *market shares of these*

competitors are 20 percent and 10 percent, respectively. *Safeway's greatest strength* lies in store *size* and concomitant *variety*. It has *greater parking capacity* and is expected to *erode* ABC's share *several points* over the next five years. Currently, no new building sights are available, so there is *little opportunity for increased competition* from new entrants. Nothing new is expected from Giant.

ABC will probably be concerned about cost containment, quality, dependability, and cost over its useful life when buying any new equipment from us. Anything to promote reducing costs will be of interest. ABC is nervous and uncertain if or by what amount its market share will be affected by the new competitors. We can appreciate the effects of a new, strong, and potentially dangerous competitor. Knowing this customer's state of affairs, our firm can communicate its empathy for its situation by planning credit terms, leases, or discounts for ABC.

Vendors and their products The account's profile should identify the other vendors (our competition) selling to this account. Who is the competition? Are their products similar or different from ours? Who is the buyer currently considering, along with us? Having answers to these questions creates a stronger sales strategy and product presentation. Identification of our competition with this customer allows us to select the best selling strategy to use against those competitors.

The account profile can address the issue of competitive vendors in a variety of ways. First could be a simple listing of who they are and where they are located. More details, such as the salespeople calling on the prospective account and length of their business relationship, would be better. Better yet would be anecdotal information about the competitors. This portion of the profile should also contain competitive vendor product information. What are vendors selling the prospect? Knowing what products the buyer currently stocks or uses from other vendors helps us plan our selling points and presentation strategy. Such an entry in the profile might be as follows:

Vendor	Branch	Salesperson	Comments
Oasis	Ohio	A.J. Kayam	Oasis is currently experiencing delivery problems and seldom delivers in less than one week. Customer needs faster service.
Ajax	Detroit	Unknown	New firm just entered market. Offering price deals to get business. Being very successful.

Selling against Oasis would require focusing on rapid delivery and excellent service. Competing against Ajax would mean price competition or selling value to convince the prospective buyer that he gets what he pays for. In either case, the salesperson knows how to customize the presentation. From such entries, the current salesperson, the sales manager, or a future salesperson has a brief on the competitors.

Business constraints Business constraints identify any restrictions the prospects' business is or could be facing. Such things as legal constraints or physical limitations are important to note.

Legal constraints include pending litigation, regulatory limitations, laws, or zoning codes. These could be local, state, or national. A liquor salesperson in Ohio, by law, can sell only to state-owned liquor stores. In Nebraska, liquor can be sold to any retailer with the appropriate license. Insurance firms selling their policies through direct marketing must abide by the laws of each state. A printer, trying to sell services to one of these firms, must know an insurance company needs numerous versions of policies to be printed and any printing mistakes are potential trouble.

Physical limitations can be, for retailers, such things as the number of retail outlets, size of the outlets, amount of warehouse space, and in-store shelf space. As another example, prospective customers may only be able to receive shipments via truck, not train.

Physical limitations result from the type of equipment customers use in their operations. The size of a drop forge, the capacity of a grinder, or the electrical service to a motor all directly affect the physical limitations of the products they buy to use with such equipment. Any type of physical limitation that can affect the purchase, delivery, storage, shipment, or use of a product is essential for the salesperson to know. The entry in the profile we are building for ABC would be:

> ABC has a *zoning problem* with a location it now occupies. Neighbors are complaining and want the zoning code changed. *ABC will probably win* this one, but it will drag out for at least *six months*. In two of the three stores, access to the rear of the store is through alleys. *Deliveries* of our equipment must be done *on short-bed trucks,* because there is not enough room for semitrailer rigs. Equipment will *need to be ammonia refrigeration,* what ABC is now using.

Section 3: Prospect's Budget

This may be the most difficult topic to work with. The ability to deal with this depends on the situation. How would a salesperson determine the prospect's budget before even getting in to see that prospect? While this is not always possible, the information is readily available in some cases. If the salesperson were building an account profile of a new account, only an educated guess would be possible.

In building an account profile of a department store, one method of "guesstimating" the store's budget for ladies dresses would be to determine the floor space allotted to those types of dresses, then make a rough count of the dresses on hand and the average price. By knowing the standard markups used in the industry, the salesperson would have an estimate of the dollar inventory on the floor. By applying the industry standard for average turns on the inventory in a season, the salesperson has estimated the store's seasonal expenditures for dresses. Is it accurate? Not totally. Is it scientific? Definitely not. Is it better than walking into the buyer's office with no notion of the money spent on the dresses? Definitely yes! Being totally accurate is just not possible in most cases. The purpose is to improve salespeople's odds of making a good presentation by being better informed than their competitor.

For industrial goods, similar applications of industry rules of thumb would work. For example, in selling industrial floor cleaners, simply knowing the square footage of floor space, the normal number of times a floor is cleaned, and the amount of cleaner used per square foot would give the salesperson a rough estimate of what the firm spends on floor cleansers. The square footage is the only unknown in this calculation. It can be obtained by asking the maintenance supervisor, measuring the building's exterior, getting a copy of the building permit from the city, or through aerial photographs.

Section 4: Buying Criteria

The last section of the account profile focuses on the prospect's buying criteria. This consists of at least two parts: timing and specifications to be met.

Timing   The salesperson wants to be ready to make the sale when the buyer is ready to purchase. Timing should be considered from both a micro and a macro perspective. The micro perspective would identify the specific days and dates the buyer sees salespeople, the details about when orders are placed, and the time allotted for a presentation. The salesperson needs to know those days and times to schedule an appointment. Dropping by at any other time or day would be a waste of time.

Timing from a macro perspective would consider seasonal buying. The salespeople who sell textbooks to college professors know book orders are placed in the spring for the fall term and in the fall for the spring term. It does little good to visit professors during the spring trying to sell books for the spring term. In the account profile we are building, a simple statement like the following would suffice for the buying criteria entry:

> The buyer for ABC sees salespeople only on *Mondays from 8:00 until noon for 15 minutes,* and *appointments* must be made a *week in advance. Secretary schedules* all appointments. Items for *Christmas promotions* are reviewed between *July and August,* with some variations allowed, depending on the nature of the product.

Specifications to be met   This includes product, shipping, packing—all specifications pertinent to the individual situation. Most firms set the product specifications for the goods they buy. The salesperson must know these if the presentation is to be effective. Specifications for industrial products involve details about size, durability, engineering performance, capacities, or tolerances. For agricultural or natural-resource products, quality grades may be specified (e.g., U.S.D.A. Choice beef or Grade A milk).

Shipping specifications may require products be shipped by truck only, loaded on 48-inch-by-40-inch oak four-way-entry pallets and stacked no more than two high. Specifications could state that products delivered in bulk be off-loadable by belt conveyors. There are endless combinations of shipping methods and requirements for the salesperson to know about. Not shipping according to the buyer's specifications means the product cannot be delivered or unloaded and the shipment may be refused at point of delivery.

Packing specifications are also common. Customers may require products to be packed in 12- or 24-unit cartons. All shipping cartons could be required to have color codes, bar codes, specific labeling, or easily identifiable warnings. Perishable products commonly have packing and minimum temperature specifications. Some packing specifications are established via regulation. For example, the government requires radioactive materials and wastes be packed in certain ways for interstate shipment. The packing is part of the product the buyer is purchasing, and to pay any less attention to this specification than to the product's specification is courting a lost sale.

Financial specifications must also be met. A firm may command such a presence in the market that it can request, and get, specific terms and conditions. For example, a firm may specify that the advertising allowance is to come off the face of the invoice, rather than be remitted in a separate check. While the vendor can specify the form of payment and the amount of any downpayments, escrowed money, or earnest deposits, preferred or new customers can often get special terms or conditions.

In our ABC Store's account profile, the following would be included:

ABC requires all *perishables* to be delivered directly to its stores *unpalletized* and at a receiving temperature of *28-32°F. Belt conveyors are used to unload trucks,* and all *drivers are responsible for unloading* their own trucks. There is an unloading dock at all stores, so trucks with *hydraulic tailgates are not necessary.*

Building a customer profile and using it are necessary steps to developing the customized presentation that is certain to win the sale. While some firms require profiles and use them religiously, others don't. However, most successful adaptive salespeople use some form of customer profiling to record and analyze purchase patterns and facts about their customers.

▶ ▶ *follow-up questions*

1. What demographic information would you collect about a business in creating an account profile?

2. What are buying criterion? What might be a new car buyer's buying criterion?

3. What makes up the description of a prospect's external environment?

Summary

This chapter was about fact-finding, the first step in precall planning. Through fact-finding, the information necessary to formulate an effective and efficient sales presentation is gathered. Fact-finding differs from qualifying in that the latter just determines if the lead meets the criteria necessary for further consideration. Many salespeople often combine the two activities (Learning Objective 1).

Fact-finding has six objectives

1. to determine the prospect's current situation,

2. to build a historical perspective,

3. to be able to anticipate the prospect's problems,

4. to anticipate problems when making the presentation,

5. to anticipate which products to offer, and

6. to determine the players in the purchase decision (Learning Objective 2).

The data gathered during fact-finding gives the salesperson information about the prospective customer that allows for customizing the presentation and building a WOTS summary. WOTS is an acronym for Weaknesses, Opportunities, Threats, and Strengths (Learning Objective 3).

Salespeople use a variety of tools to gather the necessary facts. An annual report is one such tool. It gives an overall picture of a firm's goals, directions, and performance. Annual reports are excellent sources for getting a historical perspective on a firm's track record. Usually several years worth of sales, profit, and expense figures are published in them. Commercial directories were discussed, and four of the most comprehensive and readily available were detailed. Organizational charts were discussed primarily as sources of determining authoritative or approval structures and for anticipating the number and positions of the decision makers or influencers. Asking questions and listening were both identified as two of the best fact-finding methods. Finally, making joint or team calls was discussed and its limited application and usefulness noted (Learning Objective 4).

The tools of fact-finding were followed by a brief section about when to do fact-finding. Ideally, that is whenever the most and best information can be obtained. Fact-finding can occur at any time: during qualifying and before or during the presentation (Learning Objective 5).

The chapter's final section detailed the contents of an account profile. The account profile could include any pertinent information; it is limited only by the needs of the salesperson and the firm. The basic foundation of an account profile is a description of the customer's business, its demographics, how it operates, and its financial status or health. These items can be as brief or extensive as needed.

The account profile should address the prospect's external environment. This would include illustrative facts about the customer's problems or needs, immediate, short-term, or long-term. It also would describe the customer's markets, if applicable, including geographic, psychographic, and demographic aspects. Also included would be the competition and their weaknesses, opportunities, threats, and strengths.

The external environment would include a description and details about other vendors or potential vendors and their product offerings. This could include either or both a description of what the prospect is currently buying from competing vendors or products from competing vendors that would be in direct competition with the salesperson's firm.

The customer's business constraints would conclude this portion. These constraints would include pending legislation, regulatory problems, laws, zoning difficulties, warehouse capacity, delivery facilities, or specific packaging requirements.

The third section would address the prospect's budget. This could be from data supplied by the customer, from annual reports or requests for proposals, or the salesperson's best estimate. The final section of the profile covers topics relating to buying criteria. These would typically be issues of timing, specifications, and the extensiveness of the customer's buying situation (Learning Objective 6).

Key Terms

Fact-finding The process of gathering pertinent facts about the prospective customer for the purpose of building an account profile and call planner.

Call planner A written form outlining what the salesperson will do and need during a presentation.

Demographics The vital statistics of a population or the vital statistics of a prospective business. These would include such things as number of employees, dollar sales, and number of locations.

Discussion Questions

1. In fact-finding, why it is important to determine the prospect's current situation?

2. What does WOTS mean, and how can a salesperson use it in precall planning?

3. What would be the tools for fact-finding used by someone selling aluminum siding to homeowners compared to those of someone selling industrial machinery to General Motors?

4. What type of information would a salesperson get from a company's annual report?

5. What makes fact-finding different from qualifying? What is similar about the two?

6. Which of the six objectives of fact-finding do you feel are the most important and why?

7. Why should a salesperson gather information about both the prospective customer and the competitors?

8. If a salesperson does an adequate job of qualifying, then does fact-finding becomes redundant?

9. How does the third objective of fact-finding benefit the salesperson?

10. What are three problems you would anticipate (and be prepared for) if you were demonstrating vacuum cleaners door-to-door?

11. You're making a presentation to a prospective client when the phone rings and she gets ready to answer it. What should you do?

12. How does fact-finding by the salesperson reduce cognitive dissonance on the buyer's part? How can it enhance cross-selling opportunities?

13. In a presentation you made this morning, you talked to the junior purchasing agent—the lowest one on the totem pole. This afternoon, you're going to make the same presentation to another company, but the vice-president of purchasing, the senior buyer, and three senior engineers will be there. How will these two meetings differ?

14. How valuable are annual reports to salespeople calling on small businesses or privately held companies?

15. The chapter lists several directories as sources. If you wanted to know about the largest hydraulic pump manufacturer in the United States, which one(s) would you use?

16. What are the advantages and disadvantages to making joint calls?

17. When are the three best times to do fact-finding?

18. How does making and updating an account profile benefit salespeople and their firms?

19. What is meant by the demographics of a firm?

20. If you were creating an account profile of a drug store in your area, what would you say about the market it serves? Who would you identify as its competitors? What are its constraints?

Application Exercise

Go back and reread the box about KOOL-FM and the salesperson trying to sell a joint advertising venture to Polaroid, then answer the following questions:

1. How could Julie Silver have known Polaroid and Disney (Shamrock) were locked in a hostile takeover situation?

2. Julie's idea was a good one. Even if she had known about the hostile takeover, what facts could she have gathered in an attempt to see Sortino and discuss her plan?

3. Should Julie have proceeded with the discussion, left, or pursued some other approach with Sortino?

Class Exercises

Group Exercise

You are a sales rep for a record distributor, and you have identified Sam's Music Shop as an excellent prospect for your new product line. Sam owns seven stores located in prime, high-density population areas.

Break into at least four small groups. Each group will be assigned one aspect of the WOTS summary model for fact-finding.

1. Brainstorm the questions to be answered under your group's assigned WOTS category as they apply to: product, price, promotion, customers, and distribution.

2. Assign a spokesperson to summarize the findings of your group.

3. As a class, discuss what has taken place in this exercise.

Individual Presentation

Assume you are the person in the Chapter 6 exercise who was responsible for increasing the membership of the student chapter of the Sales Executives Club.

In order to prepare a presentation on this plan, you will have to do some fact-finding. One of the objectives of fact-finding, as described in this chapter, is to anticipate the problems you may have in making the presentation to prospective customers.

1. Describe to the class problems that you may have in making this presentation.

2. Describe to the class how you would go about overcoming these problems.

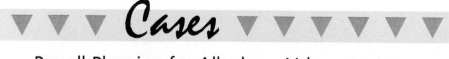

Cases

Case 7.1

Precall Planning for Allegheny Valves

Barbara Cohen is a sales rep for the Allegheny Valve Company. Allegheny's valves are major pieces of industrial equipment distributed through independently owned plumbing supply houses in the northeastern United States. The valves are used on piping carrying any type of liquid or steam. The plumbing supply houses buy the valves from Allegheny and resell them to industrial and institutional users.

Barbara has been given the assignment of contacting new prospects in the Midwest in hopes of expanding Allegheny's market. She wants to get started on this assignment as quickly as possible. Generating leads is not a problem. Although she already has the names of all the members of the national plumbing supply distributor's association she feels she needs more than that. She wants to be able to contact these distributors, gather as much information as she can, then schedule appointments to see them, but she doesn't know how to get started. She has come to you for advice. What would you tell her to do to start her new assignment?

First-Call Fact-Finding

Making the first call on a prospective customer is always a nervous affair at best. Making the first sales call in your career is even more anxiety-producing. Derek has just graduated from college and has a new job selling insurance and financial plans. He is going to make his first sales call next week. You have been watching him, noticing his apparent nervousness. You are now meeting with him to give him a little advice.

Derek says, "I'm nervous about this call. I want to make the sale and start off right. I want to have these customers feel good about buying a policy and recommend me to their friends." "Who are you going to see?" you ask. "Keven Sells and his wife," replied Derek. "They live in Centerville, have a couple of kids, and are doing okay. I guess I'm just nervous about what might happen, what they might say or do. I want to be prepared for anything they throw at me." You understand the feeling, so to calm Derek down, you ask him to explain what he anticipates their problems to be and what problems he might have in making the sale. What do you think Derek would have to say?

References

1. Edward F. Walsh, "A Primer for Planning," *Sales and Marketing Management*, 142 (1990): 75–78.
2. Adapted from Tom Hopkins, *How to Master the Art of Selling* (New York: Warner Books, 1982), pp. 157–58.
3. The Standard Industrial Classification (SIC) code is a system used by the U.S. Department of Commerce to categorize all businesses. It is based on an expandable code. For example, the broadest code is two digits, signifying major industry groups; for example, SIC code 20 is for all businesses involved in the manufacture of food and kindred products. SIC 201 includes just the meat packers in SIC 20. SIC 2011 is just the slaughterhouses of SIC 201. The more digits, the more specialized the business in its broader business group.
4. Think about who would be information sources. The dean's office receptionist would tell you who the department's faculty are, who the chair is, who the department secretary is, the location of the department's office, and its phone number. The departmental secretary could tell you who teaches selling and their phone numbers, locations, and hours. The bookstore manager could tell you whose book was used in the past and the approximate volume of sales, along with when the book orders were due from the faculty. These are just a few sources. Can you think of more?
5. This data is available from public corporations and through credit checks. It does not come as financial ratios but must be calculated. It would include such things as assets and liabilities, stock turn rates, long-term and short-term debt, and cash flow.

Chapter

8 The Preapproach: Step 2 of Precall Planning

Objectives

After reading this chapter, you will be able to:

1. Distinguish between an account profile and a sales call planner.

2. Know the benefits of writing a sales call planner.

3. Identify five questions to be answered in the sales call planner.

4. Write a sales call planner from the samples illustrated in the text.

5. Explain the purpose of the preapproach.

6. Develop a telephone script for getting an appointment with a prospective customer, including fact-finding questions and dealing with initial objections.

7. Construct a letter for getting an appointment with a prospective customer.

8. Develop a plan for an unannounced cold call on a prospective customer.

9. Practice an actual presentation of yourself and your product or service to a prospective customer.

246

The Professional Selling Question

What do you do just before making a sales call?

Sales Experts Respond

Two sales experts, James E. Lukaszewski and Paul Ridgeway, agree that successful presentations start with good preparation. No one simply walks in and wings it, then emerges with a big order. To make a good—and successful—presentation, you must do several things. First, think of yourself as a winner. If you visualize yourself closing the sale, you have the right frame of mind to do it. If you begin thinking of all the reasons the prospect probably will not buy, then you are setting yourself up to expect the worst, not the best. You should determine in advance where problems and rough spots might occur and how you will handle them if they do. If they do occur, you can take them in stride.

Plan to make your presentation as exciting as you can. Many presentations are dull, lifeless exercises. Before you make the call, review your visuals, your demonstrations, and what has worked in the past. Can they be enlivened? Have you used color to its best advantage?

Rehearse your presentation. Go over it until it is so natural it comes off like a conversation, rather than a sales pitch. Outlining what you are going to say and do will make the presentation rehearsal and the actual presentation come off much better. This is a confidence builder, and that confidence will show in the presentation.

Most important of all, do your homework. Be prepared. Know your customer's needs. If you are calling on an existing customer, review the notes you made after the last meeting and update them, if necessary. If this is a new customer, gather all the information you can. Also, use common sense; what would you need if you were the customer?

By taking the time to prepare for the presentation, updating your customer information, reviewing your presentation materials, and rehearsing, you should be prepared for anything the customer might throw at you. Preparation is the key to a great (and successful) presentation.[1]

> No one plans to fail . . . . They just fail to plan!

Introduction

No professional salesperson prepares for a call without a plan. Some salespeople write their plans down and present them to their manager. Others mentally make a plan just before making the call. All good salespeople have one thing in common: they preplan their calls.

Large-account sales for complete systems of products or services, such as telecommunications systems, computers, or a corporate advertising campaign, require extensive preplanning. Such plans often take weeks, even months, to develop. In large accounts, much is at stake, and a firm cannot afford to lose out for lack of having a well-rehearsed and well-thought-out presentation. Smaller-item sales, even something as simple as a pair of shoes, also take preplanning. Although not as much is at stake in these, the salesperson who doesn't have a good plan in mind for quickly discovering and addressing customers' needs will lose the sales.

For many salespeople, getting the appointment to see the buyer can be a major undertaking in itself. Many business executives get hundreds of requests every week for appointments. Only some salespeople get through, and these are the ones who planned a strategy for getting the appointment, who approached getting the appointment as seriously as they do making the presentation after they get in. There is a definite strategy for getting the appointment, just as there is for making the sale.

In this chapter, we center our attention on how to construct a call planner from an account profile and how to get that all important sales appointment. These activities are called the preapproach. Throughout this chapter, one theme will come through: poor call planning means a poor preapproach, a poor preapproach means no appointment with the customer, and that means no sale. In preapproach, we are making the final plans for a successful call.

Create a Call Planner Before Calling on the Customer

A **call planner** is a brief outline containing the information important in scheduling the appointment and making the sales presentation. A call planner contains pertinent, yet very brief, information about the prospect and the prospect's business, along with a few structured notes about selling techniques to use. It can be put onto a couple of note cards or sheets of paper for quick reference. The call planner is a distillation of information taken from the account profile you learned about in the last chapter.

Case in Point

A Bit of Whimsy with a Powerful Message

A route salesperson came to the fork in the road, pulled over, and stopped. A farmer came by and asked him if he was lost. The salesperson said, "I do not know which road to take." The farmer said, "Where do you want to go?" "I'm not sure," came the reply. "Well," said the farmer, "if you do not know where you want to go, any road will get you there."

Comment: Do not underestimate the value of precall planning!

▶ ▶ ▶ ▶ ▶ ▶ ▶ ▶ ▷

Learning Objective 1: Sales call planners and account profiles are noticeably different

While account profiles and call planners can be the same thing, they are usually significantly different. The account profile looks at the customer from a total business perspective. It may identify several buyers at the customer's business and a variety of products they buy. It is more global, having information about the general business conditions and environment in which the customer operates.

The call planner can be and usually is call specific, written for an individual sales call to an individual buyer. It is very explicit in identifying the precise goal the call is to accomplish, the particular product(s) to be presented, the types of objections to anticipate, and the selected closing techniques to use. The account profile represents a far more encompassing dossier on the firm and its situation. The call planner is akin to a set of review notes targeted toward a specific and single-purpose event, the sales call.

Benefits of Planning

Planning provides salespeople with five benefits:

Learning Objective 2: Five benefits of making a sales call planner

1. Preparedness
2. Efficiency
3. Self-confidence
4. Logical, organized delivery
5. Builds buyer's confidence

Preparedness   Planning prepares the salesperson for the call. Part of planning the call is having a well-defined objective in mind. Sales calls have many objectives ranging from something as simple as getting acquainted, to closing a sale, to collecting a past due bill. As simple as it is to do, many salespeople make calls without being adequately prepared.

Case in Point

Professionals Take Precall Planning Seriously

"When I go into a call," says Larry Nonnamaker of Eastman Kodak, "I know what I want to sell, how much I want to sell, what the benefits to the customer are, the objections he or she will have, how I will address those objections, a complete plan from shipping to merchandizing to advertising the product, the margins the dealer will receive, and my anticipated reorders after the initial sell-through. All sales reps have to deal with the unexpected, but by planning thoroughly before they ever enter the customer's office, they minimize the chances of failing to attain their objectives."

"One of the main purposes of a sales call to an existing account," says Dave Clark of Simmons, "is to help the retailer fine-tune her or his business plans. To enable you to achieve this objective, you need to know which of your products or promotions are working and which are not. If you are not prepared, your competition will do it for you."

"Preplanning cold calls is essential because of the very limited time you can actually spend in front of the prospect," says John Heitzenroder of Occidental Chemical. "Before ever making a call on a prospect, I try to qualify him or her as much as possible by consulting business directories, Dunn & Bradstreet reports, trade journals, and the business sections of local newspapers, as well as calling on the prospect's competitors. I will even drive to the prospect's place of

Continued

---

business without going in, just to get a feel for the operation. The more I can learn about the prospect, the greater are my chances of a successful cold call. I jot down an outline of the facts I have uncovered and review it before making my first call."

"For that call, I try to formulate an approach, such as emphasizing a particular line of coverage or benefits that may be important in his or her business. Often I do not even discuss my product with the prospect on the first call. It's better to ask a lot of questions about his or her business—after all, the prospect is the best reference source for information about the firm.

"I use an index-card file to maintain updated information about my prospects. The whole idea is to make as much of an impact as possible within the time limitation. I've watched and learned from really good salespeople—they do not make cold calls, they make hot ones!"

Source: Porter Henry, *Secrets of the Selling Masters,* New York: Amacom, American Management Association, (1987), 71–73.

A call planner helps salespeople focus on the benefits they can offer to satisfy the customer's needs. These benefits should be reviewed prior to making an appointment for the presentation. In the following dialogue, Marcus bought steam-cleaning equipment from Dominique four years ago. Dominique would like to contact Marcus again; it's about time for him to replace some, if not all, of that equipment. How will Dominique remember what benefits Marcus wanted without a planner? When Dominique calls Marcus to talk about new equipment, she can focus on his specific needs and communicate to him that she remembers him, not as a customer but as an individual. The conversation would be something like this:

Dominique: Marcus, this is Dominique from Mid-State Industrial Equipment. How are things going?

Marcus: Pretty good, Dominique.

Dominique: How's that hydraulic steam pressure system you bought as an option? Still as great as when we tested it last June?

Marcus: It is still working great!

Dominique: Marcus, I have a new model Big Bear steam cleaner I think you might be interested in. We also have a new financing plan that I think you might like to know about. Have you checked on the value of your old equipment lately? Do you know it's worth $4,000 on a trade?

Marcus: No, I didn't think it would be worth that much. But I'm not in the market for a new steam unit. The old one still does the job.

Dominique: Well, maybe so, but I thought about you when I saw all the features this cleaner has, particularly the newly designed pressure control system and the fact that with your present equipment as a trade in and this great new financing plan, we could get you a new one for only $50 a month more than you are now paying.

Marcus: Fifty a month more?

Well, you can see Marcus is on his way to owning a new steam cleaner. Look at the information Dominique had at her fingertips, and from four years ago! From their previous sales interactions, she knew the benefits Marcus wanted, remembered the date of the test, how much Marcus's monthly payments were, and tantalized him with the fact that his old equipment was worth $4,000 (an important item used to get Marcus's attention with a payment increase of only $50 per month). A planner is the key to preparedness, and preparedness is one step closer to a closed sale.

A planner helps the salesperson plan what features, advantages, and benefits to use during the presentation itself. It also aids in formulating a strategy for any demonstration. A planner should list the possible objections the prospect might raise during the presentation. By being prepared, the salesperson can determine which objections can be prevented and how to handle the others, should they occur.

Efficiency By planning, salespeople are more efficient at making presentations. Since they already have a game plan in mind, the presentation can be fine-tuned to the topics the customer raises as it progresses. By anticipating the features, advantages, and benefits, as well as the objections, the salesperson is ready for what will occur.

An updated planner tracks the events of previous calls, too. By quickly reviewing this information before making a new call, the salesperson is refreshed on what previously transpired. This eliminates the time-consuming effort of trying to remember what occurred or physically searching through records. Taking a little time to update the planner before and after each call saves time in the long run. A quick review of the planner makes more efficient use of both the salesperson's and the buyer's time. Updating and retrieving the planner are even easier if the planner is stored in a computer file.

Self-confidence Planners create self-confidence. Imagine a sports team going into a game without reviewing its game plan and scouting information about its opponent. Reviewing a planner is a final confidence builder before the presentation. A planner is like a review sheet for a test. You feel much more confident going into the exam if you know the likely test questions and answers. Using a planner makes you more successful at closing sales.

> Maintaining self-confidence was one of the ten most difficult aspects of selling, according to a survey of over 2,000 college students taking a personal selling course.
>
> Remember: Knowledge builds self-confidence, and reviewing what you have done successfully in making a sale will remind you of what works and what doesn't.

Logical, organized delivery Using a planner makes the presentation flow more logically and with better organization. The planner allows salespeople to establish a mental sequence of events to follow. They can develop an organized delivery by thinking something like, "I will lead with several situational questions, listen, then if she says this, I can follow with these benefits. She will probably object here with a 'no-need' objection, to which I will say...," and so on.

Using the planner to mentally rehearse the presentation prevents the salesperson from rambling and allows the presentation to be structured to lead the buyer to the buying, rather than the not-buying, conclusion. As a student, you can appreciate your instructor's use of a lecture plan. You likely have been in a class where the instructor seems to jump from one point to the next without any apparent sequencing. You probably came out of the lecture with notes that were little more than random collections of information and did more to confuse than clarify.

Builds buyer's confidence   Buyers form impressions of how salespeople will handle their account by the way the presentation is made and organized. If the presentation appears scattered, unorganized, and slipshod, buyers will likely assume that is how their orders will be handled.

The planner builds the salesperson's self-confidence, which, since it is contagious, builds the buyer's confidence in the salesperson. Being self-confident creates a more convincing delivery and permits answering questions more directly and with little hesitation.

Case in Point

The Computer in Personal Selling: Chrysler Spends $5 Million on Laptops

Chrysler decided to spend $5 million on laptop computers for its 600 district managers and 250 district sales managers. The computers have the ability to download almost a dozen different databases. They also will eliminate numerous reports previously done by hand by each salesperson. Through the databases, the Chrysler Corporate Representative has ready access to data about each dealer, including:

▸ The number of orders the dealer has placed, how much of that order has been produced, and the dealer's allocation of cars from the factory.

▸ The dealer's market penetration compared to other dealers and the U.S. average.

▸ Customer information, such as the dealer's customer satisfaction score (a very serious measure on which franchise renewals are often based).

▸ The dealer's financial condition.

The hand-written call planner and customer profile are quickly becoming a thing of the past for Chrysler's corporate sales force.

Source: Thayer Taylor, "Chrysler Takes the Laptop Plunge," *Sales and Marketing Management,* 136 (1986): 82.

▸▸ *follow-up questions*

1. How does the call planner differ from an account profile? Could they be one in the same?

2. Are salespeople who use call planners more confident than those who do not? Would a planner be a good tool for a novice salesperson or trainee to use? Why?

3. In what ways does a planner make the salesperson more efficient?

Five Questions Inherent in the Planner

◀ ◀ ◀ ◀ ◀ ◀ ◀ ◀ ◀

Learning Objective 3:
Questions the sales call
planner should answer

It is now time to create a planner from the account profile you learned how to construct in the last chapter. Planners can take on many formats, but regardless of format, they all address five questions:

1. Who—are the customers, buyers, users, gatekeepers, decision makers, and benefit recipients?
2. What—are the features, advantages, and benefits customers want and need to be more satisfied with your product over your competitor's? What will they be getting for their money?
3. When—do they buy, take deliveries, want promotional materials, need service or installation? When do they expect to reorder?
4. Where—do you make your presentation? Where do they want it delivered? Where will they use the product?
5. Why—should they buy from you? From your competitor? Why should they believe what you say? Why are your reasons more convincing? Why should they pay your price?

Who?

The "who" question is specific to the particular call. Examples of "Who" questions are:

Who:

▶ Is the buyer?
▶ Makes the decision?
▶ Are the gatekeepers?
▶ Influences the decision?
▶ Will be attending the presentation?
▶ Will be using the product, handling delivery problems, and so on?
▶ Already has the customer's business?
▶ Are present customers we can use as references?
▶ Referred this customer to us?

As you can see, it is not a simple matter of just thinking about the buyer. The adaptive salesperson knows how important it is to remember when making a sale that there are often many more players than just one buyer. Answering these "who" questions identifies everyone participating in this presentation or meeting. The answers should address the roles of the various attendees and how to deal with them. For a meeting with several parties from the customer's firm, the planner should develop a strategy for dealing with the group as a whole, as well as the individuals.

What?

The "*what*" question focuses on product or service alternatives and a target product. Identifying alternatives provides the salesperson and the buyer a refined list of choices from the salesperson's total product list. In most instances, some products are clearly not applicable to the buyer's needs. The salesperson should make a list of possible product candidates based on the information obtained in qualifying and completing the customer profile, discussed in the last chapter.

The salesperson should rank the list of candidate products to determine which is the most likely to benefit the customer. Following that, the salesperson develops a benefit plan for each. Such a benefit plan identifies the most appealing features, advantages, and benefits of the particular product to this specific buyer. This may sound formidable, but it doesn't have to be. Think about showing a house to a prospective home buyer who has indicated an interest in a swimming pool. The features, advantages, and benefits of the pool would be similar for all houses having a pool. Often, products share many common features, advantages, and benefits.

In writing this part of the planner, the salesperson should estimate a target sale. For example, suppose a salesperson for a hot dog maker were calling on a grocery chain with 85 stores. The salesperson estimates each store needs two cases (24 packages) of hot dogs to fill its displays, and the displays will need filling once a day. Since the chain orders on a weekly basis, the salesperson's target sale is 1,190 cases for a first order (2 cases × 7 days × 85 stores). The hot dog salesperson would strive to convince the buyer that 1,190 cases is the amount to order to prevent stock outages at the stores and to satisfy customer demand being created by a national or local promotion. The salesperson now has a goal and can logically suggest such a quantity. In this part of the planner, the salesperson must think about "cross-sold" items, also. Firms often offer a host of complimentary products to complete their full-line offering.

When?

The "when" question, like the "who" question, has many facets. "When" refers to the timing of events and occurrences related to making the sale and getting paid. Any of the following "When" questions would be appropriate for the planner:

When:

▸ Do buyers see salespeople? Schedule appointments?

▸ Do they take deliveries?

▸ Do they want our promotional materials?

▸ Do they need a callback or service or set-up after original sale?

▸ Do they normally reorder?

The planner should have details about the timing and scheduling of the upcoming call, as well as information about the order cycle and delivery schedules, if they are germane to the forthcoming call. Some call planning forms have spaces for the salesperson to enter dates and times of follow-up calls resulting from the current one. Recording the standard time periods for ordering, delivery, advertising, and so on means the salesperson knows what is normal for *that* particular client.

Where?

The basics of knowing "*where*" come from the account profile or from information taken during fact-finding or qualifying. Some of the "where" questions to answer in a planner are:

Where:

▸ Are presentations made?

▸ Do they have stores, warehouses, distribution centers, loading and unloading facilities?

▸ Do they want this shipment sent?

▸ Do they want demonstrations made?

▸ Will they use this product?

"Where" information is important in dealing with large corporate buyers because their office locations and their receiving destinations are often hundreds, sometimes thousands of miles apart. Identifying where customers will use the product helps in understanding what they will use it for and what they will expect it to do. Knowing that the accounts payable department is in a home office location far from the point of sale or delivery can explain time delays between delivery and receipt of payment. Noting this

A salesperson must know where to deliver products sold.

information in the planner tells the salesperson what is normal and what to expect when selling to this customer.

Why?

Salespeople must put themselves in the buyer's shoes when thinking about this topic. "*Why* should the prospect buy from me? What is there about my product or service that will allow this person to be satisfied, make a profit on resale, or solve a problem?"

The "why" of a planner must address two issues. The first is why prospects can effectively use more of your product or why their customers can use more of it. The second we can just call your "deal," which is the financial reasons to buy from you. Both of these issues are addressed in a good planner. They may not be labeled as such on some planning forms, but they generally are covered.

The end-use or resale plan   The **end-use or resale plan** is a strategy to help customers resell or use the product you are selling them. This should answer the question "If I buy this, what all can I use it for?" As an example, retailing a riding lawn mower to a homeowner is easier if the salesperson expands on its uses beyond cutting grass (the salesperson is creating perceived value in the customer's mind.) The salesperson creates an end-use plan by telling the customer that the riding lawn mower also bags grass, mulches leaves (making raking unnecessary), pulls aerators or two-wheeled carts, and removes unwanted thatch with an attachment. The salesperson has explained all the uses for this mower, many of which the homeowner didn't think of. In doing so, the salesperson added value to justify the $1,000 price tag. Multiple uses give multiple advantages and benefits and therefore justify the investment.

Selling to a reseller requires that the plan identify how the customer can effectively resell the product. The salesperson may offer to train the customer's salespeople in the most effective ways to sell the product to end-users. The salesperson may simply make suggestions on displays and promotions or offer complete "blueprinting" or floor-planning designs. **Blueprinting** or **floor-planning** is a plan offered by manufacturers or wholesalers to customers that diagrams the exact positioning of products in sales floor displays and how much product is needed in these displays. These plans have usually been determined through experience and research and offer resellers the greatest potential return for their investment. Blueprints and floor plans may indicate which product colors and sizes to put together and how big to make the displays. (See Figure 8-1.)

The purpose of the end-use or resale plan is to provide customers with ideas to enhance their satisfaction. By having a plan with information about the customer and by having a preliminary notion of the products that might appeal most to the customer, the salesperson can form an end-use or resale plan to easily answer the question "If I buy this, what all can I use it for?"

Formulate your "deal"   The second issue addressed by the "why" of a planner is your "deal." The planner identifies the deal you and your firm are willing to make the customer. The planner should list a brief summary of the following:

**"It's Not How *Much* You Make on *Each* Sale. . .
But How *Often* You Make it!"**

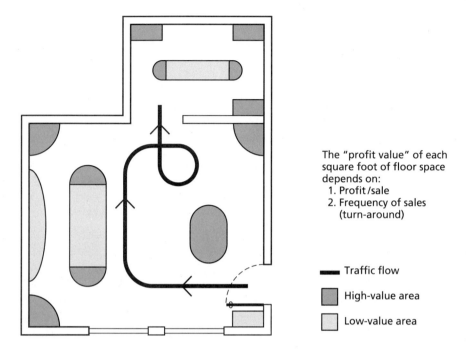

The "profit value" of each square foot of floor space depends on:
1. Profit/sale
2. Frequency of sales (turn-around)

━━ Traffic flow

■ High-value area

□ Low-value area

Each square foot of space in the retail portion of the store has a "square-foot value" based on the repeat sales (turn-around) of the product being displayed at *that* location. Should a "low-turn" product be located in a "high-value" floor space, it should be replaced by a "high-turn item." Should the store manager say he or she has no space for your product, explain the benefit of making room for your "high-profit" product by moving the "low-profit" item to another location. It works!

▶ *Price*—The list price, suggested retail price, and the price including delivery and freight charges, if applicable.

▶ *Discounts*—All the discounts and allowances you are prepared to offer: cash, seasonal, volume, trade, or promotional.

▶ *Spiffs, sweeteners*—Spiffs and sweeteners are enticements to purchase. For example, if a wholesaler agrees to buy 1,000 ceiling fans, the manufacturer may give the wholesaler a trip to Hawaii.

▶ *Markups, profits*—The standard markups and gross profits to the reseller.

▶ *Return on investment*—The customer's return on investment.

▶ *Payment plans*—All available payment plans and the one(s) most likely to appeal to this customer. An example would be "no payments for 90 days" or "90 days same as cash."

▶ *Value analysis*—The value the customer gets by buying your product, rather than a competitor's. Value analysis is extremely important if your product is clearly more expensive than a competitor's and you must convince the buyer that yours is actually worth the extra money. Examples of a value analysis are in Figures 8-2 and 8-3.

Figure 8-2 Sample Value Analysis of OURS versus THEIRS

	Ours	Theirs
List price	$1,500	$1,100
Discounts		
Cash	2%	1%
Volume	5%	5%
Seasonal	2%	–0–
Annual maintenance	$150	$250
Freight	Free	$ 50
Terms	60 months	48 months
Annual ownership cost	$423.71	$568.17

While THEIRS is $200 cheaper on the list price, after considering terms, maintenance, and delivery, OURS is actually $144.46 less per year to own!

This entire calculation would not be listed in the planner, rather simply the notes about the annual ownership cost. The salesperson would remember how to do the calculations for the customer who says, "THEIRS is $200 cheaper than yours. I do not think I can afford to spend that much more on yours." Such a calculation could be summarized by using a T-account comparison like the one in Figure 8-3.

▶ ▶ ▶ ▶ ▶ ▶ ▶ ▶ ▶

Learning Objective 4: Writing a call planner

Figure 8-4 is one example of a business-to-business call planning form. Adaptive salespeople customize and adapt it to their different customers and their unique situations, using the more detailed account profile information. Figure 8-5 is a form that has been used at Roerig Division of Pfizer and could be customized to be a quick guide to the sales call. The Roerig sales-

Figure 8-3 The T-Account Comparison Approach to Value Analysis

Price—is the dollar investment required to ultimately reduce the cost of the operation for the next time period.

Cost—is the dollar expense of the present operation, if continued for the same time period.

Should your customers tell you that they can't buy your product or service because your price is too high, let your preplanner show a cost "benefit" on this basis:

The annual cost of the operation now.	The annual cost of the same operation with your product or service
Total $ _____	Total $ _____

Business-To-Business Sales Call Planner

Source of lead _____

Company name _____

Address _____

Phone _____

Individual and title _____

Best time to see _____

Receptionist's/secretary's name _____

Is this person the decision maker? _____

Who is the decision maker? _____

If not, does this person influence decision? _____

Type of company _____

Main product, service, or type of industry _____

Approximate annual sales or purchases _____

Buyer profile _____
_____

Individuals involved in the buying decision _____
_____
_____

Greatest problem/why _____
_____

Benefits sought _____

Business environment _____

Sales presentation

▸ Special equipment needed _____

▸ Sales approach _____

▸ Features/Advantages/Benefits to stress _____

▸ Demo method _____

▸ Trail closes _____

▸ Anticipated objections _____

▸ Techniques to overcome _____

▸ Closes to use _____

▸ End-use or resale plan _____

▸ Deal offered _____

Sales made $_____   Units _____

Delivery/shipping details _____

Postsale follow-up planned/promised _____

Comments _____

Figure 8-4   **Example of a Sales Call Planner**

Source: Courtesy of Ralph Eubanks, Roerig Division of Pfizer.

Figure 8-5 **Call Planning Form Used by Roerig Division of Pfizer**

ROERIG
SALES CALL GUIDE

Physician's name _DR. SMITH_   Date _11/13/87_

Specialty _INTERNAL MEDICINE_

Objective of this call? _GET DR. SMITH TO PUT FIVE TYPE II DIABETICS ON _____ FOR SIX WEEKS TO EVALUATE EFFICACY_

If objective is achieved how will you recognize it on this call? _DR. SMITH WILL AGREE AND PLACE DOSAGE CARDS IN FIVE PATIENT'S FOLDERS._

What is your strategy, what do you plan to do? (opening, features, benefits, sales aids, etc.)

USE VISUAL AID OPENER "TIMING IS EVERYTHING"

STRESS ① LOWERING GLUCOSE LEVELS WITHOUT THE RISK OF hypoglycemia.

    _② SHOW CLINICAL FROM JOSLIN CLINIC STATING _____ IS THE ONLY ORAL AGENT THAT CONTINUES TO PROVIDE EFFECTIVE GLUCOSE CONTROL FOR OVER FIVE YEAS WITHOUT HAVING TO BUMP UP THE DOSE_

    ③ EMPHASIZE ONE A DAY DOSING FOR CONVENIENCE

What objections do you anticipate? _____ IS NOT AS POTENT AS _____ IN LOWERING BLOOD SUGAR LEVELS._

DID YOU ACHIEVE THE CALL OBJECTIVE?   Yes ☑   No ☐

If "yes" describe how you recognized it. (what did customer say or do?) If "no" what will you do to achieve it next time?

_DR. SMITH THOUGHT OF SEVEN PATIENTS TO TRY _____ ON & ASKED THE NURSE TO BRING IN THE PATIENTS FILE FOLDERS. HE PLACED DOSAGE CARDS & FILE CARDS IN FOLDERS._

Salesperson _Ralph Eubanks_

Source: Courtesy of Ralph Eubanks, Roerig Division of Pfizer, from Porter Henry's *Secrets of the Selling Masters* © 1987, p. 80.

person simply outlines a brief plan of attack for the upcoming call to the doctor. This planner answers the "who" question: "Dr. Smith." It identifies the *specific* call objective: "Get Dr. Smith to put five Type II diabetics on _____ medicine for 6 weeks." It would designate, although it doesn't here, a specific product to present to Dr. Smith. The "when" and "where" questions were not needed for this call. The "why" question is addressed in the planner's middle section, along with the expected objections. In this type of selling, there is no direct business proposition because pharmaceutical salespeople do not transact any sales with physicians. That is done between the manufacturers and the drug wholesalers. Planners can be as detailed or brief as needed. Regardless of length, the call planner outlines the attack strategy, among other things, for each call.

Case in Point

How to Use Your Call Planner

S	*Stimulate attention* Gain the prospect's attention by asking questions relating to gain, need, pride, convenience, and security.
A	*Announce benefits* you believe prospect needs (see [s] above). • _____ • _____ • _____ • _____
L	*Look at product/service features* and *relate* features to benefits. • _____ • _____ • _____
E	*Establish proof* (Better to *understate* and *overprove!*) • _____ • _____ • _____ • _____
S	*Summarize and close* (Review previous steps and gain approval.) • _____ • _____ • _____ • _____ • _____ • _____

▶▶ *follow-up questions*

1. What benefits does a salesperson get from writing and using a sales call planner?

2. What constitutes your "deal"?

3. How would you use a value analysis and what would it include?

The Preapproach and Its Purpose

How the Preapproach Fits into the Selling Process

The **preapproach** is the transition between writing the call strategy out on the call planner form and making the presentation to the customer. The preapproach is applicable to any type of selling where obtaining an appointment and/or getting through a gatekeeper is necessary. This includes most industrial and many retail sales.

The preapproach should be thought of as a prelude to the actual presentation. It is really a minipresentation in itself. Salespeople must get an appointment with the customer. This can be a tough sale in itself! Just as persuading customers to buy requires a strategy, so does convincing prospective customers, or their gatekeepers, to give the salesperson an appointment. This may well set the tone for the entire relationship to come. The first contact establishes the first impression, and a good first impression can make the difference between a presentation that is a comfortable experience and one that is, at best, a tenuous encounter. The first contact also gives salespeople a first impression of the customers and how they do business. The customers may be predisposed toward the salespeople turned off by what transpires in the preapproach.

When Things Go Right

The Champagne-and-Book Approach

"As a sales rep for a major textbook publishing company, I was working on a large sale at one of my major universities," relates Arnis Burvikovs. "The book coordinator was a very particular guy who required that appointments be made well in advance and that the books have a very specific set of characteristics. Our book was a little late, and I was afraid he would make a decision without taking a close look at it. His secretary said he was all booked up but did give a general list of the criteria a book was required to have.

As it turned out, a few days later he was attending a local convention at which our company had a booth. I took a copy of the book and tabbed all of the spots where we met his requirements (and we did so thoroughly). I then tipped a room service waiter to deliver to the book coordinator that evening the book, along with a bottle of champagne, a note, and two glasses. As a result, we got the adoption, which was worth a large five-figure sale per year to us. Not getting to see him in his office may have been one of the best things that could have happened—but being in the right place at the right time with the right product always works."

Source: Arnis Burvikovs, West Educational Publishing Company, personal communication.

Purpose of the Preapproach

The purpose of the preapproach is two-fold: (1) to get the appointment to make the presentation and (2) to rehearse what you will say and how you will do your demonstration and arrange your visual material for the greatest impact. Gaining entry through gatekeepers is the first step.

◀ ◀ ◀ ◀ ◀ ◀ ◀ ◀

Learning Objective 5: The purpose of the preapproach.

Gatekeepers are secretaries, receptionists, or anyone that controls access to the customer. Everyone has dealt with a gatekeeper. In trying to get a date for Saturday night, you may have had to deal with a parental gatekeeper just to talk to your intended and ask for the date.

Purchasing agents and management executives are often protected by secretaries or receptionists who religiously guard them from a variety of salespeople. The secretary's job is to schedule appointments but also to do the preliminary screening, separating salespeople who have something of interest to the firm from those that do not. Gaining access to the right person is vital. Getting that all-important appointment can be done in a variety of ways.

Case in Point

Don't Let Corporate Screeners Interfere with Your Job

Corporate gatekeepers are skilled in screening unwanted or suspected time wasters, but they also have a responsibility to see that information about useful products and services gets through to their managers. Some tips for getting through the gatekepers are:

▸ Find out who makes the key decisions and how they are made.

▸ Get acquainted with decision makers by joining the same associations and professional organizations they belong to; in other words, get acquainted before you make the call so the customers will let you in while they keep strangers out.

▸ If they have internal news letters, ask if you could write a piece for it; this gives you a reason to make a noninvasive, nonthreatening contact.

▸ Talk to prospects' salespeople if they have them; they can be good clues to how to get in to see the boss.

Source: Excerpted from Lee Boyan, "Don't Let Screeners Interfere with Your Job—Meet Decision Makers on Your Terms," *Personal Selling Power,* 9 (1989): 12.

Getting the Appointment

The appointment is won by using one or more of four tools: (1) the phone, (2) letters, (3) "camping out," and (4) the unannounced cold call.

The phone   The phone is the most common vehicle in the preapproach. Tom Hopkins, noted author on selling techniques, offers some suggestions on the next page for using the phone to get the sales call scheduled and gather information for the planner.

How to Find Fortune and Felicity with the Phone[2]

Be professional when you phone. First, have a legitimate offer that you are knowledgeable about. Second, call only during reasonable hours. Third, be sure you are unfailingly polite. Fourth, bring any unfavorable call to a quick and courteous close. Fifth, put any unproductive call immediately out of your mind and move to the next. In the process of making the call to gather information and as a preapproach, do the following:

1. Use the prospects' name immediately.
2. Introduce yourself and your company.
3. State the purpose of your call and ask your first question.

Example: "I'm Stephanie Mangelson with Harbor Marina. We're contacting people who might be interested in trading in their old powerboats for a new Berkeley jet boat. Do you mind telling me whether you presently own a boat?"

4. Probe for more information: "How long have you owned it?" Ask what they like about their present product (the boat, in this case), and probe for what they are unhappy with.
5. Introduce the strong selling points of your product.

Examples: "Is your delivery truck getting 35 miles to the gallon?", "Is your present supplier giving you next-day delivery?"

6. Use the windup appointment close—as you wind up the survey, thank them for their help and ask if you can mail them a brochure on your model. If they agree, they must give you their address and all particulars. Use the fast delivery of your brochure as a way of getting to see the prospect.

Example: "After talking with you, Mr. Hammersmith, I feel that you have a need to know more about this and I'm excited about that. With your permission, I'd like to drop this off to you, rather than have you wait for the mail. I'll drop it by this afternoon."

Learning Objective 6: Developing a phone script to get an appointment for a sales call

There are seven things to remember about using the phone to make an appointment:

1. Use the KISS principle.
2. Prepare an opening statement.
3. Prepare fact-finding questions.
4. Prepare for initial objections.
5. Ask for the appointment.
6. Confirm the appointment.
7. Always express thanks.

Use the KISS principle The acronym KISS stands for Keep It Simple and Straightforward! Asking for an appointment should not be a 20-minute discourse, a complete presentation, the salesperson's life history, or a compendium of facts. It should be short and simple. The phone call should be planned in advance to accomplish this. Remember the person receiving the call is busy and you want to make a good impression from the very first. Use common sense—think of the questions the secretary or receptionist may raise when you call. For example:

- Who are you?
- Who do you work for?
- Why are you calling?
- Specifically, what do you want?
- Why should we give you an appointment?

When making the call, be direct and purposeful and in control. By all means be polite, courteous, and pleasant. Remember, you are creating the first impression, so watch your language.

Case in Point

Tips on Getting the Appointment over the Phone

There are numerous ways of getting an appointment over the phone. Here are several suggestions from Janis Drew of the *Los Angeles Times*:

- Call between 9 and 11 A.M. 3 and 5 P.M. If the prospects are not there, leave your name and a *specific time* when you will be calling back. Don't just say you'll call back later.
- Call as often as necessary to get through to the customers. Call back when you say you will. It won't usually take more than three calls before customers will take the call.
- Once prospects are on the phone, introduce yourself and your company. Give them a clear purpose for your call and never give the "yes-no choice" about the appointment; work with three possible choices for the appointment, not will they or won't they see you.
- Promise you will only take 10 to 15 minutes of their time, then keep your promise.

Source: Janis Drew, cited in Porter Henry, *Secrets of the Selling Masters* (New York: Amacom, American Management Association), p. 51.

Prepare an opening statement Begin to build your initial call strategy by starting with the opening statement. The opening statement should address some, if not all, of the questions above. The following is an opening statement you could use when the first call goes to a gatekeeper secretary:

Salesperson: Hello. My name is Lance Wilson with the Mississippi Tool and Die Company. I'm calling to make an appointment with Ms. Arnett for Thursday afternoon. Would she have half an hour free so I could stop by an meet with her, at, say, 3:00 or 4:00?

The secretary now knows who the salesperson is, who he works for, and the exact purpose for his call, and he has suggested a date and tentative time. Note the question was not phrased so the gatekeeper had a "yes-no" option. Compare that with the following:

Salesperson: Hi. Is Ms. Arnett there?

Hearing this, the secretary must ask the questions listed above. Or:

Salesperson: Hi. Is Ms. Arnett there? I need to schedule a meeting with her at her convenience.

Ms. Arnett may have more convenient times than others. She may see salespeople only on Mondays. The salesperson may get an appointment for Wednesday, only to get there, be discovered to be a salesperson, and be told to come back on Monday. The salesperson has not been specific and has allowed the secretary to control the first encounter. The secretary has no idea who is calling, the firm the caller represents, or the reason for the request. Some friendly, ice-breaking conversation is always good if this is not the first time the salesperson has called for an appointment.

Regardless, however, of whether this is the first or hundredth time, courtesy, friendliness and getting to the point is always appreciated. If this call is the result of a referral, mentioning the name of the referrer as part of the opening statement is a good idea. We would modify our previous example of an opening statement as follows:

Salesperson: Hello. My name is Lance Wilson with the Mississippi Tool and Die Company. I'm calling to make an appointment with Ms. Arnett for Thursday afternoon, if possible. Henry Claven of Southern Distributors suggested I call to make an appointment with Ms. Arnett. Henry and I have done business together for several years, and he thought Ms. Arnett would be interested in our products. Would she have half an hour free so I could stop by and meet with her on Thursday, the sixteenth at 3:00 or 4:00?

If our salesperson were talking directly to Ms. Arnett, the above opening statement could be modified to be:

Salesperson: Hello, Ms. Arnett, my name is Lance Wilson with the Mississippi Tool and Die Company. Henry Claven of Southern Distributors suggested I call to make an appointment to see you. Henry and I have done business together for several years, and he thought you would be interested in our products. Would you have half an hour free to meet with me on Thursday afternoon at 3:00 or 4:00, whichever would work best for you?

Ms. Arnett has just received enough pertinent information to answer her initial questions.

When preparing an opening statement, using an interest-creating question is good idea. Many telemarketing sales agents use this technique when doing scripted presentations. An interest-creating question would be like:

Salesperson: I have noticed your construction workers using Schulmberger drilling equipment. Would you be interested in making that equipment more reliable and cutting its operating cost by 15 percent?

An interest-creating opening statement doesn't need to be long. It should focus on product benefits but could be directed toward features or advantages. Using benefits gives you ample room for creativity, and since you know your prospective customer through the account or customer profile you created, targeting the appropriate benefits should be easy.

Prepare fact-finding questions   Be prepared with fact-finding questions during this initial call. Although you may be talking to secretaries or receptionists, do not underestimate the amount of factual information they have. The facts could be of a personal nature:

Salesperson: How long has Ms. Arnett been the buyer for ABC Electric?

or

Salesperson: Is this the office that takes quotes on pneumatic equipment?

or

Salesperson: I'd like to make a presentation to your company about our X-37 postal meter. Is there a specific day the buyer sees salespeople?

You may think this will annoy secretaries or buyers by taking too much of their time. Quite the contrary. The key to success at this point is to ask only a few fact-finding questions and make them quickly and easily answered. Don't ask questions the person is not readily prepared to answer. Remember, the preapproach is like a minipresentation. After making the opening statement and asking brief fact-finding questions, be prepared to meet initial resistance in the form of objections.

Prepare for initial objections Salespeople commonly encounter resistance at this point. The busy buyer is naturally skeptical about the value of seeing another salesperson. You should expect to encounter objections. Think about how you would deal with statements like the following if you were selling for a paper wholesaler.

- ▶ "We already have enough paper vendors supplying us now."
- ▶ "We are in the process of reducing the number of vendors we deal with."
- ▶ "I don't think we need another paper vendor."
- ▶ "We just authorized a new paper vendor. We don't need another new one."
- ▶ "Ms. Binda has left word to tell inquiring salespeople that we are not in the market for paper at this time."
- ▶ "Why don't you call us again in several weeks?"
- ▶ "I'd really like to see you, but we have meetings until the middle of next week, then I'm not sure what we will be able to do."
- ▶ "Before I schedule any appointments, I must clear it with Mr. Latimer."
- ▶ "I'm awfully busy. Why don't you call me again at a later date."
- ▶ "I'd like to see you. Why don't you call me back later and maybe we can set something up. But call my secretary, she schedules all my appointments."
- ▶ "We can't afford to take on another vendor now."
- ▶ "I know what you guys charge, and it's more than we can afford."

Clearly, these objections can be tough to overcome. However, they are typical of what you will hear and should expect. You do not want to anger the prospect or gatekeeper, nor do you want to do anything else to create a bad impression. There are several approaches to dealing with objections. Try the following steps:

Step 1: Acknowledge the objection

Step 2: Reverse it, if possible, to be a reason *to* schedule the appointment

Step 3: Move the prospect away from the objection

Step 4: Ask for the appointment

Let's illustrate using these steps in the following conversation:

Salesperson: Hello. My name is Lance Wilson with the Mississippi Tool and Die Company. I'm calling to make an appointment with Ms. Arnett for Thursday afternoon, if possible. Henry Claven of Southern Distributors suggested I call to make an appointment with Ms. Arnett. Henry and I have done business together for several years, and he thought Ms. Arnett would be interested in our products. Would she have half an hour free so I could stop by and meet with her?

Secretary: Ms. Arnett is really too busy to see salespeople this week. Why don't you call back at a later date?

Salesperson: I know she is busy *(acknowledges objection)* and that's why efficiency in getting things done are important to her. That's one of the traits Henry spoke of. In fact, that's specifically why he suggested I talk with her *(reverses objection to be a reason to schedule the appointment)*. Henry's secretary said the same thing, but because I was able to meet with him, I reduced his order processing time by 20 percent, saving him money and his secretary a lot of typing time and headaches. Do you think Ms. Arnett would like to save 20 percent? I'd certainly like to offer my services to both of you. Would a Wednesday meeting be better than Thursday afternoon *(attempts to close on the meeting day)*?

In this scenario, the salesperson used all four steps while still maintaining control, and he did so in a pleasant, polite, and courteous manner. Dealing with objections to scheduling the appointment in this manner will not always work. Nothing works perfectly with every prospect every time. However, by keeping those steps in mind, and with practice, salespeople can develop effective means of handling these objections that fit their personal style and what they have to sell.

Ask for the appointment   Remember why you called—to ask for an appointment. Don't forget to do that! You may want to suggest a meeting time, as in our examples above, or you may get what you are given. In asking for the appointment, it is better to probe for alternative possibilities than asking for a "generic" appointment and getting whatever the secretary assigns. For example, which of the following gives the secretary more chances to deny the request for an appointment?

Salesperson: I would like to get in to see Mr. Holzman. What appointment times are possible?

or

Salesperson: I would like to see Mr. Holzman early next week. Would 10 A.M. Tuesday be possible, or would 9:00 on Wednesday be better?

Always ask for the appointment!

Confirm the appointment   To avoid mistakes, confirm the appointment before hanging up. Repeat the meeting particulars to the prospect or gatekeeper. Confirm the time, date, location, and persons who will be in attendance. Be sure to write this down! Confirmation should be followed up by a reminder call the day before the meeting. Things change, and sometimes prospects forget to tell secretaries to reschedule appointments. It is just good practice to call a day ahead to double check that the meeting is still on and ask about any changes that may have occurred.

Always express thanks Finally, always express your thanks for the appointment. It is only simple courtesy but often overlooked. Forgetting to thank the prospect or secretary for scheduling the meeting is the quickest way to get off to a bad start.

Letters Letters are an effective way of efficiently contacting many prospects at once. Letters are often used to make the first contact with prospects and are often the first step to scheduling an appointment. Salespeople use several types of letters. One is the lead letter.

Learning Objective 7: How to write a letter to get an appointment for a sales presentation

Lead letters are part of a direct-marketing strategy used to stimulate a prospect to make an inquiry call to salespeople so they can make the sale or schedule a presentation. The purpose of the lead letter is to stimulate interest. It should focus on the product's benefits. Lead letter may be long or short; salespeople should test different letters and determine which works best. Since letters are so inexpensive to do, the cost-benefit ratio is very favorable. Salespeople using adequately prepared and up-to-date customer profiles can create several versions of a lead letter, each customized to a set of prospects with the same general needs.

The lead letter should answer the same questions the phone call does. It is crucial that the letter be clear and concise. With a phone call, the salesperson has a chance to listen and react to the prospect, to clear up any confusion, and to expand on points of interest to the prospect. With a letter, there is no chance for personal interaction, so it must be complete. It must answer the questions that will occur to the reader.

The letter should tell prospects exactly what to do after they have read the letter:

▸ "Call this number for more information."

▸ "Mark the box beside the product you are interested in."

▸ "Return the enclosed card before December 25."

If you plan to call as a follow-up to the letter, say so. If your secretary will be calling the prospect's secretary, say so. Never leave prospects wondering what this letter wants them to do.

Personalize the letter if at all possible. The chances of getting an appointment, or any response, increase tremendously when the letter is personalized with the recipient's name, firm, and address. What would be your impression of a salesperson sending you a letter starting with "Dear M/s/r/rs. Buyer"? Personalization is easily done with most computer word processing programs. In these, information from the customer profile is merged with letter templates, and in an instant, personalized letters are on their way.

The Fine Art of Writing a Sales Letter[3]

Eight of the most common mistakes in writing a sales letter are:

1. Not focusing on your main point. Its easy to forget what you want the letter to achieve.
2. Not writing the letter from the reader's point of view. Readers aren't interested in you or your point of view as much as what they and their company need.
3. Not stressing benefits.
4. Not making the letter eye-catching and easy to read. People are bombarded with mail, so keep it brief.
5. Not creating an attention-grabbing beginning.
6. Not including a P.S. That little addendum is the most often read part of the letter.
7. Not creating the right image.
8. Not following up; it is a must.

Sending the letter via an attention-getting priority or express mail service can be very effective. While it is expensive—costing from $8 to $20 per letter—this technique does get the prospective buyer's attention. Both the urgent status automatically attached to such a letter and the curiosity on the receiver's part guarantee this approach will garner immediate attention to your letter.

Letters of introduction are useful in the preapproach. They are written by a third party to the prospect introducing the salesperson or advising the prospect that the salesperson will be calling. A letter of introduction does not

Using a priority mail service can be very effective in getting your prospect's attention.

guarantee a sale, however. Depending on who writes the letter and the prospect's respect for that person, the letter of introduction can be a very powerful door opener.

The "letter-phone combo" approach uses all of the techniques already explained. When using this combination, timing is important. Pay careful attention to when the letter is mailed, when it will likely be received, and when the follow-up phone call should be made.

The letter-phone combo affords salespeople several advantages over using just one or the other. First, the letter goes directly to the addressee, the key person they want to talk to. This means not having to thread their way through the maze of gatekeepers. Second, the letter allows salespeople to briefly present a message about a product or service written directly to the reader. This can be customized for each prospective client. The follow-up phone call is a way of checking to see if prospects have any questions. Third, the combination gives double exposure to the company, the product, and the salesperson before the appointment is even set.[4]

Camping out   Camping out is an inefficient method of getting an appointment. It is mentioned here only because it is used by some salespeople. Camping out means literally waiting in prospects' offices until they will see you. It is a war-of-nerves approach, the strategy being that you will eventually make the prospect tired of seeing you there and grant the meeting. This is not the best way to make a good first impression and can be very costly in terms of opportunities missed while you are camped out. It is a last-resort technique.

The unannounced cold call   The unannounced cold call is simply appearing at the prospect's location and asking to see the prospect. This is a common practice in many selling situations. Often prospects allow salespeople to make presentations without formally arranging them in advance. Using the unannounced call may not get the salesperson an immediate entrance, but it can be productive for scheduling appointments or for leaving samples. Many

◄ ◄ ◄ ◄ ◄ ◄ ◄ ◄
Learning Objective 8: The unannounced cold call needs to be planned like any other

When Things Go Wrong

A rep had been trying to reach the chief operating officer of a company to begin the process of selling a number of electronic components. The rep had tried everything he could think of to get to see this executive. Letters didn't seem to go anywhere and the phone always led him to an impenetrable secretary. There were internal obstacles everywhere. Finally, he had a brainstorm. He decided to park in the executive's parking space. He reasoned, if he got there early, he would park in the space, then the officer would come to work and ask the sales rep to move his car. A conversation would follow, the rep would feign ignorance of the ownership of the parking space, and this would turn into the entree to a presentation.

As it turned out, the executive saw someone in his place and notified his security staff, who then had the rep escorted off the premises and his car towed.

Source: Arnis Burvikovs, West Educational Publishing Company, Personal Communication, June, 1991.

Salespeople use unannounced cold calls to gather information as well as sell their products.

salespeople prefer the unannounced call because secretaries and prospects find it easier to say no over the phone than in person.

In summary, the four vehicles discussed are part of the adaptive salesperson's repertoire of preapproach techniques. Using them singly or in combination is dictated by the salesperson's selling situation and knowledge of customers and the customs dictated by buyer-seller relationship.

Rehearsal

▶ ▶ ▶ ▶ ▶ ▶ ▶ ▶ ▷

Learning Objective 9: Practice and rehearsal sharpens the impression you make on that first call

The final activity in the preapproach is rehearsal. No actor ever goes on stage without a rehearsal, and no salesperson should enter a presentation without one. This rehearsal ranges from a formal run-through using another member of the sales staff as a surrogate buyer to something as simple as mentally rehearsing a few minutes before the meeting what will be said and done.

Appearance The rehearsal should include a review of your appearance. How are you dressed? Is everything in order? Small things make big impressions. Not only should you take a last look at yourself but also the products you intend to show the prospect. A beat-up demonstration model will not

What Would You Do If...?

On Monday morning, your sales manager comes into your office. She says, "I want you to start calling on Sears, Roebuck. Our new line of women's and girl's jeans is not being carried by Sears, in fact, they are not carrying any of our jeans. I think if we can open the door with our women's and girl's lines, we can also get the others in! I'll work with you on this. We need to prepare for a big presentation, so you'd better get started now!"

You're thinking, "What does she want, and how in the world will I get the information she'll probably need?"

▶ Question: What would you do?

What Would You Do If...?

It's Thursday afternoon and you are making your phone calls to schedule appointments to make your presentations for the following week. You dial up the Western Plumbing Supply, and the receptionist answers the phone. After asking to speak to Mr. Simon, you are connected with his secretary. Having never called on this account before, you introduce yourself. The secretary indicates Simon is not interested in seeing salespeople. Her attitude is far less than congenial. You know Simon sees salespeople, but for some reason, she is being particularly difficult. You begin to think of what you can say to win her over and get the appointment. You also begin to hatch plans to get your message to Simon without going through her.

▶ Question: What will you do to get past this obstacle?

make a favorable impression. Always take a new model or fresh sample along, if at all possible.

Manners and customs   Rehearse your manners. How will you greet the prospect? Referring to your customer profile and call planner are the best ways to refresh your memory on this. If you are involved with foreign customers, research and rehearse the appropriate manners and customs of their culture. For example, when meeting prospects from the Far East, do you bow first, do they bow first, how long should this go on? Is it proper to shake hands or offer your business card first, and is a business card essential? Knowing the manners and customs of the prospect's culture can mean the difference between closing and losing a sale.

Check your attention-getters   Next in the rehearsal process is double-checking your attention-getters. If you are going to use visuals, make sure they are large enough, but not too large, for the space you will be working in. If your presentation will be in the prospect's office but confined to the desk, a three-foot-square conference pad will not work. Make certain the visuals are not overcrowded with information and they are arranged in order. Nothing disorganizes and disrupts a presentation more than a salesperson who keeps sorting and fishing for the right visual.

Test product demonstrations before the presentation. *Be sure they work and do what you say they will do.* Plan for all contingencies when doing demonstrations. This is only common sense, because as soon as you assume the batteries are good, they will fizzle out.

A customer tests new software at a computer shop.

▶ ▶ *follow-up questions*

1. Why is part of the preapproach like a mini-sales presentation?

2. Why would a salesperson start dealing with an objection by acknowledging it?

3. What are the benefits of using the priority mail technique in the preapproach?

Summary

In this chapter, the creation and uses of a call planner and the steps of the preapproach were considered. The account profile was discussed as the basis of information for a call planner. The planner is a summary of pertinent information a salesperson reviews before making a presentation. Call planners are call specific: they are brief summaries of what the salesperson is going to do during the presentation and of the parts of the account profile that are particularly relevant to the call. While an account profile contains both general and specific information about the customer or account, the call planner uses only information that is necessary for the call (Learning Objective 1).

Call planners make salespeople better prepared for the sales call and more efficient when making the call (Learning Objective 2). This bolsters salespeople's self-confidence. As a result of all this, call planners build customer confidence in salespeople who use them. Planners prepare salespeople to address the traditional who, what, when, where, and why questions.

The "who" question identifies the customer-participants in the sales call and what roles they play. The planner can address strategies to use on these people as a group and/or as individuals. The "what" question is answered in the planner by specifying the product(s) the salesperson plans to showcase during the presentation. The "when" question deals with the time details surrounding the presentation, such as the time, date, and duration of the appointment, or the order-cycle time. The answer to the "where" question centers on such details as the site of the presentation and the locations of warehouses, receiving plants, or stores.

The "why" question identifies the benefits that will be stressed during the presentation and the anticipated objections. It may also focus on a usage or resale plan for the customer. If the customer were to buy the product for her own use, the salesperson would want to be prepared to offer creative applications for the product. If it were being sold to a reseller, then the call planner would identify suggestions the salesperson would offer on how to better sell the product to the prospect's customers (Learning Objectives 3 and 4).

Preapproach is an important precall activity. The emphasis of the preapproach is on getting an appointment to make a presentation, then rehearsing for it. The techniques for getting the appointment revolve around preparing to make a mini-sales presentation to either the gatekeeper or the prospect. The purpose of this minipresentation is to close the person on the appointment. Just as in the full presentation itself, the process here involves preparing an opening statement, doing fact-finding, dealing with initial objections, then asking for the appointment (Learning Objective 5).

An appointment for a sales presentation can be obtained in a number of ways; the most frequent is by using the telephone. When using the phone, the salesperson should have a brief script in mind, one that amounts to a minipresentation in itself. It should answer the buyer's or gatekeeper's fundamental questions about the salesperson, the product, and the firm (Learning Objective 6). Letters can also get appointments and often are used in conjunction with the phone call (Learning Objective 7). Some people use the camping out approach to getting in to see the prospective customer, but it is not very productive or economical. Still others use the unannounced cold call. One of the oldest approaches to getting in to see the prospect, it gets mixed results. It takes a salesperson who has a well-rehearsed and well-thought-out approach to both the appointment and making the sales presentation. Although most buyers would rather have a salesperson make an appointment than a cold call, a seasoned veteran can use this technique effectively (Learning Objective 8).

Finally, all presentations and preapproach activities should be well practiced and rehearsed before they are used with a real customer. They should be rehearsed so their delivery is natural. Rehearsal should be structured to prepare the salesperson for any questions, objections, or conditions the buyer or gatekeeper could raise before agreeing to grant a sales call appointment (Learning Objective 9).

Key Terms

Call planner A brief summary of information about the customer and an outline of the selling techniques the salesperson will use during the presentation.

End-use or resale plan A strategy to help customers resell or use the product.

Blueprinting or floor-planning Merchandising plans offered by manufacturers or wholesalers to their customers that diagram the exact positioning of products in sales floor displays and how much product is needed in these displays.

Spiffs Inducements to purchase.

Preapproach The activities undertaken just prior to making the presentation, for example, scheduling the appointment, rehearsing, and testing the samples or demonstration.

Gatekeepers Anyone who controls or influences access to the key players in the buying decision.

Buying criterion The requirements or guidelines setting the standards which must be met to consummate the sale.

Value analysis Usually financial in nature, the value analysis is a comparison between the salesperson's product and the competitor's to illustrate the competitive advantage and justify the price asked.

KISS An acronym which stands for the words Keep It Simple and Straightforward.

Lead letters Letters used to encourage prospective buyers to make an inquiry call to the salespeople so they can schedule a meeting or presentation.

Discussion Questions

1. To be adequately prepared for a sales presentation, what should salespeople include in their planner?

2. How does a planner help salespeople make more efficient sales calls?

3. What is cross-selling, and why should it be part of a precall plan?

4. What are the five questions inherent in a call planner?

5. If you were going to make a call on your school's purchasing agent for computer paper, which of the "who" questions would you want answered before you got to the appointment? How would you get those answers? What are the "when" and "where" questions you would want answered?

6. What is an account profile, and why is it so valuable to salespeople and their firms?

7. What are the elements that constitute your "deal" to the customer?

8. Why should a planner include anticipated objections?

9. How does having used a planner build the buyer's confidence in the salesperson?

10. If you were going to make a presentation to a department store, hoping it would buy your brand of jeans, what would be some of the "who" questions you would consider answering in your call planner?

11. How would you do a value analysis, and what would you include in it?

12. What are the objections you might expect a gatekeeper to raise when you are trying to schedule an appointment?

13. How can salespeople make effective use of lead letters to make contacts and get appointments?

14. How would the Nabisco cookie salesperson use blueprinting or floor-planning?

15. What is the central purpose of the preapproach?

16. What would you do to get around a gatekeeper to your school's purchasing agent?

17. List the seven things to remember in using the phone to get an appointment.

18. What are some typical attention-getters a salesperson might use in a presentation?

Application Exercise

Reread the Case in Point about how Eastman Kodak salesperson Larry Nonnamaker plans a call, then answer the following questions:

1. Is the process Larry goes through transferrable to other selling situations, or is it just unique to his type of selling?

2. What type of information would Larry need to complete his call plan?

3. Suppose you were the manufacturer's rep for Levi Strauss, selling jeans to your local hometown department store. How would you use Larry Nonnamaker's process in your selling situation?

Class Exercises

Group Exercise

One of the major challenges for a salesperson is to bridge the gap between call planning and the actual presentation to the customer.

In small groups of two to four students, develop a script for a role play that will demonstrate *two* of the *four* following vehicles (use the phone plus one other) for getting the appointment for a potential sale: 1) letters, 2) camping out, and 3) cold calling.

You will be selling an office cleaning service to the manager of a building complex that has 100 offices and two large lobbies. The building manager has a secretary and an office services coordinator.

Each written set of role plays will be placed in a box from which the instructor will select *two* for presentation to the class.

1. Critique the effectiveness of both the script and the presenters. (Would they get the appointment from you?)

2. Is there *one* best vehicle in those listed above for getting an appointment? Why or why not?

3. Are there alternatives to those vehicles above? Be creative and try to think of as many as you can. There could be very different ones for different situations.

Individual Presentations

You have recently ordered, through a major distributor of cutting instruments, the Ajax knife, a highly researched product of quality steel that is self-sharpening. Its primary assets are durability and versatility. Its uses include cutting rope and heavy twine, leather crafting, fishing, camping, carving, and food preparation. In addition, it is economically priced.

Once you decide this product is salable, you plan to purchase 500 units to be sold to local hardware stores, craft shops, and individual friends and classmates. Assume you have chosen to visit craft shops first:

1. Construct a sales call planner for this task.

2. Explain how this sales call planner helps focus on product benefits important to the customer (shop owner) and to the end user (the craft shop's customers.)

▼ ▼ ▼ ▼ ▼ ▼ *Cases* ▼ ▼ ▼ ▼ ▼ ▼

How to Cut through a Diamond

Lorraine Lundstrom works for Mid-States Pharmaceuticals. Mid-States is a purveyor of "ethical drugs," that is, drugs that require a physician's prescription. It primarily makes drugs for the "cough and cold" market, including a variety of antihistamines, analgesics, and fever reducers. It is a seasonal business that, in some areas, peaks during November through March.

Lorraine has been calling on the Central City Allergy and Respiratory Clinic for several years. The clinic is a privately held corporation owned by a group of 15 physicians. Lorraine has been calling on Doctors Zikmund and Alexander, two principals in the group. About a month ago, the clinic replaced its receptionist with Ann Diamond. Ann has apparently taken it upon herself to prevent all salespeople from seeing the doctors. Lorraine has been discussing this new development with Jim Johannson, her sales manager.

"Jim, this woman is the Genghis Khan of receptionists! Getting past her is like trying to leap the Great Wall of China. When I call to get an appointment, I get roadblocks: 'The doctors are busy, please call again,' 'The doctors are not taking calls', 'I'll tell them you called, and I'm sure they'll get back to you." Jim thought about it as he listened to her tale of woe. He said, "It sounds like you've got a real stonewaller on your hands."

Lorraine said, "I know if I can get to see these physicians, everything will be okay. They may not even know she's doing this! I'm concerned: if I get to see them, do I tell them what a jerk their receptionist is being? All I would need would be to have Zikmund say, 'Oh, you mean my sister-in-law?' or something like that!"

Jim said, "Calm down. First, let's work on getting you in, then we can worry about what to tell the doctors."

Questions:

1. If you were Jim, what would you suggest and why?

2. Should Lorraine tell the doctors about their receptionist's behavior? Why or why not?

Making Jocko More Efficient

Jocko Mayer was a football star at the state university and is very well known in the city and surrounding area. Jocko is a missionary salesman for Z & Z Distributing, the local distributor for Buddies, Coos, and Mauler beers. Even though

Jocko doesn't write any sales orders himself, he still has a sales quota to meet. The idea is that if he's been doing his job, tavern and restaurant owners will be promoting Z & Z's brands and sales will go up.

Jocko hasn't been doing so well lately. His manager has told him to call on more accounts during the day, which means spending less time with each. The manager has been pressuring Jocko to call on new accounts, ones that have either never done business with Z & Z or are inactive customers. Jocko figures he's going to have to be more efficient in calling on his existing accounts and have his calls planned better when he calls on the new and inactive ones. He's never done a call planner before, but he has read about them and seen examples. Jocko has come to you for advice.

"I need to spend less time at each call. You know how the manager has been down on me lately about needing to make more calls per day. She suggests I use a call planner to get better organized. Can you help me out? I need something that is brief, quick, and easy to use, something I can get on a three-by-five card. What should I have on it to give me exactly what I need to know and no more?"

Question:

1. How would you help Jocko?

References

1. Adapted from James E. Lukaszewski and Paul Ridgeway, "To Put Your Best Foot Forward, Start by Taking These 21 Simple Steps," *Sales and Marketing Management,* 142 (1990): 84.
2. Tom Hopkins, *How to Master the Art of Selling* (New York: Warner Books, 1982), pp. 132–36.
3. Linda Lynton, "The Fine Art of Writing a Sales Letter," *Sales and Marketing Management,* 140 (1988): 51–55.
4. Adapted from Porter Henry, *Secrets of the Selling Masters* (New York: AMACOM, American Management Association, 1987), p. 51.

III

Making A Successful Sale

9 Making the Presentation, Part I: Presentation Formats and Openings

Objectives

After completing this chapter, you will be able to:

1. Identify the stages of the purchase decision.

2. Define the basic structure of the sales call in relationship to:
   ▸ Functional steps
   ▸ Message conveyed
   ▸ Information gathered.

3. Link the buying process (hierarchy of effects) to the structure of a sales call.

4. Identify and explain the four types of presentations salespeople can use along with the situations best fitting each.

5. Compare and contrast the advantages and disadvantages of each of the four presentation methods.

6. Incorporate the "4-P's" of a presentation into the structure of a sales call.

7. Select any of ten ways to successfully open a sales call.

The Professional Selling Question

Making a presentation to a customer or prospective customer is the heart of selling. What are the secrets of a good presentation?

Sales Experts Respond

Making a successful presentation is not easy because both the customer and the salesperson have inherent fears. The customer fears making a wrong decision and having to pay the price for it. The salesperson fears rejection. Presenting a product or service can be made easier if several basic ideas are kept in mind. These come from two sales experts: Arnold L. Schwartz, owner and president of a sales training firm, and Gerry Marx, head of Gamma Presentations. Both specialize in sales training and communications.

Marx offers the following advice on developing persuasive messages. He recommends salespeople take a sincere interest in their clients' position. He says that customers' needs generally fall into three areas: financial, performance, and image. To be persuasive during a presentation, the salesperson must address the area most important to the customer. He also recommends salespeople understand customers' marketing mission. They may be buying for resale or use in a product they make, so salespeople must address during the presentation how their product will fit into their customers' mission. Marx feels the good presentation includes communicating a good understanding of the client's position and providing an option analysis (what the client stands to gain or lose as a result of the buying decision).

Arnold Schwartz says that a sale is a combination of satisfying both an emotional and a rational need. He says that, all things being equal, the salesperson who can fulfill the emotional or psychological need in the buyer will get the business. Schwartz feels a presentation must build trust and eliminate feelings of threat or defensiveness. He feels that complimentary openings are particularly useful as long as they are sincere and not plastic. He says feelings of trust and rapport are cemented in a presentation if salespeople exhibit their product knowledge within the context of the customer's unique buying situation. Above all, he says, salespeople must not knock the competition.

Regardless of which presentation style salespeople use, they are still dealing with another person at the receiving end. This person has feelings as well as rational buying needs. The presentation is the vehicle that delivers the message about the salesperson's concern for the customer. All presentation styles should include concern for both the customer's rational and emotional needs.[1]

Introduction

"Am I ready to do this? I think I have done everything I can to prepare for this presentation. Now, I must decide how I want to go about actually making the presentation. There are so many alternatives to consider. Which one is best?" Janet is getting ready to make a presentation to a prospective customer. She must do a good job to make the sale. As a new salesperson, she realizes that watching the pros and reading the books can only do so much. She thinks she is ready. She is if she has done her homework well.

Now there is one last decision to make—how to construct the presentation. Ivan, her mentor, offers the following suggestion: "I start by planning my opening. I usually use a complimentary opener, followed by a question. I try to get the prospect involved and focused early on. The presentation style that works best for me is need-satisfaction. I find the formula approach tough to manage. Sometimes, I just try to keep the chitchat to a minimum, offer my best shot, and give customers a couple of alternatives. I called on a real amiable guy yesterday and ended up walking him through the decision. It all depends on who you are dealing with. Stick to your product benefits and use plenty of trial closes to test the water. Watch your words—the customer will! Stay calm and do not worry, it's not that tough. Talk to me after the presentation and tell me how it goes."

This conversation could be taking place in any office between a novice and an experienced salesperson. Ivan is well trained in adaptive selling, and Janet is on her way. She is overcome with all the choices, but Ivan seems to have mastered it, and she believes she can, too. Adaptive selling techniques are for every salesperson selling anything.

In this chapter, the adaptive selling tools for opening the presentation will be introduced. We will start by discussing the purpose of presentations in general, then go on to the four presentation formats. From there, you will learn at least ten ways of opening a presentation. After reading this chapter, you should be able to determine which presentation format is best for your situation and which opening fits your personality, selling style, and challenge.

Purpose of the Presentation

A sales call can have many purposes. A call is not always made to make a direct sale, but it is always sales-related. Here, we want to focus on the sales call where the purpose *is* to make a sale.

A purpose of the presentation is to convey information. This information should ultimately lead to persuading the prospect to start buying or the current customer to continue buying. A sales presentation is not a series of random events; rather, it is an orchestrated and structured conversation that doesn't appear so. Successful salespeople are aware of the steps they are taking. The prospect should see the presentation as a discussion flowing from one topic to the next. The appropriate bridges and transitions carry the conversation from a definite beginning, through a contextual body, to a conclusion requiring an action.

A presentation that just starts, goes on, then abruptly stops confuses prospects. Think of it like a movie: it has a beginning that sets the stage and gets the audience into it, a plot and character development, and a conclusion that resolves the story. If the movie is done well, you can follow the story and know where it is headed. If it isn't and you're left wondering "What was that all about?", then you know the feeling you want to avoid giving your customer after the presentation. You want the presentation to link the buying and selling processes so the latter tracks the path of the former.

Linking the Buying Process to Making the Sale

▶ ▶ ▶ ▶ ▶ ▶ ▶ ▶ ▶ ▶

Learning Objective 1: Stages
in the buying decision

In the buying process, the prospect arrives at a purchase decision through what is called a **hierarchy of effects.** The hierarchy of effects means a lower-level activity is a precursor to the next activity. For example, you notice a problem, that is, you get hungry at noon. That problem causes you to increase your knowledge of eating places (you search for a place to eat). From that beginning (hunger), you eventually end up eating lunch. The hierarchy of effect for most purchase decisions follows the path shown in Figure 9-1.

The sales presentation should track along the stages customers follow in deciding to buy. The presentation should start by getting their attention. Capturing their attention is easier if they see the product as a solution to a current problem, if it appears to prevent a problem they think they might have, or if they perceive they would be better off with it than without it.

Sales presentations should develop and enhance the customers' interest. This is done by enhancing their knowledge about their own situation, the salesperson's product, the competitor's product, and why the salesperson's is better than the competitor's. As customers are convinced that the salesperson's product *is* a better alternative, they move into the liking and preference stages. With their desire for the product developing, they move through the conviction stage to the final stage, action. Now the salesperson closes the sale, the customer makes the purchase, and both sides are better off now than when they started.

Figure 9-1 **The Hierarchy of Effects**

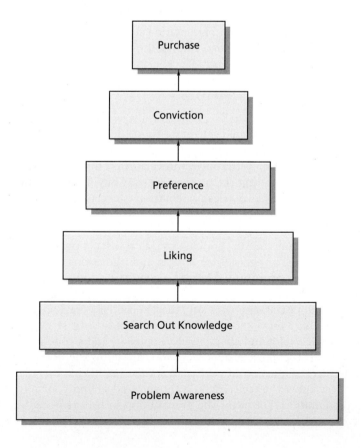

Customers are sometimes presold, so the salesperson needs only to close the sale.

Not all presentations follow this route, however. Some customers are presold, that is, they already want the product, so the salesperson needs only close the sale. Others are not so far along. Customers may be shopping—aware and interested but not convinced whose product is right for them. An adaptive salesperson's job is to determine the prospect's level or stage in the hierarchy. Once determined, the salesperson develops the presentation from there. Sales calls are structured around the hierarchy of effects—some start at lower levels than others, some at higher levels. Figure 9-2 illustrates the basic structure of all sales calls.

◀ ◀ ◀ ◀ ◀ ◀ ◀ ◀

Learning Objective 2: The structure of a sales call

During Steps 1 through 3, the salesperson develops an awareness and knowledge of the prospect's problem. In Step 4, the prospect and the salesperson mutually agree on what needs to be accomplished. The salesperson offers alternative solutions in Step 5. During Step 6, the salesperson must prove the product benefit claims. The customer needs to be convinced that the product will do what the salesperson says and that it really is better than a competitor's offering. By now, the prospect should be moving through the liking and into the preference stage if the presentation is going well.

By Step 7, the salesperson should have explained all of the product's features, advantages, and benefits. It is time to test the buyer's degree of preference and conviction. At this point, the trial close gauges the salesperson's degree of progress in the selling process and the buyer's degree of advancement toward being convinced enough to purchase. If the buyer has been convinced, he or she will authorize the purchase. If there are further questions, misunderstandings, or disbelief of the salesperson's claims, these will surface as objections (Step 8).

Step 9 involves handling those objections. At this point, the salesperson must correct any misunderstanding or overcome the objections. This can be done by showing customers that their concerns are not justified or they have incorrect information. This is also where the salesperson will be negotiating terms and making deals to overcome price objections. If it appears that objections have been successfully overcome, it is time once again to test the

Figure 9-2 **The Structure of a Sales Call**

Functional Steps	Message Conveyed	Information
1. Opening statement	—Who you are —Why you are here —Why should they listen	—Attitude —Circumstance
2. Overview (big picture)	—Discussion framework —Your product's capabilities	—Are they prospects?
3. Needs identification	—You are interested in them —What are their ideas? —You and they prioritize needs	—What are their needs? —Are they capable of buying? —What/why could they buy? —Will they buy?
4. Net out	—You listened and understood —You want to understand	—Do they understand? —Do you understand?
5. Presentation of benefits	—You want to solve the problem —You have the answer	—What specifically solves their problem? —What do they gain?
6. Support benefits with features and advantages	—You can prove the benefits are valid —Here are features that support the claim —You can show them that yours is better than theirs —You have proof —Are other features important, too?	—Does this support your claim? —Is this a needed attribute? —Is it significantly better? —Is your proof believable? —Customers' needs are broader than you thought
7. Trial close	—Are they ready to buy? —Does your product fill their needs? —Uncover objections —Trigger questions	—In commitment stage yet? —Are there hidden needs they haven't divulged? —What don't they like? —What haven't you answered?

Continued

waters, that is, do another trial close (Step 10). If there are no more objections, it is time to close the sale and start the paperwork to officially conclude the exchange.

The close, Step 11, occurs when the prospect believes purchasing is the right decision. With a retail sale, this would be as simple as filling out a sales slip or ringing up the sale. For an industrial sale or commercial sale, this is usually signaled by the buyer assigning a purchase order number for the salesperson's sales invoice.

The last and most important step is Step 12, the follow-up activities. This is the most important part of the selling process because the whole buyer-seller interaction should be looked upon as the start, or continuation, of a long-term relationship. Follow-up activity, or the lack of it, means the difference between the sale being a one-time encounter or a life-long interdependence. Failure to follow up is a major reason for buyers switching vendors. The follow-up can be as simple as checking to see if everything arrived on time, if there are other questions, or if the product is performing as promised.

Figure 9-2—*Continued*

Functional Steps	Message Conveyed	Information
8. Objections	—What is not clear? —What keeps them from authorizing the deal?	—Have you explained well enough? —Price too high? —Stalling for some reason? —Have you adequately established a need for the product? —Is there a hidden objection you don't know about?
9. Handle objections	—Can it be negotiated away? —Is there any need to worry about that? —Do you have the answer to that objection, which will make it of no concern?	—What terms are needed? —What are they stuck on? —Was there a miscommunication?
10. Trial close	—Are they ready to buy? —Does your product fill their needs? —Will it uncover objections? —Will it trigger questions?	—In commitment stage yet? —Are there hidden needs they haven't divulged? —What don't they like? —What haven't you answered?
11. Close	—How can you and they get started? —Are there no more obstacles to buying?	—What commitment can you get? —All questions and concerns have been answered or overcome
12. Follow-up	—If they have problems, you are here to help —Can you help even more?	—Are there things that occurred that you did not anticipate? —Do they want ancillary products or services? —What do they want they did not initially ask for?

When Things Go Right

Listening to the Wrong Person Makes a Sale

Stanley Paterson sold his first car in 1924, a Model T Ford. He has since retired but relates how a mistake of listening to the wrong person actually made him a sale.

"A couple came into our dealership located south of Los Angeles. After looking at a few models, they settled on a model and asked me to hold it for them for a few days. The next day, their son stopped by to look at the car. He told me it would be highly unlikely that his parents would buy the car and suggested I put it back on the lot.

Continued

Learning Objective 3: The structure of the call and the buying process are linked

The 12 steps of the sales call link the buying process and the selling process. The buyer and salesperson need to be on track together. The salesperson must be able to accurately judge where the customer is in the buying process and pace the presentation accordingly. Figure 9-3 illustrates how the stages of the sales call link up with the stages of the buying process.

▶ ▶ *follow-up questions*

1. What does the term *hierarchy of effects* mean?

2. List and explain the steps in a sales call.

Taxonomy of Presentations

Learning Objective 4: Four types of sales presentation formats

There are four types of presentation formats an adaptive salesperson uses: the *scripted presentation*, the *formula presentation*, the *need-satisfaction presentation*, and the *consultative presentation*. Each has its own specific uses, advantages and disadvantages, characteristics, and situations where it is most applicable.

In many companies, the salesperson doesn't need to make a decision regarding the presentation to use. The salesperson is trained in only one delivery style. This decision to dictate a particular style is based on a track record of success. Let's begin by discussing the oldest and most widely recognized form of sales presentation, the scripted presentation.

The Scripted Presentation

The **scripted presentation,** sometimes called a canned or stimulus-response presentation, is a format allowing little, if any, variation in the delivery. The salesperson has a script and follows it through the presentation. The script assumes there are people with similar interests or needs and those people are either ready to buy or interested in buying. They only need to be contacted to spark that interest or readiness into a sale.

The scripted presentation's distinguishing characteristics suggest its applicability. It is characterized by the "stimulus-response" interaction. The essence of the scripted presentation is a brief opening statement to stimulate and test the prospect's interest. The prospect will either give a positive or negative response, and the presentation will either continue or end at that point. Its second characteristic is a strategy of numbers: many people must be contacted to generate the necessary amount of sales. If the positive response rate is 10 percent, then a salesperson needing 25 sales per day must make 250 contacts to hit the target. In the typical outbound telemarketing sales force, where the scripted presentation dominates, the success rate is about 15 to 20 percent when the telemarketing salesperson calls a qualified prospect. When the telemarketer makes a cold call on an unqualified prospect, the success rate drops to below 10 percent.[2]

The scripted presentation is characterized by being brief and to the point. Its purpose is to elicit a positive response as quickly as possible, then complete the presentation and make the sale. When traditional scripted presentation techniques are used, salespeople do not probe the needs of the customer, nor do they try to customize the features, advantages, or benefits to

Structure of a Call		Hierarchy of Effects
1. Opening	A	
	T	
	T	
2. Overview	E	
	N	Awareness
	T	
3. Needs identification	I	
	O	
	N	
4. Net out		
	I	
	N	
5. Presentation of benefits	T	Liking
	E	
	R	
6. Support benefit claims with features and advantages	E	
	S	
	T	
7. Trial close	D	
	E	
	S	Preference
8. Objections	I	
	R	
9. Handle objections	E	
	A	Conviction
10. Trial close	C	
	T	
	I	
11. Close	O	Purchase
	N	
12. Follow-up		

Figure 9-3 **Linking the Buying Process and the Structure of a Sales Call**

the specific customer. With the use of computers, however, the traditional rote script is being replaced with a modularized script.

Case in Point

The Scripted Presentation is Alive, Well, and Growing

Scripted or canned presentations were somewhat of a standard for the selling profession in the early days of door-to-door sales. Then, selling moved to more "high touch" selling, more interactive customer involvement, needs indentification and customized presentations. The scripted presentation began to fall away. Now, it's back! A few years ago, General Electric received a $100 million order as the result of a scripted presentation used by one of its telemarketers.[3]

Telemarketing and its link to the computer is one of the newest tools firms are using to extend their ability to do personal selling. General Electric operates over 40 telemarketing centers and has over 2,000 telemarketing salespeople. Computers are now directly linked to databases, so when a telemarketing salesperson makes a connection, that customer's vital information is instantly displayed on the screen: phone number, address, name, and buying history.

The telemarketing salesperson keys in the appropriate script, which appears on the screen, and reads through it. The result is instant recognition of the customer so she can be dealt with on a first name basis. Call management is more efficient because the caller can see what and when the last purchase was made and can deal with the customer on a first-name basis. The bottom-line effect is a sales presentation just as if the buyer and salesperson were face-to-face. The big difference is it costs ten times more to make the face-to-face call than the telemarketing call. The scripted presentation is alive, well, and being used more than ever before—all thanks to computer and telecommunications technology.

The modularized script consists of numerous separate units. Prospects are probed for their interest in a particular product. If they are interested in product 1, then module A is recited. Depending on how the prospects respond to module A, modules B, C, D, or E would follow. How prospects respond to that module would lead the salesperson to use module F, G, or H. While still scripted, this modular approach allows the salesperson a great deal of flexibility in the structure of the script. This type of scripted presentation has been significantly advanced with its marriage to the computer, as described in the box below.

Scripted Presentations and Laptop Computers: A Successful Marriage of the Old and the New

Insurance companies now use scripted presentations in conjunction with laptop computers to do in-home presentations. The laptop computer, with its ability to present animated visuals, now accompanies many salespeople

Continued

Continued—to prospects' homes. The salespeople turn on the computer and the company logo appears. They probe prospects for the type of insurance they are interested in and select that type from the menu on the screen, then the show starts. The salespeople have a memorized script they follow with each visual that appears. The result has been to close sales in one or two calls where it used to take three to four. The increase in salespeople's efficiency has been tremendous as a result of the marriage of the laptop and the scripted presentation.

In a scripted presentation, the bulk of the conversation is carried by the salesperson as the stimulator, with the prospect being just a responder. In this format, the salesperson probes for product interests, then listens for the positive key-word responses needed from the prospect. Depending on the responses, the salesperson keys into another part of the script. The salesperson is in the lead, and the customer reacts to the stimuli.

The scripted presentation has its greatest applicability in telemarketing, in-home sales, sales training, and door-to-door sales. In these situations, the salesperson needs a precisely formatted presentation to readily identify interested prospects, then move them to committing to the order. The scripted presentation is often used to get trainees off on the right foot. Newly hired salespeople may not have the experience necessary to be able to adapt to a variety of customer and presentation styles. They need a presentation format that can be repeated over and over without the chance of making a mistake. This helps them develop self-confidence and self-esteem.

Case in Point

What's in a Script?

Many telemarketing experts suggest using a script, specially when a telemarketing or training program is just getting under way. Not only does it act as a guide, but it also serves as a checklist to make sure that key points are made. Once a relationship between the telemarketer and customer is established, the script will not have to be followed as closely or can be abandoned altogether.

The following are the topics in a generic script suggested by consultant Craig Tarler:

▸ Introduce yourself and your company.

▸ Establish credibility: "We are the world's largest manufacturer...."

▸ Use an attention-getter: "We are running a special on aluminum widgets."

▸ Investigate. Find out names, buying history, and so on: "Before I tell you about the special, I'd just like to ask you a few questions, if you have the time."

▸ Close by going back to the attention-getter: "Would you like six or ten dozen widgets while we have this special offer?"

Continued

▶ ▶ ▶ ▶ ▶ ▶ ▶ ▶ ▶ ▶

Learning Objective 5:
Advantages and disadvantages
of scripted presentations

Advantages and disadvantages The scripted presentation's advantages and disadvantages are:

Advantages	Disadvantages
▸ Has some guarantee of success	▸ Generally has a low response rate
▸ Quickly separates interested prospects from the uninterested	▸ Limited salesperson and customer interaction
▸ Useful training method for novice salespeople	▸ Generally not used in selling products where a long-term interactive relationship is anticipated
▸ Best used in telemarketing, in-home sales, or door-to-door sales	▸ Can't be effectively used with complicated products requiring extensive explanation

The scripted presentation may be used with other presentation formats as well. It is possible to use a scripted opening inquiry statement to separate interested from uninterested prospects. If the prospect shows significant

Scripted presentations are
used by telemarketing agents.

interest, the salesperson shifts to a more unstructured style. The scripted presentation format is the most structured and disciplined of the four presentation styles.

Formula Presentation

Less structured than the scripted format is the formula presentation. In a **formula presentation,** the salesperson subtly proceeds through the presentation in a predetermined series of steps. This format is one step up from the scripted presentation and shares some of the same characteristics. To be successful, it needs a smooth conversational delivery so prospects do not feel like they are being led through a step-by-step formula. The scripted presentation assumed there were enough prospects in similar situations that, given a similar presentation, a certain percentage would respond predictably. The formula presentation has somewhat the same approach but allows and encourages greater interaction between the salesperson and the customer. Unlike the scripted presentation, where the salesperson does most of the talking, the formula presentation is a dialog evenly divided between the customer and the salesperson.

A-I-D-A formula   The formula presentation's purpose is to proceed through a series of sequential steps in a predetermined *format,* rather than through a predetermined *script.* A number of formulas are used. The one that follows the hierarchy of effects is traditionally termed the A-I-D-A formula. The hierarchy-of-effects model says the salesperson should proceed through the presentation by stimulating *Attention* or awareness, then build *Interest,* stimulate the prospect's *Desire* to purchase, and finally close the sale with the *Action* of signing the order.

In any formula presentation, the secret to success is being able to determine where the customer is in the formula. A salesperson never wants to get ahead of the customer nor lag behind. If the salesperson gets ahead, the customer feels rushed and pressured into a decision. This may turn off some of the more timid customers. Lagging behind bores customers because they are ready to buy or ready for more information that the salesperson is not providing. Some suggestions for successfully proceeding through such a formula as A-I-D-A are listed in Figure 9-4 on page 294.

SQR³ formula   Another formula is called SQR³. This presentation formula says to *Stimulate* interest first, allow the prospect to *Question* and the salespeople to *Respond* to the question, followed by the customer's *Reaction* to the response, and finally, *Reinforce,* in which salespeople may request reinforcement to determine if they have understood the meaning of the prospect's statement, or they may reinforce the prospect's reaction to the stimulus. The stimulus could range from something as simple as an opening question to something as complicated as a rate or fee structure quotation.

An SQR³ formula's dialogue could be as follows:

Salesperson: The price of machined parts is going up every day, it seems. Our firm offers mass-produced parts that fit a variety of applications and at a 35 percent reduction in cost. *(Stimulus)*

Where is the customer in the formula? Where should the salesperson be? The following are a sampling of clues to watch for:

Stage of Formula: Attention

▶ Response to a direct question: "Are you familiar with Scroll Equipment Company?

▶ Customer volunteers awareness: "Scroll? Oh yes, I've heard about your saws and grinders."

▶ Customer admits to lack of awareness: "Scroll? Can't say I've heard of you."

▶ Facial expressions or body language communicates awareness or lack thereof.

Stage of Formula: Interest

▶ Customer asks for information, brochure, another call to be made; generally indicates a desire for more of whatever the salesperson can give.

▶ Customer leans forward in chair, arms and hands are more open, generally begins to listen more intently, makes more direct and frequent eye contact.

▶ Customer begins to handle the merchandise.

▶ Customer begins to scrutize the product closely and asks questions about it.

▶ Customer asks for input from others; expect to hear the "Well, what do you think?" question asked of a co-worker, spouse, or so on.

Stage of the Formula: Desire

▶ Customer may ask the hypothetical question, "If we were to buy this, then...."

▶ Customer asks if product will work with what he or she already has.

▶ Customer tries the product to see how it works.

▶ Customer simply expresses desire: "I'd love to see us using Scroll equipment."

▶ Customer asks for terms.

▶ Customer asks for specifics, for example, "Can you make it green?" or "Do we have to take delivery on only truckload lots or can we get less?"

Stage of the Formula: Action

▶ Customer says, "I'll take one."

▶ A delivery date is requested.

▶ A purchase order number is assigned.

▶ The customer offers to pay or asks how payment should be made.

▶ Customer asks about the paperwork to complete the deal.

▶ Salesperson is directed to the appropriate person to set up an account number.

Customer: Everybody says their parts are going to save me money, but are mass-produced parts as reliable as custom-made parts? *(Question)*

Salesperson: Our tests indicate, and our customers tell us, that the mass-produced parts we sell last 10 percent longer than the competitor's. *(Response)*

Customer: I find that hard to believe! *(Reaction)*

Salesperson: I know. Most of our customers did until they saw our parts in action. I expected you would find it hard to believe, but Hank Alleman over at his tool and die shop said he would vouch for it. Would you like to set up a demonstration? *(Reinforce)*

Advantages and disadvantages The formula presentation's advantages and disadvantages can be summarized as follows:

◀ ◀ ◀ ◀ ◀ ◀ ◀ ◀

Learning Objective 5:
Advantages and disadvantages of formula presentations

Advantages	Disadvantages
▸ Less structured; more flexible	▸ Requires greater time, therefore less contacts are possible
▸ Ensures presentation can be presented in a logical manner	▸ Salesperson must be able to recognize what stage of the buying process or stage of the formula the customer is in
▸ Can be customized to the buyer-seller interaction	
▸ Greater ability to probe specific needs and wants of the customer	
▸ Applicable to selling situations where long-term relationships and repeat buying are anticipated	
▸ Can be effectively used when calling on either new prospects or continuing customers	

As you can see, we've gone from a very rigid and structured format to one that allows greater flexibility for the salesperson. Moving along in that same direction, the third type of presentation format an adaptive salesperson uses is the need-satisfaction presentation.

Need-Satisfaction Presentation

The characteristics of the need-satisfaction presentation make it very different from the previous two. This presentation format is highly interactive and allows the salesperson to customize the presentation as it develops. This format is particularly applicable when a salesperson has many types of products or lines to offer. The need-satisfaction format, unlike the two preceding it, does not assume that success is based on finding similar people in similar situations who will respond to similar features, advantages, and benefits.

The **need-satisfaction presentation** is characterized by extensive questioning to determine the buyer's needs, prioritize them, then offer the best product alternatives. Determining the specific needs to address is accomplished in three phases: need development, need awareness, and need fulfillment. In the need development phase, salespeople direct questions to get detailed information from prospects about their problems, needs, and the ideal solution they envision. During this stage of the presentation, the customers carry the bulk of the conversation. During the need awareness stage, salespeople try to clarify and restate the customers' high-priority needs. In this phase, the conversational responsibility starts shifting to the salespeople. The final stage is the need fulfillment phase. Now, the salespeople begin presenting the features, advantages, and benefits of the most applicable product alternatives. They test buyer readiness with trial closes, then attempt to close the sale.

The key to success in using the need-satisfaction format is the listening and questioning skills of the salesperson. Since this style is so interactive, the salesperson must be fully attentive to what the customer says. This is where the knowledge of questioning techniques you learned in the chapter on sales communication comes into play. Applying the knowledge of open- and closed-ended questions to specify, analyze, and evaluate the customer's needs is vitally important.

▶ ▶ ▶ ▶ ▶ ▶ ▶ ▶ ▶

Learning Objective 5:
Advantages and disadvantages
of the need-satisfaction
presentation

Advantages and disadvantages The advantages and disadvantages of the need-satisfaction presentation can be summarized as follows:

Advantages	Disadvantages
▶ Is customized to prospect's needs	▶ Difficult for salespeople with poor listening and question skills
▶ Applicable when salespeople have a wide array of products to offer.	▶ Could be extensively drawn out, requiring multiple calls, the first being informational and subsequent ones being actual product presentations
▶ Particularly well-suited for service or relationship type sales (financial services, real estate, legal, medical, or insurance)	
▶ Well-suited to selling situations where long-term relationships are anticipated	
▶ Well-suited to sales of high-tech, expensive, major purchases that involve a significant degree of personal risk on the buyer's part	

The final presentation format adaptive salespeople use carries customization to the limit. It is often so customized that it is hardly recognizable as a presentation style at all. It is the consultative presentation.

Consultative Presentation

The **consultative presentation** is uniquely different from the previous three. As its name implies, it puts the salesperson in the role of a business consultant on the customer's complex and systemwide problems. A consultative presentation format is characterized by a lengthy presale relationship that may span weeks or even months. Such firms as computer and telecommunication companies, defense contractors, architects, and advertising agencies typically use this format. The presale activities involve lengthy and complicated studies of the prospect's problems and business. Based on these studies, the selling firm makes its product and service recommendations to the prospect.

It is common with this presentation format to find the prospect's firm inviting selected vendors to compete for the contract. For example, when Procter & Gamble or IBM changes ad agencies, several ad agency candidates will be selected and invited to make presentations. Prior to the presentation, the selected agencies spend a great deal of time with the customer learning about the problems, goals, tactics, and strategies. After each competing agency has made its particular study, the presentations are scheduled, and one agency is selected to receive the contract. The other participants are customarily paid for their time and expenses. As is typical with the consultative

Sometimes salespeople work closely with the prospective customer's business to understand their problems before a presentation is planned.

presentation, the agency winning the contract can expect many years of sustained business. In the case of defense contracting, firms like General Dynamics or McDonnell-Douglas may spend years developing a prototype airplane to fit the specifications identified by the Defense Department. Winning that contract means having exclusive rights to build and sell the new airplane to the government.

The consultative presentation is also characterized by the integration of the traditional buyer-seller roles. The salespeople act as an extension of the customer's firm, using her or his capabilities to solve its problems. The salespeople become positioned as true adders-of-value for the customer's firm. A salesperson in a consultative sales environment still has to compete to serve the customer, but once accepted, the salesperson becomes the customer's partner in profits and progress. The salesperson and the customer will know each other's objectives and strategies and will work together to achieve the shared objective.

Another common characteristic of the consultative presentation approach is that once a partnering relationship has been established, salespeople may spend more time at the customer's firm than they do at their own. This is because the complex nature of the relationship often requires salespeople to be involved in the product's delivery, installation, and daily operation and the training of the customer's employees. Medical equipment salespeople often install and service the equipment they sell as well as train physicians and others to use it. Computer salespeople get actively involved in the installation, programming, and testing of the systems they sell.

Learning Objective 5:
Advantages and disadvantages
of the consultative selling
presentation

Advantages and disadvantages The advantages and disadvantages of the consultative presentation approach can be summarized as follows:

Advantages	Disadvantages
▸ Salesperson's firm becomes intimately acquainted with customer and customer's firm	▸ Requires extensive development time
▸ Buyer-seller relationship is usually long-lived	▸ Requires extensive training of the salesperson to become familiar with the customer's firm and industry
▸ Once established as a consultative partner, it is very difficult to be dislodged by competitors	▸ Can be very expensive

While the consultative presentation is not the most frequently used, it is the format responsible for many major sales. The buildings at your school, the parking lot, the lab facilities, and even the chairs you are sitting on are probably the results of this presentation format. Most government purchases of all types are a result of this format. It is the common sales approach used for most major industrial sales.

Case in Point

Build Effective Presentations

Make up a presentation form with the following topics:

1. Purpose or topic
2. Results
3. Audience
4. Methods and media

Here's what this means:

▸ State your purpose in a word or phrase: "Training supervisors how to coach," "Introduce myself and my company," or "Obtain a loan for advertising."

▸ State your expected results: "Salespeople will understand new sales track," "Prospect will know what my company offers and contract for my services," or "Banker will lend me $15,000."

▸ Define your audience: you must not only know who they are but what they are as well. The larger the group, the more diverse the interests.

▸ Select your methods and media. Write an outline listing all your points. Organize it in a logical sequence and eliminate what is not pertinent. Decide how you will illustrate your ideas: slides, flip charts, overhead transparencies, and so forth.

Using these steps as a guideline will help you put together a presentation that effects the desired changes in your audience.

Source: John Melchinger, "Build an Effective Presentation," *Personal Selling Power* 9 (1989): 6.

Which Is Best?

You may be wondering, "Which is best? Which should I use?" The answer is simply, they are all best! Each presentation style has a particular situation for which it is best adapted. The best style to use is dictated by the product or service being sold and the type of customer. These presentation styles are all tools in the adaptive salesperson's tool kit. It is simply a matter of using the right tool for the right job to achieve the best result. Adapting to the customer is the key in all types of selling situations, but it requires modifying the presentation style.

▶ ▶ *follow-up questions*

1. What type of selling environment best suits the scripted presentation style?

2. What is meant by a formula sales presentation?

3. Could the same product be presented using several different presentation formats? Are there some products to which only one presentation style is applicable?

Case in Point

Teleconference: Making a Presentation to Thousands Without Leaving Home

Sales presentations on a one-to-one basis are still the norm, but the norm is developing interesting variations. Many companies do sales presentations to their own salespeople first. This is to introduce them to new products and get them excited about selling them. More of these internal sales presentations are being done through teleconferencing. Teleconferencing is linking a central transmitting station to remote receiving stations via telephone lines and satellites. It has been around since the early 1980s and has grown continuously. In 1983, Ford used teleconferencing to introduce its new Thunderbird to 4,700 dealers simultaneously in 40 different cities. Prior to teleconferencing, it had only been able to reach 50 percent of its dealers through its traveling "dog-and-pony shows."

While teleconferencing is too costly to do for individual customers, it holds promise for trade show presentations, annual company meetings, or any event where a single presentation can be made to hundreds or thousands of customers at once. It is an alternative to costly travel and offers the opportunity for presentations by corporate executives who might otherwise never have the chance to address the group.

The 4-P's of Presentations

The 4-P's of a presentation are *Picture, Promise, Prove,* and *Proposition.*[4] These come from successful direct marketing techniques where mailed letters must do the job of getting attention, convincing the prospects, exciting them

◀ ◀ ◀ ◀ ◀ ◀ ◀ ◀
Learning Objective 6: The four P's of a sales presentation

to action, and getting them to finally commit to purchase. The four P's apply to formulating a personal presentation as well.

P No. 1—Picture

Create the image of how the buyer will benefit. A prospect must mentally commit or "buy in" to the concept of a product or service. For example, if a woman believes spending hours over a kitchen stove cooking for the family is an expression of her love, she will not buy into the idea of a microwave oven's benefit of reducing time in the kitchen. Creating the mental picture is an essential element when selling travel, legal, or medical services and the like. Travel agents create mental pictures through the brochures they give away or the posters of Hawaii on their office wall. They say things like "Imagine, you could be on that beach in December!" The prospect's mind will do the rest.

Creating the picture means selling the benefits of the product—not the features or advantages, but the benefits. As stated in previous chapters, prospects buy solutions to problems. Solutions to problems deliver their own benefits. The prospect's mind will work in the salesperson's favor because people imagine things bigger than they really are. As the salesperson paints the mental picture, the prospect's mind will automatically amplify the picture. Create the appropriate picture, get the prospect to buy into the idea, and the sale is made.

> ### Presentation Rule
> Sell benefits, convince with proven advantages and deliver with features.

P No. 2—Promise

How will customers profit from buying? This part of the presentation builds prospects' expectations, moving from the picture to the promise. What will the product do for them? How will they be better off after buying than before? During the promise part of the presentation, salespeople make their product's performance claims. During the presentation's promise portion, the salesperson focuses on the features. *The* **features** *are the physical attributes or performance characteristics of the product.* Features would include such physical attributes as size, weight, shape, color, and the guarantee attached. Performance characteristics would be such things as a grinder's speed, a computer's processing capacity, or a car's gas mileage.

It is difficult to draw a line between picturing and promising in a presentation. Promises support and enhance the picturing process. A salesperson could create a picture and promise simultaneously:

Salesperson: Imagine yourself wrapped in the luxurious feeling of a *full-length silk dress.* A dress like this will make you feel like royalty and draw the attention of everyone who sees you in it. The *finest fabrics, the most meticulous stitching, and regal satin accents* have been combined to give you the finest dress available on the market.

In this statement, the features are in italics. Note how they weave through the fabric of the presentation. The features both communicate the quality of the dress and paint the mental picture.

It may seem difficult to separate benefits, advantages, and features. Think of it this way: the benefit is *what* the customers are in the market for, the advantage is *why* they should buy from the salesperson, and the features are *how* the advantages and benefits will be delivered. Read the following excerpts from sales presentations to recognize the features, advantages, and benefits:

Salesperson: The Steeliness T-31 file cabinet is a four-drawer *(feature)* unit totally constructed from 12-gauge steel *(feature)* and has riveted seams *(feature)*. It's four-foot height *(feature)* makes it ideal *(benefit)* for storing file folders in areas where there isn't much room *(advantage)*. The steel construction *(feature)* makes it one of the longest lasting *(advantage)* and most durable *(advantage)* cabinets on the market. If it ever breaks, our lifetime guarantee *(feature)* says we will replace it free *(benefit)* with no questions asked *(advantage)*. Because of its quality construction, it costs less to own *(benefit)* in the long run, looks good longer *(benefit)*, and will make it easier *(benefit)* for your secretary to file and recover files.

or

Salesperson: This pair of slacks is the best selling *(advantage)* we have; a pair that will keep you looking good *(benefit)* by never wrinkling *(advantage)*. That means you do not have to fool around ironing them *(benefit or advantage)*, and because they are wash-and-wear *(feature)*, you do not have to go to the cleaners all the time *(advantage)*. So you not only end up with a better looking slack *(benefit)*, but one that is easier to maintain *(benefit)* and eliminates the cost and hassle of cleaning bills *(benefits)*.

As you can see from these excerpts, there is no particular order for presenting features, advantages, and benefits. The customer in the second excerpt should be envisioning himself wearing the wrinkle-free, maintenance-free slacks. With the second P, the customer will be evaluating the claims the salesperson makes—the claims of benefits brought about by the advantages the salesperson says the product has.

When selling to resellers, the focus of the benefits, advantages, and features is often on how the product can be resold to the end user, rather than how the product actually performs. What salespeople promise in such presentations is in the marketing plan, which shows the prospects how to effectively resell the product, how to merchandise it, and how to support it with promotional materials. These promises revolve around increased sales and profits, greater inventory turns, and greater cross-selling opportunities. A Nabisco salesperson promises increased profits (the benefit) if the retailer stocks Nabisco brands. The various cookies compliment each other, so the surest way to maximum profits is stocking the complete line. The features delivering on those promises are tied to the taste, coupons, packs, and Nabisco's advertising. The Nabisco salesperson's marketing plan for a retailer would then include suggested shelf locations, the number of facings each cookie should have, where to display the point-of-purchase promotional materials, and how to build end displays.

P No. 3—Prove

The salesperson explains and convinces the buyer of the validity of performance claims through proof statements and demonstrations. Proof statements can be as simple as the salesperson saying the product will deliver on the claims. More substantial proof statements come in the form of research reports, guarantees, or testimonials of satisfied customers. Demonstrations physically prove the product's claims.

The customer's acceptance of the proof as valid depends on the credibility of the source, the timeliness of the claims, and the quantity of the evidence. Since all sources are not equally credible to all customers, salespeople like to use unbiased sources, such as government test reports, university trials, and unsolicited testimonials from influential and satisfied customers. The sources of proof must also be timely. A government report or customer testimonial several years old lacks the credibility of similar evidence only several weeks old. Finally, there must be enough evidence to support the claims. Just one testimonial letter from thousands of customers isn't going to carry a great deal of weight. However, the volume of proof must not be so overwhelming that customers grow weary of it. It is not necessary to show customers 350 letters to convince them. Show several and have the others available on request. Most customers will not request to see the others, but the fact that others are available and have been offered usually carries as much weight as if they were presented.

> **Presentation Rule**
> When proving the benefits of the product, it is always better to understate and overprove, never the reverse.

P No. 4—Proposition

The last segment of any presentation is the deal, the proposition. This should be the easiest part of the presentation. If the prospect is convinced, the deal should be little more than a wrap-up of a sale. If the salesperson has stressed the value of the product, then the price and discounts are simply details to work through, not hurdles to overcome. A successful adaptive salesperson always sells value, convinces with value, and emphasizes value.

> **Presentation Rule**
> Stress value and investment, rather than cost.

Clarity, Enthusiasm, and Sincerity Are Vital

A good sales presentation should be clear and brief. A presentation doesn't need a short time limit, but avoid wasting time with extraneous material. Follow the K-I-S-S principle.

Enthusiasm is also essential. Presentations that lack enthusiasm are a bore for everyone involved. If you are enthusiastic about your product and what you are doing, this infuses the presentation and the customer. Along with enthusiasm come a positive attitude. Salespeople need to maintain a positive attitude because like enthusiasm, it shows if you don't have it. A positive attitude is also a bulwark against rejection, which is just part of the selling business.

Good sales presentations maintain a controlled and predictable pace. The salesperson and customer should see the presentation moving along toward an end. It is obvious when it is going nowhere, when someone is just trying to fill time. When making the appointment for a sales presentation, always inform the customer about how long the presentation will take. It may take less time, but you should avoid going too far over your allotted time.

The good presenter should be sincere. Sincerity is the basis of all relationships and the salesperson who projects a sincere concern for customers and their problems will be far more successful than transparent salespeople only interested in the quick sale.

Ways to Open a Presentation

Salespeople get only one chance to make a first impression. What they do and how they do it in the first few minutes of a presentation determine, in large part, their success or failure. They must accomplish three tasks early in the presentation: removing tension, getting an early focus, and opening the presentation.

Gain Attention Early

A presentation is communication directed toward an objective. Salespeople need to put prospects in a receptive mood, get them to open up, and gain their attention early on to the purpose of the meeting. The first minute or

Steve Jobs gains the industry's attention by presenting his new computer.

two is when prospects and buyers size each other up. First impressions are being created.

Just before entering the prospect's office, the salesperson needs to double-check a few items, including the following:

▶ *How do I look?*—Is my tie straight? Makeup in order? Shoes shined? Is my appearance in order?

▶ *Am I ready for the presentation?*—Do I have my visuals, brochures, and price list in my briefcase? Are they in order so that I can find them easily? Do I have a pen and business card ready to use when needed?

▶ *Do I have just what I need?*—Do I have my product ready to demonstrate? Do I need to take my coat, umbrella, newspaper, etc., into this meeting? If not, have arrangements been made with the secretary or receptionist for storing these while I'm making the presentation?

▶ *Is there anything else that I haven't thought of?*

Having gone over this last-minute mental checklist, the salesperson is ready to enter the prospect's office and make the presentation. The salesperson should be full of confidence, having reviewed the customer's account profile, studied the sales call planner, and done the last-minute mental check. Everything should be in order. The salesperson should be excited and full of confidence about the upcoming presentation and ready to walk through the door.

Finesse the first minute   Salespeople's excitement builds when the secretary shows them into the prospect's office. This is when the challenge occurs: selling themselves as a reputable, a professional, and a dependable partner in this and future business relations. During the first minute, they must break the ice to create a receptive atmosphere.

If prospects come to the salesperson's office, display room, or show floor, the salesperson must welcome and greet them in a courteous and friendly manner. The greeting should be warm and enthusiastic but not overdone to the point of being phony and transparent. The most important accomplishment of the first minute for salespeople is selling themselves so they will have the prospect's respect and attention.

Create a good first impression   During the first minute, the salesperson communicates a great deal both verbally and nonverbally. Nonverbal messages are created in a number of ways. First is posture. Enter with an erect but not rigid or military-type posture. This projects self-confidence and professionalism. Next, remember that maintaining good eye contact is a must. Prospects do not trust salespeople who do not make eye contact. Salespeople should extend their hand to the prospect. The handshake should be firm and assertive. Nothing creates a poorer first impression than the limp-fish or wet-rag handshake. The salesperson should communicate an air of enthusiasm both verbally and nonverbally. A smile, almost to the point of grinning, is one of the best nonverbal communicators of this.

What salespeople say during the first minute can mean the difference between success or failure. They shouldn't apologize for taking up the prospect's time. They are not impinging on the prospect's time but rather are creating an opportunity for the prospect to be better off. Believing that, salespeople need make no apologies for the time they will spend. Next, salespeople must not imply that they were "just in the neighborhood" and thought they would stop by. Prospects don't want to believe they were simply an afterthought or a spur-of-the-moment choice. The salesperson specifically comes to see prospects to present them with an opportunity and solve a problem. Finally, salespeople should present their business card and introduce themselves and their company.

Now is the time to ask for or verify the correct pronunciation of the prospect's name if the salesperson does not know it or has not already asked. Few things are more annoying to people than having their name constantly mispronounced. There are a few tricks salespeople use to remember prospects' names. One is word association. **Word association** is forming a mental connection between an unfamiliar word and one that is familiar and easy to remember. When being introduced to Mr. Hafer, think "Hafer, rhymes with wafer." Another technique to remember the pronunciation of the prospect's name is to use it over and over. Something like the following is always helpful: "Mr. Maracek, I'm here with the Acme Petroleum Company...," "Mr. Maracek, we at Acme Petroleum...," "Mr. Maracek, I appreciate your taking time out of your busy day to see me this morning...," "Mr. Maracek, could I ask you a few questions before we begin?"[5]

Relax the customer and yourself   When entering the prospect's office look around for clues about family or hobbies. Photos on the wall, trophies, awards, and the general condition of the office (neat and well ordered or sloppy) give insight into the prospect's personality and interest. These can be great clues for opening conversations. Don't try to overimpress or overdo comments made about those pictures, plaques, trophies, and so on. Remember, the salesperson is not there to grill prospects about every game of their kid's baseball season.

Use a "mirroring" strategy. Ask questions and make opening conversation mirroring the tone and demeanor of the prospect. When calling on a shy person, salespeople should tone down their voice and gestures to reflect that person's more sensitive style.

Use a presentation preview. One form of relaxer that works well with certain personalities is to avoid chitchat entirely and begin with a preview of exactly what the salesperson planned to discuss before starting the presentation. Remember, not all prospects have time for relaxing, icebreaking conversation; some want to get right to it!

Use a sales promotion device as a relaxer. Salespeople give sales promotional materials, such as pens, calendars, and notepads, to relax the prospect and open the conversation. On referral calls, the conversation can always be started by mentioning the name of the reference.

Get an early focus   Relaxers and icebreakers may be essential in some situations. The ones mentioned above needn't take any longer than one to two minutes at most. How much time is spent on this is dictated by the prospect's social style. If too much time is spent, more often than not the problem resides with the prospect. If the salesperson mentions the mounted sailfish on the prospect's wall, the prospect might launch into a complete account of his two-week Florida vacation. The salesperson must graciously turn the prospect away from the vacation to the presentation's purpose. This is done

Some salespeople never quite focus their presentation on the buyer's interests.

by listening to what the prospect has to say and seizing an opportunity. The inability to get an early focus to a meeting results in wasted time and effort for both the salesperson and the buyer.

> **Presentation Rule**
>
> Don't tell the prospect all you know about your product. Cover only the points necessary to relate the benefits to him/her. Get an early focus and maintain it.

Ten Ways to Open a Presentation

▶ ▶ ▶ ▶ ▶ ▶ ▶ ▶▷

Learning Objective 7: Ten ways to open a sales call.

There are at least ten ways to open a sales presentation. They fall into three major categories: statement openings, demonstration openings, and questions as openers.

Statement Openings   Four types of statement openings are available to the adaptive salesperson: the introduction opening, the complimentary opening, the referral opening, and the premium opening.

Introductory openings   **Introductory openings** are as simple as statements in which the salespeople introduce themselves, their company, and what product or service they're representing:

Seller: Hello, Mr. Beeker, I'm Susan Houston with the Acme Tool and Die Company of Sidney, Ohio.

Complimentary openings   **Complimentary openings** range from a compliment about the prospect's business and its success to a personal affect. For example, we will add a complimentary opening to the introduction above:

Seller: Hello, Mr. Beeker, I'm Susan Houston with the Acme Tool and Die Company of Sidney, Ohio. Your plant certainly looks great with the new addition. I hear your business is really growing!

Referral openings   **Referral openings** can be used when the lead was obtained through a referral. The presentation is opened by mentioning the name of the reference and any pertinent details. We could add a referral to the opening above:

Seller: Hello, Mr. Beeker, I'm Susan Houston with the Acme Tool and Die Company of Sidney, Ohio. Your plant certainly looks great with the new addition. I hear your business is really growing! Gene Alexander of Alexander and Associates referred me to you. I've known him for quite a while and he speaks highly of your firm and all it does.

Premium openings   **Premium openings** involve handing a small gift or expression of gratitude, usually a sales promotional device, to the prospect upon entering. Ball point pens, desk calendars, business card file folders, or notepads are common premiums. Here is an example using all four openings:

Salesperson: Good morning, Ms. Koempel. I am Angelo Tucker with the Builtrite Electric Motors Company *(introductory opening)*. In coming through the gate of your plant today, I noticed what the new landscaping has done for the building *(complimentary opening)*. It's really great to see that an industrial company like yours will spend the extra money on such things *(complimentary opening)*. That indicates to me a business that's concerned with its image in the community and neighborhood *(complimentary opening)*.

   I'd like to begin by giving you one of our complimentary business card files *(premium opening)*, something that Jerry Jerkins of ABC Distributing certainly liked when I called on him last week. Jerry's company has been a customer of ours for a number of years and in fact, it was Jerry that suggested I come down and see you *(referral opening)*. I'm here today....

This brief opening took only a few seconds. The salesperson managed to weave all four openings into the initial greeting. He could have used any of the statement openings alone or in combination with any of the others.

Demonstration openings   Demonstration openings come in two subcategories, product-related and "razzle dazzle."

Product-related   **Product-related openings** focus on an initial demonstration of what the product does. They may begin by simply putting the product in the prospect's hands. A salesperson selling a food product to a retail grocery buyer would begin by giving the prospect a sample to taste. A way of letting the product start the presentation would be to say, "Our recent consumer tests of this new snack food indicate that people really love its taste. Here, try some on a cracker and let me know what you think."

"Razzle dazzle"   "Razzle-dazzle" openings require a good bit of showmanship and must come off perfectly to be effective. They must be rehearsed many times so that the salesperson is assured they will not fail. A salesperson selling unbreakable glassware might take a piece of stemware out of a briefcase and "accidentally" drop it on the floor. The prospect, not knowing it is unbreakable, would be startled and expecting the glass to be shattered. The salesperson then would pick the unbroken glass up and, with a smile, hand it to the prospect, saying, "This is our new unbreakable stemware that so closely resembles fine crystal no one can tell the difference until they drop it." The startled prospect, now with curiosity piqued, would want a much closer look at this remarkable product. The presentation would now be underway; the salesperson has captured the prospect's full attention and the sale is close to made already.

A product demonstration serves as a good presentation opener.

Questions as openers Question openings get the prospect involved at the start. They are a good way of judging the social style of the prospect, too. If the prospect responds to open-ended questions with short, choppy answers, this is a person who wants to get right to the point. The salesperson should plan the presentation style accordingly. On the other hand, if the prospect is a real conversationalist, the key to success here will be developing a friendly rapport. The four question openings most commonly used are the customer benefit opening, the curiosity opening, the opinion opening, and the shocker opening.

Customer benefit **Customer benefit openings** focus on a benefit the customer will receive from purchasing the product. In using this type of opening, always be sure the benefit mentioned will draw a positive response. Examples of customer benefit openings would be:

▶ "Mr. Fromm, what would you be doing with your spare time if you didn't have to paint your house in the summer?"

▶ "Ms. Wong, would you rather have 20 percent return on your money compared to the 10 percent you're getting from your savings and loan?"

▶ "Mr. Abdul, would reducing the down time on your production line be of interest to you?"

▶ "Mr. Quinn, would you be interested in providing for your children's education, while at the same time getting a 15 percent return on the money that you set aside for that?"

Curiosity openings **Curiosity openings** ask prospects about something that will stimulate their curiosity. The question and answer serves as a natural bridge to the presentation. Examples of curiosity openings are:

▶ "Ms. Tremanian, did you know that most businesses spend 15 percent or more on business insurance than they really need to?"

▶ "Mr. Kim, what would it be worth to you to save half the time painting machinery that you now spend?"

▶ "Mr. Janssen, what happened to the last purchasing agent here at XYZ Corporation that saved the company 50 percent on its input purchase prices?"

Opinion openings **Opinion openings** ask prospects for their opinion. The opinion question is directed toward an answer that will help the salesperson lead into the product's feature, advantages, or benefits. Examples would be:

▶ "Mr. MacPherson, what do you think will happen to the export business if the Republicans get elected in the next election?"

▶ "Ms. Lesueur, how high do you think interest rates will go this year on new home mortgages?"

Shocker openings **Shocker openings** use a shocking fact or vital statistic to grab prospects' attention by making them aware of something that could affect their life or business. Some examples are:

▶ "Mr. Vallier, did you know that statistics show that one out of every three homes will suffer fire damage before the home mortgage is paid off?"

▶ "Mrs. Feinstein, are you aware of the fact that you are paying twice the stock brokerage commissions than you really should be?"

▶ "Mr. Garcia, did you know that under the mortgage plan of most companies, you will end up paying three times the purchase price of your house before you finally get it paid off?"

Using one type of question does not preclude using any others. Through combining questions, salespeople literally have hundreds of alternatives at their disposal.

Presentation Rule

Only use questions to which you know the answers. Don't rush for an answer; give the prospect time to think about and answer; and above all, listen and hear the answer that the prospect gives.

▶▶ *follow-up questions*

1. How does a salesperson finesse the first minute of a presentation, and what must a salesperson accomplish in that time?

2. What are two icebreakers and how they are used to relax a prospective customer?

3. What are two examples of openings in each of the three major categories of openings?

What Would You Do If...?

As a college student, getting a good paying job with a prestigious company having an opportunity for personal and professional growth is pretty important. The difficulty is how to distingush yourself from all the other students who have interviewed with the corporate recruiter before you. Below are three situations. What would you do when the door to the interviewing room opens and you are asked to enter for an interview and make your "presentation opener" with:

▶ A prestigious banking firm? The firm has branch offices all around the nation and a tradition of being conservative with little inclination to do anything out of the ordinary. The interviewer is around 50 years old, has the title of vice-president, and has been with the bank for 25 years.

▶ A new ad agency that just started in business? The interviewer is 28 years old, a recent graduate herself, and is looking to get her business off to a roaring start. The agency has a good business and is growing. It specializes in some pretty off-beat campaigns and wants someone who is really dynamic, energetic, enthusiastic, and creative.

▶ An IBM sales manager?

      ▶ Question: How would you open each situation where the product you are presenting is you?

Summary

The focus of this chapter was the alternatives a salesperson has when making presentation decisions. We began by discussing the generalities of sales presentations, such as their purpose. A sales presentation is a salesperson's communications showcase. If successful, the presentation communicates the right information, emotions, and excitement in the right way.

To be successful at making a sales during a presentation, the salesperson needs to realize where the customer is in the purchase decision process. All potential customers start out at the "problem awareness" stage. Here, the salesperson must introduce these customers to the product and its features, advantages, and benefits. As customers become more and more interested, they ultimately make the purchase (Learning Objective 1).

Next, the basic structure of all sales calls was presented. The call is a twelve-step process. While all sales calls have these steps, some may be combined and many can be handled very quickly. The sales call starts with an opening statement, which may be as simple as a personal introduction. Steps that follow present the customer with the big picture or overview of the product. Then comes a needs identification process, followed by a "net out," which is simply a confirmation that the salesperson and the customer are understanding exactly what the customer's real problem is. Then comes the presentation of features, advantages, and benefits; several trial closes to test the buyer's readiness to make a decision; handling the customer's objections; and another trial closing test. If the objections have been overcome, the salesperson is ready to close the sale. The last stage is the many different types of follow-up activities salespeople do to make sure the customer is satisfied (Learning Objective 2). The steps of an effective selling process are linked to the buyer's stage in the purchase decision process (Learning Objective 3).

Four different presentation styles were discussed, along with the advantages and disadvantages of each. Those four styles were the scripted presentation, the formula presentation, the need-satisfaction presentation, and the consultative presentation. Many telemarketing firms use the scripted style. For more complex selling, the other three are most often used (Learning Objective 4). The chapter discussed the characteristics, applications, and advantage and disadvantages of each of the four presentation styles. One is neither better nor worse than another; each is the style of choice depending on the product and selling environment (Learning Objective 5).

A presentation must accomplish each of the 4-P's of a presentation: picture, promise, prove, and proposition. Creating a picture in prospects' minds is getting prospects to envision themselves as owners, to pique their curiosity to want to hear more. Promise is making the product claims. Prove is to convince buyers of the validity of those claims. Proposition is making the offer and asking for the order (Learning Objective 6).

Once the presentation is scheduled, the salesperson has at least ten alternative methods for opening it. These can be grouped into three categories: statement openings, demonstration openings, and questions as openers. These are not mutually exclusive; they can be used in concert to create dramatic and powerful openings (Learning Objective 7).

Key Terms

Hierarchy of effects   A lower-level activity has an effect that causes the activity that follows.

The scripted presentation   Sometimes called canned, a format allowing little, if any, variation in the delivery.

Formula presentation   The salesperson subtly proceeds through the presentation in a predetermined series of steps.

Need-satisfaction presentation   A format characterized by extensive questioning to determine the buyer's needs.

Consultative presentation   In this format, the salesperson act as a consultant to the prospect's firm for the purpose of solving a problem that is typically complex and systemwide.

Four P's of a presentation   Picture, promise, prove, and proposition.

Features   The physical attributes or performance characteristics of the product.

Introductory openings   Statements in which salespeople introduce themselves, their company, and the product or service they represent.

Complimentary openings   A compliment used to open a presentation.

Referral openings   A discussion of the person giving the referral opens the presentation.

Premium openings   A small gift or expression of gratitude, usually a sales promotional device, is handed to the prospect upon entering the presentation. Such things as ball point pens, desk calendars, business card file folders, or notepads are common premiums.

Product-related openings   The focus is on an initial demonstration of what the product will do.

Customer benefit openings   The focus is on a benefit the customer will receive from purchasing the product.

Curiosity openings   Prospects are asked about something that will stimulate their curiosity.

Opinion openings   Prospects are asked for their opinion as a way of starting the conversation.

Shocker openings   A shocking fact or vital statistic is used to grab the prospect's attention.

Discussion Questions

1. What would you say is the one distinguishing feature of each of the four presentation styles?
2. What makes the scripted presentation a powerful tool for novice salespeople?
3. Name three products you feel would be well suited to a scripted sales presentation?

4. Explain how to structure a presentation using the SQR³ formula.

5. What are advantages of a formula presentation?

6. Where, on a continuum ranging from totally structured to totally unstructured, does the need-satisfaction presentation fit?

7. How and why does the conversational burden shift from seller to customer when using a need-satisfaction presentation style?

8. What is the key to success in the need-satisfaction presentation style?

9. What is a consultative-type sales presentation?

10. Why and how would Boeing use a consultative style presentation when trying to sell airplanes to the Defense Department?

11. What are two advantages and two disadvantages of the consultative presentation style?

12. What are product benefits? What are the benefits a travel agent sells? A lawn care service? A funeral director?

13. What is the purpose of all sales calls?

14. What are the 4-P's of a presentation?

15. How do you create a good impression nonverbally?

16. What is a shocker opening?

17. What are the three phases in determining a customer's need when using the need-satisfaction presentation style?

18. What are two advantages and disadvantages of the need-satisfaction style presentation?

Application Exercise

Go back and reread the material on "The Structure of a Sales Call" in Figure 9-2, then answer the following questions:

1. Apply those 12 steps to a job interview you are going to have or one you have had. Can you find a place in your plan for that interview for all 12? Why or why not?

2. At some time in your educational experience, you have had to or will have to sell something to raise money for a club, the band, an athletic team, etc. Make up a call that follows this structure for selling chocolate bars door-to-door to raise money for your school band's trip to the Rose Bowl.

3. Which part of the 12 steps do you think is the hardest and why?

Class Exercises

Group Exercise

There are four different types of sales presentations suggested in this chapter. Break into four small groups in the class and complete the following assignment for each respective group:

Group 1: Prepare and present a *scripted* presentation for a telemarketing fund drive for a charity organization. The phone call should only last three to five minutes.

Group 2: Prepare and present a *formula* presentation for the sale of an antique automobile.

Group 3: Prepare and present a *need-satisfaction* presentation for a broad line of computer software packages.

Group 4: Prepare and present a *consultative* presentation of a telecommunications network encompassing many site locations.

Each class member will evaluate the presentations using the following evaluation form:

Salesperson _____
Product _____
Date _____

Evaluation of the Sales Presentation

Place a point value after each of the following sales presentation factors. 1 equals poor, through 18 which is excellent.

1. Did the salesperson know the product? . . . .
2. Did the salesperson gain the attention of the customer? . . . .
3. Did the salesperson use an *organized* sales presentation? . . . .
4. Was the salesperson's voice pleasant, well modulated, clear, projected well? . . . .
5. Was the presentation given in terms of the customer's interest? . . . .
6. Was customer agreement and approval gained as the presentation progressed? . . . .
7. Were the customer's questions answered promptly and effectively? . . . .
8. Were all objections answered to the customer's satisfaction? . . . . .
9. Did the salesperson ask the customer to buy? . . . .
10. Do you believe the salesperson made the sale or gained a favorable response? . . . .

Based on the above factors and your evaluation of each, what would be your *overall rating* of this sales presentation?

Poor   Excellent

    2   4   6   8   10   12   14   16   18

(Place a mark on this line that represents your overall rating.)

Special Comments: _____
_____
_____
_____

Individual Presentation

You are a direct marketer of industrial adhesives preparing a mailing that you hope will reach a wide range of potential customers and serve a variety of needs. Your goal is to get prospects' *attention*, *convince* them, *excite* them, and get them to *commit* to a purchase.

1. Address the problem of using the four P's of a presentation, as described in this chapter.

2. Which one of the four P's of a presentation was the easiest for you to construct? Which was the most difficult? Why?

▼ ▼ ▼ ▼ ▼ ▼  ▼ ▼ ▼ ▼ ▼ ▼

Silver Years Retirement Village

Silver Years Retirement Village is a senior citizen facility located on the outskirts of Thorndale. The city is the home of a state university with about 20,000 students. Thorndale is a very pleasant place, which accounts for its winning the status of "All American City" three years ago. Many cultural events take place there each year. Some of these are the result of the efforts of civic organizations, and others are the product of the University Fine Arts Council.

For these and many other reasons, the Phillips Corporation decided ten years ago to construct a 500 unit retirement village in Thorndale. The Corporation's original feasibility studies indicated that the area's blend of cultural, educational, and shopping opportunities could be exactly the draw needed for their target market. The market, as they defined it, was composed of individuals and couples over the age of sixty who desired a high level standard of living, transportation, group companionship, freedom from household chores, and privacy. Limited medical treatment facilities were also desired.

The Phillips Corporation had been on target. Within two years of its opening, Silver Years was completley filled and even had a sizable waiting list. The Silver Years resident enjoyed a one-bedroom apartment with daily housekeeping service and limited cooking facilities. Residents were encouraged to eat together in the main dining room area, where white linen tablecloths and flowers adorned each table. The dining atmosphere was very pleasant and guests were welcome to dine there before going to a concert or play on transportation provided by Silver Years.

For the first seven years, the food service operation at Silver Years had run very smoothly. Residents were well satisfied with the high quality of the menu and the table service. The waiters and waitresses were traditionally recruited from the students at the university and were paid the federal minimum wage.

During the past three years, Phillips Corporation has become concerned with the declining level of profitability at Silver Years. At the same time, it has noted that the facility's waiting list has shrunk due to the construction of a similar facility in the Thorndale area. For these reasons, Phillips has been very reluctant to increase the price structure at Silver Years and, instead, has focused on cutting costs.

Inevitably, the cold focus of cost cutting was cast upon the food service operation. After a quite thorough investigation, it was determined that rising costs in food services were due to the fact that the waiters and waitresses would no longer work for the minimum wage. In addition, there was a reluctance to reduce the quality of food during a period of rising ingredient prices. The first problem resulted in higher wages, and the resolution of the second problem was assigned to the head sous chef. After three years, it was clear that no progress was being made in the area of ingredient costs. The sous chef insisted that nothing could be done to lower food costs without sacrificing the quality that the residents had come to expect.

At this point, Phillips Corporation decided to hire Ken Tyler, age 25, as purchasing agent for Silver Years. While he had purchasing responsibility for the entire operation, he was hired specifically to attack the food service problem. Ken's background was in the corporate food service activities of a large hotel chain. While he lacked hands-on experience in food preparation as such, he had earned a corporate reputation as a troubleshooter who could turn unprofitable food operations into successful ones. His career had become somewhat stymied, however, by a corporate mentality that dictated the need for practical, operational experience in the hotel business for promotion to upper-management ranks. Ken was an accounting major in college, and his focus had always been on ledger sheets and net profit. Sensing his own limited mobility within the hotel chain, he had made his name available to an executive search firm that had matched him with the position at Silver Years.

Your company has been the primary full-line wholesale food vendor to Silver Years since its opening. While two other wholesalers have attempted to make inroads to the account, you have been able to retain the business due, in large part, to your close personal relationship with the former purchasing agent, Dick Foster. You spent much time and money entertaining Dick and his wife at cultural and sporting events. He stuck with your company even when some of your prices weren't the lowest in the market. Therefore, it came as quite a shock to you to find out that he had been asked to take early retirement.

During the two-week transition period between Dick and his successor, you have had a chance to talk to Dick and gather his impressions of Ken Tyler. You knew that there would be a certain degree of bitterness in his remarks.

"I feel sorry for you," he confided. "This new guy would sell out his own mother if he could save a dime. What's worse, he's a rookie in the kitchen, and all he can talk about is controlled-portion servings and minimizing ingredient costs. Eventually, it's going to catch up with him when the quality starts falling and the residents complain, but for now, he's got a honeymoon relationship with the Phillips management. I've seen his type before, with the fancy sports cars, Rolex watches, bottled spring water, and the whole works. He doesn't give a damn about loyalty, quality, or anything else that won't advance his petty little career."

You have also talked with the purchasing department's secretary, Sally Winthrop, the sous chef, and other workers in the kitchen area. Everybody appeared to be walking on eggs.

Sally Winthrop was congenial to you when you stopped by to set up your initial appointment, as requested by Ken Tyler in a letter you had recently received. When you casually asked her how things were, however, she asked what you meant by that. After assuring her that you meant with her kids in college, she said, "Fine, fine, everything's fine." When you pushed it and asked how she liked working for her new boss, she gave a glowing account of what a fine young man he was. It was as if she were reading directly from cue cards. You knew when to quit, so you wished her a good day and beat a hasty retreat.

Your meetings with the sous chef and the other kitchen workers drew similar responses. However, they made a point of telling you that they had been instructed to refer to Ken as "Mr. Tyler." He had given the instruction openly to the sous chef in front of the other workers in their initial meeting. He had also made it perfectly clear that there was no longer an "open door" policy in the purchasing department, as there had been in the past.

"Ms. Winthrop will screen all requests for appointments, and you will be notified when I can see you," Tyler had added.

The staff politely listened. After he left, however, their remarks were not kind, and morale began to sink.

Recently, you received a form letter (see below) from "Mr. Tyler" that has left you wondering about your future relationship with the Silver Years account. You are quite certain, from its tone, that things are not going to continue to be business as usual. Still, you are not in a position to give up this important, lucrative account without a fight. The appointment that you scheduled through Sally Winthrop is set for next week. You have five days to prepare for the meeting. You know that it may very well determine if you have a future with the account.

TO: All Silver Years Retirement Village Food Vendors
FROM: Ken Tyler, Director of Purchasing

I have recently assumed the purchasing responsibilities for Silver Years Retirement Village. In reviewing our files, I have noted that your company is one of our vendors of record. I am currently meeting with past and potential vendors to determine if we have a mutuality of interests.

The new operating philosophy at Silver Years Retirement Village is one focused on cost consciousness. However, we expect the same high levels of product quality and vendor service that we have experienced in the past.

For some of our past vendors, this will necessitate a reassessment of pricing policies as they relate to our needs. Potential vendors can view this as a new opportunity to deal with our firm. All vendors will be impartially judged, and I will source our business to those firms deemed most competitive.

If your firm wishes to be considered as a future vendor, please schedule an appointment with my office within the next two weeks. I would appreciate it if you were specifically prepared to demonstrate your firm's ability to compete in our cost-conscious environment.

Thank you for your anticipated cooperation.

This case was written and contributed by Robert J. Boewadt, Georgia College, Milledgeville, GA.

Questions

1. How do you plan to make your initial approach to Ken Tyler?

2. What kinds of motives are present here? How can you appeal to them?

3. How do you interest him in dealing with you?

4. What objections will Ken Tyler raise? How will you prepare for them?

Now That's Success!

"I am going to be successful!" vowed Mona Powell. She quickly scanned her customer records to locate the Emerson Company file. She mentally recited what she was going to say and how she was going to say it, then stepped out of her car.

After a brief introduction to the receptionist, she settled on the sofa in the lobby to await her meeting with the purchasing manager, Carl Padowski. Again, she rehearsed.

Carl reached for his jacket and quickly left his office to walk down the long corridor to the lobby. "Another boring and pushy sales rep," he thought to himself, "trying to get me to buy something I don't need. This shouldn't take long."

Carl: Hi, Ms. Powell, I'm Carl Padowski.

Mona: Please call me Mona. May I call you Carl?

Carl: Sure. Let's go to my office. ("That firm handshake tells me she's all business," he thought.)

Mona: Carl, I know your time is valuable and frankly, so is mine, so I'll get right to the point.

Carl: That would be fine. I'm in the middle of a heavy project and appreciate timeliness.

Mona: ("Good thing I noticed the pile of files on his desk!") May I ask two questions?

Carl: Shoot.

Mona: First, how much wire do you buy a year, and secondly, are you satisfied with your present supplier's price and service?

Carl: Well, that is sure to the point! I figured you were going to ask me the usual two questions: Would I like to buy a product that would help me make more money, or would I like to cut my inventory costs? Well, in response to your questions, I buy 15 to 20 reels at a time, which is about 30,000 to 40,000 pounds. I'm pretty satisfied with our present supplier, except their price does seem high for the quantity I buy.

Mona: Has your current supplier even mentioned to you that by bumping up your order to 25 reels, or 50,000 pounds, you'll fall into the next quantity bracket? My company buys in such volume that we can pass the extra 7½ percent cost savings directly on to you.

Carl: Well, no, I haven't been made aware of that.

The conversation continued but didn't last more than half an hour. Mona listened to Carl and made notes as he talked. She offered the price reduction on 25 reels of wire for the upcoming six months. Of course, Carl had to get management's approval to increase the order, but it looked like that would be a formality.

As Mona shook hands with Carl, gave him her business card, and left the building, she reviewed the conversation. "Whew, I'm glad I took that 'effective communications' course. It has given me more confidence and sensitivity to listening and understanding my customers' needs."

Mona's next appointment was with Georgette MacIntosh.

Mona: Nice to see you again, Georgette. It's been a while.

Georgette: A bit too long, Mona. I expected to hear from you before now.

Mona: I'm sorry I haven't kept in touch with you, but I have been monitoring your orders, and it looks like deliveries have been on time. I know that was problem with your former supplier.

Georgette: That's the truth! You're right, deliveries have been on time. I just want you to call me more often in case I need to make changes.

Mona: Sure, why don't I call you two or three days before each shipment is scheduled. Is that okay?

Georgette: That will be fine. Truth is, there are a lot of changes going on in the company, and I want to be doubly sure that my department has no slip-ups.

Mona: I understand completely. How about some lunch? My treat.

Georgette: Great! I'm starved!

Third call of the day, later that afternoon.

Mona: Hi. My name is Mona Powell with Axiomatic Industries. I'd like to meet with your purchasing manager if possible.

Receptionist: Do you have an appointment?

Mona: No, I don't. I just had a few extra minutes in my schedule and took the chance that the manager might be in. Is that a problem?

Receptionist: Well, Mr. Clausen usually receives visitors by appointment only.

Mona: Mr. Clausen? I see. Okay, well, I'll call and make an appointment with Mr. Clausen.

Receptionist: I'll be glad to make an appointment for you right now for next week.

Mona: Really? That would be great! What is your name?

Receptionist: Belinda Myers.

Mona: Belinda, you've been a great help. Thanks so much. By the way, what is Mr. Clausen's first name?

Receptionist: Colbert. C-O-L-B-E-R-T. Clausen is spelled C-L-A-U-S-E-N.

Mona: Belinda, thanks again. See you both next week. ("What a friendly and professional receptionist!" Mona thought to herself. "I must remember to send her a thank you note.")

This case was written and contributed by Alicia G. Lupinacci, Tarrant County Junior College, Ft. Worth TX, and by Tom J. Lupinacci.

Questions

1. Did Mona handle herself in a professional manner? Was she assertive, aggressive, or passive? What are the differences?

2. Do you think Carl was justified in his general attitude toward salespeople.

3. Was Mona as confident and sensitive on her second appointment? Did she react appropriately?

4. Did Mona experience success on her encounter with the receptionist?

Notes

1. Adapted from Gerry Marx, "The Hardest Sell of All," *Sales and Marketing Management,* 137 (1986): 16, and Arnold Schwartz, "Bring on the Warm Fuzzies," *Sales and Marketing Management,* 135 (1985): 16.
2. Personal conversation with B. Quinn, WATS Marketing, Omaha, Nebraska, 12 February 1990.
3. Paraphrased from Bill Kelley, "Is There Anything That Can't Be Sold by Phone?" *Sales and Marketing Management,* 141 (1989): 60.
4. Slightly modified from the original "Picture-Promise-Prove-Push" described by Max Ross in *Direct Mail Letter Copy Fundamentals* (New York: Direct Marketing Association, release 310.2, 1979).
5. Adapted from Charles Futrell, *Fundamentals of Selling* (Homewood, Ill.: Richard D. Irwin, 1984), p. 197.
6. This case was written and contributed by Robert J. Boewadt, Georgia College, Milledgeville, GA.
7. This case was written and contributed by Alicia G. Lupinacci, Tarrant County Junior College, Fort Worth, TX, and by Thomas J. Lupinacci.

10 Making the Presentation, Part II: Customizing the Presentation

Objectives

After reading this chapter, you will be able to:

1. Define adaptive selling and its role in presentations.

2. Differentiate the working of ISTEA (the adaptive selling process) as applied to new customers and to existing customers.

3. Identify the four social styles salespeople encounter.

4. Apply the specifics of a presentation, from getting the appointment through closing, to each social style.

5. Produce a short script for a "minor yes" close to probe the buyer's readiness using "tie-downs."

6. Manage the presentation environment for an effective presentation.

The Professional Selling Question

What would you recommend to a salesperson who wants to have a great presentation?

Sales Experts Respond

James E. Lukaszewski, senior vice-president of Georgson & Company, and Paul Ridgeway, president of Ridgeway Associates, say that a great presentation is more than just knockout razzle-dazzle. It starts before the salesperson even gets in the door. They offer these suggestions: concentrate on what the customer's needs are. Talking about product benefits is only important to the customer who needs them. The key is to determine the customer's needs and sell to those. Next, be prepared. Never ad lib a presentation. The presentation should be well organized; they recommend making an outline. The presentation should be rehearsed, too. This will make the salesperson feel more comfortable, and with numerous rehearsals, the presentation will actually come off more natural than one ad libbed. They also recommend salespeople plan for and develop a strategy to deal with troubles they may have in the presentation during the rehearsals. Its a good idea to have someone play devil's advocate during the presentation rehearsals. They feel that if a salesperson can visualize the presentation and making the sale, this will make it happen. Their observation is that by thinking like a winner, the salesperson will become a winner.

When actually making the presentation, Lukaszewski and Ridgeway recommend that salespeople start with the most important issue or problem facing the client. Salespeople don't want to prematurely offer a solution that turns out to only partially solve a problem.

The presentation should move at a brisk pace. Put a specific time limit on each segment of the presentation and try to finish earlier than the allotted time. This makes for a more relaxed atmosphere and allows time for questions. Making the presentation exciting creates a feeling of excitement in the customer.

To make a great presentation, make it intelligent. Customers aren't stupid, so don't treat them that way. Salespeople shouldn't lecture like they are the world's greatest authority. Be responsive and try to draw the customer into the presentation as much as possible. Be specific. Generalities, suppositions, and statements that dance around an issue without addressing a solution are a waste of time.

Bring up the price and ask for the sale. Fumbling around and not being specific about the price doesn't help the seller or the customer. Salespeople have to ask for the order, that's why they are there; the buyer knows it, and they know it. If there are objections, asking for the order will bring them up so the salesperson can deal with them.[1]

Continuous Improvement—
Texas Instruments

How does a high tech firm sell internally? As with all companies, Texas Instruments has found that it is important to convince the sales force that their products are superior. In order to do this, one of the vehicles Texas Instruments employs is a regularly televised information program.

◄ This "selling" program is shot using a professional set and equipment. The program not only discusses Texas Instrument's innovations and advantages, but also competitive information which is critical to a salesperson's success. ▼

© Texas Instruments Corporate Visual Services

▲ One tool Texas Instruments uses to educate and inform the sales force is the "Systems Flash" segments of the program. Here, the T.I. Systems Flash reporter prepares to do a new product review with one of the developmental engineers. Information from this interview will give salespeople instant, in-depth, and timely knowledge of a new product release.

▶ Home office support, through the "Systems Flash," gives salespeople instant access to information they need to sell their products, and they get that information directly from the product's designers and engineers. Using satellite and broadcast technology, T.I. efficiently and effectively demonstrates new products to its world-wide sales force.

Quality Assurance— Union Pacific

UPCAT—Union Pacific Customer Action Team, is a quality assurance program utilizing the combined talents and expertise of the train conductor, yard manager, and customer to solve that customer's specific transportation problems. The team approach improves the customer's relationship with the railroad by providing the individual attention so important in the total quality management of a service firm. More personalized service, greater attention to each customer's specific needs and the team approach have gained Union Pacific the reputation of a customer-oriented, quality-oriented transportation company.

© Union Pacific Railroad

At Union Pacific, continuous improvement is a central theme. Often known as a commitment to total quality management, this theme of UPCAT is exemplified by salespeople, management and line workers who are concerned with questions such as how they are doing and how they can do better. In order to be truly customer oriented, all UPCAT teams are trained in active listening and are encouraged to clarify all the customer's needs and problems.

UPCAT teams go beyond strict lines of responsibility to truly be helpful. Ultimately, customers are satisfied because the continuous improvement process leads to concrete action which is timely and efficient.

◄ UPCAT teams introduce new opportunities for Union Pacific employees. Often customers can turn to the trainmen themselves for insights, efficiencies and solutions to a variety of new challenges.

► Employees such as this conductor act as facilitators in identifying needs and problems and resolving them. The process is a win-win situation, since the railroad, the customer, and the employee get what they want in terms of performance, job satisfaction, and knowledge that building their relationship will benefit everyone.

Scripted Sales— Mutual of Omaha

▶ The Mutual of Omaha videotape is an excellent example of a scripted sales call in which a highly trained salesperson interacts with potential clients in an adaptive fashion. Note in this picture that because he is left handed, Steve has positioned himself to the right of the prospects. From here he will hold their attention with his sales aids.

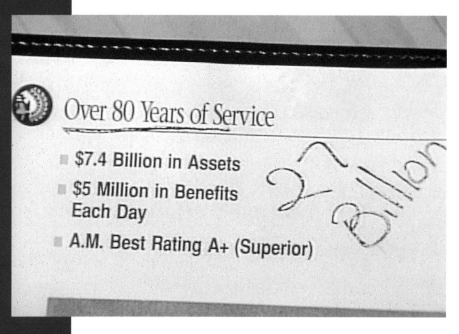

Over 80 Years of Service

- $7.4 Billion in Assets
- $5 Million in Benefits Each Day
- A.M. Best Rating A+ (Superior)

◀ Steve can use his visuals to build prospects' confidence in Mutual of Omaha. By using the binder and underlining important notes, he acknowledges and addresses their concerns along the way.

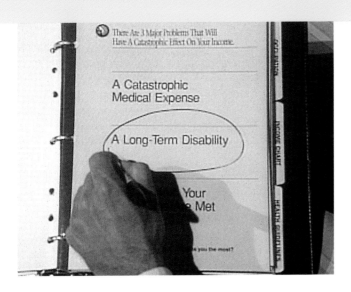

◀ Fact-finding is an important part of the communications process. In selling with Mutual of Omaha, Steve has been trained to determine dominant buying motives and to answer objections.

▼ By using well prepared visuals and asking probing questions, salespeople effectively communicate the product's features, advantages, and benefits. What does the body language of the prospects indicate in the photograph on the right as opposed to the one below?

◄ Prior to closing, a salesperson must handle objections such as those relating to a prospect's needs, desires and ability to afford the product.

◄ While the salesperson works on essential calculations prior to closing, prospects review company literature to reaffirm their decision was a good one. Well developed promotion pieces are indispensable.

► It looks like a successful close. Steve has been careful to investigate and address the prospect's needs, show how Mutual of Omaha insurance is the best choice to serve those needs, and close the sale. Steve now asks for references for further sales and has cemented the long-term relationship with the prospects. This service orientation creates satisfied customers for life.

Introduction

Being able to customize a presentation is the heart of adaptive selling. Each customer has a unique personality and social style. Some are very quick and matter-of-fact in their business dealings, while others are slow and deliberate and want every fact possible. Adapting to these different styles is this chapter's focus. Adaptive selling has been referenced in previous chapters, but now we will focus on using it in a sales presentation.

Salespeople must first recognize the buyer's social style. Second, salespeople need to understand their own style and if it is compatible with or antagonistic to the customer's. Third, salspeople must be able to adjust the presentation accordingly. Salespeople are often faced with presenting the same product to many different buyers in a single day. Different social styles, buying emotions, and reasons for buying or not buying mean the salesperson must customize the presentation to each customer.

This chapter is really about managing a presentation. As presentations proceed, they require numerous mid-course corrections. To recognize that a course correction is necessary, a salesperson first has to distinguish the signals predicting that correction. The salesperson must constantly monitor the presentation and determine what corrections or adaptations are necessary. We will discuss using trial closes to do that and how to adjust a presentation based on the customer's social style.

Adaptive Salespeople Match the Sales Situation

What is Adaptive Selling?

An adaptive sales presentation has flexibility built into it, but this does not mean it is unstructured. This chapter will provide suggestions for managing a sales presentation based on a person's unique social style. To a successful adaptive salesperson, selecting and applying the right presentation technique after determining the buyer's social style is as much a thrill as making the sale. Reading the signs and making the correct choices are what separates successful from unsuccessful salespeople. When you have finished this chapter, you will be better at doing that! To begin with, let's discuss what adaptive selling is and how it works in more detail than we have in the past.

The **adaptive selling** concept says salespeople modify their presentation strategy to the buyer's social style and the selling situation at hand. Adaptive salespeople make a judgment about each customer, the presentation's structure, and its content, then determine the best strategy to use. Even though the product may be the same from customer to customer, the adaptive salesperson keeps in mind that each customer is different and adapts accordingly.

◀ ◀ ◀ ◀ ◀ ◀ ◀ ◀

Learning Objective 1:
Adaptive selling defined

Sales effectiveness through adaptation is a process of pattern recognition. Pattern recognition means the process of deducing from clues or observations behaviors that seem to recur in conjunction with the observation. As a student, you are exposed to a variety of instructors, and you begin to recognize clues in their behavior that accurately permit you to predict future occurrences. For example, in Professor A's class, you learn that when she puts an asterisk by a statement written on the board, it always appears on the test.

You quickly recognize that pattern and adjust your note taking and studying accordingly. The salesperson must remember the repertoire of customer behaviors and how to adjust to them.

Case in Point

Adapting to the Disgruntled Customer May Mean Playing the Foil

Playing the foil means being the opposite or mirror image of something. In sales, disgruntled customers are sometimes best handled by the salesperson taking the opposite approach when dealing with them. Regardless of social style, sometimes playing the opposite part is the key to success. John Cleese, noted actor of Monty Python fame and a successful sales training consultant, offers the following suggestions for adapting to the disgruntled customer:

If the Customer Is:	Adapt By Being:
Aggressive	*Assertive*
"Your price is way out of line!"	"Comparing price to the quality improvements we've made, you'll actually be getting more for the money you spend."
Indifferent	*Engaging*
"Big deal ... if you hadn't made those changes, you'd be out of business."	"I agree, that's why more firms are switching over to us than ever before."
Upset/Confused	*Soothing/Clarifying*
"I still don't believe you have to charge that much."	"Does it really sound like so much when you consider the improvements in productivity you will enjoy?"
Upset/Silent	*Pleading*
"I don't know. What I don't undertand is why you have to charge so much."	"Your old product will not be worth more than it is today. The question you must ask is, 'Can I afford a major breakdown?' "
Resigned	*Confirming*
"I guess not . . . . "	"It sounds to me like you have made a decision to go ahead."

Source: L. B. Gscwandtner, "John Cleese Brings His Unique Body Language Savvy to the Sales World," *Personal Selling Power* 9 (1989): 12.

An adaptive salesperson soon learns to take cues from customers and their surroundings. A salesperson need only be observant to soon realize that these cues are accurate predictors of behavior. Some buyers proudly display pictures of their spouse, kids, and softball team all over the office. These are

Figure 10-1 **The *ISTEA*
Process: The Basis of
Adaptive Selling**

> **I**—Develop an *Impression* of the customer through questioning, qualifying, and precall planning.
>
> **S**—Use this information to formulate an effective presentation *Strategy.*
>
> **T**—Implement this appropriate strategy through tactics to *Transmit* messages, that is, verbal and nonverbal communication.
>
> **E**—*Evaluate* the effectiveness and appropriateness of the messages.
>
> **A**—A*djust* messages and transmission strategy as dictated by customer reaction.

cues. The salesperson soon recognizes a pattern: for example, customers who have their offices covered with these pictures like to make small talk before getting into the presentation. The salesperson who calls on a prospective customer and sees walls covered with similar pictures would be wise to develop a relationship by talking about the kids and the softball team before getting into the presentation.

Remembering the repertoire of customers' styles is a first step in sales effectiveness. The second is accurately being able to classify customers by style type. Once the customer is correctly classified, the salesperson can tailor the presentation to the style and needs of that particular customer. With proper training, the adaptive salesperson can move from call to call and from buyer style to buyer style without any difficulty. The salesperson develops alternative presentations for individuals, just as marketing campaigns are designed to appeal to different customer groups.

The adaptive selling process sequences the steps of forming impressions, selecting strategy, transmitting messages, evaluating their impact, and then adapting the presentation to the reaction of the customer.[2] This sequencing is called the **ISTEA process.** Figure 10-1 identifies the activities in this sequence of events.

The adaptive salesperson realizes that how a presentation ultimately unfolds may be exactly as planned or may even be totally different, depending on the customer's reaction. The key to success is being able to adapt to the situation and modify the presentation accordingly.

Case in Point

Selling Profit per Square Foot Increases Total Sales

Fred Bickless was a representative of a power hand tool company selling to retail distributors. When he attempted to stock a new product, the frequent comment of the distributor was, "We have no space for another product like yours." Fred soon realized that most of the buyers were analytical, no-nonsense types. These buyers were money- and profit-oriented. To get their business, Fred had to adapt his presentation to their interests.

After talking to several managers, Fred learned that each square foot of display space represented a dollar value in terms of the profit

Continued

How ISTEA, or the Adaptive Selling Process, Works

Learning Objective 2: The ISTEA process

Adaptive selling (the ISTEA process) builds on salespeople's knowledge of their customers. With repeated observations of a customer's habits and buying procedures, salespeople's learning curve grows. They learn what to do and what not to do. It's a deductive process. They narrow down the field of presentation formats to the ones they know will work. Let's look at how this adaptive selling concept would work with a new customer (a first call) and a well-known, established customer:

ISTEA Stage	New Customer	Established Customer
I—Develop *Impression*	Do fact-finding and qualifying; talk to others.	Observe how customer has done business with you in the past.
S—Formulate *Strategy*	Use sales strategies known to work with this type of customer.	Use strategy that has worked in the past with some experimentation.
T—Tactics to *Transmit* Messages	Try many different tactics that have been known to work.	Modify tactics selectively. Make no wholesale modifications.
E—*Evaluate* Effectiveness	Observe body language cues; listen for verbal cues.	Use more direct and open communication. Intention will also play major part. Use intuition based on knowledge of customer's personality.
A—*Adjust* Messages as Needed	May need to make major strategic and tactical changes as presentation proceeds.	Few adjustments necessary; only minor changes required. Already know the major strategies and tactics to use and the ones to avoid.

follow-up questions

1. Are the scripted sales presentation and adaptive selling incompatible?

2. Can retail salespeople working in department stores use the ISTEA process? What about service salespeople, such as those selling stocks and bonds, insurance, or financial services?

3. In your opinion, what is the most difficult part of the ISTEA process? Why do you think so?

Identifying and Selling to Different Social Styles[3]

Four Social Styles

Four social styles generally categorize the way people interact with each other in business. You were introduced to them in an earlier chapter. In this chapter, the focus will be on selling to these different types of people by customizing your presentation to fit their styles. Figure 10-2 briefly summarizes the recognizable characteristics of each social style.

The social style matrix is presented in Figure 10-3. Note first that low responsiveness-type buyers (Analyticals and Drivers) possess similar characteristics. Both have a need for control, are rational in their decision making,

◀ ◀ ◀ ◀ ◀ ◀ ◀ ◀

Learning Objective 3: Characteristics of the four social styles

Figure 10-2 Social
Styles and Their
Characteristics

Analyticals

Technically minded
Conservative
Awards and recognition prominently displayed on office walls
Active and work-oriented

Amiables

Very open, friendly, good-humored, affable, and good natured
Casual dressers
Relationship-oriented: pictures of family and softball team prominently
displayed
Office arranged for discussions to take place in their "personal space"

Drivers

Technicians, gadget lovers, detail-oriented
Very time-, efficiency-, and results-oriented
Conservative dressers
Office arranged so contact with salespeople is generally across the desk
"Get to the point" people

Expressives

Artsy, theatrical, somewhat eccentric, standoffish
Creative, willing to do it differently than has ever been done before
Open atmosphere in the office
Office generally cluttered and disorganized
Flamboyant, animated in their speech and body language
Tendency to exaggerate everything

Figure 10-3 **Social
Style Matrix**

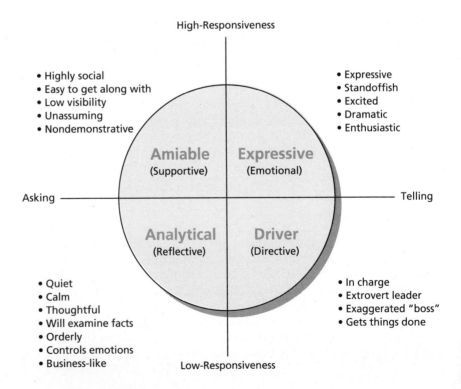

High-Responsiveness

• Highly social
• Easy to get along with
• Low visibility
• Unassuming
• Nondemonstrative

• Expressive
• Standoffish
• Excited
• Dramatic
• Enthusiastic

Amiable
(Supportive)

Expressive
(Emotional)

Asking ———————————————— Telling

Analytical
(Reflective)

Driver
(Directive)

• Quiet
• Calm
• Thoughtful
• Will examine facts
• Orderly
• Controls emotions
• Business-like

• In charge
• Extrovert leader
• Exaggerated "boss"
• Gets things done

Low-Responsiveness

and are very task-oriented. They are very independent thinkers and business-like. Drivers and Analyticals are similar in their assertiveness and competitiveness. They are not risk-averse and are very take-charge, fast-acting people.

The high responsive types (Amiables and Expressives) are open, informal, and friendly. They are emotional and relationship-oriented. On the "ask-tell" horizontal axis, Analytical and Amiables tend to be slow to act and averse to risk. They want to be cooperative and lack the Driver's and Expressive's assertiveness.

Now, note the degree of incompatibility. Analyticals are the direct opposite of Expressives, and Amiables are the opposite of Drivers. If a salesperson has just made a presentation to an Amiable and the next presentation is to an Analytical type, the presentation style will only require minor modifications. Similarly, going from an Amiable to an Expressive will require incidental variations. However, going from an Amiable to a Driver would require a major change in both the presentation's strategies and tactics. Keep in mind that if you are an Amiable, you will find it relatively easy to deal with Analyticals and Expressives but less so with Drivers.

One final note, and a cautionary one: Not everyone fits neatly into these four social styles. Still, knowing that people tend to exhibit more of one style than another is helpful in adapting to customers' personal styles. A salesperson develops a sense of a customer's social style over time and through repeated interactions. However, some people are quite easy to categorize from the very beginning. So, while categorizing can be an important and useful tool, it is only one tool and should be used along with other facts gathered about the customers and how they do business.

Case in Point

Finding the Right Personality for Telemarketing is the Key

Businesses are making greater use of technology in personal selling, and no where is that more evident than in the application of telemarketing to industrial product sales. Traditionally, this type of selling has been handled on a face-to-face basis. Now, with the typical face-to-face sales call costing over $200 while the telemarketing sales call costs only about $20, the switch is on. According to industry sources, over $100 billion worth of industrial products are sold each year over the phone. But the technology of computers and telephones and the impersonality of a phone call means it takes a special type of personality to succeed as an industrial sales telemarketer.

Bob Bucknam of NRI Data Products, a Pennsylvania-based computer supply company, attributes early failures at telemarketing to hiring the wrong people. He first had them selling the company's entire 3,000-item line over the phone. He admits this was too much for them to handle. Now he plans to use telemarketers to follow up directed mailings. Before, his problem was hiring people who were not assertive enough to close the sale. Bucknam used outside, traditional salespeople first and found they tended to concentrate on only their key accounts. This did nothing to increase business and left the smaller accounts

Continued

Case in Point—Continued

getting even less service than they were getting before. Bucknam says, "You need someone who thinks in terms of getting on and off the phone and contacting a lot of people. The outside salespeople like to get on the phone and spend a lot of time talking to one customer."

Source: Adapted from Bill Kelley, "Is There Anything That Can't Be Sold by Phone?" *Sales and Marketing Management* 141 (1989): 63.

When In Japan, Adaptive Selling Takes on a New Meaning!

Selling to a customer in or from a foreign country brings a new meaning to adaptive selling. Not only must salespeople adapt the way they would normally make a presentation, but in a foreign country, culture and customs also must be added to the equation as well. This is nowhere more evident than in making a sales call on a Japanese customer. In the United States, a good salesperson-customer relationship begins with a positive attitude toward the customer. In Japan, that is five times more important. One of the first signals a Japanese prospect looks for are signs of negative feelings about Japan or its people. Expressing negative feelings about the way Japanese do business causes instant failure.

Don't treat all Japanese the same. Although we have heard that Japan is a very homogeneous society, each person is different, just like here. There are strong regional differences, too. People from Tokyo are different from people from Osaka, just like New Yorkers are different from Californians. Japanese customers are more reserved than Americans. You will have a much harder time detecting body language signals from a Japanese customer than from an American. The Japanese shy away from exaggerated claims or actions; back slapping, vigorous hand shaking, or waving arms around will not be appreciated.

In Japan, you can never be too polite nor apologize too much. These are two aspects of Japanese communications Americans must come to terms with. Politeness and apologizing are built into Japanese customs and way of life; they are part of their communication idiom.

Finally, when selling to Japanese, put the emphasis on the relationship you will develop. In Japan, long-term relationships are tied to long-term planning, so if you want to be part of the long-term plan, you must be willing to commit to a long-term relationship even before the first sale is made.[4]

Case in Point

Customers' Social Styles Vary

Gordon Griffith is a purchasing agent who is more interested in his employees' welfare and convenience when purchasing shipping boxes

Continued

Case in Point—Continued

than he is in how the shipping boxes are manufactured. Gordon wants to know how much the boxes will weigh, whether they will be comfortable for the shipping room employees to handle, and whether they will fit the various products without the hassle of having to use expensive packing materials. Gordon is an Amiable when he considers the comfort and convenience of his people in the shipping room. However, he is a Driver when it comes to price and delivery dates; he is an Analytical with the installation of a conveyor system; and he may be an Expressive on the golf course (depending on how the ball bounces)!

The professional salesperson should be able to adapt the presentation to the social style of the customer as the selling interview progresses.

Selling to Amiables

The salesperson must understand this customer's sensitivity and need for personal assurances. Being too aggressive, assertive, or overpowering is the surest way to lose the sale and all future relationships. The following is a summary of strategies for selling to Amiables.

Learning Objective 4: Selling to the four social styles

Getting the appointment Use personal, friendly introduction letters. Referrals work well with this customer, and be sure to relate your experience with clients whom the customer may know. This reinforces the sense of relationship. Emphasize your reliability and ability to follow through on all promises, and always stress quality. Amiables don't want to worry about having made the wrong choice in a purchase, so give them the reassurances they want.

Opening the call Be pleasant and conversational. Don't begin by discussing the business at hand; your conversation should focus on your sincere interest in the customer's personal goals and work interests. Amiables like to start the call with a bit of general conversation; compliments work well, as does simply talking about business in general. Be sure to emphasize the satisfaction of past customers and reassure Amiables that they can call on those customers for references. A soft, easy opening will work well here, and it is a good idea to start the call with a relaxer opening. Complimentary, referral, and premium openings should also be considered for these customers.

Discovering the buyer's needs Don't be surprised if Amiables come up with the questions and ideas first. Amiables are relationship-oriented, so they may have questions about you and your company, how long it has been in business and how long you have been with the company. They are searching for a sense of your relationship to your company and its relationship to them. Also, don't be surprised if they are shy about expressing their needs.

Questioning is very effective as long as it is low-keyed and subdued. Be patient and allow them time to talk; they will give you an enormous number of verbal and nonverbal messages. You should respond with supportive,

Analyticals are detail oriented. (Left)

Drivers are control-oriented people. (Right)

Expressives have a "big picture" orientation. (Left)

Amiables are casual, open, and relationship oriented. (Right)

appreciative, and understanding verbal and nonverbal messages. Periodically summarizing what's been discussed is a good idea because of the rambling nature of Amiables.

Making a recommendation   It's a good idea to make your recommendations both verbally and in writing. This will encourage Amiables by showing them that you truly intend to stand by what you say. In making the recommendation, provide plenty of assurances to minimize Amiables' cognitive dissonance. Again, referrals to other satisfied customers enforce the relationship notion.

Checklist for Working with Amiables

Dos	Don'ts
1. Start however briefly, with a personal comment. Break the ice.	1. Don't rush headlong into business or the agenda.
2. Show sincere interest in them as people; find areas of common involvement; be candid and open.	2. Don't stick coldly or harshly to business; on the other hand, don't lose sight of goals by being too personal.
3. Patiently draw out personal goals and work with them to help achieve these goals; listen; be responsive.	3. Don't force them to respond quickly to your objectives; don't say, "Here's how I see it."
4. Present your case softly, nonthreateningly.	4. Don't be domineering or demanding; don't threaten them with position or personal power.
5. Ask "how" questions to draw their opinions.	5. Don't debate facts and figures; they'll get lost or shut up.

Dos	**Don'ts**
6. If you agree easily, look for possible areas of early disagreement or dissatisfaction.	6. Don't manipulate or bully them into agreeing, because they probably won't fight back.
7. If you disagree, look for hurt feelings, personal reasons.	7. Don't patronize or demean them by using subtlety or invective.
8. Move casually, informally.	8. Don't be abrupt and rapid.
9. Define clearly (preferably in writing) individual contributions.	9. Don't be vague; don't offer options and probabilities.
10. Provide guarantees that their decision will minimize risks and provide them with benefits.	10. Don't offer assurances and guarantees you can't fulfill.
11. Provide personal assurances, and clear, specific solutions with maximum guarantees.	11. Don't keep deciding for them, or they'll lose initiative; don't leave them with no back-up support.

Closing the sale. The direct hard close is unlikely to work, so ask for the order indirectly. Don't rush Amiables; give them time to make the decision, but during that time reassure them that the decision is a correct one. Again, reassure with guarantees, warranties, and testimonials from satisfied customers.

Offering contingency plans is a good idea. This will reassure Amiables that they are not out on a limb if something doesn't work. Reassure them that bringing other people into the decision is acceptable, too. They may want to get an opinion from a colleague, an assistant, or a supervisor. Do not discourage this multiple participation, but do question why. This does two things. First, it may reveal the customer is unclear about something said during the presentation. If this is the case, a simple reexplanation may do the trick. Second, you want to know who else is being brought in. You may discover at this point that you are talking to an influencer, not the decision maker. While you should not object to bringing in others, remember the fewer people you have to deal with, the easier it is to sell. More players make for more questions, more explanations, and more chances for one who is not a decision maker to raise obtuse, irrelevant, and tangential issues that can sour the sale or protract the presentation.

Selling to Analyticals

Remember that Analyticals, like Amiables, are risk-averse, slower-acting individuals. Analyticals are low-keyed buyers like Amiables. Analyticals' needs are more focused on control and tasks. Because of their rational decision-making process, the approach can be much more business-like and straightforward. Strategies for selling to Analytical buyers are as follows:

Getting an appointment As with Amiables, a letter of introduction works well with Analyticals. However, the letter should be totally business-like, omitting the friendly relationship tone that a letter to Amiables would have. The personal testimonials used for Amiables are not necessary here. Analyticals like specifics. They will want to know specific details about you, your product, and your credentials. Be sure to highlight both yours and your company's noteworthy achievements. Be straightforward and to the point in terms of what your product will do, its costs, the customer's savings, and the specific details. These same tactics apply when getting the appointment over the phone.

Opening the call   Come prepared with everything you have. This includes facts, figures, brochures, and drawings; in essence, every scrap of information necessary to answer any and all specific questions Analyticals will have. Analyticals will expect you to be an expert in your area and expect you to treat them as an expert in their area. To be successful with Analyticals, a detailed customer profile is essential, as is doing your homework prior to the presentation. Be prepared to present a very organized and logical presentation, making use of every minute. Just about any of the different types of openings you learned about in the last chapter will work with this customer. However, Analyticals are more get-down-to-business people, so judge the amount of time you spend on preliminary ice-breakers and relaxers accordingly.

Discovering the buyer's needs   Avoid small talk and follow a systematic questioning approach to uncover the buyer's needs as directly as possible. Be certain that the exchange of information is comprehensive from both your perspective and that of the prospect's. Encourage Analyticals to express their expert opinions. As when dealing with Amiables, let the conversation develop at its own time and pace. Be sure to support Analyticals' thinking, concept, and visions.

Making a recommendation   With Analyticals, cost savings and profit potential are the easiest ways to justify a purchase decision. Make a recommendation supported by all the financial data that you can muster. Be prepared for a barrage of questions from Analyticals when it comes time for you to make a recommendation. This will be a test of your expertise. When attempting to discover Analyticals' needs, be reserved and avoid flamboyance; be straightforward, decisive, and business-like. Avoid emotional appeals that might have worked with Amiables. Once Analyticals' needs are discovered, you can feel free to recommend a specific course of action. Analyticals want to get right to the bottom line and not be presented with a tremendous range of alternatives.

Asking for the business   When dealing with Analyticals, you can feel free to ask directly for the order. Do this in a nonaggressive, nonassertive, and low-keyed way. Be prepared for negotiating. Analyticals will try to drag out making a decision, rather than committing right now. Be able to prove that a positive buying decision is in their best interest. Analyticals will always be somewhat hesitant because they want more proof, more numbers, and more information. There will come a time when you must weigh the cost of getting more information and its value to the decision.

Checklist for Working with Analyticals

Dos	Don'ts
1. Prepare your case in advance.	1. Don't be disorganized or messy.
2. Approach them in a straightforward way; stick to business.	2. Don't be circuitous, giddy, casual, informal, or loud.

Dos

3. Support their principles and thoughtful approach; build your credibility by listing pros and cons to any suggestion you make.

4. Make an organized contribution to their efforts; present specifics and do what you say you can do.

5. Take your time, but be persistent.

6. Draw up a scheduled approach to implementing action with a step-by-step timetable; assure them that there won't be surprises.

7. If you agree, follow through.

8. If you disagree, make an organized presentation of your position.

9. Give them time to verify the reliability of your actions; be accurate and realistic.

10. Provide solid, tangible, practical evidence.

11. Indicate long-term guarantees, but provide options.

Don'ts

3. Don't rush the decision-making process.

4. Don't be vague about what's expected of either of you; don't fail to follow through.

5. Don't dilly-dally.

6. Don't leave things to chance or luck.

7. Don't provide special personal incentives.

8. Don't threaten, cajole, wheedle, coax, or whimper.

9. Don't use testimonies of others or unreliable sources; don't be haphazard.

10. Don't use someone's opinion as evidence.

11. Don't use gimmicks or clever, quick manipulations.

Selling to Drivers

Some of the characteristics of Analyticals also show up in Drivers. Drivers are risk-taking, fast-acting, and controlling. They are assertive and aggressive and appreciate those qualities in a salesperson, but remember that they are control oriented; don't wrestle them for control of the presentation. Drivers are competitive, so the presentation can become a competition if it gets out of hand. The strategies for selling to Drivers are as follows:

Getting the appointment   Consider avoiding introductory letters, or if used, be sure to follow up with a phone call. Drivers often see such letters as a waste of time. A phone call may work best in getting an appointment as long as it is business-like and to the point. Don't be shy about asking straight away for an appointment. Avoid all the unnecessary chitchat; be unpretentious and to the point. Ask them for the appointment; tell them what you want and schedule a meeting.

Opening the call   Establish that you have the expertise to deal with their problems and get right to the point. Be sure to stick to the point and get an early focus; Drivers have little time for chitchat or digression. Drivers appreciate formality and conservative approaches. Friendliness and cordiality are appreciated, but avoid the "warm-fuzzies" you would use with Amiables. Unlike Analyticals, Drivers want to know only the pertinent facts and information, not every detail available. They will soon become bored with minutiae and ask you to get to the point.

Drivers will tend to think, "If you cannot tell me your whole story in ten minutes, then you don't have your act together." Salespeople who are Expressives and Amiables may have difficulty in dealing with Drivers. Drivers want it brief and will make a decision; they dislike a presentation that drags on peppered with personal chitchat that doesn't relate to the business at hand.

Discovering the buyer's needs   Be sure to let Drivers feel that they are in control. Avoid telling them what you think they need. Drivers know what they need and don't appreciate you making second guesses. Asking direct, fact-finding questions is the quickest way of gathering the information that you need. If you have any questions or don't undertand statements made by Drivers, ask directly. Knowing Drivers' need for control, don't be surprised that they ask more questions than they answer. Be sure to have a clear understanding of what they need, want, and expect before going on to make a recommendation. Again, if you are the least bit uncertain about those, ask directly.

Making a recommendation   Offer Drivers a solution and let them make up their own mind. Offering alternatives is totally acceptable, but in doing so, be sure to stress the outcomes of each alternative. When making a recommendation, include all documentation stressing the facts that they need to know to make an intelligent choice. When making a recommendation, be sure to support with facts—but in summary form, not in the detail you would present to Analyticals. Drivers appreciate summaries.

Closing the sale   Don't beat around the bush; ask directly for the order. If a Driver is clearly rejecting your first recommendation, be ready to quickly and easily switch to an alternative. The soft, subtle close you might use with an Amiable will be less effective when dealing with a Driver. Close directly.

Checklist for Working with Drivers

Dos	Don'ts
1. Be clear, specific, brief, and to the point.	1. Don't ramble on or waste their time.
2. Stick to business.	2. Don't try to build personal relations.
3. Come prepared with all requirements, objectives, and support material in a well-organized package.	3. Don't forget or lose things; don't be disorganized or messy; don't confuse or distract them from business.
4. Present the facts logically; plan your presentation efficiently.	4. Don't leave loopholes or cloudy issues.
5. Ask specific (preferably, "what") questions.	5. Don't ask rhetorical or useless questions.
6. Provide alternatives and choices so they can make their own decisions.	6. Don't come with a ready-made decision or make it for them.
7. Provide facts and figures about the probability of success or effectiveness of options.	7. Don't speculate wildly on guarantees and assurances.
8. If you disagree, take issue with facts, not the person.	8. If you disagree, don't let it reflect on them personally.

Dos	Don'ts
9. If you agree, support results, not the person.	9. If you agree, don't reinforce with "I'm with you."
10. Motivate and persuade by referring to objectives and results.	10. Don't try to convince by "personal" means.
11. Support, maintain, and use indirection.	11. Don't direct or order.
12. After talking business, depart graciously.	

Selling to Expressives

Expressives are enthusiastic, flamboyant personalities. They expect you to be enthusiastic about the presentation and what you have to sell. Taking the reserved, quiet, shy approach when selling to Expressives will be far less effective than employing more showmanship and razzle dazzle. Strategies for selling to a Expressives are described below.

Getting an appointment   An introductory phone call is the best technique. Expressives, being more relationship-oriented, will want to know more about you, your product, and your experience. If you're going to use a letter, it needs to be business-like but can have more of a personal touch than you would use with Analyticals or Drivers. Remember that Expressives are interested in the "big picture." They will probably want to know how you came to know them, partly as a measure of their fame and popularity and for curiosity's sake.

Opening the call   You'll have to be fast to keep up with Expressives. Tell them why you're there, but don't waste any time doing it. Opening the call with Expressives can take time. Being people-oriented, they will want to share experiences and stories that you may both have in common. Talking about mutual acquaintances is always a good idea because it's important for Expressives to accept you into their clique of friends. Your verbal and nonverbal communication should be enthusiastic and can even border on being flamboyant and outrageous. Like Amiables, Expressives are relationship-oriented. They want to feel that they are doing business with a friend, so opening the presentation with friendship development tactics is a plus here.

Discovering the buyer's needs   Discovering Expressives' needs can be quite a trick. Since they tend toward exaggeration, a salesperson can easily mistake a minor for a major problem. Expressives' needs may be presented in a convoluted fashion; being ramblers by nature, they easily get off the track onto unproductive tangents.

Discovering Expressives' needs through questioning is the best approach and is often most effectively accomplished by brainstorming. Adaptive salespeople may have to use all of their organizational ability to keep this part of the presentation focused.

Making a recommendation   Use plenty of summarization throughout the presentation to help keep it focused; from that, you can determine the recommendations to make. It is a good idea to write out salient points as the presentation progresses to help focus and lead you to a clear recommendation. It's more productive when dealing with an Expressive to state your recommendations based on ideas and concepts, rather than on facts and figures. Analyticals and Drivers like facts and figure; Expressives like concepts and ideas. All recommendations should be made in a manner that enhances and plays to the Expressive's ego and self-esteem.

Closing the sale   The best way to ask for the business is to do it casually and informally. Expressives respond well to buying incentives. For example, "If we can agree on an order today, then we'll throw in an additional..." or "In addition to that, we also include...". The idea is to close the sale by making the purchase seem even more exaggerated and a better deal than the Expressive originally envisioned. Don't be afraid to ask for a definite commitment. However, this cannot be done in an aggressive, assertive, or hard-close manner. Don't be surprised if the Expressive closes the sale and then asks for the details—the exact opposite of the Analytical.

On closing the sale, reassure Expressives that their purchase will enhance their position, self-esteem, or ego. It's very important for Expressives to know that they made a good decision. Reassure them of this, focusing on their grand concept, grand illusion, or grand vision.

Checklist for Working with Expressives

Dos	Don'ts
1. Plan interaction that supports their dreams and intentions.	1. Don't be curt, cold, or tight-lipped.
2. Leave time for relating and socializing.	2. Don't drive on to facts and figures, alternatives, abstracts.
3. Talk about people and their goals, opinions they find stimulating.	3. Don't leave things hanging in the air, or they'll hang there.
4. Don't deal with details; put them in writing; pin them to modes of action.	4. Don't waste time trying to be impersonal, judgmental, or task-oriented.
5. Ask for their opinions and ideas regarding people.	5. Don't "dream" with them too much, or you'll lose time.
6. Provide ideas for implementing action.	6. Don't kid around or stick to the agenda too much. Be flexible.
7. Use enough time to be stimulating, fun-loving, fast-moving, entertaining.	7. Don't talk down to them.
8. Provide testimonials from people they see as important, prominent.	8. Don't be dogmatic.
9. Offer special, immediate, and extra incentives for their willingness to take risks.	

Modify Your Social Style to the Customer's

Since an individual seldom fits exclusively into only one social style, it's not uncommon to find a Driver possessing some of the characteristics of an Analytical. The same could be said for Expressives and Amiables. The adaptive salesperson must continually fine-tune the presentation to match the

What Would You Do If...?

Baxter, your West Coast salesman, is scheduled to make a presentation on Monday at a major aircraft manufacturer your company has never sold to before. His precall research and customer profile has turned up something that worries him. The purchasing agent he will meet has a reputation for heavily using facts and statistical support. He also likes to include in his team a number of technical specialists. Clearly, Baxter knows that he is in for some tough going if he is to establish credibility.

▶ Question: What would you tell Baxter to do now, before his call, in order to prepare himself for his customer's style? And how should he respond when his customer begins to pour on the data?[5]

buyer and the situation at hand. When making a presentation, you may have to modify both your presentation style and social style. If you are an Analytical or a Driver, you must reduce your assertiveness when dealing with Amiables and Expressives. Similarly, if you are an Amiable or Expressive, you must increase your assertiveness when dealing the Analyticals and Drivers. If you are an Amiable or Expressive, then plan on reducing your emotional appeal when dealing with Analyticals and Drivers. The opposite holds true if you are a Driver or Analytical dealing with an Amiable or Expressive.

▶ ▶ *follow-up questions*

1. What is meant by the statement "sales effectiveness is a process of pattern recognition"?

2. What is the ISTEA process?

3. How would you get an appointment, open the call, discover the needs, make recommendations to, and close the sale to an Amiable? What would you do differently with a Driver?

The Minor Yes and the Trial Close

Making a sales presentation is sometimes like sending up trial balloons. You try this approach, negotiate on that point, and probe for a clue as to what is on the buyer's mind. This is particularly true in trying to determine if the customer is ready to close the sale and complete the transaction. Salespeople use two proven techniques to probe the customer's readiness to buy. They are the "minor yes" and the trial close.

Testing for Readiness via the Minor Yes and the Trial Close

As the buyer progresses from unawareness to conviction, the readiness to commit increases. To effectively proceed through a presentation, the salesperson needs to probe this readiness. Trying to close before the buyer is ready can be disastrous, as can failing to close when the buyer is ready. The minor yes and the trial close are the presentation tools salespeople use to probe this readiness. What are these and how do they work?

▶ ▶ ▶ ▶ ▶ ▶ ▶ ▶ ▷

Learning Objective 5: Using tie-downs and the minor yes close

A **minor yes,** also called a minor yes close, is getting the prospect to agree on the importance or necessity of a small aspect of the product. The minor yes may be directed toward a product's feature, advantage, or benefit. The idea here is that the "big yes" is simply a summation of the minor yesses. The industrial equipment buyer may not be ready to commit to buying a crane but is moving in that direction. If the salesperson can get minor agreement on the fact that the prospect's next crane will be self-propelled, the salesperson has a definite conviction on at least one aspect of the crane purchase. Thus, testing the prospect's readiness to buy the entire crane is pursued one feature at a time. Finally, the customer realizes the crane has all the desired features and decides to close the sale. You could think of it as testing for commitment in bite-sized pieces.

Salespeople use "tie-downs" to elicit minor yesses.[6] A **tie-down** is a two- or three-word question at the end of a sentence used to elicit a minor yes. Typical tie-downs are made from a variety of word combinations listed in columns 1 and 2 below:

Column 1	Column 2
Could/Couldn't	He/She
Should/Shouldn't	It
Would/Wouldn't	You
Are/Are not	We
Is/Was/Were	They
Can/Can't	That right/wrong
Have/Haven't	You agree
Will/Won't	

Typical Combinations

Aren't they	Aren't you	Can't you
Shouldn't it	Doesn't it	Don't you agree
Don't we	Shouldn't it	Wouldn't it
Haven't they	Hasn't he/she	Isn't it
Isn't that right	Didn't it	Wasn't it
Won't they	Won't you	Couldn't they

Below are five statements illustrating how tie-downs work:

"That red color is certainly eye-catching (*don't you agree?*)."

"Everybody could use a higher return on their bonds (*couldn't they?*)."

"Safety is important to all of us (*wouldn't you agree?*)."

"You could have a lot of fun on a savings of an extra $30 a day (*couldn't you?*)."

"Quality is important (*isn't it?*)."

Tie-downs are used to probe the prospect's readiness to buy by creating a positive, "say yes" attitude. This separates buyers from their negative thoughts and leaves them with only positives.

A **trial close** is a direct question, often using a tie-down, strategically asked during the presentation as a barometer of buying readiness. A trial close is used when:

- Salespeople have just explained a particularly strong selling point in a presentation.
- Salespeople finish a presentation, having said all they think they need to say.
- Salespeople have answered the prospect's questions about a particular feature, advantage, and benefit.
- Salespeople think they have overcome a prospect's objection.
- Salespeople want to finally close the sale.[7]

A trial close can be the salesperson's best friend in a presentation. Think of a trial close like testing the temperature of bath water. You only want to put your toe in a little way to check if it's ready; similarly, the trial close makes a small test of the buyer's readiness. It doesn't ask the customer to commit nor does it attempt to finalize the sale; it simply measures readiness. Trial close techniques can be as simple as asking a direct question. Some examples would be:

"Is that something like what you had in mind?"

"Do you think these terms will pass with the senior buyer?"

"Is that a benefit you would like?"

"This seems to meet your criteria, doesn't it?"

"Are these terms agreeable to you?"

"Have I answered all your questions adequately?"

"Are you still concerned about _____?"

"What do you think?"

Case in Point

Powerful Stuff Indeed

"What are the four most powerful words in business?" I was asked by Ren McPherson, a friend and neighbor. Ren was a CEO of Dana Corporation and a dean of Stanford University's graduate school of business, and he continues to be on boards of such companies as Dow Jones, Miliken and Westinghouse.

"The words are, 'What do you think?'" Ren said. And that got me thinking. Maybe those words don't apply just to business but to almost everything else. For instance:

▶ You cannot have very effective marketing without marketing research. This involves asking prospective customers what they think they want or need.

Continued

Two trial closing techniques are augmentations of the direct question. They are the alternative advance and the porcupine. The **alternative advance** offers customers a choice of alternatives to test their readiness to buy. The alternative advance probes the customer's readiness by asking for a minor decision between two alternatives. It assumes a positive response. In the **porcupine trial close,** the customers' question is turned around to test their readiness to close. Some alternative advance examples are:

"Which do you like best, the red or the green?"
"Is a Tuesday or Thursday delivery better for you?"
"Which one will your husband like best, the extra large or the large?"

The porcupine trial close (so-called because it is sharp on both ends) is simply a rephrasing of a customer's question. It works like this:

Customer: Does it come in only black?
Salesperson: Is there another color you want?

or

Customer: Do you deliver on Tuesday?
Salesperson: Do you want us to deliver it on Tuesday?

or

Customer: Do we get a volume discount on a thousand-piece order?
Salesperson: Are you going to place a thousand piece order?

Listening to the customer's response could mean cycling back to the presentation's beginning after discovering that significant needs or problems have not been addressed. It could mean customers are not ready because they want to see more of the demonstration. They may not be sure how the benefits apply to them. They may balk at the price, wanting a lower price, better terms, more discounts, or a sweetener. What ever it might be, the trial close is the tool that measures buyer's readiness and the salesperson's progress in the presentation. Positive answers to trial closes gives the salseperson the green light to proceed.

▸▸ *follow-up questions*

1. What is a minor yes?

2. What are tie-downs, and what role do they play in minor yesses and trial closes?

3. How would you use a trial close if you were selling shoes at the local shoe store? How would you use trial closes if you were selling a mainframe computer to your school?

Adapting to and Managing the Presentation Environment

Environmental control means more than regulating the light, temperature, and humidity. It mean managing the emotional and perceptual impact of the presentation.

Environmental Control

The physical environmental Environmental control is managing the proper selling environment. When calling on prospects in their office, salespeople can do little to manage the physical environment. Many presentations, however, take place where salespeople have control over the physical environment. Showrooms, trade show booths, and display facilities can be controlled to create the proper selling environment. Ethan Allen sells furniture in room galleries to showcase the furniture and accessories. The shoppers envision their houses looking like the model rooms. Sewell Village Cadillac in Dallas, Texas, displays its cars in opulence created by an environment embellished with fresh flowers and expensive antiques. Tom Peters says it looks more like the boardroom of a Fortune 500 company with cars sitting around than a car dealership.[8]

Discount stores create a selling atmosphere targeted to their market as well. A K-Mart "Blue Light Special" is hardly appropriate for the likes of a Neiman-Marcus or Nordstrom's department store. Real estate agents often tell homeowners to heat potpourri or bake an apple pie just before holding an open house. The aroma creates a homey atmosphere visitors find appealing and comforting. What's your first impression on entering a house smelling of apple pie, compared to one reeking of stale cigarette smoke?

Demonstrate A demonstration is the quickest and easiest way to highlight a product's features, advantages, and benefits. When doing a demonstration, keep the "show and tell and show" idea in mind. This simply means to break up the demonstration with explanations highlighting different aspects of the presentation. If the salesperson follows the approach of showing features, then explaining advantages and benefits, then showing features, and so on, the product is presented in a series of digestible portions.

When doing a demonstration, ask two questions: "*Why* are you demonstrating?" and "*What* are you demonstrating?" You are demonstrating to prove your product's performance claims. *What* you are demonstrating is how the product will deliver benefits to the customer. The easiest way to accomplish this is to get prospects involved in the demonstration. Getting prospects involved—and getting them to recognize the benefits offered—requires planning.

Planning a prospect involvement demonstration requires three things. First, determine what the prospect *needs* to know. Having reviewed the sales call planner, the salesperson plans to focus on the features, advantages, and benefits uniquely appropriate to the prospect's situation. Second, plan an exercise to showcase the product's features, advantages, and benefits. Finally, in planning this exercise, make sure it will be successful. This means the

Getting a prospect involved in a demonstration is a good way to prove performance claims.

salesperson should have tried it many times before the prospect tries it once. Whether the involvement exercise is as simple as loading a casette into a tape-player or as complicated as assembling a cutting mechanism on a machining lathe, the exercise must be guaranteed never to fail.

Case in Point

George Beattie: Salesman
Known for Explosive Presentations

George Beattie is vice-president and sales manager for American Explosives, Hayden Lake, Idaho, and is well known for his explosive demonstrations. George was a mining consultant and engineer before acquiring his explosives distributorship through DuPont. His normal workday finds him a mile below ground demonstrating his explosives products against his competitor's. He regularly stays in the mines 8 to 16 hours, blasting huge slabs of rock and analyzing the quality of his demonstrations for the customers. In all his years, he has only had one demonstration go wrong: a six-foot-by-six-foots lab of rock fell on him and broke his neck. Surgery saved him from paralysis.

George uses a consultative approach to selling. He must make every demonstration count; a bad demonstration down there, and two things happen: either your product looks bad or someone gets seriously hurt. It's a case of having the demonstration be exactly right each time. Preparation time is lengthy and expensive and the results must work; there's often no second chance.

Adapted from Mark Thalenberg, "Salesmen in Dangerous Territory," *Sales and Marketing Management* 134 (1985): 55–56.

In planning a prospect involvement exercise, remember the three key words to success are: *simplify, simplify,* and *simplify*. Don't make the exercise any harder than it needs to be. Regardless of the complex nature of the product, make everything as simple as possible for the prospect. Finally, plan for problems. Remember that if the demonstration can get fouled up, it probably will. Plan accordingly.

Demonstrating what can't be demonstrated Not everyone sells products that can be demonstrated. Travel agents make the intangible benefits of an island vacation tangible—and thus create a demonstration—through posters and brochures. Physicians and lawyers demonstrate and make tangible the quality of their service through their office decor. Insurance agents demonstrate savings by showing the customer calculations of the investment value of the policy. Demonstrating what physically cannot be demonstrated takes only a bit of imagination and creativity.

▶ ▶ ▶ ▶ ▶ ▶ ▶ ▶ ▶
Learning Objective 6: A positive environment is important to making the sale

The mental environment The proper mental environment is even more important than the physical environment. The mental environment is influenced emotion. The adaptive salesperson recognizes and enhances the positive emotions of the prospect and removes the negative emotions. Prospects

Table 10-1	**Fourteen Buying Forces**
Positive emotions trigger sales; negative emotions destroy sales. Fourteen of the most powerful buying forces are:	
Color and style	Peer pressure (keeping up with
Pride of ownership	the Joneses)
Vanity	Self-improvement
Security	Health
Prestige and status	Love of family
Ambition	Family getting larger
Employment change	Family getting smaller

often buy on emotion and justify their decisions through logic or rationalizations. Table 10-1 lists the 14 most powerful buying forces a salesperson works with to make a sale.

Everything the salesperson says, verbally and nonverbally, creates or destroys the buying emotion. Knowing this, the salesperson must practice and use "go-ahead" terms, rather than rejection terms. Many of these were discussed in the chapter on communications, but a review now would be in order. Let's talk about:[10]

Ownership	Rather than	Price or cost
Initial investment	Rather than	Down payment
Monthly investment	Rather than	Monthly payment
Agreement	Rather than	Contract
Owning	Rather than	Buying
Supplying you	Rather than	Selling you
Presentations	Rather than	Pitches
Authorizing	Rather than	Signing
Transactions	Rather than	Deal
Inexpensive	Rather than	Cheap
Counselor	Rather than	Salesperson
Offer to buy	Rather than	Bid

All these serve to put the buyer in the appropriate frame of mind, the proper mental environment. Using audiovisual equipment can contribute to creating the right mental atmosphere.

Using Audiovisual Equipment to Enhance the Buying Environment

The greater the five senses are involved, the greater a person's ability to remember. Talking to a customer addresses only auditory memory. Using audio and visual aids in conjunction with an explanation addresses two senses and is more powerful than either one alone. Audiovisuals are particularly useful in trade shows, where they both inform and attract customers to the displays. Audiovisual (AV) equipment can explain with one picture what it could easily take a salesperson 20 minutes to verbally explain. When showing products that require set-up and assembly, an AV presentation is much more meaningful than a mere verbal presentation. Table 10-2 provides examples of typical AV aids and their uses.

Table 10-2 Audiovisual Aids Commonly Used in Presentations

Type	Typical Usage
Charts and graphs	Illustrate relationships, show trends, scheduling, accounting information. Typically, computer software can now illustrate any numerical schedules or tables as pie charts, bar charts, line graphs, or point-and-figure graphs. Computer printers can produce these in color or black and white; many are capable of producing three-dimensional effects. Particularly useful in showing the cumulative effects of increased sales, cost savings, territory expansions, market share increases, etc.
	A favorite of salespeople because of their portability, flexibility, and adaptability; can be reshuffled as needed during the presentation.
Photos and pictures	Used extensively in sales brochures to illustrate benefits, show designs, and highlight features and in any situation where the product or service is intangible.
	Typically used by realtors, travel agencies, car dealerships, food producers, financial services, landscapers, interior decorators, etc.
Sales manuals	Generally used to accompany scripted presentations. They often are three-ring binders that contain the whole presentation. The salesperson takes the prospect through the presentation page by page, where each page highlights, either through pictures, diagrams, or words, an important part of the presentation. They are also used in large and complex presentations where extensive amounts of data, plans, drawings, or blueprints may be used and referred back to.
	Typically used when making home presentations to consumers for such products as water softeners, interior decorating services, landscaping, etc.
Films, videotape, and slides	Require equipment to be set up at presentation site but have the benefit of offering both visual and audio imagery. Work well for group presentations where projection can be managed. Equipment is now available that can be carried in a briefcase and set up on the customer's table or desk.
	Effectively used in presentations to large groups, when the product is too large to be demonstrated or seen any other way, or when product needs to be viewed as it is being operated.
Models and samples	Very effective for explaining features and advantages of a product. Excellent vehicles for getting the customer involved in the presentation. Like slides or pictures, models can depict, in reduced size, the actual product and how it operates. Samples are a way of getting the customer and other members of the buying center involved. They have something to evaluate and try.
	Used extensively for demonstrating consumer products. Models often used for large equipment; architectural firms use models extensively for three-dimensional effect.

The more senses involved, the more a prospect remembers a presentation.

Keep the following in mind if you are thinking about using any type of AV in a presentation:

▶ AV is part of and enhances a presentation but is not a substitute for a good presentation.

▶ AV does not do the salesperson's job.

▶ AV enhances important points, but don't use it to present all of them. Too much AV is like too much of anything; it loses its impact after a while.

▶ AV takes time—time to set up, take down, and use—so plan for it.

▶ Be prepared for AV failure; bring along extra projection bulbs, extension cords, batteries, etc.

▶ Make sure your visuals are not too large, too small, crowded, dark, bright, or that you have too many.

When Things Go Wrong

Throwing a Little Light on the Subject

The room for your sales presentation had been booked at the hotel for more than three months before the meeting. A list of the necessary audiovisual equipment and a chart of the seating arrangements were submitted to the staff of the hotel. When you and your sales team arrived the first morning of the meeting, you found the room had floor-to-ceiling picture windows on three sides, which provided an unobstructed view of the bathing beauties at the pool. Rescheduling another room was impossible. What would you do?[11]

Source: Adapted from Bill Voelekl, "Ten Ways to Screw Up a Sales Meeting," *Sales and Marketing Management* 140 (1988): 46.

Be efficient in using AV and make it enhance the presentation Remember, AV should make the presentation more efficient. It should convey more in less time than if it were not used. While doing so, it should not detract from showcasing the product or some aspect of the product. A presentation has a certain flow and rhythm to it. Breaking that rhythm by wrestling with a demonstration, a projector, or pictures reduces the presentation's effectiveness.

Make the presentation simple, concise, and easy for the customer to understand. Audiovisual aids should not be used to cram more material into a limited time span; rather, they should amplify and reinforce significant benefits, features, advantages, and uses of the product or service.

The audiovisual supporting material is physically part of the presentation and, as such, should have the appropriate trial closes, questions, and anticipated objections figured in. For example, if a salesperson were showing a slide highlighting the durability of a steel container, the salesperson would ask if that is an important feature to the customer and not assume that it is. This would be a way of incorporating a trial close into the AV portion of the presentation. If the AV portion is not amenable to starting and stopping, like the slide mentioned above, the salesperson should be prepared to summarize the important points the AV highlighted. This could be done with a summary of the benefits, advantages, and features amplified in the AV presentation. The key point is that audiovisual aids should hammer home an image, fact, relationship, or facet of the product the salesperson wants the customer to remember. If customers remember only 20 percent of what they hear and 20 percent of what they see, then if they both see and hear, they should remember 40 percent!

Case in Point

Put Some Showmanship Into the Visuals You Use!

The right visuals enhance any presentation, but many are too dull or too complicated. Here are some hints for putting some life into AV-enhanced presentations:

1. Open with a real grabber. A catchy title, a cartoon, a headline, or brief quotation gets attention.
2. Make them big—the bigger the better. A few bold words filling the screen holds people's attention better and longer.
3. Use key words or, better yet, pictures, symbols, or graphs.
4. Use color, but be careful: red means stop and green means go. Make the colors you use communicate a message in and of themselves.
5. Use animation when possible. Many computer graphics programs and overhead projection devices can do animation. People always remember something dynamic better than something static.

Source: Adapted from John H. Melchinger, as cited in "Create a Picture Perfect Presentation," *Personal Selling Power* 8 (1989): 5.

▸▸ follow-up questions

1. How does a salesperson stimulate or create the right mental atmosphere?
2. What are five powerful buying forces?
3. Why do a demonstration?
4. How does a salesperson demonstrate what cannot be demonstrated? Give two examples.

Case in Point

Telefocus Marketing Supports Sales and Salespeople

Telefocus marketing and sales uses a combination of videotape and telemarketing/direct marketing. Instead of sending a prospective customer a printed brochure, firms are now sending videotapes to tell their story. The prospective customer, after viewing the videotape, calls and places an order or visits a salesperson. Since two-thirds of all U.S. households today have at least one videotape player, the availability of playback units is no longer a barrier to telefocus marketing.

Continued

Summary

This chapter explained why and how to customize a presentation. The essence of adaptive selling is to be able to present the same product in a variety of ways, depending on the customer's particular social style and buying situation (Learning Objective 1). This is done using the ISTEA process in a sales presentation. ISTEA is an acronym for Impression, Strategy, Transmit, Evaluate, and Adjust (Learning Objective 2).

To effectively do this, the salesperson must understand personal social style characteristics. Four styles were identified and explained. They were Amiables, Expressives, Drivers, and Analyticals. Amiables are open, friendly, relationship-oriented individuals who must be dealt with patiently. Analyticals are very systematic and thorough. They expect salespeople to be experts in their fields and able to answer the most detailed questions. Analyticals will be looking for facts and figures, expecting them to be presented in a straightforward manner. The Driver's style was characterized as being risk-taking, fast-acting, and controlling. With the Driver, a salesperson can and should come right to the point. Drivers can be dealt with very directly in all aspects of the presentation. Because of their controlling nature, the presentation should be structured to let them make up their own mind, rather than trying to tell them what is best. The Expressive was the last social style discussed. Expressives are theatrical, flamboyant types given to overstatement and exaggerations. They are always impressed by the big picture, the larger-than-life claim, the grand plan. Expressives are creative and have active imaginations. Salespeople can be direct with Expressives; direct questions and asking for a definite commitment will work. This, however, cannot be done in an aggressive manner, as it would be with a Driver (Learning Objective 3).

The techniques for customizing a presentation to each individual style were presented. How to work with each social style was discussed in the context of five selling activities: getting an appointment, opening the call, discovering needs, making recommendations, and closing the sale. Because salespeople have a social style that they must adapt to the buyer's style, ways to increase or decrease assertiveness and emotionalism were presented. Decreasing assertiveness results from more questioning and listening. Increasing assertiveness is accomplished by being more direct and initiating conversations. Decreasing emotionalism means relying more on factual information and rational, logical approaches (Learning Objective 4).

An explanation of trial closes followed. Trial closes test the buyer's readiness to commit and can be used any time during a presentation. Alternative advance and porcupine trial closes were also explained. The alternative advance trial close gives the customer options to select from. The porcupine trial close restates a customer's question as a question; for example, "Does it come in red?" becomes "Do you want it in red?" (Learning Objective 5.)

The final element in formulating a presentation strategy is environmental control. This was discussed relative to both the physical and mental environment. Emphasizing positive buying emotions stimulates the mental environment, and using audiovisual enhances the physical environment (Learning Objective 6).

Key Terms

ISTEA An acronym used to identify the process an adaptive salesperson uses to customize a presentation; ISTEA stands for *I*mpression, *S*trategy, *T*ransmit, *E*valuate, and *A*djust.

Minor yes Also called a minor yes close, it is getting the prospect to agree on the importance or necessity of a small aspect of the product.

Tie-down A two- or three-word contraction at the end of a sentence used to elicit a minor yes from a prospect.

Trial close A direct question, often using a tie-down, strategically asked during the presentation as a barometer of buying readiness.

Alternative advance A trial closing technique that offers customers a choice of alternatives to test their readiness to buy.

Porcupine trial close Rephrasing customers' questions back to them when, for example, they inquire about a feature, advantage, or benefit to test their readiness to close.

Discussion Questions

1. Walking into a prospective customer's office, you notice trappings that indicate a well-organized and efficient person. However, when she begins talking to you, you realize she is more of an Expressive type. How do you handle the situation where the prospective customer doesn't fit neatly into one social style or another?

2. What social style would you most likely find the easiest to sell to? (Hint: What style are you?)

3. What is the key to success when selling to a Driver?

4. How are Expressives and Drivers alike?

5. If you are an Amiable selling to a customer who is a Driver, how would you adjust to the customer?

6. What are product benefits? What are the benefits a travel agent sells? A lawn care service?

7. What are the three things required in planning a customer involvement demonstration?

8. If you were selling your calculator to someone, what would be a feature, advantage, or benefit you could use as a focal point for a minor yes?

9. What are the dangers in discussing your competition during a presentation?

10. Why would a salesperson make a call on a customer fully intending not to sell anything?

Application Exercise

I. Go back and reread the box entitled "The Right Presentation to the Right Person Yields 230 percent of Quota," then answer the following questions:

1. The vice-president of operations was convinced in ten minutes. Knowing no more than that, what social style would you guess he was?

2. What benefits would you stress if you were this copying machine salesperson and had only ten minutes to get your point across?

3. If you had to sell a duplicating machine to an Analytical, how would you approach it? What if you were selling the same machine to an Expressive?

II. In the chapter, four social styles were explained, along with how to sell to them. Another application of social styles is in handling people's complaints. If a customer (a Driver) called you to come and talk about a problem with the motor you sold him, how and what would you do to prepare for the meeting?

Class Exercises

Group Exercise

Discuss the characteristics of each social style as identified in the chapter and identify your own social style. Pick another student and identify his or her social style as best you can. Then, ask that person if your observations match what he or she thinks he or she is. Were you right in seeing that person the way he or she sees him or herself? Is the other person correct in the way he or she views him or herself, or is that the way he or she "thinks" he or she *is* or *wants* to be perceived?

Now, pick another student whose social style is opposite yours and prepare a short presentation of a familiar product to that person.

1. How effective was the presentation, in terms of the meshing of social styles? Now try a presentation with a person who has the same social style as you and do it again. Was it easier or harder to interact with that person or the first one?

2. Which presentation did you feel was the most effective? Why?

Individual Presentation

Assume you have been assigned to sell advertising in the program for the upcoming school theater production. You will be presenting to prospective individuals and organizations the benefits of gaining exposure in this publication.

It's Friday afternoon, and you have entered one of the local retailer's stores close to campus. You hope the owner will buy a nice display ad for the program.

1. Make your presentation, using at least four different tie-downs that would elicit minor yesses.

2. Make your presentation using the alternative advance and porcupine trial closes.

3. Summarize with the class what has happened.

 *Cases*

Formulating a Presentation Strategy

Samuelson Glass has been in business for over 50 years and run by the same family. Part of the glass installation process requires using industrial solvents to remove and dissolve glazing compound around the window. James Washington is the salesperson for Industrial Solvents, and he wants to make a presentation to Samuelson's management. Their account, while not extremely large, is a steady sale; they order about the same amount of solvents each month, amounting to sales of slightly less than $75,000 per year. James knows from doing an account profile and developing a call planner that Paul Samuelson, the brother responsible for purchasing, has a technical background and is very conservative. James knows he is a very results-oriented person, always seeming to be short of time and not liking to be bothered by salespeople.

Industrial solvents are a price item to most buyers. James's prices are competitive, and he knows that if he can get some of the business away from the competitors, he can probably have it all within a year or so. The meeting is set for next Monday with Paul. James is not nervous, but he does want everything to go well.

James's manager Lisa Oslund says about James: "He's a good man. He is not the most dynamic in the world, but he really cares about serving his customers and tries everything he can to accommodate them. He likes to feel a close tie to them, become their friends, get to know all about their kids, spouses, hobbies, and so on. Most of his customers appreciate this, and he has established good friendships and relationships with all the people he sells. He's not the assertive, hard-sell type, for sure. He'll do okay with Samuelson, but he's going to have to change his style a little. I've heard Paul Samuelson can be quite intimidating until you get to know him. I hope James gets the account. It's the type we like."

Questions

1. How would you classify Paul Samuelson's social style? James's social style?

2. Depending on your answer to question 1, how will James modify his social style to adapt to Paul's?

3. Suppose you are James. How would you plan your call? Be sure to include the following:

  ▸ What opener, icebreaker, or relaxer you would use?
  ▸ What presentation style would work best?
  ▸ How you would get the appointment, uncover needs, make recommendations, and close the sale?
  ▸ Since price is competitive, with everyone offering about the same, what tangible and intangible benefits might you stress?

Case 10.2

Selling Suits to Suit

As the manager of the retail men's clothing store, your job is to train new salespeople. The store carries top line merchandise and caters to a clientele that can afford $350–$650 suits. The store also carries all the accessory items, shirts, ties, shoes, jewelry, etc. Most of the customers are professional and managerial types, and the up-and-comers just entering the ranks of management.

You've been observing one of the new salespeople dealing with customers. This person has been working at the store for about two weeks and seems to be having a little trouble making a presentation of the suits to customers. He is not having the success he should be having and you have several ideas why.

Question

1. What alternatives would you suggest he consider in the following:
  ▸ Openers to use when first meeting the customer.
  ▸ The most applicable presentation format.
  ▸ Discovering the buyer's needs and tailoring the benefits to match.
  ▸ The trial close(s) which would work best.
  ▸ Determining which buying force to focus on.

References

1. Adapted from James E. Lukaszewski and Paul Ridgeway, "To Put Your Best Foot Forward, Start by Taking These 21 Simple Steps," *Sales and Marketing Management,* 142 (1990): 84–86.
2. Barton A. Weitz and Peter Wright, *The Salesperson as a Marketing Strategist: The Relationship between Field Sales Performance and Insights about One's Customers* (Cambridge, Mass.: Marketing Sciences Institute, Working Paper No. 78-120, 1978).
3. The next few sections borrow heavily from and have paraphrased the work of Roger Wenschlag, *The Versatile Salesperson* (New York: John Wiley & Sons, 1987), chapters 9 and 10. The format used here follows his because of its succinctness, ease of understanding, and parsimony. Students are encouraged to consult his book for a complete treatment of selling to different social styles.
4. Martin J. Seldman, "How to Land Lucrative Japanese Accounts...Learn Their Lingo," *Personal Selling Power,* 10 (1990): 22–23.
5. Modified from Robert E. Kellar, "How Good Are You at Negotiating?" *Sales and Marketing Management* 141 (1989): 29. (For the answer, see ibid., pp. 29–30.)
6. This section borrows heavily from Tom Hopkins, *How to Master the Art of Selling* (New York: Warner Books, 1982), pp. 21–22.

7. Adapted from Charles Futrell, *Fundamentals of Selling* (Homewood, Ill.: Richard D. Irwin, 1984), pp. 285–86.

8. Tom Peters has used this reference in many personal and TV appearances.

9. Hopkins, *How to Master the Art of Selling*, p. 47.

10. Ibid., pp. 48–49, and "Killer Words," *Better Homes & Gardens Real Estate Service*, November 1979.

11. Moral: Don't just plan ahead of time; plan thoroughly ahead of time. On-site visits, exact specifications, and written confirmations all help ensure a successful meeting. Don't leave *any* detail up to a hotel staff; always check for yourself and follow up. Often, there is no chance to make changes at the last minute!

12. Richard Kern, "Making Visuals Work for You," *Sales and Marketing Management*, 141 (1989): 46–48.

Welcome Objections

Objectives

After completing this chapter, you will be able to:

1. Define specifically what objections are.

2. Identify five categories of objections.

3. Describe the steps in the objection-handling system you can use to overcome objections.

4. Relate the rules for applying the objection-handling system to a selling situation.

5. Describe the ten techniques for handling objections, including an example of each.

6. Identify which objection-handling technique works best on each social style of buyer.

7. Explain how trial closes can be transitions to successfully closed sales.

The Professional Selling Question

What is the objection or sales resistance you encounter most often, and what have you found is the best way to handle it?

A Sales Expert Responds

Doug Rende is a senior contract marketing representative with Armstrong World Industries. He answers the question based on his years of selling experience by saying, "My responsibilities include working with the architectural and interior design community to secure specifications of Armstrong products for new construction or renovation projects and to follow the negotiation or bid process through the general contractors or subcontractors to the successful installation of material."

"As you can imagine, all of this involves dealing with many different types of people with many different areas of expertise and responsibility. The constant challenge is to be prepared for any and all objections that could be raised about your product. The key word regarding this challenge is preparation: knowing the strengths and limitations of the items you represent and the requirements of the individual you are contacting."

"This state of preparedness for a person in sales can also be described as professionalism. To keep abreast of the latest technology regarding your industry, to know your competitors' strengths and weaknesses, and to perform the service of being a consultant to those you contact gives you the credibility necessary to develop and maintain a long-term client relationship that exemplifies professionalism."

"For the person considering a career in sales, or a person new to the field, one of the major anxieties is 'How will I deal with rejection? When the door is closed on me, or when a negative concern is raised, how will I react?' The best way I have found to alleviate that uncertainty is to remember that any objection is an opportunity. Any time an objection is raised, it allows you to more specifically pinpoint the presentation, thus targeting the real reason for the buyer's objection."

"The most difficult buyer to deal with is the one who says nothing, who simply nods or occasionally mutters an 'Uh huh'! With this individual, you are shooting at your target in the dark, not knowing where to adjust your sights. Gathering the necessary information to conform to your customers' requirements can only be achieved through questioning. The best approach is the use of open-ended questions (who, what, why, etc.) which require a full answer or explanation allowing you to better present *the* item that most aptly suits the customer's needs."

"The most often heard objection is the price objection. This then typically turns the approach toward treating the product like a commodity—where the only way to satisfy a customer is with a low-cost item. With a reduced emphasis on styling, products in this area tend to look very similar. Because of this, the quality of an item is not easily recognized and thus much is sold by *apparent* value."

"When dealing with a price objection, it is necessary to do two things. (1) Qualify the objection. Cost concerns in particular typically show a want to buy, but at that point, not enough reasons have been presented to justify use of your product. When the price objection is genuine, remember that if this commodity item performs according to specification, if it does what it says it will, it is a quality item and not just a 'me too' product. (2) Differentiate yourself. What does your product offer that sets it apart from the rest? Sell your strengths. In doing so, again be aware of what features the competition offers, and in presenting your product features, always state what function it provides—offering proof of these claims. The last area of differentiation is that of the individual. Sales is, and always will be, a people business, and the last factor in any decision making, especially in a commodity business, is the perception by the buyer of the representative."

"Excitement in sales comes from the many different people encountered and the constant challenges they present. Satisfaction comes from meeting the objections raised and proving your value to your customers, to your company, and most importantly, to yourself."

Introduction

People who are apprehensive about a career in selling because they will run into objections do not understand what objections are! Knowing what they are and how they can be used creates opportunities for sales and success. Objections represent a customer's resistance to purchase. There are a variety of reasons for this resistance, but every salesperson gets objections; it is just part of the selling process. Understanding why they occur is necessary for knowing how to handle them.

Objections occur for several reasons. They may happen because of poor qualifying. If prospects have not been adequately qualified, they may not be interested and therefore can legitimately claim they have no need for the product or cannot afford it. The clue here is that many objections can be eliminated before they occur if prospects are qualified properly and thoroughly. Objections occur because customers are often uncertain about making the purchase. This manifests itself in a variety of ways. If customers are unsure about whether they really need the product, they will probably claim they do not need it or at least do not need it at this time. Customers' uncertainty about making a purchase also stems from not being clear on specific points about the product, its price, its performance, or their recourse if it does not work. Here, customers will raise objections as a way of getting the clarification they need. Salespeople welcome objections because more often than not, an objection is not a rejection but a disguised request for clarification or more explanation. Everyone, not just salespeople, have faced an objection to a request at one time or another; even getting a date can be thought of as a sales effort.

Everyone at one time or another has asked someone out for a date. Everyone has been turned down at one time or another, too! Why were you turned down? Was it because of poor qualifying on your part? Was it because of something you could not do anything about? Or was it because you were getting an *objection* and you did not know how to handle it? Getting a date and making a sale are a lot alike. In both instances, you are trying to get someone

Successful salespeople are skilled at handling objections by staying calm or presenting relevant information about the product.

to behave in a manner that will benefit both of you. In getting a date, you want the prospect to agree to go out with you. In sales, you want the prospect to agree to make a purchase.

Successful salespeople see objections as a sure sign of progress in the sales presentation. If prospective buyers are not interested, they have no need to raise objections. It is really simple: if prospects are interested, they raise questions and objections. Objections create opportunities for salespeople to explain the features, advantages, and benefits of their product or service.

Salespeople who have mastered adaptive selling welcome objections. They look upon them as challenges to their abilities to develop creative and innovative methods for dealing with them. They understand how the prospect's buying psychology works and how objections are a natural part of the decision process. Inexperienced salespeople often fear objections, which is a major reason for their failure.

People who are successful in sales and people who seem to be successful at getting dates have something in common: they both know how to handle objections! We will discuss the types of objections salespeople can expect and how to deal with each one.

What Specifically Are Objections?

Objections Versus Conditions

Is the customer's "no" an objection or a condition? This question represents the two classes of obstacles that prevent a prospect from buying. Understanding these allows salespeople to adapt their presentation to help the prospect make the buying decision. Obstacles to an affirmative decision can stem from either a truly bona fide impediment to making a purchase or a lack of understanding or information.

Learning Objective 1: What objections are

Conditions   **Conditions** are valid reasons for not being able to buy and cannot be easily overcome. They may, however, be negotiated away. They reflect a "condition" that prohibits a positive buying decision. A customer may be totally out of storage space for more inventory and thus raise this as a condition. It is a "condition" because it represents a situation which physically and actually prevents buying more products. If the salesperson can negotiate a deal where his/her firm will store the product (at a price) for the customer, then our salesperson has negotiated away the condition. The "condition," now removed, allows the customer to buy. Some conditions are transitory. They exist now but at some time in the future may disappear. While you cannot financially afford to buy that Rolls-Royce now, you may be able to buy one in the future and probably will!

Conditions are usually discovered in the qualification stage of the selling process. Conditions are total blocks to a buying decision, and the adaptive salesperson must become adept at qualifying to avoid trying to overcome a condition in the presentation.

Objections   The dictionary defines an objection as something said in disagreement or disapproval. We will define an **objection** as any opposition or resistance to a salesperson's request, usually coming from a lack of understanding or information. Objections represent an obstacle to an affirmative decision which can usually be overcome by the salesperson. Tom Hopkins, a noted sales consultant, says, "Objections are the rungs of the ladder to sales success."[1] Each rung represents an obstacle and an opportunity to reach the top. Apprehension and anxiety over objections and how to deal with them means that you do not understand how to make them work for you!

Case in Point

Why Prospects Object

A prospective buyer resists or objects for many reasons during the sales conversation. The following six appear to be the more frequent reasons:

1. Prospects do not completely understand some aspect of the proposal.
2. Prospects are unable to justify the cost involved.
3. Prospects want more proof of the claims for why they should buy.
4. Prospects want more control at the interview (they do not want to be pushed).
5. Prospects want to be part of the discussion, not merely the target of the salesperson.
6. Prospects believe that the value of the product is not equal to or greater than its cost.

Objections are Questions

If prospects objects to the price, they are not sold on value.

If they question value, they are not sold on the benefits.

Continued

Continued—If they question the benefits, the salespeople have not proven their claims.

If they question the salespeople's proof, they are not sold on their honesty.

If they question the salespeople's honesty, they are not sold on their character.

If they question the salespeople's character, the salespeople should not be in sales!

Four Facts to Keep in Mind about Objections

Fact 1: No objections usually means no buying decision   Buyers with serious intentions always raise objections and ask questions. Do not confuse questions and objections. Questions represent opportunities for further explanation, clarification, and education. Objections represent resistance to some part or all of the presentation. Objections can stem from lack of information, but a question is not always an objection in disguise. For example:

Buyer: How can we afford this?

This can be a simple question asking for clarification or financing ideas. It can also be an objection in the form of a question. Nonverbal signals would be the distinguishing clues. If there is no intention to consider a purchase, the buyer faces no risk, has no immediate need for information, and will raise no objections.

While having no objections can signal no serious intention to buy, it can also signal that the salespeople have not done their job adequately. They may find no objections because:

▶ They have not qualified the prospect adequately.

▶ They may be talking to the wrong person. The person may not have the authority to make the decision or even be part of the decision process.

▶ They may have failed to locate the buyer's needs. Buyers may have no objections to the product simply because the salesperson is trying to sell them the wrong product. This differs from inadequate qualifying in that here, the focus is on motivation to buy, while in qualifying, the focus is on physical, economic, or personal criteria.

Fact 2: Objections indicate interest   Quite simply, the prospect would not even be talking to the salesperson if there were no interest at all! Objections may be disguised requests for information or a face-saving way of communicating a lack of understanding or a misunderstanding. Why would a prospect allow a salesperson to continue if there were no buying intention or interest? Keep in mind that objections indicate interest. Be more concerned if there are no objections. Objections are a natural reflection of interest.

Fact 3: Objections may be revealing the buyer's thoughts   The type of objections raised reveals what buyers are thinking and gives salespeople the opportunity to focus their presentation on the features, advantages, and benefits that are most important to the buyers. For example, if prospect raise objections to price, they are trying to rationalize the purchase on cost savings or to figure out how to budget for the expenditure. In other words, they may be questioning the price not because of the price itself but because they cannot afford that large of a one-time expenditure. They might be able to afford it, however, if the price could be spread over monthly payments. If salespeople recognize this, they can redirect their presentation away from price and toward a payment plan.

Fact 4: Objections may reveal the prospect's true interests   The objection being raised may signal that the salesperson is trying to sell the wrong product. If prospects keep coming back to the point that they do not see any need for the product, the salesperson may be offering the wrong product. Adaptive salespeople recognize that objections often mean something different than what is actually being said. They can alter their presentations to present a different product.

Is the Objection Singular or Bundled?

Singular objections appear one at a time. Bundled objections are several all raised at the same time. Determine through questioning which of the objections is the most important to the prospect.

A bundled objection might appear as follows:

Prospect: I can get an Apple desktop or even an IBM from your competitor at a lower price *(this is a price objection)*. At your price, I would have to take it to the boss for approval anyway *(this is a stalling tactic)*

Seller: Just so that I can be clear, is it the price or something about the product that you'll have to justify to your boss that is keeping us from coming to an agreement? *(Seller is trying to probe the prospect's priority.)*

Prospect: The problem is justifying the purchase of another desktop computer at that price. *(Buyer has identified a desire to focus on price.)*

Seller: In addition to that, are there any other problems?

Prospect: We really need a rock-bottom price if we are going to add another desktop. We have to show it is economically justified.

The salesperson in the above scenario has probed the buyer's state of readiness, and the prospect has given a definitive signal that the objection is to the price. The salesperson then takes the cue and moves back into the presentation for an in-depth discussion of the price and the economic justification based on cost savings, useful life, or similar value-oriented aspects.

Case in Point

Customer's Objections Can Be Converted to Profitable Sales

The new sales representative of a pharmaceutical manufacturing company walks into the pharmacy department for the first time:

> **Rep:**   My name is Frank Baker, from W. Smith Laboratories.
>
> **Buyer:**   No use calling on me. I will never again buy from your company!
>
> **Rep:**   I'm shocked to hear that! Could it have been something the company did or the recent rep, whom I know to have been a fine person?

Continued

I would personally appreciate your kindness by telling me how we could get back into your good graces.

Buyer: I returned about $30 worth of your merchandise about three months ago, and the office never credited my account and continually billed me. I called the office, and some woman said, "That medicine was outdated and we don't give credit for such items." I told her I gave it to the salesman and he said he would take it back. She said, "That rep is no longer with us and there is nothing I can do," and hung up!

Rep: If I were you, I would feel exactly as you do. You are 100 percent justified in your attitude. Our company was not in error, but the rep *failed* by not picking it up *before* it became outdated. The office employee was thoughtless in her discourtesy to you, a good customer, on the phone.

Your store routinely sells our products A and B and you make a reasonable profit on these items.

If my sales manager approves (and I'm sure she will), I would be pleased to replace the $30 you did not get credit for with the products you now sell and will deliver them personally tomorrow if you will be in about 2 P.M.

Buyer: Well, that should do it. I'll see you tomorrow when you come to check our stock for any "outdated" merchandise.

Rep: Thank you for understanding. I feel much better now.

follow-up questions

1. Why would a prospect have no objections at all to anything salespeople might be saying about their product?

2. How can objections reveal the real thoughts of the prospective buyer about the product?

Five Categories of Objections

◀ ◀ ◀ ◀ ◀ ◀ ◀ ◀
Learning Objective 2: The five categories of objections

With training and practice, salespeople can become skillful at recognizing which category of objection they are facing and determining the best method for overcoming it. All objections fit into one of five categories: no-money or price, time or stalling, hidden, no-need, and product objection. Objections may take the form of any of the five types but actually come from deep concerns arising from a past history with or apprehensions about a firm's products, services, the salesperson, or the company itself. A buyer may be apprehensive about the ability of the new salesperson to handle the complexities of the order, doubt the validity of the service claims, or be uncertain of the firm's record of product quality.

Such concerns as these need to be ferreted out and dispelled, disclaimed, explained, or compensated for. The techniques explained below help to uncover both obvious and subtle objections.

The Professional Salesperson Should
Become an Objection Specialist

The No-Money or Price Objection

The **no-money or price objection** is frequently used and involves prospects saying they cannot afford the product, the price is too high, or they do not have the money now. The price objection comes couched in a variety of terms and phrases. It may focus on the price, the prospect's budget, costs, or inability to afford the product. This objection may be a valid request for the salesperson to show prospects how they can afford it or how they can work it into their budget. It may also be an attempt to try to get the salesperson to lower the price. Remember, it is the job of the buyer to get as low a price as possible, just as it is the job of the salesperson to make a sale that is profitable for the selling company.

In dealing with the no-money or price objection, salespeople must think about several things. First, can they handle this objection by lowering their price and should they? Lowering the price is an easy way out and one that inexperienced salespeople often fall prey to. If buyers can get salespeople to lower their price, why shouldn't they? If salespeople have a product that offers prospects true value, if their price fairly reflects their costs and a reasonable profit, and if the quality of their product or service justifies the asking price, then they should not lower it!

Second, salespeople should not apologize for their price—they should justify it instead! Their company, like the prospect's company, is in business

Prospects who cannot afford the product, or find the price too high use the no-money or price objection.

to make a reasonable profit. If they are asking a fair price for their product and the price objection arises, they should review the benefits and move on.

If prospects have a problem with the price, they will send clear signals; if not, salespeople should not create the objection in prospects' mind! Let's look at the following dialogue to see how a salesperson *created* an objection in the prospect's mind:

Prospect: I can appreciate the features of desktop publishing software, but what kind of a price are we looking at?

Seller: This software package costs $499.95. Let me explain what we can do to work this price into your budget and what we might do to make it even more attractive for you!

Prospect (thinking): At $499.95, this is competitive with the other products I have bought. Maybe I have been paying too much! I think this price is "soft" and has some room for me to work with. This guy seems willing to drop the price. I will play along and save some money.

Prospect (speaking): Well, I was thinking that the price did seem a little too high. At $499.95, it would be hard for me to justify the purchase. If we were thinking about buying, what is the absolute lowest price you could give me?

A third technique would be to handle this objection as a reflection of value. Rather than dwell on the price, move the prospect away from this objection by selling the value of the product. Curtis-Mathis, a manufacturer of home entertainment equipment, dealt with the price objection in its TV ads by openly stating that its prices were the highest in the market but its quality and dependability (as backed by its guarantee) made its products worth it. Some prospects are purely price buyers. They are not interested in quality, service, or anything other than price. Adaptive salespeople dealing with this type of buyer quote their lowest price and move to close the sale; such prospects won't be interested in anything else anyway!

The fourth important consideration in dealing with the price objection is the selling company's policies and the law. Can the salesperson deal on price? In a study of insurance salespeople asked about their ability to negotiate prices on policies, over 30 percent said they had some degree of latitude to negotiate price with prospective customers. To the horror of the company, this meant that these agents did not know that such negotiating was strictly forbidden by the company and state law! Ignorance of the law in dealing with the price objection is no excuse. It may leave salespeople and their company both liable.

Case in Point

Price and Ignorance of the Law: Go Directly to Jail, Do Not Pass Go!

Antitrust laws are complex and the management and sales staff often do not receive any preventive legal advice. Ignorance of the law is no excuse! Penalties for violating antitrust laws are severe. Fines can be imposed of up to $100,000 for individuals and $1 million for companies.

Continued

The Time or Stalling Objection

The time or stalling objection can be a real smoke screen for the inexperienced salesperson. This objection allows prospects to create the notion that they are going to buy but not during this call. Inexperienced salespeople often, but incorrectly, accept the stalling objection as a positive sign of an impending sale. This objection allows poor salespeople to rationalize their failure by claiming, "The prospect was really hot and promised to buy. Something must have gone sour. It is not my fault something soured the deal!"

The stalling objection is a frequent ploy prospects use to get rid of salespeople. Prospects can agree that the salesperson has a great product, the right price, and the features needed, but they say they cannot buy now, will certainly consider the offer, and will get back to the salesperson soon. This way, the prospect does not have to formally reject the salesperson.

This objection comes in many forms. Some of the most common are "I will have to think it over," "Next time...," and "I will have to get the approval of my superior." These forms can be handled by using a little creativity. For example:

Prospect: Yes, you certainly do have a good product there, but I will have to think it over and get back to you.

Seller: I can understand how you would want to take a little more time to consider this, but what bothers you that you'll have to think over?

or

Prospect: Well, if it were up to me, I would buy it! However, I have to get the approval of my boss to go ahead.

Seller: What kind of concerns will your boss have? If you could go ahead with the offer today, would you?

or

Prospect: It sounds good, but not this time. Maybe next time.

Seller: We certainly could wait until next time, but I would hate to see you miss out on the savings we are currently offering. You would like to save money, wouldn't you?

In dealing with this objection, keep in mind that people do make up their minds at different rates of speed. Some are very decisive and will want to make the decision today, and some people are risk-averse and will want to put off making the decision as long as possible. This may be particularly true if the product or service is new or unfamiliar to the buyer. How people adopt new or unfamiliar products can be a key to understanding how to deal with the time objection effectively.

The Hidden Objection

A hidden objection is probably the hardest type to deal with. The **hidden objection** is one the prospect does not reveal for whatever reason. The seller must try to uncover and deal with it if the sale is to be made. The very nature of the name indicates the problem with this objection.

The real objection may be of a sensitive nature and not something the buyer wants to reveal. For example, some prospects simply do not like to turn salespeople down. They feel uncomfortable saying no and will appear to be hesitant for a reason the seller cannot determine. The buyer may have been told not to deal with the seller's firm anymore. A bad experience may be the cause for the objection. There are many reasons for hidden objections; but from the seller's perspective, it is still an objection that must be overcome.

Some behaviors signal a hidden objection. A prospect's body language may offer a clue. If the prospect sits with arms and/or legs crossed, fails to make eye contact, or generally appears to be agitated or uncomfortable (the nonverbal rejection or caution signals discussed in the chapter on communication), the salesperson might suspect a hidden objection.

Hidden objections may be identified through a process of elimination. After agreeing on features, advantages, and benefits, that the price is not an obstacle, and that the person with whom the seller is speaking has the authority to buy and if the salesperson has exhausted all of the other reasons for objection, then the seller is dealing with a hidden objection.

In this case, the salesperson can ask directly if there is some objection that has not yet been handled. A direct question is a totally fair approach. Asking for honesty and candor will save a lot of time and frustration for both the salesperson and the prospect.

The No-Need Objection

Like other objections, the no-need objection can take several forms. Salespeople may hear "We are all stocked up now," "This is not our type of product," "I don't need any," or "I have all that I can use." Any of these statements can really be opportunities for them to continue their presentation. By asking how often the prospect orders, how much is generally used in a week, or when the last order was delivered, the astute seller can handle this objection and close the sale (or determine a future time to call again.)

This objection is often coupled with others. It is quite possible to hear "We don't need any at this time, try me again in a few weeks." This is tying the no-need and the stalling objections together. Another possibility might be "We don't need any because we are already satisfied with our current supplier." Adaptive salespeople would tell this prospect that they are pleased the prospect is happy with the current supplier, but they stand ready to help any time the prospect might need them.

What if prospects *really* do not need the salespeople's product? If this is the case, then the salespeople have done a poor job of qualifying the buyers and are wasting everyone's time. This is why meticulous qualifying is so important! By determining in the qualifying process that there is a need for the product, the adaptive salesperson has eliminated a major hurdle to successfully closing the sale.

The Product Objection

The product objection is an objection that specifically relates to some aspect of the product itself. The customer may object to a variety of things about the product. Possible sources of objections are:

1. Performance characteristics
2. Packaging
3. Incompatibility with present system, other products or shipping methods
4. Doesn't conform to specifications
5. Size, weight, shape
6. Color, style, design
7. Apparent difficulty in using it
8. Not what customer thinks s/he wants

In some cases, the salesperson can handle the objection with further explanation. The objection may stem from a simple lack of understanding which further explanation will clear up. It may stem from a change in the buyer's needs. The installation of a new computer system could make the salesperson's software offering incompatible with the customer's new system. The objection to the product could be strictly emotional, the customer just doesn't like the way it looks, feels, tastes, etc. It may stem from a qualifying problem on the salesperson's part as well. If the salesperson hasn't done an adequate job of fact-finding and qualifying, he/she may be presenting a product that physically won't work for the customer. There are a variety of possibilities.

When the salesperson faces such an objection, offering an alternative product is the natural solution, if possible. This may be a very simple objection to overcome or may actually turn out to be a condition the salesperson simply can't deal with and must pass on making an offering to the customer. The salesperson should always anticipate such an objection and have several alternatives in mind. An objection based on color, for example, may be simply handled. An objection based on performance characteristics or design problems could require totally new engineering and manufacture, something the salesperson's company may not be financially able or willing to consider.

▸▸ *follow-up questions*

1. What are the five categories of objections?
2. In your opinion, what is the most frequent objection salespeople face?
3. When confronted with a salesperson, which objection do *you* use the most?

Dealing with Objections

Accomplished salespeople who have become proficient at dealing with objections soon recognize objections for what they are and welcome them as challenges to their creativity. Experience is one of the best teachers when it comes to objections, but until the salesperson gets that experience, knowing some of the tools of the trade will help. In this section, we offer some proven strategies and techniques for handling objections.

Remember that a strategy is like an overall game plan; what we need to think about before getting into any specific techniques. By keeping an overall game plan in mind, recognizing and dealing with objections becomes far less intimidating than you might think.

Handle Objections Systematically[2]

Objections can be effectively handled if they are approached systematically.

Step 1: Hear Out the Prospect   Too many salespeople are impatient when dealing with objections. Listen completely to prospects. This will give you two advantages. First, the prospects may provide the answer to their own objection without even realizing it! It is always easier to overcome objections if the prospects, consciously or unconsciously, give clues to the answers.

Learning Objective 3: The steps to systematically handle objections

Second, by listening completely, you buy time to think. Don't be in a hurry to answer an objection until you are sure what the real objection is.

Prioritize the objections if they are raised together. Take a second to sort them out and plan a systematic approach to dealing with the most important one first. If you are not sure which objection is the most important, always ask.

Step 2: Restate the Objection Back to the Prospect As a Question   You can feed the objection back to the prospect in the form of a question, or you can ask a question that implies that you are uncertain as to the nature of the objection. For example:

Prospect: You have a fine copier, but I really do not need any more than the one I have.
Seller: You don't need any?
Prospect: No, I really don't. We just bought one three months ago.

The salesperson now has a clear field to continue the presentation and determine the usage rate, what the prospect likes and dislikes about the current supplier, and ask for a possible order as a trial against the competitor the next time the prospect is ready to order.

Let's look at another example:

Prospect: You have a fine product, but I really do not need any.
Seller: Do you mean you have never used this type of product, it does not fit into your operation, or you're just all stocked up?

Prospect: This is not the type of product we handle. We need a product that will...."

In this scenario, the prospect has given an objection that sounds similar to the one in the previous example, but the meaning is entirely different. Here, the seller can now either gather more information on exactly what the prospect wants in a product or simply change gears and present another product that more closely matches the prospect's specific needs. In both scenarios, the seller has been able to clarify the meaning of the objection in order to create a better presentation.

Finally, feeding the objection back to the prospect may get the prospect to expand on the objection. It is human nature to feel compelled to give an explanation when confronted with a question. Try this experiment. The next time you ask a friend to go to lunch and he or she says "I can't," simply feed it back by saying "You can't?" and you will see the explanation automatically pour forth.

Step 3: Answer the Objection   Answer the objection to the prospect's satisfaction. Watch for clues in the prospect's facial expressions, body language, and further discussion. If you feel you have been successful in answering the objection, move on. Don't dwell on it. Keep the prospect moving forward in the presentation. Always try to separate the prospect from the objection as quickly as possible to avoid getting sidetracked from the flow of the presentation.

Step 4: Confirm the Answer with the Prospect   Did you adequately deal with the objection? Were you satisfied with the answer you gave? Probe the adequacy of your answer. If you feel that the prospect is not completely satisfied that the objection has been overcome, do not be afraid to ask. If you haven't done a satisfactory job, the prospect will tell you. For example:

Seller: Does that explanation clarify our pricing structure and address your concern about our price?

or

Seller: Does that explain our warranty a little better and answer your objection?

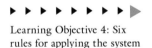

Learning Objective 4: Six rules for applying the system

Step 5: Move on in the Presentation   After the objection has been successfully dealt with, the presentation should proceed. *You are systematically eliminating all of the reasons to not close the sale.*

Rules for Applying Your System

Rule 1: *Don't Argue.*

Getting into an argument with a prospective buyer may mean that you win the argument but lose the sale, now and forever. Arguments evolve as misunderstanding increases or differing points of view surface. Everyone is entitled to their opinions, and during the presentation is not the time for you to straighten the buyer out. Arguments also reflect interactions where emotions take over and good business logic and rationale are left behind. Regardless of who is right or wrong, arguments create losers. As long as the prospect is raising objections, there is still an interest. All objections can be handled without having to resort to argument. By remaining objective and calm and by acknowledging the other persons' concerns, the salesperson can proceed smoothly with the presentation.

Rule 2: *Do Not Prove the Buyer Wrong.*

This rule is much like the argument rule; you may win argument but end up losing the account. Allow the prospect to save face and avoid embarrassment. Remove the objection as quickly as possible and refocus attention on the flow of the presentation. You should avoid statements such as:

▸ "You don't seem to understand"
▸ "You're missing the point."

and

You should say:

▸ "I don't think I have made myself clear."
▸ "I get the feeling I haven't explained it well enough."

Remember, the customer may not always be right—but the customer is *always* the customer.

Rule 3: *Maintain Focus.*

Keep the prospect focused on the presentation. Some potential buyers will try to use objections as diversionary tactics to throw you off during the presentation and break your concentration. Some, but not many buyers, will deliberately try to harass salespeople by using objections. Most prospective

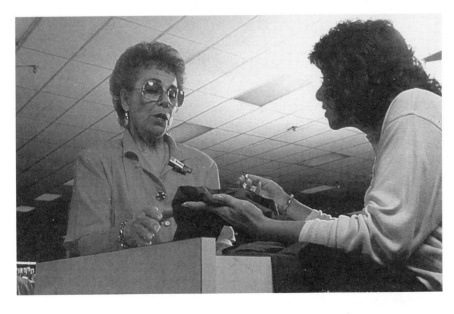

A salesperson should not argue, but remain objective and calm while acknowledging the prospect's concerns.

buyers are looking to establish a lasting business relationship with a salesperson and that is accomplished only by dealing openly and honestly. Buyers with high integrity know that the old saying "you only do business with your friends" holds true and will not try such tactics.

Rule 4: *Keep a Positive Attitude.*

Objections are not personal rejections! An objection is a natural and normal part of the selling-and-buying process. Making a presentation without getting objections is often a greater concern to a good salesperson than is a barrage of them!

Rule 5: *Deal with Objections as They Arise—Most of the Time.*

The question of when to deal with objections really has three answers. Generally, the best rule is to deal with objections when they appear. At times, you may want to deal with an objection by anticipating it.

At other times, however, it may best to postpone any attempts to overcome the objections. One such situation exists with the premature price question. Some prospects are price buyers, and before you even get started into your presentation, they want to know the price. They seem to not care about anything but price. In such a circumstance, you might want to say something like "I know price is important, but to really appreciate the value reflected in the price, let me continue to explain about the features, advantages, and benefits you would be getting for the investment you will be making."

Another situation that calls for a postponement is when the buyer uses what is called the "trivial diversion technique." For example, the buyer may ask you in the middle of your presentation how your boss is getting along or how business has been. In such a case, consider politely indicating that you will answer that after you have concentrated on solving the buyer's most pressing problem.

Rule 6: *Try to Get Them to Answer Their Own Objection.*

Prospects often explain their own objections or tell you what they want you to say without realizing it! The following scenarios illustrate this point:

Prospect: I can appreciate all of the fine qualities of your product, but I don't need any more than I already have in stock.

Seller: You don't need it now?

Prospect: Right. I have all the stock my warehouse can handle for the next six months, so I really have a timing problem on my hands.

Seller: If we could write up the order today, you could take delivery in six months when your finances and warehouse space will be freed up. How does that sound?

or

Prospect: I can appreciate all of the fine qualities of your product, but I cannot afford to pay that right now.

Seller: Oh?

Prospect: Yes, the price is several dollars more per case than I am paying now.

or

Prospect: I can appreciate all of the fine qualities of your product, but I cannot afford to pay that right now.

Seller: I may have given you the impression that the entire amount has to be paid on delivery. This is not the case. In fact, most of our customers feel that our payment terms make our offer even more attractive. If that was the impression I gave you, that was my mistake. Let's go over our payment terms, and then we can close the sale for, what do you think, ten cases?

Prospect: I understood that the payment was due in full on delivery. Terms would certainly make things easier for us.

In each of these situations, the prospect had the same objection. However, while the words were the same, the meanings were entirely different. In the first case, there was a time problem; in the second, a definite price objection; and in the third, the objection arose out of the prospect's ability to handle the payments. Each of the different meanings required handling the true objection differently. By carefully probing the objection, the seller was able to uncover the true nature of the objection and the prospect in essence told the seller how to handle that objection. Try to get the prospect to clarify the objection for you, and you will have a road map showing how to overcome it.

Objection Handling Techniques That Work

Ten techniques are used to conquer objections. Always try to adapt your style in dealing with the objection to the personality of the prospect. One technique may work on one type of buyer but not on another, even though the objections of both may be the same. First, we will discuss ten techniques, then in the next section of the chapter, you will see how they can be effectively used to overcome the objections based upon buyer's different social styles.

Technique 1. Rephrase the Objection as a Question Most objections are not too difficult to rephrase. An example of how **rephrasing** the question would work might be seen in this short vignette:

Learning Objective 5: Ten techniques to handle objections

Prospect: This price you have just quoted is a little out of line with others I have been quoted.

Seller: The price is out of line?

Prospect: Yes, your price is a little higher than the rest.

Seller: I can appreciate your concern for the investment we are talking about and how our price would seem high at first glance, but have you ever purchased a product that was initially less expensive than another, only to find that over the life of the product, its lack of dependability or quality ended up costing you more than if you would have spent a little more up front?

Prospect: Well, that does happen once in a while.

Seller: So, can we agree that what is really important is the total cost over the life of the product?

Prospect: Yes, that is a big factor in our long-term profitability.

Seller: Let me further clarify why we are asking what at first may seem to be a higher price....

The seller rephrased the objection as a question and got a clarification that the quoted price was higher than the buyer had been quoted by competitors, but the buyer indicated the price was not excessively higher. The seller moved to address the objection by obtaining agreement that life cycle cost, rather than initial price, was a key issue. Next, the seller led the prospect away from the price objection by focusing on value, not price.

Technique 2. Postponing the Objection **Postponing** the objection means you will put the objection off until later in the presentation. This must be handled carefully. If you judge from the prospect's body language or tone of voice that this is a very significant concern and one that, if put off, would endanger the success of the presentation, then it is best to deal with the objection as it arises, even though it may be out of the sequence you expected.

An unanticipated objection can come from prospects not being able to determine the product's value to them at this point in the presentation. This could reasonably occur if you had not yet discussed the product's benefits. A clue here would be if the customer was objecting to the price being too high for what appears to be the value. If it is clear the customer is raising an objection that will be cleared up after the benefits and value portion of the presentation, then postponing would be a good idea. If you are uncertain, ask for permission to postpone. Below is a vignette that illustrates the postponing technique:

Prospect: Listen, before you even get started, I have three other guys all trying to sell me the same thing you have, and I will tell you what I have told them. I cannot buy anything without approval from the board.

Seller: I understand that approval for significant purchases is the normal procedure. Could I explain our features, advantages, and benefits that I think will help you in your business and deal with your situation? After all, that really is what we need to do, isn't it?

or

Seller: I know how important a decision like this can be. But, if you'll permit me, I think I can show you how you can justify the purchase to your board after I have presented our product's unique advantages to you. You and your board wouldn't want to pass on something that could be very profitable as well as lower your operating cost by 12 percent. Would that be all right with you?

The postponing technique has several advantages. First, the objection may be automatically answered in the presentation after having discussed the features, advantages, and benefits of your product. Second, rather than risk trying to think up something on the spot and handling it poorly, by postponing, you can get the time you need to think of the answer and determine the best way to present it. Third, postponing may be the most tactful way of dealing with the prospect.

Of course, it has disadvantages as well. Prospects may perceive the postponement as a stall on your part. This could lead them to think you cannot, do not want to, or will not answer the question. Also, they could feel you do not know the answer or have the expertise to answer it. The postponing technique is very useful and effective, but its overuse may signal buyers that you cannot answer their questions and do not know what you are talking about, thus destroying any credibility and rapport you might have with them.

Technique 3. "Boomeranging" the Objection A boomerang flies off in one direction but circles back and returns to the thrower from a different angle. The **boomerang technique** means converting an objection to an advantage or benefit. This has the effect of moving the prospect from a negative thought to a positive thought about your product. Here are a couple of examples:

Prospect: Your product is really too heavy and weighs a good ten pounds more than others I have seen.

Seller: You are exactly right, and that is the way we have designed it. By being heavier, it has both more stability and a lower center of gravity. That reduces vibration and the tendency to tip over, and the fact that it is heavier indicates greater structural strength. These are the kinds of things that prevent downtime and provides greater reliability. Is that an important consideration to you?

or

Prospect: Your product seems too complicated for us.

Seller: Simplicity of operation is important, but our product is often criticized as being too complex until users realize that what appears to be added complexity is really a reflection of additional operating features that some competitors have failed to include in their products.

The boomerang technique uses reverse psychology by turning an apparent deficiency into an asset. This technique works well with a variety of objections and has the added benefit of proving the prospect's objection is really a reason to buy, rather than not buy.

Technique 4. Direct Denial The **direct denial** technique requires tactfully denying what the prospect has said as being incorrect. Prospects may have incorrect facts or may not understand the information upon which they have formulated incorrect perceptions. A direct denial requires a very delicate approach and should be used sparingly. Earlier we said the salesperson should never prove the prospect wrong. However, there are situations where the prospect is clearly incorrect and a direct denial is the only solution.

The key to successfully using a direct denial is to remember not to put prospects in a position where they lose face, become antagonized, or feel humiliated. Salespeople must have a good feel for the stage of the relationship they have with the buyer when considering using the direct technique. Here are a couple of examples. Notice how the denial is softly phrased:

Prospect: Your warranty is only for the first year.

Seller: No, our service contract is for the first year, but the warranty is for five years.

or

Prospect: Why should I buy from you today? The new models come out next week.

Seller: That is true only for the items "listed as new on special"; the rest of the line comes out this Monday.

or

Prospect: Your price per unit is twice as high as theirs!

Seller: It appears that way at first glance, but notice that we pack twice as many per case as they do, so our per unit price is the same as theirs.

The manner in which the objection is handled, along with feeling confident enough in your relationship with the buyer that a direct denial will not be taken personally, will mean the difference between success or failure. A buyer may actually appreciate a direct denial and welcome correct information so as to avoid appearing misinformed later.

Technique 5. Indirect Denial or "Yes...But" The **indirect denial** accomplishes the same objective as the direct denial but is a softer approach. The indirect approach is more diplomatic and allows both parties the benefit of making their individual points while still arriving at a new position without being antagonistic. Most people do not like to be directly contradicted, and the indirect denial approach acknowledges the prospects' positions but redirects them to the correct facts, circumstances, or conditions. It is like rolling with the punches; the blow is still there, but it is softened a bit and easier to take.

By acknowledging the possibility of the prospect's position or thought, sellers put themselves in a situation where they give a little ground and thus create an atmosphere where the prospect is more willing to do the same; both compromise a bit.

Examine the following dialog, and you will see how much softer the denial can be, compared to the direct approach.

Prospect: Your price is considerably higher than what your competitor has quoted.

Seller: At first glance, it appears that way. But it is less if you examine the total cost, including maintenance, downtime, and monthly payments.

This is a much more tactful and artful approach to convince the prospect that the objection is incorrect. By acknowledging the possibility that the prospect is correct, the presentation can continue on a positive, rather than a negative, note. Keeping things positive, even in the face of an objection that is clearly wrong, is part of an adaptive salesperson's technique in preventing the presentation from becoming a battle of opposite opinions.

Technique 6. Anticipation of the Objections The **anticipation** technique overcomes the objection before the prospect has a chance to raise it. There are often "standard" objections. Objections that could typically be anticipated would be related to operating cost, high price, or no need at this time.

Anticipating the objection has some advantages and disadvantages. One advantage is that it allows you to counter the objection in the flow of the presentation. Also, it creates in the prospect's mind the impression that you have really done your homework and empathized with him or her. A third advantage is that it gives you greater degree of control over the flow of the presentation.

One disadvantage that you must be careful to avoid is creating an objection in the process. Anticipating an objection makes the assumption that the objection is in the prospect's mind. This may be an unfounded assumption. Novice salespeople often assume the price objection will always have to be overcome. This may not be the case, and dealing with the price as though it were going to be an objection may just create that objection. Prospects do not always assume that the price you are quoting is too high and will have to be justified. Another, related disadvantage is that by assuming the objection will arise, you are not giving the prospect a chance to participate fully in the presentation. The objection, depending on how it is raised, when it is raised, the body language that accompanies it, and the actual wording of it, communicates messages about the prospect's greatest concerns. By anticipating the objection, you have denied yourself the opportunity to get a wealth of information from the prospect. Successful use of the anticipation technique comes with experience. Here is an example of how a salesperson could anticipate a price objection:

Seller: The Model X-34 floor cleaning pads come packed in boxes of 144 pads per box. Most of our customers initially think that's probably too many for a first order. However, with normal usage, that represents a six-month supply. So while it might seem like quite a few, it really means less hassle and bother reordering for your maintenance people.

The salesperson, obviously having had the no-need objection before, has dealt with it inside the presentation. Here, our salesperson has overcome the objection before it appeared.

Technique 7. Compensation for the Objection The **compensation** technique is an attempt to show the prospect that a benefit or advantage compensates for an objection. The job of the salesperson is to acknowledge the objection raised by the prospect but make it seem so unimportant or trivial that it fades away. This objection-handling technique can follow the same initial delivery as some of the others we have discussed. The objection is not denied at all. It is acknowledged, then balanced off by compensating features, advantages, and benefits. The following scenario illustrates the point:

Prospect: You have a good deal, but XYZ Company will give me a 10 percent ad allowance off the face of the invoice.

Seller: An ad allowance would certainly be helpful, to be sure. Our company does not do that. Instead, we provide you with all of the advertising material you will need to allow you to present professionally produced ads at no cost. It seems that what we are offering more than compensates for not giving a 10 percent ad allowance, don't you agree? *(tie-down)*

or

Prospect: Their packaging costs are quite a bit less than yours, so I think we will have to pass on your offer.

Seller: We don't deny that at all. In fact, their packaging costs do run 15 percent less. To compensate for that, we will let you order in smaller quantities and place add-on orders. This keeps your inventory costs down and gives you greater flexibility with a more rapid response time. We feel that represents the kind of trade-off that is more beneficial to you in the long run, wouldn't you agree? *(tie-down)*

Technique 8. Third-Party Reinforcement The **third-party reinforcement** technique uses the opinion of a third person or company to help overcome the objection and reinforce the salesperson's points.

Sources for third-party reinforcements can be either in person or through letters or documents. Calling on a third party "in person" does not mean having the person present at the time of the presentation. You can obtain permission from a satisfied customer to call him or her if the need arises or to give the third party's phone number to the prospect.

Third-party reinforcements can be testimonial letters, published documents, engineering reports, research reports, or the results of market tests. These represent the opinions of unbiased third parties.

If testimonials are expected to be part of the presentation, either in the form of letters, reports, or phone calls, have them in hand or know where you can get them quickly.

Technique 9. The Three-F's Tactic The **three-F's tactic** is useful in dealing with objections, closing, and many other selling steps. It uses the words *feel, felt,* and *found* to overcome objections.

The three-F's tactic is illustrated in the scenario below:

Prospect: I think with the prices everyone else is offering that I can make more money using someone else's product.

Seller: I can appreciate your concern for wanting to get the highest return you can. I can understand how you *feel.* Mr. Kennedy at XYZ Distributing *felt* the same way until he started stocking our line. Within two weeks, he *found* that he was not only making more than he anticipated but was noticing customers buying more of his other products as well.

The three-F's tactic is almost universal in its applicability and adaptive to all situations. The tactic is easily blended with some of the other techniques as well. It can be tied to a third-party reinforcement by saying:

Seller: I can understand how you *feel.* Several of our customers *felt* the same way until they read the government research report and *found....*

Or with the compensation technique:

Seller: I can understand how you *feel.* Several of our customers *felt* the same way but *found* that after examining our excellent credit policy, our customized delivery schedule, the quality control we use, and the ease of use, the objection you raise has been more than compensated for.

The three-F's tactic allows the salesperson a great deal of flexibility for dealing with different personality types, different objection-handling techniques, and different sales presentation situations. It is one of the most tactful and diplomatic approaches to handling even the most difficult objections in the most adversarial situations.

Technique 10. The Five-Question Sequence[3] The **five-question sequence** can be used if you have been unsuccessful in convincing the prospect to buy and it has become evident throughout the presentation that a buy decision is not coming. Figure 11-1 illustrates the five-question sequence.

The five-question sequence starts with the question "There must be some good reason why you are hesitating to go ahead now. Do you mind if I ask what it is?" When the reason is stated, you make a mental note of it and proceed directly into the second question, "In addition to that, is there any other reason for not going ahead?" You may get another objection or a condition for not buying. In the former case, you can try to overcome the additional objection; in the latter case, the condition may signal that a quick and understanding conclusion to the presentation may be the best solution.

Next comes the third question, "Just supposing you could convince yourself that.... Then you'd want to go ahead?" If the prospect gives you a positive indication, either through a direct agreement or through a body lan-

Figure 11-1 **The Five-Question Sequence**

Question 1: There must be some good reason why you are hesitating to go ahead now. Do you mind if I ask what it is?

Question 2: In addition to that, is there any other reason for not going ahead?

Question 3: Just supposing that you could convince yourself that . . . . Then you'd want to go ahead with it? (If positive response, continue selling; if negative response, go to question 4.)

Question 4: Then there must be some other reason. May I ask what it is? (Wait for response and move back to question 2. You can go directly on to question 5 or back to questions 1 and 2 again.)

Question 5: What would it take to convince you?

guage cue, you should continue selling. If however, the response is negative, then you proceed directly to the fourth question.

The fourth question is "Then there must be some other reason. May I ask what it is?" After the prospect responds to this question, make a mental note of the nature of the response (objection or condition) and go back to the second question again, "In addition to that, is there any reason for not going ahead?"

The purpose of the five-question sequence is to smoke out any and all possible obstacles to a close and deal with them. If you get a negative response to question four, then you can feel relatively certain that the prospect has finally aired all possible objections and you're set to bring the presentation to closure by either making the sale or making a tactful exit.

The fifth question, "What would it take to convince you that . . . ?" puts the play squarely in the prospect's court. The prospect must either say he or she is finally convinced and will close or tell you what is needed in order to be convinced.

After the fifth question, you may find the prospect is now willing to close. Some prospects will now tell you what you have to do to make the sales, that is, the terms they want, the price, the certain specifications, or any of a variety of things.

Here are two vignettes that illustrate the five-question sequence:

Prospect: I can appreciate all you have said, but I would rather wait and think it over for a few days. *(stalling objection)*

Seller: You must have some good reason why you are hesitating and not going ahead now. Do you mind if I ask what is? *(Question 1)*

Prospect: I just don't think we can justify the expense now.

Seller: In addition to that, is there any other reason for not going ahead? *(Question 2)*

Prospect: Well, no, not really. Justifying the expense is my biggest concern right now.

Seller: Well, just suppose that you could convince yourself that by making the purchase now, the expense could be justified in terms of the savings it would generate for you over the next two months, then would you want to go ahead with it? *(Question 3)*

Prospect: Yes, if I could see how it would save money, then I would probably go ahead. *(positive response, so sequence stops)*

At this point, the salesperson has been asked by the prospect to show how an expenditure actually creates a savings. The salesperson should now go into a value analysis or work out a plan for the prospect to illustrate the potential savings that would result from an immediate decision and the potential added expenses that would result from waiting.

Here is the second example, in which a real estate agent is showing a house to a prospective buyer.

Prospect: I'm not sure. The gutters and overhangs of this house look like they're going to need quite a bit of work.

Agent: That is possible. Remember, this is not a new house, and houses of this age generally do need some minor repairs. There must be some other reasons you seem hesitant. Do you mind if I ask what they are? *(Question 1)*

Prospect: The other reason is the driveway. It looks like it needs to be replaced.

Agent: In addition to that, is there any reason for not writing up a contract today? *(Question 2)*

Prospect: No, those are the two major concerns that I have.

Agent: Just supposing you could convince yourself that if you wrote a contract on this house today, we could get these repairs done for under $500 and it would increase the value of your new home by more than $500, then you would go ahead with it? *(Question 3)*

Prospect: No.

Agent: Then there must be some other reason. May I ask what it is? *(Question 4)*

Prospect: I don't think the house is structurally sound.

Agent: What would it take to convince you of this house's structural soundness? *(Question 5)*

Prospect: I want a structural engineer's report. If we can get that, then we'll write the contract.

When Things Go Right

ABC Collection's Fearful New Rep

ABC Collections, a company that specializes in collecting past due bills for businesses, was opening a branch in a small town near a large metropolitan area where it was already established. ABC sales reps call on businesses of all sizes to discuss what the firm can do for them, particularly when accounts receivable are over 60 days past due.

In addition to collecting, ABC also helps set up internal collection procedures if necessary, counsels on present procedures (no charge for these services), and produces prompt monthly reports of account status. The recovery rate is between 20 and 30 percent, depending on the quality of the account. The national average for recovery is 25 percent.

ABC earns its money by keeping a percentage of the dollars it receives from delinquent accounts and only charges fees on accounts collected. No upfront money from the client is necessary to start doing business with ABC.

Kathleen Piatrowski, a new sales rep, has been having problems breaking in the territory. Many companies in the small town are not using a collection agency, and although prospects will see her, she has problems handling their

Continued

When Things Go Right

ABC Collection's Fearful New Rep — *Continued*

objections. For three weeks, her standard method for dealing with such comments as "I'm afraid I will lose customers if I hire your firm" or "The price is too high" has been to immediately invoke third-party reinforcements. She tells the customer to call Mr. or Ms. X at company PQR and talk to them about ABC Collection's expertise. Of course, the prospects do not do this. She is expecting a satisfied customer to close the sale when objections have not been answered, but the prospect has no motivation to pursue the call.

Kathleen's sales manager noticed the low numbers of closed calls and offered to help her overcome her fear of dealing with the customer's concerns by developing some standard answers to the typical objections. She explained that Kathleen's job was to educate the customer in the use of a collection agency, as well as close the deal. She also pointed out that third-party reinforcement was helpful or necessary only after she had thoroughly addressed objections and the customer still seems reluctant to go ahead. Kathleen's manager instructed her in the correct use of the third-party technique, and others she could use.

One week after the conference with her sales manager, Kathleen's closing ratio improved by 50 percent. By learning how to handle objections effectively, Kathleen overcame her fear of asking for the business and was doing a much better job of helping her customers solve their problems. She had much less need to invoke the third-party technique again.

*Source: This case was provided by Barbara Schoeneberger of Schoeneberger and Associates, Omaha, Nebraska, and is an account of an actual business situation.

What Would You Do If . . . ?

You are an interior designer working with a retailer. Your company offers design services for homeowners and businesses. You have knocked yourself out to design a living room for a client, including furniture, drapes, and accessories. You know the customer will be doing the project in stages. The customer likes your work and yet you cannot seem to get a start date from her.

▸ Questions: What might be the hidden objections keeping you from getting her to close?

▸ Assuming she is an Amiable-type personality, what type of objections might you expect and how would you handle them?

▸▸ *follow-up questions*

1. How is the boomerang technique different from rephrasing the objection?

2. Why would the five-question sequence be the last technique you would employ?

Adapt Your Techniques to the Buyer's Social Style

Learning Objective 6:
Adapting objections-handling
techniques to an individual
buyer's social style

Each prospective buyer is different, and being aware of the differences can make you more successful in sales. If you are skillful and observant, you can recognize certain traits in the prospect you are dealing with and choose the objection-handling techniques that will be most effective with the prospect's personality.

Remember that there are four categories into which most people can be grouped: Amiables, Analyticals, Expressives, and Drivers. Each of these types will respond differently to the objection-handling techniques we just discussed.

Handling the Objections of Amiables

Amiables may be slow to give objections and appear very agreeable. During the sales presentation, you may be lulled into a sense of false security and think everything is going well but then be stymied by a reluctance to close.

The techniques most effective on Amiables would be indirect denials, anticipation, compensation, third-party reinforcements, and the three-F's tactic. These techniques are softer, and more relationship-oriented, which the Amiables prefer. They offer the Amiables the support they need and the feeling that you are interested in developing a relationship with them.

Handling the Objections of Analyticals

When using any of these techniques, be sure that you have your facts and figures correct because the Analytical will search for flaws. In handling the objections of Analyticals, be pleasant and remain cool. They dislike conflict, and objection-handling methods that appear to them to be antagonistic or conflict-creating will do you more harm than good! Such techniques as the three-F's tactic, third-party reinforcements, and indirect denials work well. Anticipation of objections will also be successful if you can deal with them by using facts and figures in the body of the presentation. This can be accomplished by showing (or offering to show) the "published results," "results of tests," "testimonials of satisfied customers," or any other factual or quantitative supporting documents or references. For the novice salesperson, Analyticals may seem to be raising every objection in the book, but it must be remembered that they are vigilant and cautious, so the more questions being asked, the faster the salesperson is proceeding to a close.

Handling the Objections of Expressives

Expressives are personable, enthusiastic, gregarious, and impulsive. When they voice an objection, you may get the impression that the objection is vitally important or a tremendous obstacle. Keep in mind their tendency to exaggerate. The best way to deal with the objections of Expressives is to employ any tactics that stroke their egos. Because they are competitive, avoid getting into a situation where they feel you are trying to compete with them. Since Expressives are grandiose thinkers and emulative of "the big or important people," techniques such as the three-F's tactic and third-party reinforcements work well, as long as the customers you are using as references represent the big, important people or firms. You may find that the Expressives make objections from the very start of your presentation, whereas Analyticals and Amiables may wait until you are done. With Expressives, be prepared to make a presentation in what may seem to be a slightly disorganized manner. Expresses tend to have shorter attention spans and are prone to voicing objections prematurely. To maintain an orderly flow, use postponing. Knowing the Expressive's tendency to exaggerate will allow you to be ready to boomerang and rephrase objections to determine the real strength of an objection that may be raised prematurely.

Handling the Objections of Drivers

Drivers enjoy negotiating. This is a reflection of their desire to control. They appreciate straightforward handling of objections. You can deal more directly with Drivers than the other types, that is, denial techniques can be used effectively as long as they are presented matter-of-factly. Giving Drivers the perception that you are in control and trying to dominate will generally prove disastrous.

Drivers, like Expressives, may be prone to premature objections. They may raise objections that would be expected later in the presentation simply because they want you to get on with it. This is in contrast to Analyticals, who want to know all of the details of everything. Drivers are results-oriented, interested in the big picture, and always in control of the situation. Rephrasing, boomeranging, denials, and the five-questions-sequence can be effective with drivers.

Table 11-1 identifies the different social styles and the objection-handling techniques that work most and least effectively for each.

Table 11-1 Different People Respond Better to Different Techniques	
on Amiables	**on Analytics**

Use: Indirect denials
      Anticipation
      Third-party reinforcement
      Three-F's tactic
      Rephrasing
      Five-question sequence
	Use: Five-question sequence
	      Three-F's tactic
	      Third-party reinforcement
	      Indirect denials
	      Anticipation
	      Compensation
	      Boomeranging
	      Rephrasing
	      Postponing

on Expressives	**on Drivers**

Use: Three-F's tactic
      Third-party reinforcement
      Rephrasing
      Boomeranging
      Anticipation
      Five-question sequence
      Compensation
	Use: Direct denial
	      Indirect denial
	      Rephrasing
	      Boomeranging
	      Five-question sequence
	      Compensation

▸ ▸ *follow-up questions*

1. Amiables and Drivers are very different in how a salesperson must handle their objections. What techniques would you use for each?
2. Can some of the same techniques be used for both Expressives and Analyticals?

Once You've Met the Objection, What's Next?

You have been making your presentation and answering the objections, and now the client seems to be more interested. There does not seem to be any obstacles to closing the sale now, but it's not safe to assume so. It is time to test the water. Is the prospect ready to commit? Are there still some problems you have not uncovered? The best way to test the readiness of the client is with a trial close.

Time for the Trial Close

After effectively dealing with the objection(s), it is reasonable to believe you have overcome a barrier to closing, but you need to know if the prospect has progressed to the point of being comfortable with making a decision. This can only be probed by using a **trial close.** You were introduced to the trial close earlier in the selling process. The trial close is used to handle objections as well. In dealing with objections, it is a question designed to elicit prospects' reactions without forcing them to make a yes-or-no buying decision.[4]

▸ ▸ ▸ ▸ ▸ ▸ ▸ ▸ ▶

Learning Objective 7: The trial close is used to handle objections and make the transition to a closed sale

The trial close is the transition between handling the objections and closing the sale. Trial closes may be phrased as seemingly harmless questions, such as "Have I addressed all the points you were concerned about?" A yes would mean it's time to close. A no would indicate there are still objections that need to be uncovered and overcome. Another possibility is to ask for the prospect's opinion on the product: "Does this seem to solve the problems we have discussed?" Still another possibility may come on the heels of an objection. The prospect may ask if your quoted price is your "best" price. This can be handled as an objection but also as a probe in a trial close. For example:

Prospect: Is this the best price you can give me?
Seller: We do have quantity discount for orders of 100 cases or more. Will you be ordering that much or more? *(trial close)*
Prospect: We always order at least 200 cases at a time.
Seller *(formally closes):* Then I will write the order up for 200 cases, and how about a Tuesday delivery?

Remember that the trial close is a probe, not a formal close. A second point to keep in mind about trial closes is that since they are probes to test the buyer's progress through the decision-making process, they can be used at any time in the presentation.

The trial close and the five-question sequence can be linked to probe prospects' readiness to buy. Question 2 in the sequence can be an effective trial-closing question. Suppose the prospects have raised the price objection. You can make a trial close by asking, "In addition to price, is there any other reason for not going ahead?" If the buyers say price is the only concern, then you know there is only one hurdle to overcome. This is a clear signal from them that if the price can be successfully dealt with, they are ready to buy. By the same token, if the prospects proceed to reel off a list of other concerns, you know they are a long way from making a decision and you have your work cut out for you.

If All Else Fails, Ask for the Order Anyway!

Even if you have done everything you can think of to deal with the objections raised by the prospects, even if you have tried to probe their readiness to buy with all the trial closes known to humankind, and the prospects still do not give you a buying signal or refuse to close, ask for the order anyway!

Asking for the order in the case of what appears to be certain refusal may seem silly, but remember this, if you do not ask, you certainly have given up any and all chances of making the sale. Even if you ask and get turned down, you can walk away saying you did everything possible to make the sale. You have nothing to lose by asking. All baseball players know that when you do not swing the bat, you certainly won't get a hit. If you have gone down swinging, you have at least done your part. The greatest single difference between successful and unsuccessful salespeople is that *successful salespeople simply ask for more orders than unsuccessful salespeople.*

▶ ▶ *follow-up questions*

1. Even if all seems to be failing, why should you ask for the order anyway?
2. How do objection-handling techniques and trial closes work together?

Summary

Objections should be welcomed. No objections generally mean no buying decision. Objections indicate that interest and progress is being made toward the closing of the sale but that the buyer is resisting the purchase for some reason. Objections also reveal buyers' thoughts and may be reflective of their true interests and concerns. Objections can be overcome, but conditions are valid reasons for not buying and cannot be overcome. Conditions should be identified, if at all possible, when qualifying prospects (Learning Objective 1).

There are five categories of objections: no-money or price, time or stalling, hidden, product, and no-need (Learning Objective 2). To deal with any of these, you must maintain a positive attitude toward objections, deal with them as they arise, not argue with prospective buyers, not prove them wrong, and try to get them to answer their own objections.

The five-step system for overcoming objections uses the techniques of rephrasing, postponing, boomeranging, direct and indirect denials, anticipation, compensation, third-party reinforcements, the three-F's tactic, or the five-question sequence (Learning Objectives 3 through 5).

The technique should be matched to the prospect's social style. Table 11-1 presented the ways objections can be handled with each of the four social style categories you learned about in earlier chapters (Learning Objective 6).

After objections have been overcome, they are linked to a close with a trial close. Trial closes are questions that probe the prospect's readiness to buy. The response to a trial close signals the salesperson to either move directly into a close or back up in the presentation and continue on in the regular selling sequence. Remember, regardless of your success in overcoming objections, always ask for the order anyway. Asking for the order in the face of what appears to be total rejection just might net you a sale (Learning Objective 7).

Key Terms

Objection   Any opposition or resistance to a salesperson's request, usually coming from a lack of understanding or information.

Conditions   Conditions are valid reasons for not being able to buy.

No-money or price objections   Involves prospects saying they cannot afford the product, the price is too high, or they do not have the money at this time.

Hidden objection   An objection the prospect does not reveal for whatever reason and the seller must try to uncover and deal with if the sale is to be made.

Rephrasing   Taking the objection and converting it to a question. This has the effect of stimulating the prospect to elaborate or expand on the objection.

Postponing   Putting off the objection until later in the presentation.

Boomerang   An objection is converted to an advantage or benefit.

Direct denial   Tactfully denying what the prospect has said as being incorrect.

Indirect denial   This technique accomplishes the same objective as the direct denial but is a softer approach.

Anticipation   Expecting the objection and proceeding to answer it before the prospect has a chance to raise it.

Compensation   An attempt to show the prospect that the benefits or advantages of the product outweigh the objection.

Third-party reinforcement   Using the opinions of a third party to overcome an objection.

Three-F's tactic   Using the words *feel, felt,* and *found* conversationally through the presentation to overcome objections.

Five-question sequence   A direct approach to uncover whatever reason may be standing between the seller and the close.

Trial Close   A question designed to elicit prospects' reactions without forcing them to make a firm buying decision.

Discussion Questions

1. If a customer told you she couldn't use your product the way it is currently made, would this be an objection or a condition? How would you distinguish between the two?

2. Objections can stem from concerns about products, prices, or affordability, the salesperson, the selling company, or the services offered. Make up an example of using the five-question sequence to discover the root of an objection founded in a problem the customer had with how one of your products worked in the past.

3. Discuss how it is possible to be in violation of the Federal Trade Commission Act when you are making promises to try to resolve objections.

4. What are the five points that comprise the strategy for dealing with objections?

5. At one point in the chapter, it was stated that objections should be handled as they arise, yet one objection-handling technique is to forestall, or postpone, the objection. Explain when it might be best to postpone an objection, rather than deal with it immediately.

6. Here are some of the most common forms of objections. How would you handle each?
   a. "Let me check it out with my boss and I will get back to you."
   b. "You're about 15 percent too high on the price."
   c. "Call me in a few months when our inventory gets worked down a little."
   d. "Our budget is already set for the year on your type of service."
   e. "That's more than we can pay right now."
   f. "We already carry three lines just like yours. We certainly do not need to make it four!"
   g. "We cannot do business with you."
   h. "I'm real busy. Why don't you call me in a month or two?"
   i. "No thanks, I'm just looking."
   j. "I really do not have enough information to make a decision."

7. Reread question 6, then answer items a through j for two of the social styles discussed in the text.

8. What are the steps in the systems approach to handling objections? What is meant by a systems approach?

9. How does a trial close test the waters of a prospect's readiness to buy?

10. What is meant when it is said that a condition is transitory?

11. Can conditions be overcome just like objections? Should a salesperson expect to deal with many conditions during a presentation?

12. Why do you think most novice salespeople fear objections and most experienced salespeople welcome them?

Application Exercise

Go back and reread the When Things Go Right box titled "ABC Collection's Fearful New Rep," then answer the following questions:

1. Besides the third-party reinforcement technique, what other objection-handling techniques could Kathleen have used?

2. What advice would you give Kathleen regarding the use of trial closes?

Class Exercise

Group Exercise

The class will be organized as follows:

1. The instructor will choose from among a variety of products or services—washing machines or printing services for example—then break the class into three-person groups with a person playing each of the following roles:

The Observer

This person will apply the *rules* for dealing with objections as listed in the text and record the *interactions* of the remaining group members for later reporting to the class as a whole.

The Customer and the Salesperson

A second member of the group will be the customer and create an objection to the potential sale of the chosen product or service.

The third member will be the salesperson and handle the objection as stated, using at least two of the ten techniques suggested in the text.

2. The class as a whole will discuss the observer's reports and come to some basic conclusion about the handling of sales objections.

The observer, as well as the entire class, should be looking to answer the following:

1. Were the rules for dealing with objections, as listed in the text, accurately applied? Did any additional rules surface?

2. How effectively applied were the *techniques* for handling objections?

Individual Exercise

The instructor will invite a "visiting customer" to meet with the class to conduct the following impromptu role play:

1. The instructor will ask a student to designate a product or service required for the role play.

2. From among the students in the class, a "salesperson" will be chosen to sell the designated product or service to the "visiting customer."

3. The "visiting customer" will object to the sales presentation, using one of the four buyer social styles—Amiable, Analytical, Expressive, or Driver.

4. A class member will be chosen to *identify* the social style and evaluate the "salesperson's" ability to adapt to that style.

▼ ▼ ▼ ▼ ▼ ▼ *Cases* ▼ ▼ ▼ ▼ ▼ ▼

The Growing Firm's Objections[5]

You are a young accountant with a "Big 8" firm. The partners have made it clear that advancement within the firm depends on how much business you can bring in. Your strategy has been to participate at Chamber of Commerce functions where you have an opportunity to meet likely candidates for your firm's services. Today, you are at a cocktail party hosted by the Chamber, along with over 500 other people.

You have been circulating and meeting quite a few new people, including Conrad Tanner, the owner of a business equipment company. His is a small company—only 16 employees—but he intends it to grow to over 30 employees in the next three years. He already has an accountant who helps him with his taxes.

You would like to talk with him about how your firm can help him get additional financing for the expansion and determine what profits and expenses are incurred in each area of his company, in addition to other services your firm can provide.

Questions

1. What things would be important to Conrad as his firm grows?
2. What types of problems will he need solved?
3. What objections might Conrad raise with you about doing business with your firm?
4. Assuming Conrad is an Expressive, how could you best handle those objections?

The New Contractor

You sell metal buildings and must get builders to use your products in their projects. Your company is expanding nationwide. Based in a small midwestern town, it is very well known in four surrounding states and has been around for 50 years, but hardly anyone outside of that area has heard of the company. You are opening up a new territory in the Northeast and are calling on a contractor who is bidding on a municipal auditorium. The contractor is experienced in dealing with your largest competitor but does not know you at all. You have one thing no one else has: a roof design that will enable the building to be constructed without any inside support walls, which is great for circuses, ice shows, sports events, and so on. The roof exceeds all safety standards; can be insulated to R-35, which would save substantially on heating and cooling costs; and can be constructed in about two-thirds of the time of your competitor's. You want the opportunity to give this contractor a quote so she might bid your building to get the job.

Case 11.2

Questions

1. What is important to the contractor?
2. What objections might the contractor raise?
3. Assuming the contractor is an Analytic how can you best handle her objections?
4. What are some of the important things you should remember when making the presentation to the customer?

References

1. Tom Hopkins, *How to Master the Art of Selling* (New York: Warner Books, 1982), p. 187.
2. This section borrows heavily from Hopkins, *How to Master the Art of Selling*, pp. 191–97.
3. Charles Futrell, *Fundamentals of Selling* (Homewood, Ill.: Richard D. Irwin, 1984), pp. 282–83.
4. Ronald B. Marks, *Personal Selling, An Interactive Approach*, 2d ed., (Boston: Allyn & Bacon, 1985), quoting J. Porter Henry, "The Ingredients and Timing of the Perfect Close," *Sales and Marketing Management*, 106 (1971): 30–35.
5. This case was provided by Barbara Schoeneberger of Schoeneberger and Associates, Omaha, Nebraska, and is an account of an actual business situation.

12 Closing the Sale and Building the Relationship

Objectives

After completing this chapter, you will be able to:

1. Define closing the sale.

2. Identify four ways to deal with rejection when closing a sale.

3. List and discuss the closing signals.

4. Close sales using 20 different techniques.

5. Apply multiple closes and use a three-step bridging process to link them together.

6. Apply the techniques of closing to the four different customers' social styles.

7. Give examples and discuss the procedures to wrap up a sale after the customer has committed to the order.

8. Explain at least five important customer relations rules.

The Professional Selling Question

Closing is where the sale finally comes together. What advice would you give new salespeople on how to be more effective at closing sales?

Sales Experts Respond

Ask any good professional salesperson, and he or she will tell you that closing is a natural part of the sale. Larry Nonnamaker of Eastman Kodak believes it is a natural part of the selling process to be handled very naturally. In his line of selling, he says, he does not approach a sales presentation with any set timing to close or a closing method in mind. He likes to use simple questions as trial closes to get a notion of where buyers are in their decision process. When he feels the buyer is ready to commit, he asks for the order. Larry, like all other good salespeople, would tell you that you have to ask for the order; do not be afraid to ask because buyers expect it.

Janis Drew of the *L.A. Times* newspaper echoes this thought. Buyers expect to be asked for their business. After all, that's why salespeople call on customers. She looks on closing as a way of helping the customer become more successful. The customer should always be better off with than without your product, so why not ask for the order? She says she never leaves prospects' offices without asking them to consider the *Times*. She feels that if you make it comfortable for the buyer to say yes, you will make more sales.

Jake Kulp of AMP says he must close many times to get an order. In selling his line of industrial products, his first close is to the design engineer. His job is to show the engineer that the products are made to the required specifications. His next close is to the reliability engineer, who must be convinced the product will work everyday, all day. His final close is with the purchasing agent. This close must be value- and cost-oriented. The purchasing agent must be convinced the product offers significant value over the competitor's. If the product is basically comparable, then he must focus on the delivery, service, replacement agreement, and personal assistance of the company representative.

Ralph Eubanks of the pharmaceutical division of Pfizer faces a different situation altogether when selling to doctors. Pharmaceutical salespeople do not ask doctors to buy anything. Doctors prescribe the medication, which the patient actually buys from the pharmacist. Ralph asks for a commitment that the physicians will agree to prescribe the medication. He uses the commitment-consistency law of psychology. His goal is to get physicians to commit to a trial usage; after that, the product must survive on its own merits. Eubanks says he often uses trial closes before asking for a commitment. He also says the best close for him is the summary of benefits. Since doctors are always pressed for time, they want and appreciate a sales presentation that gets to the point. Closing, regardless of the circumstances, is one of the necessary steps to helping the customer. Some salespeople take a straightforward approach, some must be more oblique. Regardless of the situation, successful salespeople keep saying one thing over and over: ask for the business and you'll get it; do not ask for it and it will not come to you.[1]

Introduction

Jack Carew, a professional sales trainer, sees closing as part of a process. "Closing is the final stage in a process where the salesperson has developed trust, credibility, and rapport. You want to look at the whole transaction in terms of the customer winning and you winning. The first thing to do is establish positive contact. You've got to adopt the language of a winner; like saying to yourself, 'Hey, I count for something. I want to be a resource to this person. I want to help. I know what I'm talking about.' Next, you have to look and act professional. Early on in the transaction, if you listen to the customers, pay attention to what they mean, reflect positive body language, acknowledge that you understand them, and attempt to really and truly come to grips with what their needs are, you will establish credibility and reliability. Follow-up and follow-through creates credibility and reliability as well.

Rapport is making personal contact with the customer. Rapport equals likability. Salespeople who are able to operate at the functional level, that is, identify the customer's needs, provide solutions, and communicate 'I care and I want to help,' are the kinds of people who get in position for a close.

A lot of people assume salespeople make one-call sales. In most client organizations, you don't close on the first call. You may work with some customers for two years before they even give you a chance to look at their business. During that time, you will have to establish your trust, credibility, and rapport, and then the question of taking or giving will be immaterial. Sometimes even closing is no more than a symbolic necessity.

Salespeople are at their very best when they are doing something good for someone else. You have to be a good person first to be a good salesperson. You can move product, but you will not build loyalty and you will not build repeat business if you're not a squared-away human being."[2]

What is Closing?

▶ ▶ ▶ ▶ ▶ ▶ ▶ ▶ ▶
Learning Objective 1:
Defining closing

What is closing? **Closing** is culminating the sale by the prospect authorizing the purchase. It can be as simple as salespeople asking customers directly if there will be anything else as they hand them the merchandise at the retail counter. It can also be complicated, requiring several types of closings after numerous presentations.

Everyone regularly closes a sale everytime they make a request, but most people do not think of their requests as being sales. When the teenage son approaches his father to ask for the car keys, he is trying to close a sale. He is trying to persuade his father to accept the request. After proceeding through the litany of reasons why he should get the car, the son ultimately ends with the question, "Can I borrow the car for this evening?" Closing a sale occurs in the same fashion. The salesperson ultimately asks the prospective customer, "Do I get the sale?"

Asking for the Order

Asking for the order is a straightforward process. Successful closers know the true art in closing is in knowing the right time to close as much as it is in knowing what to say to close the sale. In previous chapters, we discussed the mental steps a prospective customer goes through in arriving at a decision to buy. Trying to close before buyers reach the conviction or action stage can scare off some customers. It can leave them with the impression that the salesperson is too pushy or interested only in making the sale and not interested in their welfare. On the other hand, failing to ask for the order after being given numerous buying signals reduces the customer's excitement and willingness to purchase.

Successful salespeople know sales are not often closed on the first try. A successful salesperson tries to close **AT LEAST THREE TIMES,** or as many times as is necessary. If customers are ready to buy, they will communicate that readiness at the first request for the order. Being rejected at the first closing attempt does not portend failure and ultimate rejection. It simply indicates the prospective customer has not been sold on the benefits of the product or service.

Being hesitant to ask for the order negates all the efforts made in an otherwise flawless presentation. Reluctance to ask for the sale may leave the customer with the impression that the salesperson does not really want the business. Buyers like to deal with salespeople who are eager to help them solve problems. When asking for the order, the salesperson must maintain a confident, positive, and assumptive mental attitude.

Dealing with Rejection is a Reality of Closing

Closing represents a leap into the unknown. "Will they or won't they commit?" Every salesperson, no matter how experienced, feels the rush of satisfaction and the relief that comes when a buyer agrees to close. Similarly, all salespeople feel a degree of rejection when they get turned down. Fear of rejection can be debilitating if allowed to supplant the salesperson's self-confidence. Successful salespeople overcome both the fear of rejection and the feelings of rejection by maintaining the proper mental attitude. It allows them to understand the rejection, deal with it, and actually use it to become a stronger closer.

John W. Mitchell has written about rejection and how to overcome it. He says:

> As a salesperson, how do you learn to deal with rejection? Sometimes you think you're immune to it. But when it happens, inevitably you get depressed, angry, and somewhat immobilized by it. Or do you? How can you overcome these feelings? How can you climb out of that hole? You've all heard the words of wisdom, 'They're not rejecting you; it's just your product or service they're rejecting so do not take it personally!', but people do. Telling yourself it's not personal simply does not work for most salespeople. Here are four ways to get past rejection:
>
> 1. *Understand the dynamics.* Rejection is an integral part of the game you're in; like getting tackled in football. Even Steven Spielberg took his script *ET* to a major motion picture studio and was told, "It has no commercial value." Rejection just means you're out there pitching. The more prospects you try to get, the more you're going to get.
> 2. *Let somebody in on it.* Talk to somebody about your feelings after rejection, preferably another salesperson. Get those negative emotions outside of you where they belong.

◀ ◀ ◀ ◀ ◀ ◀ ◀ ◀

Learning Objective 2: Dealing with rejection when closing a sale

3. *Think about it.* Since you cannot change the rejection, the only thing you can do is learn from it. Exaggerated, negative self-talk only compounds and prolongs the problem. Steer yourself to see that in every defeat, you will find the seeds of victory.

4. *Use rejections for energy.* Average producers get defeated by rejection; top producers are energized by it. Use the rejection to give you a burst of determination. Like Vince Lombardi said to his players: 'To the victor—100% elation; to the vanquished—100% determination.' Instead of falling behind, attack.

Case in Point

Closing The Sale

One frequently sees newspaper want ads for salespeople that say candidates must be good closers. Customers seldom are ready to close on a sale until they believe they have sufficient reasons to say yes.

Don Roberts, a sales rep for the Sky Blue Paint Company, was calling on a buyer for a retail paint store:

Don: I'm Don Roberts with the Sky Blue Paint Company.

Customer: I already have a good representation of paint manufacturers in my store. I don't need another one.

Don: I'm here to help you in any way I can to increase your repeat business in today's competitive market.

Customer: We don't need a new brand of paint; we already carry over 15 brands now.

Don: Our company is instituting a unique adult class at the high school in your neighborhood—teaching the skills and money savings one can enjoy by doing one's own interior and unfinished furniture painting. Because you already carry a good selection of fine home paints, we would like to include your store in our list of paint sources. Even if you don't wish to place an order now, we will be pleased to direct our students to all paint stores in this area, including yours.

Customer: When do your classes start? I would be pleased to speak at one of your meetings. How soon could I get a small representative stock of Sky Blue on my shelves?

Don: Our warehouse is only 24 hours away by truck. Here are the items I would suggest. We also accept any unopened returns.

Customer: Send me a normal supply. This is our purchase order number.

Questions:
▸ Did Don convert or create a sale?
▸ Did Don know the customer's needs?

▸▸ *follow-up questions*

1. How many times should a salesperson attempt to close before giving up?

2. Explain two of the four ways a salesperson can overcome the psychological consequences of being rejected when closing.

Reading the Signs that Indicate When to Close

An attentive salesperson watches and listens for a customer's buying signals. Depending on the social style of each buyer, the signals may be communicated directly or subtly. Regardless of social style, all customers communicate their readiness to close. Reading the signs requires being attentive and using trial closes.

Recall from the previous discussion of trial closes that a trial close is a probing question that tests the customer's readiness to commit to the order. A trial close can be as simple as asking the customer, "Is that a benefit you feel is important?" or "Is red the color you would order?" or "That's really an economical price, isn't it?" Depending on how the customer responds, the salesperson either has the green light to proceed or must work through an objection, provide more explanation, detail a feature, or do any number of other things.

Using trial closes when closing is essential for two reasons. First, trial closes are a direct means of probing the customer's level of commitment. Second, trial closes validate suspicions. A buyer's verbal and nonverbal cues lead the salesperson to suspect the buyer is ready to commit. A trial close affirms or denies that suspicion. There are eight signs indicating a willingness to close.

The Signs to Look For

Closing signals that customers exhibit can range from doing nothing to saying they will buy. Eight signs are:

◀ ◀ ◀ ◀ ◀ ◀ ◀ ◀ ◀

Learning Objective 3: Eight closing signals

Signal 1. *No more objections* Buying results from either having reasons *to buy* or not having reasons *not to buy*. Customers raise objections when they have not reached the conviction stage in the buying process. Sales are not made until all the objections have been overcome. Clearly then, when a buyer has no more objections, the salesperson can assume the customer is sold on the value of the product or service and can attempt to close the sale at that point.

Signal 2. *Buyer asks questions* When buyers start to ask key questions, it's time to close. The key questions concern delivery dates, quantities, available volume discounts, payment terms, or after-sale service. These questions concern activities that assume the sale has been made.

Signal 3. *Changes in verbal and nonverbal signals* Buyers unconsciously give closing signals. The attentive salesperson closely monitors the buyer's verbal and nonverbal signals. When customers are mentally committed to buying, they change their verbal and nonverbal signals. Verbal signals are a more excited tone, faster pace, and generally being more conversational. Nonverbal signals are leaning forward, nodding the head in agreement, opening up the arms and hands, and moving closer. When interest and commitment grow, more eye contact occurs. The buyer will become less defensive, more cordial, show more interest, and exhibit all the go-ahead signals associated with positive nonverbal communication.

Signal 4. *Buyer solicits opinions of others* Soliciting someone else's opinion is a sign of commitment and readiness to close. This is a form of external validation that the right decision is being made. The key signal is the "What do you think?" question. The close may actually shift to another person at this point. In an industrial sale, soliciting the opinion of others could mean bringing in engineers, operators, or any other member of the buying center. In retail sales, it is common for input to come from spouses, children, or

When customers begin to closely examine the product is a good time to try and close the sale.

others when the decision is about to be made. The "What do you think?" question may be asked of several people in this situation, too.

Signal 5. *Buyer begins to closely examine the product* A subtle sign appears when the buyer begins to examine the product closely. Customers may say very little, but their nonverbal signals give away the fact they are interested in what the salesperson has told them. For example, if a salesperson were presenting a computer modem and the customer tried to plug it into the computer, the salesperson would be getting a clear buying signal. There are no set guidelines separating curiosity from a buying signal. Experience will teach the salesperson more about differentiating the two and the value of this signal.

Signal 6. *Definite statements of interest* A more direct indication is when the customer makes definite statements of interest: "I am interested if you have a model with 75 horsepower," or "We buy these packed 24 to a case. Do you pack that way?" or "I need to have ten tons by the end of the week. Do you have that much on hand?" When the salesperson hears a statement like any of these, it is time to stop selling and close the sale.

Signal 7. *Silence from the buyer* The most difficult signal to read is customer silence. Some customers give little if any sign of being ready to buy. Customers may, out of courtesy, wait for the salesperson to finish the presentation and ask for the order before they give any sign at all. When dealing with this behavior, successful salespeople work from the assumption that if the customers are *not* ready to close, they will let them know.

Signal 8. *Buyer says, "I'll take it"* This is the best signal a salesperson can get. At this point, stop selling and write the order. *Do not continue the presentation thinking you must complete its full cycle before you can take the order.* When the buyer is ready to buy, be ready to close.

The Cambridge Diet Plan is a weight-loss plan distributed through home demonstrations. Prospects are given the presentation and samples of the product to taste. The product is a water-soluble powder that mixes with milk to form a drink of milkshake consistency. It is used to replace one or two meals per day and is fortified with vitamins and minerals to be a complete meal in a glass.

Mr. and Mrs. Hinkel went to Carole's house over the noon hour for the presentation. The presentation itself takes about 15 minutes and, with questions, should take no longer than half an hour. Carole was a new distributor. After going through the presentation about the chocolate-flavored drink, the Hinkels were convinced and ready to buy. Carole said, "Well, what do you think?" Mr. Hinkel said, "It tastes pretty good. I think you have an interesting product here." Carole said, "Well, that's great!" Then she sat looking at them.

The Hinkels, figuring there was more to the presentation, said nothing. Carole then cycled back into the top of her presentation and started the whole pitch over again with the strawberry-flavored drink. At the end, the same thing occurred. The Hinkels again said nothing, thinking the presentation would cycle again for the next flavor. Needless to say, they were becoming bored and restless with the same presentation three times in a row. Carole was becoming frustrated after seeing all the positive signs but never hearing the Hinkels say they would take it. The problem was Carole didn't know how to close; the Hinkels were waiting to be asked for the order.

The moral of the story is: a 15-minute presentation does not have to take an hour if you know how to close. Recognize the closing signals and above all, *ask for the order!*

The Most Important Rule in Closing

The most important and oldest rule in closing is:

Ask for the order and shut up—the next person that speaks owns the product.

After asking for the order, it is the buyer's responsibility either to authorize the order, thus closing the sale, refuse, or bring up additional questions or objections. The following dialogue illustrates how failing to wait for the reply can cause problems:

Salesperson: Mr. Madden, I believe I have covered all the salient points and addressed all of your concerns. I would like to do business with you. Can I write up an order for 200 cases for a Wednesday delivery? *(Not saying anything, the buyer picks up the sample and closely examines it. A minute or two of silence ensues.)*

Salesperson: You seem to be hesitating. If it is the price you are concerned with....

At this point in the presentation, the salesperson has just lost the edge. The buyer was ready to say yes but now sees an opportunity to get a lower price. He didn't even have to ask for it! The buyer has been given the signal to hold out and wait for more concessions. The salesperson has brought this on by forgetting the rule: the next person to talk owns the product!

▶▶ *follow-up questions*

1. What are the eight signs that signal a buyer's readiness to close? Explain three of them.
2. How would you expect closing signals to differ when making a presentation to a group, compared to an individual?
3. What is the most important rule in closing?

When Should the Close Happen?

The obvious answer may appear to be "at the end of the presentation." However, this is not always the case. The salesperson must convey enough information in the presentation to make the customer feel confident enough to commit to a decision. The adaptive salesperson must be ready to close at any time.

Close When Signaled to Close

There are several things to keep in mind about when to close. First, close when you see the signals. When buyers are communicating they have made a decision, close. You may walk in the prospects' door to find them greeting you saying, "I've heard about your new cleaning compound. Would you send me two 55-gallon drums to try?" Closing can come when you are presenting your features, advantages, and benefits. Buyers might just tell you that your product sounds just like what they need!

Closing sales for services like those provided by small construction companies or lawn services is often done on the first visit. The homeowner adding a deck to the house may indicate right up front, "I want you to build this deck 15 feet by 25 feet, starting here." The contractor does not even have to sell the customer on the services! Whenever you see the closing signals and feel the time is right, go for the close.

Closing Signals May Come from the Decision Maker, Not the Buyer

The decision to buy is the responsibility of the person in the decision-making role. In many sales situations, buying decisions are made by one person without the aid of advice from others. A person who seeks advice from other members of the buying center is a consensus decision maker. Another decision maker uses the group as advisors: this person takes the group's opinions into consideration but ultimately makes the decision that may or may not follow the group's opinions. The third style is the autocratic decision maker. These deciders make up their own mind regardless of what the other members of the buying center think.

To sell in group situations, adaptive salespeople must carefully assess the style they face. If the decision maker has a consensus style, the salesperson closes to the group, and the decision maker follows along. Where the decider takes guidance from the other members, the salesperson closes to both the

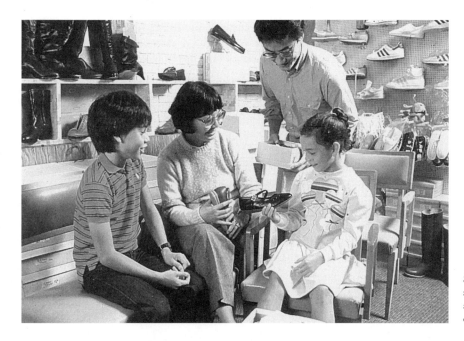

Salespeople may face situations where several people are involved in the buying decision.

influencers and the decider. With the autocratic decision maker, the salesperson closes to just that person.

▶ ▶ *follow-up questions*

1. When do closing signals usually appear in a presentation?

2. What would you do if a customer starts giving you closing signals five minutes into your 60-minute presentation?

3. What would you do when you have finished your 60-minute presentation and you have had no closing signals or objections?

Proven Closing Techniques

Purchasing magazine conducted a survey in which purchasing agents kept records of what happened when salespeople called on them. One of the questions was, "After the salesperson had explained the product or service, what did he or she ask you to do?" In an astonishing 35% of all sales calls, the answer was "nothing."[3] Customers, particularly professional purchasing agents, expect to be asked for the order.

Learning Objective 4: Twenty proven closing techniques

Just as a sales call can have a variety of goals, so too can closing. If the purpose of the call is to just introduce the salesperson, then no close is planned because nothing gets presented on which to close. If the call's goal is to present a product and schedule a field trial or demonstration, then the close in this case would be securing a firm date for the prospect to observe the presentation. Most calls are targeted toward completing a sale, so we will focus on techniques for that purpose.

Closing Techniques That Work

Closes are grouped into two categories: oral and action. In an **oral close,** the salesperson asks questions probing readiness to buy. With an **action close,** the salesperson takes an action, such as writing up the order or filling out an estimate sheet, that buyers must stop if they are not ready to buy.[4]

There are many different types of closing techniques. Salespeople are inventing new ones every day as they face challenging new buyers and situations. Few salespeople ever rely on just one technique. An adaptive salesperson prepares several closing techniques and uses them singly or in combination. Prior to making a formal close, the salesperson should mentally review the following questions:

1. Have I given the buyer enough information to make a decision?

2. Have the objections been handled sufficiently so there are no hurdles left?

3. Have I summarized the benefits and checked with the customer for agreement that the benefits solve his or her real needs or problems?

4. Have I used enough trial closes?

5. Are the closing signals there, and have they been positive?

6. Am I ready to ask for the order?

If salespeople are able to say yes to all six questions, they are ready to close the sale. What techniques should they use? There are 20 possibilities:

1. The direct close   The **direct close** is simply asking for the order. Some possibilities are:

"I would like to do business with you. Do I get an order?"

"Can I write an order today?"

"Do I get the sale?"

"Can I consider this sale closed and get the paperwork started?"

2. The assumptive close   The **assumptive close** assumes the sale is made and moves forward on that premise. Salespeople do not ask if they can have the order; they assume it's done unless the buyer stops them from placing it or writing it up. Salespeople often have such a well-established relationship with customers that asking for the order is not necessary. Some salespeople never call on customers and make presentations; they quote their prices over the phone, then wait for the buyer to call back with the order without ever asking for it or formally closing the sale. An assumptive close would be like any of the following:

"We will place the order today for a Monday delivery."

"I'll write this order up and call it in this afternoon."

"Let me have our fitter measure you for that suit and while he is doing that, I'll select some ties and shirts for you to choose from."

"What purchase order number will you use?"

By using these or similar statements, the salesperson has put the customer on notice that an action will take place unless told otherwise. This gives the buyer a last chance to stop the close, raise more questions, or voice any objections. When using the assumptive close, everything the salesperson says and does must imply that the sale has been made.

3. Alternative choice close   The **alternative choice close** gives customers a chance to say yes by giving them a choice of alternatives. The alternative choice close works well with the assumptive close, as well as by itself. This is

one of the most popular closes. In a recent survey, this technique was reportedly used at least 75 percent of the time.[5] It is a softer close than a direct close. Some examples of an alternative choice close are:

"Would you like delivery on Monday or Friday?"

"I will get you a red one or blue one. What's your pleasure?"

"We pack our product in 12 packs or 24 packs. Which would be best for you?"

"Will this be cash or charge?"

4. The minor points close The **minor points close** is similar to the alternative choice close in that it is a less threatening approach to asking for the order. The minor points close does not ask the customer to commit to the product in total and all at once. It, in essence, has the buyer commit on a very subtle, feature-by-feature basis.

The minor points close is applying the "minor yes" idea you learned in a previous chapter. Many salespeople use the terms "minor points" and "minor yesses" synonymously. The idea is to have the customer commit to the purchase decision on a sequential minor-point-by-minor-point basis. A metaphor illustrating the minor points concept is that of eating a steak dinner. For most people, the steak is easier to digest if eaten one bite at a time, rather than all at once. The minor points close can make a big sale more palatable if closed one feature at a time.

5. The written close The **written close** is an extension of the assumptive close but is a more active, less passive close. When doing the written close, the salesperson uses the order form through the presentation to record specific information. By the time the presentation is over, the salesperson has taken down all the specifics, and the order is all but authorized. This close is also called the "Let me make a note of that" close. It is called that because the salesperson uses the order form or notepad to make a note of all the specifics required by the customer: size, color, delivery dates, and so on.

The problem with the written close is that it makes customers think an order is being written up before they have authorized it, which may alarm them. This impression, however, is precisely what makes it work! The written close works like this:

Buyer: I think you have a nice product here, but I'm not sure we need it. *(No need objection)*

Seller: Let's talk more about what you are looking for in this type of product. *(At this point, the salesperson pulls out the order form and begins by writing the customer's name, firm, address, and so forth on the order. As the conversation progresses, the salesperson writes such things as the quantity the customer would need, color, and descriptions. The buyer begins to notice an order is being written.)*

Buyer: Hey, what are you doing? I haven't said I was going to buy anything. Don't be writing up an order!

Seller: Ms. Owens, I'm using the order form to record the specifics of what you need. This way I'm certain not to miss a thing, and *if* we come to an agreement, I will have everything written down just as you need. That way I'm sure to have no errors.

Buyer: That's all well and good, but you're not going to be placing any orders unless I okay it.

Seller: Ms. Owens, I wouldn't think of it. In fact, if we do not reach an agreement, I'll either give you this order form to destroy or I'll do it in front of you.

At this point, the buyer is reassured. At the end of the presentation, the salesperson can say:

Seller: Ms. Owens, I've written down everything we have agreed to here on the order. Since we do seem to have a fit between your needs and what we can do, all I need you to do is authorize this order with your initials right here and we have already started the ball rolling!

Now the close is like the assumptive close. If the buyer does not hesitate and signs, the close is made. If there are other objections, questions, or reluctance, they will surface now. Any problems are dealt with and the order changed if necessary. After that, the salesperson cycles back to asking for an authorization of the order.

6. The T-account close The **T-account close** is also known as a "Ben Franklin," balance sheet, or balancing act close. Dr. Franklin used a T-account to make decisions. He listed all the reasons *to* do something on one side of the T drawn on a sheet of paper and the reasons *not* to do it on the other. The T-account close is the same. The salesperson lists the reasons to buy on one side and the reasons the customer gives for not buying on the other. The salesperson should make sure there will always be more positives than negatives before embarking on this close. This is a close that should be used after all the objections have been overcome and there is little doubt the positives will outweigh the negatives.

A modification of the T-account close is for the salesperson to ask the customer to complete the T-account. This does two things. First, it gets the customer more involved with seeing that the benefits do outweigh the costs, and second, the customer is actually writing, seeing, and thinking about the evidence that indicates it is better to buy than not to buy.

Another alternative is a modified T-account close. In this close, only the reasons for buying are listed; the reasons not to buy are omitted.

A salesperson would work into using the T-account close like this:

Seller: Ms. Holman, we have discussed all the products features, advantages, and benefits. You have also raised good objections. To keep things straight, let's list all the reasons we should proceed with this order and all the reasons we should not proceed. Here's a tablet. If you would, write the reasons you feel we should go ahead on the left side of the T and why we should not on the right side.

Case in Point

Using the T-Account

A salesperson for a precision tool and die firm routinely calls on small manufacturing plants to sell them custom tool and die work. The small manufacturers routinely resisted having this custom work done. They figure it would be cheaper for them to do it inhouse. The salesperson decided that the best way to make the sale and serve the customer at the same time was to compare the cost of making gears and parts inhouse with having them custom-made.

Continued

The salesperson decided to use theT-account close and take the customer completely through a cost comparison. The salesperson would ask the customer or purchasing manager to check the figures for accuracy. As a result of this closing procedure, the salesperson was able to convince many new customers it would be cheaper for them to have their parts custom-made. As a result, sales increased dramatically.

The T-account close can be a very versatile and useful close with customers who need and want to see side-by-side comparisons.

7. The porcupine close   In the previous chapter on making presentations, the porcupine was described as a trial close. It can also be used as a final close. It works well with a client who is inquiring about alternatives and in the process giving positive closing signals. The **porcupine close** hinges on the buyer's statement, "Do you have it ____?" and the seller's retort, "Do you want it ____?" The porcupine close gets its name from the porcupine's quill: sharp at both ends. For example:

Buyer: Jack this is a nice printer. Do you have one that will do 200 copies per minute?

Seller: Ms. Brown, do you want one to do 200 copies per minute?

Buyer: Yes, we need that amount of capacity.

Seller: Our model 32 will do just that. Can I assume I have the order for a model 32?

8. The sharp angle close[6]   This carries the porcupine close to a higher level. Instead of answering a question with another question, the salesperson answers with one that means, if prospects reply the way their original question indicates they will, they have bought it. The **sharp angle close** involves two pivotal points: (a) the salespeople must know what benefits they can deliver and (b) they have to know how to pan the gold from that information. For example:

Buyer: If we decided to go with your product, we'd have to take delivery by June 15. Could you handle that? *(Most salespeople would be tempted to say yes. Note, the buyer has not said he would buy if the condition is met! Now the adaptive salesperson takes advantage of an opportunity.)*

Seller: If I could guarantee delivery by June 15, are you prepared to approve the paperwork and give us a 10 percent deposit today?

The seller must now sit and wait for the answer. Many demands or desires can be used in this close besides delivery. Getting an order in before a price increase takes effect is a powerful one. The sharp angle close also is a good gambit to use on pompous and antagonistic buyers who want to set conditions they think the salesperson cannot meet. This is done by some buyers as a way of harassing salespeople so they will not call again. Such antagonism can be used in the sharp angle close technique. For example:

Buyer: I like your product, but if you really want my order, you're going to have to deliver it all tomorrow.

Seller: If I can get it all here by tomorrow, are you prepared to pay COD?

The customer has tried to put a seemingly impossible condition on the sale, but the seller has used the sharp angle close by coming back with a condition of his or her own. If the buyer agrees to buy on this condition, the ball is back in the seller's court. Adaptive salespeople need to be careful when using the sharp angle close: they must be able to perform their side of the sharp angle!

9. The process-of-elimination close[7]   In the **process-of-elimination close,** the salesperson eliminates all the reasons for not completing the sale. In using this close, the salesperson says, "Is it because of such-and-such reason?" No. "Because of so-and-so?" No. In the end, buyers either have no objections to closing or must reveal their true objection for not committing to the order. In either case, the salesperson has tried to eliminate all the reasons for *not* buying, thus leaving only reasons *to* buy.

10. The think-it-over close[8]   One of the most common objections salespeople encounter is the stall. The most common stall is "I'll have to think it over." A poor closer or a salesperson who fears rejection is always tempted to say, "That's fine. I'll get back with you next week sometime, after you've had a chance to think it over." Why not turn the "I'll think it over" stalling objection into a close? The adaptive salesperson never passes up an opportunity to close and takes advantage of this stalling objection to convert it to a closed sale.

The think-it-over close is a five-step process, which works as follows:

Step 1. Agree with them.

Seller: That's fine, Mr. Malveaux. On a decision of this magnitude, I'd think it over, too. You wouldn't be wasting your time thinking it over unless you were seriously interested, would you?

At this point, buyers cannot logically say, "No, we're not seriously interested." After all, if they weren't seriously interested, what would they have to think over?

Step 2. Confirm the fact that they are going to think it over.

Seller: Since you are interested in evaluating our product benefits, I would like to give you those reports on our product to review. May I assume that you'll give them very careful consideration?

Buyer: You bet. We'll really think about what you have said today and consider how it might fit into our current operation.

Step 3. The "Get rid of me" question.

Seller: Mr. Malveaux, you're not saying that just to get rid of me, are you?

Watch for nonverbal communication cues. If buyers suddenly break eye contact, appear nervous, begin to fidget, or assume any of the negative body language postures, then the salesperson has a good idea that the buyers do not intend to think it over and are really trying just to get the salesperson out of the office.

Step 4. Clarify and squeeze.

Seller: Just to clarify my thinking, what is it in particular that you want to think over? Is it _____?"

Adaptive salespeople can fill in the blank with anything they think the buyer may be uncertain about. For example, they could say:

▸ "Is it my *price?*"
▸ "Is it my *guarantee?*"
▸ "Is it our *delivery policy?*"
▸ "Is it our *payment terms?*"
▸ "Is it our *company reputation?*"

These clarifying questions will bring to the surface any of the buyer's lingering objections or apprehensions. Notice that this part of the think-it-over close incorporates the process-of-elimination close. By systematically eliminating what it isn't, the salesperson gets a clearer idea of what it is.

When the salespeople do get to the particular hurdle that still exists in the buyer's mind, they know what they are up against and can target their presentation to overcome that problem, and thus they come to step five.

Step 5. Confirm what the problem is.

Having identified what the problem is, the focus of the sales presentation can home in on it. This is a time when a summarization of facts, features, advantages, or benefits is essential. This assures that the buyers have their facts straight and can do a fair and accurate comparison. It also gives the salespeople a chance to hit their selling points one more time. They want to be sure the buyers will carry both the correct factual information and the correct perception back to the influencers helping to "think it over."

The think-it-over close is a very powerful tool that can turn missed or postponed sales into signed orders on the spot. To use this close successfully, salespeople must execute it in a nonaggressive, nonthreatening manner. Careful attention to the buyer's nonverbal and verbal messages is essential to successfully using this close.

11. Reduce-to-the-ridiculous close   The **reduce-to-the-ridiculous close** tries to reduce the price obstacle to insignificance. This is used to close a customer who is stuck on price as the obstacle to closing. It is a very effective close, particularly for large-ticket items that might be financed over a long time; it also works on other types of products. The reduce-to-the-ridiculous close works like this:

Buyer: Joanne, I just do not think we can afford that type of a press. It's not in our budget to spend $3,000. I'm afraid we will have to pass on this one.

Seller: Mr. Cassatt, I can appreciate your feelings. Let's look at the economics of this. The only thing standing between what you want to accomplish and our press that will allow you to do it is the price of $3,000. This press will last a minimum of ten years, so we're really not talking about $3,000 but actually $300 per year, or only 82 cents a day. Do you really want 82 cents to separate us?

The salesperson has reduced the $3,000 obstacle to an insignificant 82 cents a day. The price objection has been reduced to a ridiculously low figure.

12. The puppy dog close[9]   The **puppy dog close,** if done right, works automatically. This close works on the premise that once you take a cute, cuddly puppy home and play with it, you'll fall in love with it and want to keep it. If

the client appears interested but reluctant to close, the puppy dog close is an excellent technique. This close works where salespeople have a demonstration model or sample they can leave with the client for a few days. The return visit to pick it up the model also gives them a chance to continue the presentation and another opportunity to make a sale.

Like some of the other closes we have discussed, this one has a series of steps that must be executed in sequence to be effective. The puppy dog close works in the following way:

Step 1. Offer to leave the sample or demonstration model with the customer for a few days.

Step 2. Call back in a couple of days. Do not try to close unless you are getting strong closing signals. Simply call to inquire about how things are going with the product's evaluation or if there are any questions or problems.

Step 3. Call the customer back a few days later and *make arrangements to pick up the model.*

Step 4. Return to the customer, discuss how everything went, and try to close the sale.

This close has the benefit of automatically allowing the salesperson to get two presentations. The first presentation was the initial appointment to introduce the prospect to the product, and the second one is an opportunity for a second chance at closing.

For the puppy dog close to be effective, the salesperson must be certain the buyer is totally familiar with the product before leaving it. Giving customers a product they do not know how to operate, cannot figure out, or are totally unfamiliar with only courts disaster. Whether the salesperson demonstrates the product or the customer is left with a sample to try, the product must work flawlessly every time.

13. The continuous yes close The **continuous yes close** is used to wrap things up by having the buyer agree on each feature, advantage, or benefit and give a series of continuous yesses. Rather than summarizing the benefits, features, or advantages and saying something like, "To this point, we have agreed this product will deliver the savings benefit, the safety benefit, and the profit benefit you seek. Should we go ahead with the order?", the salesperson asks about each benefit one at a time. This puts the buyer in a positive frame of mind, ready to say yes to the request for the order. The continuous yes close would sound like this:

Seller: Mr. Fuentes our X-34 industrial trash compactor gives you the space-saving benefit you want?

Buyer: Yes, it does.

Seller: And it offers you the savings you need?

Buyer: Yes, I think it will save us some money.

Seller: You do like the safety features on the X-34?

Buyer: Yes, it is one of the safest trash compactors I've seen.

Seller: Then, Mr. Fuentes, since it seems to fill the bill for you, what purchase order should we use?

This close must be used with some discretion. Salespeople will not want to use it if they were going to take the customer through a series of 15 questions. It would soon get tedious and boring. It does work well if there are only three or four benefits to summarize, or at least three of four major ones the salesperson wants to focus on. Note also in the above dialogue how the salesperson tied two closing techniques together. The continuous yes close lead to an assumptive close ("...what purchase order should we use?") to seal the deal. The salesperson didn't need to directly ask for the order; she assumed it, given all the yes responses.

14. The standing-room-only close The **standing-room-only close** tries to excite the prospect to buying because only a limited number of openings or amount of product is available. This close should not be used deceptively. It is unacceptable and unethical to induce someone to buy on false pretenses. Doing so has legal ramifications and can be fraudulent. There are legitimate circumstances when the standing-room-only close is applicable, such as when an equipment dealer receives only a small allocation of a limited-edition production model.

15. The get-on-the-bandwagon close The **get-on-the-bandwagon close** is a simple one whose purpose is to excite the customer to jump on the bandwagon. This close plays on prospects' emotional desire to be part of a group; therefore, they should get on the bandwagon along with everyone else. This is a very effective close for selling optional items or accessories to a major purchase. A good example of the bandwagon close is shown below where our salesperson is concluding the sale of a VCR to a retail customer. It works something like this:

Seller: Ms. Radke, I think you're going to really like this VCR. It's got all the features you wanted, and it has the optional feature of a remote control. For only $50 more, we will include a remote control with your unit.

Buyer: Nelly, I'm not really sure that I need a remote control.

Seller: Well, that's all right. You really do not need one, but we have found that as we have been selling these over the last couple of months, everyone who didn't buy a remote control initially usually ends up coming back and buying one later. Now, practically all our customers order a remote control when they order their VCRs. Everybody is getting them, and everybody swears by them after they take them home.

Buyer: Well, I don't know. You say there are a lot of these being sold?

Seller: You bet! Everyone is ordering them to the point where in a year or two, they'll be such standard items that not having one will be a rarity.

The seller has effectively used the get-on-the-bandwagon close by playing on the buyer's emotional need to conform. This close is effective for Amiables and Expressives, who have a strong desire for conformity.

16. The higher authority close[10] The **higher authority close** involves using a satisfied customer as a spokesperson for the salesperson, one who will give the salesperson and the product a glowing testimonial. The ideal candidate is someone who is known or whose firm is known and respected in the market. For example, when calling on a small grocer, a higher authority figure might be a major chain store buyer. With small contractors, it might be a major contractor in the area.

The higher authority close has several steps adaptive salespeople must follow. First is the ground work. They cultivate a person who will serve as their higher authority spokesperson. Second, they recruit that person and get them to agree to talk to any customer they have. They reassure this person that he or she will not be called on all the time, only when customers similar in stature are about to make a buying decision.

The higher authority close requires preplanning. In planning a call, adaptive salespeople determine the higher authority close may be necessary and contact the spokesperson to advise him or her that they might be calling to ask him or her to speak to the prospect; they also tell the spokesperson the day and about what time to expect the call.

When they are actually making the sales call on the prospective client, they say something like:

Seller: You know Mark Cade, don't you?

Buyer: Runs the shop at Finekrax, doesn't he?

Seller: That's right. He is one of our clients, too. Let me dial him up and you can talk to him about how our product performs. *(Dials the phone and gets the spokesperson, Mark, on the line.)*

Seller: Mark, I'm here at XYZ with Jasmine Henderson, and she has some questions about our product and how it performs. Let me put her on the line....

At this point, the salesperson hands the phone to the prospective customer. After the conversation, he or she uses another closing technique, such as the assumptive close, alternative choice close, or written close, and completes the deal. The higher authority close is powerful, but it must be planned for and set up well in advance. To do it without proper preparation is asking for embarrassment and failure.

17. The inducement close[11] In the **inducement close,** the customer is given a bonus or reward for closing today, rather than waiting. The inducement can be lowering the price to meet the competition, a buy-one-get-one-free deal, a special price for closing now, or any number of rewards. Magazine subscriptions are sold using the inducement close. Everyone is familiar with the TV ads that say, "If you order today, we will send you absolutely free a solar calculator." Many customers decide to purchase because of the inducement.

18. Creative price close In the **creative price close,** enterprising and imaginative ways to pay for the product are used as a close. When prospects say they cannot afford the price, it usually means they are trying to determine a way of paying for the product, but not all in one payment. Adaptive salespeople might suggest trying to split up the cost and suggest that the customer pay part in cash and part by check or credit card.[12]

Using creative pricing is a way of overcoming the price objection and closing sales at the same time. Many times, a purchase seems unaffordable, but when payments or terms are tailored to fit the buyer's situation, the close is almost automatic.

19. Summary-of-benefits close In the **summary-of-benefits close,** the seller simply summarizes the product's benefits, then asks for the order. The summary-of-benefits close can be used intermittently throughout the presentation, particularly if it is a complex presentation spanning a relatively

long period of time. Using the summary-of-benefits close would work something like this:

Seller: Mrs. Vang, let's just summarize the benefits that our printer will deliver to you. It will save you time because of its speed. It will save you money because of its unique ribbon rewind feature that allows you to get the most out of each ribbon. It will save you money on maintenance costs because of its solid-state construction. It's initial up-front cost is lower than the competition's, thus making it easier and more affordable for you initially. Is this printer then a workable solution to the problems we identified earlier in the presentation?

The summary-of-benefits close is both effective and reassuring. It keeps the benefits fresh in the buyers' mind and repeats them so they do not lose track of any. This is particularly helpful if the buyers want to stall for more time or need to talk to other people involved in making the decision. In that case, the seller must know upon departure that the prospective customer is well-versed in the benefits and hasn't forgotten any.

20. The lost sale close   The **lost sale close** is a unique and somewhat theatrical close. It is an action close that uses the customer's final rejection as a lever for one last attempt at making the sale. The lost sale close works as follows:

Step 1. Acknowledge that you have lost the sale, being sure to look and act appropriately disappointed.

Step 2. As you gather up your coat, briefcase, and product sample and move toward the door, you ask the "Where did I go wrong?" question.

Step 3. The buyer, thinking that the presentation is over and no longer needing to be on guard, will tell you.

Step 4. You say apologetically, "I didn't realize that. Let me explain . . . ."

Step 5. Deal with that objection and try to close once more.

A dialogue using the lost sale close would sound like the following:

Seller: Well, Mr. Bacon, it does not look like we can work things out today, does it? I think we have a great product, one that could work well for you. Well, maybe next time. *(Salesperson starts gathering up her things, getting up and moving toward the door, where she would ask the "Where did I go wrong?" question.)*

Buyer: Ann, I did like your presentation, but you really lost the sale when you wouldn't work with me on the price. Your price is just more than I can justify. Particularly in light of the competition being 15 percent lower.

Seller: Mr. Bacon, I didn't realize that. I was under the impression we were offering a competitive price. I probably didn't adequately explain all the amenities we include with the price. I may have made it sound like those were add-ons, when really they are free. If I could, let me just take one last second to explain what you get free.

When salespeople use the lost sale close in this manner, hidden objections surface, and they get one more chance. In the example above, the salesperson assumed the buyer was aware the add-ons were free. The buyer assumed they cost extra. As a result, both were operating on incorrect assumptions. The lost sale close brought that to light, and the sale gets completed.

▶ ▶ *follow-up questions*

1. What questions should salespeople ask themselves before making the final close?

2. How does a T-account close differ from a modified T-account close?

3. The stalling objection is frequently encountered by salespeople in all industries. Which close(s) do you think would work best against it?

Adapt the Close to the Situation

Use Multiple or Sequenced Closes

▶ ▶ ▶ ▶ ▶ ▶ ▶ ▶ ▶ ▷
Learning Objective 5:
Sequence multiple closes and bridge between each

All successful salespeople use multiple closes. A close that works in one situation does not necessarily work in another. Closes can be coupled or sequenced. When coupled, two closes are used together in the same closing sentence. For example:

Seller: Mr. Poletes, by closing this order today, we not only get you the price you wanted but can give you the additional aisle displays that will increase your sales at no extra cost. Should we set delivery for Tuesday or Wednesday?

In this example, two closes were coupled into an effective and conversational closing question. Another approach to multiple closing is sequencing. Here, the salesperson attempts one close, then waits for a positive reaction. Getting one, the order is taken. Not getting a positive reaction, the salesperson sequences into another close and again waits for a positive reaction.

Sequencing closes must be done in a conversational manner to avoid sounding like a mechanically recited script. Some possibilities could be:

Seller: Ms. Jacobsen, I think the X-152 has the profit potential, safety features, labor savings, and guarantees you are looking for. Should I write up the order? *(summary-of-benefits close)*

Buyer: Joe, I'm not sure. I think we will just have to wait and see. *(stalling objection)*

Seller: I can appreciate your situation. The X-152 does have the benefits everyone seems to want, and I have sold it to almost every firm in town like yours. *(get-on-the-bandwagon close)*

Buyer: Joe, I just do not think so. Call me next week.

Seller: I understand your reluctance, but what we can do, if you close today, is provide you with a free set of ancillary accessories. We normally do not do this, but since you have been a customer of ours for such a long time, we can add this package to your order at no cost. It's worth $150, and I think that added value makes our offer to you very attractive. *(inducement close)*

Buyer: Would that allow us to do our own repairs and minor maintenance?

Seller: Yes. Not only that, it's normally something we offer only with our larger machines, so if you wanted to trade up in the future, you would already have this package.

Buyer: That does make it seem like a better deal. How could we finance this, just in case I did decide to order?

The salesperson is now on the way to an order. As the salesperson tried one close after another, one finally struck pay dirt. If Joe had given up after the first close, the sale would not have been completed.

Planning for Multiple Closes is a Must

Being effective at using multiple closes requires planning, practice, and learning. Some transitions will work better than others. In most instances, moving from close to close is conversational, and the transitions are transparent to the customer. How do salespeople bridge from close to close if the customer is giving them signals that they have pushed a little too hard? How do they get back into the closing groove and bring the customer back to a more positive frame of mind? The solution is a three-step approach called **bridging**.[13]

Bridging step 1   The first step is to apologize or acknowledge the fact you may have come on too strong. Salespeople do this with a simple apology, like: "I'm sorry. Sometimes I get a little carried away because I know what a great deal this is, and I want everyone to be as excited as I am."

Bridging step 2   The second step is to summarize the benefits already agreed upon. Tie-downs work well here. Also, it is a good idea to try to close again on minor points. This serves to get the customer back into the proper mind set in a nonthreatening way. Salespeople might say:

> "I may have gotten a little ahead of myself. You may still have questions, but this model does have the capacity you need, doesn't it?" (Notice the 'doesn't it' tie-down.)

or

> "I'm just trying to close this sale to get you the savings you want as soon as possible. Wouldn't it be nice to start getting those savings as soon as possible?"

or

> "I see I'm pushing you. I do not want you to rush into something you do not want, that would be bad for both of us. But so many of our customers have already taken advantage of this offer and enjoy it that I would like you to give it some serious thought. Our X-134 really does a great job, doesn't it?"

Bridging step 3   The last step in bridging is to ask the lead-in question. This question moves the salesperson to another close. This lead-in question can either be more direct or less threatening, depending on the buyer's frame of mind. The customer's nonverbal and verbal cues will tell the salesperson which approach to take. Continuing on with one of the examples from above, the lead-in question would be incorporated as follows:

Seller: I see I'm pushing you. I do not want you to rush into something you do not want, that would be bad for both of us. But so many of our customers have already taken advantage of this offer and enjoy it that I would like you to give it some serious thought. Our X-134 really does a great job, doesn't it?

Buyer: I will not rush into any decision. I'll think it over.

Seller: That's all I can ask. Just as a point of clarification, we have agreed that the benefits we offer and that you need are: ..., haven't we? *(summary-of-benefits close and tie-down)*

Salespeople must plan multiple closes. Linking closes is a powerful way to culminate a good presentation.

Adapt the Closing Strategy to the Buyer's Social Style[14]

▶ ▶ ▶ ▶ ▶ ▶ ▶ ▶ ▶ ▷

Learning Objective 6: Adapt closes to different social styles

When planning closes, the salesperson must consider the buyer's social style. Using a hard close on an Amiable can be disastrous; using the wrong close is the cause of many a lost sale. The following are good ways to close each social style:

Closing Analyticals:

▶ Ask for the order in a direct but nonthreatening manner.

▶ Expect to negotiate and haggle. A closing technique explaining the details works well.

▶ Pay particular attention to pricing questions and eleventh-hour price objections.

▶ Work toward an immediate close. Avoid having the prospects or you delay the commitment. Waiting may result in them analyzing themselves right out of the commitment.

▶ Cite your track record, call on satisfied customers, stress your service record.

Closing Drivers:

▶ Be direct, ask for the order; do not beat around the bush.

▶ Be clear and factual; leave no room for assumptions or misunderstandings.

▶ Offer options and alternatives; remember, Drivers have a strong need for control.

▶ Be prepared to negotiate. Drivers like to attach special conditions just when you think they are closed (the sharp angle and porcupine closes work well with these types).

▶ Anticipate objections arising during the close.

Closing Expressives:

▶ Closing Expressives can be done more informally and casually. The assumptive close works well.

▶ Expressives are particularly keen on extras, creative pricing, and inducements. They like to feel they are getting something "bigger" than they paid for, something extravagant.

▶ Do not confuse Expressives with options. You may have to make the decision for them or tell them the product they need and why.

▶ Save the details. They are interested in details after they have decided; they may just as easily want to leave the details up to you to work out.

▶ Get a definite commitment.

Closing Amiables:

▶ Be careful not to appear too aggressive. Be discreet in asking for the order, be indirect.

▶ Stress the extras, particularly guarantees, track record, and satisfied customers.

▶ Amiables are very susceptible to buyer's remorse, so closing will require a variety of assurances that their decision was right and the risk has been minimized.

- Do not be afraid to encourage them to ask others to participate in the buying decision.
- Use the most personal closing techniques possible; remember, they want to do business with their friends.

Table 12-1 shows the 20 various closing techniques and the buyers with whom they are most effective. An unmarked closing technique does not mean it will not work with the indicated social style, only that it would be less effective than others.

What Would You Do If...?

After making a good presentation to Henry Skrip, the buyer for a national food chain, you feel it is time to ask for the order. He has been giving positive buying signals and shows interest in the product. You've known Henry for some time and have a good relationship with him. Henry's social style is Amiable. He likes doing business with people he feels are his friends, and your meetings with him have always been cordial.

Assuming this sale is closed, you start to write up the order. Henry suddenly stops you, saying, "Let's not get too hasty here, Madeline. I never said we would take this product on. It seems like it would be a good fit with what we have, but your competitor has one just like it. I cannot take both." After saying that, he just looks at you. It's your turn to speak.

▶ Question: What would you do?

Table 12-1 Match the Close to the Buyer's Social Style

| Closing Technique | Social Style of Buyer | | | |
	Analytical	Driver	Expressive	Amiable
1. Direct	X	X		
2. Assumptive		X	X	
3. Alternative choice		X		
4. Minor points	X	X	X	X
5. Written	X	X		
6. T-account	X	X		
7. Porcupine	X	X	X	X
8. Sharp angle	X	X		
9. Process-of-elimination	X	X	X	X
10. Think-it-over				X
11. Reduce-to-the-ridiculous	X	X	X	X
12. Puppy dog	X			X
13. Continuous yes	X	X	X	X
14. Standing-room-only			X	X
15. Get-on-the-bandwagon			X	X
16. Higher authority			X	X
17. Inducement	X	X	X	X
18. Creative pricing		X	X	X
19. Summary-of-benefits	X	X	X	X
20. Lost sale close	X	X	X	X

▶▶ *follow-up questions*

1. What is meant by sequencing closes?
2. After a rejection at closing, how would a salesperson bridge closes to get buyers back into a positive frame of mind?

Building the Relationship After the Close

The job of closing is really only the start of the buyer-seller relationship. Part of making the sale complete is accurately completing the details of the transaction.

The Wrap-Up Completes the Sale and Starts the Relationship

Wrapping up the sale after the close must be done efficiently and, above all, accurately. Neither the buyer nor the seller wants to waste time correcting mistakes in price, quantities, delivery dates, or any of the details that accompany writing the order and issuing the purchase order. Unfortunately, this is exactly how a good deal of a salesperson's time is spent! To avoid these nuisances, follow a five-step wrap-up sequence:

▶ ▶ ▶ ▶ ▶ ▶ ▶ ▶ ▶
Learning Objective 7: Steps in wrapping up the sale

Step 1. *Accurately complete the order form.* Recheck all arithmetic and figures for accuracy and legibility. A 7 and 1 can often look the same on the third carbon that goes to accounts payable. Math errors can be permanent if not caught and corrected in a reasonable amount of time.

Step 2. *Signatures.* Be sure all papers needing signatures have them. Check to make sure they are signed correctly. Be sure all copies have a legible signature. Payment can be delayed days or months if the clerks in the respective firms' accounting departments cannot read the authorizing signatures.

Step 3. *Payment.* Before the sale is completed, both parties must settle on the method of payment: check, cash, trade-in credit, and so forth. Both parties must agree on the terms, if any. This includes the length of the payment period and any discounts or allowances to be taken and when. Terms also encompass the handling and deducting of down payments. It is also necessary to determine when the payment(s) will be made. This could be on the spot, when the order is approved, when the products are received, or when the products are installed and working satisfactorily. If the sale is to be a credit sale, the appropriate credit documents must be completed.

An efficient and accurate wrap-up completes the sale and begins the buyer-seller relationship.

Step 4. *Cement the sale.* Be sure to attach your business card to everything you give customers. Briefly go over the benefits and terms again to guarantee total understanding. Congratulate customers on making a great decision. Reassure them. They are excited; foster and nurture that excitement!

Step 5. *Give a receipt.* Proof of purchase is always necessary, even if it is simply a note saying what was sold to whom, when, and for what amount.

Building the Relationship After the Sale

Making the first sale may be the easiest part of the buyer-seller relationship. After the first sale, the salesperson must work to keep customers satisfied, keep them from going over to the competition, and above all, *keep them as customers.* The vast majority of sales are made to repeat customers. The goal of every salesperson should not be to make a sale but to create a customer, one that returns for more frequent and larger purchases.

Learning Objective 8: Rules for building strong customer relationships

> **Important customer relations rule:** It is easier to keep an existing customer than find a new one.

Keeping customers after the initial sale is incredibly easy and can be done effectively if approached systematically. This might seem difficult if a salesperson had, say, several hundred customers, but it isn't. Porter Henry, noted author on selling, surveyed numerous "star" salespeople on the topic of post-sale customer relations. One respondent, Betty Cinq-Mars, a stockbroker for

Merrill Lynch, has systematized her postsale customer relations activities. She does the following:

1. Mails each client updates on stocks whenever there is an opinion change or any significant news.
2. Mails birthday cards to her Individual Retirement Account (IRA) customers (she has their birth dates as part of their IRA record).
3. Sends certificate of deposit (CD) holders a notice when their CD is coming due and asks them to call her to talk about current rates and alternative investments.
4. Makes a point to talk to her customers enough to recognize their voices when they call so she does not have to ask who is calling.
5. Periodically runs a computer list of all clients and their trading activity.
6. Meets periodically with her clients face-to-face to discuss investment alternatives and give them that personal touch.[16]

Part of postsale service is rectifying complaints. Complaints should always be given top priority. A complaint, no matter how small, how nagging, or how insignificant is important to the customers. If it wasn't, they wouldn't be complaining. Complaints should be handled quickly and courteously at all times. Nothing will create customers faster than handling their complaint on the spot when they were anticipating a protracted tangle of redtape, excuses, and no solution.

Postsale service is the cornerstone of a profitable seller-buyer relationship. Building the relationship means more business for you and more problems solved for the customer. Stay in touch. Calls to check on the performance of a product, the accuracy of deliveries, and the overall satisfaction mean a lot. The call shows concern and interest. Buyers appreciate that. It also keeps your name in their minds and that gives you the edge over competitors who only call when they want something or there is a problem.

Important customer relations rule: Track the customer's orders.

Tracking the customer's purchases is also important in building the relationship. Steadily increasing or decreasing orders or unexplained variances often warrant further investigation. Increasing sales can signal a customer's expanding business, greater product satisfaction, or increased usage. Decreasing sales can signal dissatisfaction, competitive encroachment, a customer's declining business, or any number of problems to which early attention could arrest and turn around.

Important customer relations rule: Be a liaison between your firm and the customer.

To build a better relationship between you and the customer, act as the liaison between your firm and the customer. As a salesperson, you are, in a way, working for both your firm and the customer. Keep up on new developments coming in your firm that could help the customer. Keep in touch with not only the buyer but the end users, asking for their comments, criticisms, and suggestions. Many new product ideas come from customers who have ideas for making the old product better. Acting as a liaison will also enable you to head off any potential problems.

Important customer relations rule: Fix problems before they become problems.

How you deal with problems can build the relationship, too. Every salesperson has troubles and problems with some sales. In business-to-business sales, problems often occur in deliveries, product performance, or pricing mistakes. Stay on top of the customer's order. Check on it until it gets delivered. By doing this, the problems are fixed before they get to the customer, and you can report to the customer that there was a problem but you fixed it. This communicates to customers that you are alert and watching out for their welfare. Too many salespeople fail to monitor orders for problems and just assume that no news is good news.

Important customer relations rule: Help the customer even if it does not directly result in a sale.

Build the relationship by helping the customer solve problems even if they do not involve your firm or product directly. Customers appreciate this "above and beyond the call of duty" performance, and they remember it. By helping customers solve problems not directly related to your product or service, you position yourself as a valued consultant as well as caring salesperson. If you cannot directly help them with one of your products or services, then helping them find a solution, even though you do not sell them anything this time, may be just as good in the long run.

Important customer relations rule: Be available all the time.

Building a relationship means being available. When customers have a problem, they want a solution and, usually, the quicker the better. Many salespeople have installed cellular phones in their cars so they can be totally available to their customers. Many times customers' problems can be handled with a quick explanation or phone call to check on their order. If handled promptly, the problem need not be a major incident for either the customer or salesperson. If, however, the salesperson cannot be reached, then the minor problem festers into a customer complaint of poor service and untimely solutions.

Important customer relations rule: Influencers and facilitators are part of the extended customer family.

Do not forget the influencers and facilitators in building the relationship. A production foreman who has significant input into the buying decision should not be left out of the loop. Paying attention to this person's input and suggestions is essential. Keeping in contact here can mean a big difference in the individual's influence on the next sale. Similarly, consideration for secretaries, administrative assistants, and any one who facilitates the relationship is extremely vital and helpful. These people are all part of the extended customer family, so leaving one out can make the next sale more difficult.

▶ ▶ *follow-up questions*

1. What postsale activities could a car salesperson use to sustain a customer relationship? What could a real estate agent do? A person who sells jets to the Defense Department?

2. What are the five steps a salesperson goes through to finally wrap up a sale?

3. Why is having the exactly correct signature on an order, bill of sale, mortgage, and so on important?

Summary

This chapter started by explaining that closing was the culmination of the sales presentation process where the customer authorized the purchase (Learning Objective 1). Closing is not a certainty and is not automatic. Salespeople get rejected every day; it is part of the job. However, rejection can be used to improve a salesperson's performance, and four ways of dealing with rejection were presented (Learning Objective 2).

To be a successful closer, a salesperson needs to be aware of who makes the purchase decision and who influences that decision. When dealing with an individual customer, knowing who makes the decision is obvious. When facing a committee or doing a group presentation, the salesperson should watch for clues identifying the decision maker and the influencers. Trying to close the wrong person is futile.

Closing must be well timed. When the buyer is ready to buy, the salesperson must be ready to close. The salesperson must be alert to any of eight signals a customer gives when ready to buy. These can range from the obvious and straightforward, such as the customer saying, "Yes, I'll take it," to a buyer's subtle and sometimes mystifying silence. When the salesperson believes a clear signal is there, it is time to ask for the order. Salespeople must always remember that once they have asked for the order, it is the customer's turn to speak. The salespeople must sit there watching and waiting, for if they speak, there's a good chance the sale will be lost (Learning Objective 3).

There are at least 20 different ways to close a sale. Some are verbal closes, like the direct close, while others are action closes, like the puppy dog close. By using any of these closes singly or in combination, the salesperson has an enormous variety of ways to close a sale. As new salespeople gain experience, they naturally narrow the field of alternatives and eventually settle in on the few that work best for them. Even though it is only natural to settle on several favorites, however, an adaptive salesperson never forgets any of the others. Having the ability to draw on any of them means the difference between a lost sale and a closed sale (Learning Objective 4).

Sequencing closes was also explained. A salesperson seldom uses just one close during a presentation. Often several are linked. A technique called bridging was explained, and the steps to make it successful were outlined (Learning Objective 5).

Different types of closing techniques are more effective on some social styles that others. Drivers and Analyticals require somewhat different closes than do Amiables and Expressives. However, some closes work regardless of the customer's social style. Different closes were presented for the different social styles (Learning Objective 6).

The sale is only closed when the wrap-up details have been completed. A sale is not a sale until it legally becomes so. In most commercial sales, that is, business-to-business sales, a sale is not officially completed until after a series of 5 activities is finished. These involve the paperwork details most salespeople dislike but nonetheless are essential. Completing a sale after closing primarily involves five steps. First, accurately completing the order form is essential. Second is getting the appropriate and accurate signatures. Third is agreeing on and documenting the form of payment. At this point, it is vital for the buyer to know how large and how frequent payments will be. Fourth, cement the sale with a gracious and sincere expression of appreciation is both good manners and good business. Finally, give the customer a receipt or proof of purchase. (Learning Objective 7).

The closed sale is just the start of a business relationship. Service after the sale is where a salesperson creates future business. Given that, the salesperson must always look upon the close as the start rather than the culmination of a sale. How a salesperson performs customer relations tasks after the sale affects future business with that customer. The chapter presented numerous customer relations rules that ranged from how to handle complaints to remembering that the customer has an extended family of influencers, gatekeepers, deciders, and others who need to be considered in postclosing interactions (Learning Objective 8).

Key Terms

Closing   Culminating the sale by the prospect authorizing the purchase.

Oral close   The salesperson asks questions to close the sale.

Action close   The salesperson takes an action, such as writing up the order or filling out an estimate sheet, that buyers must stop if they are not ready to buy.[17]

Direct close   Simply asking for the order.

Assumptive close   The salesperson assumes the sale is made and moves forward on that premise.

Alternative choice close   This close gives customers a chance to say yes by giving them a choice of alternatives, such as product features, delivery dates, and payment plans.

Minor points close   This close does not ask the customer to commit to the product in total and all at once. In essence, it has the buyer commit on a very subtle, feature-by-feature basis.

Written close The salesperson uses the order form through the presentation to record the specific information. This close is also called the "Let me make a note of that" close.

T-Account close The salesperson lists the reasons to buy on one side of a T drawn on a sheet of paper and the reasons the customer gives not to buy on the other.

Porcupine close This close hinges on the buyer's statement, "Do you have it ____?" and the seller's retort, "Do you want it ____?"

Sharp angle close The salesperson answers the buyers' question with one that means, if they reply the way their original question indicates they will, they have bought it.

Process-of-elimination close The salesperson eliminates all the reasons for not completing the sale.

Think-it-over close A five-step process for turning a stalling objection into a close.

Reduce-to-the-ridiculous close This close tries to reduce the price obstacle to insignificance.

Puppy dog close This close works where salespeople have a model or sample that they can leave with the client, then call back in several days to either close the sale, make one last attempt, or retrieve the model.

Continuous yes close This close wraps things up by having the buyer agree on each feature, advantage, or benefit, thus giving a series of continuous yeses.

Standing-room-only close This close tries to excite the prospect to buying because only a limited number of openings or amount of product is available.

Get-on-the-bandwagon close A simple close whose purpose is to excite the customer to jump on the bandwagon along with everyone else.

Higher authority close This close involves a satisfied customer acting as a spokesperson for the salesperson, one who will give the salesperson and the product a glowing testimonial.

Inducement close The customer is given an inducement, bonus, or reward for closing today, rather than waiting.

Creative price close Enterprising and imaginative ways to pay for the product are used as a close.

Summary-of-benefits close The seller summarizes the benefits of the product or service and asks for the order.

Lost sale close An action close that uses the customer's final rejection as a lever for one last attempt at making the sale.

Discussion Questions

1. What impressions do buyers form of timid closers?
2. Discuss two behavioral outcomes resulting from closing anxiety.
3. How do trial closes make final closing easier and more effective?

4. Compare an oral to an action close.

5. Compare the minor points and continuous yes closes.

6. What is the assumption of the assumptive close?

7. When doing a written close, what will be the customer's most likely reaction? How will you deal with it?

8. What are the five steps of the think-it-over close?

9. How is the think-it-over close like the process-of-elimination close?

10. How would you use the reduce-to-the-ridiculous close to deal with this buyer's statement: "I cannot afford the $150 difference between these two suits."

11. How does the puppy dog close work?

12. How is the standing-room-only close different from the get-on-the-bandwagon close?

13. What is the objective of the lost sale close? (Do not say, "To close the sale!")

14. When bridging between several closes, how does a salesperson make the closes flow from one to another?

15. What are the first three things a salesperson must do after the customer has agreed to buy?

16. Pick the two customer relations rules you think are the most important. Why did you picked them?

Application Exercise

Go back and reread the box about the Cambridge Diet Plan presentation, then answer the following questions:

1. When should the salesperson have closed the sale?

2. What buying signals were the prospects exhibiting?

3. What closes would you have used?

4. Were these prospects presold, that is, really ready to buy when they came for the presentation?

5. How effectively did the salesperson use trial closes to test the readiness of the prospects to commit to a closed sale? What trial closes or tie-downs would you have used?

Class Exercises

Group Exercise

The situation involves the selling by a real estate firm of the final block of time in a time-share vacation condominium. The class will be divided into four groups.

Session #1:

Each group shall develop a scripted role play to illustrate two buying signals preselected by the instructor during the first interface between the seller and the buyer.

Session #2:

Dyads will be chosen at random to role-play for the class the script developed in Session #1. One member shall assume the role of the buyer, and the other member shall assume the role of the salesperson.

As a result of the given buying signals in the script, the salesperson member of the dyad shall be assigned to choose and role-play *two* of the chosen closing techniques as illustrated by the text.

The class shall then evaluate the dyads in terms of: 1) identification of appropriate buying signals, 2) the ability of the salesperson to pick up on the signals, and 3) the effectiveness of the salesperson's closing techniques.

Individual Presentation

From the group exercise above, the individual student shall develop for presentation a *multiple-close sequence* that will produce a sale for this time-sharing condominium.

 Cases

The Buyer Who Cries Money![18]

Symco is a major designer and marketer of software for industrial and financial applications. As the salesperson for Symco, it is your job to sell the predesigned products in the company line, along with custom-designed orders.

You suddenly find yourself in the following situation with the buyer from Haggerty Manufacturing:

Buyer: You'll have to cut your price by $5,000 or more. The software is inadequate.

Seller: Our price is fairly firm, I'm afraid. But we can surely make some software adaptations for you.

Buyer: But there are hundreds of pages of technical specs. It would be a lot easier for both of us if you would just reduce your price by $5,000—we will deal with the software.

Seller: We have dealt with a lot of software specifications. Let me show yours to my design people. There's no question they can satisfy your needs.

Buyer: I do not have the authority to hand our specs to outsiders. Sorry. We either have to get an agreement between us on price right now, or I'll be forced to go back to the committee for approval on this. What do you say? Are you going to drop your price or not?

It's obvious you have a pushy buyer interested in price more than anything else. Your problem now is compounded: how to close the sale without concessions, how to convince the buyer the product is worth the additional $5,000, and how to defuse this ultimatum?

Questions:

1. What would be your plan for dealing with this buyer's questions?
2. The buyer has said several key words that should be clues for you to use in planning your close. What do you think they are, and what do they tell you to do?

The Rambunctious Car Salesman

Emily went to the local Honda dealer to look for a new car. Her old one had seen its last days, so she decided to buy either a Honda or Toyota. After she looked over the models on the showroom floor for several minutes, Larry came up to her and introduced himself. Emily said she was just shopping around, comparing features and prices. Larry asked several questions and determined Emily's interest was centered on the Honda Civic.

She seemed interested, so they went for a test drive. Everything went well; she liked the way the car handled and was satisfied with its performance and its ride. After they returned to the dealership, Larry invited her into this office. There he proceeded to show her the available options and talk about their prices. At that point, he took an order form from his desk and started writing down her name and asking her for her address, place of employment, and other details. She seemed shocked, almost startled. She told Larry, "I do not want to buy a car today. I just want to look and compare." With that, Emily thanked Larry for his time and started to get up from her chair.

Questions:

1. What mistake(s) did Larry make?

2. If you were Larry, how would you get Emily to sit back down so you could try to close the sale? How would you repair the damage? Suppose you were Larry's sales manager watching this transpire. What guidance would you give Larry to improve his closing techniques?

References

1. Excerpted from Porter Henry, *Secrets of the Master Sellers* (New York: American Management Association, 1987), chapter 13.
2. Excerpted and paraphrased from Jack Carew, "Closing Is Part of a Process," *Personal Selling Power*, April 1989, pp. 22–29.
3. Henry, *Secrets of the Master Sellers*, p. 208.
4. Ibid.
5. "Eight Techniques to Close More Sales," *Personal Selling Power*, November/December 1989, p. 33.
6. Taken directly from Tom Hopkins, *How to Master the Art of Selling* (New York: Warner Books, 1982), p. 219.
7. Henry, *Secrets of the Master Sellers*, p. 214.
8. Hopkins, *How to Master the Art of Selling*, pp. 228–29.
9. Ibid., pp. 235–37.
10. Ibid., pp. 224–25.
11. Henry, *Secrets of the Master Sellers*, p. 216.
12. Ibid., p. 221.
13. Hopkins, *How to Master the Art of Selling*, p. 223.
14. The following has been adapted from Roger Wenschlag, *The Versatile Salesperson* (New York: John Wiley & Sons, 1987), pp. 187–94.
15. This is a common technique interviewers use. The purpose is to see how candidates react and if they can think on their feet. When interviewing for a sales position, keep this scenario in mind. What are three closes you could always fall back on as being the easiest and most effective to work with?
16. Henry, *Secrets of the Master Sellers*, p. 256.
17. Ibid., p. 208.
18. Robert E. Kellar, "How Good Are You at Negotiating?" *Sales and Marketing Management*, (1989): 32. The answer to handing this case can be found in this article.

13 Negotiating Sales Agreements

Objectives

After completing this chapter, you will be able to:

1. Define the concept of negotiating.

2. List the sources of power in negotiating.

3. Identify the characteristics of a successful negotiator.

4. Construct a matrix relating win-loss outcomes and five major negotiating styles.

5. Create a planning pyramid for negotiating the sale of a product or service.

6. Describe at least five negotiating tactics and give examples using each.

7. Counter at least three buyer's negotiating tactics.

8. Describe briefly the ethical and legal aspects of negotiating.

The Professional Selling Question

What is the most important piece of information you could pass along to a new salesperson about negotiating an industrial, business-to-business, or governmental sale?

A Sales Expert Responds

Bill Voelkel, a creative director for Porter Henry & Company, a New York-based sales training firm, says that sales negotiating is a distinct process but not separate from the selling process. Negotiating is working out the details of such things as prices, terms of payment, optional features, or delivery schedules.

Voelkel offers numerous suggestions for the new negotiator. First, he says, determine throughout the selling process what the important issues are to your customer. Are the issues price, payment terms, service, reputation, or maybe product quality? Then focus on the most important ones. There will probably be more than one, so you will need to prioritize them. If the issues are irresolute, they cannot be negotiated, but if they can be modified, they are negotiable.

Second, know what is of real value to your customers, and not value just in terms of money. Do they really value safety or security? It could be convenience or recognition. The emotional or intrinsic values often outweigh the economic and rationally calculated extrinsic values. If the firm prides itself on its status in the marketplace, then it is willing to pay more for products that give it not only good performance but also an incalculable status bonus.

Third, keep in mind the customer's limitations. This gives you negotiating power. All firms have their limits; their budgets are not unlimited, they are limited in what they can get from other vendors, they may be facing a tight deadline. Everyone operates under some form of constraint, and that constraint is a source of negotiating power for you.

Fourth, Voelkel says, do not react too quickly to competitor's proposals or give in too soon on the little things. This is does not leave you any room to maneuver on the big items. Get closure on the major points, then negotiate on the little items to fine-tune the deal.[1]

Introduction

In negotiating a sale, the salesperson works out the details with a customer. They make arrangements for optional features, how the customer will pay for it, when and where it will be delivered.

Salespeople are always negotiating. In some industries, formalized negotiations are the standard mode of operation. In most selling situations, however, negotiations are neither that formalized nor structured.

Formal negotiations are more common in commercial sales, that is, business-to-business sales, than in consumer sales. It is common for professional buyers to negotiate on price, delivery dates, transportation alternatives, insurance, quantities, and discounts. In retail sales, negotiating occurs infrequently. U.S. consumers pay the price marked on the price tag. They seldom haggle over price, quantity, or delivery dates. In other cultures, even the smallest retail sales are negotiated.

Negotiating is the oldest and most widely practiced form of selling in the world; if there is an oldest profession, then negotiating predates it. The Garden of Eden is often cited as the first location for a formal negotiating session. Formalized and lengthy negotiations are a standard selling practice in many nations. U.S. businesspeople trying to do business in the Middle East, the Far East, and Latin America must become acclimated to lengthy negotiations. A presentation and completed sale, which may take two or three meetings and span two weeks here, would commonly take the greater part of a year in China or Japan. The successful international salesperson is not only aware of the importance of negotiating but is keenly attuned to the customs and traditions surrounding negotiations with a foreign customer.

This chapter will examine negotiating as a separate but integral part of the selling process. While negotiating can occur in both commercial and retail sales, the focus of this chapter will be on the commercial or business-to-business negotiation.

Negotiating—A Powerful Tool

Learning Objective 1: Defining the concept of negotiating

What does the term **negotiating** mean? The dictionary defines it as conducting communications on the basis of agreement; coming to terms on some matter; making arrangements for an exchange or transaction; surmounting or traversing (as in *the horse negotiated the fence*). Negotiating is a secret weapon to salespeople who know how to prepare and execute a negotiation; who know what is and isn't negotiable and the operational latitudes in which they may maneuver. If negotiating is the oldest form of selling, why is it a

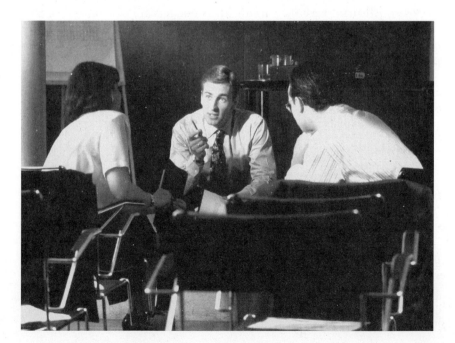

Successful salespeople are skillful negotiators.

secret weapon? The answer to that question lies in the fact that few people on either side of the desk are properly prepared for it.

Who's secret weapon is it? Whichever negotiator is best prepared and most adequately trained. Through negotiations, the buyer and the seller arrive at an alternative acceptable to both. Read the following dialogue and note how the sales rep negotiates her way through a pricing problem:

Sales Rep: Sorry, I cannot really lower the price. That would have to go through the product manager and the marketing director.

Buyer: Well, your price is too high.

Sales Rep: Let us talk to your engineering manager. Maybe we could make some changes to the product to save you money overall.

(fifteen minutes later with the engineering manager on hand)

Sales Rep: Do we really need all six belts on this model, or could you accept four belts if we could save you some money?

Engineering Manager: We could easily go for four, if you install the next larger size.

Sales Rep: That is certainly possible. We will take $100 off the price.

Buyer: That is not enough. We need $200 off.

Sales Rep: I understand your high quality standards. Could we take a short break while I make a phone call?

(ten minutes later)

Sales Rep: We can give you $112 off if two belts are regular size and two are the larger size.

Engineering Manager: That is fine. That is fine.

Buyer: Yes, that's fine.

Sales Rep: And for backup, why don't you take an extra inventory of heavier belts? You will always have them for emergencies.[2]

In this scenario, the sales rep managed to reduce the price of the machine, but not by $200. She reduced the price by $112 but also sold the heavy-duty belts for their inventory. The buyer won; he bought the machinery at a lower price. The salesperson won; she made the profit from the machine sale and the additional sale of the heavy-duty belts. This salesperson cleverly negotiated a reduced price on the primary redesigned item but made an added sale of two secondary items.

Formal and Informal Negotiations

Negotiations follow a three-step cycle of planning, negotiating, and following through. A successful salesperson seldom thinks in terms of just one negotiating episode. Since most sales are made to repeat customers, the negotiating cycle is repeated as well. In Figure 13-1, we see how the follow-through of one sale should overlap with planning for the next session.

Negotiating is both an art and science. It is a science in its structure and process and an art in its application. While it is adversarial by its very nature, the process of negotiating seeks to improve everyone's welfare. Realistically, buyers want more for less and sellers want to sell more for more. Somewhere in the middle is the mutually beneficial solution where the negotiations settle.

Formal negotiations   Formal negotiations, such as that done in labor unions or by governments, is guided by a structure influenced by laws or regulations. **Formal negotiations** have a structured format and a formal agenda.

Figure 13-1 **The Nego-
tiation Cycle**

Source: Robert E. Kellar, *Sales
Negotiating Handbook* (Englewood
Cliffs, N.J.: Prentice-Hall, 1988),
p. 168.

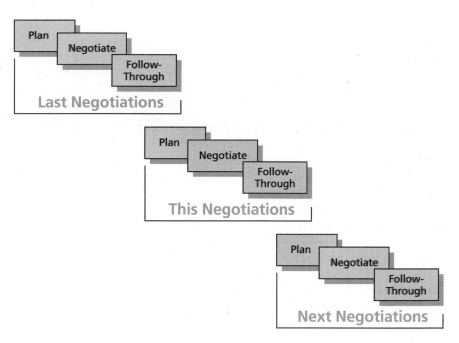

All participants know the purpose of the ensuing meetings is to negotiate.
The first agenda item is often deciding and negotiating the issues to negotiate! Formal negotiations are often carried out by negotiating teams.

Informal negotiations Informal negotiations are the most common.
When buyers and sellers are haggling over prices, they are informally negotiating. Even though informal negotiations lack the structured approach of
formal negotiations, laws dealing with misrepresentation and anticompetitive practices still apply.

In service sales, such as real estate, legal, consulting, construction, or
home services, informal negotiation is the standard practice. Such services
often lack a formal market where competition influences prices. Sellers have
unique talents and expertise that they price accordingly. The price (real estate commissions, for example) and services offered to a homeowner by a real
estate agent are negotiated before the listing agreement is signed. Regardless
of whether the negotiations are formal or informal, all salespeople need to
understand the specifics and nuances of negotiating. Understanding negotiating means understanding power relationships. There are numerous sources
of power in negotiating. These are discussed next.

Balancing Power Relationships[3]

Power is the ability to exert influence and cause changes in another party's
behavior. The perception of power is more significant than its actual possession. Your opposition will tell you what they perceive your power to be in
their tone of voice, body language, and gestures. Salespeople are often in a
rush to close sales and, in doing so, give the negotiating power to the buyer.
Salespeople who willingly discount the price rather than negotiate for a
trade-off come home with a closed sale but less profit. Worse, they have just
taught the buyer how to negotiate for a lower price.

Well chosen suits can enhance your power image.

◄ ◄ ◄ ◄ ◄ ◄ ◄ ◄

Learning Objective 2: Sources of power in negotiating

Power source 1: Appearance   The perception of power is created through appearance. Wearing "power colors" enhances the perception of power. Table 13-1 lists examples of such combinations that enhance the perception of power and credibility.

The list of power colors for women exceeds that for men as a result of tradition and custom more than anything else. Men in warmer colors, for example, shades of brown, are not perceived as carrying the same authority and power as those dressed in the cooler, more powerful colors. Neckwear adds to the image. String and bow ties detract from the image. Excessive jewelry also detracts from the power image.

Table 13-1	Dressing to Enhance Your Power Image
Colors That Enhance a Power Image	
Men's Suits	*Women's Suits*
Dark grey	Solid grey
Light grey	Medum-range blue
Light blue	Navy blue
Dark blue	Charcoal grey
Pinstripe in dark	Medium-range grey
Blue or grey	Camel
	Dark brown
	Beige
	Deep maroon
	Deep rust
	Black
	Steel grey

Source: Gary Karras, *Negotiate to Close* (New York: Simon and Schuster, 1985), p. 43.

Power source 2: The competition   What the competition can and cannot do enhances the salesperson's power to negotiate. For example, if a buyer wanted to book a hotel banquet facility for 3,000 people, she would be very limited in her choices of hotels. If the hotel salesperson erroneously assumes the buyer can go to many competing hotels to book the rooms, he has just given the buyer tremendous bargaining power, which she will use to get a discounted price and extra services. If he was aware that no competitor could handle such a large group, he would have her over a barrel. The competing hotels that cannot handle such a large crowd give negotiating power to all that can.

The competitor's price, quality, and delivery performance give salespeople power. The fact that the competition offers the lowest price in town but has the poorest delivery record gives the salesperson power to offset any price discounting. If salespeople assume that their competitors are as good or better than they are, they have given all their power to their competitor and the buyer.

The competition is an endless source of power in negotiating. If a competitor has failed to deliver on any promise to a customer, this is a source of power for your firm. A summary thought on competition: "The buyer will always want to buy the most reliable product from the company with the best reputation—but at the price of the most unreliable product from the most unreliable seller."[4]

Table 13-2 lists several questions salespeople can use to realize the power their competition gives them. The answers to these questions will help identify chinks in the competitor's armor and opportunities to gain negotiating power. For example, salespeople might question the competition's warehouse capacity and in researching the answer to the question find it has its own warehouses filled and has rented all the available local storage it can get. This would give the salespeople negotiating power because it allows them to offer delayed deliveries, their own storage, or smaller shipments, knowing the competition has no place to store large shipments. This can be part of the package offer and a justification for a higher price.

Power source 3: The perception of legitimacy   The power emanating from the perception of legitimacy cannot be overvalued in negotiating. Legitimacy is created through documents, testimonials, technical reports, and even something as simple as a business card. The power of legitimizing symbols creates tremendous command when negotiating. Salespeople's appearance, their business card, and the quality of their briefcase are legitimizing symbols. People believe salespeople are successful if they display the trappings of success.

Power source 4: Knowledge   The more knowledge salespeople have, the greater their power to influence outcomes. The knowledge a salesperson must have, which was discussed earlier in this book, encompasses product, company, competitive, legal, and social style-recognition expertise. In the following Case in Point is a list of questions to which a salesperson selling to an industrial firm would like to know the answers. As you read them, think of what power the answers to these questions would give you if you were going into a presentation with the firm's purchasing agent. Think about how many of them could be answered by using the sales call planner. The updated and current sales call planner becomes an important tool in preparing for negotiations.

Table 13-2 Questions to Help Determine the Salesperson's Source of Power Against Competitors	
Question:	What's their capacity to produce?
Source of the Salesperson's Power	They are at full capacity; can take orders but must backlog them—"How long will you wait to get your order?"
	They have excess capacity; why do they have such excess? Maybe nobody wants their product—"Maybe the reason nobody wants theirs is technical obsolescence. Do you want what nobody else does?"
	They have adequate capacity; where they have the capacity may not be convenient—"I'm sure they can handle your order, but their plant is four days away, and ours is here."
Question:	What's their capacity to deliver?
Source of the Salesperson's Power:	They only deliver on Monday—"We deliver every day, thus keeping your inventory to a minimum."
	They deliver every day—"That's great for service, but do you want your people doing the same paperwork everyday that they could be doing just once a week?"
	They have had a spotty delivery record—"Their price is great to, be sure, but how much is it worth to save money on the price and lose money because your customers can't be served due to a delivery delay or mistake?"
Question:	What do they do with prices?
Source of the Salesperson's Power:	They have the lowest prices—"Their prices are low, but does the price reflect quality and service?"
	They have the highest prices—"Their price and quality go hand-in-hand, but for this job, do you need to pay the price of a Cadillac when a Volkswagen is all that's needed?"
	Prices are the same—"Our service and quality make us the logical choice."

Case in Point

Examples of Questions That Would Give an Industrial Salesperson a Negotiating Edge

What do the buyer's engineers think of our product?

How much of a risk-taker is the buyer?

Have they had any bad experiences with us before?

Continued

The power of knowledge has two aspects:

1. Taking the time and making the effort to collect as much information as the salesperson can about the buyer and his or her organization.

2. Staying in tight control of the flow of information to the buyer about the salesperson's organization.[5]

These two have important long-term negotiating implications. First, salespeople want to know all they can about their customers; their needs, wants, aspirations, constraints, and business practices. Second, salespeople want their customers to know only what they need to know about the selling firm; they should know only the good aspects of the firm, its products, and their performance. The buyer doesn't need to know about the seller's problems; adaptive salespeople tell them what's great and keep the bad news to themselves.

Power source 5: Time   Time devoted to gathering information is time invested, not spent. Being in too much of a rush reduces negotiating power. Successful salespeople know that a little more time invested in thinking, planning, and gathering more information than the competition pays big dividends.

Taking time to ask questions pays off in two ways when negotiating. First, asking the buyer questions reveals more information useful in the negotiation. Second, taking the time to verify a price, terms, or package deal with the salesperson's own sales manager makes the salesperson a stronger negotiator.

Time is an asset both sides use. Buyers pressure salespeople for quick decisions, often threatening to back out if they do not get an immediate answer. More often than not, this is a gambit to fluster the salesperson into making a deal benefiting the buyer far more than the seller. When using time as a negotiating tool, remember that being pressured into a deal is capitulating to a bad deal.

Table 13-3	**Characteristics of a Successful Negotiator**

1. Intrinsically motivated. Negotiators must be motivated to enjoy the feeling of success that comes from a successful negotiation. Extrinsic rewards may not be as immediately forthcoming as some people would like.
2. Willing to take reasonable risks. Taking reasonable risks is part of the job. The successful negotiator doesn't take risks without a sound knowledge of what and how high the risks are.
3. Patient and confident. Patience and confidence are cornerstones in negotiations. Hurrying means making mistakes, and that means losing. Showing lack of confidence gives the other side an advantage.
4. Able to anticipate the other side's tactics, targets, and strategies. Negotiators who can anticipate the opposition's tactics can plan accordingly.
5. Students of the opposition. They learn everything possible about the opposing negotiator.
6. Able to separate real bargaining power from assumed power. Many times in negotiations, a good deal of bluffing goes on. Successful negotiators do their homework well enough to know what the opposition can and can't do and what power they have and would like others to think they have.
7. Detail-oriented. Successful negotiators document the details, define and clarify all modifications to the agreement, and build the relationship for the future.
8. Keenly aware of keeping things in perspective. They do not win the battle, then lose the war; they do not let little things side track the purpose of the negotiations. They know what they can give in to and what they must stand firm on.

Salespeople also use time to their advantage. They can stall a pushy customer, take time out to ask questions and thus get more information, or speed up the negotiations if they seem to drag without coming to closure. A customer that wants to close a sale too quickly can be as much a sign of trouble as a customer who won't close and wants to drag out a negotiation.

Characteristics of Successful Negotiators[6]

While all salespeople are negotiators, some are better than others. Negotiating ability, like selling, is a combination of talent, training, and practice. In most sales negotiations, neither buyers nor sellers get adequate training to think like negotiators. What they know is the result of experience. Successful salespeople become successful, in part, through their ability to handle the face-to-face negotiations of everyday selling. The characteristics of a successful negotiator are listed in Table 13-3.

◀ ◀ ◀ ◀ ◀ ◀ ◀ ◀

Learning Objective 3: Characteristics of a successful negotiator

Case in Point

Negotiating in the Global Arena

Frank Sergey is in marketing and sales for General Tire Company and experienced in negotiating with foreign customers. Regarding doing

Continued

The selling profession has taken on global proportions.

Case in Point—Continued

business in foreign countries, he recommends that "if you don't have local contacts, you may face bureaucratic and union problems.... Not knowing the country, being on your own, dealing with the bureaucracy and trade unions, a lack of local know-how, these are all areas to consider." He stresses a key point in international negotiations is not to negotiate "formal controls" but rather "substantial controls."

Mr. Sergey goes on to say, "Regardless of the level of sophistication, experience or expertise, it has little bearing on the quality of negotiation or the character of negotiation. The problem is, nearly every business person negotiates every day, and since they do it every day, everyone thinks they do it automatically. But negotiating isn't based on what you know about specific businesses or industries, it is based on psychology, strategy, preparation, and relationships. In other words, you can't negotiate in Tokyo the same way you negotiate in Los Angeles."

Source: Excerpted from "Gaining a Global Outlook," *Sales and Marketing Management* 144 (1992): 52–55.

▶▶ *follow-up questions*

1. Which characteristic of a successful negotiator do you think is most important and why?

2. Why does a successful negotiator need to focus on both the long- and short-term outcomes of a negotiating session?

3. If you are selling against competitors, how do you gain negotiating power from them?

4. What are some of the symbols a salesperson could use to create the power of legitimacy?

5. How can negotiating be adversarial by nature yet both sides win? Shouldn't there be a winner and loser?

Winners, Losers, and Problem Solvers: Negotiating Styles

A sales presentation is a negotiation. Planning has been stressed throughout this book. Effective negotiators plan for all possible scenarios that might unfold when they make their presentations and negotiate their agreements. They are never caught off guard.

Your Style May Predict Your Success As A Negotiator

▶ ▶ ▶ ▶ ▶ ▶ ▶ ▶ ▷

Learning Objective 4: Different win-loss outcomes and five negotiating styles

Salespeople's personality and social style affect the way they orchestrate sales presentations and how customers react to those presentations. These are very important for the salesperson to know, along with the customer's negotiating style. A negotiator's style is influenced by two primary concerns: for the

What Would You Do If...?

You are making a routine sales call on a key customer. When the secretary lets you in to the buyer's office, the following conversation occurs:

Customer: You've got one heck of a nerve coming in here to try to sell me something at a time like this! Boy, did you people ever screw me up! What I'm sending you back with is not a purchase order but a claim for $15,000.

Sales Rep: I heard about the problem, Perry. That's why I'm here. I think we can help get this sorted out.

Customer: Send me a check for $15,000. That will sort it out.

Sales Rep: Perry, you've been buying from us for over ten years. You know we won't damage you. You're a key account with us.

Customer: Cut the sales pitch. You've already damaged me.

Sales Rep: Perry, I grant you, we should have put the additional instruction labels on that shipment. But your night shift should never have tried to use our material in that kind of application.

Customer: Nonsense! How could they have known that?[7]

▶ Questions: What would you do to calm Perry down?

▶ Who is at fault here, the salesperson's firm for not providing instructions or the buyer's workers for using the materials in the wrong applications? *(How would your answer here affect the probability of the buyer's firm paying the claim?)*

relationship, which has or will develop as a result of negotiating a sale, and for achieving personal goals. A matrix of possibilities, shown in Figure 13-2, illustrates how these two concerns interact.

The matrix shows the continuum of possibilities from one to nine, with nine representing the most concern. A salesperson or customer highly concerned about the relationship coming from the negotiation but having little concern for his or her personal goals would fall into the upper-left quadrant.

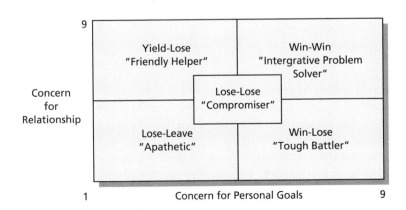

Figure 13-2 Win-Loss Outcomes and the Different Negotiating Styles

Source: Adapted from A. C. Filley, *Interpersonal Conflict Resolution* (Glenview, Ill.: Scott, Foresman, 1975).

As to exactly where that person would be in that quadrant is a matter of judgment. Trying to be more exact would be difficult because there is no standard of comparison. However, it would be fairly easy to distinguish between someone in the lower-left quadrant and a person in the upper-right quadrant. Just as salespeople need to be aware of the four social style types, they also need to know their own negotiating style to be successful when negotiating a sale.

The lower-right quadrant (9,1) is a win-lose negotiator. To this person, winning is everything. Losing reflects inability, loss of self-image, and both personal and professional failure. To these people, negotiating occurs only because the opposition fails to see that they are right. To be considered a success, this "Tough Battler" must win and the opposition must lose.

Opposite from the "Tough Battler" (9,1) is the "Friendly Helper" (1,9). This person is willing to relinquish any and all concern for personal goals to maintain and enhance the buyer-seller relationship. Such people are generally underachievers and, as customers, will buy whatever the salesperson recommends. While seemingly easy to sell to, these people avoid confrontation and discussing differences. The hidden objection frequently occurs with these customers because they don't want to raise an objection that could hurt the salesperson's feelings. In negotiations, this person is a capitulator and frequent loser. A salesperson with such a negotiating style finds the customer calling all the shots. Salespeople like this are frequently backed into corners trying to fulfill price and delivery-of-service promises they should not have made in the first place.

The lower-left quadrant (1,1) represents the person who sees any conflict, disagreement, or negotiation as a hopeless, useless, and punishing experience. When differences arise, these "Apathetics" mentally remove themselves from the disagreement by apathetically complying or becoming totally noncommittal. These people are only suited to order-taking-type sales positions. As customers, they are frustrating to work with and have no loyalty to any vendor.

The fourth quadrant (9,9) represents the "Integrative Problem Solver." These negotiators are strongly and equally committed to both the buyer-seller relationship and their own personal goals. They realize that differences are a natural, normal part of doing business. They look upon these differences as a creative challenge and understands the politics, social dynamics, and turf-protecting that naturally occurs in coming to closure on a business deal. These people are committed to a fair and equitable problem solution that seeks to integrate the needs of the buyer within the limited capacity of the salesperson to meet those needs.

The final negotiating style is the "Compromiser" (5,5). Such an individual looks for win-win solution when negotiating. This person's approach differs from that of the (9,9) "Integrative Problem Solver". While the latter looks at melding side A and side B to create a synergistic C solution, the "Compromiser" approaches a solution as a series of trade-offs until an optimal solution results. For side A to get something, it must give up something to side B and vice versa.

The "Compromiser," in effect, creates a lose-lose situation. The buyer didn't get what he or she wanted, and the salesperson had to give up something, too. Reaching a final settlement just in itself could be considered a win, but that's relative to which side made the greatest sacrifice to get any settlement at all.

▶ ▶ *follow-up questions*

1. If the buyer is a "Compromiser" and the salesperson is a "Tough Battler," what is likely to be the outcome of this selling negotiation?

2. What types of negotiators would probably work best against each other? Which ones do you think would be the worst combination to have together?

3. Do you think people, salespeople or buyers, can be easily categorized on such a matrix? Why or why not?

Negotiating Tactics[8]

Two key elements must be well thought out in formulating negotiating tactics. First are the demands, and second are the concessions. Demands are what the salesperson wants from the buyer (and, of course, what the buyer wants from the salesperson.) Concessions are what the salesperson (or the buyer) is willing to give up to get the deal.

Goals First, Tactics Second

When formulating tactics for a sales negotiation, adaptive salespeople must determine their goals. We have discussed this in earlier chapters. Goals can be stated as scenarios: What would be the best thing we could get? What is the worst we would settle for? What would be acceptable? It is useful to create a **planning pyramid** when planning the negotiating tactics. The pyramid can be upright or inverted. An example of a planning pyramid is shown in Figure 13-3 for two separate negotiating plans. In one pyramid, the salesperson plans to negotiate with the customer for everything at first, then back down to the core product as necessary. In the other, the salesperson uses the opposite approach, that is, selling the core product and adding extras.

With such a plan, a salesperson has a road map to follow through the negotiation. If the plan is to follow the upright pyramid, a salesperson progresses by adding more features and the buyer makes concessions. If the plan is to follow the inverted pyramid, just the opposite occurs. A salesperson could form a negotiating strategy by saying, "I'm going to ask for everything possible right up front, but if the customer shows signs of refusal, I

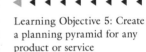

Learning Objective 5: Create a planning pyramid for any product or service

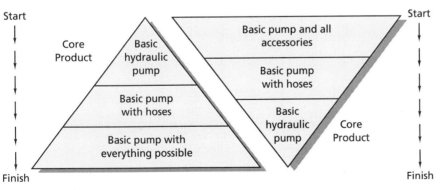

Figure 13-3 Using a Pyramid to Plan Negotiations

will quickly give up most all the small items and a few major ones and settle for a quick sale of the core product." Another salesperson could say, "I'm going to ask for everything up front and I won't give in on even the slightest detail until they have made a significant concession." These two strategies are equally valid. Their success depends on the customer and the situation.

Tactics for Successful Negotiating

There are ten negotiating tactics for successful negotiating. They are:

1. Opening demands
2. Authority
3. Information
4. Tough guy
5. Changing the package
6. Adding extras
7. Diversion
8. Changing people
9. Time
10. Ego building

Opening-demands tactic Opening demands are initial propositions. Seldom is it prudent for a salesperson to "demand" anything. Some novice salespeople hesitate to take the initiative and would rather wait for the customer to take the lead. This puts the customer in the most powerful negotiating seat. If salespeople have a good offer at a reasonable and fair price, they are in a better position to negotiate. By the salesperson being aggressive and stating the product's features, advantages, and benefits, then selling to the value they offer, both parties are at a starting point for negotiations.

Some people will say, "Start high and work down." While this strategy has merit, it is a better strategy to start high and work the customer up. The important point to remember is simply do not acquiesce too early and do not make too large a concession early.

Authority tactics Two variations of **authority tactics** are used in negotiations. The first is the "no authority" tactic and the second is the "higher authority" tactic. The no authority tactic is used when a customer is asking for a concession. The salesperson simply states that she or he "has no authority to sanction that concession." The buyer can try to exert pressure but realizes it would be futile to do so. A slight variation is the no authority-higher authority combination. A salesperson would plead no authority but will ask a higher manager who does. This is the application of the stalling objection by the salesperson, rather than the vendor.

Buyers will use the no authority tactic, too. It is important for a salesperson to be negotiating with the highest authority possible. A good rule to remember is to negotiate with the highest level possible and keep the customer from negotiating with anyone higher than you.

Information tactic Information is a powerful asset. Not having it can be used in salespeople's favor, as well. When entering a negotiation or presentation, if salespeople find they need time, data, or a review session with their management, asking for a recess to get more information is a clever and useful ploy. A salesperson can ask for time to gather more information on the grounds that the time spent will provide better answers and benefit the customer more than simply giving an educated guess based on limited information. Asking for a recess to get more information can be effectively used in a number of selling situations.

Another way of using the **information tactic** is to request justification or validation of the buyer's information. This is particularly useful on damage claims or negotiations involving engineered items. When the customer is claiming losses or costs that seem out of the ordinary, asking for proof or validation is not only a good negotiating tactic but simply good business. Using this tactic will quickly foil any bluffs the buyer could try.

Tough-guy tactic Not all customers feel salespeople are their partners in progress. Some use hardball tactics by making excessive demands and threatening to cancel orders or stop doing business. To handle these unpleasant situations, adaptive salespeople need to have their own set of hardball tactics.

When using the **tough-guy tactic,** salespeople want to avoid engaging in head-to-head confrontations with the customer or the buyer's negotiator. The secret to using tough-guy tactics is to bring in a neutral party, such as an accountant, manager, or engineer who is not directly related to the sale, who assumes the role of being almost unreasonable in the negotiations. The purpose is to make the salesperson's original offer become very attractive in light of what the "tough guy" wants to do or will not concede to. This makes the salesperson appear as a hero to the buyer, rather than an adversary. The result is the salesperson makes fewer and smaller concessions.

The success of this tactic lies in the perception of power. When the salesperson's tough guy creates a perception of a tough, uncompromising, and extremely powerful influence, the buyer is much more likely to want to deal with the more reasonable and less powerful salesperson. The idea is to make buyers think they are really getting a better deal with the salesperson than they would get if the tough-guy gets involved. Using tough-guy tactics are the exception rather than the rule, but in the sales industry, one must be prepared for dealing with tough-guys by using tough guys.

Changing-the-package tactic   The most common negotiating tactic salespeople use is **changing-the-package** by adding or deleting items in the deal. For example, a furniture salesperson would be willing to swap out one set of lamp shades for another if it meant the difference between a lost sale and a successful close.

The adding-extras tactic   This tactic is similar to the one above. As the name implies, the salesperson adds some little items *at the end*. This should not be confused with giving the customer something for free. While that can be done, it is just as common to have the "little extras" be high-profit items. When a copier salesperson closes the deal on the machine, the customer will always need paper, and the profit margin on the paper may be higher than on the machine. In 1989, when Seiko-Mead entered the desktop color copier market, it considered selling its copier below cost because there was so much profit in selling the paper (which customers could only get from Mead). Since the paper for the copier was patented and controlled by Mead, a negotiating strategy initially considered was to make tremendous concessions on the price of the copier to get them in as many offices as possible and therefore lock out the competition. Once accomplished, the profit would come from the continuous sales of paper.

Diversion tactic   The **diversion tactic** changes the focus of a negotiation. A diversion tactic might go something like this:

Customer: Price is the big item here. You are going to have to drop your price by 10 percent. Otherwise, there is no point in proceeding.

Salesperson: I certainly understand your position and I'd like to do something with the price, but I'm afraid that to cut the price, we would have to be talking about a minimum shipment of at least two carloads. Shall we talk about your ability to handle two cars at this time?

In this conversation, the salesperson diverts the buyer away from price by bringing up the specter of a large delivery and inventory as a trade-off for the cheaper price. The salesperson's tactics are to make the customer realize that demanding a significant price reduction would end up costing more than the reduction would save.

Changing-people tactic   In some negotiations, there are people who simply do not work well together. They can be on the seller's team, the buyer's team, or both. A reasonable tactic to use when this occurs is simply to **change the people** involved, either by replacing them or adding others with specialized skills.

Time tactics   Patience is the key when using time tactics. One of the oldest rules in negotiating is "Plan to concede in very small pieces and very, very slowly, if you must concede at all."[9] Table 13-4 lists several guidelines for making concessions. As you read them, think about situations you have been in where you made concessions, only to wish later that you had not acted so hastily.

Another time tactic is simply to call a time-out. This is done to regroup and reevaluate offers made and concessions asked for. There is nothing wrong with asking for a delay to think about what has been accomplished (or not accomplished) and to plan what to do next.

A final time tactic is being patient. If it is a good deal today, it will be a good deal tomorrow. Novice salespeople are sometimes pressured by customers for an immediate answer. Responding without adequate thinking time can be very expensive. The negotiator with the greatest patience will ultimately win out in the long run; do not be in a hurry to negotiate.

Ego-building tactic   The final tactic a salesperson can use is **ego building.** This doesn't mean gushing flattery so transparent it insults the buyer; instead, it means using compliments on valid points. The buyer may have an outstanding record of accomplishments in his or her company, he or she may be a firm but fair negotiator, or the firm may have made notable strides in growth or sales. Everyone likes receiving compliments, and customers are no exception. Robert Kellar, an experienced negotiator and author on the subject, says, "For every dollar you gain in economic value, plan to give your buyer a dollar's worth of ego value in return."[10]

In summary, these tactics, when properly employed, make the adaptive salesperson a better negotiator. With practice, training, and good timing, all can come to play in closing sales. Like the techniques used to close a sale, negotiating tactics can be used singly or in concert with one another. Table 13-5 summarizes the negotiating tactics as a handy checklist. Remembering these will allow the adaptive salesperson to deal with all negotiations, from the

---

Table 13-4   Guidelines for Making Concessions

▸ Buyers' satisfaction often depends more on how they got the price than it does on the price itself. They can feel better about a $10 price that they feel they negotiated than a $9 price that came too easily.

▸ How and when to concede can be more important than what to concede.

▸ Concede in small and diminishing increments—a little at a time.

▸ Give in slowly.

▸ Give yourself room to negotiate.

▸ Do not think you must give tit for tat or split the difference.

▸ Do not mishandle a ridiculous offer; treat each offer seriously.

▸ Do not be the first to concede on major issues.

Source: Gary Karras, *Negotiate to Close* (New York: Simon and Schuster, 1985), pp. 145–46.

Table 13-5	**Summary of Negotiating Tactics**

Opening Demands
    Strike first; acknowledge their demands and hold firm

Authority
    Plead no authority
    Negotiate at their highest level; avoid bringing in your highest authorities

Information
    Recess to gather more; ask them to justify theirs

Tough Guy
    Use a supporting "tough guy" to force a tough issue

Changing the Package
    Offer inexpensive changes and concessions

Add Extras
    Add some little high-profit extras at the end

Diversion
    Use the "I'd like to, but…" approach
    Divert their attention

Change the People
    Bring in some new faces: an expert, a partner, another team member

Time
    Use patience
    Use small, slowly paced concessions
    Use planned but temporary deadlocks to gain more time
    Give the other side time to sort things out

Ego Building
    Help the buyer save face
    Stroke the buyer's ego; be sincere, not phony
    Make the buyer look good

Source: Robert E. Kellar, *Sales Negotiating Handbook* (Englewood Cliffs, N.J.: Prentice-Hall, 1988), p. 76.

easiest to the most difficult. We must now look at the other side of the coin: the buyer's tactics and how to counter them. Just as salespeople plan their tactics, so do buyers.

What Would You Do If…?

As a national meat buyer for the largest grocery store chain in the country, you are accustomed to making large, negotiated purchases. In your company, the buying process works through a person called a meat merchandiser. Each

Continued

What Would You Do If...?—Continued

of the company's eight divisions has a meat merchandiser whose job it is to determine the retail prices and amounts for each division to order. Those orders are funneled to you, and as the buyer, you shop the national suppliers for the best price and service.

In one of the divisions, a merchandiser ordered a truckload of a frozen meat item from the largest meat packer in the nation. After two years, only 10,000 pounds of the original 40,000 pounds has sold. The rest were still setting in her freezer, taking up valuable space and getting freezer burn. Your conversation with the merchandiser (who is your superior in the company hierarchy) goes like this:

Merchandiser: John, we still have a slug of those things left in the warehouse. Call Armour and have them come and get them and give us our money back.

Buyer: Catherine, we have had those for two years. They won't come and get them, let alone give us our money back!

Merchandiser: John, I guess I didn't explain it to you: get them gone and get our money. Do I need to draw you a picture?

▶ Next day

Buyer: Bruce, Catherine wants you guys to pick up those meatballs you sold us two years ago. Can you do it?

Salesperson: Sure, no problem. How much is left, ten or fifteen boxes?

Buyer: Bruce, we have 30,000 pounds left. We want you to come get them and give us our money back.

Salesperson: Be serious. We won't do it! You guys bought them in good faith, didn't merchandise them very well, and now you want us to take the fall on this. The answer is no way!

Buyer: Bruce, we have been doing a lot of business with you guys for a long time. I wouldn't want to see that jeopardized over this.

Salesperson: John, I cannot do it. And besides, I won't do it.

Buyer: Bruce, I know this is a bad deal all the way round. I do not have any choices here, if you know what I mean and who I mean. Let us get your branch manager, you, and I together and try to work something out.

Salesperson: John, I'll see what I can arrange, but realize my manager isn't going to have the best attitude when we talk. This is the most ridiculous thing I have ever run into!

▷ Questions: What are your alternatives?

▷ What is going to be your negotiating environment?

▷ What are your demands? Concessions? What is your goal for this negotiation?

Case in Point

**Fifteen Tactics Essential to Success
When Negotiating with the Japanese**

There are really four problems American sales negotiators have when trying to negotiate business agreements with the Japanese. First, they don't understand the Japanese culture. Next, they are not prepared when they go into a negotiating session. Third, they lack clarity on their overall goal. Finally, they fail to handle conflicts within their own team. Below are 15 key points for negotiating with the Japanese:

1. They always refrain from taking the initiative; they want you to make the first move.

2. Cultivate relationships on a personal level; socializing after hours is a must with the Japanese.

3. Try to learn even just a few words of Japanese; they will appreciate your trying. Also, be sure to have your business cards printed in Japanese, as well as English.

4. Never negotiate alone with a team of Japanese. The more associates you have, the bigger your entourage, the more important you and the negotiations must be.

5. Bring your own interpreter.

6. Winning the confidence of the entire Japanese negotiating team is important; don't just concentrate on the leader.

7. The Japanese will test your patience at every step of the negotiating process. They will never make a quick deal.

8. Always try to act less informed and less skilled than you really are. Underplay your knowledge.

9. "Yes" doesn't mean you have a deal. "Yes" to Japanese may mean nothing more than "I understand what you are saying."

10. Expect your proposals to be submitted to their home office for complete scrutiny—another reason for lengthy periods of apparent inactivity before the deal is made.

11. Just because they entertain you and treat you lavishly, don't think for a moment that you have won them over.

12. Once you make a concession, that now becomes the baseline—don't expect a counterconcession on their part.

13. If you don't get a response from your request, remain silent. It is the other side's turn to talk, so wait them out.

14. They will often use the "tough guy" tactic unless you make one more concession. Don't!

15. They will often test you by agreeing to big orders to get price concessions, then after getting the concession, order only very small amounts and try to get the same price.

Source: Gerhard Gschwandtner, "Selling and Marketing in Japan: A Blueprint for Success," *Personal Selling Power* 12 (1992): 50–51, citing John Campbell, director of the University of Michigan East Asia Business Program.

Negotiating customs are highly varied around the world.

Countering Buyer's Tactics[11]

Buyers have and use negotiating tactics just like vendors. Knowing this, adaptive salespeople can plan for anything buyers may throw at them. When dealing with countertactics, an overriding necessity is patience. Patience is needed to avoid making foolish concessions.

Market conditions affect the seller's (or the buyer's) ability to make demands or give concessions. In a buyer's market, the buyer has the strongest negotiating position. If this condition exists, salespeople will usually find the buyers wanting to drag out the negotiations or open them with demands totally favoring their position. If there is balance in the market, that is, the market affords neither the seller nor the buyer an upper hand, buyer's tactics can be balanced by the seller's countertactics. A balanced environment favoring neither side offers the best situation for developing creative and innovatively negotiated solutions. Finally, if the market favors sellers, they are in a position to extract more and better concessions from buyers. This can be beneficial in the short-run, but every salesperson should remember that getting and keeping a customer for the long run is preferable to a short-term negotiating victory. Unfair, pretentious and overbearing demands for concessions always come back to haunt you in the long run.

Six typical tactics buyers use are time pressure, high opening demands, information barrages, changes in the package, authority-level issues, and diversions or traps. We will explain and discuss each in turn along with the seller's countermeasures.

Buyer's tactic 1: Time pressure   Buyers will try to stress the negotiations by stalling, demanding time ultimatums, or threatening to break off the presentation. Stalling is common and was discussed in the chapter on objections. They can use a number of approaches to stalling, for example, "Come back and see me next week," "I'll have to get back to you," or "I'll have to check it out and talk it over with my people." The time ultimatum is done by requiring the seller make a firm offer in a specified period of time. For example, "You have until noon to get back to me with a firm offer." This tactic is used to try to force the seller into making a major concession to meet the deadline rather than lose the sale. Finally, threatening not to deal unless the concessions are met has much the same tone as the time ultimatum, for example, "Unless we get at 25 percent discount, we cannot do business with you."

When faced with time-pressure tactics, the salesperson has several alternatives. One is to change the package. Creative pricing, innovative delivery schedules, or adding sweeteners works to counter these tactics. Another approach is to remind the customer of the seller's financial position in the deal and how a major concession like the one demanded could be done once, but such a concession could seriously impact the potential for future business.

Several other approaches are possible. One possibility is to make a minor concession. Adaptive salespeople might show the buyers they are willing to move a little if the buyers are willing to back off a little. Another approach is to appeal to a higher authority. Finally, the most nonadversarial approach is the probe. "What is the reason behind the noon deadline?", "Why would you want to break off the negotiations when you already have so much time invested and we are so close to an agreement?", or "Is noon today so critical that another day would keep our agreement from coming together?"

Buyer's tactic 2: High opening demands   High opening demands come in several forms. They can be an unacceptable price requirement, unreasonably stringent specifications, or service requirements that cannot reasonably be met. These would be similar to "conditions" discussed in the chapter on objections. Here, the buyer is starting by trying to establish conditions that will be impossible for the salesperson meet. In reality, they are not conditions at all but a gambit to gain negotiating advantage. When salespeople meet with such "conditions" during a sales presentation, they should not take them at face value without probing deeper into their source. Conditions can be negotiated away in many instances.

When salespeople are faced with high opening demands, a host of countertactics can be used. Getting emotional is one. Appeal to the buyer's sense of fairness, and express how frustrating it will be for everyone to start the discussion from such a demand. Another alternative is to stand firm—make no concessions but simply say the negotiations cannot proceed if that demand is firm. Probing and delaying also work here. Probe the reason for the high demand, or stall the negotiations by seeking time to "check it out" with your manager. The tough-guy tactic will work, but not repeatedly. Of course, the final possibility is to make a minor concession.

Buyer's tactic 3: Barrages or voids of technical information   This tactic will appear with either the customer wanting a barrage of technical information (all the time having no intention to really use it) or burying the salesperson with such information. This is just another stalling technique in the form of a disguised objection whose purpose is to buy time and gain negotiating advantage. Burying the salesperson with information is generally done to try to convince the seller of the relevance and rationale for the opening demands. The buyer can use a void in the technical information as an excuse to prolong the negotiations, for example, "We cannot proceed until you produce the data on the product's performance under high temperature stress."

Three countertactics can be used in this situation. First, deny the relevance of the information—"Yes, it is important to have such data, but in your application, high temperature operation is not possible." The second is to bring in experts. Refer the data request to experts to determine its relevance. Finally, probe the need for such data. Customers may mistakenly believe such data is necessary because they have misunderstood something in the presentation.

Buyer's tactic 5: Changes in the package   Buyers, like salespeople, can use the tactic of changing the package. They may want additional options added at the last minute or some removed. They may want to change delivery dates, quantities, or any number of things. For the salesperson, the countertactics are to simply offer creative alternatives to the changes or investigate the possibilities of trade-offs—"We can do that if you can do this...". Of course, the probe of asking why the changes are necessary is always effective at countering the tactic or uncovering its source.

Buyer's tactic 6: Raise authority-level issues   Authority-level issues come in the form of questioning the salesperson's authority to ask for concessions or to make demands. This tactic can be used to stall the discussion as an ego play for the buyer—"I'm too important to be talking to you," or "You're not high enough in the hierarchy to be talking to me." The customer can also use this tactic as a stall—"I do not have the authority to authorize any agreements" or "It's my boss's responsibility to okay any final terms."

One of the best and most nonthreatening approaches to countering this tactic is to patiently probe the customer's perceived desire to talk to the salesperson's superior. Salespeople can reassure the customer of their authority, qualifications, and experience. If the buyer uses this tactic to stall, probing the company's authorization process will flush out the true nature of the customer's tactic. The buyer may really not have the authority. If this is so, then the salesperson needs to do a better job of qualifying to determine who the proper authority is.

Buyer's tactic 7: Diversions or traps   Buyers will commonly try to divert salespeople when negotiations get sticky. It is a way of changing the focus in hopes of catching the other side off guard. Buyers sometimes get themselves into corners and try to extricate themselves by throwing the blame on to the salesperson. For example, the buyer may have purchased the wrong product, tried to use it in a manufacturing operation, and upon discovering the mistake, try to claim the salesperson sent the wrong product, therefore entitling the buyer to a full refund. The buyer, having made the mistake, now needs a way to get free of this situation, so the strategy is to make the salesperson appear to be at fault.

When faced with diversions or traps, salespeople can use face-saving tactics, stand firm on their position, or probe the reason for the diversion. In the example above where the buyer ordered the wrong product, a face-saving tactic would be to give the buyer credit for the unused portion of the product that is returned and drop the issue. The alternative is to stand firm: the buyer ordered the wrong items, the salesperson delivered them, and thus the salesperson is not responsible for the error.

As you can see, buyers use as many tactics as salespeople. The important thing when confronted with any of these tactics is to first recognize which are being employed. Next is to stay calm and be patient. Finally, before taking any countermeasures, it is a good idea to use inquisitive probes to try to discover the reason for the tactic. In many cases, the buyer's tactics can be the result of a miscommunication or lack of understanding. In Table 13-6, the buyer's tactics are listed and the appropriate countertactics appear opposite. By knowing how to effectively deal with buyer's tactics, the adaptive salesperson will be able to handle a greater number of situations successfully.

▶▶ *follow-up questions*

1. What would you do to counter a buyer using a time delay strategy?
2. If you were selling residential real estate, what tactics do you think buyers would use most often and how would you counter them?
3. What is a planning pyramid? How does a salesperson use it to determine a concession strategy?

Table 13-6 **Countertactics Checklist**

Tactic	Countertactic
Time pressure	Change the package Make minor concessions Appeal to higher authority Probe
High opening demands	Emotionalism Stand firm Make minor concessions Probe Use tough-guy tactics
Barrages or voids of information	Deny relevance Refer to experts Probe
Changes in the package	Offer creative alternative Offer trade-offs Probe
Authority-level issues	Probe Appeal to higher-ups Change the package
Diversions or traps	Probe Save face Stand firm

Source: Robert E. Kellar, *Sales Negotiating Handbook* (Englewood Cliffs, N.J.: Prentice-Hall, 1988), p. 140.

4. What is the difference between the tactics of adding extras and changing the package?

5. What are several ways to use the information tactic?

Negotiating, Ethics, and the Law

Professional salespeople must remember that the person with whom they are negotiating is a customer. Because they will want to continue doing business with this customer, ethical dealings on both sides are a must. Ethics will be dealt with briefly here.

Learning Objective 8: The legal and ethical aspects of negotiating

Ethically dealing with a customer means bargaining in good faith. Professional salespeople do not make promises they cannot fulfill, and they do not make unwarranted demands. While there is certainly nothing wrong with hard bargaining, lying, deceiving, and threatening are not acceptable. Fair and honest dealings are ultimately the best source of negotiating credibility and success.

Negotiating ethics are affected by laws. It is illegal under the federal Robinson-Patman Act to offer special concessions to some customers and not others. Any special deals must either be offered to all or be justifiable on a cost or service basis. Knowingly offering a special price to one customer that will give that customer a competitive advantage so great it will severely impact another customer is both unethical and illegal.

Using threats or deceptive claims to intimidate a customer (or salesperson, if done by a customer) is unethical and illegal. Such activities constitute fraud and unfair trade practices, both of which are or can be illegal and certainly are not conducive to extended business relationships.

Bait-and-switch is another unethical and illegal practice in some states. Negotiating on a product through a low-price inducement, then switching the customer to higher-priced products because the lower-priced ones are out of stock, or delivering and billing for a higher-priced product can be grounds for legal action.

In summary, salespeople and buyers are known through their industries by their reputations. The reputations they build comes from their credibility and fairness in dealing. An ethical standard that is above reproach is one of a salesperson's best assets.

▶▶ *follow-up questions*

1. How does the Robinson-Patman Act affect sales negotiations?

2. Using deceptive product claims in negotiating is illegal. Is this true or false, and why?

Summary

Negotiating is something salespeople do everyday. They deal in formal negotiating sessions as part of teams, and they deal individually with buyers on minor points. Most salespeople, and buyers for that matter, are not well versed in negotiating. They approach it without a plan or preparation. They have little concept of a formal strategy and as a result deal in reactive negotiating; they react to propositions and requests for concessions, rather than plan for them.

Concessions are half the negotiator's tools; the other half are demands. Both sides realize they have needs and wants that must be met, but on some points, they are willing to give in. Negotiating, whether formal or informal, is a three-step cycle; planning for the negotiation, negotiating, and following-up. It is a cycle because planning for the next negotiating session should occur before the follow-up activities of the previous one have been completed (Learning Objective 1).

Negotiating is a contest of power. The side with the greatest power or that can create the greatest perception of power argues from the strongest position. Trying to balance the power relationships is a demanding task. The perception of power is enhanced through such things as appearance, the power the salesperson gets from competitors, commitment, legitimacy, and using time advantageously (Learning Objective 2).

Successful negotiators are characterized as reasonable risk-takers. They calculate the consequences of their terms and concessions and pursue negotiations accordingly. Patience and confidence are the hallmarks of good negotiators. They must have the patience and confidence to wait out difficult buyers, ask for more time, and, in general, use a planned, well-paced approach. They seldom make knee-jerk decisions or act spontaneously. A good negotiator is able to anticipate the actions of the opposition. This comes from experience, homework, observations, and planning. Finally, successful negotiators are characterized by thoroughness with details and a long-range perspective. They seldom are willing to trade a short-run gain for a long-run loss (Learning Objective 3).

How people react to and deal with negotiating differences can be depicted on a negotiating style matrix. Five styles were identified in this chapter. The "Friendly Helper" has a high concern for the buyer-seller relationship but far less for personal goals. As a result, this negotiator tends to negotiate poorly, ultimately yielding and losing. The "Apathetic" has a lower concern for both the relationship and personal goals. These people avoid disagreement by distancing themselves from the situation or simply agreeing with whatever is said. The "Tough Battler" is a win-lose negotiator. This person is compelled to win at the expense of the opposition. The "Integrative Problem Solver" looks to creative solutions for win-win outcomes. This person searches for the synergistic, novel, and innovative answers, realizing that conflict and differences are a normal and natural part of doing business. Finally, there is the "Compromiser," who attempts to extract solutions through trade-offs; everyone must lose a little for the sake of closure (Learning Objective 4).

Negotiators use ten tactics: opening demands, authority, information, tough guy, changing the package, adding extras, diversion, changing the people, time, and ego-building. These tactics have applications in all types of negotiating situations. Some, such as changing the package and adding extras, are very common. Others, such as the tough-guy tactics, are used very infrequently (Learning Objectives 4, 5, and 6).

There are a variety of ways to counter negotiating tactics. Time pressure, high opening demands, and barrages or voids of information are frequently used. Some negotiators counter tactics in other ways. These can be through changing the package, bringing up authority-level issues, and creating diversions (Learning Objective 7).

In conclusion, ethics and high standards of behavior are essential to having a good reputation and being a successful negotiator. Unfair, coercive, or threatening tactics are both unethical and often illegal. Using such tactics weakens a negotiator's bargaining position in the short and long run. Such tactics as bait-and-switch, deception, and fraud not only are illegal but also lead to poor business relations. They should be avoided as both a matter of principle and good judgment (Learning Objective 8).

Key Terms

Negotiating The creative orchestration of alternatives ideally benefiting both the buyer and seller; the art and science of working out compromises through demands and concessions.

Optimal solution A solution that may not be the best solution but is one both parties can live with within the constraints imposed by either or both; one where both parties benefit but may not get all they wanted.

Minimum requirements The minimally acceptable conditions; the conditions below which terms are not negotiable.

Constraints Any limitations one negotiating side imposes.

Authority tactics Used by negotiators to bring in persons with more negotiating influence or to stall a negotiation by claiming lack of power to make a decision and needing to wait for the senior person.

Information tactic One negotiating side claims lack of information to stall for more time or to take the time to get the necessary information.

Tough-guy tactic Seldom used, it pits the salesperson's "unreasonable tough-guy," usually a third party brought in who could influence the terms of the sale, against the unreasonable and abrasive buyer or negotiator.

Changing-people tactic One or both sides changes the personnel involved in the negotiation. This is done if it appears a personality problem may be hindering the negotiations, more expertise is needed, or for any number of reasons.

Diversion tactic Any tactic that diverts the customer away from the current negotiating discussion.

Ego-building tactic Building up the opposition's ego during negotiations. This might lead to better concessions or a more pleasant atmosphere. Ego-building tactics cannot be phony or overused, or they will soon lose any effectiveness they might have.

Discussion Questions

1. Why is negotiating a salesperson's secret weapon?
2. Why are services so often negotiated?
3. What is meant by "the perception of power?"
4. Negotiating power comes from commitment. What types of commitment does a salesperson draw on to gain negotiating strength?

5. There are several ways a salesperson gets negotiating power from legitimacy. What are some of the ways a salesperson creates legitimacy?

6. In negotiating, knowledge about the buyer and his or her knowledge about you and your firm is not a two-way street. What does this mean?

7. What are the aspects of time that make it the greatest source of negotiating power?

8. What do you consider the most important element in goal setting and why?

9. When planning a sales negotiation, having enough of the right information is vital. If you were negotiating the sale of a fleet of cars to Hertz, what type of information would be the "right" information to have?

10. What is considered essential financial information for a negotiator?

11. Why is it as important to plan your timetable for conceding as it is to plan what items on which you'll concede?

12. Why would a salesperson want to use the tough guy tactic?

13. If you were a car salesperson, what would be some diversionary tactics you could use on a person who is bent on arguing price?

Application Exercise

Go back and reread the section on negotiating tactics. Suppose you have a grade dispute with your instructor. The test you took had a question that would make the difference between a grade of A or B for you on the test and between and A or B for your total course grade. Answer the following questions:

1. Of the ten negotiating tactics, which of them do you think would work best and worst? Rank them in order of "most probable to succeed" to "least probable to succeed."

2. After looking at the matrix of negotiating styles, where would you place yourself? Where would you place the instructor you have for this class?

3. Think of another instructor you have. Place him or her in the matrix. Would you alter your ranking of the negotiating tactics?

4. Prior to entering this grade negotiation, what would be your demands and what would you be willing to concede?

Class Exercise

Group Exercise

Session 1:

Break into groups of five students:

1. Two members will act as the sellers and create a planning pyramid for negotiating the sale of a product or service they choose. They can use either the upright or inverted pyramid form.

2. The same two members will choose at least *three* specific tactics for negotiating the sale of the product or service in number 1 above.

3. Another two members of the group will act as *buyers* and develop *three* negotiating tactics of their own.
4. Finally, the selling group will counter the *three* buyers' negotiating tactics.
5. The remaining member will act as observer and recorder.

Session 2:

1. The observer and recorder for each group will summarize the group's activities.
2. The class as a whole will discuss the importance of negotiating the sale and rank the group's performance on how well they defined and carried out their plans and tactics (did they in the final analysis make or lose the sale?).

Individual Presentation

1. An individual will be chosen at random by the instructor to negotiate the "sale" by the class to the instructor of the following proposition:

    A final exam in this course that will be required only for those who wish to take it.

2. The instructor will leave the room until a negotiating strategy is worked out by the class and the individual chosen as the chief negotiator. When the instructor returns, the negotiation session will begin.

▼ ▼ ▼ ▼ ▼ ▼ *Cases* ▼ ▼ ▼ ▼ ▼ ▼

Take It or Leave It[12]

Harris, an earnest but inexperienced salesperson, is on the phone. "Boss, they've hit me with this take-it-or-leave-it stand. They'll pay 50 cents a pound, they say, and not a cent more. And there's something else, too. Instead of Rollins and her assistant being here, a guy named Wilson showed up. Says that the others are tied up today, and he was asked to sit in for them. What's going on, anyway? I'm not sure what I should do next!"

Questions

1. What should Harris's response be to the customer's take-it-or-leave-it opening?
2. What would you tell him is probably behind the mysterious appearance of Wilson?

The "Reasonable" Salesperson[13]

Williams Construction had a major contract delayed due to equipment failure. With a deadline fast approaching, the company called Rogers, a salesperson for Alliance Equipment Supply, and requested that he arrange for immediate delivery of replacement supplies so the construction firm could meet its promised deadline.

Rogers, eager to break into this new account, agreed to generous credit terms and to absorb air freight charges to get the equipment to the customer as quickly as possible. The concessions, however, reduced the company's usual net profit from 20 percent to below 10 percent.

Rogers's rationale was: "I felt I needed to be reasonable with this account. I wanted their business in the future. I was there when they needed help, the deal was struck quickly, and they'd remember and thank me later with new business. I think the concessions were justified."

Question

1. How would you respond to Rogers?

The Audio/Video Problem[14]

Last week, Pat Tonnonaka wrapped up a very profitable negotiation with Audio Corporation, a contract for eight packaging machines at $13,000 each, plus a three-year service account and an increase in her share of Audio's supply orders over the next year. The increase would be from 60 percent to 80 percent.

It had been a doubly tough (and rewarding) negotiation. Tonnonaka had faced a conflict between Audio's purchasing department, which wanted to buy from Tonnonaka's main competitor at a slightly lower price, and its manufacturing department, which liked Tonnonaka's offer because of her track record of getting better service for her customers.

In the end, Tonnonaka was able to trade some minor price concessions for a longer service contract (which produced higher profits than the equipment itself). Both purchasing and manufacturing at Audio were pleased. But a new twist came up:

> **Tonnonaka:** We committed a 12-week delivery to Audio. Now they're in a pickle and need four machines as soon as possible. The moment I said I'd have to get back to them, their purchasing reps contacted our main competitor, who promised immediate delivery—and asked for an increased share of the supply order as part of the deal.
>
> **Service Supervisor:** We will try to find a way to help them, but we do have them under contract for eight machines plus the service and supplies, right?
>
> **Tonnonaka:** Well, there's one technicality. Everybody at Audio had signed but the vice-president. They're just waiting for her to get back from Europe.
>
> **Service Supervisor:** You think they would actually back out on the contract at this late date?
>
> **Tonnonaka:** They could, under pressure, if we cannot get them four machines quickly.
>
> **Sales Supervisor:** I think the line is running at capacity. And every machine for the next two months is committed to another customer, Video 202. We get a 5 percent premium on supplies from Video 202. And they buy nearly as much from us as Audio.
>
> **Tonnonaka:** "Video, 202. That is Pat Pinelli's account isn't it? So what do I say to Audio?

Question

1. What would you suggest Tonnonaka do to get out of this dilemma?

References

1. Adapted from Bill Voelkel, "Help Yourself Negotiate the Sale," *Sales and Marketing Management,* 139 (1987): 97–98.
2. Robert E. Kellar, *Sales Negotiating Handbook* (Englewood Cliffs, N.J.: Prentice Hall, 1988), pp. 107–8.
3. Much of the information in this section comes from Gary Karras, *Negotiate to Close* (New York: Simon and Schuster, 1985), pp. 37–81.
4. Ibid., p. 43.
5. Ibid., p. 77.
6. Kellar, *Sales Negotiating Handbook,* pp. 6–7.
7. Adapted from Kellar, *Sales Negotiating Handbook,* p. 53.
8. Adapted from Kellar, *Sales Negotiating Handbook,* Chap. 5.
9. Ibid., p. 71.
10. Ibid., p. 72.
11. This section paraphrases much of the material in Kellar, *Sales Negotiating Handbook,* pp. 130–40.
12. Robert E. Kellar, "How Good Are You at Negotiating?" *Sales and Marketing Management,* 141 (1989): 30. (Kellar's recommended solutions are included in this article, where this case originated.)
13. Ibid., p. 33.
14. Ibid., p. 30.

IV

Additional Dimensions of Selling

14 Selling in Nonprofit, Not-For-Profit, and Service Firms

Objectives

After completing this chapter, you will be able to:

1. Compare the sale of services (intangibles) to tangible products.

2. Compare nonprofit to not-for-profit organizations in relation to the sales task.

3. Describe four types of relationship sales (marketing) strategies.

4. Outline a five-phased plan for managing a customer's service sales encounter.

5. Define the enhanced role of the firm's image in the selling of services.

6. Explain the relationship between a salesperson's credibility and the firm's image.

The Professional Selling Question

How has your company approached the problem of selling the intangible service?

A Sales Expert Responds

The answer to this question comes from Jim Lagowski, who was assistant manager of marketing for Detroit Edison in 1986, when the Fermi II nuclear power plant was coming on line. At the time, Lagowski faced a major challenge. There was little demand for the extra electricity the new plant would generate, Detroit Edison had stiff competition from gas companies, and it was his job to make sure the electrical utility was selling 40 billion kilowatts by 1990. To do this, he needed a plan to aggressively sell electricity, but he had a salesforce of "industrial marketing engineers" (IMEs) who handled mostly billing complaints and technical problems; they didn't sell.

The IMEs had to be retrained in consultative selling, generating leads, and qualifying prospects. The competition from gas companies was stiff, and the only way to beat them was by offering better service and more concern for customers. To be successful, Lagowski needed a new type of salesperson to sell electricity. He and the consultants hired by Detroit Edison created a computerized sales support system that linked the IMEs, other electrical service reps, and economic development consultants (EDCs) together. Since then, this sales team has worked to keep area businesses from relocating and has provided such nonelectrical services as advising businesses on finances, real estate activities, and job training. This seemingly tangential approach was all part of the total service package offered to hold and attract new business.

The sales team members reported on the computerized system everything about a call they made on a client or prospect. This data were updated daily. Being able to see what had transpired with their accounts each day allowed team members to stay abreast of any new problems or opportunities. Service selling for the electric company has come a long way from just providing electricity. Selling electricity for Detroit Edison has meant more than just trying to convince a customer to use electricity over gas. It has meant a total commitment to business customers' success by giving them more than just electricity; that's all part of the service for Detroit Edison.[1]

Detroit Edison changed from selling electricity to selling service.

Introduction

Service, nonprofit, and not-for-profit firms offer unique selling challenges. These are distinct organizations with specific goals and objectives that make the job of the salesperson different from, yet similar to, a traditional selling position. The uniqueness of sales in these organizations is that often there is nothing to sell! Nothing tangible, that is. These types of enterprises sell experiences, relationships, education, prevention from one thing or another, but rarely something tangible. This is not to say what they are selling is not valuable. It simply means that the salesperson in a service or nonprofit organization must be particularly good at creating and managing the message and impression since there is little, if anything, to put in the customer's hand.

Hospitals are hiring salespeople to recruit physicians and technical experts. Hospital salespeople also sell the hospital's services and capabilities to health maintenance organizations and large businesses. The college or university you are attending has salespeople, though they seldom are called that. They are called recruiters or admissions counselors, and it is their job to travel to high schools selling graduating seniors on the notion of attending your college or university. They also sell high school guidance counselors on the university's or college's benefits in hopes that they will recommend the school to undecided students.

The art and techniques of selling for a service, not-for-profit, or nonprofit organization require focusing on the relationship to be created and nurtured. In this selling arena, as in all selling, perception is a key factor. How the salesperson creates the proper perception and builds the relationship is essential to success and a happy, satisfied customer.

Imagine yourself in the position of a recruiter for your school. What would be your target market segments? Who in those segments would you target? What would you want to know about them before you gave them your presentation? What would be your selling points, that is, your features, advantages, and benefits? What objections would you expect to deal with? As you can see, the questions revolving around this type of selling are no different than those in selling a tangible good. In this chapter, you will learn that in service, nonprofit, and not-for-profit firms, salespeople come in many forms. You will also learn how the method of selling differs from selling tangible goods. You will read about specific strategies for relationship selling and how to plan the customer's service encounter so everything comes off flawlessly. In the end, you should be able to formulate a plan for selling a service by applying the suggestions this chapter has to offer.

Salespeople Come in Many Forms

The three cornerstones of selling are identifying the customer's needs, proving you are offering the best value, and then persuading the customer to close the sale. These are also the cornerstones of a variety of occupations not customarily considered sales positions. Many seemingly nonsales occupations are actually selling jobs in disguise. Salespeople come in many forms. Many businesses and professions are adopting selling techniques. Professionals such as lawyers and physicians sell their services. If a salesperson from a health maintenance organization (HMO) has contacted you, then you have experienced someone selling professional services. Salespeople are also selling legal services to people who have no immediate need for them. Lawyers are going to target marketing. They are establishing retail storefront offices and advertising on the radio and TV and in the newspaper. Innovative selling techniques are being used to promote legal services, and a firm called Prepaid Legal Services is a good example. Like an HMO, Prepaid Legal Services allows clients to make installment payments for legal services. When the clients finally do need the service, they have already paid for it and get no bill from the lawyer.

"Within the next decade, more and more lawyers will be looking to professional marketers of prepaid legal plans to supply them with business. 'Today, all doctors work for insurance companies, and lawyers are eventually all going to work for prepaid legal plans,' says James Sokolove, a Boston attorney who runs a "boutique" that supplies client leads for 25 area law firms.

Lawyers are being forced to consider new ways to deliver their services simply because there are so many of them. The United States has 650,000 today (compared to Japan's 16,000), and with some 42,000 joining the bar each year, the total is expected to reach an even million by the mid-1990s. Prepaid legal plans got their start nearly 15 years ago when an Oklahoma sharecropper's son named Harland Stonecipher got burned by a lawyer's bill and saw a need for affordable legal service. He founded Prepaid Legal Services (PLS), now the largest of the prepaid plans, with 500,000 subscribers in 28 states and revenues of over $42 million.

Spokesman Hen Magner says PLS is signing up members at the rate of 5,000 a week and forecasts a 100 percent annual growth rate for the company and $1 billion in sales by 1992. And the more individuals PLS enlists, the wider it casts its marketing net. It uses a multilevel marketing system, a la Amway, in which all 163,000 of its "sales associates" are also plan subscribers.

One thing is fairly certain, prepaid legal plans will eventually become a mainstream product. 'These plans will do for the legal profession what the assembly line did for manufacturing," says lawyer-marketer Sokolove. 'There will be great advantages for both the supplier and consumer.' "[2]

You are in a sales position when you interview for a job. You try to persuade someone you are the right person for the job. You may have tried to sell yourself to a prospective date, and you probably have tried to sell your parents, teachers, friends, and classmates on your ideas. If you were not as successful as you think you should have been, you may simply need to sharpen your selling skills! The basis of sharpening your selling skills is understanding a basic tenet: to successfully complete the sale, both parties need to come away with something valuable. A sale is an exchange, and as a salesperson, your job is to facilitate the transaction and leave the customer better off after the exchange than before.

▶ ▶ *follow-up questions*

1. When you go to your dentist's office, who is the salesperson?
2. Could the pastor of a church be considered a salesperson?

Selling in Service, Nonprofit, and Not-for-Profit Firms

A profit-driven firm thrives through its profits. It provides products and services to its customers, whereby it makes a profit. Different types of businesses have distinct rates of profit that reflect the risks they take. For example, the pretax gross profit on most groceries is less than 30 percent, while for fine jewelry, it is often over 500 percent.

The distinction between profit-driven or commercial firms and other organizations can be thought of this way: commercial firms target profits at what they consider to be a reasonable level; nonprofit organizations try to maximize the delivery of their specific services; and not-for-profit enterprises try to maximize revenues. There are many examples of nonprofit organizations, but some common ones are the YMCA, the YWCA, public radio and television, and your local symphony. Many social service organizations and hospitals are in the not-for-profit category. They try to maximize their revenues to counterbalance their operating costs. They get no support outside the revenues they generate. Any profits generated do not get distributed to shareholders or owners but rather are held as operating reserves or plowed back into the organization to allow for lower charges to users.

People selling services are marketing intangibles. The managers of YMCAs spend a good part of their day contacting businesses to persuade them to subscribe to a corporate fitness program. They talk to civic groups to encourage them to participate in a variety of programs, and they solicit memberships through phone calls or direct mail campaigns.

Selling Services is Different from Yet Similar to Selling Tangible Products

Selling services requires the same mechanical skills as selling tangible products. There is still prospecting, qualifying, making a presentation, handling objections, and closing, but the nature of what is being sold is markedly different. Table 14-1 compares the characteristics of services and tangible products.

Table 14-1 Services and Tangible Products Compared

1. Services are experienced; they cannot be evaluated by all five senses, as can tangible products.
2. Services cannot be inventoried or stored for later use; they tend to be "manufactured" and "consumed" simultaneously. Tangible products can be held until demanded.
3. Services are produced on the spot, not made in one place and transported to the point of consumption. Because of this, consumers and producers together are often directly involved in making the product.
4. Distribution decisions frequently center on the location where the service will be made and the times that location will be open for the buyer to come in and consume the service.
5. Personal attention by the salesperson may be the most vital element in the customers' satisfaction with the service. This is different from some tangible products, where dissatisfaction with the product may be difficult to communicate to the manufacturer and can stem from poor manufacturing, improper delivery, or inadequate retail service. In other words, the customer can be dissatisfied with a variety of aspects involving the use of the product, many of which have nothing to do with the product itself. With the service, manufacture, delivery, and installation are often one in the same operation from a single point source.
6. Demand must be managed since services cannot be stored in times of low demand and pulled from inventory when demand is high, as is the case with tangible products.

Source: Christopher H. Lovelock and Charles B. Weinberg, *Marketing for Public and Non-profit Managers* (New York: John Wiley & Sons, 1984), p. 287.

Learning Objective 1: Selling intangible services is similar to yet different from selling tangible products

Selling services focuses on selling the customers on the expected experience they will have. Your insurance salesperson focuses on the peace of mind you will have knowing your family is safe and secure in times of disaster. Your stockbroker sells you on the speed with which the brokerage will execute your orders or the knowledge and quality of the information its research staff will be able to provide you. The kid next door who wants to mow your grass must try to convince you it would be easier and cheaper for him to do it than you.

Service salespeople cannot physically demonstrate their product very easily, but they can demonstrate the results of their work. They must create images in the prospective customer's mind of what experiencing the service would be like. Your travel agent cannot have you touch, taste, smell, or hear the ocean but can exhibit pictures of the beach and people enjoying it. Through those pictures, the agent tries to create the sensations in your mind.

Although services and tangibles are different, they are also alike in several ways. In a study of industrial service users, the five most significant factors in choosing a supplier were:

1. usefulness of the service (filling the needs of the customer),
2. quality,
3. understanding the client's problems,
4. firm's reputation, and
5. qualifications of key employees.[3]

Travel agents sell a service resulting in memorable experiences.

These are the same factors customers of tangible products look for in a supplier. From customers' perspective, the important factors have little to do with whether the product is a tangible or a service, as long as it solves the problem they have!

Making the intangible tangible and the tangible intangible   Services are intangible and physical products are tangible. Selling either one requires all the salesperson's creativity. Remember that with both services and products, customers are buying the promise that the product or service will deliver benefits. This means the salesperson must try to make the intangible tangible or the tangible intangible. When a hotel sales manager sells a convention organizer on the benefits of staying at the hotel, he or she will try to make these benefits tangible by providing the organizer with pictures of the rooms, the restaurant, the pool, and the hotel's surroundings in the city. Since the manager cannot bring a sample of the hotel to the organizer, he or she must try to create the feeling of being in a room, eating at the restaurant, and swimming in the pool. In this way, the encounter is vicariously felt, tasted, seen, and heard by the organizer, just as if it were a tangible product.

When the salesperson is selling tangible products, the buyers experience the sensations from their five senses. They often can feel the weight and size of the product, see exactly how big it is, hear it in operation, and know what it smells or tastes like. Salespeople make what is tangible intangible by creating sensations of the benefits that the product provides: "Think about what a night out wearing this perfume would be like!" or "After seeing how our mattresses are made, imagine what waking up totally refreshed would be like."

Selling services is selling an encounter. People experience services, rather than consume them, so it is important to create tangible sensations in the presentation. Pictures, descriptions, or audiovisual aids create these sensations. Services get sold on a more emotional basis than products and should

What Would You Do If...?

You have been planning a very special night out for yourself and your companion, and the focus is dinner at a very plush restaurant. Upon arriving ten minutes ahead of your reserved time, you check in with the maître dê. He confirms your reservation and tells you it will be about 15 minutes; you can have a drink in the lounge and he will call you when your table is ready.

You and your companion proceed to the bar and order what you feel are very expensive drinks. After 20 minutes, you have not yet been called, so you order another drink. Forty-five minutes have now passed, and you are finally called and seated at your table.

The waiter gives you the menus and explains the specials. Ten minutes pass and you are ready to order, but the waiter doesn't come by your table. Ten more minutes pass, still no waiter. FInally, the waiter arrives and takes your order. Half an hour passes with no meal in sight, yet you have seen your waiter serving other people who came in after you did.

▶ Question: What would you do as the customer at this point? After leaving? If you owned the restaurant?

take advantage of the human mind's ability to create the same sensations from intangible cues as it does from tangible product's actual sensations. You don't have to lose 20 pounds to imagine how your life would be if you were 20 pounds lighter!

> Remember this rule: The more intangible the product, the more the judgment about it is made through the packaging, that is, how it is presented, how it is sold, and the effectiveness of the process of making it tangible.

What Is a Nonprofit and a Not-for-Profit Organization?

Learning Objective 2:
Nonprofit and not-for-profit firms are different

A **nonprofit organization** is one that exists for the good of society and does not depend on profits to survive; it often has tax-exempt status. Art museums, charities, some hospitals, arts organizations, and religiously sponsored businesses are in this category. There are two classes of nonprofit firms. The first is "donative": the firms' revenues come from grants and donations, like the American Cancer Society. A distinction between selling and soliciting needs to be understood when talking about not-for-profit and nonprofit donative firms. Soliciting is not selling for our purposes here. Soliciting is synonymous with canvassing for funds or in-kind gifts. While the distinction often gets blurred because of the various ways organizations offer premiums for memberships or gifts, we want to concentrate on selling and not on this form of revenue acquisition by nonprofits and not-for-profit firms. While this may seem to be the type of firm where personal selling is not needed, this is far from the case. The second class of nonprofit firm is the "commercial nonprofit firm": revenue comes from the prices charged for services, such as with an art gallery or symphony orchestra.[4] It is not uncommon to have a firm operating as both a donative and commercial nonprofit firm. This means it actively sells its products (e.g., tickets or other services), and it solicits funds through donations and memberships.

Nonprofit firms differ from for-profit firms in many ways.[5] One of the most significant is in the nature of their products. Nonprofit firms market services and social behaviors. Examples of social behavior marketing would be a representative of the local Civil Defense or Red Cross organization "selling" tornado safety guidelines to your local school and the local fire department encouraging people to do fire safety checks in their homes. In the former, the behavior being sold is public safety, and in the latter, it is fire prevention techniques.

What both nonprofit and for-profit enterprises have in common is that they are selling something, and because of this, someone is a salesperson. In the case of a traditional for-profit firm, such as Sears, J.C. Penney, or your local car dealership, the salespeople are obvious and easily identifiable. In the nonprofit firms, the salespeople may not be quite as apparent.

Not-for-profit organizations are somewhat different than nonprofit organizations, even though many people use the terms synonymously. Many hospitals are not-for-profit, as are many professional organizations. They differ from nonprofit organizations in that they attempt to maximize their revenues. Your local chapter of the American Marketing Association is an example. It tries to collect as much as it can from dues, charges, and dinners.

A church-sponsored bingo game is another example. The church tries to collect as much revenue as possible to offset costs. However, surpluses are not considered profits and are not distributed to anyone. They are retained against future unexpected costs. At the end of the fiscal year, the for-profit commercial firms have money to distribute to owners, the nonprofit firms have a zero balance, and the not-for-profit firms may have a positive balance but must retain it as carryover to the next fiscal year.

▶▶ *follow-up questions*

1. What is the most important difference between services and products? How does that difference affect the ways each is sold?

2. How do you make tangible the quality of your service if you are the sales manager for an architectural firm?

3. Is your college or university a nonprofit, not-for-profit, or for-profit organization?

Selling Services Is Relationship Marketing

Relationship marketing is the management of the customer's total relationship experience with the firm. In relationship marketing, the goal is to create a dependent relationship between customers and vendors. This means the vendors want customers to perceive them as more than just providers of services or products; rather, as partners with the customers in their enterprise. With relationship marketing, the ideal situation has been achieved when customers look to the vendor as a trusted friend, someone who will offer advice and watch out for them, someone who will go beyond giving them just what they want to advising them as to what is best for them. The firm identifies a core product or service of most interest to the customer, then expands from

Relationship marketing is the central theme in banks' selling strategy.

that to its ancillary products or services.[6] Four relationship marketing strategies accomplish this.

Relationship Marketing Strategies

Core product focus
Service augmentation
Customize relationship
Relationship pricing

Four Strategies of Selling Service Relationships

Learning Objective 3: Four
types of relationship selling
strategies

Focus on core products The first strategy is to focus on a **core service.** The basis and strength of the relationship comes from the core service. This is the salesperson's central offering and is the most important: it focuses on the customer's greatest needs. For a bank, the core service would be a checking account; for a lawyer, it could be wills, divorces, or real estate contracts.

Salespeople may have several core products at their disposal, depending upon the customer's needs. Different target markets have distinct needs centering on separate core products. For the hotel sales manager trying to sell to the convention director, the core may be room availability and convention

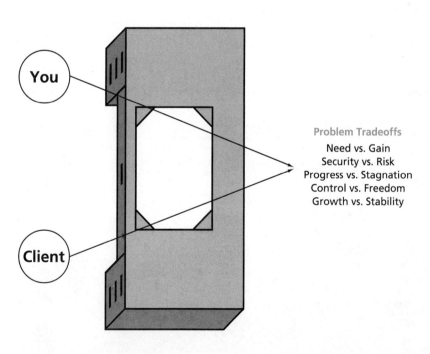

When the Salesperson (You)
and the Client Look at a Problem *Together*—
You Both Become Part of the *Solution*!

You

Client

Problem Tradeoffs
Need vs. Gain
Security vs. Risk
Progress vs. Stagnation
Control vs. Freedom
Growth vs. Stability

This is *Relationship Marketing*
(an excellent way to reduce your competition!)

facilities. For you and me, it may be inexpensive rooms and weekend mini-vacations. The core product is the base to which all other services or products are subordinate.

Customize the relationship   The second strategy is **relationship customization.** Can a relationship be customized to fit the unique needs of the individuals experiencing it? The answer can be simple or complex. American Express provides its business card holders a quarterly printout of all their charges, in addition to regular monthly statements. American Express knows that for tax purposes, business expenses must be accurately accounted for and documented. It also knows that most business card holders are too busy to tally each and every receipt at the end of the month, quarter, and year. American Express customizes the relationship with its business clients by offering this special service that is not available to nonbusiness card holders. It promotes the service as a custom feature for business card holders and as a reason to get a business card in addition to the personal card.

Augment the service with unexpected extras   A third strategy is **service augmentation** and refers to the unexpected extras vendors can provide. Hotels offer such things as free newspapers in the morning and turndown services at night. These are not promoted at the time customers make the reservation; they are unexpected luxury extras to which customers soon become accustomed and enjoy. The customers see these "extras" as beneficial and come to expect them from all hotels. This creates the image that customers are getting more than they paid for. It creates unexpected and appreciated value that cements the relationship. After all, everyone likes someone who gives them unexpected gifts more than someone who gives them nothing.

Use relationship pricing   The fourth strategy is **relationship pricing.** Customers receive price incentives to consolidate their business with one supplier. The airlines have frequent flier programs and video rental stores offer movie clubs as price incentives to continue and cement the relationship. Regardless of the form relationship pricing takes, the objective remains the same: to encourage customer loyalty by rewarding it.[7]

▶▶ *follow-up questions*

1. What are the different aspects of relationship marketing strategies?
2. What would be the core product of a hotel and what would be the ways that core product could be augmented?

When Things Go Right

Why Bankers Can't Sell

Almost every bank president and marketing executive I've ever spoken to wants his public-contact staff to sell more products and services to customers. With one voice these executives lament spending large sums on various advertising and sales promotion campaigns only to see the resulting valuable sales opportunities squandered by the new account sales staff.

Continued

Why Bankers Can't Sell — Continued

Unlike such manufactured products like hammers, cheeseburgers and VCRs, banking services often require the accurate completion of multiple forms in order to be activated. You don't just ring up another checking account on the cash register at check-out time as you do for a gallon of milk. In some banks this process can encompass up to five separate forms and may take 15 to 30 additional minutes to complete.

Bank employees who are busy, or feel overworked and underpaid, and who are not measured or rewarded for sales results will take the path of least resistance, and not try to sell the additional product or service. They'll take the customer's order and open up the desired account, but they won't cross-sell any more accounts because it would add to their clerical burden.

The more complex reason for the poor sales performance of bankers lies in banking's roots. For decades, bank management has been primarily concerned with operational accuracy. Employees are screened, hired and promoted for their clerical competence, rarely for selling.

In the late 1970's banks turned to sales training programs to try to improve their sales ability, only to learn that sales training alone, unsupported by massive organizational changes, doesn't work. They've got to organize for sales, measure sales effectiveness, reward sales results, hire competent sales managers and train public-contact employees in sales skills.

In the aftermath of deregulation, it has become increasingly important for banks to evolve into sales organizations. The competition for consumers' deposits and increasingly for their loan business, promises to escalate as more and more retail banks convert to stock-ownership structures.

So don't be too surprised when sometime in the future, you go into your friendly local bank and are greeted by a happy, smiling face looking up at you. The teller will politely ask if you would like to transfer your checking account to his/her bank, or, possibly, if you would like to consider paying off your high-cost loan with a lower-cost home equity line of credit?

*Source: K. Elia Georgiades, "Why Bankers Can't Sell," *Sales & Marketing Management*, 138 (1987): 42.

Everyone Is a Salesperson

Selling in service, nonprofit, or not-for-profit firms is the responsibility of everyone. Since customers' purchases of services are experiential, anything and anyone that enhances or detracts from their total buying experience affects sales. In this section, we want to explain how everyone is a salesperson even though there are few people ever designated specifically as salespeople.

Five-Phased Approach to Selling Services

In services, the key selling ingredient is the management of all the facets of the customers' dealings with the organization and any of its personnel. Because managing the service encounter is essential for success and since everyone having contact with the customer is in part a salesperson, there should be a consistent behavior for everyone that focuses on maximizing customers' satisfaction with the buying experience. One way to make everyone an effective services salesperson is to have a plan for dealing with customers. This plan should actually start before the customers' experience begins. Let us now look at a model plan for dealing with customers using a bank as an example.

Planning and Managing the Service Encounter

Five Phases of Encounter Management
1. Precontact information gathering
2. Initial encounter
3. Introduction of product lines
4. Sales presentation
5. Conclusion

Precontact information gathering The plan begins before making any customer contact. It starts with investigating what buyers want and expect. It is also important to research what they do not want and what would cause them to be dissatisfied. In a bank, this is management's job. It can be done through survey research, focus groups, and indirect customer questioning. Tracking specific customer complaints is also valuable to determine if there is a pattern to the complaints and if they can it be traced to a particular aspect of their encounter. An example would be determining that over the noon hour, customers get tired of standing in line to make deposits. The solution would be to create an express line or to have more tellers available at noon.

Learning Objective 4:
A five-phased plan for managing the customer's service encounter

Initial encounter Next is the beginning of the customer-salesperson encounter. When a customer enters the bank, alert tellers and receptionists should look for any signs of confusion. If the patron goes directly to the teller window, there is no problem. If the customer appears to be looking around for something, a person designated to make the first contact should ask if assistance is needed. This person should take the customer to the proper bank officer or specialist. That person becomes the second salesperson in this chain of events. It is the responsibility of this second person to carefully and completely see to the needs of the customer. It is important at this point to make the service tangible. Pamphlets, brochures, displays, or simply the salesperson's knowledge of the products available accomplishes this. It is important that the salesperson convey the impression of offering specialized service and genuine concern. This is the point where relationship marketing becomes important. The encounter the customer has with this person will mean the difference between creating a lifelong or short-term relationship.

Introduction to product lines At this point, adaptive service salespeople have the opportunity to develop the relationship based upon the core product, though they can cross-sell here as well. For example, the customer may have asked for a checking account. A VISA card that is available to holders of checking accounts enhances the checking account's importance. Financial planning services may be available at reduced cost to holders of both checking and savings accounts. The adaptive salesperson will try to cross-sell these products. By cross-selling, the banker has not only sold more of the bank's service—a benefit to the bank—but also may have sold the customer products to make financial management easier and possibly cheaper—a benefit to the customer. Thus, the customer went into the bank for one thing but came out with three and a higher level of satisfaction than he or she might have had from just opening a checking account. The customer has also been impressed with the concern shown and with the knowledge that he or she has actually saved money by buying all three products as a package.

The sales presentation   The customer encounter with the bank's salesperson should have consisted of three activities. The salesperson should have

1. made the service tangible when possible,
2. emphasized organizational image, and
3. used external references.

The banker made the service tangible through the use of brochures, pamphlets, and so on. This created the perception of concreteness about something that is actually experiential. The banker emphasized the organizational image through his or her appearance, approach, responsiveness, and courtesy. The banker used external references by inquiring about how the customer came to be acquainted with the bank and possibly by using testimonials by referring to the fact that many people like the customer are taking advantage of the plan being offered.

Conclusion   The conclusion phase is the point of departure when the customer has completed the interaction and service encounter. This is as important (if not more so) as any other phase. The parting and concluding activities are freshest in the customer's mind and often serve as the basis of any reflections on the entire encounter. The departure should be prefaced by questions to ensure everything went well. Courtesy is extremely important. Thanking customers, making sure they have not forgotten anything, and escorting them out seal the relationship and conclude the sale.

As with any type of sales, after-the-sale follow-up is important in the service sales model. Checking back to make sure everything is as it should be, determining if other problems have come up, and generally showing concern for the customer's satisfaction are vital.

What Would You Do If...?

As the marketing person for your local art gallery, you are responsible for maintaining the interest of the local community in visiting the gallery. In addition, you want to try to stimulate others to visit for the first time, hoping to make them repeat visitors and potential contributors. On Monday, you have a meeting scheduled with the employees to discuss how they can do a better job of promoting the gallery to visitors and to people who have never been to the gallery.

▶ Questions: What will you say when they ask you to explain what you mean by "promoting the gallery"?
▶ When they say they thought you were hired on as the marketing director and that selling the gallery is your job, not theirs, how would you respond?

▶ ▶ *follow-up questions*

1. How could an airline use the five phases of the plan for dealing with service customers?
2. How did the last movie theater you attended attempt to emphasize its organizational image? If it didn't, what would you suggest for it?
3. What are the phases of the service selling model?

Projecting the Right Image is Vitally Important When Selling Services

In service, nonprofit, and not-for-profit firms, the image the salesperson projects is as important, if not more so, as in product marketing firms. The salesperson is the personification of the company and its intangible product. The ability of the salesperson to project the attributes of quality, dependability, and problem-solving expertise is the difference between making or losing the sale.

The strength and clarity of the firm's image is often the factor that draws the prospective buyer's initial attention. Merrill Lynch attempts to create a strong clear impression by using the bull in its advertising. Prudential Insurance has used the rock of Gibraltar to accomplish the same thing. Some companies spend millions to create and establish their image. Humble Oil spent over $100 million to change its name and image to Exxon.[8]

Case in Point

Wells Fargo's Salesforce Tames the Wild West

Aggressive selling? Commissions? At a bank? Concepts that were considered taboo at financial institutions just a few years ago are now the hot words in a deregulated banking industry that invites out-of-state competitors and encourages K-Mart to peddle CD's.

"When I first came here a year-and-a-half ago, all we talked about were the major bank competitors," says Gregory Mazares, who left Carnation as a group product manager in charge of breakfast foods to guide the marketing efforts at First Interstate Bank's retail branches. "Now we talk about savings and loans, Citicorp, Chase Manhattan, Sears and supermarket chains offering loans and financial services. The competitive set has widened, and you've got a new type of marketing person coming into the banks, bringing in new techniques that are more aggressive."

"The problem is that banking products, unlike say, office copiers or automobiles, are pretty much the same from bank to bank. All are selling services related to the commodity of money, and all are affected by the same swings and shifts in [interest] rates," says Lona Jupiter, Wells Fargo's director of corporate communications.

Nowhere, perhaps, is this concept better understood than among the 29 members of Wells Fargo's commercial lending sales force, hailed

Continued

Why Is Projecting this Image so Important?

A firm's image is the perception customers have as a result of their experiences with that firm, their knowledge of it, and their beliefs about it.[9] Since service, nonprofit, and not-for-profit organizations must rely on the experiential nature of their customers' encounter, the image projected by salespeople is vital to their success.

Learning Objective 5: The salesperson enhances the image of the firm

The image projected by the salesperson is important for several reasons. First, memory is cue-dependent, and relevant cues stimulate recall.[10] This means the salesperson's verbal and nonverbal signals bring back memories of the customer's experience with the service. This is one of the reasons IBM salespeople were very restricted in their dress only being permitted to wear certain colors. This sameness in dress went with the stable image the firm was trying to create. It also served as a cue to the customer to remember IBM and the quality and service it strove for. In the same way, every time you see the Merrill Lynch bull, you are reminded of the bullish nature of the company.

Second, repetition enhances both learning and recall. The more times a salesperson projects the same image, be it through verbal and/or nonverbal cues, the greater the repetition and customers' association of the image with their experience. You may have learned through repetition that the person in the physician's office with the white coat is the physician. By the same token, customers will judge the quality of their experience with a service, nonprofit, or not-for-profit firm by the people they encounter.

Projecting the proper image to the customer is essential in all selling careers.

The third element is **interactive imagery.** The image projected by the salesperson must interact with the image being created by the firm and vice versa. The salesperson's image is simply a fraction of the company's image. The images of both become linked in the customer's mind and can powerfully reinforce each other. This has a very positive effect if the linkage is to a positive experience or a very negative one if it was not. The customer will form an opinion of the company based upon the briefest of encounters.

Case in Point

Image

I went to my favorite service station and asked if my wheels needed balancing. The mechanic said that the best place in town was Ozarks Tires, a few blocks away. There, the service technician was very cordial, carefully removed the decorative wheel rims, did a superb balancing job, washed the wheels before he put them back on, and thanked me for coming to Ozarks Tires. He even took the car for a test drive to be sure all wheels were properly in balance. I'm sure I'll not only go back to Ozarks when I need new tires but will tell my friends about the service. The "competitive edge" just may be the image this employee created.

How Does the Salesperson Contribute to That Image?

Salespeople contribute to the image in the way they deal with customers. It is helpful to understand how customers evaluate service salespeople and the firms they represent.

Physicians sell a service they customize to each patient.

First, consumers of services seek and rely more on information from personal sources than from nonpersonal sources. Service salespeople should understand this and be willing and able to spend more time with customers because they are the major source of customer information. A poor source of information (ill-prepared service salespeople) will create a bad image of the firm.

Second, service customers often judge quality on the basis of price and atmosphere. Service salespeople are part of the atmosphere the firm tries to create. For example, the waiter at your favorite restaurant helps to create the atmosphere of the restaurant and reflects to you the image of the establishment. Service salespeople who use price discounting as a selling tool may be damaging the image of the firm.

Third, consumers perceive greater risks when buying services than when buying tangible products. Clearly, the salesperson for a service will have a greater responsibility to try to reduce the consumer's risks. The salesperson will positively affect the firm's image by helping customers understand the risks associated with a purchase.

Finally, consumers are less likely to change from one service provider to another than from one product provider to another. People tend to stay with the same physician, attorney, and so on, as long as they perceive they are getting adequate service. If the service salesperson creates and nurtures this positive relationship, it can be sustained for many years. The other side of this means it is far easier to create and keep a customer than to take one away from another firm.[11]

Credibility Is a Key Factor

▶ ▶ ▶ ▶ ▶ ▶ ▶ ▶ ▷

Learning Objective 6: The salesperson's credibility relates to the firm's image

The most important asset salespeople have is credibility. This is true regardless of the type of product or service they sell. Credibility is an important factor not to just those who sell services but to all salespeople. It is, however, for service salespeople, often the only evidence the customer has to make a purchase decision. For salespeople selling tangible goods, such as computers, there is the actual tangible machine customers can watch perform and evaluate. The salesperson could be a poor one, but as long as the machine works and does what it is supposed to do, chances are the customer will be satisfied at least with the machine's mechanical operation. When a person selects a physician, attorney, architect, or insurance agent, that person makes the choice in part based upon the perception of credibility; there is no tangible machine to observe or mechanical operation to evaluate. The customer often has little to go on other than the perceived credibility of the service salesperson and the firm. The customer perceives the salesperson's credibility based on four factors.[12]

Components of Credibility

1. Honesty
2. Knowledge and expertise
3. Prestige
4. Referent affinity

Honesty The first source of credibility is honesty. Service salespeople, in particular, must be perceived as being genuinely honest and interested in customer satisfaction with the service. Sellers lose their credibility if customers perceive that the sellers' objective is intentional manipulation. If you sense the insurance salesperson's main objective is to sell any policy just to make the sale, then the salesperson's ability to persuade you to buy a policy is greatly decreased.

Knowledge or expertise The second factor is knowledge or expertise. Credibility is directly related to the seller's knowledge of the service. Imagine going to the emergency room of a hospital and asking several employees for directions and getting incorrect information from all. What would you think of a hospital where the employees did not know the emergency room's location? The greater the customer's belief in the seller's expertise, the greater the persuasive ability of the seller. This is why it is extremely important that all customer contact persons in service firms either know the answers to the customer's questions or know how and where to find them.

Expertise is a key factor in selling services.

Prestige Credibility is generated when the customer knows and respects the salesperson's or the firm's prestige. This is the reason firms will use well-known and respected movie stars, industrialists, or athletes as testimonial speakers to promote their products. The prestige of the salesperson has a halo effect on the product and vice versa. Service firms try to create the perception of prestige and status through the design and decor of their physical facilities and the conduct of their customer contact personnel. If your banker dressed like your garage mechanic, would he or she have an easy or difficult time convincing you your money would be safe?

Referent affinity Referent affinity means being able to relate to someone in a harmonious way; a feeling of cooperation, empathy and rapport. People tend to trust people to whom they can relate. Salespeople build greater credibility if they can relate to their customers and the customers to them. Service salespeople use a variety of verbal and nonverbal cues to create referent affinity. Their dress, speech, phrases and mannerisms communicate credibility. Salespeople who can convey an understanding of the customer's problem generate credibility as customers perceive a greater referent affinity.

Everything mentioned above is designed to create, enhance, and nurture customers' image of the organizations they are buying from. In selling intangible services, the only real tangible item immediately accessible to the customer is the salesperson. How salespeople present themselves, what they use to reinforce the image their firm wants to project, and how the total customer's buying experience is managed determine whether that customer will return. Experiences can and should be managed. Nothing should be allowed to just *happen* during the customer's encounter. The trick here is to manage the encounter so it doesn't appear to the customer to be managed at all! The organization that is conscious of relationship marketing, the one that trains its customer contact people in the techniques of selling, and the one that totally embraces the concept and application of relationship selling in this high-touch atmosphere will be the successful organization.

▸▸ *follow-up questions*

1. How does a service salesperson build credibility with a customer?
2. Is the image of the firm part of the "total product"?

Summary

In this chapter, the focus was on the similarities and differences between selling services or intangibles and selling tangible products. Selling services is selling something that is experiential. Services cannot be stored for later use and are generally created by the salesperson specifically for the customer at the time of purchase. Such is the case with medical, housecleaning, and banking services, for example (Learning Objective 1).

Selling in nonprofit, not-for-profit, and service firms has some similarities to selling in for-profit firms. In service, nonprofit, and not-for-profit firms, the demarcation between who sells and who does not is not as clear as it is in firms manufacturing and marketing tangible products. In service firms, everyone who has any customer contact is, in essence, a salesperson. In service firms, the management of the customer's encounter with the service provider determines the customer's image of the firm. Not-for-profit firms sell services and/or desired social behaviors, such as public safety, fire prevention, or cholesterol control (Learning Objective 2).

A core product or service was explained as being the center of successful relationship marketing, a key feature of selling services, just as in selling tangible products. Ancillary products or services are marketed through cross-selling, relationship customization, service augmentation, and relationship pricing (Learning Objective 3).

The relationship can be managed and planned through a multiphased process, beginning with the investigation of customer's needs and continuing on to planning the encounter from initial contact through conclusion. Managing the phases means managing precontact information, then the customer's initial encounter, how the customer is introduced to the products, how the product is presented, and finally how the service encounter is concluded (Learning Objective 4).

You have read how consumers of services perceive greater risks when buying services and that salespeople dispel this apprehension through their honesty, knowledge or expertise, prestige, and referent affinity. These contribute to the firm's and the salesperson's image in the customer's mind, and it is through interactive imagery that customers learn to judge the quality of the intangible product (Learning Objective 5).

Salespeople in service, nonprofit, and not-for-profit firms operate in a unique environment. The key to success is an understanding of the unique nature of this environment. With this understanding, customers' encounters with the firm can be managed in such a way that the experience will seem totally free of established procedures. That's the secret of selling in service, nonprofit, and not-for-profit firms: selling without appearing to be selling; creating a relationship, not a sale. While the outcome may be the same, the way you get there can be very different (Learning Objective 6).

Key Terms

Nonprofit organization   A firm that exists for the good of society and does not depend on profits to survive; often has tax-exempt status.

Relationship marketing   The management of the complete customer relationship, from identifying a core product to expanding to the ancillary products the firm offers.

Core service   The service upon which the customer relationship can be built.

Relationship customizing   The ways in which a service relationship can be customized to fit the unique needs of the individuals experiencing it.

Service augmentation   The unexpected extras vendors can provide that augment or add to the core service. An example would be including a VISA card as an extra no-cost option for new checking account customers at a local bank.

Relationship pricing   Customers are given pricing incentives to consolidate their business with one supplier.

Interactive imagery   The image projected by the salesperson must interact with the image being created by the firm and vice versa.

Discussion Questions

1. If you were going to buy a cruise from your travel agent, what would be the "total product"?

2. Selling a service is selling an encounter. How could an opera house sell its service by managing the customer's encounter?

3. Think of two services you buy. What are their core products? What are their ancillary products?

4. Make a flowchart illustrating the service encounter you have when making a bank deposit. Who are the people you encounter? How could you improve the encounter?

5. How does your physician create the perception of a quality product? How does he or she create an image?

6. What are the four sources service salespeople (or any salesperson, for that matter) use to create credibility?

7. What is impression management?

8. What are the three cornerstones of selling?

9. Are physicians "salespeople?" If so, what do they use to sell their expertise?

10. What would you say is the most significant factor distinguishing tangible products from intangible services? How does that affect how you would sell the two?

11. How does cross-selling apply to the products of banks? Stock brokerages? Lawn-care companies?

12. How does the image projected by a firm help a salesperson sell, and how does the image projected by the salesperson help the firm?

13. Why would consumers perceive greater risks when buying services than when buying tangible products? How can the service salesperson dispel the consumer's apprehension?

14. How would a hotel use relationship customizing?

15. Hilton Hotels has an "Honors Club" for selected patrons who receive privileges regular guests don't get. What relationship marketing strategy is the hotel firm using?

Application Exercise

Reread the Case in Point about Wells Fargo's salesforce, then answer the following questions:

1. If you were a Wells Fargo salesperson, what characteristics would you look for in a business prospect?

2. As a Wells Fargo salesperson, how would you apply the five phases of dealing with service customers?

3. Would Wells Fargo's salespeople have a problem with the customer's image of Wells Fargo? Why?

Class Exercises

Group Exercise

The class will break down into appropriate sized groups of no less than three members. The service to be sold will be lawn care. Each group will represent a company sales team focused on a different socioeconomic market segment: upper class, upper-middle class, and lower-middle class.

Each group (student team) will report to the class the four-step strategy of selling services, as denoted in the chapter under "Relationship Marketing," to effect the sale to their assigned market segment.

The class will then discuss the results and choose the best team approach to the sale of the lawn service.

Individual Presentation

Each student will, prior to the class meeting, choose a particular service to sell to the class.

Each student will then prepare a sales plan for this service, applying the five-phased approach to selling services (encounter management), as denoted in the chapter.

The instructor will call on selected individuals to present their plans.

The class will then evaluate the plans as presented in regard to: 1) thoroughness, 2) organization, 3) clarity, and 4) originality.

▼ ▼ ▼ ▼ ▼ ▼ *Cases* ▼ ▼ ▼ ▼ ▼ ▼ ▼

The Three Cases of the Struggling Stockbrokers

The following information applies to the three cases that follow:[13]

The A. J. Hogle Company is a medium-sized stock brokerage located in a major midwestern city. Jim Nielsen had been the manager of the 11-person firm for the past three years. Although the firm was profitable, Jim was concerned about expanding the customer base. Increased competition from a new E.F. Hutton office and a shift of some customers away from his firm to discount brokers had him concerned about the future growth of his firm. In an attempt to explore new market opportunities, Jim came across a study conducted a year earlier.

This study on public attitudes toward investing concluded that the vast majority of brokerage firms had penetrated several market segments quite deeply. These included experienced older investors, experienced traders, and conservative, upscale clients. The study suggested that clients and prospects have different financial goals, attitudes, and opinions about investment opportunities, expectations about performance of investments, willingness to take risks, and knowledge about investment possibilities.

Two segments were identified as having excellent potential. These were first the affluent blue-collar segment comprising 14.8 million households. This is the largest and most affluent segment of people who have never owned securities. In this segment, most are employed full-time, largely in skilled craft jobs or as labor supervisors. Fewer than 20 percent attended college, and 85 percent are young, married, and have children.

The second segment consists of both single and married working women. Women constitute more than half of all the millionaires and more than half of all adult stockholders. The study also indicated that 36 percent of women who play an active role in their financial affairs do not enjoy making these decisions. Those who do not participate in financial decisions feel they lack the education to make proper judgments, are afraid of losing money, and do not know whom to trust.

Four significant barriers in the marketing of securities to these two groups were identified. One, many in these two groups can be reached only in their homes. Two, brokers have consistently used language and other interpersonal cues to show their lack of interest in these potential clients, especially in the blue-collar segment. Three, these potential customers fear investments and are ignorant of opportunities. Four, account representatives do not feel comfortable dealing with these prospects.

Jim called a meeting of the 11 brokers in his office, and a unanimous decision was made to more aggressively pursue both of these market segments. When additional training was suggested to deal with this new approach, the brokers all expressed confidence they knew all there was to know about selling securities and that additional training would not be necessary.

After a two-month effort, Jim was not pleased with the progress most of his salespeople were making in tapping these two target groups. He decided to question some and listen to other's conversations to evaluate how they handled their sales presentations.

Roger Clark had been a broker with the firm for just over six months. Prior to joining the firm, he had sold waterless cookware door to door using the referral system. He was convinced that using referrals and contacting prospects in their homes was a great way to reach the working women segment he had been told to pursue. After the last few unsuccessful attempts to sell a retirement program to the secretaries of a nationwide insurance company, Roger was more than a little discouraged. He had made over ten presentations to these secretaries in groups of between three to six at each meeting, which was held in the home of one of the women. His approach was to spread a dark purple velvet cloth on the floor as soon as he entered the home and place a prospectus from the mutual fund he was selling in a golden-colored pouch. He began his presentation by removing the prospectus from the pouch and asking each of the young secretaries if they wanted to be as poor when they retired as their parents were today. Then he would explain the benefits of a no-load mutual fund that operated like an annuity fund. He always asked if there were any questions, and because no one ever asked any and he knew he spoke slowly, he was convinced that all potential questions were handled in the presentation. To help close the sales, he would pass around the contracts for each woman to sign as he offered a free plastic rain bonnet to each who signed up right then.

Questions:

1. How would you coach Roger to improve his presentation?
2. What type of image is Roger creating in the customers' minds through the techniques he is using?
3. If Roger presented securities to you in this fashion, what would you think?

Bob and Sally Wise were both in their early thirties. Bob was a foreman at a local castings company. They had contacted the A. J. Hogle Company to see what they could do with part of their savings to earn more than the 5 1/4 percent they were currently earning. They came to the office late one Friday afternoon and asked to see someone. Because Monique Adams was the next broker to receive a walk-in customer, they were directed to her desk by the receptionist. Monique finished discussing her plans for that evening with another broker, and after a brief introduction by the receptionist, Bob and Sally sat down. After Monique noticed Bob's soiled hands, she said, "Well, what can we do for you?"

Bob replied that they thought they might be interested in earning more than 5 1/4 percent on their savings. Monique said, "The A. J. Hogle Company has some excellent investments, and the sky is the limit. Don't worry about a thing. I helped another couple just like you earn a lot more than just 5 1/4 percent on their money. How much money do you have to invest?"

Just then the phone on Monique's desk rang. When Monique finished the call, she turned back to where Bob and Sally were sitting and discovered they were gone.

Questions:

1. How did Monique bungle this encounter?
2. Why did the customers leave?
3. What would you suggest to Monique to improve her impression management technique?

Brent Wilson was a specialist in financial estate planning. He had been with A. J. Hogle for 12 years. He consistently was the sales leader in his office. Most of his clients were successful businessmen and many had been with him for 11 to 12 years. Brent was not happy with the pressure placed on him to sell more to the working women segment, but he decided to give it a try to keep the manager off his back.

Brent's office wall was covered with sales awards he had won over the past 12 years. He was proud of these accomplishments and felt he could be successful in selling his services to anyone. One of his clients who was a vice-president of sales at a large printing firm told him that his company president was very much into the stock market. The president's name was Chris Turner, who Brent was shocked to learn, was a woman. Brent was going to ask her to come to his office but decided it might be best to meet her at her firm. An appointment was made, and Brent began to plan his strategy.

Brent was prompt for his appointment and began by saying, "I understand you do a lot of trading in the stock market. Because most of my clients speak highly of me and my skills in helping them manage their accounts, I thought I might be of service to you."

Chris came right to the point and asked, "What can you do for me that my current brokers cannot do?"

"I have been a broker for 12 years and most of my customers seem very satisfied."

Chris indicated she used a number of different brokers, and because she did her own evaluations of the securities she purchased, all she needed a broker for was to transact the order. Any of the discount brokers could do that very well, she said, and for a lot less money than Brent's firm charged.

Brent made a few more attempts to convince Chris he was a good broker, but Chris indicated she was busy and asked him to leave.

Questions:

1. Why was this encounter unsuccessful?
2. What could Brent have done to make this successful?
3. What did Chris really want from Brent that he failed to address? What could Brent have done to uncover what Chris's real needs in a broker were?

References

1. Adapted from "Electroshock at Detroit Edison," *Sales and Marketing Management,* 137 (1986): 20.
2. Alan Urbanski, "Lawyers Go to Mass Marketing," *Sales and Marketing Management* 138 (1987): 32–34.
3. A. Parasuraman and Valerie Zeithaml, "Differential Perceptions of Suppliers and Clients of Industrial Services," *Emerging Perspectives on Services Marketing,* ed. Leonard Berry et al., (Chicago: American Marketing Association, 1983), pp. 143–145.
4. Modified from Henry B. Hansman, "The Role for Nonprofit Organizations," *Yale Law Journal,* 89 (1980): 835–901.
5. Christopher H. Lovelock and Charles B. Weinberg, *Marketing for Public and Non-profit Managers* (New York: John Wiley & Sons, 1984), pp. 32–36. A lengthy and more complete discussion can be found here.
6. Leonard Berry, "Relationship Marketing," *Emerging Perspectives on Services Marketing,* ed. Leonard Berry et al. (Chicago: American Marketing Association, 1983), p. 27.
7. Ibid.
8. "Humble 'Exxon' In; and Esso Out," *National Petroleum News,* June 1972.
9. David L. Loudon and Albert J. Della Bitta, *Consumer Behavior* (New York: McGraw Hill, 1979), p. 337.
10. Edward Grubb, "Consumer Perception of 'Self-concept' and Its Relationship to Brand Choice of Selected Product Types" (Unpublished diss., University of Washington, 1965).
11. Valerie A. Zeithaml, "How Consumer Evaluation Processes Differ Between Goods and Services," *Marketing of Services,* ed. James H. Donnelly and William R. George (Chicago: American Marketing Association, 1981), pp. 186–91.
12. Loudon and Della Bitta, *Consumer Behavior,* p. 410.
13. William George, J. Patrick Kelly, and Claudia Marshall, "Personal Selling of Services," *Emerging Perspectives on Services Marketing,* ed. Leonard Berry et al. (Chicago: American Marketing Association, 1983), pp. 66–67.

15 Legal and Ethical Aspects of Personal Selling

Objectives

After reading this chapter, you should be able to:

1. Identify and give examples of the types of laws that affect the salesperson-buyer relationship.

2. Explain what constitutes a contract and what remedies salespeople and customers have if contracts are breached.

3. Define the basic legal aspects of selling, storing, and shipping goods.

4. Briefly describe the product liability conditions for which salespeople are liable.

5. Relate the concepts of restraint of trade, price discrimination, and deception to the selling process.

6. Evaluate ethical situations between salespeople and their employers, their customers, and their competitors.

7. Identify the legal and ethical issues of sexual harassment and several alternatives for dealing with it.

The Professional Selling Question

Most people are ethical in their business practices, but sometimes difficult ethical problems arise. What do you think influences the ethical behavior of salespeople, particularly new salespeople?

A Sales Expert Responds

William Finn, founder of W. T. Finn and Associates, a management and sales training firm in New York, says that most people face ethical situations on their sales jobs at one time or another. The guidance they get in handling the situation builds their ethical foundation for the business deals that follow. Finn cites three reasons why salespeople act unethically when they face a moral dilemma: 1) their manager's influence; 2) the pressure to perform against unrealistic expectations; and 3) the corporate or business structure they work in.

According to Finn, a major source of unethical role modeling is the salesperson's immediate supervisor. If managers condone unethical behavior, if they do not discourage it, or if they are seen as sometimes taking the unethical route themselves, then the people working for them see such behaviors as OK for them, too. After all, if the boss does it, it must be acceptable for everyone else, too. A survey by the American Management Association found the influence of one's immediate supervisor to be the most frequently cited basis for unethical behaviors.

Regarding the second reason for unethical behavior, Finn says that local managers who are pressured to make higher and higher sales quotas—and to do so at whatever cost—may opt for putting ethics on hold to make the sales rather than lose their jobs.

Finally, the company chain of command also affects ethical behavior. Should the salesperson go over the manager's head to report or question ethical situations if the immediate manager condones unethical behavior or even encourages it? This is a dilemma for the field salesperson. After all, the manager has the most direct control and influence over the salesperson's job and career. To further complicate matters, how does the salesperson know that the manager's boss does not support and condone such actions?

Finn cites sales training, including ethics training, as one of the best ways to prepare people to handle ethical situations on the job. Ethics training must be part of all training programs, he says, but training is not enough. Ethics must be incorporated into the company policy as a code of conduct. This code of conduct, he says, must be more than just written, it must be enforced—and from the top down. Top managers should set examples for lower-level managers, who then set examples for all employees. Ethical behavior cannot simply be discussed during training; it must be seen as permeating the company and enforced at all levels.[1]

Introduction

Sooner or later, everyone in business faces an ethical or legal dilemma requiring a decision of right or wrong. That decision is the product of a personal value system, a firm's policy on the issue, and the legal system. The legal system is complex and made more so by the intertwined labyrinth of federal, state, and local laws. Salespeople cannot be expected to be lawyers or to know all aspects of the laws that govern their behavior in commerce. However, lack of knowledge is no excuse.

Ethics is more complicated than law. It does not have the technical framework like the law, but it requires a person to make judgments balanced between the desire to get ahead and be successful and between what is right and wrong. Ethical dilemmas involve such questions as: Who will be hurt? Will anybody really know? Will anybody really care? Will it make any difference anyway?

The purpose of this chapter is to make you more aware of the laws that regulate the day-to-day dealings of salespeople. Also, some of the typical ethical situations salespeople face are discussed. It is not the purpose of this chapter to tell you what is right or wrong. It is merely to present you with what the law, as well as many companies, identify as right and wrong. You must make the appropriate decisions for yourself.

We will begin the chapter with a discussion of the legal system, some aspects of the Uniform Commercial Code, and the federal laws that try to keep competition fair. We will end the chapter with a presentation about ethical problems salespeople deal with each day.

The Legal System in Which Salespeople Work

Selling involves the legal transfer of ownership. A product is not legally sold unless an exchange agreement between the buyer and seller is reached, be it for money or barter. The transfer of ownership means laws must be followed and the appropriate documentation created.

Structure of the Legal System

The purpose of the legal and judicial system is to create and enforce the rules of conduct for society. These rules are the written laws. Laws spell out what can and cannot be done and the penalties for breaking them. They are often vague: "Any price is lawful if it is made in good faith to meet competition." What is "good faith"? How broad is the definition of competition? Courts interpret the law as it applies to each individual situation. Table 15-1 is a brief overview of the legal aspects of selling that will be covered in this chapter. While it is by no means complete, it does highlight the legal issues a salesperson should be aware of.

Public law deals with the relations between the government and private citizens or businesses. An example is a public law is a sales tax. **Private law** spells out the rules individuals must follow when dealing with each other. For example, when you sign a contract agreeing to make monthly payments, you are bound by law to do so. A major subset of private law is the law of

◀ ◀ ◀ ◀ ◀ ◀ ◀ ◀

Learning Objective 1: Types of laws that affect the salesperson-customer relationship

Table 15-1	Legal Highlights	

Public law — government's relationship with individuals and businesses

Private law — individuals' relationships with each other
    Tort law — duties one person has to another
    Contract law — rules governing agreements
    Agency law — rules governing one person acting on behalf of another
    Partnership and corporation law — rules of business organization and behavior

Legal Aspects of Business Communications

Slander

Libel

Defamation

Disparagement

Legal Aspects of Promises Made

Fraud

Component of Contracts

Agreements

Consideration

Free will

Legality

Aspects of Sales Law

Transfer of ownership

Aspects of Storage

Bailments
Bailee's duties

Aspects of Product Liability

Express Warranties

Implied Warranties

Liability

Agency Functions

Agent's and principal's duties to each other

Aspects of Federal Laws Salespeople Must Know

Restraint of trade

Price discrimination

Deception

torts. *Tort* comes from the old French word meaning a wrong or injustice committed by someone on someone. **Tort law** spells out the duties a person has to another person. Automobile accidents are the most frequently occurring infringement of tort law. The law says you should not crash into someone else. Compensation is the significant feature of tort law. Salespeople enter the realm of tort law when the product they sell fails to perform. If your hair falls out after you use a bottle of hair coloring, you may have a tort case against the manufacturer.

Contract law is another type of private law that involves salespeople. Every time a salesperson accepts a purchase order, a contract is created. **Contract law** establishes the rules governing the agreements people make. Contracts dictate who will do what for whom. A whole host of laws govern what constitutes a contract and who is obligated to do what by a contract.

Other types of laws affecting salespeople are agency law, partnership and corporate law, and regulatory law. **Agency law** deals with the relations one party has on behalf of another. This directly affects salespeople because their job is to sell on behalf of the firm they represent. The independent sales representative for Procter & Gamble is acting on behalf of the company and is therefore its agent. **Partnership and corporate law** regulates the behaviors and organization of business enterprises. Such laws designate the limits of liability, the rules about how and when businesses should be taxed, and the businesses' responsibilities.

The regulatory environment Regulatory agencies are responsible for guaranteeing that the functions they oversee are carried out in accordance with the existing laws. **Regulatory law** is a part of public law that establishes and enforces the rules of regulatory bodies, for example, the Federal Trade Commission, the Securities and Exchange Commission, and the Federal Aviation Administration, to name a few. States also have regulatory agencies. Nebraska, for example, has a regulatory body that governs the insurance industry. All policies sold in Nebraska must conform to the state's laws as enforced by this agency. Similarly, most states have liquor control commissions, departments of transportation and taxation agencies.

Agencies enforce laws Agencies, such as the ones mentioned above, are mandated to enforce the laws. They do not have the power to create laws; only legislatures can do that. Agencies are creations of laws. For example, Congress created a law saying monopolies are illegal. The Federal Trade Commission was created by a companion law and empowered to enforce the anticompetitive practices laws. Regulatory agencies enforce their regulations by imposing fines or other penalties on violators; charges of violations are litigated in the courts or in internal agency adjudication procedures.

Laws: Governing Who, What, and How

The legal system governs the behaviors of society. In the United States, the legal system is adversarial. If customers feel they have been sold a defective product and want to be compensated for damages it caused, they bring suit against the manufacturer, vendor, or salesperson. The person (or firm) initiating the complaint is the plaintiff. The person (or firm) who is the target of the complaint is the defendant. Only the person or firm that can show injury has standing to sue. For example, if your neighbor's house burned down because of a faulty gas stove, you cannot sue the stove's maker because you were not aggrieved.

Suits are generally brought by a person or firm claiming damages against another. Lawsuits may also be class actions, in which a group of persons claim similar damages. For example, a group of concerned citizens could bring suit for all the citizens damaged by a firm charging unfairly high prices.

1. What category(s) of law would a customer's refusal to pay for delivered goods fall under?
2. If laws apply to everyone, what is the difference between public and private law?
3. How do federal or state agencies enforce the laws?

Basic Law for Salespeople

Business Communications and the Law

Business communications are a quilt of verbal and nonverbal communications often comprising explicit and implicit terms. Explicit terms specifically state what will occur. Implicit terms infer or insinuate what will occur. The greatest areas of concern for salespeople lie in three areas: 1) what they say about competitors; 2) what they promise buyers (or what buyers think they have been promised); and 3) what is specifically written in business communications.

What you can and cannot say When a salesperson makes unfair or untrue oral statements about competitors or their products to a third party, then **business slander** has been committed. If competitors feel such statements have damaged their reputation or ability to do business, then a suit can result. **Business libel** occurs when the unfair or untrue statements are written, as in a letter, brochure, ad, or sales literature.

Salespeople should be particularly careful in their conversations to avoid statements that could be considered personally defamatory. Such statements would include:

▸ Saying that your competitors are always being sued for one thing or another or that they routinely engage in unfair business practices when they do not.

▸ Saying competitors generally do not live up to their contractual responsibilities (ship faulty goods, deliver the wrong orders, etc.) when they do not.

▸ Making untrue statements about competitors' financial dealings or general financial condition.

▸ Making untrue statements about the owners or managers of competing companies.[2]

Such conversation becomes legally actionable when it results in personal or business damage.

Claims about products can lead to lawsuits as well. **Product disparagement** is the result of untrue or unfair claims made about a competitor's product. Such unlawful communications might claim a competitor's products will not perform when in reality they will. A similar concept, but opposite in its object, is claiming your own product will do something it will not. It is one thing to claim a competitor's product *will not* do something when it will; it is another thing to claim yours *will* when it really will not.

Case in Point

Ten Tips to Avoid Misstatements That Can Get You Sued

Customers rely on what a salesperson says as being statements of fact and, in some cases, warranties. Salespeople, though, are guilty of puffery: expanding on the superlatives. There is a fine line between facts and opinions. Opinions cannot be relied upon as a basis for legal action, but facts or factual-sounding statements can. If you say, "Our service department is one of the best in town," that is opinion. If you say, "Our product will make widgets as fast as anybody's widget maker," that can be taken as fact (even though it really may be the salesperson's opinion). The less knowledgeable the customer, the more the court will interpret a loose statement as taken as fact by that customer and thus as actionable. To stay out of trouble, follow these ten tips:

1. Know the distinction between praise, opinion, and fact. "This freezer will keep your food frozen even in the most intense heat." This is an actionable statement of fact for the customer, even though it may be only the salesperson's opinion.

2. Educate customers. Tell them what is fact and what is your opinion. Tell them all you can about the product's performance. Just because they do not ask is no reason not to tell them.

3. Be totally accurate in all product claims. Do not tell customers what you think the product will do; tell them what field tests have shown.

4. Know all the technical specifics of what you sell. If you do not know a fact, look it up, find out, and call back or get someone who does. Do not make a claim.

5. Make no exaggerated claims about safety.

6. Be totally familiar with the federal and state laws regarding warranties and guarantees.

7. Know the performance characteristics of what you sell: what it will do at top speed; if it shimmies, whirrs, or vibrates when it runs, and so on.

8. Be aware of all design changes and incorporate this information into your sales presentation.

9. Do not give opinions when customers ask for specific facts.

10. Never go beyond what you are absolutely sure of.

Source: Steven Mitchell Sack, "Legal Puffery: Truth or Consequences," *Sales and Marketing Management* 137 (1986): 59–60.

What you can and cannot promise   Salespeople should be careful to communicate only what they, their company, or their products can actually do. Products are often sold with an explicit promise to perform. Fraud and misrepresentation are the results of incorrect or false representation, whether with or without intent. **Fraud** is a misrepresentation of fact to the point where it has had a moving influence on the contracting party. Telling someone a house is green when it is blue is not fraud, but telling someone a house is green when it is blue and thus causing the people being told to decide not to buy the house because they believe it is green is misrepresentation. The false representation of the house made a significant difference in their decision, thus misrepresentation occurred. The defining issue is intent to deceive.

Silence can also be fraudulent. It is a misrepresentation to *not* inform a buyer of faults, defects, or malfunctions. For example, suppose an equipment salesperson knew an engine being sold had a leaky radiator and the customer said, "I suppose everything is in good working order?" If the salesperson simply remained silent, knowing the prospective buyer was under the impression that the radiator was without malfunction, then fraud by silence would be the result.

Promising a buyer something can also constitute an oral contract. If salespeople say, "We will give you 10 percent off the list price...," they have made an offer, and an oral contract exists. For the salespeople to later claim it was not valid because it was not written anywhere makes no difference. It is generally considered that there must be a "meeting of the minds for a contract to exist." This means both parties must understand that an offer to do something has been made and that some form of consideration and reward will result. It is extremely important for salespeople to understand that what they say, offer, or promise during a sales presentation can be considered a contract.

What you write is what you mean   When a document, such as a contract, is signed, the minds of both parties are said to have met in agreement, and thus a contract exists. What is stated in writing often deals with the price and terms of payment. The sales invoice given by the seller's firm and the purchase order issued by the buyer's firm constitute the paper that each uses to consummate the sale. These pieces of paper are also where mistakes occur most often. For example, the salesperson quotes a price of $45 per unit to the buyer, but when the invoice was typed, the price was listed as $4.50 per unit. The buyer could try to hold the salesperson to the $4.50-per-unit price, but this is clearly a mistake, so the seller can rescind the mistaken price. It is generally accepted that a customer is not permitted to profit from such a mistake. Most courts would allow the seller to withdraw the offer if the seller acted in good faith, without gross negligence, was prompt in giving notice of the mistake, and will suffer as a result of the mistake and if the customer's status (well-being) has not been greatly changed. If, on the other hand, the salesperson failed to catch the mistake and waited an unreasonable period of time to call it to the buyer's attention and if the buyer had already disposed of the goods at, say, a price marked up on the basis of $4.50 rather than $45, it would be an entirely different matter. For this reason, salespeople must always monitor their written communications and sales paperwork. What you write is generally considered to be what you mean.

What Constitutes a Contract?

▶ ▶ ▶ ▶ ▶ ▶ ▶ ▶ ▶

Learning Objective 2: What constitutes a contract and the remedies available if the contract is breached

"A **contract** is a promise or set of promises for the breach of which the law gives remedy, or performance of which the law in some way recognizes a duty."[3] The Uniform Commercial Code[4] states, "Contract means the total legal obligation which results from the parties' agreement as affected by the

Act and any other applicable rules of law." (U.C.C., Sect. 1-201 [11]). Salespeople get involved in three major types of contracts: real estate, service, and sale of goods. To have a contract, four elements must exist:

1. there is an agreement;
2. there is a consideration;
3. the agreement is legal; and
4. both parties entered into the agreement of their own free will.

Salespeople are involved in three major types of contracts: real estate, service, and sale of goods.

Agreement An agreement consists of several components. An agreement must have an offer. An offer is a willingness to enter into a bargain. In essence, the offer says, "I will do this for you, if you do that for me." The offer must be communicated, that is, both parties must know promises are being made. If you put a for-sale sign in your yard and I come along and say I will buy your house, we have a communicated offer. If you come to my house and say, "Congratulations, I will be glad to sell you my house," but I did not know about the deal, it was not communicated to me, so there was no contract. The agreement must have definiteness; that is, sufficient terms must be spelled out so both parties understand the promises made. Finally, an agreement *may* have duration, which is a specified time period to complete the promises made in the contract. Real estate offer-to-purchase contracts are the best example of duration. They state the offer of the prospective buyer and give the seller a certain time period in which to respond or the contract is voided. Duration is not a requirement for an agreement but is often included.

Acceptance is the last feature of an agreement. The person to whom the contract is offered must accept it for there to be an agreement. Acceptance may be in writing, verbally, or by silence. Silence is a special case. If the agreement said, "If I do not hear from you by noon, we will assume you have accepted our terms," and the recipient did not respond, then the offer has been accepted by silence.

Consideration The second component of the contract is consideration. Consideration is the mutual financial promise the buying party makes to the selling party. If Jean says to Armand, "I will give you this car," and Armand accepts, this is no contract. Armand has agreed to no reciprocal promise. If Jean says to Armand, "I will give you this car if you give me $400" and Armand agrees, this is a contract. Armand has promised Jean a consideration of $400.

Legality The third component of the contract is that it must be legal. The contract must not violate any rules of law or force one party to violate a rule of law in its completion. An agreement between two competitors to fix prices to drive a third out of business is an illegal contract. If competitor A fails to perform and does not hold to the agreed price, competitor B cannot sue A; the contract was illegal.

Free will entry Finally, both parties must have entered into the contract of their own free will and knowing about the mutual responsibilities each holds to the other. Contracts made under threat, undue persuasion, misrepresentation, or fraud are not valid.

Failure to discharge—not doing what was agreed When both sides of the agreement do what they agreed to do, the contract has been discharged. If one party fails to complete his or her side of the bargain, there is a **breach of contract.** Numerous conditions may make breach of contract legal or illegal. For example, the contract may be impossible or impractical to discharge. Death of one of the parties makes the contract impossible to discharge. If you contract with Jack to paint your house on Tuesday, but it is snowing on Tuesday, the contract is impractical to discharge. In the case of impossibility or impracticality, a breach has *not* occurred. However, if Jack only paints half your house and will not do the rest, a breach *has* occurred.

Breach can usually be avoided if both parties fully understand their obligations to each other. Breach can also be avoided if both parties renegotiate the contract to alleviate the cause creating the breach. Since breach of contract is a very serious matter, consultation with a legal expert regarding the contract, its environment or situation in which it was formulated, and the degree to which it was discharged is imperative.

Remedies salespeople and buyers have If a contract is not upheld, either in total or in part, the aggrieved party may receive a remedy for the failure to perform. Remedies can come in the form of awards for damages, specific performance, or restitution.

Damages are monetary awards to the injured party. The amount of damages recovered depends on what the injured party is due. This can be the sum of the amount of money the injured party expected to receive but did not and other inconsequential losses caused by the breach, less the amount of money the injured party did not have to spend as a result of the contract not being completed. If you sold 300 TVs to Carmichael Distributors, but delivered only half and refused to deliver the rest, Carmichael could not refuse to pay you for what you had sold and it had accepted. However, because of your breach, Carmichael did not get the $6,000 profit it expected. Instead, it realized only half that amount, or $3,000. Since it usually sells a $100 antenna with each TV, it realized only $1,500 from antenna sales, rather than $3,000. However, since it did not have enough TVs to sell, it *did not spend* $1,000 on advertising. All totaled, Carmichael can sue for $3,000 plus $1,500 minus $1,000, or $3,500.

Punitive damages are awarded by the court to punish the wrongdoer. Each state has its own laws on punitive damages. The following Case in Point illustrates an award of punitive damages.

Case in Point

Punitive Damages Run into the Millions

In California, a roofer fell off a roof while performing his work. He injured his back but not so seriously that he could not get around. His injury was serious enough, however, that he was unable to work. He had recently taken out an insurance policy that he thought would pay

Continued

Specific performance is a legal remedy when contracts are not fulfilled. **Specific performance** is a mandate from the court to carry out the specific promises of the contract yet unfilled. Suppose you were selling mainframe computers and as part of the deal, you and your company agreed to provide the maintenance. If you said to the customer that your firm was no longer going to provide maintenance on the computers it sold, that customer could sue for specific performance. The court could say you had to do the maintenance or provide the customer with maintenance services at your expense.

Restitution is the third type of remedy. Restitution is restoring to one party what he or she gave to the other. If you sell a piece of machinery to a customer and that customer gives you $1,000 as a deposit but you fail to deliver the machinery, the customer can ask for restitution, that is, the $1,000 back. The customer may also ask for damages, but more often than not, restitution ends the dispute.

Sale, Storage, and Shipment of Goods

Along with knowing about contracts, salespeople must be aware of the laws governing sales, storage, and shipment of the goods they sell.

Learning Objective 3: Legal aspects of selling, storing, and shipping goods

Sales law   Sales law is a type of contract law dealt with in the baic set of laws that govern commercial transactions in each state. Sales law deals with sales, which are different from gifts, bailments, and leases.

▸ A **sale** occurs when the title passes from a seller to a buyer for a price.

▸ A **gift** is a transfer of title without expectation of consideration (payment).

▸ A **bailment** transfers possession but not ownership; when you park your car in the parking garage downtown, the garage owner creates a bailment, not a sale.

▶ A **lease** is a fixed-term arrangement for possession and use but not ownership.

Salespeople sell goods and services. The law clearly defines a "good." The Uniform Commercial Code says that "goods are all things...which are moveable at the time of identification to the contract..." (U.C.C. Section 2-105 [1]). Services are another matter entirely. The law has always had a problem distinguishing or separating goods and services. When you buy a sofa, it is clearly a good, it is tangible and moveable. If you are selling paint for commercial application and it does not stick, was the good (the paint in this case) at fault or the service (the painter's application)? Paint and its application are difficult to separate. When the product and service are sold as one, it is called a mixed transaction. Salespeople should know that when making a mixed transaction, they are responsible for both the service and the tangible component of the sale.

The terms of sale are important. They must be fair and not obscure. This means that all parties must understand what they are getting into and that the agreement is free from "unfair surprise." Sales agreements should be free from obscure, small-print, confusing verbiage. The saying "let the buyer beware" is now accompanied by "let the seller beware." Contracts may be modified, remedied, or nullified by courts on the basis of the seller having clauses that "unfairly surprise" the buyer. This has forced some sales contracts, particularly home sales, to be accompanied by a form signed by the buyer stating that he or she has read and understands everything he or she has just signed.

Transfer of title   Title can pass between buyers and sellers in any manner and on any conditions upon which both parties agree. When the title transfers, the ownership transfers. When the ownership transfers, the buyer has the obligation to pay the seller. The big question becomes, *when did* the transfer actually occur? This is particularly important for salespeople to know when servicing customer's claims for damages of goods on delivery.

Transfer of title can occur at time of shipment (this is called a **shipment contract.** If firm A (the seller) has a shipment contract with firm B (the buyer), transfer of ownership occurs when firm A loads its goods on a truck bound for firm B. Ownership transfers when the goods are turned over to the trucker. If the trucker is loading the goods on the truck and breaks some, the loss is the buyer's, not the seller's, even if that truck has not pulled away from the loading dock. If the loaders are the employees of Firm B and not the trucker's or the buyer's, the loss is carried by the seller. Salespeople commonly deal with this type of situation. A destination contract is similar to a shipment contract but merely says the transfer of title occurs when the buyer accepts the goods.

Transfer of title can also occur when a "delivery of documents of title" takes place. This usually occurs in conjunction with taking physical possession but does not have to. Ownership is transferred when the customer accepts the title to the goods, regardless of whether the customer takes immediate physical possession. A house buyer owns the house when he or she signs the closing documents, not when he or she actually moves in.

FOB FOB stands for "free on board." FOB is stated as "FOB origin" or
"FOB destination". "FOB origin" means the buyer pays the freight
charges and accepts the risk of losses from the point of origin on. The
ownership transfers when the goods leave the seller. Losses in transit are
born by the buyer. "FOB destination" means the seller pays the freight
and suffers any losses until the goods are accepted at the buyer's destination. Ownership transfers when the goods are delivered.

FAS FAS means "free along side." It designates where the seller's
obligation to deliver ends. This is a term used when transporting via ship.
The term "FAS vessel" in a sales agreement means the seller has the obligation for the delivery cost and risk of loss until the goods are delivered
"along side the ship." When the seller gets a delivery receipt from the
shipping company indicating the goods have been delivered along side,
the seller's obligation ends. If the goods are damaged loading them onto
the ship, it is the buyer's, not the seller's, problem.

Ex-ship This is the opposite of FAS. This term in a sales agreement
means the seller is responsible for the goods and any losses until they are
delivered to the buyer's location.

CIF and CF These are price terms that in effect make a sales agreement also a shipping contract. If the salesperson quotes a price "CIF destination," that means "cost, insurance, freight to the destination." It is the
seller's responsibility to arrange shipment, load the goods, buy the necessary insurance, and tender whatever commercial paper (invoices, bills of
lading, etc.) to the buyer. If the agreement reads "CF destination," the
seller is responsible for everything mentioned above, excluding the insurance. It is the buyer's responsibility to insure the goods while in shipment.

Performance by the seller and by the buyer In sales law, since a sale is an
agreement or contract, both the buyer and the seller have an obligation to
perform their promises to each other. In the absence of any terms specifying
details, the seller is obligated to deliver the goods in a reasonable time to the
buyer's place of business, unless otherwise specified, and how specified
(shipment contract, destination contract, etc.). The Uniform Commercial
Code does not deal with failure to specify how to deliver. In the case of any
omission regarding delivery time, location, and method, the salesperson
should assume nothing and always get a definitive statement from the buyer
specifying these conditions.

The buyer also has obligations to perform as part of a sale. The buyer
must pay for goods accepted. Under the Uniform Commercial Code, the
buyer has the right to inspect the product for conformity against what was
ordered. The buyer can accept the goods by words, silence, or action. "By
words" means the buyer says he or she will accept the product. "By silence"
means acceptance is assumed if the buyer fails to reject the goods after having
a reasonable opportunity to inspect them. "By action" means physically
taking possession or doing something like reselling the goods. Finally, the

buyer has the obligation to pay the seller "in any manner consistent with the current business customs." Payment is due on acceptance of the goods or taking the title to the goods, unless otherwise stated. In most business sales, payment is handled through billing, with the bill specifying the payment option ("Due on receipt," "2/20 net 30", etc.).

Lack-of-performance claims have a statute of limitations of four years under the Uniform Commercial Code. If the terms of the contract are not fulfilled and either party fails to sue or rectify the situation within four years, then it is assumed that a reasonable time has passed, and claims cannot be made.

Storage of goods When salespeople or customers store a product they own, the risk of loss is theirs. When they store something they do not own, they take on the responsibilities of what is called a bailment. A **bailment** is taking possession and responsibility for something which is not yours. When salespeople agree to store products for customers until they can take possession, the customers are the rightful title holders, but the salespeople are putting their company in the position of being a bailee. This means the selling firm must afford the goods "ordinary care under the circumstances." Problems occur when the goods are damaged in storage. The selling firm, in this example, is responsible for the safekeeping of the goods. The danger salespeople must recognize is that their company's insurance may not cover stored goods that are not owned by the company. A novice salesperson is wise to check the company policy on storage before making such offers, even in good will.

Product Liability

Learning Objective 4: Salespeople must know about product liability and warranties

Product liability is not a type of law but a type of claim. For the salesperson, product liability usually revolves around a product not living up to the claims made for it; it also arises in resale situations when a product does not perform and the final customer raises a claim against the second seller, who then

Storing products for customers creates a legal obligation as a bailee.

What Would You Do If...?

Milt Waldman has been one of your best customers for about five years or so. He has been a regular buyer of the cleaning supplies your firm sells. Since his plant is one of the largest in town, he buys his solvents and detergents from you in 55-gallon drums. His typical order is always around 50 drums a week. That represents about $10,000 a week and makes him one of your most valuable customers. Since your commission is 10 percent, he is a customer you can ill-afford to lose.

It's about ten in the morning, and you are just getting back to the office from an eight and a nine o'clock call when the secretary hands you a phone message. It reads, "Your shipper ran into a bus on the way over to the storage facility on Jones Street. Need the 50 drums of solvent replaced ASAP. Call me with details."

You get out the purchase order, the invoice, and the bill of lading to see what the damage amounted to. Since this is a major account and a major accident, you figure you had better tell Margaret, your sales manager. Going into her office with the paperwork, you recount the story.

Margaret looks at the bill of lading and says, "What is the Jones Street business? The bill of lading and everything else says Apple Street. What is on Jones?" You say, "I do not know, they probably have some storage warehouse they use for temporary storage, I suppose. When can we get this replaced for Milt?" Margaret says, "We will replace it for him today. But he's going to have to pay for both the replacement load and the lost load, you know." Totally shocked, you say, "He is not going to stand for that! He was not responsible for the accident. It was our truck that hit the bus! It is not Milt's fault!" Margaret says, "Read your bill of lading. We were supposed to delivery to Apple Street, not Jones. Even though it was our truck, we are not liable for anything other than getting the load to Apple Street. We are not going to kiss off $10,000 for something we are not responsible for. You handle Milt any way you want to, but that is the policy."

▶ Question: Now you have to go talk to Milt. What would you do?

makes a claim against the original vendor. Product liability involves the laws of consumer protection, fraud, deception, and several others. We will only deal with two aspects of product liability here: warranties (promises made) and liability (who is at fault).

Warranties of all kinds Express warranties can be written or verbal, but in either case, the seller promises what the product or service will do. It is part of the bargaining process and expressly states the performance of the product or establishes the conditions under which the buyer can seek redress from the seller. The **express warranty,** or guarantee, does not have to use the term "guarantee." For example, the label on a weed killer does not have to say it is guaranteed to kill weeds; the fact that it is labelled as a weed killer is enough.

Express warranties do not have to be written and can be conveyed by the seller to the buyer verbally in the terms of the normal presentation. An express warranty comes into existence by virtue of an affirmation of fact or promise made by the seller to the buyer that relates to the goods and becomes part of the basis of their bargain. These statements by the seller create an

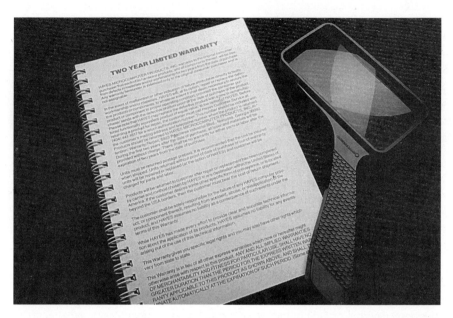

Warranties are promises of performance.

express warranty that the good will conform to the seller's affirmation or promise.

An express warranty can be made in a variety of ways. One of these is for the seller to make a factual statement, such as, "The engine has 500 horsepower." Another is to make a direct promise with respect to the goods, such as "This grass seed is free from weeds." An express warranty can also be based on the instructions of the seller on the use of the product.[5]

During the normal sales transaction, an implied warranty can be created. **Implied warranties** are promises that are obviously and legally present unless clearly disclaimed or negated.[6] The purpose of the implied warranty is to require sellers to purvey goods that are reasonably safe for the purposes for which they are intended. This is why it is extremely important for salespeople to not make claims of performance they are not absolutely certain the product can fulfill.

Be Specific in Making a Warranty

When a salesperson makes a warranty (promise or assurance), it can be written or orally conveyed. Only written warranties are covered by the federal Magnuson-Moss Act, but states have a variety of warranty laws. A salesperson should be sure to do the following when making a warranty:

▶ Be clear and understandable and use terms with which the customer is familiar and can interpret correctly.

▶ Avoid extravagance, puffery, or exaggeration.

▶ State specifically what the product will do, but more important, state what it *will not* do.

▶ Set time limits or use limits, if applicable; everything wears out and breaks if not treated properly or used as intended.

▶ Limit the company's liability by sticking to the company policy, product specifications, and the usage applications the product was designed for.

Liabilities   In product liability, the plaintiff (injured party) bears the burden of proving the product was defective. In many cases, the product was not defective, but the buyer operated it, assembled it, or used it incorrectly. Salespeople should know that they or their firm is liable under only certain conditions:

▶ *The product has been sold in a defective condition.* Since the Uniform Commercial Code does not deal with services, it is difficult to assert a defectiveness in a service, thus the growth of malpractice cases.

▶ *The product is "unreasonably dangerous."* To be considered unreasonably dangerous, the product must present a danger beyond what would be contemplated by the ordinary consumer who buys it with ordinary knowledge common to the community as to its uses and attributes.

▶ *Physical harm has been done to the direct purchaser.*

▶ *Physical harm has been done to the ultimate user where the product has not been substantially changed.* The seller is liable only to the extent the product reaches the ultimate user without substantial change in condition. The lead ore mine is not liable for the death caused by a bullet made from the ore because it has been substantially changed.

▶ *The product is defective.* The seller may still be liable even though he or she has "exercised all due care." What matters is the product being defective, not all the care the manufacturer, vendor, wholesaler, or retailer took. A defective product is a defective product.

When You Act as an Agent or Have an Agent Act For You

Agent's duties to principals   Many selling positions are agent positions, for example, real estate agents, insurance salespeople, and stockbrokers. As agents, salespeople have a special legal relationship with their customers and parent company. An **agent** is a person who legally acts on the behalf of another. In a normal contractual situation, the two parties' duties to each other are bound by the contract. Neither party owes any responsibility to the other beyond what is stated in the contract. Each party is equal under the contract. Under an agency agreement, however, the agent is responsible to subordinate his or her interest to that of the principal, regardless of whether their contract states that to be true or not.

Salespeople acting as agents may not lawfully profit from a conflict between their personal interest and their principal's interest in the same transaction.[7] For example, if you were acting as a manufacturer's rep selling pipes, valves, and fittings to XYZ Engineering, you could not sell those pipes through your brother-in-law's dummy corporation in direct competition with the firm you represent.

Agents act as members of their parent company and as such have a duty under the law to maintain and preserve the confidentiality of information. Parent companies typically reveal their marketing strategies, pricing structures, trade secrets, customer lists, design innovations, and corporate tactics to their agents. These agents have a duty to hold such information in confidence. Agents also have a duty to give information to their parent company. Part of the reason a firm hires agents is to get access to market information in the trade area served by the agent.

As an agent, a salesperson has a duty to keep and render accounts. This simply means the agent is responsible for keeping accurate records of his or her dealings on the parent company's behalf. The agent has a duty to obey and act only as authorized. The parent company authorizes, through its policies, its agents to do and say only certain things. Agents have a duty to not go beyond their authorizations.

Principal's duties to agents Just as the selling agent has duties and responsibilities to the parent firm, so the parent company (principal) has duties to the agent. In general, the principal's responsibilities to the agent run parallel to the agent's duties to the principal firm. For example, the agent's business and reputation are no less valuable than the principal's, thus the parent company must treat the agent in a reasonable, fair, and consistent manner. One area of distinction is the principal's duty to **indemnify**. This means the principal is obligated to reimburse the agent for the expenses incurred in getting it business and making sales on its behalf.

▶ ▶ *follow-up questions*

1. What is the difference between an express and an implied warranty?
2. When merchandise falls off of the truck during shipment to the customer's store, who is responsible for the loss?
3. What duties does the agent owe the principal (parent company)?

The Regulatory Environment

Numerous regulatory agencies of the federal and state governments make their presence felt in the day-to-day activities of business. Some are charged with enforcing the laws governing three important business-related activities that we will focus on here: restraint of trade and concentration of power (monopoly behavior), price discrimination, and deception. Many of the laws discussed here were written in the early part of this century and the last of the nineteenth century. They exist to maintain and protect competition; they also carry heavy penalties for infractions.

Restraint of Trade

Learning Objective 5: Salespeople must know about and guard against restraint of trade, price discrimination, and deception

The **Sherman Act** (1898) made restraint of trade illegal. "Restraint of trade" is not well defined in the statute, so the courts have to decide if the actions of a person in business restrain the competitiveness of a market or another business. The **Clayton Act of 1914** is an encompassing piece of legislation that forbids price discrimination and selling a commodity to a customer on the condition that the customer agrees not to do business with the seller's competitors. Finally, the Federal Trade Commission Act forbids unfair methods of competition and unfair or deceptive practices in commerce. Some of the specific Federal Trade Commission prohibitions are listed in Table 15-2.

Price Discrimination

Knowledge of the law concerning price discrimination is of utmost importance to salespeople. Sales are made many times a day by a single salesperson.

Table 15-2   Aspects of the Laws Preventing Restraint of Trade

▸ *Agreements to fix prices are illegal.* Two competitors cannot come together and agree to charge the same prices. They may by market conditions or circumstance charge the same prices, but to agree to do so is a restraint of trade.

▸ *Exchanging price information may be illegal, depending on intent.* Not every exchange of price information is illegal; however, if that exchange has been done for the purpose of restraining trade and has that result, it is illegal.

▸ *Competitors cannot agree to control output to restrict supply.* Each competitor can choose to limit its own production, but the industry cannot come together and agree to limit production as a group.

▸ *Competitors cannot come together and allocate territories or customers between themselves.*

▸ *Boycotting is illegal.* In the case of the *Eastern States Lumber Dealers Assoc. vs. the United States,* the lumber trade associations published a list of wholesalers and warned their retail lumber dealers not to do business with the wholesalers on the list. The courts held this practice to be an illegal restraint of trade.

▸ *Exclusive dealing contracts are illegal.* Exclusive dealing contracts are ones that say, in essence, "I will sell to you if you agree not to buy from my competitor."

▸ *Tying contracts are illegal.* A tying contract says, "I will sell 100 cases of A to you, but you have to agree to buy 150 cases of B as a condition to getting A." The tying of one product's sale to another is not allowed because it prohibits the free trade of other competitors selling the same product.

The price that is quoted can be illegal and carry a heavy fine. The laws concerning price discrimination are very specific and unforgiving.

The Robinson-Patman Act is a subdivision of the Clayton Act mentioned earlier. It was enacted to prevent the large trusts of the early 1900s from selling at prices below cost to drive small competitors out of business. The heart of the act reads:

> "It shall be unlawful for any person engaged in commerce...to discriminate in price between different purchasers of commodities of like grade and quality...where the effect of such discrimination may be substantially to lessen competition or tend to create a monopoly in any line of commerce, injure, destroy or prevent competition with any person who either grants or knowingly receives the benefits of such discrimination, or with customers of either of them." Robinson-Patman Act, Sec. 2(a).

Note several things about this: First, it makes buyers as guilty as sellers. If a buyer knowingly enters into an agreement to buy goods whose prices have been set in a discriminatory fashion, he or she is just as guilty as the seller. Second, the goods must be of like grade and quality. Pricing Grade A eggs to one grocery store at a dollar a dozen does not prevent the vendor from selling Grade B eggs at a different price. However, in the markets served by that vendor, the vendor must charge all Grade A egg buyers the same price but can adjust for additional costs to serve the customers.

Deception

Deceptive practices are the meat and potatoes of the Federal Trade Commission. Whether deception is accidental or deliberate, it makes no difference to customers who feel they have been deceived. All salespeople should be aware that deception is in the eyes of the beholder and because of that, disclosure of all pertinent facts to the customer is vitally important.

Deceptive practices come in many forms. We will only present the most pertinent. One of the first mistakes a salesperson can make is failing to disclose pertinent facts. An important fact, claim, or piece of information about a product and its performance is important, regardless of whether or not the customer asks about it.

Product descriptions can be deceptive. Describing to a customer (in writing or orally) that a product will "permanently seal that radiator leak" or "guarantee you a healthier more vibrant complexion" is bordering on deception unless the product will do just exactly what is claimed.

Misleading price and saving claims can also be deceptive. The guidelines for quoting a sale price and comparing it to a former price are: 1) the former price must have been offered for a substantial period of time in the near past, 2) the comparison must involve truly comparable products (in saying "This mattress would cost you $500 down the street," the salesperson must really be comparing the exact model and make of the mattress), and 3) false claims of "limited-time offer," "giant moving sale," or "going out of business sale" are deceptive unless they truly reflect the claim.

Bait-and-switch is illegal, as are some free offers. To advertise or promote one product at a low price, then switch the the customer to a more expensive one is bait-and-switch. Free offers are not free if the free product is available only by buying something else at an inflated price. The question becomes, which of the two products in a buy-one, get-one-free deal is the customer really paying for?

▶▶ *follow-up questions*

1. How is price fixing a restraint of trade?
2. What is the difference between price discrimination and deception?
3. What is bait-and-switch?

Ethics and the Salesperson's Integrity

In business today, ethical standards are not what they used to be. What is legal and what is ethical are two separate but sometimes overlapping areas.

Ethics Defined

Ethics is the set of moral principles people have and use to guide their actions in separating right from wrong, fair from unfair. Each person has his or her own perception of what is right and wrong, but in addition, firms and trade associations spell out the ethical standards to which they hold their members. Some firms have considered ethics such an important area of their business that they have established ethics committees and corporate directors of ethics to oversee the creation and administration of ethics policies. As the following Case in Point illustrates, even the most diligent efforts to instill ethical behavior in employees does not always work.

Case in Point

Ethics at General Dynamics

More and more companies are developing and implementing ethical standards. General Dynamics in 1987 had a 20-page code of ethics for salespeople to follow. To oversee a strong commitment to ethics in the salesforce, it established a corporate steering committee to review the

Continued

Dealing with Customers

Learning Objective 6: Ethical situations can arise with customers, employers, and competitors

Salespeople face numerous ethical challenges in dealing with customers. The ones most often encountered are bribery, gifts, influence, and threats.

Bribery Bribery and kickbacks are the everyday stuff of business in some countries. Bribery exists when a salesperson (or buyer) offers an inducement to the buyer (or salesperson) to grant a favorable decision. Bribes occur as outright cash payments or goods and services.

Bribery is both an ethical and a legal issue. In most states, the laws tend to focus on the bribery of public officials, but lately, the legal sanctions around bribery have broadened. Now, people who take a bribe and do not declare the income on their tax return face federal penalties for income tax evasion.

Gifts This is one of the most difficult and common ethical issues that affect salespeople and buyers. When does a gift constitute a bribe? Salespeople often want to express their thanks at the end of the year with a present to the customers that have given them good business. How do they accomplish their goal of expressing thanks and not appear to be bribing the buyer? Also, many purchasing agents expect to get a gift during the holidays.

The problem of the gift can be handled several ways that avoid the ethical (and legal) entanglement. First, the best way to express gratitude is through good service to the customer. Beyond that, salespeople should review their company's policies regarding gifts to customers. Tell buyers they want to express their thanks for the business but they do not want to create any problems and ask what the buyers' company policy is, and follow the policies of both companies. A simple card expressing thanks followed by a phone call will often do more good than any gift.

Influence Salespeople are in the influence business. They try to influence customers to select their products over their competition's or one product over another. Exerting influence is of questionable propriety when it is done in a malicious manner, one that is intended to do harm or gain unfair advantage.

Salespeople represent large, extremely powerful corporations and businesses. Corporations with international connections and billions of dollars in assets have significant economic and political power. In an industrial or business-to-business situation, salespeople should avoid trying to influence buyers' decisions by even hinting that the power of the company will come down on the customer who does not buy. Such "punishment" tactics can be refusing to sell a full line of products, deliberately shipping late or incorrectly, or pressuring others to avoid the customer's products. These actions are an unethical use of influence, and most are illegal under federal law. A threat to cease dealing or refuse to sell should never be made in even the most subtle terms.

Threats Threatening a customer is bad business from any perspective. Customers who buy under duress will be looking for a new vendor at the first opportunity. Threats are an unethical way of getting and doing business. There are many types of threats. Aside from threatening bodily injury, an actionable threat can be threatening to instigate criminal or civil prosecution and to breach a contract. For example, if Francis bought drilling equipment from Clem and found it to be bad equipment, Clem could refuse to give Francis his money back. If Francis says to Clem, "If I do not get my money back right now, I will have my lawyer eat you up in court," this constitutes no threat. If, however, Francis says, "If you do not give my money back now, I will go to the Consumer Protection Agency and tell them you have been using counterfeit parts and tell them you told me I could have my money back whenever I wanted it," this constitutes a threat because Francis has fabricated charges against Clem that are not true. Even though Clem could defend against the suit and probably win, his reputation would be damaged by the accusation that he is a crook.

Salespeople must be aware that there are unethical buyers who will threaten them. They will threaten to cease doing business, to spread lies through the trade, to reject the product based on trumped-up claims of the product being out of specification, and to pass information along to competitors. In such a situation, the salesperson is faced with a dilemma: to buckle under and succumb to the threat or to refuse and chance losing the business. It is better to risk the latter. Threatening buyers are unscrupulous, and if they can do it once, they know they can do it again. To give in is to put yourself on their level.

Dealing with Employers

Ethics are also important in salespeople's dealings with their employer. Salespeople represent their company to the customers. In doing so, they also have a moral obligation to be fair and ethical in dealing with their employer. Four frequent ethical problems are falsifying reports, padding the expense account, moonlighting, and kickbacks or commission splitting. Unfortunately, some salespeople begin their employer-employee relationship unethically by lying on their job applications, a practice the following Case in Point discusses.

Case in Point

Lying From the Start: Falsification of the Job Application

Career fraud is an ethical problem faced by employers and employees alike. If a person would lie about the information on a job application, what else would he or she lie about? Data gathered by Krakower/Brucker International, a major executive search firm, indicates that salespeople are three to four times more likely to practice career fraud than others. It found that over the last 20 years, almost half of the job applicants lied about their salaries and job responsibilities with prior employers. Nearly one-third lied about their educational background.

Some firms check employment application information, some do not. Many executive recruiting firms ask for the applicant's W-2 form. They feel it is the only way of getting accurate income information.

Is dishonesty encouraged? The answer is often yes. One reason is a shortage of competent employees, says Alan Coppage of Industrial Security Analysts. He recounts the stories of firms who have hired "cokeheads," embezzlers, and admitted child molesters who lied on their applications.

Source: Adapted from Liz Murphy, "Did Your Salesman Lie to Get His Job?" *Sales and Marketing Management* 139 (1987): 54–56.

Falsifying reports Many salespeople operate outside of a formal office structure. They work out of their homes or call on accounts in their territories at their own discretion. Sales managers ask for periodic reports identifying who has been called on, how much time was spent, and the outcome of the call. These are called call reports. Some salespeople want to look like they are working harder than they are, so they embellish such reports. This may be as simple as adding a couple of calls that they did not make or staying at home and making telephone calls and counting them as face-to-face calls. Some will even get customers to cover for them by saying a call was made when it was not.

Sales managers are aware of this and often ride with the salesperson through his or her territory. Sales managers who suspect such fraud commonly call customers and ask how a salesperson is doing or, while riding with the salesperson, ask questions about the last call made. The managers quickly learn from the customer's verbal and nonverbal communication cues if the information in the call reports is valid. Turning in fraudulent call, sales, or activity reports often results in firing or formal warnings with subsequent occurrences resulting in termination.

Padding the expense account   The most common unethical behavior is padding the expense account. This is when the salesperson records greater expenses than were actually incurred and involves doing anything from reporting completely false expenses to inflating real ones. Padding expense accounts is unethical and illegal. However, some salespeople rationalize it by saying they really deserve the money because the company pays them so little anyway.

Some firms cleverly make padding the expense account its own penalty. They do this by paying salespeople on net commission, that is, profits from the sale less expenses incurred in getting the sale. This method quickly teaches salespeople that padding simply reduces their reward; therefore, there is no gain from doing it.

In an agent-principal relationship, where the salesperson is a contract agent for a parent firm, the firm has an obligation to pay the salesperson for expenses incurred in selling. If, however, the salesperson is reporting non-existent expenses or inflating true expenses, then the parent firm can take legal action against the agent for fraudulent expense reporting. This is tantamount to embezzlement, which is a criminal offense. Finally, if the padded amounts can be proven, the salesperson could face charges of income tax evasion if the padded amounts were not reported as income.

Appropriate management of an expense account is an ethical responsibility.

Moonlighting Moonlighting is when a salesperson holds down a second job at night or on the weekends. Some companies forbid their employees to work for other firms. At other firms, it makes little difference. In department store or grocery retail sales, little is made of working for another company at the same time. In telemarketing, most of the telephone sales agents only work part-time and hold full-time jobs elsewhere.

Moonlighting becomes a serious ethical concern when the salesperson's second job is with a competitor or customer. An "arm's length" association is best maintained at all times between vendors and customers. Working for a competitor or customer creates a division of loyalty and a conflict of interest. Termination is a frequent remedy employers use to solve the problem.

Kickbacks and commission splitting A **kickback** is an unethical and often illegal payment from a salesperson to a buyer or from a buyer to a salesperson. Consider this example: you come home one night to find your basement full of water. The rains over the last few days saturated the ground and that water has started to seep through your foundation. Your insurance agent tells you to get an estimate of the damages and turn it in. When the repair company's salesperson makes the estimate, he makes you a deal. Since your insurance company only pays 80 percent, he will overestimate the job by 20 percent so you really do not pay anything and he gets the job. This is unethical and is defrauding the insurance company. In most states, kickbacks are illegal. They can also be a violation of the federal anticompetition laws.

Commission splitting is when the salesperson agrees to split his or her commission with the buyer in return for the order. In real estate, for example, a salesperson might offer to split the commission with the seller to get the listing or sell to a certain buyer. This violates the real estate agents' code of ethical behavior and can be a legal violation, depending on the state's laws. It also is contrary to the arm's-length relationship concept.

Dealing with competition The laws define which types of competitor-to-competitor activities are illegal. Making false statements about a competitor or the competitor's products is illegal and unethical. Salespeople must remember that unethical behavior toward a competitor can get their reputation spread around their own industry with dramatic short- and long-term effects. Buyers and sellers work together. A professional purchasing agent works with many salespeople in the same industry. Through the normal flow of commerce, these buyers get to know who the unethical and unprincipled salespeople are. Purchasing agents will work with such salespeople only as a last resort. In the long run, salespeople with a bad reputation for running down the competition may want to change jobs in the same industry, but they may find few job opportunities because of their bad-mouthing.

Dealing With the Opposite Sex: Sexual Harassment

What is sexual harassment?   The victims of sexual harassment can be both sexes, though most predominantly they are women. Sexual harassment is usually considered to encompass all direct sexual advances, including unwanted touching, putting the victim in a compromising situation, and directly attaching job-related rewards to sexual favors (such as, no sex, no promotion). Sexual harassment is more than the overt, unwanted advances from a manager or fellow worker. A sexually offensive atmosphere in working conditions can constitute sexual harassment. Jokes, comments, and the posting of sexually offensive cartoons, among other practices, are forms of sexual harassment. In companies that have federal contracts, such offenses can cause them to lose their contracts or be severely fined.

Sexual harassers tend to fit a general profile: they are married, tend to drink too much, and often have a reputation among fellow workers as not being "well balanced." They come from a background that is sheltered or socially deprived, giving them a narrow mind-set about people in general and the role the opposite sex should play.[9]

◄ ◄ ◄ ◄ ◄ ◄ ◄ ◄
Learning Objective 7: The legal and ethical issues surrounding sexual harassment

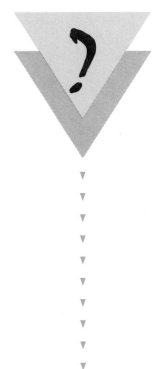

What Would You Do If...?

The Dilemma of Sexual Harassment[10]

A few years ago, Linda, who sells industrial labels in the Midwest, opened a sales office in a suburb of Chicago. One evening, when she was alone in the office packing up for the day, her manager approached her. After some amiable and innocuous conversation, without warning he said, "Kiss me."

"No," she replied.

"Kiss me," he insisted, moving closer to her.

"I am a married woman," she said, backing away.

"So what? I am married, too."

Linda began to feel frightened. Before she could escape, he had her pinned against a wall.

"Kiss me," he said again.

▶ Questions: What would you do if you were new on the job and needed it very badly?

▶ Is a little kiss all that big of a deal?

▶ If your boss made the advance, who would you tell?

▶ What would be the outcome if you were believed? If you were not? Is this incident worth reporting?

Sexual harassment is both offensive and illegal.

How to professionally handle the sexual harassment situation Handling a sensitive situation like sexual harassment can be perplexing. If you are going to complain to the boss, you will need specifics: times, dates, number of occurrences, specifics of who said what or did what. You just cannot waltz into the manager's office and make accusations without proof. Should you decide to go straight to your local federal Equal Employment Opportunity Commission (EEOC) office to file a charge, proof also will be required. If your case is considered and you cannot prove it, a countersuit for defamation of character is always possible. There are several ways to deal with the milder forms of sexual harassment that are direct and get the message across to the offender:

1. *The Direct Approach*. Simply telling the offender to stop and never do it again works. If said forcefully, directly, and while looking the offender straight in the eye, the message comes across loud and clear.

2. *Handle It with Humor*. While it is not a humorous matter, humor often sends just as clear a message as the direct approach. In the box above, the woman approached by her puckering predator simply said, "If I kiss you, I expect you to drop your wife, I will drop my husband, and we'll get married. The only man I kiss is my husband." The woman providing the story stated, "He was out of the office like a bolt of lightning!" [11]

3. *Simply Leave*. When sexual harassment is encountered, a good way to deal with it is simply to state the reason for refusing to continue the encounter with the offender and leave.

4. *Avoid Drinking Alcoholic Beverages*. When drinking, you can lose control of the situation or at least be perceived as losing control.

5. *Don't Listen to Their Sob Stories*. Sexual harassers often use the sob story as a way of inducing sympathy to let them get closer.

6. *Don't Get Too Friendly*. Another preventive measure is not to get too friendly with the potential offender. Keep everything on a business-like basis and avoid the after-hours meetings and dinners.

7. *Avoid Being Alone*. Have someone walk you to your car; do not stay in the office after hours alone; arrange for someone to be at the office or store with you at all times. If a dinner is in the offing, ask the other person to bring his or her spouse along. Overt sexual harassment seldom occurs in the presence of others.

8. *Maintain Independent Transportation*. By having your own transportation and arranging to meet, rather than being driven, a potential arena for sexual harassment is quickly eliminated.

▶ ▶ *follow-up questions*

1. As a salesperson, you want to send your best customers gifts at Christmas as a token of your appreciation. What should you do before sending the gift?

2. What is the difference between kickbacks and commission splitting?

3. Do you feel moonlighting is unethical? Explain why or why not?

4. How would you define sexual harassment? What would you do if it happened to you?

Summary

This chapter has introduced you to some of the many laws and ethical issues salespeople deal with daily. The purpose was not to make you a lawyer or an ethical judge but to give you a glimpse of the broader side of selling, namely the legal and ethical implications of making a sale. Most salespeople get little if any training in the laws that govern their actions in commerce. Unfortunately, most salespeople find out about the laws the hard way, when they or their company faces a suit.

In this chapter, both private and public law were discussed. Private laws govern the actions and relationships between individuals. Public laws govern how salespeople do their business in general. Under private law, torts were explained. The Uniform Commercial Code was cited several times as being the body of laws most affecting commerce (Learning Objective 1).

Contracts and the many aspects of contract law were explained. What makes an agreement a contract, what the obligations of the parties are to each other, and what are the remedies for nonperformance were all presented along with examples. Breach of contract occurs when one party will not carry out his or her end of the bargain. These are important points for salespeople. They make contracts every time they close a sale, yet few salespeople know anything about contract law (Learning Objective 2).

Some of the more commonly occurring legal aspects of the sale, shipping, and storage of goods were introduced. Salespeople are constantly called by customers complaining of incorrect shipments or damaged goods for which they want restitution. Salespeople must know what their company is and is not responsible for in transit (Learning Objective 3).

Liability was presented in terms of product liability and what the salesperson's company would be liable for when a customer complains about a product's lack of performance. Again, as with shipping problems, salespeople are always dealing with customers who claim the product did not do what was promised. Salespeople must know what their responsibilities are to effectively handle such problems (Learning Objective 4).

We concluded the legal portion of the chapter by presenting only the briefest of descriptions of the regulatory environment. Salespeople are under the umbrella of federal and state regulations, particularly in pricing policies and methods and the agreements they enter to do or not do business with customers. The areas of greatest concern to salespeople and their firms are discriminatory pricing and unfair trade practices (Learning Objective 5).

The chapter concluded with a presentation of some of the ethical situations all salespeople confront at sometime in their careers. Expense account padding, falsifying reports, moonlighting, and bribery are all too common occurrences in the selling profession (Learning Objective 6).

A less common occurrence but one of serious personal, legal, and ethical consequences is sexual harassment. A good portion of this section of the chapter was devoted to identifying what it is and how to handle it. This problem was presented so you will understand that it has absolutely no place in a professional sales organization. The legal and personal ramifications for the firm, the harasser, and the person being harassed are far greater than most people realize (Learning Objective 7).

Key Terms

Tort law   The legal duties a person has to another person.

Contract law   The rules governing the agreements people make.

Business slander   Unfair or untrue oral statements made about competitors or their products to a third party.

Business libel   Unfair or untrue statements about competitors or their products that are written in a letter, brochure, ads, sales literature, or other forms.

Product disparagement   The result of untrue or unfair claims made about a competitor's product.

Fraud   Misrepresentation of fact to the point where has a moving influence on the contracting party.

Contract   A "promise or set of promises for the breach of which the law gives remedy, or performance of which the law in some way recognizes a duty." [12]

Breach of contract   One party fails to complete his or her side of the bargain.

Damages   Monetary awards to the injured party. Punitive damages are awarded by the court to punish the wrongdoer.

Specific performance   A mandate from the court to carry out the specific promises of the contract yet unfilled.

Sale   The passing of a title from a seller to a buyer for a price.

Gift   A transfer of title without expectation of consideration (payment).

Bailment   A transfer of possession but not ownership.

Lease   A fixed-term arrangement for possession and use but not ownership.

Shipment contract   Transfer of title occurs at time of shipment.

Agent   A person who legally acts on the behalf of another.

Ethics   The set of moral principles people have and use to guide their actions in separating right from wrong, fair from unfair.

Kickback   A kickback is an unethical and often illegal payment from a salesperson to a buyer or from a buyer to a salesperson.

Sexual harassment   Direct sexual advances: unwanted touching, putting the victim in a compromising situation, or directly attaching job-related rewards to sexual favors. A sexually offensive atmosphere can also constitute sexual harassment.

Discussion Questions

1. Differentiate between libel and slander.
2. What are five ways to avoid misstatements that could get you sued?

3. What four elements must be present for an agreement to be a contract?

4. Is a verbal agreement a contract? Explain.

5. What is meant by "acceptance" when writing and closing a contract for a sale?

6. If a customer signs a contract, is he or she bound by its terms? Explain your answer.

7. When is a contract invalid? Are all contracts enforceable?

8. What is an example of an "implied contract?"

9. What conditions must occur for a contract to be discharged?

10. What would be good examples of "specific performance" and "restitution?"

11. When does a salesperson officially transfer title to a customer?

12. What would it mean if you wrote a contract and quoted the price "FOB origin"? FOB destination? CIF? Who would pay the freight in each case? If you were the customer, which of the above would you want? If you were the salesperson, which would you want?

13. How can a customer accept goods "by silence"?

14. If your firm agrees to act as a bailee for goods you have sold to a customer, what are some of your firm's obligations?

15. Who is liable if you sell a product to a customer and it does not work right?

16. What obligations does a real estate agent have to his or her customers? To his or her agency?

17. Is price discrimination illegal? Explain why it may and may not be.

18. What is the difference between a gift and a bribe?

19. How can creating a sexually offensive environment can constitute sexual harassment?

20. What are some ways to handle a sexual harassment situation?

Application Exercise

Go back and reread the Case in Point about General Dynamics, then answer the following questions:

▶ Are such extensive efforts, like the ones General Dynamics took, really necessary? Why or why not?

▶ What could a small business, say a real estate agency, do to deal with its ethical issues?

▶ Can a firm place so many restrictions on its employees to "legislate their ethical conduct" that the restrictions and guidelines become ineffective?

▶ How would you react if you were a newly hired salesperson for General Dynamics and you were handed a 20-page code of ethics?

▶ Make three random calls to businesses in your area and ask them if they have a written code of ethics for their salespeople. If they do, ask them to send you a copy, then compare what they say. If they do not, compare what your classmates were able to get. Keep track of the number of firms that do and do not have a code of ethics.

Class Exercises

Group Exercise

The class will be divided into the three groups listed below and be asked to choose one of the topical areas under the group's heading:

1. Customer
   Bribery
   Gifts
   Influence
   Threats
   Lying

2. Employees
   False reporting   Padding the expense account
   Moonlighting   Kickbacks or Commission Splitting
   Sexual harassment

3. Competitors
   Price discrimination
   Spreading rumors

The groups will discuss the assigned topic and develop a short plan to deal with it.

The class as a whole will then reconvene to discuss the overall issue of ethics in selling.

Individual Presentation

Assume the role of a lawyer and be prepared to give a short lecture on the section in the chapter titled "Business Communications and the Law."

Emphasize the following, using a specific product or service as an example:

1. What you can and cannot say.

2. What you can and cannot promise.

3. What you can and cannot write.

The class can then evaluate the presentation itself for its clarity, organization, and usefulness.

Cases ▼ ▼ ▼ ▼ ▼ ▼ ▼

The Case of the Cafeteria Plan

Ben Whittaker was an annuity salesman for the American Annuity Company for nine years. Recently, he left American Annuity and accepted a similar position with the Benefit Annuity Company. While with American Annuity, Ben had put in place a tax-deferred retirement program for Central Servicing Corporation, a not-for-profit student loan servicing corporation. William Morris, head of Central Servicing, has been very pleased with the returns received on the money invested with American Annuity and now wants to expand the benefits offered to his employees. He called Ben about the possibility of offering benefits through a tax code-approved IRS 125 cafeteria plan, a program designed to offer benefits on a pretax basis. Ben met with Morris and explained that although American Annity offered no such program, Benefit Annuity did and could serve as the third-party administrator for the total offering of a full range of benefits. While discussing the cafeteria plan, Ben also mentioned that Morris might be interested in considering a change in the retirement program currently in effect. Ben explained that Benefit Annuity was currently paying an interest rate that was one and a half points higher than American Annuity's and that over the long term, this would mean significantly more retirement money for the Central Servicing employees. Also, if both programs were with Benefit Annuity, the fee of seven dollars a month per employee for the 125 plan would be waived.

After careful consideration of the two proposals, Morris decided to install the cafeteria plan and to exchange the retirement program for the Benefit Annuity's program. The main consideration in changing retirement programs was the difference in the interest rates. He felt that the increased rate would offset other features of Benefit Annuity's plan that were not as good as American Annuity's.

All the necessary paperwork was completed over the next three days by Ben and submitted to Benefit Annuity. Upon receipt by Benefit Annuity of the retirement portion of the paperwork, Ben was advanced commissions on the sale in the amount of $5,800, with the balance of $4,200 and the commissions on the 125 cafeteria plan to be paid upon receipt of the first monthly deposits, which were due in 45 days.

Two weeks later, Ben was notified by Benefit Annuity that, due to economic conditions, interest rates on the retirement annuity would be lowered by 1 percent, effective in 60 days.

This case was written and contributed by Charles Burney, San Jacinto College South, Houston, TX.

Questions:

1. Should Ben inform Morris about the pending interest rate change, which will come after the start of the new retirement contract with Benefit Annuity? What factors should Ben consider in making this decision?

2. If Ben decides to disclose the pending interest rate change to Morris, what should his recommendation be regarding the retirement program? The 125 cafeteria plan?

Don't Worry, Ours Works With Their's, So It Will Work in Your Operation

Case

15.2

Marshall Reese buys equipment for Western Slope Sausage Company. It is a small company employing about ten people that specializes in ethnic sausage sold primarily to the Denver market. It only produces about 100,000 pounds of sausage per week, but over its last ten years in business, it has seen sales grow from 500 pounds per week to its present output. And business is still growing. Western Slope wants to expand, but it is limited by its stuffing machine's capacity.

The firm has been shopping for another stuffer. These are quite expensive, large machines imported from Switzerland or Germany. There are domestic manufacturers, but Western Slope's management is leaning toward the imported machines. Marshall let it be known that Western Slope wants an additional machine, and salespeople started calling for appointments to talk to him. After about three weeks of listening to salespeople, Marshall settled on the Magnastuff, a $76,000 machine. Harry Zickler, salesman for Magnastuff, said he thought the Magnastuff would run in tandem with the VEMAG stuffer Western Slope was now using. "After all," said Harry, "I've been in this business for a long time and haven't seen a stuffer the Magnastuff wouldn't work with or outperform." Marshall hadn't either. Marshall had no personal knowledge of this type of machinery and told Harry so when they were closing the deal. Harry was anxious to make the sale and had cut the price by 13.5 percent for Marshall. This price was significantly less than all other vendors were quoting. Harry assured Marshall that the new machine would keep up with its other machine and work well with all the other equipment Western Slope was now using. The Magnastuff would work, Harry assured Marshall, and not to worry, the company would stand behind it.

After two months of operation, the Magnastuff was not keeping up. In fact, it worked so poorly with the existing equipment that it frequently caused stoppages and breakdowns. Marshall called Harry and said Western Slope was dissatisfied. He said it wanted its money back, and if it did not get it back, Western Slope would sue Harry's company.

Questions:

1. If you were Harry, what would you do?
2. Does Marshall have grounds for a suit in your opinion?
3. Did Harry make a (some) mistake(s) in what he told Marshall?
4. What could Harry have done to avoid this whole mess?

To Feather Your Nest or Not? That is the Question!

As a young buyer for a national grocery store chain, Michele had just come from a three-year apprenticeship in one of the company's stores that she had started in straight out of college. Being a buyer was a heady job for the 24-year-old. On an average day, she would spend $300,000 of the company's money buying meat and poultry for the company's divisions around the country. For all this responsibility, the pay was less than fantastic, however; she was making only $13,000 per year.

After two years, she became the poultry buying specialist. Her job was to buy approximately 150 truckloads of poultry per week for the company's many divisions. One day the phone rang. "Michele, how are things going? This is Randall from Southern Poultry. I am going to be in town on Wednesday. Let's get together for lunch, OK?" Michele said, "Sounds great. I will see you then."

On Wednesday, the lunch went off as planned. During lunch, though, Michele got a proposition she did not know how to handle. Randall made her an under-the-table offer. For every load of chickens she bought from Southern, Randall would deposit $150 in a bank account in Michele's name in Arkansas. Michele calculated that at the rate of 50 loads per week (what she was buying from Southern now), that came to $39,000 a year. And there was no risk! No one would know. She wouldn't have to change her buying pattern or do anything that would raise suspicion. She also figured that with her salary of $13,000 and the $39,000, she would be making $52,000 per year. This is more than she would ever make with this company, even as a branch manager in the biggest branch!

Questions:

1. Would you take the offer if you were Michele?
2. What should Michele do? Should she tell his boss, report it to the Federal Trade Commission, or just let it go by as if nothing happened. What would she say if she turned Randall down and Randall went to the company and said *she* asked for $150 per load and he refused?

References

1. William T. Finn, "How to Make the Sale and Remain Ethical," *Sales and Marketing Management*, 140 (1988): 8.
2. Steven Mitchell Sack, "Watch the Words," *Sales and Marketing Management*, 136 (1985): 56–58.
3. Jethro K. Lieberman and George J. Siedel, *Business Law and the Legal Environment* (New York: Harcourt Brace Jovanovich, 1985), p. 144.
4. The Uniform Commercial Code is the body of laws in each state that govern most business transactions. While each state has differing statutes in the code, they tend to be fairly uniform across all states. In this chapter, we will abbreviate the code as the U.C.C. Be sure if you ever have any questions about the code to check with an attorney or read the code in your state.
5. Robert N. Corley and William J. Roberts, *Principles of Business Law* (Englewood Cliffs, N.J.: Prentice-Hall, 1979), p. 314.
6. Ibid., p. 315.
7. Jethro K. Lieberman and George J. Siedel, *Business Law and the Legal Environment* (New York: Harcourt Brace Jovanovich, 1985), p. 812.
8. "General Dynamics Unit Ex-Aide Pleads Guilty to Getting Kickbacks," *Wall Street Journal*, 16 June 1989, p. B-6.
9. Linda Lynton, "The Dilemma of Sexual Harassment," *Sales and Marketing Management*, 141 (1989): 68.
10. Ibid.
11. Ibid., p. 69.
12. Lieberman and Siedel, *Business Law and the Legal Environment*, p. 144.
13. Case provided by Charles Burney, San Jacinto College.

Chapter

16 Managing the Salesforce

Objectives

After reading this chapter, you should be able to:

1. Describe the sales manager's role in the firm's administration and salesforce.

2. List the steps in setting up sales territories.

3. Explain the various tools managers use to motivate their salespeople.

4. Explain how sales managers recruit, select, and train new salespeople.

5. Describe the three major compensation plans for a salesforce, including the advantages and disadvantages of each.

6. Explain why performance evaluations are necessary.

7. Conduct a performance evaluation with an employee that will avoid EEOC problems.

The Professional Selling Question

Sales managers sooner or later run up against the maverick sales-person. How should a manager deal with that person who just won't follow the rules but is a top performer?

Some Top Managers Respond

Mavericks, by their nature, tend to do things their own way, regardless of what managers say. Most managers will agree that the mavericks have tremendous energy and are usually among the best performers on the salesforce. They are, however, prone to be overly independent. Bud Boughton of Legend Technology in Florida says they cannot be allowed to just roam at will; they must be managed. Doug Clayton, a manager for Hershey Chocolate, feels that managers who have mavericks must try to direct their energy; mavericks can be frenetic, but helping them focus their energy will prove rewarding.

The key issue, managers say, is not that mavericks are rule breakers but what rules they are breaking. Gene Russell of Soundesign in New Jersey says that breaking financial rules must be stopped immediately. This can be done through direct intervention, coaching, and retraining. If the broken rules are procedural, many managers feel that may be a signal to review the procedures; they may be outdated and need changing. When faced with rule-breaking mavericks, Terry Gibson of Perceptics Corporation in Tennessee follows four procedures:

1. ask the mavericks if they knew about the rules,
2. work with them on determining both the positive and negative outcomes of breaking the rules,
3. determine what actually will or did occur as a result of the broken rules and implement the necessary corrective action, and
4. monitor to determine if the mavericks have a rule-breaking pattern.

Finally, managers generally feel that mavericks, while they may provide short-term gains, are generally not worth keeping around if they are going to be a sustained problem and make other people have problems. If the mavericks do not eventually conform to the rules and procedures, their actions begin to infect others. Terry Gibson feels that persistent rule breakers won't have the respect of their fellow workers; they can be an undue burden on their co-workers and create dissatisfaction by leading others to question why they should follow the rules. Mavericks can be a source of high productivity, but when their actions become detrimental to customers, the company's image, and other salespeople, they have to go.[1]

Introduction

Sales managers are responsible for everything their salespeople do and for getting them to do it. A sales manager's position is personally and professionally rewarding and often the first step for a salesperson interested in moving into top management. Sales managers are usually selected because they can transfer their knowledge and experience to the salespeople working for them.

The sales manager is the front-line administrator who must see that the salesforce-customer interaction is smooth, trouble-free, and mutually profitable. Sales managers often direct as many as 15 salespeople, who, in some types of sales, may be posted across the nation. The sales manager performs a variety of tasks, most related to administering the firm's policies. Sales managers are accountable for achieving the goals established by top management.

Sales managers have a controlling and evaluating function. They analyze sales and costs and evaluate the people working for them. Such analyses form the basis of their day-to-day decisions, which directly affect their employees' lives, futures, and daily activities. Being a sales manager is rewarding and challenging for anyone whose goal is success, promotion, and professional growth. In this chapter, you will learn about sales managers' responsibilities and how they fulfill them.

The Role of the Sales Manager

Sales managers have many roles: administrators, coaches, trainers, recruiters, disciplinarians, mentors, and salespeople themselves. **Sales management** involves planning, organizing, staffing, directing, and controlling the activities of the salesforce to achieve the firm's goals and enhance the business relationship with customers. The manager's job is to make it possible for salespeople to accomplish their missions and to make sure they understand what their mission is. The sales manager's primary task is to implement the firm's sales program through the salesforce within the constraints of the environment.

Sales Managers Manage but also Usually Sell

Learning Objective 1: Sales managers have a variety of roles

Many, if not most, sales managers were full-time salespeople before going into management. To be tapped for management roles, salespeople must demonstrate the ability to successfully sell and get others to accept their ideas. Firms often identify the salesperson who has the consistently highest sales as a prime candidate for management. Unfortunately, the best salespeople often do not make the best managers. Many salespeople like selling for its freedom—the ability to do it the way they think is best. While some salespeople are good at selling, they do not have the necessary talent for working through others.

A good manager must be able to delegate responsibility to work through subordinates. The firm's sales goals will be achieved only through the cooperation of its salesforce. The two major factors in the sales management success equation are being a good salesperson and being able to communicate effectively so subordinates willingly accept responsibility for performing the duties assigned.

Sales managers usually sell as well as manage, handling only the largest local accounts, often called "house accounts." Managers devote a significant amount of time to these vital accounts and still have time to devote to their salesforce.

Success as a local sales manager typically leads to a regional sales management position. Regional sales managers work less directly with individual salespeople and more with local sales managers. The regional sales manager is responsible for the region's sales goals and the broader operation of numerous local sales branches.

Regional sales managers may still call on some selected customers, particularly large national corporate accounts that have headquarters or major buying offices in the region. Many firms feel it is necessary for their regional managers to deal with large accounts for two reasons. The first is a matter of diplomatic relations. Buyers for large national accounts want to feel like they are dealing with a salesperson "on their own level." They sometimes feel a local salesperson just does not have a broad enough view of the whole picture. Like a foreign secretary of state negotiating with a local town mayor, the same deal may be accomplished, but on the whole, it is better done by peers. Business politics must be played as astutely as governmental politics. Having a local salesperson deal with a large corporate or governmental customer

A Typical Career Path for Outstanding Salespeople

could be interpreted as viewing that customer as insignificant, worthy of no more than low-level attention.

Regional managers deal with the large national customers for a second reason. Large, important customers may need or want special consideration that local sales managers do not have the authority to grant. Large customers commonly ask for special volume price discounts, or they may want special packaging or handling. Japanese car importers can ask for and get special rail cars and port modifications. Such requests are outside the authority of local managers to grant.

The highest level of sales management is that of national sales manager, or vice-president (VP) of sales. The national manager or VP of sales is responsible for setting companywide policy and sales goals and dealing with and through regional managers to accomplish the corporate goals. The national sales manager or VP of sales rarely deals directly with local salespeople or small customers.

Like the regional manager, the national manager will only deal with the largest customers. Even then, the national manager may only get involved in establishing the home-office-to-home-office relationship and negotiating the policies of how the firms will work together, while leaving the day-to-day regional or local account servicing to the field managers.

The national sales manager or VP of sales is one of the firm's most important positions. Subordinates usually reflect or react to management's attitude, style, and vision. National sales managers, then, are the top corporate-level influence on their firm's entire salesforce. They set the tone and direction for the entire salesforce. The national sales manager is one of the firm's most important and influential people. He or she is responsible for the firm's most vital function: generating its income.

The progression discussed here is a typical professional sales career track for a large, national corporation. Most smaller firms do not have so complicated a structure. Many have just two levels, salesperson and manager. In such a small firm, the sales manager would perform all the managerial functions discussed above. The layers of management come about as a firm grows and the number of people reporting to a single manager becomes too large for one person to coach effectively. When the salesforce grows to the point where several sales managers are required, then a person is needed to manage the sales managers, and so it goes. It is important to realize that there is no one best or even most common structure in sales management. The structure and the number of management layers a firm has reflects its needs to direct the salesforce and effectively and efficiently serve customers.

Sales Management Is a "Boundary Position"

Sales managers occupy a boundary position in the firm. They are both managers and salespeople. Occupying a boundary position means the sales managers perform activities that are defined by the expectations and demands of other people. They must try to satisfy the expectations of the firm and the salespeople while responding to the needs and demands of customers or suppliers.

Environments   Sales managers operate in the internal company environment and the external market environment. In the internal environment, top managers, production managers, advertising managers, and the salesforce place expectations on the sales manager. Externally, the sales manager faces the expectations of customers, suppliers, regulatory agencies, and competitors. The job of sales managers is to balance these for the salespeople they supervise, interpret the firm's goals and policies for implementation by the salesforce, and coach salespeople through the maze of the marketplace.

Role perceptions   In this boundary position, sales managers must clearly communicate to the salesforce their role so they accurately perceive what they are supposed to do. **Role perception** is the individual's understanding of what the job entails and how to do it. Research repeatedly has shown that people with inaccurate role perceptions are less satisfied with their jobs and are poorer performers. The manager's job is to translate to each salesperson what the company expects, how to do it, and what the rewards or penalties will be for performance or lack of performance.

Managers coach salespeople on how to deal with the conflicting demands of the company, customers, and family. For example, a customer wants a volume discount and will cancel the order if she does not get it, but the company policy says no discounts. A spouse demands less travel, but increased travel and promotion to manager go hand-in-hand. The manager must help salespeople resolve such conflicts.

Managers need to be good communicators to facilitate everyone's understanding of what needs to be accomplished, how, and when. Doing this also involves their control and evaluation functions.

Control and evaluation   Sales managers span the boundary between salesperson and administrator when carrying out control and evaluation tasks. Managers are charged with monitoring interim sales and cost figures and seeing that below-par performance is corrected, which may involve imposing sales quotas and cost control measures.

Sales managers evaluate salespeople for annual raises, promotions, transfers, demotions, disciplinary actions, or terminations. The company, as well as common sense, dictates that certain behaviors are rewarded while others should be punished. Being late to work and late to appointments must be dealt with firmly and quickly. Dealing with such behaviors is seldom pleasant, but it is part of the job.

Sales managers perform numerous control and evaluative tasks. Two important ones are establishing territories and administering the compensation system. A common way of organizing a salesforce is to define discreet sales territories and assign salespeople to them. By creating specific territories and monitoring what salespeople do in them, sales managers directly track and control their salespeople's performance over specific sets of customers. Territories can be designed around specific products, markets, or geographic areas (the most common basis). Setting up territories is a five-step process, as shown in Figure 16-1 on the next page.

To design and establish sales territories, sales managers first select the control unit, usually counties, cities, or groups of states that form regional sales territories. Before final territorial boundaries are established, the managers estimate the potential or total possible business in that territory that all the competitors will be after. They must design a territory so it has enough business to be worthwhile and support the salesperson. When sales territories

◀ ◀ ◀ ◀ ◀ ◀ ◀ ◀

Learning Objective 2: Five steps to setting up sales territories

Figure 16-1 **Five Steps Used to Design Territories**

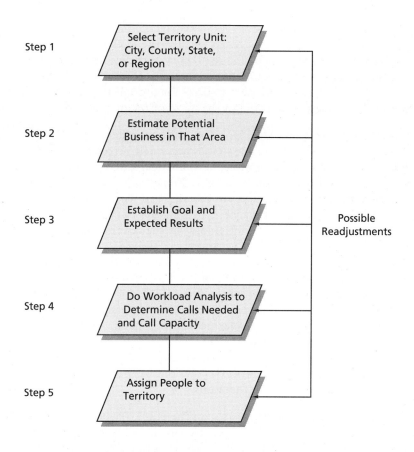

Step 1 — Select Territory Unit: City, County, State, or Region

Step 2 — Estimate Potential Business in That Area

Step 3 — Establish Goal and Expected Results

Step 4 — Do Workload Analysis to Determine Calls Needed and Call Capacity

Step 5 — Assign People to Territory

Possible Readjustments

are too big, either because of inaccurate design or growth, either more sales-people need to be added or the territory needs to be redefined. A territory too big for the salesperson to handle causes frustration for the salesperson and inadequate account service. Both lead to lowered performance, job dissatis-faction, and lost opportunities. A territory with too little business potential will not generate enough sales to be profitable.

Next, sales managers set specific objectives or results that should come from a territory. These could focus on sales volume in units or dollars, ac-count penetration, new accounts, or attacking the competition. The goals for the territory should encompass both long- and short-term objectives. A short-term objective might be an monthly sales quota. A long-term objective could be a targeted share of the market within three years. Managers often set more than one goal for the salespeople in the territories. Multiple goals focus the salespeople's activities on several tasks the firm needs carried out. A typical such set of goals would include sales volume, number of new ac-counts, and calls per day.

After establishing goals, managers perform a workload analysis to deter-mine how many salespeople they need. This involves making three important policy decisions. The first is how to categorize the accounts in the territory. Most often, they are categorized by their sales potential, with A accounts being the largest and C accounts the smallest. Specific target customers are placed in each category. The second control decision is determining call frequency. Managers decide how frequently accounts in each category should be visited. Typically, large accounts are given more attention than small ones. The third decision is setting the policy on call duration. Managers determines how long a typical call on each category account should last. These three decisions tell the salespeople in the territory how to manage their time. By multiplying the number of accounts by call frequency and duration, managers know the necessary workload, or how much time will be needed to adequately cover a territory. At this point, managers may elect to enlarge the original territorial boundary or reduce it.

The final step is to determine how many people are needed to cover the territories. This is done by dividing a salesperson's capacity to make calls into the number of calls needed. Managers must take into account such things as travel time, lunch time, and account diversity when estimating capacity. Clearly, a pharmaceutical salesperson working in Wyoming wouldn't be able to call on as many doctors as a salesperson in Manhattan. An example of a workload calculation is shown in Figure 16-2. After completing the workload analysis, sales managers assign specific people to the territories.

Managers also make control and evaluation decisions in administrating the compensation system and evaluating the salesperson's performance. Later in the chapter, you will read about a variety of compensation systems and how to do a performance evaluation. For now, you should know that sales managers use the firm's compensation system to control the salesforce. Control can be exercised through the amount and frequency of bonuses, sales contests, or merit raises. Rewards, when tied to accomplishment of specific objectives, such as quotas, are powerfully effective in directing and controlling what salespeople do and do not do.

Figure 16-2 Sample Workload Calculation

1. *Categorize accounts by size (A = biggest, B = medium-sized, C = smallest)

   A accounts = *520;* B accounts = *1,020;* C accounts = *1,750*

2. *Determine call frequency

   A = *12* calls/year; B = *6* calls/year; C = *4* calls/year

3. *Determine call duration

   A = *1* hour/call; B = *1/2* hour/call; C = *1/2* hour/call

4. Calculate calls needed

   A accounts: 520 accounts × 12 times/year × 1 hour/call   = 6,240 hours
   B accounts: 1,020 accounts ×   6 times/year × 1/2 hour/call = 3,060 hours
   C accounts: 1,750 accounts ×   4 times/year × 1/2 hour/call = 3,500 hours
                                                    Total = 9,800 hours

5. *Calculate salesperson's call capacity

   Salesperson works 2,000 hours/year but only 70 percent of time is spent in selling; the rest is in travel, meetings, etc. Thus, salesperson has a call capacity of *1,400 hours.*

6. Calculate number of salespeople needed

   9,800 hours needed/1,400 hours of capacity = *7 salespeople needed* for that territory

*Determined by manager as policy or expectancy guideline

Managers Influence Salespeople Through Their Bases of Power

As we noted in earlier chapters, the power to influence comes from referent power, coercive power, reward power, expert power, and legitimate power. It only makes sense, and research supports this, that noncoercive power is directly related to positive performance, while coercive power (managing through threats, deceit, evasion, and subterfuge) is associated with negative performance and the loss of the salesforce's respect for the manager. Such managerial tactics are returned by similar ploys from the salesforce.

▶▶ *follow-up questions*

1. What is a "boundary position"? How does your definition fit the description of what a sales manager does?

2. Do good salespeople make good managers? Why or why not?

3. When salespeople go into sales management, what aspects of the personal selling role do they give up? What aspects of management do they take on?

The Basics of Sales Management[2]

Basic No. 1: Control quality on incoming hires and most management problems won't appear.

Basic No. 2: Don't adhere to "typical profiles" of successful or unsuccessful salespeople in recruiting, hiring and promoting. While the "typical profile" gives an average, everyone is different; be flexible.

Basic No. 3: As a field sales manager, you must get out into the field. Managing from a desk does not work.

Basic No. 4: You must be an internal salesperson first. Everything—policies, procedures, products and programs—must first be sold to the salespeople before they will embrace it and use it.

Basic No. 5: If you want to do something with the whole salesforce, try it out on one or two people first. A small test run often points to problems you do not want to have on a grand scale. It's better to look silly in front of one or two people than everyone.

Sales Managers Are Responsible for Productivity

Sales managers are responsible for achieving the sales, cost, and activity goals set out by top management. They must see to it that the salespeople are well informed on what needs to be accomplished. Top management commonly gives sales managers a target sales figure, then lets them figure out the best way to achieve it.

Who Determines the Goals and How Are They Set?

Productivity goals are generally set in broad terms by top managers. They may simply state the company's goal as being a 2 percent increase in market share or a 10 percent increase in sales. Field sales managers must translate that to individual salespeople. Sales managers use a variety of ways to determine and set individual goals.

Quotas   One way of setting goals is by using quotas. **Quotas** are sales, activity, or profitability thresholds or targets. They may be directed at certain products, a general level of sales revenues, specific territories, or a combination of all three. They may be defined for any combination of specific time periods as well. Activity quotas can be used to manage such activities as setting up displays, calling on new accounts, or making prospecting calls.

Quotas should serve as sales motivators and have a definite reward linked to them. Such a reward could be a bonus, an increased rate of commission, or any of many nonfinancial rewards (promotion, companywide recognition, time off with pay, etc.). It is through this reward that the quota has an impact on salespeople's incomes and motivation. If the reward is highly desired and the probability of getting the reward through attainment of the quota seems reasonable, then salespeople will expend the effort to achieve or surpass the quota. Thus, how high a firm sets its quotas directly affects its salespeople's income, motivation, and morale.

Across-the-board increases   The simplest way to set a sales goal is through an across-the-board increase. This is simply passing along top management's productivity goals in tact to the salespeople. For example, if management says the goal is a 10 percent sales increase, then the field sales manager could simply say everyone in the salesforce must increase his or her sales by 10 percent as well. This might prove easy for someone starting from a small base but very difficult for the top salesperson with a large territory and high sales volume.

Objective-task method   Borrowed from advertising budgeting, the **objective-task method** involves setting goals based on the objective and the tasks needed to carry them out. Going back to our mandated 10 percent sales increase, using the objective-task approach, field sales managers could examine each salesperson's territory potential business and compare it to the actual business coming from it. They would then assign individual performance goals accordingly, based on the salesperson's ability and the existing potential business in the territory.

Management by objectives   Management by objectives (MBO) is a cooperative effort between managers and salespeople. When using MBO, managers let the salespeople participate in determining their own sales quotas or production estimates. The manager could ask each salesperson to estimate what the potential sales would be in his or her respective territories and how much of that he or she would reasonably expect to get. The manager and the salesperson would then meet to establish a mutually agreeable goal, one which meets the company's stated requirements, reflects what the salesperson feels he or she can do and what the manager thinks the salesperson can do. With such a method as MBO, salespeople do not feel the goals set for them have been arbitrarily determined because they have had input into the process. As a result, they will be more committed to achieving the goal. In the process, the salespeople have an opportunity to state their case and managers have an opportunity to explain their own and the firm's requirements. Both are better able to understand each other's position, and they have arrived at a decision both are committed to seeing accomplished.

How Do Managers Instill Productivity?

▶ ▶ ▶ ▶ ▶ ▶ ▶ ▶ ▶

Learning Objective 3:
Managers use a variety of
motivational tools

Managers motivate their employees to be productive. **Motivation** is the amount of effort a salesperson is willing to expend on the job. Some people are more internally than externally motivated. People who are motivated by the satisfaction they get from doing a good job or meeting a challenge have **intrinsic motivation.** People who are motivated by the material rewards they expect have **extrinsic motivation.** Most people are motivated to some degree by both intrinsic and extrinsic rewards; in fact, without intrinsic rewards, people usually become dissatisfied with their jobs, regardless of the type or amount of extrinsic rewards. Sales managers use a variety of methods to motivate their salespeople. Compensation is the prime motivator.

Compensation and incentives   Regardless of how much a person makes, he or she must feel that the system for allocating rewards across members of the salesforce is fair. Fair does not mean everyone must get the same thing. On the contrary, it means people who excel should get significantly higher rewards than those who do not. A system that rewards everyone equally would create a salesforce whose goal would be doing only enough to get by and no more. The details of compensation plans and their administration will be discussed later in this chapter.

Incentives are another form of compensation being used by more and more firms. **Incentives,** which may be financial or nonfinancial, are rewards for accomplishing certain specific goals. Here are two examples of how incentive programs have been successfully used: The Armstrong Tire and Rubber Company spent $2 million a year on prizes for its salespeople and dealers. For selling a prescribed number of tires, salespeople received a comparable number of sweepstakes tickets that increased their chances to win the grand prize of a new Chrysler Laser. Dealers were eligible for prizes ranging from a trip around the world to a Porsche 928. Armstrong salespeople and dealers certainly had a great incentive to increase their sales.[3] A second example is Amerisource, a nationwide computer retailer. Amerisource required its salespeople to simply hit 100 percent of quota to receive a three-day, two-

Salespeople who excel should
be rewarded more than those
who perform only adequately.

night trip to a vacation resort.[4] In the following When Things Go Right segment you can see what happens if incentive programs are not carefully designed and evaluated.

Company X Finally Gives Everyone a Chance

The following case history, based on actual events, illustrates how a special incentive program that has lost its impact can be revitalized by making some critical changes. The company manufactures and sells various lines of office supply, clerical, and related mechanical and paper products. A national salesforce of more than 500 representatives sells all product lines to large, medium, and small corporate and institutional accounts, distributors, and chain and local retail outlets. Product demand varies by region, depending on the concentration of mainline corporate customers (banks, insurance companies, etc.), distributors, and chain retailers.

Current special incentive programs are funded through budgets controlled by product-line managers who establish virtually all program parameters. They use the special incentive programs to compete for the time and attention of the salesforce to accomplish their product-line goals. Most programs pay a fixed amount for each unit of product sold during a defined period or offer a prize or trip to sales representatives who sell the most units or dollars of product during a defined period.

Recently, management has become concerned because a large percentage of the salesforce is not responding well to the special incentive programs. Many salespeople believe that the probable winners for most contests can be identified the day the programs are announced. Since the likely winners vary somewhat by contest, many of the salespeople who stand a chance choose between contests, rather than giving every program their best effort.

Conversely, some of the sales representatives believe they are effectively excluded from all contests. Some have ignored special incentive programs; others carry a deepening resentment that, despite their best efforts, they have little chance of getting into the winners' circle.

After analyzing the special incentive programs, management concluded that significant changes were needed. While sensitive to the product managers' need to get adequate time and attention from the salesforce, management decided the special incentive programs could be best managed in the field. Consequently, these changes were implemented:

▸ Funds for special incentive programs were collectively transferred from product-line management to the sales function.

▸ Specific product-line objectives were included in the goals of the sales function, with senior sales management performance rated in part against product-line achievement.

▸ Regional sales managers, with senior sales management guidance, were given responsibility for developing regional special-incentive programs tailored to regional needs for specific product emphasis.

▸ Performance of regional sales managers was measured, in part, on their success in achieving product-line objectives.

Continued

Nonfinancial Rewards Go a Long Way at Amway[5]

Every rung on Amway's sales ladder is betokened by recognition. To start with, *everybody* gets a pin, no matter how highly or humbly placed in the direct distributor sales force. "It's got to be close to 100% recognition," says Randy Preston, vice president of special projects. "It's an integral part of managing our field sales representatives. Otherwise, who knows they're out there and what they're doing?"

An understandable view, considering that Amway, a marketer of home and industrial products, sells through more than 1 million independent distributors in 40 countries. Most are husband-wife teams who sell directly to homeowners. To handle the far-flung field force, Amway marks every sales step with a sales pin. The higher in rank the salesperson climbs, the more striking and jewel-encrusted the identifying pin. Amway even names the rankings after the emblems: Ruby Direct Distributor, Pearl Direct Distributor, and all the way up the jewelled staircase to the recognition given at their sales pinnacle, the five-diamond pin blazing on the lapel of the Crown Ambassador Direct Distributor.

As the sales achiever's rank increases, so do the kinds of recognition plusses. These are paid speaking engagements, front-page spreads or profiles inside the 700,000-circulation Amway monthly, *Amagram,* publicized business cruises on the 126-foot company yacht *Enterprise II* with an Amway executive host couple, and even a formal portrait in the Amway Hall of Achievement back at headquarters in Ada, Michigan.

Managerial and organizational policies affect motivation   Salespeople's motivation is affected by their manager and the organization as much as it is by any reward system. Two managerial factors shown to be directly related to motivation are closeness of supervision and frequency of communications.[6]

Attaining the right amount of closeness of supervision depends on the person supervised. People whose "locus of control" is internal, meaning they are self-motivated, only need to be given their objective. Then they want the manager to stay out of their hair. Salespeople who have an "external locus of control" want someone to tell them what to do. They are people who need guidance, supervision, and direction. Most people fall somewhere in the middle; they want and need some degree of supervision but do not want the sales manager breathing down their necks.

Frequency of good communication effects motivation   The salesforce that feels its manager is keeping it informed will be more motivated than one that is kept in the dark. Salespeople do not need or want to be inundated with information that does them no good. Frequent communication increases the accuracy with which salespeople interpret their role and helps them understand the tasks and activities they are expected to perform. This reduces role problems, a major factor in job dissatisfaction, quitting, and low performance.

Three organizational factors influence motivation: (1) span of control, (2) influence over standards, and (3) recognition rate. A manager's **span of control** is the number of people he or she supervises. As the span gets too broad, not enough time gets devoted to each individual. This reduces the frequency of communications and the closeness of supervision. Too broad a span of control can have a demotivating effect on the salesforce. Managing a group of eight to ten people is considered normal, but some managers have more and some less.

The second factor affecting motivation is influence over establishing standards of performance. Theory says that the more input individuals have in determining the standards by which they will be judged, the more they will buy into the standards and put out the effort to meet them. In reality, salespeople can only have a limited degree of input. This is particularly true in large corporations where the spans of control can be large and the sales objectives come straight from the top. So, while this is beneficial from a motivational standpoint, in practice, it is sometimes difficult to implement.

The third factor is the recognition rate. The **recognition rate** is the number of times a person gets recognized and saluted for his or her accomplishments. Everyone likes to receive the accolades of his or her peers for a job well done. This is a powerful intrinsic motivator. Like the others discussed, it can be done to excess. Overuse of recognitions, such as the "Salesperson of the Month" distinction, can have a decreasing effectiveness. If a person is

Frequent effective communication from management helps motivate salespeople.

What Would You Do If...?

You have been a sales manager only six months now. You have been familiarizing yourself with the salespeople and their territories and with the policies and procedures of the former manager. She started running monthly sales contests 14 months ago, and since you have been in the job, you haven't changed this.

During the time the monthly sales contests have been in operation, M. F. Maxwell has won them 10 out of 14 times. After looking over the sales figures, you observed that for the first few months of the contests, everyone's sales increased. After Maxwell won the contest for the first four months in a row, you noticed that his sales had stabilized and remained fairly constant. Also, the sales of the other people increased for a while, then fell off. They are now showing little response.

▷ Questions: What has happened to cause the contest to fizzle?
▷ Why do you suppose the previous manager let things go on like that?
▷ What will you do about this?

always recognized as the "Salesperson of the Month," the recognition loses its sparkle. It also has a demotivating effect on those who are not recognized.

Sales managers are constantly looking for new motivational techniques that will spark that extra productivity from the salesforce. There are as many possibilities as there are creative managers. Professional assistance is also available from incentive and motivational companies that specialize in providing motivational speakers and designing contests and incentive sales programs.

▶▶ follow-up questions

1. What are quotas and how do sales managers use them?

2. What is the difference between intrinsically and extrinsically motivated salespeople?

3. How are span of control and frequency of communications related?

Sales Managers Recruit, Select, and Train

▶ ▶ ▶ ▶ ▶ ▶ ▶ ▶ ▶
Learning Objective 4: Sales managers are often responsible for recruiting, selecting and training new salespeople

Sales managers recruit, select, and train salespeople. Done correctly, recruiting and selecting prevent many long-range personnel problems. It is far easier to spend more time up-front in recruiting and selecting than it is to try to correct problems caused by a person who is wrong for the job. Many managers feel recruiting and selecting form the real heart of their job. Often, however, managers are not trained in these functions and are under pressure to fill a position as quickly as possible. The combination of these two deficits results in hiring someone who managers *hope* will turn out OK.

Recruitment and selection decisions are the most important and far-reaching a manager makes because its people are the most important asset the firm has. Every CEO, company president, and general manager started out as someone's new hire, so when making a hiring decision, a sales manager may be hiring a future CEO!

Recruiting and Selecting Salespeople

Recruiting and selecting need to start out right and proceed correctly to achieve the desired end. **Recruiting** is the process of soliciting names for the candidate pool. **Selecting** is the process of screening the candidates in the pool to find the best one(s). These are two distinct and separate functions that must work in concert to be effective. Table 16-1 lists the steps in recruiting and selecting that will be discussed in detail.

Step 1. Review organizational goals and objectives The first step is to **review the organizational goals and objectives.** The purpose of the review is to make sure the newly hired people will fit into the firm's long-range development plans. For most managers, this takes minimal time and effort because they are already familiar with the goals and objectives. If a firm is looking to expand its product offering, increase its penetration into new markets, or develop a specialized area, such as an international market, then a review is in order.

Step 2. Do a job analysis **Job analysis** is the systematic investigation of a job's tasks, duties, and responsibilities, along with the review of the knowledge, skills, and abilities needed by someone to fill the job. Many job analyses are simple; the sales manager determines what the new salesperson will be held responsible for and outlines the tasks necessary for success.

Job analyses should be done periodically, since the specifics of most jobs change over time. The analysis should reflect what the job currently entails and what will be needed in the future. All too often, the job analysis is done to match what the existing person in the job is doing, not what the person *should be* doing. Without the long-range perspective fully in view, job analyses can, over time, result in jobs changing from their original purpose to what their occupants make them into.

Step 3. Do a personnel audit A **personnel audit** compares the number and type of people currently in the job to the type of person who should be in the job. The purpose of the audit is to continually ask the questions, "Do

---

Table 16-1	**The Steps in Recruiting and Selecting**
Step 1.	Review Organizational Goals and Objectives
Step 2.	Do a Job Analysis
Step 3.	Do a Personnel Audit
Step 4.	Write, Review or Update a Job Description
Step 5.	Post Job Announcement
Step 6.	Eliminate Unqualified Applicants
Step 7.	Screen Candidates
Step 8.	Interview the Prime Candidates
Step 9.	Make the Offer
Step 10.	Complete the Paperwork to Close the Hiring Process

we need more of the same type of people in this job, or do we need something different?" Technological changes and new applications might dictate a person in the job have good computer skills and a familiarity with medical terminology, both of which current people in the job do not have.

Step 4. Write a job description   A **job description** is a written summary of the tasks, duties, and responsibilities of the job. Job descriptions are important because they outline the job holder's role. Unclear, ambiguous, and vague descriptions are a major cause of role problems for new hires and ultimately a reason for some of the personnel problems managers have.

Job descriptions form the basis for evaluating a person's work performance. A person's performance should be evaluated against the details of the job description. Managers can get into trouble if they hire someone who understands the role and nature of the work through the job description but is later required to do things not listed in that description. The employee may be rated poorly at evaluation time because he or she didn't perform adequately in the manager's eyes, even though he or she may have been doing exactly what the job description stated.

Job descriptions result from job analyses. If job analyses are not done and periodically updated, the job descriptions will be inaccurate and obsolete. Inaccurate and obsolete job descriptions are often the basis for judgments against employers or managers in discrimination suits. Thus, for the good of the employee and the manager, job descriptions need to be very clear, specific, and functionally oriented.

Step 5. Post job announcement   To get enough names into the applicant pool, the job must be adequately posted. **Job posting** means advertising and informing all possible qualified applicants of the job's availability. The posting should be adequate to ensure that everyone who is qualified and might be interested in the job is informed. Job posting can be done internally and externally. Many firms open the application process to internal candidates before going to the outside. Newsletters, bulletin boards, and personnel department hot-lines are common ways of informing internal candidates of an opening. External posting is usually done through newspaper and trade magazine ads, word of mouth, professional associations, or school placement offices. The extent of the response depends largely on the reach and frequency of the ads.

Posting sales job announcements can be a double-edged sword. Firms with government contracts, public institutions, and governments must follow the spirit and letter of federal, state, and local affirmative action laws and federal Equal Employment Opportunity Commission (EEOC) regulations. This assures nondiscrimination and that access into the pool of applicants has been open to everyone. However, widespread posting often has the effect of generating such a large number of applicants that it chokes the recruiting process.

Job posting should generate a large enough pool to provide a high-quality, representative group to choose from but not one so big that the process cannot be efficiently carried out. The solution to this dilemma lies in the job description. If written specifically, the job description will target the key skills, experience, talents, and education applicants need. A job announcement built from this should draw the right type of person and discourage the unqualified. If the description is written so generally that anyone fits the bill, the manager will be flooded with applicants, most of whom won't qualify. This wastes everyone's time and money.

Step 6. Eliminate unqualified applicants   This is the simple process of comparing the qualifications set forth in the job description against what applicants have to offer. Managers do this on a cursory basis first. If the job announcement calls for a college degree, then everyone who applies and has no degree is eliminated on the first pass.

Step 7. Screening candidates   Screening candidates is done through five vehicles: application forms, face-to-face interviews, reference checks, physical examinations, and formal testing. We will take a detailed look at the interview in the discussion of Step 8.

Application forms   The first screening is through the application form. A person must fill out an application form to be considered. Many potential candidates are eliminated immediately because they incorrectly complete the application. Others are eliminated for spelling or grammatical errors. Still others omit entire sections of the application so the manager has no alternative but to reject the applicant for failing to follow directions or submitting an incomplete form.

Reference checks   Reference checks should be done on all applicants but most certainly on the finalists. While reference checks can be time-consuming, they allow managers to probe into the work behaviors and previous experience of applicants. Also, it is an unfortunate fact that some people lie about previous work experience, job responsibilities, and education. Such people operate under the assumption that nobody checks references so they think they can just make some up, and of course, the better sounding they are, all the better the chances to get the job. Reference checks quickly uncover such deceptions.

Case in Point

Checking References: Should You or Shouldn't You?

Managers and recruiting specialists generally agree that checking references should be part of the hiring process. Anyone doing the checking must know what to do and how to do it. The law protects applicants from unfair inquiries, just as it protects them from unfair hiring practices. Keep the following in mind:

▶ Applicants must be considered as they "presently exist." You cannot ask an applicant's physician about previously existing ailments. You cannot ask if someone has been arrested, but you can ask if the applicant has any previous convictions.

▶ Asking about age or national origin is discriminatory and should be avoided.

Continued

Physical examinations   Some sales jobs have physical limitation requirements and require physical exams because insurers won't pay for preexisting conditions. In some fields, physical examinations are necessary to identify a person's susceptibility to or existing conditions involving certain diseases. In industrial sales, certain allergies or asthma may be disqualifying factors if the job entails working in the dusty conditions of a mine, factory, or assembly plant.

Formal testing   The battery of tests an applicant takes could include intelligence, aptitude, or personality tests. Intelligence tests attempt to measure the ability of people to learn, reason, draw conclusions, and express their general knowledge. Aptitude tests seek to measure specific skills or abilities. For example, people being considered for the job of a computer salesperson might be tested for their ability to think logically and sequentially from a set of facts down to a specific conclusion. This would give the recruiter an indication of the applicants' innate talent for understanding computer logic and systems design. Personality tests are often used to determine if the applicant's personality is conducive to working with certain types of people or working situations. Some sales jobs require salespeople to be part of a team, while others require the person to be an individual who is able to work alone. Putting people in an environment not suited to their personality type spells trouble for both them and their manager from the very beginning.

There is a strong and continuing debate over the ability of such tests to predict success. Tests have come into and out of favor over the years. Some firms believe strongly in their use, while others do not.

What a manager should recognize about formal testing is that regardless of what test is used, the testing process must be fair and equitable. The results must be consistently interpreted, and the tests must be uniformly applied to all applicants. Similarly, passing scores must be the same for all applicants for the same job. While the EEOC does not ban testing, it does require that if testing is going to be part of the screening process, it be part of the process for everyone.

Personal interviews may be highly structured or very informal

Step 8. Interview the prime candidates The interview process may be as simple as an informal discussion with the candidate or as complicated as a three-day process involving interviews with managers and corporate executives, plant tours, and customer visits.

Personal interviews may be highly structured or very informal. Managers should be prepared with a list of questions to be answered by the applicant. In the **structured interview,** managers use a list of standardized questions to get the same information from all applicants. In **nondirective interviews,** managers ask applicants broad general questions for the purpose of getting them to talk about themselves or the job. The results of nondirective interviews are harder to interpret than those of structured interviews because of the nature and variety of answers. With such interviews, comparability between candidates is difficult to assess. Nondirective interviews are often merely a cover-up for an ill-prepared interviewer or one who is untrained and simply does not know what specific questions to ask.

The **stress interview** is designed to create anxiety in candidates to test their response to pressure and ability to think on their feet. This is a poor interviewing technique producing little, if any, good information. It generally backfires and creates such a negative image for the interviewer that good candidates are driven off. Some managers think it is a way to weed out the faint of heart, but in reality, it simply creates ill-will and bad feelings from the start.

Step 9. Make the offer Once the ideal candidates are identified, managers need to make the formal offer. This should be in writing and should outline the terms of the employment arrangement and provide the candidates with specific information. It should tell them when they will start, where they should report for their first day, who they should report to, and what will be their compensation and benefits package. While a verbal offer is almost always extended in advance of a formal written offer, having everything written out protects both parties.

Step 10. Complete the paperwork to close the hiring process There is always paperwork to complete that closes the hiring process. This is simple and usually amounts to having the new hire complete insurance, retirement account, and income tax forms. Many firms will send these papers to new hires before they even report for the first day of work. Others have new people complete all the paperwork on their first day of work. Once this step is completed, the hiring process is over; the job is listed as filled with the personnel office and removed from the posted list.

Field Sales Training

Sales managers do a significant amount of training in most companies. Many new hires go to company sales training sessions that feature formal classroom instruction on such things as product knowledge, company policy, and selling skills. After this, sales managers give these people their indoctrination in field sales. During this training, new salespeople get to apply what they learned in formal training sessions. The training continues while the new employees gain actual selling experience under the watchful eye of the trainer or manager. The trainees usually are on their own part of the time and with the trainer the other part. Through such an approach, trainees gain the experience necessary yet have the assurance that an experienced salesperson is backing them up.

In some large field sales offices, someone other than the sales manager is the designated trainer. Some firms have taken the innovative approach of using retired salespeople, many of whom have been trainers, to do field sales training. Navistar International Transportation (formerly International Harvester) used "recycled salespeople" to train its salesforce and in doing so was able to close six very expensive training facilities.[7]

 *follow-up questions*

1. Why should sales managers do a job analysis before recruiting? Should a job analysis always and only be done before recruiting begins? Explain.
2. What are the ways a manager screens job applicants?
3. Why is a stress interview dangerous for a firm to use?

Sales Managers Administer the Compensation Package

▶ ▶ ▶ ▶ ▶ ▶ ▶ ▶ ▶
Learning Objective 5: Compensation packages typically include straight salary, straight commission, or some combination of salary and commission

In sales, the paycheck may only be part of the salesperson's total compensation package. The **compensation package** represents the sum of all the financial and nonfinancial rewards given to salespeople for accomplishing the objectives defined by the firm. In many companies, the value of the nonfinancial rewards may equal the financial rewards.

Components of a Compensation Package

Benefits Rewards vary with the selling job. Financial rewards may be direct or indirect. Many firms provide their salespeople with a car, extensive health and life insurance, and tuition reimbursement. Contributions to retirement plans may also be part of the total compensation package. Some

Table 16-2   Benefits Typically Given to Salespeople

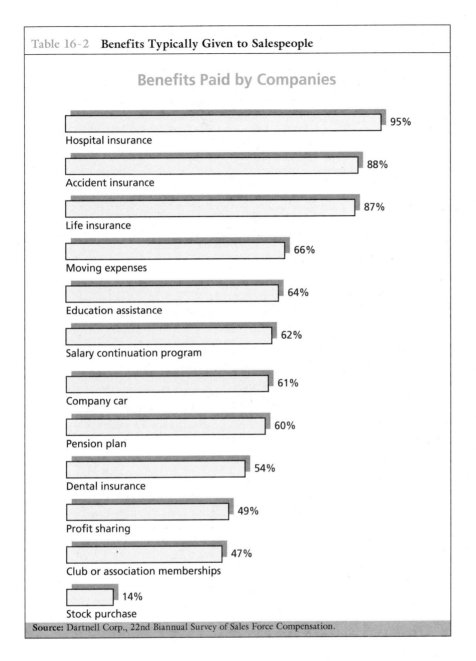

Benefits Paid by Companies

Benefit	Percentage
Hospital insurance	95%
Accident insurance	88%
Life insurance	87%
Moving expenses	66%
Education assistance	64%
Salary continuation program	62%
Company car	61%
Pension plan	60%
Dental insurance	54%
Profit sharing	49%
Club or association memberships	47%
Stock purchase	14%

Source: Dartnell Corp., 22nd Biannual Survey of Sales Force Compensation.

typical benefits provided to salespeople are shown in Table 16-2. Typically, benefits are worth about 25 percent of the salesperson's annual income. Health insurance alone can be worth thousands of dollars a year.

Six Principal Objectives of a Compensation Plan

1. *It should provide income and security.* Today, job security is becoming as prominent a negotiating item as pay.
2. *It should be an incentive itself.* The plan should motivate employees.

Continued

3. *It should be understandable.* A compensation plan with numerous goals, contests, levels of commission, and so forth can become so cumbersome that salespeople may not know how much of their pay came from what part of the plan. Plans that cannot be understood can cause problems.

4. *It should be flexible.* A plan should allow for changes in business conditions.

5. *It should be economical.* From the firm's perspective, it should reward the salesperson, but it should reap more in profits than it costs.

6. *It should be fair.* Everyone need not make the same as everyone else, but salespeople should be rewarded in a way that is commensurate with their performance.

Compensation Methods

Compensation plans are usually one of three types:

1. straight salary,
2. straight commission, or
3. some combination of salary and commission.

Other compensation tools will also be discussed later; the three mentioned here comprise the most common plans. Over the years, the trend has been away from both straight salary and straight commission and toward combination plans. Table 16-3 identifies the various methods of compensation across five industry groups.

Straight salary   Straight salary plans pay a fixed sum of money to salespeople at regular intervals. Salaries are annually adjusted up or down, after managers reflect on the entire sum of each salesperson's annual performance. Sales trainees who lack experience and who may not yet have had the training necessary to be successful at some type of commission selling usually start with straight salary. Straight salary is common for salespeople primarily engaged in:

▶ Servicing accounts

▶ Opening new accounts

▶ Selling products that have long sales cycles

▶ Missionary selling

▶ Consumer packaged-goods industry and retail sales where advertising and sales promotion carry most of the actual selling job

▶ Team selling

Straight salary plans have the following advantages and disadvantages:

Advantages

▶ Easy to manage; the firm knows what it has to pay each month, and the salespeople know what they will get each month.

▶ Provide security and freedom from fluctuations that can occur when earnings are based on a percentage of sales.

Table 16-3   Methods of Compensation by Industry Group

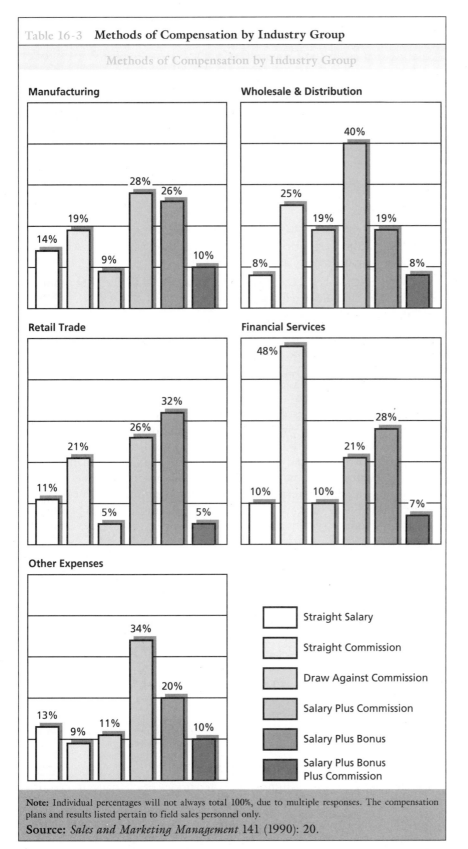

Methods of Compensation by Industry Group

Manufacturing

14%   19%   9%   28%   26%   10%

Wholesale & Distribution

8%   25%   19%   40%   19%   8%

Retail Trade

11%   21%   5%   26%   32%   5%

Financial Services

10%   48%   10%   21%   28%   7%

Other Expenses

13%   9%   11%   34%   20%   10%

☐ Straight Salary

☐ Straight Commission

☐ Draw Against Commission

☐ Salary Plus Commission

☐ Salary Plus Bonus

☐ Salary Plus Bonus
   Plus Commission

Note: Individual percentages will not always total 100%, due to multiple responses. The compensation plans and results listed pertain to field sales personnel only.

Source: *Sales and Marketing Management* 141 (1990): 20.

- ▸ Provide a general and diffused type of motivation. Salespeople may sell a broader, more profitable mix of products.
- ▸ Salary expenses for the firm are easy to forecast and budget.
- ▸ Salespeople can shift from territory to territory or market to market secure in knowing what their income will be.
- ▸ Selling costs as a percentage of sales are low when sales are high (which is, of course, reversed when sales are low!).
- ▸ Reward nonselling activities, such as servicing, missionary sales, and prospecting, that may be a big part of the job.
- ▸ Attractive to people just starting out in sales.

Disadvantages
- ▸ Reward time spent, not necessarily performance.
- ▸ Limit the incomes of high-performing salespeople, who might sell more if their pay were directly related to their sales.
- ▸ Salary expense is a fixed cost to the firm, unaffected by the sales or profits generated by the salesperson.
- ▸ Tend to be favored by underachievers.
- ▸ May be a demotivator for good salespeople as they see underachieving salespeople being paid the same as they are.
- ▸ No incentive to improve performance, only to maintain performance.

Straight commission   In a **straight commission** plan, pay is a predetermined percentage of a "base." This base can be sales (the most common base), profits, or units of product. With straight commission, salespeople's earnings are directly tied to their productivity. This direct link makes it the compensation plan preferred by the best salespeople and their managers. In selling real estate, stocks and bonds, and many industrial products, straight commission is a popular form of compensation. Commission rates vary by product and industry but range from under 5 percent to over 20 percent.

Straight commission plans have the following advantages and disadvantages:

Advantages
- ▸ Commission furnishes a direct and powerful incentive.
- ▸ Easy to administer.
- ▸ Firms know what their selling cost as a percentage of sales will be.
- ▸ Attractive to the best performers on the salesforce.
- ▸ No ceiling on earnings.
- ▸ Cost is variable and thus can allow for a lower breakeven point.

Disadvantages
- ▸ Incomes of salespeople may fluctuate dramatically.
- ▸ Do not reward for nonselling activity.
- ▸ Not attractive to people starting out in sales.
- ▸ Salespeople may resist realignments in territories or changes in territorial assignments due to potential changes in sales and thus their earnings.
- ▸ No floor on earnings.

▷ Turnover tends to increase when business conditions are poor.

▷ Salespeople may see themselves as independent and have less loyalty to the firm.

Case in Point

Commission Selling Spreads to Department Stores

"There has been some shift in the past few years" from straight salaries "to more incentive pay plans, and we expect the trend will continue and may accelerate," says Phil Johnson, personnel vice president of Marshall Field's. The chain experimented with higher commissions last Christmas. Bloomingdale's switched to commissions three years ago.

Merchants see a double gain. Commission spurs "sales associates," as the store prefers to call them, to offer better service. And they help attract better personnel. It's not unheard of for successful salespeople to earn more than $60,000 a year, says Patricia Chadwick, manager of Bloomingdale's Chestnut Hill, Massachusetts, store. Neiman-Marcus contends that, with its commission structure, it rarely looses sales associates to other stores.

Source: *Wall Street Journal,* 21 March 1989, p. A-1.

Combination plans Many firms use a combination of both salary and commission. When the sales position requires little creativity or deals with simple types of products that do not require any technical expertise and have a short selling cycle, salary makes up the largest portion of the combination. Selling greeting cards or candy to retailers would be good examples of this.

When selling involves more complex negotiations, greater creativity and technical expertise is required, so the tendency is to have more of the compensation based on commission than on salary. By using a combination of salary and commission, the firm can reap the benefits of both while minimizing the problems with either.

Drawing accounts The drawing account is still another compensation plan. The **drawing account** is a periodic monetary advance to salespeople to be deducted from the commission they will eventually earn. In this system, the company in essence "loans" salespeople money until their commissions are large enough to pay the company back. In industries where sales are cyclical or seasonal, the drawing account assures the salespeople of a steady income. From the company's perspective, it pays the same amount on sales regardless of whether it is in the form of commission or draw. For the salespeople, the draw represents a minimum guaranteed income. Let's see how a drawing account works.

In the following example, three salespeople's performance in June and July are listed. They all receive a 5 percent commission on sales or a $300 draw against future commissions, which ever is larger. This means their firm, XYZ Inc., pays either the calculated commission, or $300 per month, whichever is larger. If a salesperson's commission totals $150 for example, XYZ would "loan" that person $150 to come up to the $300. In the next month, if the salesperson's commission were $800, XYZ would deduct the $150 it loaned.

Drawing Account Calculations

Allen	Brown	Cooper
June sales = $6,000 Commission = $300 Is commission greater than or equal to $300 draw? Yes	June sales = $0 Commission = $0 Is commission greater than or equal to $300 draw? No	June sales = $5,000 Commission = $250 Is commission greater than or equal to $300 draw? No
Allen gets $300 commission check and no draw.	Brown gets a $300 draw against future commissions.	Cooper gets $250 in commissions and $50 against future commissions.
July sales = $10,000 Commission = $500 Is commission greater than or equal to $300 draw? Yes Allen gets $500 commission check and no draw.	July sales = $12,000 Commission = $600 Is commission greater than or equal to $300 draw? Yes Brown pays back $300 loaned in the form of a draw and for July gets a $300 paycheck.	July sales = $10,000 Commission = $500 Is Commission greater than or equal to $300 draw? Yes Cooper pays back $50 and for July gets a $450 check.
XYZ has paid out $800 on $16,000 in sales, or 5 percent of sales.	XYZ has paid out $600 on $12,000 in sales, or 5 percent of sales.	XYZ has paid out $750 on $15,000 in sales, or 5 percent of sales.

What if the salesperson quits before ever making enough in commission to repay the draw? Firms can either sue the salesperson for the money or absorb the loss as a cost of doing business. Most firms do the latter! To conclude the explanation of drawing accounts, let's identify their advantages and disadvantages:

Advantages

▶ Stabilize salesperson's income at least at a minimal level

▶ Protect salesperson from unexpected downturns in business

▶ Represent a variable cost to business, thus helps keep the break-even point low

▶ Easy to manage

▶ Easy to understand

Disadvantages

▶ Salesperson gets paid even for poor performance

▶ Firm must absorb the amount paid out in draw if salesperson quits without generating enough commissions to repay the firm

▶ Doesn't provide a strong incentive to improve performance, particularly if draw is set too high

Individual bonus Another form of financial reward is the individual bonus. A **bonus** is a lump-sum payment to the salesperson for accomplishing a predetermined level of sales. The amount of the bonus may be predetermined by management and communicated to the salesforce, or it may be subjectively administered. In the former case, the salespeople would know that accomplishing a certain level of sales would get them a particular bonus; in the latter case, the bonus would be a surprise. By using a bonus in conjunction with a salary, companies selectively reward individual performance and overcome some of the problems of the straight salary system.

Expense allowances **Expense allowances** are provisions for travel and other business expenses incurred by salespeople. Some firms elect to pay expenses on a per diem basis. This means they pay a fixed amount per day for expenses. Should salespeople spend more than the per diem, it will come out of their pocket. This encourages salespeople to control expenses carefully and affords the company a rigid control on its costs of selling.

Another form of expense allowance is payment for predetermined expense items. Some firms only pay for meals and lodging and not for entertaining. Other firms will pay for entertaining as well. In selling jobs requiring extensive travel, firms commonly pay for all airfare and accommodations, plus any other travel-related expenses. For sales jobs requiring extensive travel in a local territory, firms usually provide a car at no cost to the salesperson and pay for all of the fuel and maintenance. Some firms provide a mileage allowance to salespeople for using their personal car on the job. There are many variations, and each firm will have its own policies for expense allowances.

Special prizes **Special prizes** are monetary amounts or valuable merchandise used to reward the winners of sales contests and other special competitions. The use of prizes varies from firm to firm; some never use them, while others use them continuously. Special prize awards are excellent motivators for very short-run efforts or can be used as long-term motivation tools when awarded monthly, quarterly, semiannually, or annually. The variety is endless.

Profit sharing **Profit sharing** is a system where company profits are divided among eligible recipients. To be eligible for profit sharing, most firms require employees attain a managerial level position and serve a prescribed number of years with the company. Profit-sharing plans usually are offered to the best salespeople and offer a long-term motivation. They are often seen as a way to build up a retirement fund.

▶ ▶ *follow-up questions*

1. What is generally included in a salesperson's compensation package?
2. In your opinion, what is the biggest advantage of straight commission plans? The biggest disadvantage? Justify your answer.
3. Why would a firm use a drawing account, and why would salespeople want it?

Evaluating Salespeople— The Hardest Part of the Job

Performance management is the ongoing process of setting goals, evaluating performance against them, and giving the coaching necessary to both motivate people and keep them on track. The evaluation process is the vehicle for performance management. Evaluating salespeople is a tough job. No one likes to deliver bad news, yet every sales manager has to do it sometime. Delivering good news, such as a significant raise, a promotion, or a bonus, is a rewarding experience for managers and employees.

Evaluating salespeople must be done correctly and with several things in mind. First, all employees need periodic reviews to confirm they are on the right track. Second, most people appreciate a review that tells them if they are not. No one likes to put in extensive sales time only to find out that his or her performance is not what the manager wanted or expected. Third, people generally want to do a good job and see progress in their careers.

Why Managers Don't Like to do Performance Evaluations[8]

1. Most people do not like to sit in judgment.
2. Managers risk offending someone whose cooperation they need.
3. If managers' people fail, it is partly the manager's fault.
4. Managers fear EEOC complaints and their accompanying investigations.
5. Tasks are often hard to measure or quantify.
6. Managers usually have had no input into the system used for evaluations, and it may be highly flawed. The company dictates the system used.
7. There could be a poor match between what the appraisal systems focuses on and what the person really does.
8. Managers often must evaluate people they have very little contact with.
9. Only 25 percent of managers doing performance appraisals have ever had any training in doing them.

Why Periodic Evaluations Are so Important

Learning Objective 6:
Numerous reasons for doing performance evaluations

Part of every manager's job is to develop his or her employees and groom them for career advancement. Performance evaluations are usually done once a year, but this is *not* when they *should* be done. Performance evaluations should be done throughout the year to monitor an employee's progress. If done periodically, say quarterly, they reduce role problems, act as vehicles in developing the career, and form the quantitative foundation for later personnel decisions.

Periodic evaluations reduce role problems   Role problems occur when people do not understand what behaviors and activities are expected of them. Role problems stem from:

1. People not knowing what they are expected to do;
2. There is disagreement about what to do; and
3. People not understanding correctly the behaviors and activities they should be doing.

Most of these problems are communication-based. With frequent performance evaluations, managers can correct any misperceptions and take the

Sales Management and Technology

▲ Sales managers occupy a boundary position as both managers and salespeople. They are responsible for achieving the sales, cost and activity goals set out by top management. To do this, they often sell product as well as manage the recruiting, training, and motivational activities of their sales units.

◄ A manager will often foster a team approach with a group of salespeople and will motivate the team to achieve the firm's goals.

► Most salespeople need some degree of supervision, but do not want the sales manager to micromanage their activities. This manager schedules regular meetings with her team to keep them informed and focused on their goals. This increases sales productivity and reduces morale problems.

▲ Recognition from one's peers is a powerful intrinsic motivator.

▼ The sales manager assumes the responsibility for the team if things do not go well. The aftermath of an unsuccessful presentation and a lost account will require earnest effort to reestablish a high level of motivation.

◀ Managers recruit, select and train the sales force. Many companies require formal instruction on things such as product knowledge, company policy, and selling skills.

▶ With the rapid changes in technology, skills and information must frequently be updated. At times such continuing education is done in a large seminar, while at other times it is done through small group meetings.

◀ Once the initial training is complete, the salesperson is ready to go out into the field. Periodically, managers accompany sales representatives on calls to evaluate job performance and selling skills.

◄ Periodic performance evaluations confirm to the salesperson that he is on the right track, doing a good job, and his career is progressing satisfactorily. A good evaluation interview also sets clear, obtainable objectives, identifies the essential performance factors, and establishes an employee development and performance plan.

◄ Census data is available on CD-ROM disks. This information will become an integral part of the sales databases and provide geodemographic information at the touch of a few computer keys, enabling salespeople to satisfy more customers in less time with a higher level of efficiency than ever before.

► Highly trained and motivated support personnel who manage information systems are invaluable to a company's success.

▲ Telephone sales support persons set up appointments, do off-site account service after the sale, handle requests for information and track down and qualify leads. In the future, telemarketing will probably be the primary tool to generate and qualify leads.

▲ The computer will produce numerical and graphic reports, pinpoint areas or products deviating from established targets, generate otherwise tedious reports, and free the salesperson to obtain accounts, close sales, and service accounts.

▲ Teleconferencing is already used to replace expensive travel to meetings. It allows firms to reach their salespeople anywhere there is a satellite dish and a television set. It may not replace the necessary salesperson-customer contact, but can be used effectively for seminar selling and mass presentations, and in sales training.

▶ Cellular telephones are commonplace with real estate and insurance agents, industrial salespeople and many service providers. Car phones continue to have a tremendous impact on the salesperson's responsiveness to customers.

▶ Increased competitive pressure means salespeople must make use of all their available time. Being able to carry a laptop computer makes good use of air travel time. When the laptop is connected through a modem or fax machine to the firm's mainframe, entire files, reports and orders can be transmitted either way.

◀ This sales presentation requires the use of charts and graphs placed on an easel; such presentation materials are often awkward and bulky to carry about.

▶ This presentation also requires the use of charts and graphs, but this is done through the computer overhead. Other uses for the computer will include electronic mail, electronic employment applications, and computerized sales training.

▲ The ease and speed of global communication makes markets around the world more accessible than ever before. Telemarketing, the entry of small businesses into the international arena, and free trade agreements will all change the ways in which businesses view sales and marketing.

▲ In the future, the salesperson will find increased foreign and domestic markets tougher competition for human resources. Expanded opportunities for multilingual people, decreased market share monopolies and more demanding, sophisticated customers will make the salesperson's and the sales manager's jobs more challenging.

opportunity to coach the salespeople on exactly what activities are expected. Research has repeatedly shown that role problems are directly related to low job satisfaction, quitting, and a host of negative behaviors. Through better communications, managers can accurately define salespeople's role and the salespeople also can express their understanding of what should or should not be done. Periodic performance evaluations increase this two-way communication and reduce role problems. Figure 16-3 is a copy of the work sheet Kraft General Foods (KGF) gives to its managers as a guide to evaluating their salespeople's performance. The four "competencies" of KGF's leadership wheel focus on a much broader set of skills than just sales performance. Note, too, how the competencies overlap. Kraft's philosophy is one of coach-

KRAFT GENERAL FOODS COMPETENCIES WORKSHEET

Figure 16-3 **Kraft General Foods Competencies Worksheet**

Source: Kraft General Foods. Used with permission.

OVERVIEW

The Competencies reflect skills and abilities that were found to be critical to success at the management level in Kraft General Foods. They are driven by the Business Style characteristics from the mission. The competencies are reflected in an effectiveness wheel which is made up of Leadership, Interpersonal Effectiveness, Personal Effectiveness, and Conceptual Effectiveness dimensions. The wheel is comprised of many parts, and no one part is paramount.

LEADERSHIP

The Leadership dimension includes the ability to get things done through others. It begins with the creation of an idea and encompasses the ability to implement effectively and efficiently, to galvanize others toward action, to delegate, influence, monitor, and adjust in order to bring work to completion.

INTERPERSONAL EFFECTIVENESS

The Interpersonal Effectiveness dimension includes the abilities to communicate effectively with others, build relationships, present ideas effectively, and develop people to support business goals.

PERSONAL EFFECTIVENESS

The Personal Effectiveness dimension includes that combination of personal skills and abilities which enable the individual to make a difference in the organization's success. It includes such competencies as initiative, aggressiveness, risk acceptance, innovation, and openness and honesty.

CONCEPTUAL EFFECTIVENESS

The Conceptual Effectiveness dimension includes those skills and abilities necessary for idea formulation, planning, and decision making. This dimension is essential in determining the future direction and business plan of the organization.

ing people to become leaders, not just high-performing salespeople. Its holistic approach allows salespeople to be evaluated and thus coached in sales-related and personal improvement areas.

Case in Point

Having Them Appraise You Will Help You Appraise Them

One of the surest ways to obtain feedback on your performance as a sales manager is to ask your subordinates to formally appraise you.

The appraisal can take many forms but boils down to either a set of questions or a rating scale of some sort. Examples of specific questions that could be asked are:

▶ Are my goals for the sales group clear?
▶ Are my goals for you as an individual clear?
▶ Am I supportive of your effort?
▶ Am I fair and equitable in assigning and appraising work?

A rating scale could be as follows:
  On a scale of 1 to 10, how would you rate my:

1. clarity of goals?
2. supportiveness?
3. fairness?
4. team building ability?

Keep in mind when using such a system that it is important to support openness in the comments by employees and definitely take action on suggestions made.

Career path The career path is the road map to career advancement that a firm designs for its employees. It may be formally stated, such as "Sales managers are promoted from the ranks of the field salesforce only after five years of experience and having attained an MBA." The company's organizational chart informally charts the path as well. It shows the levels and positions people customarily advance through as they move up in the firm. The performance appraisal system keeps salespeople in touch with how they are proceeding on that career path.

Quantitative basis for personnel decisions The increasing emphasis on equality in the workplace demands that managers use quantitative measures when evaluating personnel. Performance evaluations are becoming more important as evidence of fair or unfair personnel decision making.

The performance evaluation compares actual performance (activities and behaviors) against a set of goals or objectives. If a person has performed up to the required level of performance, then that person is entitled to the same treatment that his or her co-workers receive for similar performance. If the person has outperformed them, commensurate rewards are in order. Managers get into trouble with discrimination lawsuits and EEOC complaints because they fail to do performance evaluations regularly, fail to establish clear objectives, or evaluate employees against objectives unknown to the employees.

The Steps in a Good Evaluation Interview

Performance evaluations with employees are the culmination of a properly designed and executed performance management system. Four steps lead to a well-executed performance evaluation interview:

Step 1. Set clear, obtainable objectives

Step 2. Identify the essential performance factors

Step 3. Establish the employee's development and performance plan

Step 4. Evaluate the employee

The steps listed above may strike you as being in a curious order. What you must keep in mind is that steps 1, 2, and 3 are done with employees for next year's work. Step 4 is done this year against the objectives, or development and performance plan, agreed to last year for this year.

Step 1. Set clear, obtainable objectives   Objectives should be set with the firm's overall goals and what the employees are capable of doing in mind. The employees' personal capabilities and sales territory potential are considered when setting objectives. Next, the objectives should be as specific as possible; an objective stating "a 5 percent increase in units sales" is better than one stating "a significant increase in sales is expected."

Step 2. Identify the essential performance factors   Specific performance factors must be identified. Salespeople need to know if they will be judged on dollar sales, unit sales, new accounts opened, or number of calls made. If there are multiple factors, they should be identified and agreed to by the managers and the salespeople. These will be the basis for next year's performance measure. Clearly, the more specific the performance factors are, the better for the salespeople. For managers, trying to identify all the things salespeople could be evaluated on could become a Herculean task. This is why managers usually focus on only key measures, such as sales, profits, or call activities, then use a generic phrase like "and other measures appropriate to the job."

Step 3. Establish an employee development and performance plan   This calls for the managers and the salespeople to establish specific areas where the salespeople should focus their attention. These can be broad or specific. Company policy might state that to be eligible for a management position, salespeople must have an MBA degree. In the development plan, managers and employees might agree that employees should take two night courses at the local university. This would develop the employees' qualifications for a promotion. The performance plan might specifically identify how the salespeople would accomplish the 5 percent sales increase objective discussed above. Such a plan could state that the employees will call on more prospecting accounts, get three more displays set up during the week, and drop their dormant accounts.

Step 4. Evaluate the employee   The final step is to carry out the evaluation interview with the employees. This is often done in two phases. First, the employees evaluate themselves against the objectives, and the development and performance plan they agreed to for this year. In the second phase, the managers do the same thing. In the evaluation interview, both sides discuss actual performance against what was planned. The reasons for success or failure in meeting the objectives become part of the next year's planning process.

Remember, the evaluation interview is normally done once each year, but it should be done formally or informally throughout the year. Some managers provide performance feedback through weekly or monthly sales progress reports, others meet face-to-face on a quarterly or semiannual basis, and some, unfortunately, do not do it at all.

Case in Point

Eight Reasons Why Managers Have Trouble with Performance Evaluations

1. They have failed to adequately define standards.
2. They focus only on the most recent performance, rather than looking at the long-run performance.
3. They rely on instinct for their rationale and reasoning.
4. The employees didn't understand standards in the first place.
5. There is little or unclear documentation.
6. They do not allow enough time to meet with employees, thus rushing the evaluation and not giving the employees time to talk, ask questions, or get clarifications.
7. They do all the talking.
8. No follow-up plan was ever developed for employees to use to do self-development.

Source: Adapted from William S. Swan, *How to Do a Superior Performance Appraisal* (New York: John Wiley & Sons, 1991), pp. 31–32.

In Figure 16-4, KGF managers are given guidelines for conducting the performance review meeting. In Figures 16-5 to 16-8, a sample of a KGF employee's written performance appraisal is shown.

Note how KGF stresses to its managers the importance of concentrating on factual rather than conjectural information. Also note that KGF emphasizes that through interim reviews, the year-end performance evaluation should present no surprises.

In its performance evaluation guidelines, KGF instructs managers *not* to discuss rewards when doing the performance evaluation. These are separate but related issues. Performance evaluations are based on how the salespeople do their job. Rewards are also based on that criteria, as well as the financial performance of the firm. The performance evaluation will serve as the basis for the reward, but the actual calculation of the annual raise or bonus can only be done *after* top management has determined the total amount for the salary or bonus pool budget.

In Figure 16-5, we see the goals Chris Zooler, a manager in KGF food service sales, has set for herself. The important thing to observe about the KGF goals form is the specificity of the direction: the users must list their objectives *in order of importance*. Next, they must indicate how success will be measured. This prevents them from writing esoteric, immeasurable goals

Figure 16-4 **KGF Plan for Conducting the Performance Review Meeting**

Source: Kraft General Foods. Used with permission.

CONDUCTING THE PERFORMANCE REVIEW MEETING

The performance review meeting is the time when all previous discussions between managers and employees are pulled together. At this meeting, as with interim feedback and mid-year reviews, managers should concentrate on the facts and specifics of performance and present a balanced view of accomplishments and shortcomings.

If frequent review sessions have been conducted during the year, the formal performance evaluation should present no surprises. This does not necessarily mean that employees will agree entirely with the managers' evaluations of their performances, but it is more likely they will understand why managers made the decisions they did. Also, if subordinates believe that managers are sincerely dedicated to their success, they can more readily accept disappointments.

Arranging the Meeting

The manager should advise the employee in advance of the meeting to allow him/her time to prepare since the employee is expected to be an active participant in the performance review meeting. Next, the manager should arrange a block of uninterrupted time (usually 1 - 2 hours) for the two to meet and review the form. If all approval signatures have been obtained before the meeting, then the manager can share the overall rating. If the approvals have not been obtained, it will then be necessary to have two meetings: one to review the individual sections of the performance appraisal form without discussing the overall rating, and a final brief meeting to share the overall rating once approvals have been obtained.

What is Covered in the Meeting

The employee should be given time to review the completed performance appraisal form before the discussion begins. Since the manager is responsible for "calling the meeting," he/she should take the lead in the discussion but continually encourage the employee to take an active role in the discussions of goals, results against specific responsibilities or objectives, Affirmative Action commitment, and plans for performance improvement.

The performance review meeting discussion focuses on what results were achieved during the review period, how those results were achieved (or could have been achieved more effectively), and what the individual needs to do in the current job to increase personal effectiveness. The annual performance review is **not** time to discuss rewards. Compensation and other reward discussions can often be very emotional and impede attention being directed toward the actions that must be taken to move the business forward by improving personal performance. Reward discussions should be held separately form annual performance review discussions.

Of course, performance and rewards are related. KGF believes very strongly in a pay for performance standard in which the most effective performers are recognized and rewarded for their extraordinary efforts. Thus, reward standards should be discussed thoroughly during the preparation of the performance goals and then modified as business conditions change throughout the year. If that is done, translating performance into merit increase recommendations will be easier to decide, explain and accept.

Employee Comments

If the employee disagrees with the overall rating or item(s) referenced in the performance appraisal, or wishes to include explanatory comments, he/she can submit a written statement for inclusion in the permanent record.

that cannot be traced to specific tasks or outcomes. The final sentence in the instructions indicates that KGF realizes that it is impractical to hold people to their stated goals if business conditions change and make it impossible to achieve the goals.

As Figure 16-6 indicates, Chris's manager has met at mid-year with her to check her performance. This is done to make sure small problems are identified and corrected before they grow out of proportion. We see that Chris's only area of concern was in her sales of Kraft-produced products. Note that her review identifies the necessary corrective action and that a new goal has been added.

Finally, as Figures 16-7 and 16-8 show, Chris and her manager have met at the end of the year. After her performance has been discussed, she has been given her *written* year-end performance appraisal. She has done an adequate job in her affirmative action efforts, and she has "fully met

KRAFT GENERAL FOODS

GOALS

Managing &
Appraising
Performance

For year __199—__ or other period from _____ to _____

__Chris Zooler__   __General Manager__   __111-22-3333__
name   title   social security no.

List in order of importance the major responsibilities and objectives for the forthcoming time period. Indicate how success will be measured. Include Affirmative Action goals. Goals may need to be revised during the year as business conditions change.

ROLI and District Income: Achieve ROLI plan of 36% and District Income of $3.6 million.

Increase District sale of Kraft produced products by 15% vs. year ago.

Improve management personnel development by reviewing, approving and monitoring MAP goals set by each staff member; assure that qualified personnel fill all Dept. head positions by year-end.

Meet Affirmative Action goal of hiring 1 minority and 1 female for available supervisory positions by end of 2nd quarter.

Improve sales personnel performance by establishing a district training program which emphasizes product knowledge, Hq operations, and F/S guidelines; have all sales personnel complete the program by year-end.

_____   _____   _____
manager   title   date

performance requirements." Her performance has been noted on the "Overall Performance Rating" line, and the definitions of the terms on the rating line have been supplied by KGF to ensure uniform and consistent understanding by all managers.

The Legal Aspects of Performance Evaluations

Performance evaluations, if not done properly, carry serious legal consequences. Because of EEOC rules and appeal provisions, many managers are intimidated by the prospect of doing a performance evaluation. The EEOC simply asks managers to keep the evaluation process, and what those evalu-

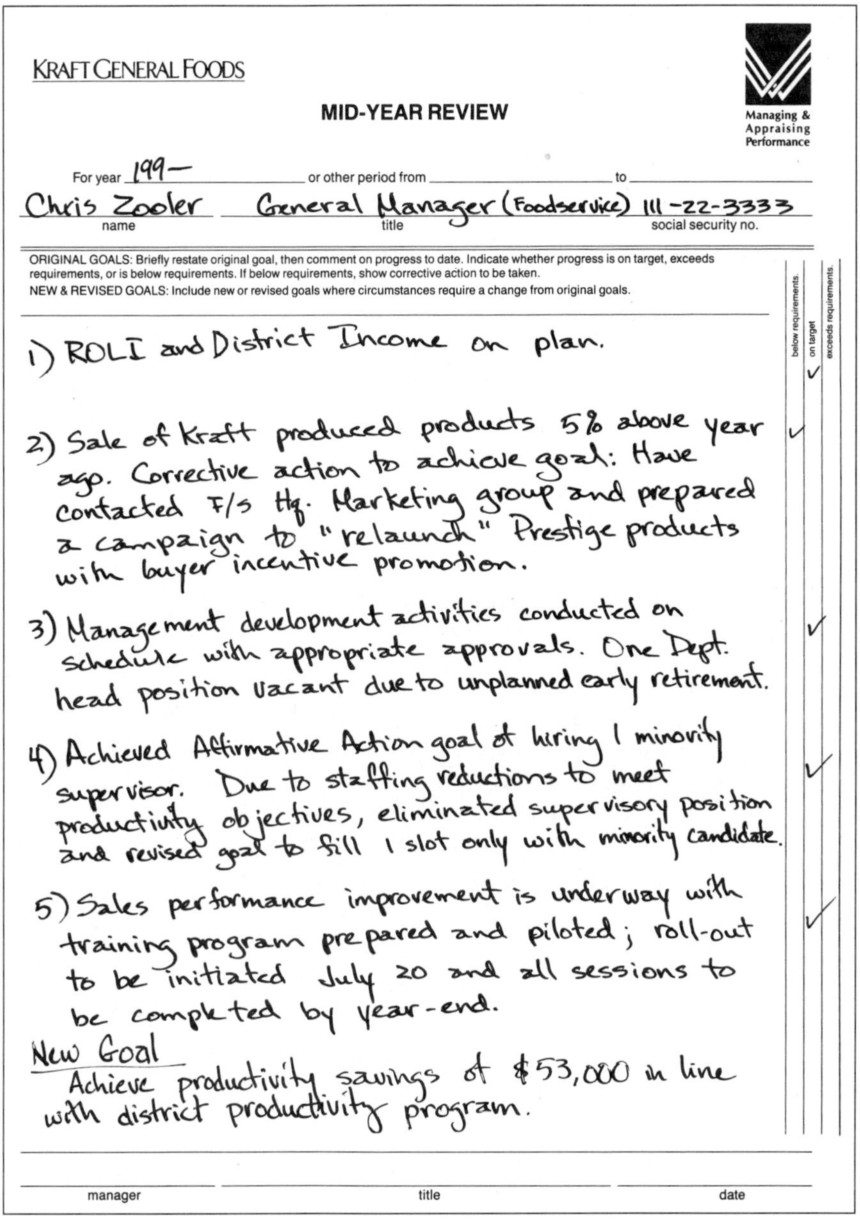

Figure 16-6 **KGF Manager's Mid-Year Review**

Source: Kraft General Foods. Used with permission.

KRAFT GENERAL FOODS

MID-YEAR REVIEW

Managing &
Appraising
Performance

For year _199—_ _____ or other period from _____ to _____

Chris Zooler _____ _General Manager (Foodservice)_ _111-22-3333_
name   title   social security no.

ORIGINAL GOALS: Briefly restate original goal, then comment on progress to date. Indicate whether progress is on target, exceeds requirements, or is below requirements. If below requirements, show corrective action to be taken.
NEW & REVISED GOALS: Include new or revised goals where circumstances require a change from original goals.

(column headings, vertical: below requirements | on target | exceeds requirements)

1) ROLI and District Income on plan. ✓ *(on target)*

2) Sale of Kraft produced products 5% above year ago. Corrective action to achieve goal: Have contacted F/s Hq. Marketing group and prepared a campaign to "relaunch" Prestige products with buyer incentive promotion. ✓

3) Management development activities conducted on schedule with appropriate approvals. One Dept. head position vacant due to unplanned early retirement. ✓

4) Achieved Affirmative Action goal of hiring 1 minority supervisor. Due to staffing reductions to meet productivity objectives, eliminated supervisory position and revised goal to fill 1 slot only with minority candidate. ✓

5) Sales performance improvement is underway with training program prepared and piloted; roll-out to be initiated July 20 and all sessions to be completed by year-end. ✓

<u>New Goal</u>
Achieve productivity savings of $53,000 in line with district productivity program.

_____   _____   _____
manager   title   date

ations are used for, grounded in job relevance, accuracy, and documentation. The EEOC can periodically audit a business to check for compliance and levy serious penalties for noncompliance. Good documentation of the performance or lack of performance is the key evidence the EEOC looks for.

Avoid EEOC problems by following these guidelines for doing performance evaluations:

◄ ◄ ◄ ◄ ◄ ◄ ◄ ◄

Learning Objective 7: Guidelines for doing performance evaluations that will avoid EEOC problems

Guideline 1: Read and follow your firm's affirmative action plan.

Guideline 2: Avoid using stereotypes in discussions.

Guideline 3: Clearly understand and define the performance factors and objectives agreed to by the manager and the employee and ensure that they are based on realistic expectations. The actual evaluative interview with the employee should revolve around these.

Guideline 4: Maintain a positive rapport with the employee when discussing his or her performance. Avoid getting emotional, even though the employee may. Focusing on actual versus expected performance that is supported by quantitative information leaves no room for emotions to interfere.

Guideline 5: Do not get into a discussion based on a person's attributes that reflect on his or her membership in a protected group. If Mary said, "Being a woman and 50 years old, it's harder for me to lift

Figure 16-7 **KGF Manager's Year End Appraisal, Part 1**

Source: Kraft General Foods. Used with permission.

KRAFT GENERAL FOODS

YEAR END PERFORMANCE APPRAISAL

Part 1

Managing & Appraising Performance

For the year 199 _____ or other period from _____ to _____

Chris Zooler   General Manager F/S   111-22-3333
  name   title   social security no.

PERFORMANCE AGAINST GOALS: Considering both original and revised goals, briefly restate each goal and indicate results. Also comment on how the results were achieved; i.e., what skills and competencies this person used or failed to use in addressing this goal.
OVERALL PERFORMANCE: In addition to specific goals, and considering both routine responsibilities and special situations, how well did this person handle the total responsibility of the job? Comment on overall effectiveness, affirmative action effectiveness, self-improvement initiative, and strengths and improvement areas.

1) Exceeded District Income plan by $302,400 and achieved planned ROLI. Designed and implemented a cost savings program which assured goal results. Attended Finance for Non-Financial Managers Course to improve personal understanding of financial fundamentals.

2) Sale of Kraft produced products increased 18% vs year ago due to buyer incentive promotion and improved computerized order entry/warehouse distribution system.

3) Oversaw the development and execution of challenging, significant MAP goals for all staff; initiated Team building activities as new staff joined the District staff; filled Dept. head vacancy with female manager.

4) Achieved revised goal of filling 1 supervisory position with minority candidate. Exceeded revised goal by filling Dept. Head position with minority female manager. Also approved District representation at KGF Affirmative Action Conference and encouraged conference information to be shared in new employee orientation program.

5) Sales training program completed with 100% attendance. Program evaluations averaged 4.33 with 5.00 scale.

6) Exceeded total productivity program goal by $7,000 for a total savings of $60,000.
Overall responsibilities handled with dispatch, attention to detail, and demonstrating good analysis and planning. Interpersonal effectiveness has improved with confidence in the role of the G.M. Improved sense of competitiveness throughout

Continued

Figure 16-7 — *Continued*

the District as evidenced by inter-team, inter-function competitions and improved understanding of the customers.

Improvement area: Although goal of increasing sale of kraft produced products achieved, a better understanding of marketing fundamentals should result in even greater accomplishments. Attendance in external Marketing Strategies workshop should be sufficient.

Due to District changes (i.e. both personnel and procedures,) Team Building activities should continue to foster improved morale and better working relationships.

Problem-solving abilities of District staff can be improved through stronger District attendance in STEPS program (i.e. only 1 District representative attended this year; should have 6-8 attend in the upcoming year).

these sample cases," it would be appropriate for you to point out to her that lifting sample cases is expected of everyone.

Guideline 6: During the performance evaluation, discuss only what is necessary to assess the salesperson's performance. Keep that discussion focused on the person's attainment of his or her goals and objectives. If Mary again brought up her age as a reason for lackluster performance, a discussion of her age-related problems would not be in order. She should be reminded of the requirements for the job.

The best way to avoid the legal issues in performance evaluations is to stick with the basics. This means managers need job descriptions that are up-to-date and set reasonable expectations with employees. They also must evaluate employees against the same criteria, for example, attainment of quotas and number of calls made. They need to stick to the facts they have documented, not what they think the employee did.

Managers Must Evaluate Problems and Take Corrective Actions

Some salespeople are problems, and their managers must deal with them quickly and effectively. Some people show up late to work, some do not do necessary reports, and some won't make the required number of calls. Managers faced with problem salespeople should ask three questions, then use one of several strategies to handle the problem.[9]

The first question is, "Is there a problem?" A problem is a variance from expected performance. Is Jack doing what he should be doing? Is it really a

Figure 16-8 **KGF Manager's Year End Appraisal, Part 2**
Source: Kraft General Foods. Used with permission.

KRAFT GENERAL FOODS

YEAR END PERFORMANCE APPRAISAL
Part 2

Managing & Appraising Performance

For the year 199 — _____ or other annual period from _____ to _____

Chris Zooler
name

General Manager
title

111-222-3333
social security no.

PERFORMANCE RATINGS:
AFFIRMATIVE ACTION EFFECTIVENESS: See reverse side of this page for Affirmative Action rating definitions.

☐ Below Requirements   ☒ Satisfactory

OVERALL PERFORMANCE RATING: Place "X" on scale. If on the line between two categories, the lower one will be recorded as the rating level. This rating is to be based on performance in the present job for the entire review period. Potential for another position should not have impact on this rating. See reverse side of this page for Overall Performance rating term definitions.

Unacceptable performance | Marginally meets performance requirements | Fully meets performance requirements | Exceeds performance requirements | Significantly exceeds performance requirements

SHORT TERM DEVELOPMENT AND IMPROVEMENT PLANS: What training, work assignments, or other actions, which have been discussed and agreed upon with the employee, will be done before the next appraisal to help this person improve job performance and prepare for future assignments?

See page 1 for full details.

- Attend Marketing Strategies Workshop (external) by end of Q1.

- Continue Team-Building activities

- Promote better District attendance in STEPS and encourage post-session application.

Appraised by: manager _____ title _____ date _____

Approved by: manager's manager _____ title _____ date _____

SIGNATURES—PERFORMANCE APPRAISAL INTERVIEW

employee _____ manager _____ date _____

The manager and manager's manager both sign the Appraisal indicating support for content. The employee's signature indicates that the appraisal has been reviewed and discussed with the manager. It does not necessarily indicate agreement. Employees may add comments on a separate sheet, which will be attached to this Appraisal.

problem or only a one-time minor occurrence? If Jack's behavior is significantly different from what he should be doing, then the manager must ask the second question.

The second question is, "Is it worth solving?" Everyone has little problems at one time or another. Most people know when they have made a mistake or are not doing what they should. Problems arise when such behaviors are consistently repeated. Managers must first decide if there really is a problem or if the difficulty is only temporary and the employee will correct it.

The third question is, "What caused the problem?" This is a difficult question to answer. Sometimes it is the person who has the problem, but sometimes the manager caused it. The problem can come from trying to follow company policies or trying to do what a customer asks. Problems can be related to ability or motivation. Ability problems are solved with training and coaching. Motivational problems are much more difficult.

Managers use six strategies to get people to do what they should. Let's look at an example that illustrates these strategies.

Example You are the manager of a branch office and one of your better salespeople, Bruce, has for some reason, decided not to answer his phone. He lets it ring until the caller hangs up. You know these calls are coming from prospective and active customers, and you know this is losing you business. What should you do? Here are six strategies you could use:

▶ **Strategy 1. The Polite Request**

"Bruce, would you please answer the phone before it rings so many times? Thanks."

▶ **Strategy 2. Praise Appropriate Behavior**

Watch Bruce and when he does answer the phone, say something like this:

"Bruce, thanks for answering the phone so quickly. That's really important to us and to the customers. Keep up the good work!"

▶ **Strategy 3. Assert Yourself**

You are the manager and sometimes assertion of your position is necessary.

"Bruce, I want you to answer the phone before it rings so long. We're losing business because you won't answer the phone."

▶ **Strategy 4. The Sandwich Approach**

The sandwich approach is layering criticism between two layers of praise. It works like this:

"Bruce, you've really done a good job for us. We're pleased with your accuracy and efficiency. It is also important to answer the phone and not let it ring so long. You are good at working with customers. Those are probably customers calling, too. If you can be quicker at answering the phone, it will only improve your already good performance."

▶ **Strategy 5. The Problem-Solution Approach**

This strategy lays a problem (Bruce's problem) out in front of him and asks him for a solution.

"Bruce, I have had some calls from some of our customers saying they have been trying to call in to place orders, but some of our reps are not answering their phones. I need your help on this one. What should we do?"

▶ **Strategy 6. The Causal Analysis Approach**

This is where you and Bruce sit down and have a heart-to-heart conversation.

"Bruce, I want to talk to you about your performance on the job. Are you having some problems that we can work on? You are not answering your phone, and this is affecting your work, your sales, and your attitude. We need to get this corrected, and to do that, I want to help you with any problems you may be having."

These strategies can be useful in dealing with all types of problems. Some are subtle, some are very direct. Whatever the problem is, sales managers must effectively handle it tactfully yet efficiently.

▶ ▶ *follow-up questions*

1. What type of role problems occur when managers fail to do periodic performance evaluations?
2. Why is the quantitative portion of a performance evaluation so important?
3. In your opinion, what are five major reasons sales managers foul up performance evaluations?

Summary

Sales managers are both salespeople and administrators. They often find themselves in boundary positions, that is, caught between upper management and their salespeople. In their job as the administrator of company policy, they are responsible for communicating that policy to the salesforce, then controlling and evaluating the salespeople (Learning Objective 1).

Part of the sales manager's role may be to establish or redefine sales territories. This has an important impact on salespeople because it affects their potential earning power. When designing territories, sales managers are often faced with deciding whether they need more or fewer salespeople. The process starts with selecting the territorial unit (usually county or state boundaries are used), then, estimating the potential business in the initial territorial boundary. Managers then establish sales goals for the territory and do a workload analysis. Managers may have to go back and rethink the first design, given the results of the workload analysis. Finally, they assign salespeople to the resulting territories (Learning Objective 2).

In their managerial capacity, sales managers must motivate their people to generate the sales as defined by the company's goals and objectives. To achieve these, sales managers establish quotas or sales targets. To motivate their people, managers rely primarily on incentives and the compensation system. Incentives may be either financial or nonfinancial. Motivation also stems from how managers work with their people. Closeness of supervision, frequency of communication, and span of control are areas under the manager's control (Learning Objective 3).

Managers spend a portion of their time recruiting and selecting new salespeople. Recruiting is the solicitation process that generates a pool of names, and selecting is the screening of applicants to find the best candidate(s). Recruiting and selecting is a ten-step process that starts with the review of the organization's goals and objectives. This is followed by a job analysis, a personnel audit, and the writing of a job description. Then the position opening is posted, or advertised. Eliminating the unqualified applicants and screening the rest leads to a small group of select individuals who get interviews. The chapter pointed out that throughout the recruiting and selecting process, care must be exercised so it isn't discriminatory (Learning Objective 4).

Sales managers administer compensation plans and often design them. Compensation plans typically include a package of benefits (insurance, retirement, and/or tuition reimbursement programs). The direct compensation usually comes from straight salary, straight commission, or a combination of the two. Drawing accounts are also popular. Other options include bonuses, expense allowances, special prizes, and profit sharing plans (Learning Objective 5).

The Equal Employment Opportunity Commission (EEOC) was discussed as the governmental watchdog agency that investigates and settles discrimination complaints. Its rules govern such areas as what can and cannot be asked on job application forms and in reference checks and how tests or examinations can be used. Its purpose is to assure that all applicants for a position are treated fairly.

Evaluating salespeople through a formal performance evaluation was discussed. While most managers do not like doing performance evaluations, periodic appraisals are necessary. Four steps in doing a good performance evaluation were presented, along with six guidelines for avoiding problems. The key to successfully completing a performance evaluation is to start with proper goals and objectives, then have carefully documented evidence of performance to ensure the utmost objectivity in the evaluation process (Learning Objectives 6 and 7).

Key Terms

Sales management Planning, organizing, staffing, directing, and controlling the activities of the salesforce to achieve the firm's goals and enhance the business relationship with customers.

Role perception The individual's understanding of what the job entails and how to do it.

Quotas Sales, activity, or profitability thresholds.

Objective-task method Goals are set based on the objective and the tasks needed to carry them out.

Motivation The amount of effort a salesperson is willing to expend on the job.

Intrinsic motivation Motivation that occurs because of the satisfaction of doing a good job or meeting a challenge.

Extrinsic motivation Motivation coming from the material rewards expected.

Incentives Rewards for accomplishing certain specific goals.

Span of control The number of people a manager supervises.

Recognition rate The number of times a person gets recognized and saluted for his or her accomplishments.

Recruiting The process of soliciting names for the candidate pool.

Selecting The process of screening the candidates in the pool and offering the job to the best one(s).

Job analysis The systematic investigation of a job's tasks, duties, and responsibilities, along with the review of the knowledge, skills, and abilities needed by someone to fill the job.

Personnel audit A comparison of the number and type of people currently in the job to the type of person who should be in the job.

Job description   A written summary of the tasks, duties, and responsibilities of the job.

Job posting   Advertising and informing possible applicants of the available job.

Structured interview   An interview in which the interviewer uses a list of standardized questions to get the same information from all applicants.

Nondirective interview   An interview in which the interviewer asks applicants broad general questions to get them to talk about themselves or the job.

Stress interview   An interview designed to create anxiety in candidates to test their response to pressure and ability to think on their feet.

Compensation package   The sum of all the financial and nonfinancial rewards given to salespeople for their work.

Straight salary   A fixed sum of money paid at regular intervals.

Straight commission   Pay is a predetermined percentage of a base, such as sales or profits.

Drawing account   A periodic monetary advance to the salesperson to be deducted from the eventual total commission earnings.

Bonus   A lump-sum payment to the salesperson for accomplishing a predetermined level of sales.

Expense allowances   Provisions for travel and other business expenses incurred by salespeople.

Profit sharing   A system where the profits of the company are divided among eligible recipients.

Performance management   The ongoing process of setting goals, evaluating performance against them, and giving the coaching necessary to both motivate people and keep them on track.

Discussion Questions

1. What differentiates activity quotas from sales quotas?
2. Why would a manager use a sales quota on an experienced salesperson and an activity quota on a new recruit?
3. Can an improperly set quota be a demotivator? Give an example.
4. What are the benefits and drawbacks of across-the-board raises?
5. What is the objective-task method of goal setting?
6. How does equity theory relate to compensation and motivation?
7. When a person's locus of control is internal, how would he or she respond to extensive close supervision? What about someone whose locus of control is external?
8. How are frequency of communications and such problems as job dissatisfaction, quitting, and low performance are related?
9. What are three organizational factors that influence motivation?
10. How are span of control and frequency of communication related?

11. Is recognition rate an intrinsic or extrinsic motivator?

12. How can the way a salesperson's territory is designed or redesigned be a motivating or demotivating factor in sales management?

13. Does a "group norm" influence behaviors in a salesperson? How can a sales manager affect this?

14. What is generally included in a salesperson's compensation package?

15. When salespeople refer to their benefits package, what are they talking about?

16. What are the principle objectives of a compensation plan?

17. Straight salary is a good plan for salespeople engaged in what kind of selling activity?

18. What are three advantages and disadvantages of a straight salary compensation system?

19. Why would the most productive salespeople tend to favor straight commission compensation over straight salary?

20. Why do most firms use a combination of salary and commission?

21. How does a drawing account work?

22. What are the advantages of a drawing account to a firm and to the salesperson?

23. What is the difference between recruiting and selecting?

24. Why is it legally important to have up-to-date job descriptions?

25. How does a job analysis differ from a job description?

26. What are the ways a manager screens job applicants?

27. When checking an applicant's references, what types of questions can be asked and what types should be avoided?

28. Should formal testing, such as intelligence and personality tests, be used to screen out undesirable applicants? Would you only want to test the "undesirable people"?

29. What are the benefits of a structured interview over an informal one? What are the benefits of an informal interview over a structured one?

30. What are some of the common training areas sales managers focus on?

31. Why do managers dislike doing performance evaluations?

32. What types of role problems occur when managers fail to do periodic performance evaluations?

33. What are the four steps in doing a performance evaluation interview?

34. What does EEOC stand for? What is it?

Application Exercise

Go back and reread the boxed feature titled "Nonfinancial Rewards go a long way at Amway," then answer the following questions:

▶ Why would nonfinancial rewards work so well?

- ▶ Would you say that generally speaking, Amway distributors are intrinsically or extrinsically motivated?
- ▶ Which type of reward do you think has the greatest motivational power, financial or nonfinancial? Why?

Class Exercises

Group Exercise

Separate the class into triads. One member of the triad will be an observer/evaluator, one will be the sales manager, and the third will be the salesperson.

The situation involves a multilocation metropolitan real estate brokerage firm. The sales manager is responsible for a salesforce of 15 agents. Every sales agent is expected to sell at least $1 million of residential real estate annually. This is the third year that the salesperson has been at the brokerage. The salesperson has yet to meet that $1 million quota (last year's sales were $835,000; the first listing year was $250,000, and year 2 was $675,000).

Role play a performance evaluation between the sales manager and the salesperson. The observer shall then report to the class concerning the effectiveness of the appraisal (according to the steps outlined in the text), make recommendations for improvement, and review probable consequences.

The class shall then discuss the group findings and make appropriate recommendations (conclusions).

Individual Presentation

As the sales manager in the above situation, you are preparing to interview candidates for a new sales agent position. Prior to class, prepare for a structured interview by making a list of at least ten questions you will ask candidates. The class will then evaluate the questions and their relevance (i.e., are they based on getting you the proper response for the information desired?).

Cases

16.1

Heat From the Top?

In the office of Accurate Communications, Inc., Irene Epson was looking over applications for the sale job she had advertised in the Sunday paper. Accurate Communications designs custom software for private firms and the U.S. Army.

The firm's human resources department had administered intelligence tests to four of the six candidates and personality profile questionnaires to five of the six. The sixth person, the daughter of the regional manager who was Irene's boss, was told by her father to apply for the job and that "Irene would take care of her."

All of the candidates, including the boss's daughter, were equally qualified in terms of their experience, education, and general qualifications. The only differences came in their test scores and personality profiles. Three candidates were female and three were male. The highest-scoring person was a minority female. A close second was a 52-year-old male.

As Irene was pondering the situation, the regional manager called and said, "Good afternoon, Irene, I was just about to call my daughter. When should I tell her to report for her first day of training?"

Questions:

1. If you were Irene, what would you say to him?
2. What problems appear in this scenario?
3. If you were Irene, what action would you take in this immediate situation and to make sure this does not happen again?

The Withdrawing Drawer

In reviewing the sales and cost data for the month, Bill Anzone, sales manager for Enterprise Distribution, was examining the performance of each of his sales-people. Ann Cline, a new salesperson, was becoming a concern. Ann was hired three months ago and given a three-month probationary period. She had some experience in selling plumbing supplies, Enterprise's major product. Bill decided that Ann showed promise, but he also knew that, as with any salesperson starting with a new company in a new territory, she would need a certain amount of start-up time. Bill put Ann on a draw of $450 per month against commissions. Enterprise paid a straight 8 percent commission on all sales, with the appropriate deductions taken for merchandise returned.

Over the last two months, Ann hadn't made enough sales to get any commissions, so Enterprise was out $1,350. Bill had begun hearing from some of Ann's customers who wanted to know where she was. They wanted to place orders and were doing so with the secretary at Enterprise because they couldn't find Ann or she hadn't been to see them to take the order. Ann's three-month performance evaluation was coming up, and Bill was getting prepared to do it.

Questions:

1. What should be Bill's strategy in planning Ann's evaluation?
2. How would you conduct Ann's evaluation?
3. Should Ann be given more time to prove herself?

References

1. Adapted from Kerry Rottenberger, "How to Handle the Maverick Salesperson," *Sales and Marketing Management,* 143 (1991): 16–23.
2. Adapted from Jack Falvey, "The Absolute Basics of Salesforce Management," *Sales and Marketing Management,* 142 (1990): 8–10.
3. Heidi Waldrop, "Armstrong Dreams Up Something for Everyone," *Sales and Marketing Management,* 135 (1985): 78–89.
4. "Why Amerisource Went West," *Sales and Marketing Management,* 135 (1985): 90–104.
5. *Sales and Marketing Management,* 134 (1985): 85.
6. See Gilbert A. Churchill, Jr., Neil M. Ford, and Orville C. Walker, Jr., *Sales Force Management* (Homewood, Ill.: Richard D. Irwin, 1981). Later editions of this book contain the same information. Also, the authors have published extensively on this topic in the marketing literature.
7. P.G. Kuchuris, "Need Expert Trainers? Consider Retired Salespeople," *Sales and Marketing Management,* 142 (1990): 123.
8. Adapted from William S. Swan, *How to Do a Superior Performance Appraisal* (New York: John Wiley & Sons, 1991), pp. 5–10.
9. Adapted from Myron Glassman and R. Bruce McAfee, "How to Turn Problem Salespeople into Winners," *Personal Selling Power,* 11 (1991): 58–60.

17 The Future of Selling and Sales Management

Objectives

After reading this chapter, you should be able to:

1. Explain geodemographic marketing and its application by salespeople in the future.

2. Define data base marketing and its role in the future of marketing goods and services.

3. Give an example of how an overlay map is used as a selling tool.

4. Understand how telemarketing will increase in importance to salespeople and their firms.

5. Identify technological tools that will change the way salespeople do their jobs.

6. Identify and explain the ways computers will be used in recruitment, selection, and salesforce management.

7. Describe the "new breed" of salesperson who will be the future of selling.

8. Identify the future training needs of sales managers.

9. Explain the concept of globalization of sales and marketing and its ramifications for the total sales environment.

Looking into the next 10 to 15 years, how do you see the profession of selling changing?

A Sales Expert and Corporate CEO Responds

A glimpse into the future of selling is provided by Richard G. Holder, president and CEO of Reynolds Metals Company. Holder says, "Historians, looking back at the decade of the '80s, will find dramatic changes in the relationships among producers and customers, suppliers and customers, buyers and seller. The role of the salesperson has evolved into that of a business consultant. Over the next decade, this trend will not only continue but accelerate."

"Selling is the most important thing a company does. The best management, the most skilled workers, the finest raw materials, the highest level of production technology—none of it means anything if the product doesn't get sold."

"Today, more than ever, selling means understanding the customer's business and providing solutions to his or her problems. We find that only 30 percent of a salesperson's time is spent on a face-to-face presentation. The majority of the time is devoted to planning, market intelligence, product and price analysis, problem solving, and travel. The members of customer companies who make the buying decisions are busy people, and a successful salesperson must be well-prepared with a written agenda to ensure that the customer meeting will be focused and productive."

"There is an old saying that 80 percent of your business comes from 20 percent of your customers. That equation was never more true. In most companies, the trend is toward closer relationships with fewer suppliers. For example, at one time, we were buying a service from over 200 suppliers; today, we have reduced that number to 12."

"We have close relationships with our suppliers under arrangements we call 'partnering.' Partnering means open and candid two-way communications on matters such as price projection plans and forecasting plans, cost improvement strategies, and a whole spectrum of other activities that formerly would have been proprietary information. These close arrangements with few suppliers mean long-term agreements—three to five years is not unusual—with cost-saving opportunities to both partners, high quality production and business stability for both customer and supplier. Among the many results of these new partnering relationships is the concept of team selling—providing solutions to a customer's problems is not the responsibility of the salesperson alone. Design, production, engineering, research and development, and even financial departments are part of the team."

"The successful business of tomorrow must be customer-oriented. At Reynolds, the sales transaction is the end result of many people and many departments—a team effort dedicated to satisfying our customers. All our efforts, in each of our operations, are directed at providing our customers

with the highest quality product and service at a fair price that gives good value to both parties."

"Selling today, and in the future, requires broad and deep knowledge of customer requirements, his or her equipment and product specifications, and an ability to fit customer needs to your company's strengths and capabilities while providing favorable margins."

"The salesperson must have a keen sense of the industry, with an understanding of business trends and a thorough knowledge of what the competition is doing. He or she must know the customer's business goals and direct his or her own company to satisfying future customer requirements. Selling is like playing a team sport. It requires individual initiative and dedication to achieving a personal best, while at the same time focusing on and supporting the ultimate objectives of the whole team." [1]

Introduction

The place of the salesperson in the history of business is evolving today into an even more important role than it has been in the past. The old images of the door-to-door salesperson, the carpetbagging peddler, and the fast-talking huckster died many years ago. Selling is a professional occupation. It is because it has to be. Competition hovers over every salesperson and product. Retail stores can just as easily buy their shoes from a company a thousand miles away as from their local shoe wholesaler. An Asian steel company can descend into a domestic salesperson's market and sew it up in the blink of an eye.

According to Howard Anderson, founder of the Yankee Consulting Group, a worldwide research and consulting group with offices on five continents, selling has progressed through three operational modes and is about to enter the fourth.[2] The first was the *consultative mode,* which started around 1900. This was about when salespeople started trying to understand their customers and come up with innovative solutions. Prior to that, salespeople received little, if any, training in how to sell. They were given products to sell and told to do whatever it took to make the sale. Images of the carpetbagger and the itinerant peddler come to mind. George H. Patterson of Dayton, Ohio, founder of the National Cash Register Company (now NCR Corporation), was the first to introduce the idea of "scientific selling." This consisted of training salespeople to use scripted presentations and to develop the art of making a pitch and closing a sale through the use of a tried and proven series of steps. Salespeople were trained in how to discover a customer's needs, then use the specific scripted presentation appropriate for that customer. However, beyond the salesperson's own intelligence, there was little outside help available. Through this period, industrial and nonretail sales have evolved into relationships or consultant-client interactions. Salespeople have become "consultative specialists," offering their knowledge about products, services, displays, education, and doing more business to the customers. Kraft General Foods salespeople are considered "category specialists" by many of their customers. This means they offer consultative help to grocery store managers on how best to display Kraft's cheese products, as well as all the rest of the managers' products. They have developed this expertise through the research and data bases created by Kraft over the years. Kraft hopes that by providing this free advice, its customers will be more profitable, do more volume, and thus be able to handle more of Kraft's products.

The second mode, which started around 1975, could be called the *modest tools mode*. The salesperson began to discover and use computers and software to do simple prospect management, pricing, call reporting, and relatively straightforward sales analysis. The consultative mode has expanded to include the use of these tools. Salespeople can use laptop computers to verify order shipments, check inventory availability for customers, and access data bases to develop an even stronger consultative relationship with customers.

Case in Point

Today's Skills Are Only the Beginning for Tomorrow's Salespeople

Ed Young is one of the new breed of professional salespeople who view themselves as orchestrators of the final sale of their products or services. In order for people such as Ed to fulfill their role, their training must be oriented toward team building with emphasis on problem-solving and facilitation skills. Many companies, such as AT&T, use sales assessment evaluation before hiring job candidates. Under this system, the candidates move through a series of simulated sales experiences using role playing and videotape playback. These companies are seeking a new breed of salesperson who will need to exhibit, either through such screening evaluations or background checks, such characteristics as empathy, ability to work with others, good listening skills, and willingness to develop oneself.

About 1988, the third mode, the *powerful tools mode,* began. This was the integration of demographic, psychographics, a person's values, attitudes, and lifestyle preferences and geographic information with a customer's buying history so the salesperson could target high-probability prospects. This came about because the technology was available and economics dictated that salespeople make more successful calls in shorter times using less money to do so. We are about to enter the fourth mode, probably around 1995.

The fourth mode will be *integrated customers and vendors*. The data of buyers and vendors will be merged in such a way that each will be able to monitor the other's production, usage, inventory, and costs. This will link customers and their suppliers closer than ever before and will usher in long-term commitments and working together for mutual gain. Bar-coding on grocery store items and scanning at the cash register allows both store managers and the salespeople who call on them to work closer together to share information and more carefully manage the wide array of products carried. In doing so, both benefit—the grocery store manager by being able to adjust inventory and product offerings to specifically match the changing needs of the shoppers, and the salespeople by pinpointing the products most likely to sell, monitoring what is selling, and avoiding trying to sell something the data shows won't move in the local market.

Purchase orders and invoices will be processed automatically so production will not be interrupted. Both partners will profit from the marriage. As firms integrate, they will begin to act as one, allowing them to be much better marketers and far more responsive to changes in the market than has ever been possible. The salesperson will not become obsolete in this era; to the contrary, the salesperson will take on an even more important role, that of innovator, entrepreneur, contract negotiator, and information gatherer.

Electronic selling is finding its way into consumer markets and increasingly into industrial markets. The salesperson of today has to be sharp, alert, intelligent, and professional. The salesperson of the future must be all these plus a computer whiz, data base manager, and expert communicator.

In this chapter, we are going to be futuristic. We will look into the haze and speculate on what will appear. Changes will occur at an increasing rate. For salespeople, technology is about to take an unprecedented leap forward. Those who embrace and use it will prosper. Those who don't will languish in mediocre selling careers and dote on the past.

The Rise of Geodemographic Marketing and Sales Support

Geodemographic Marketing is Micromarketing

In geodemographic marketing, the "geo" part refers to a location database reference. This is a ZIP code, census track, postal carrier route, county, or city. The "demographic" part refers to an individual's or household's vital statistics and psychographics. **Geodemographic marketing** is integrating demographic and geographic information to design highly specialized marketing plans for niche markets. The old strategy of exposing a high number of people to the message to find the small percentage who will respond has been replaced with the new strategy of exposing a specific set of highly qualified potential buyers to a message tailored to them. It is a strategy of going after a lot of business from a few, rather than chasing a little business from many. Geodemographics is being used by more salespeople everyday to pinpoint prospects and reduce the qualifying time spent with each. By comparing the known characteristics or qualifications of existing buyers to target groups of suspected potential customers, salespeople can quickly and efficiently eliminate the unqualified ones without having to spend time asking them qualifying questions. This saves salespeople time and money and the unqualified suspect the annoyance of a call.

Learning Objective 1:
Geodemographic marketing allows the targeting of more customers more effectively

The most rapidly advancing technique in marketing, selling, and sales support is geodemographic marketing. Geodemographic marketing uses relational data bases to pinpoint target customers geographically and demographically. A relational data base is comprised of component data bases that in some way relate to each other. For example, a relational data base could contain data bases on the number of children in a household, their ages, their grade in school, their favorite TV programs, the ages of their parents, and their parent's income. Having this relational data base would allow the salesperson selling toys to retailers to pinpoint the children's age brackets on which various stores in different communities should focus. Claritas Corporation offers a psychographic coding system to marketers based on the clustering of like characteristics in relational databases. Its PRIZM system has

40 categories based on income, age, life-style, interests, and occupations. Table 17-1 lists an abbreviated PRIZM descriptions of several. This is just one example of how geographic, demographic, and psychographic data from different data bases can come together to produce information highly useful to salespeople.

When advertising was based on the notion of "spray and pray," the strategy was mass coverage. Customers were sprayed with TV, radio, and print ads. The notion was simple: someone out there will buy, and enough people will buy if a broad enough field is covered. The technique was straightforward: tell everyone the same thing, then rely on a certain percentage to react. The ability to target to the individual was not possible before geodemographic marketing; targets were broad and only roughly defined, if at all. With geodemographic marketing, salespeople and sales support activities can be precisely focused on individuals with similar needs and wants, to the exclusion of all the rest.

Case in Point

What Will Be Different About Selling and Marketing in the 1990s

Tremendous changes in sales and marketing will make sales managers' job more complex. They will be responsible for more objectives, and how they are achieved will be very different in the 1990s than in the 1970s and 1980s:

In the '70s	In the '90s
Volume was sold by direct sales	25 percent of all sales will be through telemarketing, distributors, sales agents, and others
There were territory reps, district managers, and regional managers	The sales manager will manage territory reps, key account reps, national account reps, sales support reps, customer service reps, telemarketing reps, administrative assistants, sales trainers, district managers, and industry specialists—all in the same salesforce
The marketing approach was mass-marketing to one type of customer	Targets will be very selective, specialized
The performance expectation was increase volume and minimize turnover	Performance expectations will be to generate volume in strategic markets with strategic products, increase and manage margins, and decrease the cost of making sales and recruiting top sales performers

Source: William A. O'Connell and William Keenan, Jr., "The Shape of Things to Come," *Sales and Marketing Management* 142 (1990): 38.

Table 17-1 How Marketers See Us. An example of a relational data base produced by geodemographic data.

Blue Blood Estates

1.1% of U.S. households
Median household income: $70,307
Age group: 35–44
Wealthy, white, college-educated families; posh big-city townhouses

Characteristics: Buy: U.S. Treasury notes; Drive: Mercedes-Benzes; Read: *The New York Times, Gourmet;* Eat: natural cold cereal, skim milk; TV: *David Letterman.* **Sample ZIPs:** Beverly Hills, Calif. 90212; Potomac, Md. 20854; Scarsdale, N.Y. 10583; McLean, Va. 22101; Lake Forest, Ill. 60045

Money & Brains

0.9% of U.S. households
Median household income: $45,798
Age group: 45–64
White families, singles; college graduates; Big-city townhouses

Characteristics: Buy: classical records, imported champagne; Drive: Jaguars; Read: *The New Yorker;* Eat: whole-wheat bread; TV: *Cheers,* the *Today* show. **Sample ZIPs:** Georgetown, Washington, D.C. 20007; Grosse Pointe, Mich. 48236; Palo Alto, Calif. 94301; Princeton, N.J. 08540; Park Cities, Dallas 75205

Furs & Station Wagons

3.2% of U.S. households
Median household income: $50,086
Age group: 35–54
New money in metro suburbs, White, college-educated families

Characteristics: Belong to country clubs; have second mortgages; Drive: BMW 5 Series; Read: *Gourmet, Forbes;* Eat: cold cereals; TV: *The Tonight Show.* **Sample ZIPs:** Plano, Texas 75075; Reston, Va. 22091; Glastonbury, Conn. 06033; Needham, Mass. 02192; Pomona, Calif. 91765; Dunwoody, Atlanta 30338

Urban Gold Coast

0.5% of U.S. households
Median household income: $36,838
Age group: 18–24, 65-plus
Upscale urban high-rise, college-educated, white singles

Characteristics: Travel by train, buy Treasury notes; Drive: Jaguars, Mercedes-Benzes; Read: *Atlantic Monthly;* Eat: fresh chicken; TV: *Nightline, Entertainment Tonight.* **Sample ZIPs:** Upper East Manhattan 10021; Upper West Manhattan 10024; West End Washington, D.C. 20037; Fort Dearborn, Chicago 60611

Pools and Patios

3.4% of U.S. households
Median household income: $35,895
Age group: 45–64
Upper-middle-class white couples with grown children

Characteristics: Travel by cruise ship, use health clubs; Drive: Alfa Romeos; Read: *The Wall Street Journal;* Eat: natural cold cereal, skim milk; TV: *Newhart.* **Sample ZIPs:** Fairfield, Conn. 06430; Morton Grove, Chicago 60053; Catonsville, Md. 21228; Mission, Kansas City 66205; La Crescenta, Calif. 91214

Two More Rungs

0.7% of U.S. households
Median household income: $31,263
Age group: 55-plus
Multi-ethnic suburbs; families, singles; multi-unit housing

Characteristics: Travel by chartered plane, cruise ship; Drive: Audi GTs; Read: *Money, The New York Times;* Eat: liquid nutritional supplements, frozen entrees; TV: *David Letterman, Nightline.* **Sample ZIPs:** Skokie, Ill. 60076; Flushing, N.Y. 11365; Fort Lee, N.J. 07024; Rancho Park, Calif. 90064; Bexley, Columbus, Ohio 43209

Young Influentials

2.9% of U.S. households
Median household income: $30,398
Age group: 18–34
Yuppies, white singles, childless couples; inner-ring suburbs

Characteristics: Buy: investment property, Irish whiskey; Drive: Acuras; Read: *Barron's;* Eat: yogurt, low-fat milk; TV: Sunday morning interview programs, *Cheers.* **Sample ZIPs:** Glendale, Colo. 80224; North Side, Atlanta 30339; Greenbelt, Md. 20770; Redondo Beach, Calif. 90277; Westheimer, Houston 77603

Young Suburbia

5.3% of U.S. households
Median household income: $38,582
Age group: 25–44
White college-educated; upper middle class; Child-rearing families

Characteristics: Buy: Swimming pools, mutual funds; Drive: Mitsubishi Galants, Toyota vans; Read: *World Tennis;* Eat: frozen waffles; TV: *Cheers, Night Court.* **Sample ZIPs:** Eagan, Minn. 55124; Dale City, Va. 22193; Pleasanton, Calif. 94566; Smithtown, N.Y. 11787; Ypsilanti, Mich. 48197

God's Country

2.7% of U.S. households
Median household income: $36,728
Age group: 25–44
Upscale frontier boomtowns; White college-educated families

Characteristics: Buy: Investment property, microwave ovens; Drive: Saabs, Subarus; Read: *Inc., Food & Wine;* Eat: canned meat spreads; TV: *Kate & Allie.* **Sample ZIPs:** Woodstock, N.Y. 12498; Plainsboro, N.J. 08536; Corrales, Albuquerque, N.M. 87048; Lake Arrowhead, Calif. 92352; Aspen, Colo. 81611

Table 17-1 Continued

Blue-Chip Blues

6.0% of U.S. households
Median household income: $32,218
Age group: 25–44
White families, high-school educated; Wealthiest blue-collar suburbs

Characteristics: Use CB radios, belong to unions; Drive: Chevy Sprints, Buick Rivieras; Read: *Golf, 4 Wheel & Off Road*; Eat: natural cold cereal, frozen pizzas; TV: *Entertainment Tonight.* **Sample ZIPs:** Coon Rapids, Minn. 55433; S. Whittier, Calif 90605; Mesquite, Texas 75149; Ronkonkoma, N.Y. 11779; St. Charles, St. Louis, Mo. 63301; Taylor, Detroit, Mich. 38180

Bohemian Mix

1.1% of U.S. households
Median household income: $21,916
Age group: 18–34
White-collar college graduates, singles, racially mixed

Characteristics: Buy: wine by the case, common stock; Drive: Alfa Romeos, Peugeots; Read: *GQ, Harper's*; Eat: Whole-wheat bread, frozen waffles; TV: *Nightline.* **Sample ZIPs:** Greenwich Village, N.Y. 10014; Dupont Circle, Washington, D.C. 20036; Cambridge, Mass. 02139; Lincoln Park, Chicago 60614; Shadyside, Pittsburgh 15232; Haight-Ashbury, San Francisco 94117

Levittown, USA

3.1% of U.S. households
Median household income: $28,742
Age group: 55-plus
High-school-educated white couples, post-war tract subdivisions

Characteristics: Watch ice hockey, go bowling; Read: *Stereo Review, Barron's*; Eat: instant iced tea, English muffins; TV: *Newhart, Sale of the Century.* **Sample ZIPs:** Norwood, Mass. 02062; Cuyahoga Falls, Ohio 44221; Donelson, Nashville, Tenn. 37214; Stratford, Conn. 06497; Cheswick, Pa. 15024

Gray Power

2.9% of U.S. households
Median household income: $25,259
Age group: 55-plus
Upper-middle-class white couples, retirement communities

Characteristics: Use movie projectors, sail; Drive: Cadillac DeVilles; Read: *Golf Digest*; Eat: canned corned-beef hash; TV: *Good Morning America.* **Sample ZIPs:** Sun City, Ariz. 85373; Laguna Hills, Calif. 92653; Hallandale, Fla. 33009; South Yarmouth, Mass. 02664; Danville, Va. 24541; Sarasota, Fla 33577

Black Enterprise

0.8% of U.S. households
Median household income: $33,149
Age group: 35–54
Black achievers, intelligentsia; High educational levels

Characteristics: Use cigars, malt liquor; Drive: Yugos; Read: *Ebony, Ms*; Eat: frozen dessert pies; TV: *American Bandstand, Nightline.* **Sample ZIPs:** Capitol Heights, Md. 20743; Auburn Park, Chicago 60620; Seven Oaks, Detroit 48235; Mount Airy, Philadelphia 19119; South De Kalb, Atlanta 30034; Cranwood, Cleveland 44128

New Beginnings

4.3% of U.S. households
Median household income: $24,847
Age group: 18–34
Middle-class, urban apartment dwellers; some college education

Characteristics: Use slide projectors, jazz records; Drive: Mitsubishi Mirages, Hyundais; Read: *Scientific American, Rolling Stone*; Eat: bottled water, whole-wheat bread; TV: *David Letterman, Who's the Boss?* **Sample ZIPs:** Bloomington, Minn. 55420; Northeast Phoenix 85016; Reseda, Los Angeles 91335; Englewood, Denver 80110; Parkmoor, San Francisco 95126; Park Place, Houston 77061

Blue-Collar Nursery

2.2% of U.S. population
Median household income: $30,007
Age group: 25–44
Blue-collar white families; High-school educated

Characteristics: Use campers, belong to unions; Drive: Ford EXPs, Chevy Chevettes; Read: *Mother Earth News*; Eat: canned stews; TV: *Newhart.* **Sample ZIPs:** West Jordan, Utah 84084; Maryville, S.C. 29440; Princeton, Texas 75044; Richmond, Mich. 48062; Haysville, Kan. 67060; Magnolia, Houston 77355

New Homesteaders

4.2% of U.S. population
Median household income: $25,909
Age group: 18–34
Middle-class boomtowns, white families; some college education

Characteristics: Use microwave ovens, cruise ship travel; Drive: Chevy Sprints, VW station wagons; Read: *Harper's Bazaar, Car Craft*; Eat: Mexican foods, canned meat spreads; TV: *Super Password, 60 Minutes.* **Sample ZIPs:** Loveland, Colorado 80537; Alamogordo, N.M. 88310; Redding, Calif. 96001; Yuma, Ariz. 85364; Pocatello, Idaho 83201; Billings, Mont. 59101

New Melting Pot

0.9% of U.S. population
Median household income: $22,142
Age group: 55-plus
New-immigrant urban areas; White collar, college educated

Characteristics: Buy mutual funds, Latin records & tapes; Drive: Chevy Impalas; Read: *The New York Times, Metropolitan Home*; Eat: yogurt, English muffins; TV: *David Letterman.* **Sample ZIPs:** Los Feliz, Los Angeles 90027; Jackson Heights, N.Y. 11372; Rogers Park, Chicago 60660; Geary, San Francisco 94121; Little River, Miami 33138

Source: Adapted from *The Clustering of America* by Michael J. Weiss, also © Copyright 1989, *USA Today.* Reprinted with permission.

Census data will become an integral part of a salesperson's strategic planning.

The use of geodemographic relational data bases gives salespeople a better chance of being successful. They can know more specifically what the prospect will and will not buy. Geodemographic marketing will result in a higher rate of success per customer contacted. Because geodemographic marketing allows for more knowledge about specific target customers, salespeople will be able to more effectively qualify potential customers and thus increase their sales success ratio.

Lack of access to the necessary census data made such finely tuned geodemographic marketing impossible until just recently. The data existed but were beyond the affordable and technological reach of most sales managers.

Census data is currently available in three forms: in hundreds of printed volumes in most public libraries; on computer tapes usable only on mainframe computers, and through computer service bureaus that can produce reports that are highly customized but generally too expensive and slow for salespeople or their managers to use.

Starting in 1992, the census data will be available to anyone on CD-ROM disks. This means the entire census will be in such a condensed form that a sales manager could carry it in a jacket pocket. CD-ROM players, like CD players for music, are inexpensive computer accessories.

Using a variety of data bases along with the census information, salespeople will look up the number of Cadillac owners in the United States, the number of households with children in college, and the population of Milwaukee with the push of a computer button. These will be merged into a relational data base, then combined with a list of phone numbers, addresses, and incomes from other data bases, and all before finishing the morning's first cup of coffee, they will have a prospect list of Milwaukee Cadillac owners with kids in college, including their names, addresses, and phone numbers.

Geodemographic marketing permits salespeople to know what products to present before ever going to make the first cold call. The cold call will be cold only from the standpoint of it being a first meeting. By the time salespeople have applied geodemographics, they will have narrowed the product presentation list down to items with guaranteed success. The result: more profitable sales, less up-front qualifying time, and more efficient use of salespeople's time. Salespeople will be able to satisfy more customers in less time and with a higher level of efficiency.

To take geodemographics one step further, data from such data bases will be used with artificial intelligence programs that will suggest the best selling techniques to use. The artificial intelligence programs will take data from related data bases (relational data bases), cross-match complimentary data, and then analyze it to produce a list of dos and don'ts for the salesperson about the new prospect.

Data Base Marketing

Most firms have data they do not use. Their sales invoices and orders are only used to create gross summary reports or for accounting purposes. Such data are now being captured by marketers and salespeople to build customer profiles and to compare such profiles to census information to uncover new potential customers. When such data bases are the focus of marketing and sales efforts, it is called data base marketing.

Future accounting and sales departments will work to create data bases from this normally occurring paperwork. For example, as a sale is processed through the accounting department, the invoice data will be automatically entered into the firm's data banks and made instantly accessible to marketing and salespeople around the world.

The firm's records will tell the salespeople the profile of frequent buyers, bad credit risks, seasonal buyers, and customers whose business is expanding. Ordered items will go into a product-purchasing profile. The salesperson's identifying code number will be used by the sales manager to track that person's performance. Finally, the amount of the sale and the cost of goods sold will produce a customer and salesperson profitability analysis. This will be cross-referenced with geographic information to produce a territory-by-territory performance index.

Learning Objective 2: Data base marketing will change the way salespeople identify new customers

Case in Point

Monsanto Salespeople Get Data Each Day

Monsanto had a data base system installed as early as 1985 and was feeding data to its salespeople on a daily basis. Its system, called OACIS (On-line Automated Commercial Information System), gives the salesperson daily updates on accounts, products, and performance.

Being a menu-driven system, salespeople need to do nothing more than log on to the company mainframe through any terminal or modem, then use the menu to review the customers for the day. Data are available about the customer's purchase history by date and/or product and cumulative sales to date by month and year-to-date. Salespeople can request order status reports so they can report to the clients just exactly where their orders are in the shipping queue.

The system also helps salespeople be better self-managers. It can compare the actual sales to a customer against the forecasted amount of sales the salesperson anticipated at the beginning of the year.

The OACIS system is putting Monsanto in the forefront of computerization in the salesforce.

Source: "A Daily Dose of Data for Monsanto Salespeople," *Sales and Marketing Management* 135 (1985): 70.

Commercially produced data bases will be as much a part of the salesperson's selling strategy as the knowledge of the product's features. Trade association data bases, mailing lists, and statistical information on consumer's and business' buying habits will be part of the data bank accessible by every salesperson. Commercially available data bases will tell the Levi sales rep exactly the type of person that buys "501" jeans. Coupling this with demographic data bases will produce an instantaneous sales projection for a store in any given location in the nation, state, or territory.

Glen Garrett

Case in Point

Selling With New Technology

Glen Garrett is a college textbook sales representative based in Tennessee. After several successful years, Glen was honored by West Educational Publishing in January of 1992 as the Co-Rep of the Year for a 28 percent dollar volume increase over the previous year. Glen feels that changing technology has had a major impact on the role of the sales representative and will continue to do so in the future. How does Glen see technology changing the way you do business with your customers and the company?

"Videodisk, CD-ROM, hypercard, and customized publishing are technologies that were not readily available when I started in college publishing in 1987. West outfitted the college sales force with Compaq laptops in 1990. Almost all reports that were done by hand are now generated on the computer and sent via E-mail. Memos that might have taken several days to reach their destination through the mail can now be sent and received the same day. This is especially helpful in obtaining competitive information as textbook adoption deadlines approach.

Sampling has been streamlined significantly. Rather than filling out computer forms in red ink and sending them to the home office for data entry, I now enter all sampling information myself, and then transmit this information to the mainframe by modem. This can cut the arrival time of examination copies to professors by as much as three weeks. Computer supplements, WESTEST,™ and software packages are becoming part of almost every course. These additional products increase the amount of product knowledge required of each sales representative, but also provide an additional avenue to create interest in those products. Successfully demonstrating accompanying software to a professor greatly enhances the chances of obtaining an adoption.

The next few years promise to be exciting in that emerging technology will continue to streamline the way we do business. The effect of customized publishing, and the extent to which computers are integrated in the classroom, decreasing the need for "traditional" textbooks, are issues which college publishers must successfully deal with in order to remain competitive."

The Overlay Map—One of Selling's Newest Tools

▶ ▶ ▶ ▶ ▶ ▶ ▶ ▶ ▶

Learning Objective 3: Overlay maps combine marketing and census data into maps salespeople can use for more effective selling

Geodemographics and data base marketing will yield a new sales planning tool, the "overlay map" or "overlay grid." The **overlay** map will be a graphic representation of a relational data base's output. Software programs are available that draw scale maps of any state, county, or city in the nation. Overlay maps will pinpoint geographic areas of highest and lowest probability of success, market potential, and competitive neglect. With this information in hand, salespeople and their managers will plan their market penetration strategy. They will know the areas of the salespeople's territory that have the greatest potential and the least. They will also know the areas in which they are already selling the most and the least amount of each product.

What Would You Do If...?

Your manager is sending you to do a market analysis of the New Jersey market for "501" Levi jeans. She told you she wants a geodemographic profile of the typical "501" buyer, then an overlay of the retail stores serving the top five markets in the state.

> ▸ Questions: What type of geographic information would you want?
> ▸ What type of demographic data would be helpful?
> ▸ How would you put them together to show her where the greatest market potential is?

Using the Census of Manufacturers,[3] the industrial salesperson will pinpoint businesses by their SIC codes, which tell the salesperson about that industry's number of employees, value of shipments, size of facilities, and much more. Having such information available in graphic form will make the salesperson more effective, efficient, and successful.

▸ ▸ *follow-up questions*

1. Explain how a company would use geodemographic marketing if it were making and selling industrial equipment. What would be the demographics of such a potential customers firm?

2. Could geodemographic marketing apply to selling services? Explain and give examples.

3. What is the concept behind the overlay map?

Telemarketing and the Salesperson

Telemarketing as a Sales Support Tool

Telemarketing will be the major sales support tool in the 1990s. Telephone sales support persons will set up appointments, do off-site account service after the sale, handle requests for information, and track down and qualify leads. Inbound telemarketing sales support staff will direct calls coming from 800 numbers to the salesperson responsible for that geographic area. The cost of having a salesperson track down every inquiry, then make a face-to-face call is becoming prohibitive, with no sign it will ease in the future. For simple requests, the sales support person will handle it on the spot. For more complicated problems, the salesperson would be notified via electronic mail, cellular phone, page, or fax to make the necessary on-site visit. And that salesperson will arrive totally prepared with information about the customer's purchasing history and service record, all supplied instantly via computer or fax.

Telemarketing sales support staff will make sales to accounts too small for a salesperson to economically service now totally accessible. Many accounts are orphaned each year because they are too small to deal with, given

◀ ◀ ◀ ◀ ◀ ◀ ◀ ◀ ◀
Learning Objective 4:
Telemarketing will significantly change the way business reach and sell to their customers

the cost of making the personal call. Telemarketing will increasingly be used to keep those small accounts active. This would hold market share while generating a small, but still positive, profit. Telemarketing will serve as the vehicle for the small orders or items, and face-to-face selling can take over the big jobs. Telemarketing will have a tremendous impact on another phase of sales support, that of generating leads. This was discussed earlier in the text, but now we focus on it in greater detail.

Telemarketing Will Generating More Leads

Telemarketing will be the primary tool to generate leads. Small companies will hire telemarketing firms to make the first inquiry call either as a cold call or from a hot-lead list. Larger firms will have their own in-house people doing lead generation for the field salesforce.

The benefits of having an outside lead generation service will lie in the numbers of leads generated and cost savings. Sellers will save money by using outside firms because they are a variable cost. Sellers will use them to generate a predetermined number of leads, then come back only when more leads are needed. Another cost-saving alternative is contracting with the lead generation service on a dollars-per-lead basis. The seller pays for only hot leads and not for dead-end phone calls.

Case in Point

Telemarketing Supports Face-to-Face Selling

Manufacturer's agents use telemarketing techniques to support their face-to-face selling efforts, according to a survey done by the Manufacturer's Agents National Association. The study found:

- Eighty-one percent of the agents use the telephone for cold-call prospecting.
- Ninety-six percent use the phone to qualify leads, and most respondents said their sales productivity was much better as a result of using the phone.
- Ninety-three percent use the phone to maintain contact with prospects.
- Ninety-one percent use the phone on a regular basis to keep in touch with their customers.

Source: *Sales Managers Bulletin,* 30 September 1990.

While telemarketing will have a tremendous impact on selling and sales support, it will not be without its problems. It can easily generate more leads than a salesperson can follow up. Some firms will go overboard using telemarketing. They will turn their salespeople off to telemarketing, as well as the prospective customers who are promised a call by the salesperson and don't get one. This will pose an interesting problem for management: cut back on the leads (which are potential business) or hire more salespeople to chase the leads telemarketing has generated (which increases cost without the guarantee of success)?

Interactive Inbound and Outbound Calling

Computerization will allow for interactive inbound and outbound calling. This will cause a major shift in some salesforces from being outside to being inside. **Interactive inbound calling** operates in the following way: When the incoming call is received by the computer, it identifies the caller's phone number. Simultaneously, it searches the company data bases for a match with a current customer file. When the salesperson picks up the phone (which is linked to the computer), the caller's account information is displayed on the computer monitor. The salesperson can verify that the person is the previous customer and the address is the same and can make conversation about how the products previously sold are working out. From here, the customer's problem can be solved or a sale closed.

Interactive outbound calling operates in much the same fashion. With interactive outbound calling, the computer records the number of the person being called, then searches the data bases for any information. It then displays geographic, demographic, and psychographic information about this specific person or about a "typical" person from that telephone exchange.

Telemarketing will create more inside sales jobs handling business-to-business products. In fact, the real growth will occur in business-to-business sales. Much of what business-to-business salespeople sell is supply items or routinely purchased products. These will be more efficiently handled over the phone. As a result of this, the list of products an outside salesperson has to sell will change dramatically. Sales of low-value, repetitively purchased items will go to the inside salesforce. This will free outside salespeople to make more profitable calls and calls requiring their expertise. The inside salesforce will do order taking, and the outside salesforce will focus on

Computers will link buyers' and sellers' firms data bases for better service and greater cost savings.

getting orders. The Union Pacific Railroad currently uses telemarketing agents to sell its services to small accounts (it defines small as customers with under half a million dollars in billings!).

Clearly, telemarketing will lead to greater specialization. In a survey by *Sales and Marketing Management* magazine, 192 sales managers were asked to rate the options that will be available to increase productivity in the 1990s. Sixty-nine percent said "integrating new technologies" (laptop computers, electronic mail, fax, and car phones) would be their number one priority, and 45 percent indicated telemarketing would be a significant force for improving productivity.[4]

Computers Will Create Greater Specialization

The future activities of salespeople will be different from what they are today. In the old days, salespeople had to do it all. They had to find the prospects, chase the leads, do the qualifying, make the cold calls, make the presentation, and service the customer after the sale. All of that accounted for only the selling activities of their job; the nonselling administrative activities were reserved for late at night or weekends.

Traditionally, activity quotas directed and call reports logged the salesperson's day-to-day activity. Managers assigned activity quotas and sales quotas and monitored salespeople's efforts and results. Reports have always been the bane of salespeople. Reading, analyzing, and making decisions from them has been time-consuming for managers. Much of this drudgery will fall on the computer. Reports will be generated directly from the sales orders salespeople submit through their laptop computer or call in via their cellular phone. Salespeople will be relieved of writing the monotonous call reports, and managers will be relieved of the tedium of sorting through page after page of paper. The computer will produce numerical or graphic summary reports by product, territory, week, month, and year. Built-in decision rules will pinpoint areas or products deviating from established targets.

Specialization means salespeople will do what they do best: get accounts, close sales, and service accounts. Since much of the prospecting and qualifying will be done by the telemarketing operation, the salesperson's job will be devoted to more directly profitable endeavors. Saving just one hour a day translates to 250 to 300 hours per year more selling time. Sales reps who use laptops save 4.4 hours per week on travel, reduce clerical errors by 20 to 25 percent, and save two to three hours per week in selling and servicing time.[5]

Retail and service selling will become more personalized and customized. Department stores and grocery stores now do instant credit checks at the cash register. The clerk inputs the customer's name and bank account number, and the company computer checks this data against its bad-check file. Services will be more specialized for the customer. In a travel agency, for example, data bases will allow travel agents to check the caller's file before they even pick up the phone. The customer's record will contain the customer's preferences for rooms, flights, and seats on the flights. Thus, the caller will get more customized service because of the computer.

Teleconferencing Will Replace Traveling To Meetings

Teleconferencing has come a long way from the original conference call. Teleconferencing is being used to replace expensive travel to meetings with far more flair than was possible with the old-fashioned conference call. The conference call is essentially a party-line call, and for small numbers of participants, it remains a viable alternative to meeting face-to-face.

But how do you make a presentation of your new equipment to over a thousand prospective customers in one afternoon? That was the problem Zimmer, Inc. solved with teleconferencing. Zimmer, a manufacturer of medical equipment, used video-teleconferencing to present and demonstrate its new arthroscopic surgical instruments to over a thousand orthopedic surgeons at 26 locations around the nation in one three-hour live broadcast. The American Dental Association used teleconferencing to reach its 6,000 members at 35 locations for a three-and-a-half-hour broadcast that included 45 minutes of questions and answers with panelists thousands of miles away.[6]

Teleconferencing allows firms to reach their salespeople anywhere there is a satellite dish and a television set hooked to it. Many businesses are now replacing costly travel to meetings with teleconferencing as a means of quickly and efficiently reaching large numbers of salespeople at a relatively inexpensive price. While not cheap—a one-hour presentation can cost up to $100,000 to produce and transmit—when compared to the cost of travel and lodging and the opportunity losses incurred while salespeople are away from their territories and not selling, teleconferencing can be a bargain. While teleconferencing will not replace the field salesperson for the necessary individual customer contact, it can be effectively used for seminar selling or mass presentations like the one Zimmer did.

▶ ▶ *follow-up questions*

1. Think about the data your school has on you. What could it use to create a profile of your school's "typical" student? Could it use that data in a telemarketing effort to recruit more students? How?

2. With telemarketing taking on so many of the sales support functions, will salespeople really be needed to do such things as qualifying, prospecting, or generating leads?

3. In what types of industries will telemarketing not be applicable? Why?

4. Will specialization of the salesforce benefit the customer? If yes, how and why? If no, why not?

The Mobile Office and the Paperless Salesperson

Many technological tools just coming into their own today will be commonplace for the salesperson of the future. Here, we shall discuss just a few.

Facsimile, or fax, machines are new but already becoming quite common. They will be an ordinary selling tool by the year 2000. Orders, invoices and contracts will be faxed between customers, vendors, and company departments as easily as they are mailed today.

◀ ◀ ◀ ◀ ◀ ◀ ◀ ◀
Learning Objective 5: New technological tools will make the salesperson's job easier, more effective, and more profitable

Fax is now, and will be more so in the future, a necessity in doing long-distance business, such as international sales. Since a fax machine can send a message to another fax machine which can store it in its memory until recalled, business transactions and communications will no longer be governed by time zone considerations. Orders placed by fax will get into the vendor's office, logged on the computer, and verified directly back in a matter of minutes. Fax machines literally will replace the mail for transmitting paper documents. Through fax machines, world markets will be only minutes away from each other.

Laptop Computers

Laptop computer are totally portable. When linked to mainframe computers, they become the vehicle for ordering, making order inquiries, reporting on delivery status, and backordering. They will allow the salesperson to place orders directly into the home office's computers. Salespeople with laptops will enter orders directly into the production schedule, manage inventory, or schedule transportation. Firms will issue laptops to salespeople right along with their business cards and car the first week of work. When the laptops are connected through modems or fax machines to mainframes, entire files of reports, communications, and customer orders will be transmitted instantly.

Case in Point

Laptops Heralded for a Range of Benefits

Laptop computer are being heralded for benefiting numerous aspects of selling. They:

▸ *Strengthen Sale Support:* DuPont's Remington Arms can role out a promotion and answer all salespeople's questions within 24 hours using E-mail (electronic mail) and laptops.

▸ *Gain Competitive Advantage:* Hercules Chemical's fragrances and food ingredients group uses laptops to outline applications of its products to its customers. Salespeople have the advantage of getting samples to customers for tests ahead of competitors. There is a high correlation between who gets the sample in first and who gets the contract.

▸ *Anticipate Future Problems:* Anaquest uses laptops to do cost and value analysis for physicians and hospitals. Laptops show the long- and short-run cost implications of Anaquest's products relative to its competitors.

▸ *Improve Call Planning and Presentations:* Coast Envelope uses laptops to access customer profiles. It also keeps bulky price catalogs on computers. Salespeople access prices during presentations without having to page through catalogs while the customer waits.

Source: Thayer C. Taylor, "Laptops and the Sales Force: New Stars in the Sky," *Sales and Marketing Management* 138 (1987): 50–53.

The traveling salesperson will use laptops for transmitting orders and correspondence and linking to the company's client data bases. Imagine a salesperson sitting in a hotel room in a distant city the night before a big presentation. The salesperson needs an update on the customer she is going to visit tomorrow. By simply turning on the laptop, connecting the phone jack, and pushing a couple of keys, everything from the customer's file is on the screen for the salesperson to review. In the future, the main function of the briefcase will not be carrying order forms or documents but carrying the salesperson's computer. There will be no need for all that paper and paraphernalia.

Case in Point

Survey Finds Laptops Doubling in Popularity, Desktops Declining

Two hundred and seventy-nine firms responded to the *Sales and Marketing Management* Survey of Selling Costs in 1989, and the trend was obvious. Firms that implemented PCs into their salesforces reported a median increase in productivity of 20 percent (it ranged as high as 78 percent).

The salesforce used them primarily for customer correspondence, maintaining customer profiles, time and territory management, doing call reports, and electronic mail.

For the first time in the history of the survey, respondents indicated they would buy more laptops than desktops. The number indicating they would buy more laptops doubled the 1987–88 percentage to 18.8 percent, while the number indicating desktop purchases fell from 73 percent to 61 percent.

Source: Thayer C. Taylor, "PCs Make Inroads, Yet Holdouts Persist," *Sales and Marketing Management* 141 (1989); 119.

Cellular Telephones

The greatest communication innovation for the salesperson is, and will increasingly be, the cellular phone. The cellular phone provides crisp, clear communications without being tied to a wire line in an office. Cellular phones are already commonplace with real estate agents, insurance agents, and industrial product salespeople, as well as such service providers as contractors, lawyers, stockbrokers, and physicians. Cellular phones put salespeople and their customers in direct contact at all times. Cellular phones will eliminate the annoyance of telephone tag.

The cellular phone will have a tremendous impact on salespeople's responsiveness to customers. In the time it would take to drive from one account to another, the salesperson can handle another customer's delivery problem or installation question without having to miss the upcoming appointment or schedule another trip to the calling customer's business. This degree of customer responsiveness will become the standard.

Cellular telephones, laptops, and fax machines will make the salesperson's briefcase a mobile office. The salesperson will be able to act on a customer's order instantly while closing the sale. The customer will get an order confirmation and shipping ticket before the salesperson leaves. The invoice

Cellular phones will be in common usage allowing salespeople to be in constant contact with customers no matter where they are.

(faxed, of course) will be handed to the customer and with all the necessary paperwork needed to complete the sale and issue a check against. Gone are the days when the salesperson's secretary types invoices.

Electronic Mail

Electronic mail links the salesperson's computer with any company branch or individual. Unlike the fax machine, electronic mail will not transmit hard copy without the aid of a printer. Electronic mail is simply linking a message in one electronic file (the sender) to another (the receiver). Electronic mail is fast, easy, and verifiable. Senders can request the computer advise them when receivers open and read their electronic mail.

Customers and vendors will be able to tap into each other's company's electronic mail. Buyers will be able to leave questions and orders with salespeople through the network of electronic mail. Salespeople will confirm orders and provide product information or shipping details the same way. These interbusiness links will be made possible through the phone system, along with local and wide area networks.

Local area networks   A **local area network** (LAN) links several computers to a central computer. LANs link computers in the same office or within a whole department. LANs allow one software program to serve many users at the same time, which saves time and money. The company needs to buy only one copy of the software program, rather than one for each user.

Wide area networks   A **wide area network** (WAN) is the LAN concept on a grander scale. Through WANs, entire companies can use the same software, send electronic mail, and make their data bases accessible. An even broader expansion of the WAN concept is linking different companies' computers, software, and electronic mail capabilities together. Such linkages will make data and file transmissions and communications easier. Such systems are available to some degree through subscriber services, such as CompuServe and others.

▶ ▶ *follow-up questions*

1. Is a LAN and a WAN the same thing? How would they benefit vendors and customers?
2. Of all the technology discussed in this section, which one do you think will have the greatest impact on the profession of selling in general? Why?
3. How will the cellular phone make the salesperson more efficient and better?

Electronic Recruiting and Training: The Newest Innovations in the Profession of Selling

Electronics and the computer will change the way salespeople are recruited and hired. One change will be in the way people apply for jobs.

The Electronic Application Will Prevail

Here's the scenario for your next job interview: You go to the campus recruiting office and ask to register for the fall term interviewing schedule. A secretary takes you to a small cubicle and sits you in front of a computer. You push the key labeled "Enter" and an electronic form appears. You complete it and go home. The next day, the placement office advisor says you have four firms interested in talking to you. You wonder, "How did they find out about me so fast?" The answer is simple: the placement office is wired in to a nation-wide recruiting search service. When you finished the form in the placement office and pressed the "End" key, your data was instantly put into a national data base for all subscribing employers to search. Your job interest profile, academic preparations, and geographic interests all matched the "ideal" of four firms. You go in the next day and pull up each of those four firms' electronic job application forms on the school's PC. You complete each one, and voilà, the interested firms have your application. Electronic recruiting has just eliminated the paper form.

Learning Objective 6: Computers will be used to help sales managers do their recruiting and selection

The electronic application will have several advantages. First, it will be instantly available to anyone wishing to review it. Second, the electronic form will be more accurate. Since the process will be interactive, inputting information incorrectly will prompt the computer to ask the applicant for the correct response. For example, if the form asks the applicant's age and the applicant enters 1948, the computer will ask again for the age in years, not the year the applicant was born.

The third benefit of electronic recruiting will be the information it sends the personnel department about the applicant's ability to complete the application itself. This will constitute an electronic interview. The computer will monitor the time taken to complete the form. This will tell managers about the applicant's ability to read, understand, and follow directions. The more time required to complete the form, the higher the probability of lower literacy or computer illiteracy. Finally, the computer will monitor the number of mistakes made in typing and the information entered. The computer will monitor spelling, grammatical errors, and completion time. All of these measures will be stored in the data base and correlated with the profiles of the successful and the unsuccessful salesperson. Using such a correlation, the manager will get a preliminary projection of the applicant's chances for success. The manager will be able to sort the data base for prospective applicants by their probability of success and then interview the best ones.

This electronic interviewing will permit faster candidate evaluations by more people, so better salespeople will be hired. The personal interview will not become a thing of the past, but preinterview preliminaries will be done with far greater speed, saving time and money.

This type of interviewing will be particularly useful to firms hiring inside or telemarketing salespeople. Since much of these salespeople's time is spent working with a computerized customer list, product list, and scripted presentations, their ability to use the computer must be measured accurately and quickly. The person who can complete the electronic form correctly without help will require less training and start-up time. Thus, the application and electronic interviewing processes become the first form of screening.

A Portion of Sales Training Will be Done by Computer

Training salespeople will also change in the decades to come. The computer and highly technological training tools will become a normal part of the training regimens of even the smallest companies. Training costs are high, and that will not change. Massachusetts Mutual Life Insurance Company, which spends over $130,000 per person in recruiting, financing, and training new hires until they become productive, thought enough of electronic training to spend $1.7 million on 125 interactive video training units.[7]

To reduce the time and expense of training, firms will move to interactive videos and computer simulations. Though interactive training systems can cost over $20,000 each, they will be the training tool of the future. Interactive video and computer simulations will present role-play situations where the conditions change and the trainees must react. Different customer's social styles can be programmed into the video or simulation. Without interactive video, a real person would have to play opposite the trainee and take on the different roles. This would be costly and would not offer trainees the instant review that a video system provides. With electronic training, the same situation can be repeated as many times as it takes to get the trainee to do the presentation exactly right.

Training Will Go Global Through Television

One of the newest and most revolutionary advances in sales training will be the result of global communications and satellite technology. Sales trainers will be training hundreds if not thousands of salespeople simultaneously over BTV. BTV, or business television, is becoming the communications tool of the future for businesses with widespread salesforces. Already, more than 60 private television networks carry programming for their business owners or may be rented for private, short-term use.[8]

Decreasing satellite costs mean beaming a training session to sales branches thousands of miles away is becoming a reality even for small companies. Firms see several advantages of satellite training. First, a program can be done live and interactively. Salespeople viewing the training sessions can call during the session to ask specific questions, just as in face-to-face training. In doing so, many trainees with the same or similar question can get

Teleconferencing and tele-training will be common for the globalized salesforce.

their answer all at once. Second, satellite transmission can bring the company's top executives into each sales branch. This not only makes such seldom-seen figures more human and accessible, but it is great for morale. These policymakers can explain what directions the company will be taking and why and what they expect each employee to do to help make it happen. This is far more effective than the impersonal, computer-generated form letter and more practical than having such people personally visit each branch, a physical, financial, and temporal impossibility in most instances. The third benefit is cost savings. Texas Instruments broadcasts a Monday morning show to all its sales branches. The cost is about $4,000 per show, but the firm figures this is cheap compared to the expense of bringing 800 salespeople together every Monday to bring them up to date and train them. A Wharton School of Business study found videos increased retention by 50 percent, compared to the same material presented in printed form.[9]

With decreasing costs and improved communications abilities through satellites and the rising cost of in-house training, more firms will use satellite training. Training at the corporate offices will be reduced, and much of what salespeople will learn in the classroom may come from the television set. Sales training is leaping into the use of space-age technology.

▶ ▶ *follow-up questions*

1. What are the benefits of electronic job applications and interviewing to the prospective salesperson? To the hiring firm?

2. What are the some of the negative aspects of interactive computer training and simulation?

3. For what types of selling jobs do you think interactive computer training would work the best? The worst?

A New Breed of Salesperson

▶ ▶ ▶ ▶ ▶ ▶ ▶ ▶ ▶
Learning Objective 7: The
salespeople of the future will
be significantly different than
those of today

Many things about selling will change. The greatest change will be in the salesperson. As a student reading this book, that means you! You are far more advanced in your skills and technical knowledge than any of your predecessors. The people coming up behind you will be even farther advanced than you are by the time they are your age. The salesforce of the future will be smarter, have more expertise, and be better educated before going into selling than ever before.

Case in Point

Death of a Salesman—A Certain Type of Salesman

The process of selling has started to emerge into a team effort. The fast moving, in-front-of-the-wave companies have realized that selling is a new game and the customer has made it so. *Smart Selling* is replacing the traditional notion of the salesperson out there making sales, riding from account to account, getting the sale and moving on to the next customer. Smart selling means making the selling effort an integrated part of the entire marketing program all the way through product development, pricing and advertising, all phases of anything having to do with products, services and customer satisfaction. Is this a new revolution? The answer is yes and no. What has taken businesses away from their customers and caused salespeople to focus on making the sale rather than developing a relationship with the customer has been scientific management, according to William A. Band, a customer satisfaction specialist with Coopers & Lybrand. He says, "The new theories emphasized narrow expertise and specialized functions inside companies...we forgot how to serve our customers." As companies grew, they moved away from the spirit of entrepreneurship that built their success on serving customer's needs.

Source: Christopher Power, Lisa Driscoll, Earl Bohn, "Smart Selling, How Companies Are Wining Over Today's Tougher Customers, *Business Week*, Aug. 3, 1992, pp. 46–47.

Smart Selling—How To Do It

▶ Focus the entire organization, from manufacturing to finance, on sales and customer service.

▶ Smart selling requires managerial involvement from the CEO on down. CEOs regularly call on customer with salespeople and they do sales training.

▶ Build relationships with customers, abandon "slam dunk sales."

▶ Smart selling requires salespeople help solve customers problems... problems that may or may not be related to the products or services sold.

Continued

Continued—▸ Change the compensation picture. Commissions reward short-term performance which actually be at the expense of long-term survivability.

▸ Forge electronic links. Link your computers to theirs. Use electronics to track customer relationships, service, delivery and overall performance. Let them order directly into your computer system and track the progress of their own orders.

▸ Pay unceasing attention to customers. Constant contact, not just when you want to sell something or not just when they have a problem is appreciated.

Who's Leading the Way

▸ **DU PONT** Pioneered team selling 10 years ago: Groups of sales reps, technicians, and factory managers work together to solve customer problems, create and sell new products.

▸ **MERCK** Tops in turning salespeople into experts. Merck trains its reps over 12 months in pharmaceuticals and trust-building sales techniques. Continuing refresher courses are mandatory.

▸ **REYNOLDS METALS** A model of perseverance and innovation. Spent 25 years cultivating Campbell Soup before winning an aluminum-can contract. Has developed team selling to educate customers such as auto makers on new uses for aluminum.

▸ **WAL-MART STORES** Built customer confidence by selling the basics: everyday low pricing, items always in stock, cashiers always available. Demanded simplified selling from vendors such as Proctor & Gamble in the form of data linkups and coordinated inventory management.

▸ **NORDSTROM** Proving that department stores need not die. Intense, personalized attention to the customer pays off in high shopper loyalty and steady growth.

▸ **HOME DEPOT** The boss as salesman-in-chief. Founder Bernard Marcus preaches smart selling and follows up with endless training.

▸ **DELL COMPUTER** How to sell a complicated product by phone and mail. The secret: Advanced technology to keep track of the customer and intense training.

▸ **TOYOTA MOTOR** Lexus luxury line uses customer satisfaction as a key measure for setting dealer compensation, turning Lexus showrooms into the new standard for U.S. auto dealerships.

▸ **GENERAL ELECTRIC** Revamping selling on many fronts: It's training salespeople to work long-term with customers, experimenting with team-based compensation, assigning staff full-time to customers' factories, and forging deep relationships with its own suppliers.

▸ **VANGUARD GROUP** A mutual-funds marketer that has perfected the low-key sell. Uses reliable customer service, easy-to-understand products, and superlow fees to lure investors who don't like the hard sell of brokers looking to earn hefty commissions.

Source: "Business Week," 8/3/92, pg. 48.

More Sophisticated

College students will be better educated. They will have had exposure to a broader range of subjects and be better prepared to use computers. They will produce more and better work than past students, and they will have sophisticated data analysis, presentation, and statistical tools at their disposal. When they are hired, they will expect at least the same to be provided for them. The firm that cannot meet such expectations will find it hard to recruit quality people.

The person coming into the ranks of the professional selling force will look on it as a profession, not a last resort. Some people still look at selling as a last resort. The future salesforce will be an elite corps. A college degree will be mandatory, and for the more prestigious selling positions, even the entry level positions will require a master's degree.

The field of selling will become more scientific and involve the study of psychology and human behavior. Knowledge of exactly what to say and how to say it will be required. This will entail using all the psychological and behavioral tools available. Knowing the psychological effects of different paper colors, opening sentences, key words, and presentation styles will be required.

A more sophisticated salesforce creates a need for better managers. There will be more competition for managerial slots. The salesforce's increased level of sophistication will require equally sophisticated managers. Managers of the future will need to be excellent salespeople and problem solvers. They will also need the same computer and human relations skills and background in psychology the new salesforce will require.

More Demanding

Because the people coming into the salesforce will be better educated, they will demand more from their managers and companies. They will expect to have the hardware and software they "grew up with" in college and at home. They will demand access to more data bases to help them do a better job planning and selling. They will require more sales support in the form of telemarketing, promotions, and qualifying.

Greater mobility will give future salespeople more options. A generation of young people has grown up in households that moved frequently. The salespeople of the future will no longer look at their present city as the geographic limit of their employability. The ability and willingness to relocate mean the new generation salesperson will be more selective and say, "If I cannot get the terms I want here, I will simply go somewhere else."

Cross-functional Team Selling Will Find Its Way into Numerous Selling Environments[10]

Cross-functional team selling takes the approach that numerous types of expertise are needed to make the sale. Cross-functional team selling is common in high-tech industries. Because salespeople often do not have the necessary engineering knowledge or technical sophistication, engineers and designers become part of the selling team.

Team selling will increase in popularity. A large school bus company uses the team approach when selling its busses to large school districts. In addition to salespeople, the team includes financial experts and regional distributors.

Team selling will find its way into marketing situations where salespeople face complex or customized products or services, products requiring extensive postsale service or support, or prospects who use a buying team or buying center approach to purchasing. Product sophistication will make the team approach a necessity. The lone salesperson cannot have enough technical information readily accessible to quickly and efficiently deal with the myriad technical questions customers and their buying team members raise.

To be successful, the sales team will need to be managed differently than a single salesperson. First, it will need to be trained as a team and to communicate as a team. Individual stardom has to give way to a team approach. Salespeople see technical people as "techies" or "nerds," while technical people often see sales people as hustlers.

Second, the team must be trained in major account sales strategy, identifying what the individual member's roles are when dealing with major accounts and how the technical people can use their knowledge to influence the buyer's technical people to support the whole selling effort.

Third, each team member must be firmly grounded in product and service knowledge. The team's technical people need to attend sales training sessions and the salespeople need to attend the technical product training sessions with the technical people. The technical people will learn how salespeople use technical information in their selling efforts, and the salespeople will learn the intricacies of and differences between engineering specifications and functional operation.

Finally, the team approach to incentives will make the manager's job more complex. Salespeople are often more motivated by money than technical people, who tend to be more interested in recognition and promotion. Incentives may have to be custom-designed for each team, taking into account the make up of the team. On this issue, the manager overseeing a team selling system may do well to simply ask the team for extensive input here. What works for one team may not work for another.

The cross-functional team approach to selling will result in more and better service to the most important customers, but it does present management difficulties. Through training, work, and solidarity, it can be successful. Managers will have to realize that a sales team, like an athletic team, soon learns to function as a single unit and think with a single mind. Team socialization will be a major consideration for managers and team members alike.

▶ ▶ *follow-up questions*

1. How will a more sophisticated salesforce require greater sophistication from managers?

2. In your opinion, what will be the most significant demand new salespeople will make of their firms in the 1990s?

Managers Will Require Greater Training in Employment Issues

▶ ▶ ▶ ▶ ▶ ▶ ▶ ▶ ▶

Learning Objective 8: Sales managers will need to be knowledgeable about more than just selling

Managing will be more complicated. Greater emphasis will be put on performance evaluations, legal matters, affirmative action and equal employment opportunity. Salespeople and their managers will need more and better training in a variety of areas, but two of the most important will be employment issues and human relations. Salespeople will demand more feedback on their performance, and managers will need to be acutely aware of the laws and issues surrounding hiring, firing, and promoting.

Performance Evaluation Training

Salespeople will be better prepared through their experience and schooling to perform self-analysis. The computer will help here, too. Salespeople will get computerized performance reports on themselves. From these, they will read how they are performing relative to their cohorts, their assigned quota, and their own performance of last year, last month, and last week. This means they will be better prepared for their performance reviews with their manager. Performance reviews form the basis for merit raises, promotions, transfers, demotions, and terminations. Having the computing skill to do self-analysis will make the salesperson of tomorrow much more of a self-manager than has been the case in the past.

Performance evaluation training will be part of every sales manager's job. With the cost of recruiting and training being so high, firms will need to concentrate on keeping and developing their salespeople. To do so effectively will involve structured and scheduled performance reviews. Performance evaluation training also will be imposed indirectly through the legal system. The days of terminating at will are over. To terminate, promote, transfer, or provide merit raises will require a record of documented evidence for justification. The performance evaluation will be the tool for providing that evidence. It will be part of every sales manager's training. An improperly completed evaluation can invalidate any paper trail being created as evidence for termination or promotion.

Performance evaluations compare salespeople's performance to their stated job description. The evaluation criteria must coincide with the job description. This will create better managers, more specific criteria, and less problems with role ambiguity, a major cause of job dissatisfaction and turnover. The use of performance evaluations should reduce the costs associated with turnover.

Commercial and Employment Law Training

The laws affecting salespeople will become more complex as new court cases modify, extend, or repeal them. Salespeople will learn more about the law than they ever have before. They will need a greater working knowledge of product safety and consumer protection laws and the the Uniform Commercial Code. They will need to know more about contracts and warranties and what can and cannot get them sued. Since the courts are holding individuals as well as companies responsible, salespeople will need to be fully aware of what can and cannot be done or promised.

Sales managers will need to be better versed in the law than their salespeople. When salespeople have a potentially legally sensitive problem, they will naturally turn to their manager for guidance. Sales managers will not become legal experts, but they will be asked to respond to more and more legal and ethical issues.

Large and small companies are growing into the international markets, which will require greater knowledge of exporting and importing laws. Small firms, in particular, will find wider possibilities in the international market place. Unlike the larger firms with their cadres of international lawyers, the small firms must develop their ability to recognize their own legal problems with foreign customers. Sales managers will be called on to answer questions surrounding pricing, distribution, contracts, and payments in foreign markets. Both salespeople and managers will gain a first-hand knowledge of international legal complications either by design or experience. The first, of course, is preferable.

Affirmative Action and Equal Employment Opportunity Training

Greater training in the application of the laws and guidelines surrounding affirmative action and equal employment opportunity will be necessary. Affirmative action and equal employment opportunity procedures are the federal, state, and local guidelines and rules of conduct employers must follow when recruiting, hiring, promoting, disciplining, and terminating employees to avoid discriminating against anyone. The federal laws and rules are administered through the Equal Employment Opportunity Commission (EEOC). EEOC complaints range from sex discrimination in hiring to age discrimination in retirement. Managers could spend a significant amount of time dealing with such complaints, or they could simply doing everything right and avoid such problems. To do everything right means proper training, and firms in the future will opt for more training over compliance problem litigation.

▶ ▶ *follow-up questions*

1. How do job descriptions and performance evaluations go hand-in-hand?
2. What is the EEOC? How does it affect salespeople and their managers?
3. It is not uncommon for job descriptions to go unrevised for five to ten years. What is the danger in this?

Selling in the Global Market

This chapter concludes by addressing the globalization of selling. The ease of global communications, as we have already mentioned, will make markets in Europe and Asia as easily accessible as the next state over. Salespeople will find themselves becoming international marketers by desire and necessity.

Salespeople Will Make Sales Around the World

Learning Objective 9: Globalization means selling on a worldwide basis and will totally change the way businesses view sales and marketing

Four significant trends will globalize the selling function:

1. Telemarketing will expand to global proportions. The technology is already there; it simply needs greater application in more firms.

2. Small businesses will grow to become global marketers by expanding their inside salesforces. This goes along with number 1 above. It is worth mentioning again because it will mean that international marketing and sales will no longer be the domain of only the largest firms. There will be greater competition for the global market.

3. Free trade agreements and greater access to foreign markets will create the need for a more international salesforce. Liberalization of trade policies will make access easier. This will expand the salesperson's job and require a greater depth of knowledge than in the past.

4. Promotion opportunities will expand significantly for multilingual salespeople. This is the natural outgrowth of the first three items listed above. Salespeople who can converse in several languages will have a natural advantages over those who cannot.

For the student today, the signal should be clear: the more one is knowledgeable about international relations, history, and languages, the more attractive one is to a prospective employer. Students must look beyond the short run and broaden their experiences to qualify for the selling positions of the future. Employers will turn to more than just business schools for their salespeople, seeking people who have a broad liberal arts background along with a strong preparation in business disciplines.

Competition Will Get Tougher

The salesperson of the future will find more opportunity but also greater competition. The future salesperson will encounter six major changes in competition:

Change No. 1: Increased market competition   Not only will our markets expand as more domestic firms go international, but the competition for the U.S. market will increase. As the economies of Asia and Eastern Europe expand and move away from being centrally planned to market-driven, nations that have not previously traded to any degree with the United States will begin to appear in the marketplace. United States salespeople will be forced to compete against traditional rivals and a host of new teams.

Change No. 2: Invaders and defectors   U.S. salespeople will see competition from foreign salespeople invading their territories and their best colleagues going to work for the foreign competitor selling in the United States.

Change No. 3: Tougher competition for talent   Competition will get tougher for human resources. The opportunities for salespeople to work for foreign firms selling in the United States will grow. At the same time, loyalty toward United States firms will fade. Salespeople of the future will be as willing to work for a British firm selling in the United States as for a Brazilian or United States firm. Firms are becoming so global in both their focus and operations that their country of origin will have little meaning.

Good firms from all over the world will be looking for good salespeople. It is totally reasonable to believe that firms will get their salespeople from a variety of countries. If they cannot get the caliber of person they need in one country, they will go to another. The talent pool for good salespeople will be as globalized as the markets they serve.

Change No. 4: Decreased market-share monopolies Competition will get tougher for market share. Future salespeople will find increasing numbers of competitors in their market. Customers will buy from vendors offering the highest quality and service. They will consolidate their sources of supply in just a few vendors, but they will demand a heavy toll for this. Vendors will have to agree to specific and stringent terms, adhere to strict quality standards with zero defects, and pay dearly if they fail even once to uphold their end. Their reward will be guaranteed business with volumes they may have only dreamed about before. Both parties will become interdependent: when one prospers, so will the other, but when one falters, the other will come down, too. Salespeople, their firms, and their customers will have to weigh these serious trade-offs.

The firm wishing to maintain market share will have to be more and more skillful at servicing the customer better than the competitor. It will be up to the field salesperson to deliver that service in innovative, creative, and economically efficient ways.

Change No. 5: More demanding and sophisticated customers Competition will get tougher because customers will demand more on every aspect of the deal. The increasing number of competitors and the concomitant decrease in loyalty will put the customer in a stronger bargaining position. The more competitors, the greater customers' ability to extract terms specifically tailored to their needs.

Change No. 6: Customer satisfaction will remain the name of the game Competition will get tougher, and competitors will become craftier, but the bottom line will still be the same: the competitor that does the best job of satisfying the customer's needs will always get the business.

Customers will place demands on salespeople to be more professional than ever before. The same tools salespeople will be using to be more successful in selling will also be used by customers as well. Both will tap into the same data bases, and both will be sharing information. The customer will place greater demands on salespeople for assistance in solving problems that may not even involve the salespeople's products. Customers will in essence be saying, "The more services you can give me, the more business I can give you."

Being able to serve customers' needs will be a hallmark of the successful firm in the 1990s and beyond. The 1990s will find industrial and business-to-business sales managers searching for trainees who can learn to understand their industry and its products, competitors, and complex relationships, along with the customer's industry and competitors. A sample of what buyers will be expecting more from salespeople is given in Table 17-2.

The profession of selling will become more challenging. The challenges will come from directions not even anticipated today and will make selling an even more dynamic and stimulating career. It will get tougher and require more expertise, but it will also be more rewarding as the demand for quality

Table 17-2 What Buyers Expect from Salespeople

Buyers will be doing business with salespeople who:

1. Orchestrate their firm's resources to yield a level of service above the competition
2. Provide extensive counseling and consulting services in addition to their normal product and services
3. Are creative and innovative problem solvers, not just product peddlers
4. Are impeccably ethical and honest
5. Will stand up to their own firm to be an advocate on the customer's behalf
6. Are well prepared for all sales calls, meetings, and demonstrations

Source: Thomas Ingram, "Improving Sales Force Productivity: A Critical Examination of the Personal Selling Process," *St. John's Business Review* 3 (1990): 6.

people increases and the markets for the products and services they sell expands. Globalization will directly or indirectly affect all aspects of selling, be it industrial or retail. The salespeople of the future will have a challenging and exciting experience ahead of them. Focusing on customer service will be the name of the game, and it will require using all the strategies and tactics we have discussed in this text and more that will need to be developed as the buyer-seller relationship changes.

▶▶ *follow-up questions*

1. What is meant by the term globalization, and how will it affect the individual salesperson?
2. Among the career openings posted in your school's placement office, how many of the firms are foreign owned? Does it make a difference to you?
3. How will telemarketing and computing make the salesperson of tomorrow a globalized marketer?

Case in Point

Tom Peters Looks into the Future

Tom Peters, noted managerial consultant and advocate of excellence in business as a cornerstone of competition, makes the following observations on the requirements for business success in the future:

1. *Organizations will need to become flat structured, rather than pyramids:* people on the front lines will have to be given the power to make decisions without having to ask for permission.
2. *Continuous improvement and learning will be necessary, demanded, and the norm.* People's education will only have begun when they have graduated from school. Continuing formal education for managers and workers alike will be essential for competitive survival.
3. *Information technology will change the way we do everything.*

Continued

Summary

This chapter speculated on how selling will appear in the future. Rapid technological and competitor-forced market changes make defining the future difficult at best. Here, the approach was to extrapolate the future from current events.

Geodemographic marketing was identified as a major new direction for marketing and sales. Geodemographics will result from pulling together data bases and customer lists to form relational data bases. These will pinpoint sales targets down to units as small as the individual household or business. Government data, such as the census, will be combined with proprietary data from firms and commercial data bases to give the salesperson the ability to prospect and customize sales presentations and promotions like never before. The overlay map, the natural off-shoot of geodemographic marketing, will produce geodemographic data in either numeric or graphic form (Learning Objectives 1–3).

Telemarketing will also revolutionize personal selling. It will have great significance in both the actual selling process and sales support. Telemarketing will support outside salespeople in several ways. It will keep small, traditionally low-profit accounts alive so the salesperson can focus on more significant accounts. Telephone sales support people will handle inquiry calls and some simple requests for information. Telemarketing will evolve into the primary vehicle for generating and qualifying sales leads. It will be able to generate more leads than a salesperson can follow up on, so a strategy of quality and quantity must evolve together (Learning Objective 4).

The technology of interactive inbound and outbound telemarketing will enhance the personal touch in telemarketing. Linking the telephone to the computer and relational data bases will make customer contact far more effective. The interactive nature of telemarketing coupled with relational data bases will provide telemarketing sales reps and sales support people with access to customer data to a greater extent than ever before. The ability to know which customer is on the other end of the line along with that customer's purchasing and service record will make the telephone sales agent and the sales support personnel an integral part of the firm's total selling efforts (Learning Objective 5).

Selling will become more specialized. Computers, data base marketing, and telemarketing will help salespeople do what they do best—make presentations, close sales, and service accounts. Much of the tedious work involved in prospecting, qualifying, report writing, and monitoring will be done by computers. Interfacing sales records with marketing data bases will create a variety of selling subspecialties.

The paperless office and the mobile office will become more prominent. Fax machines, cellular telephones, electronic mail, and laptop computers will permit salespeople to carry their entire compliment of office machinery in a briefcase. Memos, letters, invoices, billings, and purchase orders will all be handled as electronic communications, rather than on paper. Laptop computers have already been shown to increase a salesperson's efficiency by over 50 percent; there is no reason to suspect anything will reverse that. LANs and WANs will become increasingly popular. These networks will help the salesperson of tomorrow communicate with cohorts and customers on a basis undreamed of only a few years ago.

Technology will change the job application and interviewing process. Candidates will complete computerized job applications and respond to computer-generated interview questions. The computer will monitor applicants' answers and generate a success probability evaluation (Learning Objective 6).

Future salespeople and managers will have more sophisticated knowledge and technical skills than their predecessors. Their training will extend to greater depths in psychology and human behavior. Necessity will force them to develop greater expertise in evaluating performance and the use of EEOC rules. This sophistication will come from better, more demanding educational preparation and high-tech training tools (Learning Objectives 7–8).

Finally, the most long-run change of all will be the globalization of the selling function. Technology will literally give every salesperson in the world access to every major market. This will mean greater competition for products, services, customers, and human resources. The salesperson of the '90s will find selling more challenging and rewarding than it has ever been (Learning Objective 9).

Key Terms

Geodemographic marketing   Using relational data bases to pinpoint target customers geographically and demographically.

Overlay map   A graphic representation of relational data base's output; it represents the distribution of a population that has a set of attributes in common.

Interactive inbound calling   Linking incoming telemarketing calls to relational data bases to produce on-screen data for the telemarketing salesperson.

Interactive outbound calling   Customer data is displayed on-screen for the telemarketing salesperson when the person being called answers the phone.

LAN   The acronym for local area networks, which are hardware links through a central computer allowing several computers to share software, transfer data, and carry electronic mail.

WAN The acronym for wide area network, which is simply the LAN concept applied on a grander scale from company office to office, regardless of geographic location.

Discussion Questions

1. What does the term geodemographic mean?
2. How does geodemographic marketing differ from mass marketing?
3. How will having the census on CD-ROM benefit salespeople?
4. What is data base marketing?
5. What is a census overlay map and how it will be used by salespeople in the future?
6. In what ways will firms use telemarketing to support salespeople?
7. How will telemarketing change what and how salespeople sell?
8. How will interactive inbound and outbound telemarketing increase sales?
9. How will technology cause greater specialization in the salesforce?
10. Why will fax machines gain widespread use in the salesforce?
11. What benefits do laptops computers bring to the salesforce?
12. Why would salespeople resist using laptop computers?
13. How will cellular phones and electronic mail be used by salespeople?
14. What is a LAN? A WAN? What are their benefits to salespeople?
15. Why would a firm implement an electronic recruiting and interviewing system?
16. What characteristics will distinguish the sales recruit of the future from the recruit of today?
17. Why will performance evaluation training will be added to the sales manager's training?
18. What aspects of the globalization of sales and marketing will impact salespeople?

Application Exercise

Go back and read the Case in Point about Monsanto, then answer the following questions:

1. As a Monsanto salesperson using the OACIS system, what information would you want about a client before going to make the first call?
2. How would you use the information in the OACIS system to improve your prospecting and qualifying?
3. As a salesperson for Monsanto, your manager has given you the following assignment: "Use the data in OACIS and go to Denver where we are opening a new branch. We have no customers there at all. It's your job to get us some business as quickly as possible." What would you do to handle such an assignment?

Class Exercises

Group Exercise

Divide the class into four groups.

Group I will discuss and evaluate personal selling in 1975.

Group II will do the same for 1990.

Group III will do the same for 2005.

Group IV will do the same for 2020.

Topics that each group should focus on should include:

1. *Communication technology*— availability and sophistication of salesforce and customers
2. *Impact trends* in customer conduct and service
3. *Demographics*
4. *Organizational characteristics*
5. *Computer technology*— impact of it compared to paperwork skills
6. *Skill requirements* of the salesforce
7. *Global market interdependence*
8. *Other areas* as deemed relevant

The groups will then summarize their findings and conclusions for class presentation. The class will evaluate the findings in terms of *personal* and *organizational* implications.

Individual Presentation

Looking toward the year 2000, each student will formulate his or her individual career goals and *action plans* for attaining those goals. Be prepared to discuss not only *goals* and *action plans* but also the *skills* required to attain those plans.

 **▼ ▼ ▼ ▼ ▼ ▼** *Cases* **▼ ▼ ▼ ▼ ▼ ▼**

 Case **17.1**

Laptop Lamentations

At the Sales and Marketing Executives International meeting, an interesting conversation was in progress. Jan was saying to Peggy, "I do not really know how I ever got along without them, my laptop computer and cellular phone. I use both so much now I would be lost without them." Peggy lamented, "I wish my manager wasn't so stingy. She makes Scrooge look like Donald Trump. She will not spend a dime for anything. Your boss can see the time the cellular phone and laptop saves. My manager says we have done okay without that stuff so far, so doing without it for a while longer will not hurt anything."

Jan told Peggy, "I know what you mean. The trick is to build a case for how much time it will save and then convert that to dollars. By doing that, you can convince your boss that these are worthwhile investments." Peggy thought that was a good idea and decided to start building her case the next day.

1. What would be the selling points Peggy should use on her boss?
2. If you were going in to convince Peggy's boss, what are the F-A-B's (Features, Advantages, Benefits) you would use?
3. What objections would you anticipate Peggy's boss having, and how would you overcome them?
4. Assume a laptop computer would cost $2,500 and a salesperson makes $45,000 per year. What would be the breakeven point for the laptop? (Hint: Use the savings percentages for laptops given in the chapter as a starting point.)

The Future Dilemma

Kay was the new sales manager for VAXC Account Management Corporation, which specializes in helping firms create data bases and selling the software to use them. Kay called Roger into her office and asked him to go see the Future Company. Future, which is owned by Jack Future, specializes in the maintenance of food service equipment for hotels, bars, and restaurants. Jack Future had a growing business and wanted to keep expanding, but he needed a way to manage data to help his salespeople do their jobs better. Also, since his business was growing so fast, he needed a way to quickly analyze what was going on with the firm's sales. He was open to any suggestions.

Kay told Roger he needed to talk to Future and help him out. Roger asked Kay what Future had for data. She said she could not be of any help because, since she was new in town, she had no real knowledge of the firm's operations. Roger went back to his office to begin planning the questions he might ask Jack Future. After an hour of work, he has come to your office and says, "I have been thinking about this Future account. I have a list of possible questions, concerns, and ideas for Future. I need your ideas, too. If you were in my shoes, what would you do to prepare to go talk to Future?"

Questions:

1. What suggestions would you give Roger regarding Future's existing data?
2. What suggestions would you give to Roger in general regarding the establishment of a data base for Future?
3. Is a data base really of any use to a small local service firm like Future? Why or why not?

References

1. Richard G. Holder, president and CEO of Reynolds Metals Company, personal correspondence, January 1991.
2. The four modes discussed here were adapted from an interview with Howard Anderson, founder of The Yankee Group, a marketing research and consulting firm with offices in the United States of America, United Kingdom, Japan, and Australia, printed in *Sales and Marketing Management,* 141 (1989): 48–53.
3. The Census of Manufacturers is one of the many specialized censuses produced by the U.S. Bureau of the Census.

4. *Sales and Marketing Management* 142 (1990): 41.
5. Thayer C. Taylor, "How the Best Sales Forces Use PCs and Laptops," *Sales and Marketing Management,* 140 (1988): 71.
6. Paul E. Gillette, "Picture This Presentation," *Sales and Marketing Management,* 132 (1984): 57–58.
7. Al Urbanski, "Electronic Training May Be in Your Future," *Sales and Marketing Management,* 140 (1988): 46.
8. Kerry J. Rottenberg, "Sales Training Enters the Space Age," *Sales and Marketing Management,* 142 (1990): 46–50.
9. Ibid., p. 48.
10. Cathy Hyatt Hills, "Making the Team," *Sales and Marketing Management,* 144 (1992): 54–57.

Glossary

Action close The salesperson takes an action, such as writing up the order or filling out an estimate sheet, that buyers must stop if they are not ready to buy.

Activity quota The number of calls per day, prospecting calls, displays set up, cold calls, and so on a salesperson is expected to make. It is a target level for a specific selling activity.

Adaptive selling Adaptive selling is an approach to the sales interaction, focusing on the premise that in order to be successful a salesperson must recognize and adapt to each customer type. Adaptive selling means managing selling behaviors and selling resources, while adapting to the buying task of the customer and the nature of the sales relationship.

Advertising allowances Discount awarded to retailers for advertising the product.

Agent A person who legally acts on the behalf of another.

Alternative advance A trial closing technique that offers customers a choice of alternatives to test their readiness to buy.

Alternative choice close This close gives customers a chance to say yes by giving them a choice of alternatives, such as product features, delivery dates, and payment plans.

Amiables A social style of person who depends to a great degree on personal relationships and trust when making business decisions.

Analyticals A social style characterized as being critical, detail-oriented, and wanting to know all the facts and analyze them before making a decision.

Anticipation Expecting the objection and proceeding to answer it before the prospect has a chance to raise it.

Assumptive close The salesperson assumes the sale is made and moves forward on that premise

Authority The power to influence derived from opinion, respect, or esteem.

Authority tactics Used by negotiators to bring in persons with more negotiating influence or to stall a negotiation by claiming lack of power to make a decision and needing to wait for the senior person.

Bailment A transfer of possession but not ownership.

Barrier to communication Anything that blocks the flow of the message or makes its meaning difficult to transmit and/or understand.

Bird dogs Persons hired to get leads for the salesperson to follow up on.

Blueprinting or floor-planning Merchandising plans offered by manufacturers or wholesalers to their customers that diagram the exact positioning of products in sales floor displays and how much product is needed in these displays.

Bonus A lump-sum payment to the salesperson for accomplishing a predetermined level of sales.

Boomerang An objection is converted to an advantage or benefit.

Breach of contract One party fails to complete his or her side of the bargain.

Business libel Unfair or untrue statements about competitors or their products that are written in a letter, brochure, ads, sales literature, or other forms.

Business slander Unfair or untrue oral statements made about competitors or their products to a third party.

Buying criterion The requirements or guidelines setting the standards which must be met to consummate the sale.

Buying life cycle The cycle of time the buyer is in the market and actively purchasing.

Call planner A brief summary of information about the customer and an outline of the selling techniques the salesperson will use during the presentation.

Cash discount A discount the seller gives to buyers for paying their bills early.

Center of influence Anyone who can exert a degree of influence on or predispose a prospective customer to buying.

Changing-people tactic One or both sides changes the personnel involved in the negotiation. This is done if it appears a personality problem may be hindering the negotiations, more expertise is needed, or for any number of reasons.

Closed-ended questions Questions that direct the person responding toward a specific direct answer.

Closing Culminating the sale by the prospect authorizing the purchase.

Closing selling environment In the closing approach, the customers usually know about the products and their features. The basic function of the salesperson is to close the sale.

Cold calling Calling on a prospect with whom no previous contact has been made.

Commitment and consistency A principle of influence that means people are hesitant to be inconsistent with either a previously made decision or stay committed to a decision in order to avoid having to repeat the decision-making process required to change.

Communications channel The conduit or vehicle that carries the message.

Company Policy The rules the company has established to guide its employees in selling and management tasks.

Compensation An attempt to show the prospect that the benefits or advantages of the product outweigh the objection.

Compensation package The sum of all the financial and nonfinancial rewards given to salespeople for their work.

Complimentary openings A compliment used to open a presentation.

Conditions Conditions are valid reasons for not being able to buy.

Constraints Any limitations one negotiating side imposes.

Consultative presentation In this format, the salesperson acts as a consultant to the prospect's firm for the purpose of solving a problem that is typically complex and systemwide.

Consultative selling environment In consultative selling, the function of the salesperson is more like that of a business consultant whose main function is to solve a complex problem by offering a variety of alternatives or solution.

Consumer sales promotions The coupons, free samples, contests, buy-one-get-one-free deals, and demonstrations you see all the time in stores and newspapers and on packages.

Continuous yes close This close wraps things up by having the buyer agree on each feature, advantage, or benefit, thus giving a series of continuous yeses.

Contract A promise or set of promises for the breach of which the law gives remedy, or performance of which the law in some way recognizes a duty.

Contract law The rules governing the agreements people make.

Core service The service upon which the customer relationship can be built, the company's main product.

Creative price close Enterprising and imaginative ways to pay for the product are used as a close.

Curiosity openings Prospects are asked about something that will stimulate their curiosity.

Customer benefit openings The focus is on a benefit the customer will receive from purchasing the product.

Customer relations Customer relations means keeping in touch, making sure that everything is working smoothly and simply expressing concern that there are no problems.

Damage allowance An automatic deduction for damaged goods used only in a few industries.

Damages Monetary awards to the injured party. Punitive damages are awarded by the court to punish the wrongdoer.

Decoding The way the receiver of a message draws meaning from the melange of signals communicated by the sender.

Demographics The vital statistics of a population, or the vital statistics of a prospective business including such things as number of employees, dollar sales, and number of locations.

Direct close Simply asking for the order.

Direct denial Tactfully denying what the prospect has said as being incorrect.

Direct rebate Cash allowances paid to customers with proof of purchase.

Direct response A prospecting tool used to generate a reply from a potential client directly from an ad, mailed letter, magazine tip-in or bind-in card, or telephone solicitation.

Display sales In display sales, the salesperson focuses on keeping the buyer in stock and making sure the price and convenience concerns of the buyer are met.

Diversion tactic Any tactic that diverts the customer away from the current negotiating discussion.

Drawing account A periodic monetary advance to the salesperson to be deducted from the eventual total commission earnings.

Drivers A social style characterized by a desire for control, a bottom-line orientation, and a greater interest in results than process.

Effective demand When customers have the need, the ability to buy, and the authority to make the purchase.

Ego-building tactic Building up the opposition's ego during negotiations. This might lead to better concessions or a more pleasant atmosphere. Ego-building tactics cannot be phony or overused, or they will soon lose any effectiveness they might have.

Emotional motives Buying motives stimulated for emotional reasons, some of which are sentimental, the result of cognitive stimuli, subconscious needs or wants, or such pure emotions as love, hate, fear, despair or belonging.

Empathy Empathy is being able to put yourself in the other person's shoes and see the problem from that perspective.

Encoding The interpretation of the message by the sender.

Endless chain referral A process in which one customer provides names of more prospects.

End-use or resale plan A strategy to help customers resell or use the product.

Enthusiasm Enthusiasm is a strong excitement for an activity.

Ethics The set of moral principles people have and use to guide their actions in separating right from wrong, fair from unfair.

Exchange Exchange is when a buyer and seller agree to make a trade. It can be barter or the exchange of goods and services for money.

Expense allowances Provisions for travel and other business expenses incurred by salespeople.

Expressives A social style identified as being flamboyant, emotional, even theatrical. People with this style are futuristic and holistic thinkers who want to see the big picture more than the details.

Extensive problem solving Decisions putting the buyer under stress, usually due to price, risk, or lack of familiarity with the product.

Extrinsic motivation Motivation coming from the material rewards expected.

Fact-finding The process of gathering pertinent facts about the prospective customer for the purpose of building an account profile and call planner.

Features The physical attributes or performance characteristics of the product.

Feedback The verbal or nonverbal way the receiver responds to the sender's message.

Five-question sequence A direct approach to uncover whatever reason may be standing between the seller and the close.

FOB price FOB stands for "free on board." The price is related to who will pay the shipping costs. "FOB destination" means the seller pays the freight charges; "FOB origin" means the buyer pays.

Formula presentation The salesperson subtly proceeds through the presentation in a predetermined series of steps.

Four P's of a presentation Picture, promise, prove, and proposition.

Fraud Misrepresentation of fact to the point where it has a moving influence on the contracting party.

Gatekeepers Anyone who controls or influences access to the key players in the buying decision.

Geodemographic marketing Using relational data bases to pinpoint target customers geographically and demographically.

Get-on-the-bandwagon close A simple close whose purpose is to excite the customer to jump on the bandwagon along with everyone else.

Gift A transfer of title without expectation of consideration (payment).

Hidden objection An objection the prospect does not reveal for whatever reason and the seller must try to uncover and deal with if the sale is to be made.

Hierarchy of effects A lower-level activity has an effect that causes the activity that follows.

Higher authority close This close involves a satisfied customer acting as a spokesperson for the salesperson, one who will give the salesperson and the product a glowing testimonial.

House list A list of customers the firm already has.

Incentives Rewards for accomplishing certain specific goals.

Indirect denial This technique accomplishes the same objective as the direct denial but is a softer approach.

Inducement close The customer is given an inducement, bonus, or reward for closing today, rather than waiting.

Information tactic One negotiating side claims lack of information to stall for more time or to take the time to get the necessary information.

Interactive imagery The image projected by the salesperson must interact with the image being created by the firm and vice versa.

Interactive inbound calling Linking incoming telemarketing calls to relational data bases to produce on-screen data for the telemarketing salesperson.

Interactive outbound calling Customer data is displayed on-screen for the telemarketing salesperson when the person being called answers the phone.

Intrinsic motivation Motivation that occurs because of the satisfaction of doing a good job or meeting a challenge.

Introductory openings Statements in which salespeople introduce themselves, their company, and the product or service they represent.

ISTEA An acronym used to identify the process an adaptive salesperson uses to customize a presentation; ISTEA stands for *I*mpression, *S*trategy, *T*ransmit, *E*valuate, and *A*djust.

Job analysis The systematic investigation of a job's tasks, duties, and responsibilities, along with the review of the knowledge, skills, and abilities needed by someone to fill the job.

Job description A written summary of the tasks, duties, and responsibilities of the job.

Job posting Advertising and informing possible applicants of the available job.

Kickback A kickback is an unethical and often illegal payment from a salesperson to a buyer or from a buyer to a salesperson.

KISS An acronym which stands for the words Keep It Simple and Straightforward.

LAN The acronym for local area networks, which are hardware links through a central computer allowing several computers to share software, transfer data, and carry electronic mail.

Lead A lead is a person or business that might become a prospect.

Lead letters Letters used to encourage prospective buyers to make an inquiry call to the salespeople so they can schedule a meeting or presentation.

Lease A fixed-term arrangement for possession and use but not ownership.

Liking A recognition and acceptance based on a degree of personal similarity or mutual need; the "chemistry" of a relationship.

List price The normal standard price charged to all customers.

Lost sale close An action close that uses the customer's final rejection as a lever for one last attempt at making the sale.

Market share The target percentage or share of the total business in the market.

Marketing Marketing is a system that is responsible for the distribution, pricing, promotion, and creation of products or services that households, individuals, and businesses buy. It ultimately sets the standard of living in a country.

Markup Also called margin, it simply is the profit.

Maslow's hierarchy of needs A theory of motivation suggesting people strive to achieve five basic needs in a hierarchical order. Those needs are physiological, safety needs, acceptance, esteem, and finally, self-actualization.

Message The intent or meaning the sender attempts to convey.

Minimum requirements The minimally acceptable conditions; the conditions below which terms are not negotiable.

Minor points close This close does not ask the customer to commit to the product in total and all at once. In essence, it has the buyer commit on a very subtle, feature-by-feature basis.

Minor yes Also called a minor yes close, it is getting the prospect to agree on the importance or necessity of a small aspect of the product.

Missionary salespeople Missionary salespeople do not take orders directly from customers but persuade them to buy from the distributors and wholesale suppliers they work for.

Modified re-buying A modified re-buy is a variation of what was bought before, but still basically the same product.

Motivation The amount of effort a salesperson is willing to expend on the job.

Need-satisfaction presentation A format characterized by extensive questioning to determine the buyer's needs.

Negotiating The creative orchestration of alternatives ideally benefiting both the buyer and seller; the art and science of working out compromises through demands and concessions.

Net price The price the customer actually pays; the list price minus any discounts, allowances, and refunds.

New buying New buying situations exist when the buyer is in the market for products not previously purchased.

No-money or price objections Involves prospects saying they cannot afford the product, the price is too high, or they do not have the money at this time.

Noise Anything that distorts or interferes with the transmission of a message.

Nondirective interview An interview in which the interviewer asks applicants broad general questions to get them to talk about themselves or the job.

Nonprofit organization A firm that exists for the good of society and does not depend on profits to survive; often has tax-exempt status.

Objection Any opposition or resistance to a salesperson's request, usually coming from a lack of understanding or information.

Objective-task method Goals are set based on the objective and the tasks needed to carry them out.

Open-ended questions Questions that direct the responder to expound and tell his or her story.

Opinion openings Prospects are asked for their opinion as a way of starting the conversation.

Optimal solution A solution that may not be the best solution but is one both parties can live with within the constraints imposed by either or both; one where both parties benefit but may not get all they wanted.

Oral close The salesperson asks questions to close the sale.

Organizational buyer Buyers for businesses, institutions, or government.

Overlay map A graphic representation of relational data base's output; it represents the distribution of a population that has a set of attributes in common.

Paralanguage What people convey simply by the way they speak, that is, through intonation, pitch, rate of speech, and so forth.

Patronage motives Motives stemming from the relationship between the buyer and the vendor. People get comfortable buying from the same salesperson or company and want to patronize that firm.

Performance management The ongoing process of setting goals, evaluating performance against them, and giving the coaching necessary to both motivate people and keep them on track.

Personnel audit A comparison of the number and type of people currently in the job to the type of person who should be in the job.

Persuasive communication A communication that has only one goal—to change someone's attitude or behavior.

Physical distribution Physical distribution is the actual transportation and storage of products.

Point-of-purchase material The banners, window signs, displays, shelf coupons, floor stands, dump displays, inflatable characters, in short, all of the promotional materials used to encourage interest at the point of purchase.

Porcupine close This close hinges on the buyer's statement, "Do you have it _____?" and the seller's retort, "Do you want it _____?"

Porcupine trial close Rephrasing customers' questions back to them when, for example, they inquire about a feature, advantage, or benefit to test their readiness to close.

Postponing Putting off the objection until later in the presentation.

Postpurchase anxiety Also called buyer's remorse, it is the feeling that the wrong purchase decision has been made.

Preapproach The activities undertaken just prior to making the presentation, for example, scheduling the appointment, rehearsing, and testing the samples or demonstration.

Premium openings A small gift or expression of gratitude, usually a sales promotional device, is handed to the prospect upon entering the presentation. Such things as ball point pens, desk calendars, business card file folders, or notepads are common premiums.

Process-of-elimination close The salesperson eliminates all the reasons for not completing the sale.

Product disparagement The result of untrue or unfair claims made about a competitor's product.

Product Knowledge Facts and operating characteristics of the product or services sold; a major component of sales training programs.

Product-related openings The focus is on an initial demonstration of what the product will do.

Profit sharing A system where the profits of the company are divided among eligible recipients.

Prospect A qualified lead.

Prospect control or lead management system A system for recording modifying, and recalling prospect information.

Proxemics The way people use space around them.

Puppy dog close This close works where salespeople have a model or sample that they can leave with the client, then call back in several days to either close the sale, make one last attempt, or retrieve the model.

Quantity discount A reduction from the list price given to encourage buying larger quantities.

Quotas Sales, activity, or profitability thresholds.

Rational motives Rational motives involve such attributes as dependability, durability, efficiency, economy, flexibility, or performance characteristics.

Receiver The person to whom the message is directed.

Recognition rate The number of times a person gets recognized and saluted for his or her accomplishments.

Recruiting The process of soliciting names for the candidate pool.

Reduce-to-the-ridiculous close This close tries to reduce the price obstacle to insignificance.

Referral openings A discussion of the person giving the referral opens the presentation.

Relationship customizing The ways in which a service relationship can be customized to fit the unique needs of the individuals experiencing it.

Relationship marketing The management of the complete customer relationship, from identifying a core product to expanding to the ancillary products the firm offers.

Relationship pricing Customers are given pricing incentives to consolidate their business with one supplier.

Relationship selling In the relationship selling approach, the goal is to develop and manage a relationship.

Rephrasing Taking the objection and converting it to a question. This has the effect of stimulating the prospect to elaborate or expand on the objection.

Retail sales Retail sales are the sales made to the final consumer.

Role perception The individual's understanding of what the job entails and how to do it.

Routine problem solving Purchase decisions made on a regular basis requiring little risk, search effort, or information on the buyer's part.

Rule of reciprocal concession If you make a concession to people, they feel obliged to make a concession to you.

Rule of reciprocation We try to repay, in kind, what another person has provided to us.

Sale The passing of a title from a seller to a buyer for a price.

Sales forecast The projection a company or sales branch makes for its expected sales.

Sales management Planning, organizing staffing, directing, and controlling the activities of the salesforce to achieve the firm's goals and enhance the business relationship with customers.

Sales quota A minimum amount of sales required, usually expressed as a target amount of either dollar or unit sales for the upcoming year.

Scarcity The scarcer something is, is thought to be, or could become, the greater its value; people will be more motivated to act if something they want is perceived as scare, rather than abundant.

Seasonal discounts Reductions used to encourage off-season purchases.

Selecting The process of screening the candidates in the pool and offering the job to the best one(s).

Selective perception The bits of the message the receiver's brain chooses to admit for processing and interpretation according to any criteria, bias, past experience, or rational or irrational method it chooses.

Selective reception The brain's selection of only the parts of the message (or signals) it wants to receive.

Selective retention What the receiver's brain chooses to remember.

Selling cycle The time span from initial contact to completion of the sale, which may extend beyond signing the order to include all of the after-sale service.

Selling to resellers Selling to resellers is done by manufacturers who sell to wholesalers and retailers, and by wholesalers who sell to retailers. It is the sale of goods destined for resale to another customer in the marketing chain.

Sender The person or firm that has a message to convey.

Service augmentation The unexpected extras vendors can provide that augment or add to the core service. An example would be including a VISA card as an extra no-cost option for new checking account customers at a local bank.

Sexual harassment Direct sexual advances, unwanted touching, putting the victim in a compromising situation, or directly attaching job-related rewards to sexual favors. A sexually offensive atmosphere can also constitute sexual harassment.

Sharp angle close The salesperson answers the buyers' question with one that means, if they reply the way their original question indicates they will, they have bought it.

Shipment contract Transfer of title occurs at time of shipment.

Shocker openings A shocking fact or vital statistic is used to grab the prospect's attention.

Social proof A principle of influence that says people are influenced by what they see as acceptable in their society; if everyone is doing it, it must be okay.

Social style A combination of the effects of thinking, feeling, and behaving.

Span of control The number of people a manager supervises.

Specific performance A mandate from the court to carry out the specific promises of the contract yet unfilled.

Spiffs Inducements to purchase.

Standing-room-only close This close tries to excite the prospect to buying because only a limited number of openings or amount of product is available.

Straight commission Pay is a predetermined percentage of a base, such as sales or profits.

Straight salary A fixed sum of money paid at regular intervals.

Stress interview An interview designed to create anxiety in candidates to test their response to pressure and ability to think on their feet.

Structured interview An interview in which the interviewer uses a list of standardized questions to get the same information from all applicants.

Summary-of-benefits close The seller summarizes the benefits of the product or service and asks for the order.

T-Account close The salesperson lists the reasons to buy on one side of a T drawn on a sheet of paper and the reasons the customer gives not to buy on the other.

Telemarketing Using the phone through either inbound or outbound calls to generate leads or make sales.

The scripted presentation Sometimes called canned, a format allowing little, if any, variation in the delivery.

Think-it-over close A five-step process for turning a stalling objection into a close.

Third-party reinforcement Using the opinions of a third party to overcome an objection.

Three-F's tactic Using the words *feel, felt,* and *found* conversationally through the presentation to overcome objections.

Tie-down A two- or three-word contraction at the end of a sentence used to elicit a minor yes from a prospect.

Tort law The legal duties a person has to another person.

Tough-guy tactic Seldom used, it pits the salesperson's "unreasonable tough-guy," usually a third party brought in who could influence the terms of the sale, against the unreasonable and abrasive buyer or negotiator.

Trade discounts Suggested reductions from a retail price the manufacturer thinks the product should sell for. The discounts are based on the normal costs of channel members.

Trial close A question designed to elicit prospects' reactions without forcing them to make a firm buying decision.

Universal functions of marketing The universal functions of marketing are the activities that create and deliver satisfying products and services to customers.

Value analysis Usually financial in nature, the value analysis is a comparison between the salesperson's product and the competitor's to illustrate the competitive advantage and justify the price asked.

WAN The acronym for wide area network, which is simply the Local Area Network concept applied on a grander scale from company office to office.

Written close The salesperson uses the order form through the presentation to record the specific information. This close is also called the "Let me make a note of that" close.

Zone price All customers in the same geographic zone are charged the same price for a product.

Index

iii © Greg Pease/Tony Stone Worldwide; **xii** Courtesy of Mary Kay Cosmetics, Inc; **xxii** © Peter Stoddart; **xxiv** © Performax, Performax, CT; **0** AP/Wide World Photos; **1** © Jean-Claude LeJeune/Stock, Boston; **2** Courtesy of KnowledgeWare; **5** © Peter Menzel/Stock, Boston; **10** Courtesy of Lockheed; **15** © Stacey Pick/Stock, Boston; **22** © David Young-Wolff/PhotoEdit; **31 clockwise from left** © 1991 PhotoResource; © Phil Cantor/SuperStock; © John Henley/The Stock Market; **32** © John Henley/The Stock Market; **33** © Tim Brown/Tony Stone Worldwide; **37** © David Young-Wolff/PhotoEdit; **42** © 1991 PhotoResource; **50** © David Young-Wolff/PhotoEdit; **50** Robert York; **53** © Dick Luria/Photo Researchers, Inc.; **62** © Phil Cantor, SuperStock; **67** Hugh Carver Group, Inc.; **68** Michelin; **72** © Ulrike Welsch/PhotoEdit; **74** © Rhoda Sidney 1989/Stock, Boston; **77** © David Shaefer/PhotoEdit; **85** © David Young-Wolff/PhotoEdit; **96 top left** © Elena Rooraid/PhotoEdit; **96 top right** © Blair Seitz/Photo Researchers, Inc.; **96 bottom left** © Rob Kinmoth; **96 bottom right** © Rob Kinmoth; **104** © 1991 PhotoResource; **106** Courtesy of Mary Kay Cosmetics, Inc.; **117** © Gregg Mancuso/Stock, Boston; **124** © 1992 Rhoda Sidney/Stock, Boston; **142 clockwise from top left** © Hazel Hankin/Stock, Boston; © Ulrike Welsch 1989/PhotoEdit; © Barbara Alper/Stock, Boston; © Rhoda Sidney/PhotoEdit; **143** © Hazel Hankin/Stock, Boston; **148** © Bachmann/PhotoEdit; **154** PhotoEdit; **158** © Jim Whitmer/Stock, Boston; **159 top** © Jeffrey W. Myers/Stock, Boston; **159** © Patricia Hollander Gross/Stock, Boston; **168** © Barbara Alper/Stock, Boston; **178** © Ulrike Welsch 1989/PhotoEdit; **188** © Hazel Hankin/Stock, Boston; **192** © Jon Feingersh/Stock, Boston; **194** © AP/Wide World Photos; **216** © Rhoda Sidney/PhotoEdit; **219** © Robert Brenner/PhotoEdit; **231** © Albert Trotman/Allford Trotman; **237** © 1992 Star Tribune/Minneapolis–St. Paul; **246** © Barbara Alper/Stock, Boston; **255** © Will/Deni McIntyre/Photo Researchers, Inc.; **270** Courtesy of Federal Express Corporation, All Rights Reserved; **272** © 1989 Spencer Grant/Stock, Boston; **274** © Hazel Hankin/Stock, Boston; **280 clockwise from top left** © Norman R. Rowan/Stock, Boston; **(middle)** © Rhoda Sidney/PhotoEdit; © Howard Grey/Tony Stone Worldwide; © Tom McCarthy/PhotoEdit; © 1991 Mug Shots/The Stock Market; **281** © Norman R. Rowan/Stock, Boston; **285** © Chester Higgins Jr./Photo Researchers, Inc.; **292** © 1991 Cunningham/Photo Resource. All Rights Reserved; **297** © Charles Gupton/Stock, Boston; **303** AP/Wide World Photos; **306** © Joe Baker; **307** A/P Wide World Photos; **319** © Howard Grey/Tony Stone Worldwide; **322** © Video Arts; **330 top left** © Elena Rooraid/Photo Edit; **330 top right** © Blair Seitz/Photo Researchers, Inc.; **330**

bottom left © Rob Kinmoth; **330 bottom right** © Rob Kinmoth; **341** A/P Wide World Photos; **345** © Bruce Ayres/Tony Stone Worldwide; **354** © Rhoda Sidney/PhotoEdit; **357** © Explorer/Photo Researchers; **362** © Anthony Mills/Allford Trotman; **369** © Bob Daemmrick/Stock, Boston; **388** © Tom McCarthy/PhotoEdit; **394** © 1989 Guy Gillette/Photo Researchers, Inc.; **397** © Ken Lax/Photo Researchers, Inc.; **413** © Ian O'Leary/Tony Stone World-wide; **422** © 1991 Mug Shots/The Stock Market; **424** © Frank Herholdt/Tony Stone World-wide; **427** © 1991 Jon Feingersh/The Stock Market; **432** © Arnold Adler; **443** © 1992 Comstock; **454 clockwise from top left** © 1992 Comstock; © Performax/Performax CT; © Pete Southwide/Stock, Boston; © David Young-Wolff/PhotoEdit; **455** © David Young-Wolff/PhotoEdit; **456** © Mike Mazzaschi/Stock, Boston; **460** © Michael Newman/PhotoEdit; **463** © Peter Stoddart; **471** © Benelux/Photo Researchers, Inc.; **472** © Gale Zucker/Stock, Boston; **473** © Frank Siteman/Stock, Boston; **481** © Pete Southwide/Stock, Boston; **489** © George Haling/Photo Researchers, Inc.; **494** © Shambroom/Photo Researchers, Inc.; **496** © Tony Freeman/PhotoEdit. All Rights Reserved; **505** © Liane Enkelis/Stock, Boston; **508** © Barbara Alper/Stock, Boston; **516** © 1992 Comstock; **526** © Frank Herholdt/Tony Stone Worldwide; **529** © Bruce Ayres/Tony Stone World-wide; **535** © 1992 Mary Kate Denny/PhotoEdit; **562** © Performax/Performax, CT; **570** © Bureau of U.S. Census; **575** Albert Trotman/Allford Trotman; **580** © Dean Abramson/Stock, Boston; **583** © 1992 Comstock

Color insert II   2 top © Mutual of Omaha Companies, 1991, All Rights Reserved; **2 bottom** © Frank Herholdt/Tony Stone Worldwide; **4 middle and bottom** © SuperStock; **5 top** © SuperStock; **5 middle** © Tim Brown/Tony Stone Worldwide; **6 middle** © Mutual of Omaha Companies, 1991, All Rights Reserved; **6 bottom** © 1992 SuperStock; **7 top** © Tim Brown/Tony Stone Worldwide; **7 middle** © Neil Selkirk/Tony Stone Worldwide; **7 bottom** © Jim Pickerell/Tony Stone Worldwide; **8 top** © David Frazier/Tony Stone Worldwide; **8 bottom** © Bruno de Hogues/Tony Stone Worldwide

Color insert III   1, 2 © Texas Instruments Corporate Visual Services; **3, 4, 5** © Union Pacific Railroad; **6, 7, 8** Mutual of Omaha Companies, 1991, All Rights Reserved

Color insert IV   1 top © Tim Brown/Tony Stone Worldwide; **middle** © 1992 SuperStock; **1 bottom** © 1992 SuperStock; **2 top** © 1992 Uniphoto; **2 bottom** © 1992 Uniphoto; **3 top** © Joseph Pobereskin/Tony Stone Worldwide; **3 middle** © Chuck Keeler/Tony Stone Worldwide; **3 bottom** David Frazier/Tony Stone